...Women

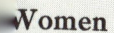

...ieth Constitutional
...biting Women

...Temperance, Prohibi-
...he Methodist Episcopal

...ONTENTS
PAGE
...g out the use of
...imply that the
...contempt of

STATISTICS

OF THE

COMMITTEE ON
ADMISSIONS

OF THE

ASSOCIATION
OF THE

OF THE CIT...
OF NEW YOR...

Compiled at the dinner given in
Committee at the University

|  | COLLEGE | CLASS | STATUS | NECKTIE | CHILDREN | AGE | POLITICS | CHURCH |
|---|---|---|---|---|---|---|---|---|
| COLE | H | '70 | M | W | 1 | 51 | R | E |
| SEXTON | H | '84 | S | B | 0 | 40 | D | E |
| ANDREWS | W P | '86 | M | B | 2 | 35 | D | R |
| HASLAM | Y | '90 | S | B | 0 | 33 | R | U |
| WORCESTER | Y | '76 | S | B | 0 | 43 | R | A |
| HUGHES | B | '81 | M | W | 3 | 37 | R | B |
| GULICK | P | '89 | S | W | 0 | 34 | R | P |
| VAN SINDEREN | Col. | '81 | M | W | 0 | 39 | R | E |
| ALEXANDER | H | '87 | S | B | 0 | 34 | D | E |
| WILLIAMS | Col. | '81 | W | W | 0 | 39 | D | E |
| MOFFAT | H | '83 | M | W | 2 | 38 | D | E |
| HOUGH | D | '79 | S | W | 0 | 41 | R | E |
| HARRISON | V | '70 | M | W | 0 | 49 | D | E |
| MARTIN | Y | '75 | M | W | 3 | 45 | R | P |
| BYRNE | H | '77 | M | W | 2 | 43 | D | C |
| ELY | Y | '82 | M | W | 2 | 40 | D | R |
| KIRCHWEY | Y | '79 | M | W | 4 | 43 | M | U |
| EUGENE SMITH | Y | '59 | M | B | 4 | 60 | R | P |
| DUNNING | P | '77 | M | B | 5 | 43 | M | R |
| BREWSTER | H | '79 | M | Absent |  |  |  |  |
| POTTER | Absent |  | M |  |  |  |  |  |

Audrey Cohen College

5 0664 01005459 3

AC
8
M376
1993

**DATE DUE**

AUDREY COHEN COLLEGE LIBRARY
75 Varick St. 12th Floor
New York, NY 10013

DEMCO

# SPINACH AND ZWEIBACK

# The Writings of

*Newell Martin*

# SPINACH AND ZWEIBACK

## The Writings of Newell Martin

Edited and Compiled by
## Cynthia Parsons

Grinnell and Lawton Publishing
Millbrook, New York

AUDREY COHEN COLLEGE LIBRARY
75 Varick St. 12th Floor
New York, NY 10013

Copyright © 1993 by
## Grinnell and Lawton Publishing
Front Street, Box 918, Millbrook, NY 12545

All rights reserved
Printed in the United States of America

**Library of Congress Cataloging-in-Publication Data**

Spinach and Zweiback, Writings of Newell Martin.
Edited and Compiled by Cynthia Parsons.
Introduction by Schuyler M. Meyer, Jr.

p. cm.

includes index.

1. Martin, Newell, 1854 - 1941.

2. Writings of Newell Martin.

3. Martin, Dr. William Alexander Parsons (father)
19th Century Missionary and Educator in China.

4. Spinach and Zwieback (English sp.).

ISBN 0-9635190-1-8          LC 93-73174

# SPINACH AND ZWEIBACK
## The Writings of
## Newell Martin

INTRODUCTION - Schuyler M. Meyer, Jr.

TIMELINE - Gregory Audette

### ONE — **THE DUTY OF REBELLION**
    Duty of Rebellion . . . . . . . . . . . . . . . . . .10
    Extracts from the
        Confessions of a Timid Old Man . . . . . . . . . .17
    The Water Bill . . . . . . . . . . . . . . . . . . .22
    Letters to Molly . . . . . . . . . . . . . . . . . .28
        February 20, 1935
        April 18, 1936

### TWO — **WETS AND DRYS**
    The Yale Commencement . . . . . . . . . . . . . . .34
    Draft Not Used . . . . . . . . . . . . . . . . . . .54
    Wine and Women . . . . . . . . . . . . . . . . . . .56
    Petition to Bannard . . . . . . . . . . . . . . . . .59
    Coolidge and the Bible . . . . . . . . . . . . . . .64
    Tests for Leprosy . . . . . . . . . . . . . . . . . .80
    Letter to R.R. Bowker . . . . . . . . . . . . . . . .89
    Aqueducts Are Unlawful . . . . . . . . . . . . . . .91
    On Drinking Alone By Moonlight . . . . . . . . .94

## THREE — WAR AND PEACE

Paper Umbrellas . . . . . . . . . . . . . . . . . . 98
From Washington's Farewell . . . . . . . . . . . 107
This is a Tract . . . . . . . . . . . . . . . . . . . 111
Letter to Major-General Robert Alexander . . . 114
Letter to Molly
    August 12, 1938 . . . . . . . . . . . . . . . . 118
War List of an Ordinary,
    Harmless American Family . . . . . . . . . 119

## FOUR — BUSINESS AND BUSINESSMEN

Martin's Bank Balance . . . . . . . . . . . . . . 124
A Deplorable Occurrence . . . . . . . . . . . . 129
Spinach and Zweiback . . . . . . . . . . . . . 131
Bad News: A Letter to
    Frederick A. Stokes, Esq. . . . . . . . . . . . 135

## FIVE — HYPHEN-BEARERS

Hyphen-Bearers . . . . . . . . . . . . . . . . . . 141
A Private Letter . . . . . . . . . . . . . . . . . . 144
The Book of Revelation
    and the University Club . . . . . . . . . . . 153
Copy of a Letter to a Publisher . . . . . . . . . 154
Armenoids . . . . . . . . . . . . . . . . . . . . . 159
Jews and Philistines . . . . . . . . . . . . . . . 165
Jews . . . . . . . . . . . . . . . . . . . . . . . . 172

## SIX — POVERTY AND WEALTH

Eugene Meyer, Jr., and the
    War Finance Corporation . . . . . . . . . . . 174
The Siamese Royal Commission . . . . . . . . 180
The Farm Surplus . . . . . . . . . . . . . . . . . . 195
Harrington Extra . . . . . . . . . . . . . . . . . . 196
Warning Against Some of the
    Effects of the Slump . . . . . . . . . . . . . . 197
Letter to Molly
    February 7, 1936 . . . . . . . . . . . . . . . . . 199

## SEVEN — PROGRESS AND REGRESS

Wireless Activity . . . . . . . . . . . . . . . . . . 202
Extracts From a Diary . . . . . . . . . . . . . . 207
Magauk! Magauk! . . . . . . . . . . . . . . . . . 210
Condolence - 1932 . . . . . . . . . . . . . . . . . 214
Letter to Molly
    March 12, 1933 . . . . . . . . . . . . . . . . . . 214
Letter to Molly
    December, 1934 . . . . . . . . . . . . . . . . . 215
Grammar . . . . . . . . . . . . . . . . . . . . . . . . 218

## EIGHT — GOD, BIBLE, AND HEREAFTER

Football and Prayer . . . . . . . . . . . . . . . . 221
Letters to Bear, 1935 & 1936 . . . . . . . . . . 223
Wrigley's Cathedral . . . . . . . . . . . . . . . . 227
Letters to Molly, 1932 - 1934 . . . . . . . . . . 228
Letter to "Ferncliff" . . . . . . . . . . . . . . . . 234

## NINE — FAMILY

From the Family Tree . . . . . . . . . . . . . . . . 236
Autobiography . . . . . . . . . . . . . . . . . . . . . 237
Geneological Data . . . . . . . . . . . . . . . . . . . 239
Letters from Newell
   to His Brothers . . . . . . . . . . . . . . . . . . . 240
Letters to and About the Family . . . . . . . . 251
Letters to the Grandchildren . . . . . . . . . . . 257
Words That I Had With Molly . . . . . . . . . 266
Molly's Will . . . . . . . . . . . . . . . . . . . . . . . 270
Some Advice As to In-Laws . . . . . . . . . . . 272
Recommendation for Schuyler
   from Phelps . . . . . . . . . . . . . . . . . . . . . 274
Pleonasm or Crime? . . . . . . . . . . . . . . . . . 275
Recommendation for Molly
   to Stokes . . . . . . . . . . . . . . . . . . . . . . . 277
A Summing Up . . . . . . . . . . . . . . . . . . . . 281

## TEN — FRIENDS

A 1922 Christmas Card . . . . . . . . . . . . . . 284
Facts, as to Dr. A.T. Osgood . . . . . . . . . . . 289
Seconder's Letter for Pell W. Foster . . . . . . 295
On Behalf of George Corning Fraser . . . . . . 297
As to W. Morgan Shuster . . . . . . . . . . . . . 304
Memorial of Charles Robinson Smith . . . . . 309
The Climenole . . . . . . . . . . . . . . . . . . . . . 313

## ELEVEN — NEIGHBORHOODS

Letter to Molly, January 1, 1936 . . . . . . . . 320
Not Even the Town Clerk Knows . . . . . . . . 320
Harrisburg Analytical Laboratory . . . . . . . . 321
A 1935 New Year's Card . . . . . . . . . . . . . 324

## TWELVE — **CHARACTER**
    Scots . . . . . . . . . . . . . . . . . . . . . . 328
    Rough Notes . . . . . . . . . . . . . . . . . . 332
    English Merchants . . . . . . . . . . . . . . 334

## THIRTEEN — **EAST AND WEST**
    To a Few Friends and One or Two Foes . . . . . 340
    Democracy's Crusaders . . . . . . . . . . . . . 345
    Korean Christians . . . . . . . . . . . . . . . . 372

## FOURTEEN — **PEAKS AND PEOPLE**
    Modern Haste on the Hilltops . . . . . . . . . 414
    Six Summits . . . . . . . . . . . . . . . . . . 418
    Great Adirondack Climbs . . . . . . . . . . . . 430
    Washing a Shirt on the Gothic . . . . . . . . . 433
    Two Great Adirondack Guides . . . . . . . . . 437
    Charlie Beede . . . . . . . . . . . . . . . . . . 442
    Helen Martin to Newell Martin . . . . . . . . 445
    Letter to Myra After Reading "Camp Six" . . . 446

## FIFTEEN — **SELECTED LETTERS**
    To Samuel R. Betts, Esqre. . . . . . . . . . . . 450
    To Myra . . . . . . . . . . . . . . . . . . . . 451
    To Grinnell . . . . . . . . . . . . . . . . . . . 457
    To Laura . . . . . . . . . . . . . . . . . . . . 458
    To Molly . . . . . . . . . . . . . . . . . . . . 459
    To Janet . . . . . . . . . . . . . . . . . . . . 471
    Merry Christmas, 1935 . . . . . . . . . . . . . 478

## SIXTEEN — **APPENDIX**
An Appreciation of W.A.P. Martin . . . . . . . . 480
Relations . . . . . . . . . . . . . . . . . . . . . . . 490
Phelps' Tribute to W.R. Martin . . . . . . . . . . 494
Memorandum as to Reverend W.W. Martin . . . 499
Dirck C. Lansing, D.D. . . . . . . . . . . . . . . 504

## SEVENTEEN — **A FINAL WORD**
Letter to Molly, August 12, 1939 . . . . . . . . . 510

# INTRODUCTION

Newell Martin was my grandfather. We called my Grandmother "Gomby," so quite logically he was "Other Gomby."

Other Gomby was born in Ningpo, China in 1854, where his father, Dr. W.A.P. Martin, was a Presbyterian missionary. Arriving in China in 1849, Dr. Martin spent his life there as a missionary and educator. He became president of Tun Wen College in Peking in 1867. [See Section Seventeen.]

My grandfather's first visit to the United States was in 1868, when the Martin family moved to New Haven, Connecticut, for a brief stay. Other Gomby remained in New Haven to attend grammar school and then Yale University, from which he graduated in 1875.

Other Gomby's Yale career was clearly not without incident. Our favorite tale was of his final escapade that deprived him of participation in the graduation ceremonies. As punishment, his degree was mailed to him! We were told that at a reunion he had removed the red trousers from a Harvard graduate, shinnied up the steeple of the Congregational church on the New Haven Green, hung the pants on the top and greased the steeple all the way down on his return trip to the ground. Reportedly it took the New Haven fire department of 1875 two weeks to remove the grease and to retrieve the trousers.

In 1877, Newell Martin graduated from Columbia University Law School and began practicing law in New York City. He soon formed his own law firm with George C. Fraser, which my father, Other Gomby's son-in-law, later joined. The firm is still in existence in New York City under the name of Seward & Kissel.

Some of my earliest and happiest recollections are of visits to the Milford farm with its winding driveway, its lawn sloping down to ponds at the bottom of a hill, and of course its animals. The house had a cupola, an especially intriguing place for a six-year old boy to explore.

My parents and grandparents moved to Huntington, Long Island, in 1928. Gomby and Other Gomby built a house just behind our's. My sisters, Molly, Janet, and Helen, and I felt especially privileged to grow up living so close to our grandparents. The other grandchildren, our first cousins, children of Uncle Grinnell, Myra, Jane, and Laura, lived nearby and shared these happy years with us, Gomby and Other Gomby.

From 1921 until his death in 1941, Other Gomby devoted much of his time to the writings published here. We have found almost 80 tracts — some as small as a single sheet, a few almost the size of a small book. We also have included a number of letters preserved by grateful grandchildren, because we have found them both entertaining and thoughtful. His choice of words and phrases are a delight. Even the most serious tracts are sprinkled with flashes of humor. Some are just great fun. We've insisted that the editor retain as much as possible Other Gomby's punctuation, spelling, and syntax, but we asked to have footnotes provided in order to elucidate the more obscure references in the texts.

When we were away at school or college, we could always count on receiving the latest outrageous sentiment or philosophy or even a personal humorous/serious note or letter. They were never signed "Other Gomby" or "Grandfather"; he either signed his full name or just his initials.

I once gave Other Gomby a pair of ear muffs. His thank-you letter was short. "Thank you for the ear muffs. In winter they will keep my ears warm. In summer, they will keep out the noise of the Fascists whom I hate. Newell Martin."

I've always been intrigued by one of his last Christmas cards. It was sent just before the start of the war in Europe and was printed with a black border. The words "merry" and "happy" were crossed out. On the reverse were the words:

> I send you this not because any man is dead but because the leaders of the world are asses, which is worse.

We chose the title "Spinach and Zweiback" for this compilation of his writings because the 1925 tract with that name neatly blends two comic vignettes with a serious message.

Almost all his serious tracts offer some encouragement to rebellion. We find one of his most thoughtful and challenging is "The Duty of Rebellion." He cites the Eighteenth Amendment (the Volstead Act), a target in many of his tracts, and reminds us of the Boston Tea Party. He asks what is the duty of rebellion? "Is submission to any law a moral obligation?" He answers, "surely not unless submission carries with it the personal conviction of rightness, which makes it moral." He continues:

> If we rebel, we produce social disorders; but if we obey, the peril is even greater, for we not only surrender the principle of free-will and our priceless freedom, but we must go through life hating ourselves for cowards and hypocrites, our citizenship nullified at the moment it was about to become an urgent thing.

Other Gomby would scorn our easy acceptance of self-serving politicians and rampant greed.

The targets of Other Gomby's wit and anger are legion, including Prohibition, wire-tappers, Ku Klux Klanners, some forms of taxation, discrimination, English merchants, slavery, and others. People and events earn his scorn, such as the Kellogg-Briand Pact in his essay "Paper Umbrellas"; which, he says, are fine until it rains! His wide-ranging reading and love of the classics pepper these tracts, leading the researcher on, what he calls, "many a merry chase."

The tracts have been compiled by Cynthia (Cynie) Parsons, former education editor of *The Christian Science Monitor*, who made this a labor of love (That's what she says!) for some five years — editing, researching, weaving. Cynie is a most extraordinary teacher, writer, and educational reformer for whom my entire family has the most enormous admiration and affection. If she had fun reading, studying, and laughing over Other Gomby's efforts, all of us have had equal pleasure in sharing them with her. And were it not for the most unusually capable and expert research done by Gregory (Greg) Audette of Hanover, New Hampshire, these writings would have been left in storage. Readers will marvel at the work he has done. He, too, says it was a labor of love. I guess he did have fun, but Other Gomby's descendants owe Greg a deep debt of gratitude. With Cynie's and Greg's help, Other Gomby's ideas come alive.

None of the family has any idea who might be attracted to reading these. We have to admit our prejudice. Yet, we can guarantee every reader will get not only a sense of life in America in the 1920s and '30s but be mentally stretched by reading what interested a remarkable, philosophic, scholarly, articulate, mountain-climbing rebel. But best of all, there is many a chuckle.

Schuyler M. Meyer, Jr.

Dover Plains, New York
December 1993

# TIMELINE
# The Writings of Newell Martin

**1854**  Newell Martin born in Ningpo, China
W.A.P. Martin publishes *Evidences of Christianity*
Commodore Perry opens Japan

**1856**  Second Opium War begins in China
Crimean War ends

**1857**  Dred Scott decision by U.S. Supreme Court

**1859**  John Brown raids Harper's Ferry
Darwin publishes first volume of *Origin of Species*

**1860**  The Martin family leaves Shanghai on the *Golden Rule* for furlough in the United States

**1861**  American Civil War begins

**1862**  Newell, brother Claude, and parents return to Shanghai via an 85-day trip aboard ship

**1865**  American Civil War ends
Lincoln assassinated
Taiping Revolt crushed in China
University Club founded in New York City

**1867**  Suez Canal completed
Seward purchases Alaska
Marx publishes first volume of *Das Kapital*
W.A.P. Martin becomes president of Tun Wen College, Peking

**1868**  Martin family returns aboard ship to U.S.; locates in New Haven, Connecticut

**1869**  U.S. transcontinental railway completed
W.A.P. Martin, alone, returns to China

**1870**  Franco-Prussian War begins

**1873**  Anthony Comstock founds New York Society for the Suppression of Vice

**1875**  Newell graduates from Yale

# TIMELINE

| | |
|---|---|
| **1876** | Custer defeated at Little Bighorn |
| **1877** | Newell graduates from Columbia University Law School; commences law practice in New York City |
| **1879** | Edison invents electric light |
| **1880** | W.A.P. Martin makes two-year visit to U.S. |
| **1882** | Newell's brother, Pascal, dies in China |
| **1890** | U.S. Bureau of Census officially notes closing of American frontier |
| **1893** | Anti-Saloon League founded in U.S. Newell's mother, Jane, dies in U.S. |
| **1894** | Captain Alfred Dreyfus convicted of treason in France Newell climbs six Adirondack peaks in one day |
| **1895** | Marconi transmits first long-wave signal |
| **1898** | Spanish-American War begins |
| **1899** | Boer War begins in South Africa John Hay formulates Open Door Policy for great powers in China First International Peace Conference held at The Hague |
| **1900** | Boxer Rebellion begins in China W.A.P. Martin lectures in U.S.; writes *Siege* in Peking |
| **1901** | Queen Victoria dies |
| **1903** | Wright Brothers fly at Kitty Hawk |
| **1904** | Construction of Panama Canal begins Russo-Japanese War begins Operation of London's New River Company transferred to Metropolitan Water Board |
| **1905** | Einstein publishes special theory of relativity |
| **1907** | Second International Peace Conference held at The Hague |
| **1908** | London Naval Conference adopts Declaration of London Helen Martin climbs Dent de Satarma |

| | |
|---|---|
| **1910** | Japan commences empire by officially making colony of Korea<br>American Society for the Judicial Settlement of International Disputes founded<br>House of Lords disestablished in Great Britain<br>Morgan Shuster takes charge of Persian exchequer |
| **1911** | Carry Nation dies |
| **1912** | China becomes a republic<br>Balkan Wars begin<br>"Piltdown Man" discovered |
| **1913** | Japan makes Twenty-One Demands on China<br>W. F. Mannix publishes fictitious life of Li Hung Chang |
| **1914** | World War I begins<br>Construction of Panama Canal completed |
| **1915** | President Wilson sends U.S. troops into Mexico<br>Chapel of Intercession completed in New York City<br>Newell's brother, Winfred Robert, dies |
| **1916** | W.A.P. Martin, Newell's father, dies in China |
| **1917** | U.S. enters World War I<br>Nicholas II abdicates in Russia; Bolsheviks seize control |
| **1918** | World War I ends with abdication of Kaiser Wilhelm II and collapse of Austro-Hungarian Empire<br>Allies commence intervention in Russia<br>Taraknath Das convicted in New York City |
| **1919** | Versailles Treaty signed<br>League of Nations founded<br>Eighteenth Amendment enacts prohibition in U.S. |
| **1920** | Jewish state established in Palestine as British protectorate<br>Nineteenth Amendment enacts women's suffrage in U.S. |
| **1921** | Washington Naval Conference limits warships of great powers<br>Schuyler M. Meyer, Sr., heads investigation into New York City government |
| **1922** | Mussolini marches on Rome<br>Teapot Dome scandal in U.S. |

# 8  TIMELINE

**1923**  Hitler attempts "beer-hall putsch" in Munich

**1924**  U.S. Immigration Act of 1924 severely limits non-Nordic immigration
Dawes Plan reorganizes German war reparations
Lenin dies

**1925**  Scopes trial held in Tennessee
*New York Times* publishes Newell Martin's decline of dry Yale reunion invitation

**1926**  Reverend John Norris shoots interlocutor

**1927**  Kellogg-Briand Pact outlaws war
Lindbergh flies Atlantic
Western powers intervene in China
Waldorf Astor declares Prohibition Will Win

**1928**  Chinese Nationalists begin Northern Expedition
Wee Willie Sherdel leads Cardinals to pennant
TransAtlantic measles

**1929**  U.S. stock market crashes, initiating worldwide depression
St. Valentine's Day massacre in Chicago

**1931**  Japan invades Manchuria

**1933**  Franklin Delano Roosevelt launches New Deal
Prohibition repealed
Nazi Party comes to power in Germany
First Everest Expedition mounted

**1936**  Edward VIII abdicates in England

**1938**  Munich Pact gives Germany Czechoslovakia's Sudetenland
Hurricane of '38 devastates New England

**1939**  Germany invades remainder of Czechoslovakia and Poland; World War II begins

**1941**  Newell Martin dies in Huntington, Long Island
Japan bombs Pearl Harbor; U.S. enters World War II

# ONE

# THE DUTY OF REBELLION

The Duty of Rebellion . . . . . . . . . . . 10

Extracts From the
    'Confessions of a Timid Old Man' . 17

The Water Bill . . . . . . . . . . . . . . . . 22

Letters to Molly . . . . . . . . . . . . . . . 28
    February 20, 1935
    April 18, 1936

# The Duty of Rebellion
[1924]

*"Intolerance produces efficiency."*

*The 14-page tract states on its cover that the author is one "George W. Martin," and that the enclosed essay is "Reprinted from the Groton School Quarterly." Neither, of course, is true. Newell Martin wrote and published the essay, placing the following message on the inside cover: "Respectfully Dedicated to the Memory of John Stuart Mill."*

*Groton, founded in 1884 as a preparatory school for such colleges as Yale and Harvard, was then and still is a highly-selective private school in Groton, Massachusetts.*

*The essay's subtitle is given in French -- Si j'etais Roi. A footnote at the bottom of Page 1 of the tract states, "This title was adopted in order to make certain that the address would not be attributed to the Headmaster of Groton School or interpreted as reflecting his sentiments."*

*On the final page is a quotation Martin attributes to Lord Acton,[1] "The great question is to discover, not what governments prescribe, but what they ought to prescribe; for no prescription is valid against the conscience of mankind."*

### Si j'etais Roi
*"This above all: To thine own self be true."*

When I look round at the faces of you with whom for five or six years at a time I have been associated as school master, I am impressed with the fact that you are grown up. Many of you are now older than I was during the continuance of that relation, many of you are doubtless wiser than I shall ever be. Many of you have had experience of men and things which lie outside the ken of a country school master; and so I make bold to confess to you a certain bewilderment which has come on me of late.

I am naturally a conservative. Like Lord Falkland, I believe that "when it is not necessary to change, it is necessary not to

---

1. John Emerich Edward Dalberg Acton, First Baron Acton (1834-1902), English historian and political philosopher, best known for the (usually misquoted) remark that "all power tends to corrupt; and absolute power corrupts absolutely."

change"[2] yet when I have been convinced that changes were necessary I have, I think, not hesitated to put them into operation. Nevertheless, I am now troubled in my mind.

With the advent of the Great War [WWI] certain fundamentals of the old order were destroyed and will not be seen again by any of us here. We learned of the "will to win", of the use of propaganda, of the necessity in war time to suppress free speech and public assembly, of the regulation of the lives of all of us for the great end. For a time, liberty was suspended. The individual's rights were eclipsed by the intensity of our common effort.

It was necessary. It was right.

But as we emerge from the shadow of that menace, and as we resume the old ways and the old life, where now is gone our ancient freedom? When come these fetters which we bear, these inquisitions, these regulations, these prohibitions? Upon what meat hath this, our Government, fed, that it is grown so great?

Intolerance produces efficiency; and efficiency is essential in war time. But in time of peace the poisonous by-products of intolerance far outweigh any compensating efficiency. Troops are not yet quartered in our homes, but auditors are; truculent political accountants who sit at our desks, use our pens, examine our books, and ostentatiously doubt our explanations. We dare not throw them out for fear they will bear false witness against us to the Government. And so, like cowardly hypocrites, we greet them with honeyed words.

Any collector of internal revenue can subpoena a citizen to come to him from anywhere in the United States. If the Government does not like your tax return, it makes one up for you out of whole cloth, and then you must pay the tax and sue to get it back again. If you recover a judgment you must wait till Congress appropriates money before you can be paid. Within a relatively short time 70,000 statutes, State and National, have been passed for our education, guidance, and government; and the greatest of these is the Volstead Act.

Under this statute liquor advertising has been eliminated, saloons greatly reduced,and drinking considerably curtailed. But to drink or not to drink is not the question. The statute is founded on a lie: that more than half of one per cent alcohol is intoxicating. It is enforced by a lie: that one offense constitutes a nuisance. It

---

2. Lucius Cary, Second Lord Falkland (1610?-1643); quotation from *Discourse on the Infallibility of the Church of Rome*, published 1660.

tortures the ancient equity practice into police court procedure solely in order that those accused may be deprived of a jury trial, that palladium of our civil rights, by the previous issuance of an injunction, whilst it impresses the unwilling landlord into the police force by threats of padlocks. It is enforced against the weak, but not against a person like the Cunard Line, which has the British Government back of it — although I am informed that every time the *Mauritania* enters the Port of New York she violates the act, and would render herself liable to confiscation if Great Britain had not bought immunity for her by the Twelve-Mile Agreement.[3] It is enforced as war is waged, by lying propaganda, by stool-pigeons and spies, by John Doe search warrants, by unlawful breaking into homes, by putting poison in spirits that those who will not conform may drink — and die.

The answer which is made to the recital of these wrongs is instant and resounding. We are told that all that those who disagree with the principle of this law have to do is to accept defeat, to recognize themselves in the minority, and to obey the law. This is, indeed, the course which I have pursued myself, and urged up others till now. I have always supposed that majority rule was the essence of American government. I have tried to inculcate obedience to law in my boys at school.

But it is coming to me that the question is not so simple as that. The power which we have to consider now is the power of random majorities collected and directed by organized propaganda. These majorities are produced by the conjunction of organized publicity and an incomplete education. The opinions of these majorities, for which such vast power is claimed, are not spontaneous judgments. As Mr. Lippmann says, "They are worked up, stoked up, arranged and calculated by men, some of them sincere and some of them insincere, who have discovered this great and ominous fact: that popular education has made it possible to reach people with printed matter, but it has not prepared those people to discriminate as to what they receive from printed matter. The fundamental way to build up that resistance is to clear our own minds of the sophistry, of the democratic fallacy, that there is any peculiar righteousness in majorities."

---

3. On January 23, 1924, Great Britain signed a treaty with the U.S. granting the reciprocal right to search any vessel within the 12-mile limit. Since the U.S. sought the treaty to prevent American-owned ships under British registry from transporting intoxicants — and wanted to extend the limit from three miles to twelve — British liners were spared search and seizure to secure Britain's consent to the outer limit.

I think this becomes plainer if we examine further into the possibilities. If, for instance, a cowardly Congress, composed of what Jefferson called "demi-lawyers", in response to what a majority supposed was a controlling *bloc* of the electorate, and pursuant to a new amendment, passed a statute prescribing nationalization of women, or female infanticide, or a 100% capital levy, we should none of us obey it for one instant, any more than we should the Anti-Evolution Law passed by the Tennessee Legislature. There is a silent referendum in the hearts and minds of men on every important enactment by a Legislature and on every important decision by a Court which involves a fundamental principle of civil liberty. Without a favorable issue in that referendum, the statute and the decision alike are written in water. As President Butler has said: "It must not be forgotten that law is but one form or type of social control. And certainly there can be no more distressing and no more disintegrating form of lawlessness than that which arises from the resistance of intelligent and high-minded people, on grounds of morals and fundamental principle, to some particular provision of law."[4] For truth, for beauty, for friendship, for the things of the spirit, you do not go to the greatest number, for if you do you will not find them.

I have considered these matters anxiously and long, particularly in view of the confidence which many of you have shown in sending your sons to me to educate. Shall I tell these boys to obey, or to rebel? Or shall I tell them nothing?

I have examined the trial of Socrates, and observed how the duly constituted authorities of Athens offered him freedom and honor if only he would be silent. I note that he chose death rather than conform, being convinced that the duty laid on him to speak, and so to rebel, was greater than life itself, and that to remain silent was to pour poison into the very veins of the body politic.

I observe that Christ refused to conform to those that "sit in Moses' seat", but drove the money-changers from the Temple with a whip. I note that Peter, after a moment of faltering, chose to be crucified head downwards for preaching what he believed, and I believe, was and is the truth.

Coming down to the Anglo-Saxon times I remember that

---

4. Nicholas Murray Butler (1862-1947), president of Columbia University 1902-1945. The quotation comes from an address, "Law and Lawlessness," given before the Ohio Bar Association in 1923, and reprinted the following year in *The Faith of a Liberal* (New York: Scribner's, 1924), p.124. Butler adverted particularly to the unfeasability of the Fifteenth Amendment and the Volstead Act.

*Magna Carta* was obtained by rebellious Barons; and in the great birth of Constitutional Liberty I recollect Pym, Cromwell, Ireton, Sir Harry Vane, and John Hampden:[5] "When he drew his sword he threw the sheath away."

Ah, Hampden, Hampden! *Vindex fortissimus libertatis*, seen riding, mortally wounded, from Chalgrove Field "before the action was done, which he never used to do, and with his head hanging down, and resting his hands on the neck of his horse."

I recall Franklin, Washington and Patrick Henry. I see William Lloyd Garrison[6] led through the streets of Boston with a rope round his neck, Col. Higginson[7] discovered at midnight at the door of the Court House at the head of a mob trying to rescue Burns, the fugitive slave, Amos Lawrence[8] shipping rifles to Kansas, and Lincoln with the Dred Scott decision staring him in the face.[9] I see the Fifteenth Amendment[10] nullified in the South, and no man in his senses proposing to enforce it. I see the Atlantic Seaboard setting itself for a long struggle to nullify the Eighteenth Amendment. I see the navy gathered off Sandy Hook as if to blockade the Port of New York, armored cars roaring through the Adirondacks, nightly battles on the Canadian border, hijackers and bootleggers waxing rich on murder, the green slime of corruption spreading ever further, and the United States Attorney for the Southern District of New York resigning from all his clubs on the day he takes office.

I see you all here, my boys, and I know that it is only out of polite consideration for my often expressed sentiments that cold water alone is seen on the table. Were I not present it would have been otherwise.

In my perplexity I have turned to my Church, -- but there are few or none who are intellectually capable of considering whether

---

5. All major political figures of the Puritan Revolution in the 1640s.
6. (1805-1879), American abolitionist. The incident mentioned took place in 1835.
7. Thomas Wentworth Higginson (1823-1911), one of the leaders of the unsuccessful attempt to free the fugitive slave Anthony Burns from the Boston Court House on the night of May 26, 1854; subsequently, Higginson commanded the First South Carolina Volunteers, the first regiment of former slaves mustered into the U.S. Army.
8. (1814-1886), son of a textile manufacturer, Abbott Lawrence, backed the antislavery movement in the settlement of the Kansas Territory.
9. The 1857 Supreme Court decision ruling that a slave is not a citizen.
10. The Fifteenth Amendment guarantees that "the right of citizens of the United States to vote shall not be denied or abridged by the United States or any state on account of race, color, or previous conditions of servitude." Martin presumably alludes to the pernicious effect of carpetbaggers' government.

*Vox Populi* is really *Vox Dei*, or what constitutes Public Opinion, or when is a majority, or whether right and wrong can finally be determined by political fiat. I know it is not wrong -- not even forbidden — to drink. The very traffic is only *malum prohibitum* and not *malum in se*.[11] Yet the Church, in control of those Elder Statesmen who have much to lose by radical change or disorder, will not face the real problem. On October 21, 1925, at the General Convention in New Orleans, in the House of bishops, the following resolution was unanimously adopted: "That facing the danger of the spirit of lawlessness in American life, we welcome the renewed attempts of the Government of the United States to enforce strictly and impartially the Prohibition law and the Anti-Narcotic law, which are so widely and cynically disregarded, and we call upon the people of our Church to set a good example of obedience to law, without which no democracy can endure."

How the calculated cunning of linking Prohibition with the traffic in narcotics slaps one in the face! Observe the smug admission in the opening lines that fear of danger and not interest in right is the prompting motive! Note the anxiety in the closing words for the continuance of the *status quo* (in which they are Bishops) without inquiry or thought as to whether a form of government in which such things can be is a democracy at all, or in any way worth preserving! The fear of God is the beginning of wisdom. the fear of men is the grave of freedom.

"Suppose," says Dean Inge of St. Paul's, "that the state has exceeded its powers by prohibiting some harmless act, such as the consumption of alcohol. Is smuggling, in such a case, morally justifiable? I should say, Yes: the interference of the state in such matters is a mere impertinence."[12]

And now suppose Dean Inge is Elijah, a small minority, but *right*; and the House of Bishops turns out to be the 450 prophets of Baal * * *

Is submission to any law a moral obligation? Surely not unless the submission carries with it the personal conviction of rightness which makes it moral. Plato said that the good life is not the life one *ought* to lead, but the life that, after solemn reflection and self-examination, one really *wants* to lead. To be moral is to

---

11. The Roman Catholic Church distinguishes that taken to be evil as involving defiance of proper authority from that taken to be evil in itself.
12. William Randolph Inge (1850-1954), dean of St. Paul's 1911-1934, known for his writings on a variety of social and political issues.

know what one is doing. It is false that man is meaningless except as part of some social whole. Our first duty is to be true to our conscience, the Inner voice of Socrates, the Still Small Voice of Elijah. *Jus est quod jussum est*[13] is the wail of men too tired to go on thinking any longer.

Of course, we may have to pay the penalty; but unless we do that which lies in us to do, we also have to pay the penalty. If we rebel, we produce social disorders; but if we obey, the peril is even greater, for we not only surrender the principle of free-will and our priceless freedom, but we must go through life hating ourselves for cowards and hypocrites, our citizenship nullified at the moment it was about to become an urgent thing.

Whatever the requirements of legal theory, in fact no man surrenders his whole being to the state. He has a sense of right and wrong. If the state, or its instruments, goes too consistently against that sense, he is pricked into antagonism. The state is for him sovereign only when his conscience is not stirred against its performance. Whatever, therefore, concerns the conscience of man, whatever brings its activity into operation, must, for the state, be sacred ground. As for the state itself — even where the opposition is small, it is probable that more is gained by the possession of that energy of character which is willing to offer challenge than by destroying it. For a state which oppresses those who are sincerely antagonized by the way in which government interprets its purposes is bound to drift slowly into despotism.

To postulate for the state a kind of centralized infallibility is to confer upon ourselves too vast a relief from thought. Man's destiny is to think, or become a dumb beast — no matter how willing the amiable Bishops are to relieve us from the strain.

Well, my period of indecision is ended. For years I have tried to teach boys to live the truth as I saw it. I should also have tried to make them live the highest truth as they saw it. I have told them the answers. I should also have told them to examine critically the basic assumptions of life for themselves. I should have placed more emphasis on intellectual integrity. Instead, I have stressed conformity to the current moral code which I considered noblest. I have taught the importance of obedience. I have neglected the duty of rebellion.

The old order changeth. I call you to a new consecration: let us dedicate ourselves to the fearless utterance of the highest truth

13. "That is just which is commanded or according to usage."

each sees; knowing that, let what may come of it, only thus can one play one's right part in the world — knowing that if one can effect the change one aims at — well; if not — well also; though not so well.

"The lights begin to twinkle from the rocks:
The long day wanes: the slow moon climbs: the deep
Moans round with many voices. Come, my friends,
Tis not too late to seek a newer world.
Push off, and sitting well in order smite
The sounding furrows; for my purpose holds
To sail beyond the sunset, and the baths
Of all the western stars, until I die."[14]

❧ ❧ ❧

# Extracts from the 'Confessions of a Timid Old Man'
[undated]

*The original pamphlet (4.5" X 7.5") consists of only three pages of type (about 400 words), and begins with "Chapter III," as though there were a larger document from which this was an extract.*

### CHAPTER III.

There is a legend, report or fable, not without its moral, now that freedom of speech is more nearly dead than ever before, that once, during the Ten Days,[1] when John Reid[2] was at the Smolny Institute,[3] there entered to him the Chairman of the Committee on Free Press.[4] He fondly showed to Reid a new decree, damp from the

---

14. The quotation is ll. 54-62 of Tennyson's *Ulysses*.

---

1. Roughly the time of the Bolshevik seizure of power in Petrograd in 1917, climaxing with the capture of the Winter Palace the night of Oct. 24-25 (Nov. 6-7 in the modern calendar). *The Ten Days That Shook the World* is the title of John Reed's book.
2. John Reed (not Reid) (1887-1920), radical American author and war correspondent best-known for his activities in and reportage on Russia during and immediately after the Bolshevik Revolution.
3. School in Petrograd for the daughters of the nobility, used as a headquarters and assembly room by the Central Executive Committee and the Second All-Russian Congress of Soviets during the Bolshevik Revolution.

18    THE DUTY OF REBELLION

printer.

'You know already,' said he 'what these Kerensky[5] hypocrites have done. They pretend to worship Milton's *Areopagitica*.[6] Yet they have published a decree, suppressing our Bolshevik newspapers, and they have sent police to shut them up. I'll show them that they can't abolish freedom. Here's our decree, suppressing their Menshevik[7] newspapers, and we have sent Red Guards to shut them up.'

[Editor's Note: Chapter XI of Reed's *Ten Days That Shook the World* tells of an incident, similar to this reference by Martin which took place in July and August, 1917. Kerensky had, in fact, shut down several Bolshevik newspapers in Petrograd, an act denounced by (the Bolshevik) *Izvestia* as a "filthy provocation." Then on the night of October 23, Kerensky's general staff responded to the Bolshevik Military Revolutionary's committee's initial seizure of power not by attacking Smolny and the unit commissars, but by sending cadets to shut down the two leading Bolshevik newspapers. (Armed detachments reopened them the next day.) After the capture of the Winter Palace, the Bolsheviks shut down several Menshevik newspapers and the entire bourgeois press for "slandering the Soviets," the most massive reprisal against the press in Russian history to that date. As Lenin put it in the subsequent debate at Smolny, "He who now talks of 'freedom of the press' goes backward." It was following this debate that the Mensheviks left the party, giving the Bolsheviks a free hand.

## CHAPTER IV.

Ellen La Motte's[8] books are a tonic for timid old people who have forgotten how to be angry when they see truth forever in the dock; wrong forever on the bench.

---

4. There was no such committee.
5. Alexander Feodorovich Kerensky (1881-1970), moderate socialist who became provisional premier of the Russian government in July, 1917.
6. Milton's impassioned defense of freedom of the press, published in 1644.
7. The word "Menshevik," literally means "minority." The minority wing of the Russian Social-Democratic Party, so called after being outvoted on matters of policy by a brief-lived majority at the 1903 party congress. The majority, or Bolsheviks, favored confining party membership to a small, disciplined elite and immediately fomenting revolution; the Mensheviks sought a party organized on mass lines as in western Europe, and a policy of gradualism in Russia that would accommodate an interim bourgeois or democratic regime.
8. (1873-1961), American author who served as a nurse with the French army 1915-1916; traveled in the far East 1916-1917. In 1922 succeeded in laying before prominent

THE DUTY OF REBELLION    19

## CHAPTER V

The American Defense Society[9] has appealed to Congress to help Kolchak,[10] Tchaikowsky[11] and Kaledine,[12] who are trying to bring back as much as may be of the old black despotism of the Romanoffs[13] and the Okhrana;[14] but, nevertheless, I am glad that I have been enrolled in the American Defense Society, because, if I were not, the people I love would not ask me to dine with them.

---

members of the British government exhaustive evidence she had gathered concerning the sale of opium in the British crown colonies and in India; was decorated by the Chinese government for this and other efforts against the opium trade. Regular contributor to *The Atlantic, Harper's, The Nation.* Her books include *The Tuberculosis Nurse* (1914); *The Backwash of War* (1916); *Peking Dust* (1919); *Civilization* (1919); *The Opium Monopoly* (1920); *The Ethics of Opium* (1924); *Snuffs and Butters* (1925).

---

9. The American Defense Society (ADS) was formed in 1915 as a political offshoot of the National Security League, aimed at promoting military preparedness and universal military training. Madison Grant, who from 1922-1937 was the vice president of the Immigration Restriction League, was one of its trustees. (See Section Five — "Copy of a Letter to a Publisher") After the U.S. entry into WWI the ADS became a notorious persecutor of all things German in American life, from churches, schools, societies, and language teaching to food and music; these activities extended to demands that German-Americans demonstrate their loyalty at mass public rallies. Between the Bolshevik Revolution and the disbandment of the ADS in 1919, it conducted a limited amount of anti-Bolshevik agitation. In December, 1918, a circular letter was sent to ministers asking that they preach sermons on the need of action by Congress to help Kolchak, and a demand was made in June, 1919, for recognition of Kolchak by the American government.
10. Alexander Vasilievich Kolchak (1874-1920), Tsarist naval officer who headed the Manchurian White Russian armies in 1918-1919, and was recognized 1919-1920 by the Whites as ruler of Russia. Was summarily executed by the Bolsheviks after falling into their hands early in 1920.
11. Nikolai Vasilievich Tchaikovsky (1850-1926), relative of the composer Peter Ilyich Tchaikovsky, was a right Social Revolutionary (i.e., moderate liberal in Western terms), and former member of the Constituent Assembly, who was set up by the British as the largely signatory head of a local Russian government in Archangel in August, 1918. In September he and five of his ministers were kidnapped by a group of former Tsarist officers and removed to Solovetski Island in the White Sea. Was there only a few weeks, and carried on with a somewhat reorganized government until January 1919, when the British replaced him with a White general Yevgenii Miller. Even though Tchaikovsky spent most of his life agitating against and otherwise opposing the Russian monarchy, and was arrested and tried, though not convicted, by the Tsar's government, he died peacefully in England.
12. Alexi Xaximovich Kaledine (1861-1918), Russian imperial army officer and hetman or chief of the Don Cossacks, who was one of the first to organize military resistance to the Bolsheviks after the October Revolution. Military reverses led to his committing suicide.
13. Ruling dynasty of Russia for more than three hundred years from 1613-1917.
14. Russian acronym for Department for Defense of Public Security and Order. Russian secret-police organization founded in 1881 to combat terrorism and revolutionary activity.

## CHAPTER VII.

It has been said, often, that there are lies, dam [sic] lies, statistics, diplomatic denials, communiques, and statesmen's formulas. These formulas are sometimes so acrid and cynical, so compact with contempt for credulous mankind, that they move the saddest of us to delighted laughter. Wilson[16] and Ishii[17] are high in the art of polishing such jewels. But there are others.

Sir George W. Buchanan[18] lectured before the Philosophical Institute, at Edinburgh, March 25, 1919, and urged invasion of Russia by an English volunteer army. Any cause sacred enough to justify the horrors of war is sacred enough to justify conscription. But let that pass. Sir George said, inter alia, (Natl. Rev. May, 1919, 347): 'In 1907 an agreement was signed at St. Petersburg that constituted the first step toward a Russo-British understanding ...That agreement was restricted ...to maintaining Persia's integrity and independence and to declining the respective spheres of influence of Great Britain and Russia in that country.'

[The continuation of that quotation reads: "That agreement, however, restricted as it was to maintaining Persia's integrity and independence, and to delimiting the respective spheres of influence of Great Britain and Russia in that country, did not remove all causes of friction between the two Governments, as they frequently disagreed as regarded the mode of its application." The article, "Great Britain and Russia," describes Bolshevik atrocities (300,000 murders; 80% of them workers and peasants) and goes on to recommend Western military intervention. "I have never attempted to defend the old autocratic regime, which was not only harsh and oppressive in its methods, but constituted a bar to the progressive development of the uneducated Russian masses. The Emperor, however, was far from being a bloodthirsty tyrant as his executioners represented him, and under his rule Russia was a happier and more prosperous country than it will ever be under the merciless tyranny of the present *de facto* Government...Had such crimes as those of which the Bolsheviks have been guilty been

---

16. Woodrow Wilson (1856-1924), President of the United States 1913-1921.
17. Ishii Kikujiro (1866-1945), Japanese statesman and diplomat
18. George William Buchanan (1854-1924), English diplomat, ambassador to Russia 1910-1918, friend of the Tsar, who initially advocated a policy of conciliation toward the Bolsheviks, but reversed his stance after the destruction of the Constituent Assembly and the murder of the Tsar.

committed under the Empire a storm of indignation would have swept through our country."]

Further particulars in regard to that agreement can be found in Morgan Shuster's *Strangling of Persia*.

[Editor's Note: William Morgan Shuster (1877-1960), government official and publishing executive. The Persian government, on the verge of bankruptcy, appealed in 1910 to President Taft for an able American to take charge of its exchequer, and Shuster was appointed. *The Strangling of Persia* (New York: Century, 1912) describes Shuster's appointment of a Major C.B. Stokes of the British army, whom Shuster saw simply as much the most qualified man available, as head of the Persian tax-collecting force. Whitehall initially acceded to Stokes' request that he be allowed to resign his commission to take the post. Russia, however, charged that the appointment constituted an interference with certain unnamed interests it held in northern Persia; and on learning of Russian opposition, the British government reversed its position on Stokes' appointment in flagrant violation of a 1907 treaty between England and Russia guaranteeing their common respect for Persia's integrity and territorial independence. Combined with Whitehall's blockage of a four million English pound loan Shuster had been negotiating, this measure, in Shuster's words, "practically nullified all hope of my accomplishing any constructive financial work on behalf of the Persian government"; and in December, 1911, he left the country. The Persian Nationalist government shortly thereafter collapsed in the face of an armed Russian intervention.]

## CHAPTER IX.

Taraknath Das has in him the soul of Patrick Henry and Nathan Hale; but I am afraid to speak up for him and too mean to subscribe for his defense.

[Editor's Note: Taraknath Das (1884-1958) was an ardent, lifelong supporter of Indian nationalism who came to the U.S. in 1906 and shortly thereafter became a U.S. citizen, working extensively in this country for the cause of Indian independence. His views caused him to take a pro-German stance during WWI, and upon U.S. entry into the war, Das went to Germany and there became a member of the German Indian Independence Commission. The commission was formed by the German government late in 1914. It maintained connections with disaffected Indian nationals throughout southeast Asia, China, Japan, and America and fomented activities ranging from agitation to, in Burma, the outright training of paramilitary forces by German officers.

In 1918, he was indicted by a U.S. court both for having misrepresented himself as an accredited representative of the Indian Nationalist Party and for having been party, prior to the U.S. entry into the war to a conspiracy to violate U.S. neutrality by helping organize an armed expedition by Germany to overthrow British rule in India. Das, who was in Japan at the time, returned to this country voluntarily in order to clear himself of the charges but was instead convicted and served a 22-month prison sentence. To the end of his life he maintained that he had been an innocent victim of war hysteria.

He did, however, undeniably advocate a military alliance of Indian nationalists with Russia and Germany at a public speech in New York City in 1920, and support Japanese claims in the Pacific immediately prior to WWII. In later life, Das lectured on international affairs at various American universities including New York University and Columbia.]

# The Water Bill
[July 14, 1927]

*Where the populace rise at once against the
   never-ending audacity of elected persons,
Where fierce men and women pour forth as the sea
   to the whistle of death pours its sweeping
   and unript waves,
Where outside authority enters always after the
   precedence of inside authority,
Where the citizen is always the head and ideal,
   and President, Mayor, Governor and whatnot,
   are agents for pay.*
Walt Whitman

Walt Whitman (1819-1892), was born in West Hills, Huntington, Long Island, N.Y. The lines above are from verse 5 of "The Song of the Broad-Axe" (Leaves of Grass I).

THE DUTY OF REBELLION          23

*As so often happens in one of Martin's tracts, we range far and wide through time and geography and, with Martin's help, meet London's New River Company formed in 1609-13 by Sir Hugh Myddelton (1565-1613), who guided the waters of the New River into a reservoir near Islington Green. The New River Company held exclusive London water rights throughout most of the seventeenth century.*

*Sir Hugh, unfortunately, ruined himself financially in the enterprise, and called on James I for assistance. The King took half the 72 shares for himself and sold the rest to "adventurers." To Sir Hugh, an annuity of 100 pounds was awarded.*

*Within 25 years, each adventurer's share was worth four figures. By the year 1700, a single share paid around 200 pounds a year, and by 1766 sold for 8,000 pounds. In 1873, a quarter-share was sold for 12,240 pounds; in 1891, a 1/20th share sold for 700 pounds, and in 1893 a single share sold for 94,400 pounds, at a time when the British pound had remained virtually unchanged in purchasing power for the better part of a century.*

*In 1904, the operation of the New River Co. was transferred to London's Metropolitan Water Board; the company having been purchased for more than six million pounds, plus contingency rights estimated at some five million pounds. The tract begins:*

Huntington, 1927, July 14, Bastille Day

Editor of Commerce and Finance:
Sir:

In an orchard, on Long Island, in Huntington, I built a house, so small that it is almost imperceptible. My first water bill was so large that I thought it was a statement of the price of the plant and good-will of the Huntington Water-Works Corporation. I sent it back, explaining that I did not wish to buy any water-works and suggesting Dillon, Read & Co., H.L. Doherty and H. Hobart Porter as possible purchasers.[1] Subsequent bills have not lessened my

---

1. Dillon, Read & Co. New York City investment banking house, one of the earliest in the U.S., formed in 1921 when Clarence Dillon (1882-1979), an employee of William A. Read & Co., went into partnership with the firm.

Henry Latham Doherty (1870-1939), industrialist, president Cities Service Co., formed for the reorganization, financing, and management of public utilities companies; at zenith of his business career director of some 100 corporations.

Henry Hobart Porter (1865-1947), public utilities official, director of numerous transit and utilities corporations. Member, with Martin, of both the Century and University Clubs.

astonishment. I paid them, under protest, and said to a lawyer:
"If these pipes ran with champagne, $168 would be too much."
"The water habit", said he, "is insidious. Before you know it, you drink to ruinous c---s. Have you ever seen a picture of the insides of a confirmed water drinker? Horrible. And how about fountains? The Versailles fountains cost so much that the Parisians run them only once a week. And how about lawns? The turf at Compton Wynates[2] costs three thousand a year."

"I have no fountains", said I, "And no turf and only four bathrooms. My linen is sent out, to be washed by a Confucian laundry or its Christian competitors. If my house were in New York, my water-bill would be one tenth of $168. Please retain engineering experts and apply for some injunctions and mandamuses.[3] How about a writ of *nemo me impune lacessit?*"[4]

"Protest and revolt", said the lawyer, "never did anybody any good. Boston rebelled against a small tea tax. Quebec paid it, with pride and joy. Result, Boston has no freedom of any kind and Quebec has always been liberty's home. And a lawsuit will do you no good. The courts have a procedure that is not intended to encourage little people cluttering up the big wheels of business with petty contentions. You are old [73]. Before your suit is reached for trial, on our crowded calendars, you will have died and gone to a place where there are no water-works, but plenty of directors of water-works companies. Tell your troubles there, to them. And be careful, in this world, not to complain, or the water-works will have the law on you, for slander."

Therefore, Mr. Editor, I make no complaint. But I ask you to invite your Huntington readers to join me in a sweep-stakes. On Long Island we have many horse-races, which is absurd, because horses are slow and no longer used for carrying letters and passengers. Nobody has any but an artificial or traditional interest in the competitive exhibition, by obsolete animals, of their various degrees of sluggishness. But every man is keenly interested in the speed of his water-meter. Mine seems to have the speed of light,

---

2. Tudor seat of the Marquis of Northampton in Warwickshire, England, scarcely changed since its completion in 1520.
3. Writs issued from a high court to an inferior court, corporation, public official, etc., commanding some specified act.
4. "No one provokes me with impunity." Motto of, among others, the order of St. Andrew in Scotland, but not a legal term.

THE DUTY OF REBELLION    25

which, Einstein says, is the greatest of possible speeds. Einstein says, also, that light is not straight. But let that pass. It is irrelevant. I propose that I and 29 other Huntington house-holders deposit with the Suffolk Bulletin[5] $200 each. At the end of a year, the Bulletin will hire an engineer to test our water-meters. From the $6,000, the Bulletin will take $1,000 for expenses. The residue will be divided among the three of us that have the swiftest meters, in proportion to the speed of our meters.

I wrote to the Public Service Commission, because $168 a year is too much for water for two old women and their few dependents. It answered:

"The Public Service Commission has no jurisdiction over water companies. The best procedure to follow in obtaining the services of an engineer and the testing of your meter, would be to write to the company who manufactured the meter."

"That commissioner" said the lawyer, to whom I showed this letter, "is a master of irony. Lafe Gleason, Tom Platt, Dean Swift,[6] could not have spoken more neatly,. He says that, if you are such a chump as to move into a town which is so slack as not to own its own water, no law can help you. Mr. Brisbane[7] and everybody except you seem to know the ancient Chinese story of Confucius and the tigers. Confucius, traveling through a jungle district, was moved to pity by a widow whose father, husband and son, had been killed by tigers. 'Come to Chefoo,[8] said he, 'Where we have no tigers'. 'How about your Chefoo taxes and water rates?' said she. 'Our water rates', began Confucius, 'have been jacked up a bit, to enrich some influential mandarins, but —' 'Say no more', said the widow. 'I stay

5. Independent Republican weekly newspaper, founded 1847, published in Huntington, circulation 4,000 in 1927.
6. Lafayette Blanchard Gleason (1863-1937; Yale '85), lawyer and political leader; head of the permanent staff of the New York Republican headquarters for 31 years; general secretary of seven Republican national conventions. Described by the NCAB as "a veritable encyclopedia on political matters; noted raconteur, trenchant wit." University Club member.
  Thomas Collier Platt (1833-1910; Yale '53), Republican senator from New York 1897-1909. Delegate to every Republican national convention from 1874 on. Reputedly a poor public speaker. His 1910 autobiography, to which Martin presumably alludes, is described by the Dictionary of National Biography as "a curious farrago of fact, fiction, naivete, and denunciation."
  Jonathan Swift (1667-1745), Dean of St. Patrick's, Dublin, and known as the greatest of English satirists.
7. Arthur Brisbane (1864-1936), editorialist for the Hearst syndicate. His columns were said to be read by more people than those of any other living man. Famous for the extent of his reading, universality of his interests, and rapidity of his mental operation.
8. City in Shantung Province, northeast China, on the Pohai River. In Kung-fu-Tse's time called Yentai.

here and take my chances with the tigers'. Your grumble about a water company that buys thousands of meters from a machine company. The Commissioner, with delicious accuracy, writes that your best remedy is to write to one of these companies and ask whether either of them regards itself as in the same class with porch-climbers. To err is human and water-meters, like gas-meters and electric meters, are almost human in their fallibility. But I doubt whether your meter is in error. Water companies do not need any metrical error. They can charge as much as they please; and 'what are you going to do about it?' They have to pile up exorbitant profits so as to show a high value when the impatient populace takes their property by force of eminent domain. That is your remedy. Wait till popular fury boils over, as it did in London. The New River Company was founded, under Charles the Second, to pipe water into London.[9] It became a Golconda.[10] The rate-payers, with unusual speed, became impatient of extortion, and set up city water-works, about the time that the rotund figure of Edward VII became a feature of the British horizon. Not even a water-company can count on the patience of rate payers, for more than two hundred years. I assume that nobody in Huntington desires to sell any more land to confiding newcomers. Are there the usual sign-boards on the rim of the town? I suppose they say: 'Build your home in Huntington. Wheatley may have high hills.[11] We have high water bills. Long Island's fastest-growing water-rates'. Keep on hammering at the water company and you will get some reform. America got decimal coinage, out of our Revolution. The water company may stop charging by the cubic foot and may begin charging by the cubic centimeter. That will make the bills more exact. Terrify the water company by using substitutes. Get your thirty tax-payers together and buy a secondhand tank steamer and import your water from Labrador. The water company or the government or somebody might, perhaps, clap on a thirty-five percent ad valorem tariff,[12] but water is cheap in Labrador. Rouse your townsmen to use mineral water in their baths. Write a tax-payers Marseillaise, a commuters'

---

9. The New River Company was formed in 1609-13, at least a half-century before Martin's date.
10. A city, now deserted, in India, which flourished c. 1500-1700; its diamond trade made it a by-word for wealth.
11. Wheatley is a town in north central Long Island, some ten miles west-southwest of Huntington. While Wheatley may have "high hills," Huntington has Jayne Hill, a favorite haunt of young Walt Whitman, and Long Island's highest at 401.5 ft.
12. A customs tax levied on goods at a rate proportionate to their value.

## THE DUTY OF REBELLION 27

chorus. Allons, enfants de la patrie, On ne boit pas cette eau maudite.[13] No, that will never do. Try this: Allons, enfants de la patrie. None of this over-charged water for me. Hire some poet to lick that into the form of a lyric. The battle of Valmy[14] was won by a song, a dance, and a neat three-word slogan, that asked for three impossibilities. Lead the passionate burghers of Huntington and the petroleuses[15] of Suffolk County to dance the carmagnole around the water-works. Inscribe on their red banners, 'Clean yourself with Clysmic,'[16] and 'Wash not, want not.'"

I have drunk high-priced water in all parts of the world; in Guatemala, where the pipes are dislocated by frequent earthquakes, and in Peking, where a Belgian water company is embarrassed by frequent revolutions, and at the Ausable Club,[17] where icy mountain brooks are curbed for the use of luxurious cottages; but nowhere have I seen water more pure and sparkling than that of the Huntington Company. The meters moreover, of the Huntington company are, without doubt, exact and comply precisely with the law. I am sure that the company never does anything illegal. But the most grievous forms of oppression are those that fall within the law. I intend to be meek and to buy stock in the water company. I am made timid by one of our family traditions, that tell of a mild Jew that lived in West Goshen,[18] in 1491 B.C. I have reason to believe that he was an ancestor of mine, of about one hundred and thirty generations ago. He was called to the door of his mud hut by one of Pharaoh's foremen. The foreman threw open his coat and showed his copper badge of office. "Here is my warrant" said he, "You are assessed $168 worth of work. Or do you prefer a hundred and sixty-eight strokes of the kurbash?" A kurbash is a sharp whip

---

13. A *Marsaillaise* parody, "Arise, children of the fatherland, no one should drink this cursed water."
14. The victory of the Republican Army over the Prussian at Valmy in 1792 halted an invasion threatening the French Revolution. The song: the *Marsaillaise*; the dance: the carmagnole; the slogan: *Liberte, Egalite, Fraternite*.
15. "Petroleuses": Female incendiaries using petroleum; figures of the 1871 Paris commune.
16. The Clysmic Spring Co., suppliers of bottled spring water, located at 251 Fifth Avenue, New York City.
17. Home of the Adirondack Club at the southwest end of Keene Valley in the Adirondacks. Said water propelled Martin over six summits in less than 24 hours! See Section Fourteen — "Martin the Mountaineer."
18. Goshen was the fertile part of Egypt occupied by the Israelites during their bondage, as per Genesis 47: 4-6. The date 1491 B.C. is the date assigned by Bishop Ussher to the Exodus.

of rhinoceros hide. It has been an effective collector of taxes in Egypt for several thousand years. "Go with the man, quietly," said my ancestor's wife, "and work on his silly old pyramid. $168 is nothing." My ancestress was right and Moses, the Bolshevik, was wrong. A discreet Jew said to me, the other day, "All the sorrows of Israel flow from our cardinal error, the Exodus. We should have stayed in Egypt where we eat by the fleshpots' and 'did eat bread to the full'.[19] We should have been polite to Pharaoh and submissive; and we should have used our spare money in squaring the tax collector and in buying stock in irrigation companies."

This hamlet is saved from obscurity by being the birthplace of the man that wrote a poem about the insolence of elected persons. But the elected persons of Huntington are polite and gentle. The insolence that I complain of is that of water-works persons whom nobody elected. Let us ask our elected persons to take over the water-works, if possible, at a price that, I hope, will be unsatisfactory to the water-workers. Any man that is not utterly servile would rather pay two hundred dollars to his town than one hundred to an uncontrolled private monopolist.

*Newell Martin*

## Letters to Molly

February 20, 1935.

Dear Molly:

Thank you for the wipe and your thoughtful letter. I am sorry you have been having so much trouble with your eyes.

Your father will now feel better day by day and younger year by year. He won't like becoming an octogenarian. Being an octogenarian is enough to make anybody sick.

---

19. The quotation is from Exodus 16:3, where the Israelites complain against Moses and Aaron in the wilderness.

# THE DUTY OF REBELLION 29

Hilda Stowe has asked me to send money to one of her charities. As you go thro life, whenever you are out of money some rich man will ask you to give alms to one of his dependants. It is a policy to give, in such cases, and to say that you like it.

I am sending you Punch, page 650.[1] Don't return it. To Hell with the Pope.

Affectionately,

*Newell Martin*

&a &a &a

---

1. What he sent was "The Word War" from *Punch* magazine (December 12, 1934) by Alan Patrick Herbert (1890-1971). In this essay, Herbert calls on his readers to go to war with him over words which are "piratical, ruffianly, masked, horrible words." His initial skirmish is over the phrase "to sabotage the peace issue," and from there the fight accelerates over "liquidate," "reaction," "reactionary," and "sophistication."

Herbert had a degree in jurisprudence from Oxford, but never practiced law; served with distinction in the royal Naval Division in WWI; joined the staff of *Punch* in 1924, having been writing for it since 1910; and was a Member of Parliament from 1935-1950. Published more than 50 books. Newell Martin, in a letter to Myra, Dec. 25, 1938, states that "there is no statesman that is more agreeable than A.P. Herbert in *Punch*."

30    THE DUTY OF REBELLION

*His April 18, 1936 letter to Molly, and others, had the following note at the top of the page:*

Before reading it, you may throw away this copy of a letter which has been sent to Mr. Stokes.[2]

Huntington, L.I., N.Y.
April 18, 1936.

To:
Miss Molly Meyer
Major General Robert Alexander
Mrs. Grinnell Martin
Miss Janet Meyer
Miss Margaret D. Whitney[3]

When the Pe Wees meet again and talk about the surprises that skillful card-players can spring upon an incautious visitor, talk to them about the stupendous surprises that will break upon all of us, in 1946, reported to us from the 200 inch glass of the new California telescope.[4] For another surprise, let them read two pages, 471 and 472, if they have leisure for such continuous studies, in the *Fortnightly* for April, 1936. Then they will learn that in February, 1936, 4 Shakespeare plays, *Othello, Twelfth Night, Lear, and Romeo and Juliet*, were running, in the theatres of Moscow.[5] Never before, in London, Chicago, New York, Berlin or Peking, or in any city on

---

2. Frederick A. Stokes (1857-1939; Yale '79), publisher. Briefly studied law, then entered Dodd, Mead & Co. Subsequently formed his own firm (Frederick A. Stokes), publishing, among others, the works of H.G. Wells, Stephen Crane, Robert E. Peary, and Maria Montessori. Author of *College Tramps* and editor of *The Poems of Sir John Suckling*. See Section Ten — "A 1922 Christmas Card."
3. Margaret D. Whitney (1867-1945), sister of E.B. Whitney. In charge of the music department of the Boston Public Library 1906-1907. For many years an invalid, but reportedly nonetheless retained a great interest in and was a champion of liberal causes. Martin called Miss Whitney his "literary advisor" claiming they had been "writing to each other since 1868" - a bit of a puff, as Miss W was only a year old at that date. See Section Ten — "The Climinole."
4. The Mt. Palomar telescope, proposed and funded in 1928, was currently undergoing construction. It was not completed for another 12 years.
5. *Fortnightly* article by London theater critic Hubert Griffith (1896-1953), titled "Moscow Turns to the Classics." At the same time the Moscow stages were also hosting Sheridan's *The Rivals*, Fletcher's *The Spanish Curate*, Schiller's *Don Carlos*, Shaw's *The Devil's Disciple*, Dumas' *La Dame aux Camellias*, and adaptations of Dickens and Balzac.

Ironically, at the beginning of 1936, the Second Moscow Art Theater — the former theater of Mikhail Chekhov — and the Leningrad Young Workers' Theater were shut down. Griffith's article and Martin's letter actually coincided with the end of the enormous variety and innovativeness of the 20th century Russian stage. The greatest of Russian stage directors, Vsevolod Meyerhold, would die in the camps three or four years later; many others involved in these productions shared his fate under Stalin.

THE DUTY OF REBELLION 31

earth, were 4 Shakespeare plays shown at once. 'One is amazed', says the Englishman who reports all this and who is no Bolshevik — 'One is amazed at the wealth and variety of the Moscow stage.' 'The Moscow stage is easily the first in Europe.'

I came to town this morning for a brief *ante mortem* dissection and diagnosis by W. W. Herrick,[6] whom I recommend to all morituri.[7] On my way home I did lunch at the most agreeable club in the world.[8] There Manuel set before me a jar of French mustard. It bore this label:

Dessaux Fils<br>
Orleans<br>
Maison fondee en 1789.[9]

1789. What a year to choose for launching a new capitalistic industry. Making mustard, when all France was rousing itself to make an end of all churches and dynasties. Founding a mustard mill when the merry Parisians, addicted 'to light wines and the dance' were pulling down the Bastille. Consider the calm courage of the Dessaux family, making mustard, *per tot naufragia*.[10] Since they began selling mustard: Two Napoleonic dynasties have risen and fallen.

The Tsing dynasty[11]<br>
The Hapsburg dynasty[12]<br>
The Hohenzollern dynasty[13]<br>
The Bourbons of Spain[14]<br>
The Bourbons of Naples[15]<br>
and the Romanoff dynasty[16]

---

6. William Worthington Herrick (1897-1945; Yale '02, M.D. Columbia '05; Number one in his class). Lifelong connection with the Columbia College of Physicians and Surgeons, in addition to his private practice. Century Association member.
7. Those about to die.
8. Presumably the Century.
9. Still being manufactured in Orleans. Business founded in 1789.
10. Through so many shipwrecks.
11. The Tsing (Chin or Tsin) ruled China 262-420. Martin certainly meant the Ch'ing or Manchu dynasty which ruled 1644-1912.
12. Dynastic rulers of Austria and numerous Austria-held territories, 1282-1918.
13. Dynastic rulers of Prussia c.1200-1918; rulers of Germany 1871-1918.
14. The French house of Bourbon commenced its rule of Spain with the accession of Philip V to the Spanish throne in 1700; with some short interruptions it lasted, at least in name, until the founding of the Spanish Republic in 1931.
15. The former kingdom of Naples occupied the Italian peninsula south of the papal states; it was ruled by a branch of the Spanish Bourbons beginning 1759, and ending with Italian unification in 1861.
16. Ruling dynasty of Russia 1613-1917.

have been abolished, and Riza Shah Pehlevi[17] and Ataturk Kemal[18] have set themselves in high places. (I am delighted to say, also, that, in a few months I can add to our list of fallen monarchs, that peculiarly disgusting lord of slave-dealers, Haile Selassie.[19] Nothing vexes me so much as American applause for Selassie.)

It would not be entirely inaccurate to add to our list of great empires that have broken down, the United States; because,

(A) The United States is the richest empire that ever existed, and

(B) The United States has allowed 20 million of its people to become destitute.

True, our government is not allowing these destitute people to starve. But, if a man is destitute, he does not really desire charity. He would rather have chloroform. Reading that mustard jar, I lost all appetite.

*Kewell Martin*

ta ta ta

---

17. (1878-1944), absolutist Shah of Iran 1925-1941, founding a dynasty after heading a coup d'etat.

18. (1881-1938), founder and first president of the Republic of Turkey, 1923-1938.

19. (1891-1975). Crowned Emperor of Ethiopia in 1930, Selassie was actually deposed by the invading Italians within a month of Martin's writing, but would return in 1941 to rule nearly until his death. Menelik II (1844-1913) had made Ethiopia an empire through a policy of conquest and depredation, and Selassie merely continued his predecessor's methods: "The pagan peoples of the south and west were treated with wanton brutality unequaled even in the Belgian Congo. Some areas were depopulated by slavers; in others Abyssinian garrisons were permanently quartered on the people, whose duty it was to support them and their descendants.... Justice, when executed at all, was accompanied by torture and mutilation in a degree known nowhere else in the world; the central government was precarious and only rendered effective by repeated resort to armed force; disease was rampant." Evelyn Waugh, *Waugh in Abyssinia* (New York: Longmans, 1936), pp. 24 & 32.

# TWO

# WETS AND DRYS

The Yale Commencement . . . . . . . . 34

Draft Not Used . . . . . . . . . . . . . . 54

Wine and Women . . . . . . . . . . . . . 56

Petition to Bannard . . . . . . . . . . . 59

Coolidge and the Bible . . . . . . . . . 64

Tests for Leprosy . . . . . . . . . . . . . 80

Letter to R. R. Bowker . . . . . . . . . . 89

Aqueducts Are Unlawful . . . . . . . . 91

On Drinking Alone By Moonlight . . . 94

## The Yale Commencement
[1925]

*Obituary, Newell Martin, November 15, 1941,* The New York Times:

Mr. Martin...attracted attention in 1925 when he wrote a letter to *The New York Times* declaring that he and some of his classmates planned to celebrate their semi-centennial commencement anniversary that year at Montreal instead of New Haven because the Yale authorities objected to wine at the dinner.

*Martin's letter in opposition to prohibition appeared in the May 25, 1925, issue. A response from the then president of Yale, James R. Angell, appeared the following day.*

*In addition, Martin printed three tracts regarding his decision not to attend his 50th reunion in New Haven. The first is dated May 15, 1925, and has a note at the top before the title: "Draft for an open letter. Shall I publish it or burn it?" The second is dated May 17, and states at the top: "Draft. Canceled and altered and not used. See Times, May 25." As is the first one, the pamphlet is headed: "REGRETS".*

*Subsequently Martin printed a third pamphlet, much longer than the others, dated June 12, 1925. We've chosen to reprint, with footnotes, the first half of the May 15, 1925, draft, and the full text, with footnotes, of the June 12, 1925, letter. We reprint, though without footnotes, the two letters which ran in* The New York Times.

### THE YALE COMMENCEMENT

#### An Old Graduate gives His Reasons for Refusing to Attend

Under President Angell, at New Haven, a novelty in deportment has been invented that deserves advertisement. After inviting the graduates, in the usual way, to the commencement dinner, the college has sent out unusual instructions, telling the graduates what will be expected of them in the way of manners. Among the men so invited and so instructed are the survivors of the Yale class of 1875, who are to walk near the head of the commencement procession, in commemoration of the fifty years that have passed since they left New Haven. I am one of the few survivors. None of us will offer any advice out of our vast experience. Aged men should be silent, if possible, occasionally, as to politics, religion, education and science. But old men, if they had not lived in seclusion, should know something of manners. I bow before Dr. Angell and his office; but his is young; and I may bend, from the frosty pinnacle of my great age, to speak to him, with paternal frankness, as to certain matters of ceremony.

I must decline Dr. Angell's invitation because it has been hinted that we old men are not desired beneath the elms. The college secretary has permitted a public statement that the college officers fear that the returning graduates will drink, unlawfully and riotously. An official college paper tells us also that the college authorities wish the visiting graduates to refrain, in New Haven, from any public or private breach of the law. These flattering suggestions have been published in many newspapers. Dr. Angell thus seems to say: "I deplore your coming. I am anxious lest you set a bad example to our young people. I am afraid that you will break a law which I love and respect, and get us in discredit with the police. I am afraid that you will get drunk on my doorstep."

I have no respect for law, merely as law. It is the duty of every citizen to show his contempt, so far as is convenient and seemly, for any laws that seem to him contemptible. But I lay aside that patriotic duty when I am the guest of a man who thinks all laws are sacred; and, I do not drink to excess in public; though I do not share Dr. Angell's horror of wine and those who deem a mild use of wine appropriate to social as well as religious ceremonies. I would have my grandsons study Rabelais, Montaigne, Ben Franklin and Li Tai Po, rather than William Jennings Bryan. Nor do I despair of students who, at times, unbend. They may become lovable conservatives, pillars of state, like Samuel Johnson and Pepys. Samuel Johnson "was a ringleader, in every mutiny against the discipline of his college." When Pepys became the most illustrious son of Magdalen search was made for his college record. The only entry found against his name was that of a fine imposed on him for being "scandalously over-served with drink."

Dr. Angell's deans, secretaries, and proctors seem to have joined the new fanatics, telling us to abstain from thought and wine. Those who make a living out of the new ethics have to say such things; but the officers of a richly endowed university do not need to earn their salaries by intoning the foolish credos of the newly established State religion of the United States. They should be of the school of Socrates, who "heartily enjoyed social pleasure and deemed it unworthy of a man capable of self-control to abstain from innocent gratification through fear of falling into excess."

There is another reason for avoiding Dr. Angell's dinner. Here is an extract from a recent newspaper:
"MEDIUMS OF EMPLOYMENT"
"The mediums of employment thoroughly exemplify the versatility of the Yale students of today. A recapitulation of student employment for the past term shows how students earned part of their tuition. *** Five became detectives, being used by private detective agencies to secure evidence later used against New Haven saloonists who sold liquor."

[Editor's Note: On March 11, 1925, Albert B. Crawford, Director of the University Bureau of Appointments, released figures on student employment which included five students who earned $11 each as detectives (twelve earned $6.50 each as butlers).]

Spies and detectives are all very well in their place. Nathan Hale is Yale's chief glory. He lost his life as a war spy, devoted to disobedience of the law and to the overthrow of his Government by violence. But our body politic is now rotten with espionage. If, in 1875, a prophet had unfolded to me the far off future, my joy in seeing electric lights and flying, and other miraculous gifts of the gods, would have been beyond words. But that joy would have been clouded if the prophet had told me that, in 1925, America would have more spies than all the rest of the world; especially, if I had been told that my own college would boast of its achievements as a school of spies.

In Japan they have a list of five or more "vile callings." You may know when invited to a Japanese dinner that no follower of one of these callings will sit at your side. But in New Haven we have no such safeguard. When I sit down at the college dinner, is one of these detectives, perhaps, to sit beside me?

Even a polite invitation is not too tempting when it asks one to banquet on water, in the company of professional prohibiters. Some of us, therefore, intend to celebrate our Yale anniversary in Montreal, with discreet and well-ordered dinners, such as are customary and lawful in civilized societies, and by staying away from New Haven.

NEWELL MARTIN
Huntington, May 25, 1925

ぉ ぉ ぉ

## The Yale Commencement

### President Angell Replies to the Objections of Newell Martin.

To the Editor of *The New York Times*:

You print in your issue of this date a letter from Newell Martin of the Yale Class of 1875, to which I beg leave to reply briefly.

To my knowledge, the university has no commencement dinner and has certainly sent out no written instructions regarding such a dinner. The reunion classes hold their own dinners and conduct them as seems to them best. The President of the university has made no statement regarding these dinners, as Mr. Martin appears to believe, and certainly I am quite unaware of any statement of the university Secretary, such as Mr. Martin refers to.

The only formal action to my knowledge which has been taken about the conduct of these alumni class dinners originated from the alumni themselves. The class reunion committees in 1923 voted to favor "a strict compliance with the law with reference to the liquor question." This action was transmitted to the corporation of the university, which endorsed the action, and requested the reunion class committees to submit the action to individual members of the reunion classes and urge upon them their support and cooperation. Later on the resolution of the class reunion committees was approved by the Alumni Advisory board, an organization which represents the various alumni clubs throughout the country. In March of 1925 the class reunion committees again passed a resolution similar to that of 1923. I think it must be apparent from these statements that the entire initiative in this matter has come from the alumni themselves, to whom Mr. Martin should carry his protest.

I am not able to determine whence Mr. Martin secures his impression about my views as to the use of wine. I certainly do not entertain the opinions which he attributes to me, but this is a personal matter which need not be discussed in your columns.

With this assurance that Mr. Martin will be quite able to conduct himself in any way that seems to him good and with the knowledge that the control of his class dinner is entirely in the hands of his classmates, we shall all hope to see him here at commencement, where he will be most welcome.

JAMES R. ANGELL
Yale University, New Haven, May 25, 1925.

ﺎ ﺎ ﺎ

On May 30, The Times *ran a letter supporting prohibition from a Roger B. Hull of Pelham Manor, N.Y.*

Smart and satirical communications from a Yale graduate of fifty years standing, about Yale prohibition and law enforcement are undoubtedly entertaining. But there are those of us — also Yale graduates — who feel that such a letter as that of Newell Martin is in decidedly bad taste, to say the least.

If a graduate of the class of 1875 prefers, as Mr. Martin frankly says he does, to celebrate his fiftieth anniversary in Montreal with a 'discreet and well ordered dinner,' that is his business....

More power to this movement to make commencement reunions at New Haven and in other college towns more nearly what they might become with the loyal and whole-hearted support of a clean-thinking, law-abiding body of alumni who go back to their college for pleasures and memories that cannot be found in Canadian cafes.

*On June 11, 1925, E. S. Martin (no relation), editorializing in "Life," wrote:*

Yale might well confer a degree of some sort on Newell Martin, who wrote a letter to *The Times* assailing President Angell and the Yale authorities for their somewhat inhospitable concern that graduates returning to commencement should be scrupulous in their observation of the Volstead act. Dr.[sic] Martin's letter was so penetrating and so amusing that it brought out instantly an admirable reply from President Angell denying that either he or the authorities of Yale were responsible for the notice given to graduates to go scrupulously dry at commencement, but that the admonition derived altogether from the Yale Alumni Association. Neither did Dr. Angell submit to Dr. Martin's imputation that he was himself a Volsteader by conviction and opposed to the use of wine. "I certainly do not entertain the opinion which he attributes to me," said Yale's president, and went on to advise Dr. Martin to carry his protest to the Alumni, and for himself invited him heartily to come to commencement "where he will be most welcome."

Really the governing boards of the colleges ought to get together to abate the organized alumni, who nowadays surpass the undergraduates in rash exuberance and rank first among the embarrassments with which the responsible college officers have to contend.

See now what Dr. Martin has accomplished by taking his mouth in his hand and stepping in where angels would fear to tread! He denounced the warning that had issued from Yale by the officiousness of its alumni, and drew out President Angell's prompt and comforting letter which leaned visibly in the direction of the recent public declaration of President-Emeritus Hadley that contemporary Prohibition was a "marked infringement of personal liberty...that must be fought on some ground or it will be dangerous in the future." This partial clearing up of the Yale reputation was the more timely since the admission of Dean Inge[1] that in all the three weeks in which he talked in the United States no one had offered him a drink. When one recalls that most of his deliverances were in New Haven, the words of Dr. Angell and Dr. Hadley fall all the gladder on the ear.

Mr. Baldwin,[2] the British premier, says of Trotsky, that he "is slowly and reluctantly discovering what Mr. Sidney Webb[3] discovered two years ago -- the inevitability of gradualness."

Slowly and reluctantly our prohibitionists are

---
1. William Randolph Inge (1860-1954), dean of St. Paul's 1911-1934, known for his writings on a variety of social and political issues. Inge had visited the U.S. the preceding April. On the 20th he gave a lecture, introduced by President Angell, in the Lyman Beecher course at Yale as a feature of the 16th convocation of the Yale Divinity School. In an interview just previous, Inge spoke favorably of an editorial in the *Yale Daily News* calling for legitimation of light wines and beers, and also alluded in the lecture itself to "the citizens of today, surrounded by the products of the printing press, which world residents of former centuries lacked, sitting in an arm chair, feet on the fender, fortified by such creature comforts as the country allows." In the then current clerical view, these words made Inge a wet.
2. Stanley Baldwin (1867-1947), British conservative party leader, three times prime minister.
3. Fabian social reformer and author Sidney Webb (1859-1947) was elected to the House of Commons in 1922; in 1924, in the first Labour government, he was sworn of the Privy Council as president of the Board of Trade. After the general election of Oct., 1924, he told his constituents he did not intent to stand again.

making the same discovery.

*A postscript in Martin's original (May 17, 1925) pamphlet deserves inclusion here.*

If I am wrong in thinking Yale men to blame for seeking to enter one of the most prevalent and lucrative of American occupations, you should set our spy department in the forefront of our Commencement parade. Let each spy wear a badge of honor, the design to be an open keyhole and a watchful eye.

In the Yale anthem, we affirm chorally that our work and sports are "For God, for Country, and for Yale."

Harvard men scoff at this stirring line. They say it is bathos, anti-climax. We can correct that error. Put the spy group in front of the cheering section and let them set forth their college aims, in an order of rising value, in a swelling crescendo. Let them sing, "For God, for Dryness and for Kale."

Respectfully,
Newell Martin

&.   &.   &.

Draft for an open letter. Shall I publish it or burn it?[4]

## REGRETS

James Rowland Angell, LL.D.,[5]
President of Yale.

My dear Doctor Angell:
You have invited the survivors of the Yale Class of 1875 to march, in June, near the head of the Commencement procession. Fifty swift years have passed since they first marched, in a procession of graduates. I am one of those survivors.[6] To realize the solemnity, for me, of this occasion, contemplate the abyss of time that lies between the graduates of 1925 and their reunion in 1975.

---

4. Statement placed on top of first page of a six-page pamphlet dated May 15, 1925.
5. Son of James Burrill Angell (1892-1916), who was president of the Universities of Vermont and Michigan. James Rowland Angell (1869-1949) taught psychology at the University of Chicago 1894-1920, and was there dean 1911-1918 and acting president 1918-1919. President of Yale 1921-1937; and subsequently educational counsellor to NBC (National Broadcasting Corporation).

Perhaps, in 1975, no college will be here, or anywhere; or our colleges may be scattered about on mountain tops and visited by flying students; or there may be such changes in manners that the 1925 men will take no pleasure in the world of 1975.

We, of 1875, are few, but, with all our modesty, we have a sense of our importance and dignity. We are by no means nobodies. We come back to you with wealth and wisdom and white heads. We have received fortunes for our medical advice, mostly erroneous and now obsolete; and fortunes for having followed a system of law that is still more obsolete. The humblest of us is a doctor of divinity who has won international fame by preaching obvious error to spell-bound multitudes, in all parts of the world.[7] One of us, for whom I have an especial affection, has been president of the Comstock society;[8] a society that leads in the debasement of our literature. We do not presume, however, on our splendor. We have little advice to offer. Aged men should be silent, if possible, occasionally, on politics, religion and science. But old men, if they have not lived in vain, should be experts in manners.

I bow before the dignity of your great office. But you are young; and I may bend from the frosty pinnacle of my old age to

---

6. Martin was secretary for the class of 1875 from 1900 to 1915, and also served on the reunion committees. His wife's brother, Frank Grinnell, was in the same Yale class as Martin, and first of the class to die, having been struck in the base of the neck by a baseball September 7, 1875, dying on September 11. The last was a Eugene Bouton, who died in 1951 a few weeks past his 100th birthday.

7. Reuben Archer Torrey (1856-1928; Yale'75; B.D. Yale '78 ). Studied at Leipzig and Erlangen in Germany. Pastorates in Ohio and Minnesota; became superintendent of Chicago's Moody Bible Institute upon its foundation in 1889, later superintendent of the Chicago Evangelization society. In 1901 the Bible Institute sent him on a trip around the world, during which it is estimated he preached to more than 15 million persons, converting some 30,000. On a tour of Great Britain in 1903-1905 he held meetings in all the principal English and Scottish cities, including one of five months' duration at the Royal Albert Hall during which he converted 17,000. From 1912-1924 was dean of the Bible Institute at Los Angeles, and from 1915-1924 pastor of the Church of the Open Door in that city. Author numerous books, among them: *The Wondrous Joy of Soul-Winning* (1914); *How To Be Saved and How To Be Lost* (1923); *Why God Used D.L. Moody* (1923); and *Death Defeated and Defied* (1923).

8. Anson Phelps Atterbury (1854-1931). Entered Yale 1871, left in '73-'74, returned '75-'76 but did not graduate. Studied at Andover Theological Seminary 1876-1878, Union Theological Seminary 1879; Ph. D. New York University 1893. Entered the Presbyterian ministry in 1880; pastor of the park Presbyterian Church in New York City 1879-1918. President of the Greater New York Federation of Churches and of the Clergy Club; director of Union Theological Seminary. Century Association member. And president − in a largely titular position − of the NYSSV (New York Society for the Suppression of Vice) from 1919−death. He was succeeded by William A. Parsons, Yale class of '80; Parsons had been treasurer since 1912. [Audette states that to locate the Rev. Mr. Atterbury he scoured the *Times* index for 1910-1925, after comparing 98 names in the class of '75 in vain with both *Who Was Who* and the *National Cyclopedia of Biography*.]

whisper to you with paternal frankness as to certain matters of ceremony.

My granddaughters are already preparing for me a dinner in honor of my golden wedding. It is to be at Montreal. There we shall eat just enough to justify a rapturous but discreet indulgence in vintage wines. If those charming girls, however, were to write to me, telling me how to behave at their banquet, self respect would compel me to send a mournful refusal to their invitation.

Likewise, with deep regret, I must decline your kind invitation. It has been hinted that we old men are not really desired beneath the elms. The secretary of your college has permitted a statement to be published to this effect: "We look with anxiety on the return of the alumni; we fear that some of them will drink and make scandals that will embarrass us." One of your spokesmen, the Yale Alumni Weekly, has published a request from the college authorities, that the visiting graduates, while in New Haven, refrain from any public or private breach of the law. These unflattering suggestions have been reprinted in newspapers throughout the land. You, our honored friend, have invited us to our old home, of which you are the custodian, but you have seen fit thus to couple your invitation with words that carry no welcome. You seem to say: "I deplore your coming. I am anxious lest you set a bad example to our young people. I am afraid that you will break the law which I love and respect, and get us in discredit with the police. I am afraid that you will get drunk on my doorstep."

This unusual form of invitation issues from a place that is a school of manners as well as morals. This confirms my fear that good manners vanished from America when America's social life died a violent death. You and your associates used to be kindly and polite. This lapse from courtesy must be owing to the fact that, in the present deplorable state of our country, even educated men lose their sense of balance, deportment and decorum.

I have no respect for law, merely as law. It is the duty of every citizen to show his contempt, so far as is convenient and seemly, for the laws referred to in your messages. But it is not my custom to indulge in unlawful practices when invited to a friend's house or college or hotel and I do not drink to excess in public.

Your horror of wine and of those who deem a mild use of wine appropriate to social as well as religious ceremonies seems morbid. I would have my grandsons study Rabelais,[9] Montaigne,[10] Ben Franklin[11] and Li Tai Po,[12] rather than William Jennings Bryan. Nor do I despair of students who, at times, unbend. They may become lovable conservatives, pillars of state, like Samuel Johnson and Pepys. Samuel Johnson "was a ringleader", "in every mutiny against the discipline of his college"[13]. When Pepys became the most illustrious son of Magdalen search was made for his college record. The only entry found against his name was that of a fine imposed on him for being "scandalously over-served with drink."[14]

You have advertised that it is your policy to inculcate total abstinence and obedience to a despicable law. Whitney,[15] Gibbs,[16] Sumner,[17] used to teach us philosophy and civil liberty. If you spent more time on their books and less with the New Fanatics you would not consent to issue orders that corrupt the mind of youth. Our old teachers were of the school of Socrates, who heartily enjoyed social pleasure and deemed it unworthy of a man capable of self control to abstain from innocent gratification through fear of falling into excess.

≈ ≈ ≈

9. The Prologue to Rabelais' *Gargantua* begins, "Beuveurs tres illustres..."
10. Montaigne, in his essay "De l'Yvrongnerie" (II,2), recommends wine in moderation.
11. Franklin's *Autobiography* lists as the first of his "Thirteen Rules for Arriving at Moral Perfection," "Eat not to dullness; drink not to elevation."
12. Li Tai Po (722-846 A.D.). Classical Tang dynasty poet sometimes compared to Anacreon, perhaps best known in the West as the author of several of the texts set in German translation by Mahler in Das Lied von der Erde (e.g., #5, "the Drunkard in Springtime"). Newell Martin's father, W.A.P. Martin translated the works of Po into English. See "On Drinking Alone By Moonlight."

13. Boswell, in his *Life of Johnson*, includes among the material for 1729 a letter from the Bishop of Dromore stating, "The pleasure [Johnson] took in vexing the tutors and fellows has often been mentioned....I have heard from some of his contemporaries that he was generally seen lounging at the [Pembroke] college gate, with a circle of young students round him, whom he was entertaining with wit, and keeping from their studies, if not spiriting them up to rebellion against the College discipline, which in his maturer years he so much extolled."
14. The entry in the Registrar's book of Magdalen College, October 21, 1653, is not the College's only record of Pepys, but is the only record of his having been in disgrace.
15. William Dwight Whitney (1827-1894), philologist, professor of Sanskrit, head of the Department of Modern Languages at Yale's Sheffield Scientific School.
16. Josiah Willard Gibbs (1839-1903; Yale '58), professor of mathematical physics, most famous for achievements in the field of thermodynamics.
17. William Graham Sumner (1840-1910; Yale '63), professor of sociology and economics, exponent of social Darwinism and of the view, expounded in his *Folkways*, that cultural differences are normatively decisive.

June 12, 1925

JAMES ROWLAND ANGELL, LL.D.
President of Yale

My dear Doctor Angell

"There is a vanity which is done upon the earth; that there be just men unto whom it happeneth according to the work of the wicked. Then I commended mirth because a man hath no better thing under the sun, than to eat and to drink and to be merry: for that shall abide with him of his labor all the days of his life which God hath given him under the sun." Ecclesiastes 8: 14, 15.

In contempt of the Holy Writ and under a pretense of hygenic reform, dryness has been foisted on us; and it has become the foundation of a new false religion, which has been made our established State religion. Well-meaning fanatics, of various religions have devoted themselves to it, hushing their sectarian hatreds so far as they interfere with dryness. They have, thus, gained political dominance. In this, they are backed by an incongruous but irresistible alliance of the strongest powers at the top of our industry with the most corrupt powers at the bottom of our society. In this, they are buttressed by an impregnable constitutional amendment and are allied with the Ku Klux,[18] a religious and political secret society with a long record of successful and brutal conquest, that has never allowed any clause of the constitution or any law to stand between it and victory. In this, they exercise a malign influence and no small degree of control over the federal government. In this, they use land forces and navies, and the police and the national machinery of both the great parties.

The separation of church and state, one of the precious safeguards of freedom, has been wiped out. That is the chief evil of the dry laws. To throw the intruding fanatics out of these new intrenchments will take a few centuries of civil war.

The state is now wedded to a religion of sacred Taboo; the sort of religion that springs up and flourishes in rude and superstitious societies. By grace of Taboos and their enforcement, theocrats now have a strangle hold on our government and politics. The smallest politician, beginning in a rural primary, must show a creed and

---

18. The Ku Klux Klan's program did include smashing stills and beating or otherwise harassing distillers and bootleggers.

conduct that will please their inquisitors. We have gone back to the days of Cotton Mather, back to Philip and Mary.[19] A theocracy is hateful. It is not less hateful when my own church shares in its power and in its profits. The issues of our contest with these usurpers are graver than those of our former civil war. This is a matter of fighting for our own freedom, not that of other men. While the contest goes on, we must be content to forego many forms of social enjoyment, in the States, and, to a great degree, rational conversation on interesting subjects. Our talk must be of the great taboo. Negligence brought us to this pass. My acquaintances, quite properly, used to complain of being bored when I reminded them that eternal vigilance is the price of not getting the whole place messed up. I spoke about this fearlessly, in private, to not less than eight persons, while the black plague of the 18th Amendment was spreading; and they answered that the rich men interested would take care of the crisis; and I merely got myself disliked.

I speak with all due love and respect of clergymen and churches. Such of them as are in this evil work stray from their duty. It is as if I found my grandson's favorite Sunday-school teacher butting in on the management of my house and my shop.

I mourned over the policy of the college in dealing too gently with the powers of darkness and my sorrow was sharpened by three newspaper items. I enclose copies of them. I mislaid two of those items while I was engaged in a work of moral uplift among the Volstead-lovers and Darwin-haters of Carolina. That caused my delay in answering your kind letter. For that delay I apologize, humbly.

I am delighted with E[dward]. S[anford]. Martin's editorial in "Life" of June 11 and am convinced that it, taken in connection with your letter, shows that there is no need of my arguing about the origin of my distressed feelings.

I add, however, a few words on that point, merely because you asked two questions; one, in regard to our "instructions", and the other, in regard to the Secretary.

In your oration of May 30, 1923, you said: "I count as far more insidious than any radical assault yet delivered the wide and rapidly spreading virus of disrespect for law.

["]When the individual citizen begins to decide for himself what laws he will obey and what disregard, the beginning of the end

---

19. Philip II of Spain (1527-1598) and his wife, Mary I of England (1516-1558), noted for religious persecution.

of free constitutional government is at hand. * * * If it is the 18th Amendment which invites disrespect today, it may be the statutes * * * concerned with homicide the next day."

On June 18, 1923, the Alumni Advisory Board made this declaration: "President Angell, in his Memorial Day Address, declared the disregard of law to be our greatest national menace. He referred specifically to the disregard of the 18th Amendment. * * * The Yale Alumni Advisory Board[20] supports President Angell and the corporation in urging strict observance of the law."

I do not know how that board is chosen or what are its powers or whether it has ever uttered an expression of opinion that the Corporation does not desire. It is in close touch with the Corporation. "The Yale Corporation has on its regular docket every month a specific place for reports from the Alumni Advisory board." (Dr. Angell, in *Yale Alumni Weekly*, April 18, 1924, page 877.)

The *Yale Alumni Weekly*, to which you refer me, shows that the Corporation, by resolution, set up a Committee, to consist, each year, of "representatives of Reunion Committees," with curiously vague duties. What the Corporation intended those duties to be is shown by the Corporation's resolutions approving the resolutions and receiving the reports of that peculiar annual committee. The acts of the Corporation made this otherwise utterly unauthorized committee its Major Domo, its Master of Ceremonies, — for obvious reasons I do not say, its Butler,[21] — for the advising of reunionists.

As the Corporation, when it created this committee of representatives of reunion committees of reunion classes, neglected to give it any short title, and as its most notable activity has been the advising of Volstead obedience, I shall, for my own convenience, refer to it hereafter as the Scape-goat Committee. Probably one of the members of the committee is a member of my class. He has no authority to speak for me on that committee. My class, five years or ten years ago, appointed a man to prepare a dinner in 1925, and

---

20. "In 1904 Secretary [Anson Phelps] Stokes suggested that an Alumni Advisory Board made up of men elected by the various Yale clubs scattered around the country would help to bring into Yale a wider viewpoint than could be encompassed by the small and necessarily eastern-oriented [Yale] Corporation. Since that body was meeting with increasing frequency, it was impossible for men from far away to be members of it....The board was officially authorized by the Corporation in February, 1906. It was intended to 'meet the desire of Yale graduates in different parts of the country for representation on the councils of the University.' Unfortunately, like so many groups at Yale, it tended to be dominated by men from the college, for they were most active in the local Yale clubs." Brooks Mather Kelley, *Yale, A History* (New Haven: Yale University Press, 1974), pp. 325-326.

21. Allusion to Nicholas Murray Butler (1862-1947); president of Columbia University 1902-1945.

to engage rooms, and tickets for a reunion. He has performed these duties with rare generosity. But I am quite sure he was given no authority to express any opinions for us as to the Volstead Law. Anything of that sort that he may have done is quite ultra vires,[22] as to us. He might just as well assume to speak for us on the dogma of the virgin birth. The member of our class who is on that Committee certainly had no authority from me to belong to that Committee or to vote, as my representative, on Volsteadism, with men that I did not choose. He has no authority to issue declarations or advice as my representative on any matter that is involved in religious, moral and political dispute.

He is made a member of that Committee by act of the corporation and when he and his associates on that Committee speak as a committee they speak for the corporation. That Committee is, in this matter, one of the College agencies.

The College, forgetting that it created that Committee, now desires the public to think that the Committee's messages are the declarations of the College's guests and that the College, in this, is a mere spectator. Your letters, of May 25 are of great value as showing that the College takes a new view, but, in justice to me, it will be observed that, before May 25, there was noting to dissociate the College from the out-givings of the Committee and the *Yale Alumni Weekly*. Before May 25, 1925, there was no disclaimer by the College except the "editorial note" in the Weekly of May 22, to which you refer me. If that is the voice of the college, then the editorial in the *Weekly* of April 10 is the voice of the College, and the instructions given in that editorial are instructions from the College. And, if, on the other hand, the "Editorial Note", of May 22 is not the voice of the College, then the College never said anything, before May 25, to dissociate itself from the various instructions that emanated from the Committees, indorsed [sic] by the Corporation.

The hand of the Committee may look like the hand of Esau, but the voice is the voice of Jacob.[23] The bluff and blunt old wine-bibbers of my day would have thought it inexpedient for a great college to hide behind a small committee.

In this connection, the words of Mr. W.E.S. Griswold, Vice-Chairman of your Alumni Advisory Board, are instructive.[24]

22. Legal terminology for an act beyond the agent's power or competence.
23. The words of the blind Isaac, deceived by Jacob into giving him, instead of Esau the first-born, his blessing (Genesis 27:22).
24. William Edward Schenck Griswold (1877-1964; Yale '99), New York City lawyer, subsequently businessman. Chairman of the Yale University Alumni Fund 1922-1924.

Last year, speaking in Battell Chapel, he named two reunion classes of graduates and spoke of them thus: "If, by a gentle politeness, one is allowed to expurgate from the reunion list the ordinarily riotous * * * gatherings of the "X and Y" classes, they are not represented on this program; nor are they, perhaps through an instinctive and wholly undeserved wisdom of their own, represented largely in this audience."

Mr. Griswold presided this year at a meeting of the Scape-goat Committee which is described in the *Yale Alumni Weekly* (April 10), about this: "The Corporation recently decided that it would be advisable to call a meeting annually hereafter of representatives of the Reunion Classes of a given year, so that matters of common interest * * * could be discussed beforehand and steps taken to carry out changes that would seem to be for the better. * * * Such a meeting was held on * * * March 24, the Vice-Chairman of the Alumni Advisory Board presiding, * * * Minutes: * * * The Chairman, Mr. William E. S. Griswold, explained the action of the Yale corporation in requesting that a meeting of this character be held annually for the purpose of considering matters of common interest to the Reunion Classes. * * * The following action was taken * * * the meeting discussed thoroughly the question of drinking at Class Reunions, and the following resolutions were adopted;

["]Resolved, that this meeting recommend to the reunion Committees of 1925 the strict compliance by the Committees with the laws of the nation and of the State of Connecticut with reference to liquor.

["]Resolved, that the Chairman of the meeting be asked to notify all the 1925 Class Reunion Committees of the action with reference to liquor at reunions and ask them to co-operate in carrying out the resolution.

["]It was the sense of the meeting that the foregoing resolutions be published in the *Yale Alumni Weekly*."

The Committee also declared "the sense of" the meeting as to "methods of preventing objectionable public exhibitions by individual members of reunion classes."

The very copy of the *Yale Alumni Weekly* in which these resolutions were sent out to us, by order of the Committee, by editorial, warned the college's guests against "individual opposition on the part of those reunionists who object to being told what to do about the Volstead Act. * * * Obey it. * * *" "Thoughtless graduates, bent on having an old fashioned good time * * * can undo the efforts * * * of the University."

"It should become impossible for any Yale man to return * * * for his reunion and spoil it for others, without losing caste, * * * and being made to realize his mistake afterwards." * * * "It may give a certain type of graduate a 'better' time. But it leaves an aftermath."

The Secretary of the College has a well-earned reputation for talent and tact. But he has been reported to be not without frankness. The Herald-Tribune says that at the Hartford meeting of February 11, 1925, he spoke thus: "'As to morality it was not necessary to talk about it in the old days and it is not now. * * * Returning alumni give us the only problem. The undergraduate is too busy studying to make a fool of himself, but when the graduate returns, that is all he has to do.'"

You caution me, justly, as to accepting newspaper reports. It is quite possible that each and every impression conveyed to me by the sort of words I have quoted is quite wrong; and that not one of these reports that I have quoted from is correct.

The President and the Secretary are under heavy burdens and cannot indeed "catch up" with all erroneous reports; but they could not fail to know that a great many graduates have formed an anxious and disappointed feeling of the sort that I have tried to describe as my own; and the authorities could not fail to know the nature of the reports that created that feeling. One word from the authorities could have dispelled that feeling; and in the absence of that word, the authorities cannot regard that feeling as unjustified.

The authorities permitted these public statements to go uncontradicted and uncorrected.

The College, like a respectable borderland neutral, now finds itself caught, in a civil war, between drys and wets, and exposed to the violence of the bushwhackers from both sides.

It may be a counsel of perfection but it would be a happy solution of a reunion problem is a college officer would speak thus to the reunion graduates:

> The *New York World says: "We have seen the incredible, the absurd, the impossible and the ridiculous actually carried into law."*

And Dr. Nicholas Murray Butler,[25] on June 3, in what must be the most mournful message ever given to an outgoing class, used these words:

> Laws enacted through fanaticism or in crass ignorance, bid fair to make of law-breaking a cardinal virtue. Such laws are killing respect for law. What was merely a Boston Tea Party in 1773 is now a nation-wide revolt against tyranny and statutory folly. Hysterical attempts at lawless and law-breaking enforcement of one particular law only add fuel to the flame.

It would gladden me, if that ideal officer would then say:

> We, the officers of this College, share these views, clearly set forth by men of weight. Nevertheless we must say to the graduates that it is unsafe and uncomfortable to drink wine in New Haven, and that good wine in New Haven is not procurable. There are, however, graduates who would like to dine in the company of such persons as Reverend Clement G. Clarke, of Portland, Oregon,[26] William Burnett Wright, Jr., of Harrisburg,[27] and Mr. Gundelfinger,[28]

---

25. See Footnote 21. In that Columbia commencement address, Butler attacked those who would enforce doctrines for no other reason than their being held by a majority, and the spinelessness of those in positions of power and influence who properly should have been resisting such measures.
26. (1869-1940; Yale '95), Congregational minister, at that time minister of the First Congregational Church, Portland, Oregon. Clarke, having received a letter from the chairman of his class reunion committee that -- in deference to "the wishes of the large, large majority of the class" -- liquor would be served, had written President Angell, Wright, and others in an attempt to prevent such lawbreaking.
27. William Burnett Wright, Jr. (1870-1946; Yale '92), at that time special counsel on law enforcement to Governor Gifford Pinchot of Pennsylvania (President of the Yale Alumni Association of Buffalo 1915-1917). On June 6, 1925, Wright had given the press copies of a letter he himself had written Angell (after hearing from Clarke) charging that the college's neutral policy on this issue implicated it in "a deliberate conspiracy...to violate the fundamental law of our country." (See excerpt from *The New York Times* of June 7, 1925, following the close of Martin's pamphlet.)
28. George A. Gundelfinger (?-?; Yale '06, Ph.D. '09). Instructor at Yale's Sheffield Scientific School 1909-1913; taught briefly at the Carnegie Institute of Technology, and then retired to Sewickley, Pennsylvania. In 1915 Gundelfinger published *Ten Years at Yale* (N.Y.: Shakespeare Press), detailing what he saw as the triviality and anti-intellectuality of Yale's undergraduate life, the excessive ease of Yale's academic requirements, the low social standing and salaries of Yale instructors (i.e., as compared to professors), and the looseness of the entire Yale moral fabric. *Ten Years at Yale* concludes, "[The freshmen's] faces are still ruddy with the bloom of youth, and the

of some other place. Graduates who are of that way of thinking will take pleasure in dining in New Haven. Others will surely find better dinners in Montreal.

No graduate could be hurt by a simple statement of fact like that.

There used to be an atmosphere of affection and ease at Chapel and College Streets; now, at the hallowed corner, I quake with thoughts of civil war, of conflicts between private law breakers and official law breakers, with fears of police and detectives and pillories. Some one man in my class might commit some one felony or some one misdemeanor or some on breach of decorum. I fear the whole class would then be denounced by Mr. Griswold by name and number, and excommunicated, with book and bell in Battell Chapel.

I am told that I did wrong in speaking of the student detectives, because the offense was a small one. Those misguided boy-spies were paid only fifty-five pieces of silver.

The *Herald-Tribune* may have been wrong in quoting the secretary. I hope not; for what he is said to have said about us was neat and funny and in some measure, true. Any secretary might well say that any visiting graduate who dines in New Haven is indiscreet; and he might go further, and say that, if any graduate anywhere uses his leisure in trying to induce other colleges to adopt so ardent a love of liberty as prevails at Columbia, then that graduate should have his head examined.

Sincerely, [unsigned]

ᴥ ᴥ ᴥ

---

essence of manhood is as yet unpoisoned within them. Let us trust that their united strength and action shall form a mighty wave to wash away the stains, however black and deep, which former classes have left upon their Alma Mater. Let us pray that God has sent them as an army of ardent and fearless reformers to win the victory in their strenuous and unyielding fight for a new and cleaner Yale." (p. 215)   Gundelfinger subsequently founded New Fraternity publications and a magazine, *Interquadrangular*, both dedicated to proving, in the title of one of his numerous pamphlets, "Why the Bulldog is Losing His Grip." In 1941 he was convicted and served a sentence of a year and a day for sending through the mails a pamphlet judged obscene, "Yale's New Fraternity vs. Roman Catholic Fascism." Gundelfinger ended his intellectual career in 1944 with a short book including all the anti-Gundelfinger remarks which had appeared in Yale periodicals over a stretch of three decades, with the long title, *The Storm of Protest "Which Will Never Come": 30 Years of Yale's "Tragic Silence" In Regard to Her "Amazing" Son "That Fellow Gundelfinger."*

[Editor's note: *Final word is from the June 7, 1925* New York Times, *p.5; quotation (final paragraph) is attributed to William Burnett Wright, Jr. (Yale '92).*]

## CHARGES 'CONSPIRACY'
## FOR DRINK AT YALE

### Graduate Attacks President Angell's Position and Demands Ban on All Liquor at Commencement.

"The time has come in my judgment, for the great majority of Yale men, loyal, law-abiding, and God-fearing, to be recognized. No longer should the feeling of those who flout the law and the Constitution be considered. In behalf of that great body of alumni who believe in God, their country, and in Yale, I appeal to you, as President, to see that action is taken immediately to advise the graduate body that no returning alumnus unwilling to respect the Constitution of his country, will be made welcome by the university authorities; and that they will take positive and effective action to see the law is observed."

ta ta ta

[*Editor's note: We have no authoritative report as to the number of "wets" at the '75's reunion; but we did find the following statement regarding the reunion of Yale's Sheffield Scientific School's Class of '75, held in New Haven on the same date in the Yale Alumni Magazine.*]
"Fifty years of the responsibilities of life is a fair day's work, and the completion of the task should entitle the laborer to a holiday.... We boarded a real man of war for a pleasant ride to the summer home of Dr. Lindsley, who had invited his classmates for their golden anniversary dinner. The exhaustion amongst the boys, due to the tiresome game and the tedious ride into town was plainly evident on their arrival at the shore and prompt measure only, probably saved many of the lives. The class physician pro tem, appreciating the condition, had a prescription immediately compounded, which after one or two doses had a desirable effect, and there were no casualties."

[Editor's note: Martin did not attend his 50th reunion in 1925, but his brother-in-law, George Bird Grinnell '70, did attend his 55th that year.]

## Draft Not Used

*Imagine if you will an off-white sheet of paper 6 3/4" wide and 6" long folded in two forming a tract 3 3/8" wide and 6" long. The words "Draft Not Used" are handled like a title, and flushed to the left margin is the greeting: "Editor of the* New York World."

*We found no evidence that the* New York World *newspaper ever received or used Martin's 400-word "letter." We do, though, know what triggered this pamphlet.*

*Emory G. Buckner (1877-1941), U.S. District Attorney South District of N.Y. for 1925-1927, by appointment of President Coolidge, was made a special assistant attorney-general New York State with the charge to investigate and prosecute city officials 1927-1929.*

*In the spring of 1925, Buckner requested four young lawyers to visit all-night restaurants and dance halls and to attempt to buy liquor. The evidence obtained resulted in the padlocking of fourteen such establishments. This, at the height of prohibition (1920-1933).*

*One of the four lawyers, a Leo Gottlieb, employed in Elihu Root's law firm, had applied in June for membership in the American Bar Association shortly after carrying out Buckner's request. He had Root's backing.*

*But several American Bar Association members served notice that when Gottlieb's application came up for consideration on Oct. 13, they would vigorously oppose it on the grounds of his conduct.*

*Buckner himself defended his actions, pointing out that not one of the fourteen restaurants and dance halls had objected to his methods. Gottlieb was admitted. The vote was not made public, but a spokesman said that the motion for denial was "overwhelmingly lost" (a 20% negative vote would have sufficed for rejection).*

Huntington, October 10, 1925
Telephone, 1484 Huntington

**Draft Not Used.**

Editor of the New York World:

Often some youth employed in the aid of our vigilant police, disguises himself as a man of pleasure and persuades some poor girl to take him to her room, where he arrests her. He does this to earn a living and to enforce a law that has some measure of popular approval and to protect a community that has always frowned on fornication. Nevertheless, to the least fastidious, he seems guilty of a worse offense than that of his victim. Men who have such achievements to their credit are not thought admissible to any society, high or low, anywhere.

Spies play a great part in America, but even here spies have no social status; and provocative agents are, of all spies, those that are held in the deepest contempt.

It has been stated in the papers that, some months ago, several young men, disguising themselves as gentlemen dining out and taking with them one or more women, at the request of Mrs. Emory R. Buckner, tempted waiters in various eating places to break the Volstead Act,[1] and that these young men then became informers; and that it has become known that a candidate for admissions to the city Bar Association is one of these young men.

Our modern newspapers are curiously accurate; but, in this, they must have been misled. It is hard to believe that such an offense could have been committed by any young man whom even an unskilled waiter could mistake for a gentleman; that any member of the bar in good standing would stoop be be a provocative agent; that any reputable lawyer would propose a spy for the Bar Association; and that any Committee on Admissions would favor his candidacy. Your paper, however, seems to say that such skepticism is mistaken, and that on Tuesday, the 13th, the Association will be asked to refrain from blackballing a man who has rendered public services of the sort that I have described.

Forty-five years have passed since I became a member of the Bar Association; and, in that time, new morals and new manners have been brought in fashion by Mr. Wayne B. Wheeler[2] and by Mr. Anderson,[3] lately of the Anti-Saloon League, and by various gentlemen from Nebraska.[4]

---

1. This Act provided the means to enforce the 18th Amendment.
2. (1869-1927), lawyer and prohibitionist. Until 1917, general counsel to the Anti-Saloon League; subsequently its legislative superintendent.
3. William Hamilton Anderson (1874-1959), state superintendent (N.Y.) of the Anti-Saloon League. Convicted of and served a term for forgery in connection with League funds.
4. Possibly a reference to "Pussyfoot" Johnson, "The Good Templar from Nebraska," who served as an agent provocateur for the Anti-Saloon League, and William Jennings Bryan, orator and strong supporter of Prohibition.

Men who cannot give up their love of obsolete manners should resign, and The Bar Association and its library of ethics and the besmirched marble of its stately corridors should be left to the young man who now offers himself as our companion; and to his friends.

Newell Martin

ια    ια    ια

FIFTH LARGE PRINTING

# Wine and Women

## A Proposal for a Twentieth Constitutional Amendment, Prohibiting Women

Dedicated to the Board of Temperance, Prohibition and Public Morals of the Methodist Episcopal Church

TABLE OF CONTENTS

                                                  Page

A. Arguments for wiping out the use of wine necessarily imply that the prohibitor has a contempt of sacred texts . . . . . . . . 2

B. A fundamentally prohibitive mind will balk, however, at no such obstacle . . . . . . 2

C. The public welfare demands new measures of prohibition that are justified by authoritative precedents . . . . . . . . . . . 3

From prehistoric times, wine has been used for social joy, to strengthen the weak, and as a part of our solemn religious ceremonies. Today, in every church, we enter into formal communion with our Lord, by drinking wine, in obedience to his farewell command.

The Lord tells us that the Good Samaritan revived the man who fell among thieves by "pouring wine" into him. (Luke 10:34). Three lines of Scripture are the foundation of Melchizedek's fame. He earned it by being the first of record to open wine for his friends.

"And Melchizedek, King of Salem, brought forth bread and

wine; and he was the priest of the Most High God." (Genesis 14:18).

Wine is distasteful to modern reformers, but it was not distasteful to their Creator.

"In the holy place, shalt thou cause the STRONG WINE to be poured unto the Lord for a drink offering." (Numbers 28:7). "Should I leave my wine, which CHEERETH GOD and man?" (Judges 9:13).

But clear-eyed modern wisdom has swept away the errors of the ignorant writers of the Inspired Canon. God was mistaken in telling us to drink wine and in giving us wine. In his short-sighted, impulsive way, he forgot that he was exhibiting a bad example by ordering us to set up strong wine before him and by telling us that he found it cheering.

Prohibitionists tell us that God now sees his youthful error and has reformed; that he has sown his wild oats and drinks no more. Sounder doctrine than that of the Bible and facts which the Creator, in Bible times, had not yet learned, are set forth by the prohibitionists in the public school physiologies. Because alcohol has been used to excess by men of weak will, we have taken away alcohol from everybody. A wise minority have contrived a law that changes the ancient customs of the majority.

There are few precedents for reforming the habits of a whole people by decree. This novelty, however, will last, and will be the first of a long series.

Prohibitionists have set down tobacco as the next evil that must be extirpated by those who know that grown men should eat and drink only what their dry-nurses think is good for them.

But I know of a much more desirable prohibition that should be the next and that can be supported by every one of the arguments that carried the 18th Amendment.

All association by men with women should be prohibited.

Women, like wine, have their merits, and their uses. Many of us have found them agreeable and improving and essential to social pleasure.

The most ancient writings praise their goodness and their charm.

A vast literature, in many languages, tells of the high delights of the soul that flow from our love of women. But remember Eve, Delilah, Jezebel, the W. C. T. U.,[1] Messalina,[2] Catharine the Great.

---

1. Women's Christian Temperance Union.
2. (c. 22-48), corrupt Roman empress, wife of Claudius I, who was executed after a particularly serious scandal.

The most prevalent of European religions judiciously teaches that women bring more harm than good and that the man whose chief wish is to lead a pure and holy life will abjure women. Even followers of the lofty-minded Sakya Muni[3] have taken this view. Buddhist monasteries teach that the first turn of the path to Heaven is to be found by turning away from women; and our own monasteries show that the practice of the highest virtue requires total abstinence from the society of women. Those who know that social pleasure is the seductive path to hateful vice, those whose watchword is verboten [forbidden], tell you that you will be more contented than ever when you have got used to the strait-jacket. Forswear old-fashioned domestic happiness to gain efficiency and peace of mind. Worldly wise men, who care nothing for virtue, have learned this lesson and bar women from the best clubs, knowing that, for true pleasure, no less than true piety, men should flock by themselves.

Women have been all very well in their place, or as companions, in moderation, of men of strong will and solid sense.

But there are men who cannot be trusted to resist, of their own accord, all feminine temptations.

The sin and sorrow caused by the misuse of wine are infinitely surpassed by those overflowing portions of sin and sorrow that would not exist in this nation, if this nation were without women.

We have tried to get rid of the evils that are traceable to the misconduct of women, by punishing the vicious. That method has failed. As we did with wine, so must we do with women. We must cut out the evil at the root.

The customs of the United States must be modified, with the thoroughness that is needed in a nation of children and morons. Our reform must be so conducted that weak men and silly men and self-indulgent men shall have nothing to misbehave with.

Men must be forbidden to go near bad women, who are worse than whiskey; men must be parted from good women, as they are from Clos de Vougeot;[4] and, above all, men must be barred away from charming women, as they are from vintage wines.

An incidental advantage of this new prohibition will be that it will stimulate domestic affection. A man who now neglects his

---

3. " Wise man of the tribe Sakya," a name for the Buddha.
4. The great vineyard of the Clos de Veugot has the most resounding reputation in Burgundy.

home, will go to it persistently and with a delightful sense of adventure and of resisting tyranny if, by the new law, the possession of his own latchkey is made presumptive evidence of criminal intent and if, under that law, he can visit his own family only surreptitiously and after squaring [bribing] somebody.

It is not necessary to consider, now, such inconveniences as might arise if the world adopted this reform

The 18th Amendment shows that we need not hesitate, from considerations of inconvenience, to abolish, beginning in America, ancient and universal customs.

If, because of the 20th Amendment, population diminishes, a few chaste foreigners can be imported. But there will be no material diminution of population, because the upper classes will continue to behave exactly as before, though at greater expense and with less publicity.

Newell Martin
December, 1923

I wish you all a Sober Christmas and a Totally Abstinent New Year.

ɞ ɞ ɞ

## Petition to Bannard
[October 22, 1926]

Otto T. Bannard, Esq.,[1]
Dear Bannard:

You ask me to vote for Mills[2] and Wadsworth[3] because they

---

1. Otto Tremont Bannard (1854-1929; Yale '76), lawyer and banker, president New York Trust Co., Fellow of the Corporation of Yale, onetime member New York City Board of Education, Republican candidate for mayor of New York in 1909.
2. Ogden Livingstone Mills (1884-1937; Harvard '05, L.L.B. '07), elected to New York Senate 1914 and 1916. New York representative in U.S. Congress 1921-1927, Secretary of U.S. Treasury 1932-1933. Unsuccessful (defeated by some 250,000 votes) Republican candidate for governor of New York against Alfred E. Smith that November – 1926.
3. James Walcott Wadsworth (1877-1937; Yale '98), member of New York State Assembly 1904-1911, speaker of the house 1906-1910. Elected to U.S. Senate 1914-1927; U.S. House of Representatives 1933-1951. Unsuccessful Republican candidate for U. S. Senator from New York against Robert Wagner that November – 1926. Both Mills and Wadsworth temporized if not precisely reversed their previous stands on Prohibition in their 1926 campaigns out of clearly political motives. Mills had actually favored a diminution of Prohibition restraints as early as 1921; Wadsworth had voted for the Volstead Act twice, once to secure passage over President Wilson's veto.

were taught at Harvard and Yale. It may be said for them, also, that they are shrewd, experienced, powerful and ambitious. Above all, they are rich. We like to look at rich men, to talk about them, to talk to them, to vote for them, and to drag their triumphal cars. Any doormat prefers to be trodden on by a polished boot. The most morose of us underdogs wags his tail "at the sight of a concrete specimen of the envied class. Millionaires are haloed and the nearer you come to the centre of power, the brighter shines the halo."[4]

But Wadsworth voted for the Volstead Law and Mills is a leader of the Carrie Nation army. The issue joined between Dry and Wet is graver than any question fought over in our civil war. It is kindred to the issues that, for a few happy years, seemed to be settled by the American and French revolutions. It is the question whether church and state shall be kept separate; whether the Methodist Committee, enthroned in its Washington lobby-palace, shall be permitted to continue to be an un-elected, self-appointed, supremely potent and irremovable part of our government. We are engaged in the early skirmishes of a long war. Bitter, it will become, before peace comes again, with the bitterness of civil war, and ruthless, with the ruthlessness of a religious war. We used to think that we had seen the last of the religious wars and our last civil war. The rich backers of the prohibitionists have changed all that. This war is still fought, on our side, with votes and arguments; but our oppressors have already, with chicane and money, and through our softness and sleepiness, enlisted against us, the armed force of the temporal power. It is for us to awaken to a hatred that is our duty and to be unforgiving to our domestic enemies and to everybody that has betrayed us into their hands.

Ninety years after the hanging of Major Andre[5] your nurse taught you to clench your tiny fist and curse, when you heard the name of Arnold. Even if Arnold's treachery had prospered, America would not have suffered as she suffers now. Englishmen under Lord North[6] were more free than Americans are under Clarence Wilson[7]

---

4. Unable to locate source of quotation.
5. John Andre (1751-1780), British spy in the American Revolution hanged after negotiating with Benedict Arnold for the betrayal of West Point.
6. Frederick North (1732-1792), English statesman, prime minister 1770-1782. His record in office was one of vacillation and complete subservience to the king.
7. Clarence True Wilson (1872-1939), Methodist clergyman; national secretary of the Temperance Society of the Methodist Episcopal Church; general secretary of the Board of Temperance, Prohibition and Public Morals; campaigner for prohibition candidates.

and Wayne Wheeler;[8] and the Church of England is a milder establishment than the Stigginses[9] that hold us in thrall. Here bogus freedom "waves the flag in mockery over slaves." Nevertheless, if B. Arnold were living now he could not persuade us to choose him for our senator.

A politician that betrays us to keep himself in power should not be forgiven even if he has reputation, lineage, education, vast estates, social rank, or any other kind of gilding. In my youth, any man that ever, under any temptation, or from any real or pretended sense of duty, had helped to enforce the Fugitive Slave Law, was forever barred, even from social intercourse, by northern lovers of freedom. In Dublin, Sir Hamar Greenwood,[10] prince of the Black and Tans, could not run for office today, on any pretense of repentance. One should never again vote for a Wadsworth; even if, as he cunningly suggests, the mischief he has done is so complete that no Smiths[11] and Wagners[12] can undo it. One should never again vote for a Wadsworth; even when he ingeniously argues that a vote for him may be interpreted as a vote against the Anti-Saloon League. Wadsworth has betrayed us once, by what he now admits to have been a miscalculation in policy. He will betray us again. Wadsworth, seven years ago, would have had no trouble in deciding that it would be an offense against the Constitution to make Mormonism our State Church or to enact into law the Mohammedan taboo of pork or the Hindoo taboo of beef; and he would have no trouble in deciding that devoting his power to such a taboo would be impolitic, even if the Mormon, or Hindoo or Mohammedan vote were important to him. He knew, just as well, that it was an offense against our institutions, to make into law the new taboo of the new religion, by enacting that wine and beer are sinful. But a great body of organized and consolidated Methodists,

---

8. Wayne B. Wheeler (1869-1927), lawyer and prohibitionist. Until 1917, general counsel to the Anti-Saloon League; subsequently its legislative superintendent.
9. From *The Pickwick Papers* — Stiggins was described as a "prim, red-nosed man, with a long thin countenance, and a semi-rattlesnake sort of eye — rather sharp but decidedly bad."
10. Hamar Greenwood (1878-1948), First Viscount Greenwood. Politician, last chief secretary for Ireland in the British cabinet. Formed the notorious Black and Tans detachment of the Royal Irish Constabulary in an effort to suppress the Irish Republican Army. The Black and Tans' adoption of the IRA's own violent and undisciplined methods defeated the government's object. Sir Hamar was a teetotaler.
11. Alfred E. Smith (1873-1944), governor of New York 1919-1921 and 1923-1929. Consistent opponent of national prohibition; in his second term as governor, secured repeal of the Muller-Gage state prohibition enforcement act.
12. Robert Ferdinand Wagner (1877-1953), U.S. Senator from New York 1927-1949. Consistent and outspoken opponent of prohibition.

Baptists, Presbyterians and Lutherans convinced Wadsworth that they had been welded into a new religious union under devotion to the new fetish, a sacred taboo, and that the fanatics of the new religion formed a compact, relentless, crusading, irresistible block. This persuaded Wadsworth that Volsteadism was, for him, the most politic of politics. I do not care whether he thought it good policy or good morals so to betray civil liberty and so to sell us into slavery to these churches and this new religion. I do not care whether our oppressor has been a crafty hypocrite or a fanatic, when we are asked to give new power to Wadsworth, Mills, Mabel Willebrandt,[13] Kukluxers, Wayne B. Wheeler, the Dry Andersons[14], Lincoln C. Andrews,[15] Emory C. Buckner,[16] or Smedley G. Butler.[17] Harvard and Yale tried to teach Mills and Wadsworth political integrity and a love of civil liberty; but when political temptation came, in its most persuasive form, they threw away their schoolboy ethics and sold us out to a band of fanatics, most of whom are vulgar and all of whom are superstitious.

When new religions, like Mormonism and Volsteadism, are brought into politics, strong hates are engendered. These hates will grow stronger. I ask men like you and Henry Taft[18] to begin to apply hatred and the boycott to men who deserve to be hated. No tortuous apology, no crafty late repentance should deter you. You should blackball and boycott, forever, any man, however "proud his name, boundless his wealth" who has done the bidding of the Methodist Committee for compelling dryness and other forms of pious abstinence. The time will come when men of your training will have no forgiveness for any man or woman who has had anything

---

13. Mabel Walker Willebrandt (1889-1963), lawyer (who drew Martin's wrath more than once), appointed U. S. assistant attorney-general under Harding in 1921, and resigned in 1929. Had jurisdiction over all questions of policy, appeals, and directions to federal attorneys in taxation and prohibition cases.
14. William Hamilton Anderson (1874-1959), New York State superintendent of the Anti-Saloon League. Convicted of and served a term for forgery in connection with League funds.
15. Lincoln Clark Andrews (1867-1950), army officer, retired in 1919, appointed assistant secretary of the Treasury 1925-1927 by Andrew Mellon to undertake reorganization of treasury agencies for the enforcement of prohibition.
16. Emory G. Buckner (1877-1941), U. S. District Attorney South District of New York 1925-1927, by appointment of President Coolidge.
17. Smedley Darlington Butler (1881-1940), known as "the Fighting Quaker." Marine officer who, on leave of absence, became director of public safety in Philadelphia, and in two years plus, won a national reputation for eliminating corruption in law enforcement.
18. Henry Waters Taft (1859-1945; Yale '80), New York City lawyer with a special interest in anti-trust cases. Commissioner of Education in New York City 1896-1900, member of commission on reorganizing New York State government 1925-1926.

to do with passing or enforcing the Volstead Law, and no amicable dealings with such enemies of civilization. You will be as friendly with them as County Cork used to be with informers. Wadsworth and Mills and their allies have made a poor dull thing out of American Society. The remnants of that society should desire revenge. It is for men like you to exert yourselves to diminish the happiness of the powerful reformers that have extirpated [eliminated] cheerfulness.

In a few years a resentful community will ask you to join them in requesting our Wadsworths, Cristmans,[19] Lowmans,[20] Millses, Lusks,[21] to sell their inherited principalities and to move into some state that will applaud their practices.

Melancthon Witherspoon[22]

October 22, 1926

*[The following appeared on the final page of the pamphlet:]*

At lunch I used to drink a pint of Chateau Yon Figeac, St. Emilion.[23] Yesterday, at lunch, I drank a pint of Poland Water. Because of Wadsworth. As I cursed him, silently, I remembered that Ezekiel foretold Poland Water and Mills and Andrews and Buckner, 2500 years ago, in a prophecy that, hitherto, has puzzled commentators:

Thou shalt drink also water, by measure:
Thou shalt drink water by measure and with astonishment.[24]

19. Franklin W. Cristman (?-?), Independent Republican dry candidate for U.S. Senate in 1926; campaigned on the view that Wadsworth's reversal was politically motivated.
20. Seymour Lowman (1868-1940), lawyer, businessman, and politician. Lt. Governor of New York 1925-1926; assistant secretary of the U.S. Treasury 1927-1933.
21. Clayton Riley Lusk (1872-1959), lawyer and politician. Republican member of the New York Senate 1919-1924.
22. Martin signs several pamphlets with the pseudonym "Melancthon Witherspoon." Since the topic of this tract is the Volstead Act — over which Martin was engulfed in melancholy — perhaps the first name is a play on "black bile." Or perhaps he slightly misspells the name of the German Protestant reformer, Phillipp Melanchthon (1497-1560). And adds to that "Witherspoon," from John Witherspoon (1723-1794), signer of the Declaration of Independence who was an American clergyman and educator born in Scotland. In the pamphlets carrying the name "Melancthon Witherspoon," there is always a sadness over some loss of independence.
23. A St. Emilion bordeaux, "one of the better of its class."
24. The break between Ezek. 4:16 and 5:13, has Martin omitting such further penalties as fathers eating their sons, sons eating their fathers, a third part of Jerusalem dying of pestilence, a third by sword, and a third scattered to the winds.

Thus shall my anger be accomplished.
 I will make thee an astonishment unto the nations that are round about thee.
 So will I send upon you evil beasts and they shall bereave thee. (Ezekiel: 4; 11, 16: 5; 13, 14, 15, 17.)

❧ ❧ ❧

# Coolidge and the Bible

*We have located three undated tracts, two of which are titled, "Coolidge and the Bible," and one carrying the title "Cautionary Advice as to the Bible." All three are addressed to Calvin Coolidge, President of the United States (1923-1929). Apparently, all three were written in reaction to a statement about Bible teaching made by Pres. Coolidge the early part of April, 1927. Since some of the text is repeated, we have grouped the three together, but fairly warn the reader that two of the essays take diametrically opposed standpoints, regarding the Bible respectively as exclusive and inclusive.*

Confidential: not to be shown to any respectable person, other than the President.

### COOLIDGE AND THE BIBLE

"We believe in the Scriptures of the Old and New Testaments as verbally inspired by God, and inerrant in the original writings, and that they are of supreme and final authority and life." (Point One, of the Fundamentalists' Creed.)[1]

To the President of the United States:

Sir:
 About the first of April, 1927, writing, in urgent

---

[1]. According to Ernest R. Sandeen in *The Roots of Fundamentalism* (University of Chicago Press, 1970), there was no Fundamentalists' Creed as such, but various collections of five, seven, nine, and fourteen articles of Fundamentalism. All these collections, however, listed the inerrancy of scripture as their first point.

commendation, to an organizer of Bible classes, you said: "It would be difficult to support (the foundations of government and society) if faith in Bible teaching should cease to be practically universal in our country ***. It seems as though a popular familiarity with the Scriptures is not so great at the present time as it has been in the past."[2]

But Thomas Jefferson, one of your heretical predecessors, would ask you to modify this handsome indorsement of the Bible. If his ghost could advise you, he would speak thus: "It was to prevent this sort of thing that we did cut out religion when we put together this nation. Speaking from the chair of the Chief Magistrate you advise reading the Bible. Such official advice must give pain to many of your pious subjects, among whom are three million Jews who dislike the New Testament and many Mohammedan Moros[3] who worship the Koran. Such advice, moreover, may seem imperfect, to four hundred thousand Latter Day Saints, among them Senator Reed Smoot[4] and Senator King,[5] who base their ethics on the Book of Mormon, delivered, through the angel Moroni, to Joe Smith.[6] Many educated men, also in your jurisdiction, think, as I do, that the lessons of the Bible do not make for good morals. I like the story of Elisha and his bears but I do not like to read that God used to delight in the massacre of Philistine babies. It is bad to tell children that the Lord's hero was David, an unscrupulous polygamous bandit. It is bad to teach them self-restraint from an inspired Book of Proverbs, written by a man who kept 300 concubines. Your Bible says, 'Thou shalt not suffer a witch to live.' [Exodus 22:18] I do not know of any other eight words that contain so much bad morals. Sitting in Washington you forget that European Christians have been only a fragment of human society. Plato, Aristotle, Socrates, Seneca, Confucius, Asoka.[7]

---

2. This is a quotation from a letter written by Coolidge to Eugene E. Thompson, organizer of the Bible class of the Church of the Epiphany in Washington, D.C., March 31, 1927. Coolidge's letter declined an invitation to Thompson's class. The original read: "Sometimes it seems as though a popular familiarity with the Scriptures is not as great at the present time as it has been in the past in American life. It would be difficult to support [the foundations of our society and our Government] if faith in [the teachings of the Bible] should cease to be practically universal in our country."
3. Members of a group of Moslem natives of the Philippines and Borneo, who were converted to Islam in an Indian missionary movement of the 15th and 16th centuries.
4. U. S. Senator from Utah 1903-1933.
5. William Henry King, U.S. Senator from Utah 1917-1941.
6. The angel Moroni revealed the location of the metallic plates on which was inscribed the Book of Mormon to Joseph Smith (1805-1844) in a vision at Palmyra, N.Y., in 1823.
7. Asoka (d. 232 B.C.): Emperor of India who made Buddhism its state religion.

Bentham,[8] Spencer, Darwin, Marcus Aurelius, John Stuart Mill, Diderot,[9] did not think that ethics depends on the Bible. The best precepts in the Bible, as to loving foreigners and dealing gently with Magdalens and sharing your wealth with the poor, have been uniformly and judiciously rejected by Christendom. Your own government has sent men to jail for handing out the Sermon on the Mount. It is bad to tell children that the basis of their morals is the Bible story and then, when they reach high school age, to tell them that there was no Garden of Eden, no Adam, no fall of man, and no need of redemption. Every child should learn, at his mother's knee, the story of Ali Cogia of Bagdad;[10] but I would not found a social system on the Arabian Nights. Do I make children moral when I tell them that God found it expedient to create a devil and to invent a hell? You, yourself, know all about Hammurabi,[11] who has been dug up since my time, and you know that the God who regulates millions of universes never wasted his time sitting behind a rock on Mount Sinai and carving Commandments on stone slabs. Any God who had to carve his own commandments would have been less prolix [wordy; verbose] in the second and fourth commandments. You have higher motives for your own virtue than a false fear of a false hell. Is it, then, right for you to recommend, as the basis of morals, a book of fiction, on the theory that its fictions are wholesome for uneducated people? There is no place for fiction in any true system of ethics. A system of ethics founded on a book of

---

8. Jeremy Bentham (1748-1832), English philosopher and economist who, according to Webster's Second College Edition, "held that the greatest happiness of the greatest number should be the ultimate goal of society and of the individual."

9. Denis Diderot (1713-1784), French philosopher.

10. In the *Arabian Nights*, Ali Cogia, a merchant of Bagdad, left a jar containing 1,000 pieces of gold with a fellow merchant while he was on a pilgrimage to Mecca, concealing the gold beneath a layer of olives. Ali Cogia was away for seven years. Near the end of that time, the merchant with whom he had left the jar decided to examine the jar's contents. He discovered the gold, removed it and the olives, and filled the jar with fresh olives. On his return, Ali Cogia discovered the theft, and hailed the merchant before the tribunal of cadi, who refused to take action after learning that Ali had no witnesses. But the caliph, Haroun-al-Raschid, wandering incognito among his subjects – as he often did – saw several boys acting out the trial; and one of them, playing the part of the cadi, called on fellows playing olive merchants to prove that olives could not keep longer than two or three years – hence the fresh olives in the jar proved the theft. Haroun-al-Raschid brought the boy to court and had him try the case, using the testimony of actual olive merchants. He, the caliph, condemned the merchant who had taken the gold to death. Thus, as Haroun-al-Raschid put it, the cadi could learn from a child to be more exact in the performance of his duties.

11. The collection of legal pronouncements that is the most enduring work of Hammurabi (c. 1792-1750 B.C.), king of the first dynasty of Babylon, was discovered inscribed on a Stele at Susa in Iran in 1901.

fiction is immoral."

Respectfully,
Cubricus Witherspoon

❧ ❧ ❧

## CAUTIONARY ADVICE AS TO THE BIBLE

To the President of the United States:

Sir:

From the Zend-Avesta[12] to the Book of Mormon, "sacred writings" have become fetishes, to be used with caution by teachers of morals. The Rev. Dr. Theodore H. Robinson, in his admirable *Outline Introduction to the History of Religion* ([N.Y.] Oxford Press [1926]), says (p. 19) that "There is, as a matter of fact, hardly a vice or crime which has not been, at one time or another, not merely permitted, but even enjoined by religion." You, Mr. President, under the Constitution, are the commander in chief of our army. In this you are like Naaman, who was "captain of the host of the King of Syria". You have often, therefore, read with peculiar interest, the story of that prosperous office holder, and you, undoubtedly, disapprove of the Machiavellian bad morals taught by the Fifth Chapter of the Second Book of Kings. The Bible there teaches our children to practice religious hypocrisy when it is needed to hold a place of power and profit. It approves Naaman and sets him up as an example to our young men, when he says: "I know that there is no God in all the earth, but in Israel. * * * Thy servant will henceforth offer neither burnt offering nor sacrifice unto other gods, but unto the Lord. In this thing the Lord pardon thy servant, that when my Master goeth into the house of Rimmon to worship there and he leaneth on my hand, and I bow myself in the house of Rimmon, when I bow down myself in the house of Rimmon, the Lord pardon thy servant in this thing."[13] Any intelligent school child

---

12. Scripture of Zoroastrianism, founded by the Persian religious leader Zoroaster (628-551 B.C.).

13. Briefly, II Kings, Chapter 5 describes how the prophet Elisha cured Naaman, commander of the army of the king of Syria, of his leprosy, requiring him to dip himself seven times in the river Jordan. When he was healed, Naaman begged Elisha to accept a gift. He refused. Then Naaman asked to memorialize the event by taking away two mules' burden of earth upon which, many commentaries explain, to build an altar to Elisha's God — the Lord of Israel. Yet Naaman also requested Elisha's permission to accompany the king of Syria to the temple of his god, Rimmon. And Elisha is reported

knows that school teachers and clergymen and editors and governors must bow down in various houses of Rimmon or lose their jobs. My prudent neighbors and I teach our children to bow down before Rimmon and not to seem queer in matters of belief; but you and I and our school teachers should be careful to keep the Second Book of Kings away from all children because it demoralizes them by telling them that, in this matter, the Supreme Ruler of the Universe has a standard of morals no higher than our own.

Respectfully,<br>Cubricus Witherspoon

ja ja ja

Third Draft

## COOLIDGE AND THE BIBLE

An affectionate letter, advising an unusual political expedient. From an advocate of fundamentalism.

"We believe in the Scriptures of the Old and New Testaments as verbally inspired by God, and inerrant in the original writings, and that they are of supreme and final authority in faith and life." (Point One, of the Fundamentalists' Creed.)

To the President of the United States:

Sir:

About the first of April, 1927, writing, in urgent commendation, to an organizer of Bible classes, you said: "It would be difficult to support (the foundations of government and society) if faith in Bible teaching should cease to be practically universal in our country * * *. It seems as though a popular familiarity with the Scriptures is not so great at the present time as it has been in the past." These are golden words.

There have been teachers of morals who believed the Bible

---

to have said: "Go in peace." Some commentators maintain that "Go in peace" is a corrupt text, properly reading, "Go with a possession of Israelite soil." (Elisha's servant, Gehazi, followed after Naaman and accepted of him two talents of silver and two festal garments, for which act Elisha cursed Gehazi and his descendants with Naaman's leprosy.)

story to be bogus and who, nevertheless, honestly thought it right to sell a fairy story to the public as a system of ethics. Such teachers are at the moral level of a mother who frightens her babies with stories of hobgoblins. There may have been, somewhere, some time, some high officer who, for his own advantage, would say that our government and society rest on the Bible, although he, himself, did not believe in it. But you would not so betray the confidence of your people. Heretofore indeed, you seem to have felt yourself compelled to obey Wayne B. Wheeler.[14] No man can do that without disobeying and dishonoring the Bible. He who disobeys the Bible gives proof that in his heart he does not believe it. But your new declaration persuades me that you are ready to forsake Mr. Wheeler and his abominations and to prove by your acts the faith that you preach. Surely, you are sincere when you exhort your subjects to Bible study. Surely, then, at a fitting time, you will teach a Bible lesson to sanctimonious meddlers who advertise their pretended belief in Biblical cosmogony [Webster's: "origins of the universe."], but when enthroned in their committee rooms, sneer at the morality that the Bible inculcates. I beg you to send out another message, to enlarge that "popular familiarity with the Scriptures" which you deem important.

The lessons of the Bible are set forth in two methods, first, by the recital of selected facts of four thousand years of history, and secondly, by precepts, commandments and prophecies that are interwoven with the sacred story. That history has been written by inspired authors so that we may see on whom divine authority has visited its punishments and so that we may avoid the sins of ancient malefactors.

In Bible history, the creator has visited on men three great punishments, two of them substantially universal, the third covering a continent. The first came with the fall of man. The inhabitants of Eden were thrown out of paradise and for their sin the whole race was condemned to bitter toil in this world and to eternal punishment in the next, a universal curse which was only modified afterwards by the redemption of the small company of the Elect.

The second great punishment fell upon this whole race except

---

14. (1869-1927), lawyer and prohibitionist. Until 1917, general counsel to the Anti-Saloon League; subsequently its legislative superintendent.

one family. In 1,656 years man became vile.[15] "Every imagination of the thoughts of his heart was only evil continually. And it repented the Lord that he had made man on the earth and it grieved him at his heart." "And the Lord said, I will destroy man whom I have crated from the face of the earth." [Genesis 6:5-7 to;]. He drowned everybody except his favorite, Noah, and Noah's family.

A lesson was divinely set for us in these two divinely-appointed catastrophes. Tell Tennessee,[16] whose rulers make a fetich of Genesis but are contemptuously deaf to its precepts, that the crimes for which these universal punishments were inflicted were committed by teetotalers. The curse that threw our first parents out of paradise and damned their descendants was a penalty that fell on two sinful water drinkers. The curse of the universal Noachian Deluge wiped out a race of water drinkers. For 1,656 years the human race had been drinking nothing but water and the minds of the race had become unendurably foul. This will not surprise any one who has observed teetotalers for even 60 years. It grieved Yahveh and, after 16 centuries of patience, he resolved to make a third experiment, this time with wine drinkers. The Creator had made two experiments in maintaining a wineless world and both were failures. In Genesis, we have His own lucid statements to that effect. Wine was unknown until after the Noachian Deluge. It is only since the Deluge that we have learned to be sociable, gentle, polite and cheerful and to have those charms and virtues which, among water drinkers, are found only in a rudimentary form; and, since the Deluge and, since our receiving God's gift of wine, God has never had to use on any of us any wholesale punishment. When God repented of having created the vicious and repulsive race of water-drinkers that he exterminated, with an appropriately world-wide excess of water, he chose Noah to be the ancestor of the new race and he conferred on us two great favors.

The ninth chapter of Genesis tells of these two cheering events in our history. God created the rainbow, so that it might remind him never again to drown the world in a fit of anger and he inspired Noah to invent wine and discovered some of the uses of

---

15. Samuel Rolles Driver (1826-1914), English scholar. In his commentary, *The Book of Genesis* (London: Methuen, 1904), the Hebrew text gives 1,656 years as the time span from the creation to the flood; according to the Samaritan text it was 1,307; and according to the Septuagint it was 2,262. The differences depend on the different ages given for the patriarchs.
16. Allusion to the 1925 Scopes trial re: creationism.

alcohol. "My bow shall appear in the clouds"; "and I shall see it and shall remember my covenant"; "and there shall no more be waters of a flood to destroy all flesh" (Genesis IX, 16, 15, 14). [Actually quotations come in order from Genesis 9: 14, 15, 16.] This great Ninth Chapter then goes on to describe the invention of wine.

I need not remind you, a thoughtful student of biblical literature, that the best commentary on Genesis is that of Elwood Worcester, D. D., the saintly and learned rector of St. Stephen's.[17] The pious purpose of that commentary is set forth by Dr. Worcester: "I have tried to express my deep sense of the inspiration of Genesis by exhibiting the true grandeur of the book." I quote Doctor Worcester's discussion of Noah's great discovery. ("Worcester's Genesis", 323.) "We come now to the great story of the Deluge, which, after the narrative of the Creation and Fall of man, is the portion of Genesis that has had the greatest effect in shaping the thought of the world." "Noah was a just man and perfect. Noah walked with God." "Noah found grace in the eyes of Jahveh" (Genesis VI. 8.9). [As quoted is Gen.6:9,8.] "Noah was a farmer. He made the discovery of the wonderful properties of the grape and began its culture. That was an important step in human progress."[18] (Worcester's "Genesis", 484.) Noah's birth is told in the fifth chapter of Genesis. The first, second and fifth chapters of Genesis are the three front trenches of fundamentalism. In the fifth chapter are five histories, the creation of man, the translation of Enoch, Noah's pedigree, Noah's birth and the prophecy, by Lamech, of the invention of the beverage that made Noah famous. The creation of man and woman is told in 21 words and the birth of Noah and Lamech's inspired prophecy as to Noah in 36 words. "In the day that God created man, in the likeness of God made he him; Male and female created he them." "And Lamech begat a son and he called his name Noah, (which means 'The comforter') saying: 'This same will comfort us for our work, for the sore labor of our hands which comes from the ground which Jahveh has cursed'."[19] Lamech's prophecy is given more space than the creation of man,

---

17. Elwood Worcester, D. D. (1860-1940), clergyman and author, rector of St. Stephen's in Philadelphia 1896-1904; of Emmanuel church in Boston 1904-1929. *The Book of Genesis in the Light of Modern Knowledge* (NY, McClure, 1901). Martin undoubtedly with tongue in cheek calling Worcester's commentary "the best."

18. Worcester's original continues: "That was an important step in human progress, but as our Jehovist loves to show us, every step man takes in this direction is beset with danger, and Noah becomes the victim of his own discovery."

19. Quotations are from Genesis 5:28-29. The curse occurs in Genesis 3:17. "Cursed is the ground because of you; in toil you shall eat of it all the days of your life."

because without the fulfillment of Lamech's prophecy, life is not worth living. Dr. Worcester studies this prophecy with the care demanded by its eminence, blazoned, as it is, on the very title page of human history. "How was this prophecy fulfilled? Certainly not by Noah's escape from the Flood in his ark. That brought little comfort to Lamech, for Noah saved only himself and his immediate family.[...] Moreover the building of an ark has nothing to do with the hardships of a farmer's life, of which Lamech so bitterly complained. This obscure saying of Lamech's, however, becomes clear in the light of the fact that Noah discovered the use of wine and first planted the grape. In antiquity generally and also in the Old Testament, the vine was always regarded as one of the choice gifts of Heaven and as expressly intended to mitigate the hardships of man's lot. 'Give strong drink [says the Proverb] to him that is ready to perish and wine to those that be of heavy hearts. Let him drink and forget his poverty and remember his misery no more' (Proverbs xxxi. 6,7). Among the best blessings Isaac could invoke on his first born was 'plenty of corn and wine' (Gen. xxvii. 28). The Psalm speaks of 'wine that maketh glad the heart of man' (Psalms civ. 15)."

In the Old Testament,[20] "the wine and grape are praised as good gifts of God, not only for their own sake, but as a symbol of a peacable and settled life. So Noah is represented as making this discovery by which the prophecy of his father Lamech was fulfilled. This seems to be very plain * * * The story of Noah and the vine [...] is quite consistent with the notice of Noah's birth.[21] Lamech prophesies that Noah will bring comfort to his contemporaries in their hard struggle with the earth and Noah fulfills the prophecy by causing the earth to bring forth wine which Jeremiah calls "the cup of consolation" (Jeremiah xvi. 7) (Worcester's "Genesis", 484-486).

Worcester's exegesis of Lamech's prophecy is that adopted by all competent commentators. "Noah is regarded as mitigating * * * the curse of Genesis iii, 17 * * * by becoming * * * the founder of a new epoch. * * * Budde, Stade, Gunkel[22] * * * consider that the allusion is to the refreshment, after toil, afforded by wine. (Ps, civ.

---

20. The full sentence reads: "Although the terrible effects of the abuse of wine are truthfully displayed in the Old Testament, yet the wine and grape are praised as good gifts of God, not only for their own sake, but as a symbol of a peacable and settled life."
21. Original sentence from Worcester reads: "The story of Noah and the vine has nothing to do with the Flood, but it is quite consistent with the notice of Noah's birth."
22. Three German Biblical commentators.

15; Pr. xxi. 6), the art of making which is in Gen. ix 20-27, referred to Noah as its inventor." (This is from page 78 of the classical commentary on Genesis of S. R. Driver, D. D., Regius Professor of Hebrew and Canon of Christ Church, Oxford, which you will remember, is one of the Westminster Commentaries, edited by Walter Lock, D. D., Ireland Professor of the Exegesis of Holy Scripture.)[23]

From Wayne B. Wheeler I appeal to the inspired Jeremiah. He was no merry-maker. He was not a convival Jew. But he lights up the gloom of his jeremiads by telling us that wine is the cup of consolation. From Ella Boole,[24] and her shrill mandates, I turn to the more alluring, plump, old-fashioned girl of the second chapter of Canticles [Song of Solomon], who murmurs, "stay me with flagons,[25] comfort me [with apples]." From Clarence T. Wilson, of the Methodist Board,[26] I turn for relief to the sacred figure of Jacob, the father of the Chosen People. Jacob is prophesying of Judah. Judah has a sublime place at the end and at the beginning of Israel's story. St. John, In Patmos heard a voice, saying, Behold the Lion of the Tribe of Judah [Rev. 5:5]. Judah became the guardian of the Temple. Jacob prophesies, of him, in a dithyrambic that must be painfully offensive to Dr. Wilson (Gen. xlix. 10).

"The sceptre shall not depart from Judah,
Until Shiloh come:
He hath washed his garments in wine,
And his vesture in the blood of grapes:
His eyes shall be red with wine."

The Bible is careful to tell us that Noah, after he began to drink, lived 350 years, reaching the distinguished age of 950. Thus Scripture fits in with Raymond Pearl's theory that judicious drinking goes well with longevity.[27]

---

23. (1846-1933), first general editor of the *Westminster Commentaries* on the Revised King James. Appointed in 1895 Dean Ireland's professor of exegesis of the Holy Scripture, Magdalen College, Oxford.
24. Ella Alexander Boole (1858-1952), temperance leader. Vice-president National WCTU (Women's Christian Temperance Union) 1915-1926; president 1926-1933. Treasurer World's WCTU 1920-1928; vice-president 1928-1931; president 1931-1947. In 1920, Prohibition Party candidate for U. S. Senate from NY.
25. Various translations use "flagons," "flowers," or "raisins."
26. Clarence True Wilson (1872-1939), Methodist clergyman, national secretary of the Temperance Society of the Methodist Episcopal Church, general secretary of the Board of Temperance, Prohibition and Public Morals, campaigner for prohibition candidates.

After the two world-wide punishments of mankind, came a third great judgment, the last of the three greatest punishments in history. This damnation did not fall upon all men. It damned Africa and the negroes.

When Noah invented wine, he became drunk, dead drunk. Neither the Bible nor the Holy Fathers blame him for this. The edition of the Douay Bible approved by Cardinal Gibbons[28] has this note: "Noe, by the judgment of the fathers, was not guilty of sin, in being overcome by wine because he knew not the strength of it." Noah had never seen wine before. Nobody had. He had to make this laboratory experiment for our guidance. He was 600 years old and presumably not strong enough to carry his wine gracefully. He was the first sailor, coming ashore and taking his first drink after an adventurous voyage. Landing, he found that all his old cronies were dead and that he was reduced to association with his own family. He had not had a drink for six hundred years. I myself, in Noah's place, would not have wished to interrupt the momentous experiment. Even Canaan did not blame him or sneer at him. What Canaan did, seems to us mild and dignified. Irving Fisher,[29] Carrie Nation,[30] Herbert Hoover[31] or Judge Gary[32] would have done

---

27. Raymond Pearl (1879-1947), biologist; author of *Alcohol and Longevity*(N.Y.: Knopf, 1927), which concluded on the basis of extensive animal experimentation and observation of human subjects that "moderate steady drinkers exhibited somewhat lower rates of mortality and greater expectation of life than did abstainers."

---

28. The Douay Bible was the first official Roman Catholic translation of the Bible; first published at Douay in France in 1610, but numerous Latinisms compelled its subsequent revision. James Gibbons (1834-1921) became the second American cardinal in 1886.
29. (1867-1974), political economist specially concerned with U.S. national health, which he believed could be promoted by reducing alcoholic intake. Became president of the Committee of Sixty on National Prohibition in 1917.
30. Carry Amelia Moore Nation (1846-1911), U.S. agitator for temperance. We can only assume Martin did not know of a celebrated Yale undergraduate prank played on Carry Nation, or he might have referred to it here. In 1903, students invited the temperance agitator to Yale under the pretext that college authorities were debauching the student body by forcing it to consume ham with champagne sauce. She toured the campus, snatching pipes and cigarettes from the mouths of onlookers, and then made a public address -- roundly cheered -- from the steps of Osborn Hall. Subsequently she was interviewed by a group of students posing as representatives of the *Yale Record*, "the college Temperance Paper." Photographs of Carry taken during this visit hung for years on the walls of Mory's Tavern. Apparently she went into her grave never knowing she'd been duped.
31. Hoover might be characterized as a "mild dry" in his personal views though his wife is known to have walked out of any room the moment alcohol was introduced. At the time this tract was written, Hoover was Secretary of Commerce (1921-1929), and was not directly involved with Prohibition enforcement. In his book *American Individualism* he wrote, "The crushing of the liquor trade without a cent of compensation, with scarcely even a discussion of it, does not bear out the notion that we give property rights any headway over human rights." In his presidential acceptance speech he declared, "Our

something ruder. The Bible does not blame Canaan for telling his brothers that the old man was drunk. The first drunk in history was an event worth reporting. Canaan's only offense was that he went out of the tent and did not throw a blanket over the old soak. These two things taken together were construed by Noah as showing a cold disapproval of Noah's drinking. They showed Canaan in three successive curses. (Genesis, Chapter Nine.)

Verse 25: Cursed be Canaan. The meanest slave let him be to his brothers.

Verse 26: Let Canaan be the slave of Shem and Japeth.

Verse 27: God enlarge Japeth and let him dwell in the tents of Shem and let Canaan be their slave.

The descendants of Canaan are the descendants of Ham. They became the inhabitants of Africa. No other prophecy has ever received so complete a fulfilment. This curse upon the descendants of Canaan, who was thus divinely punished for being the first reprover of wine, has been in force now for 4,275 years. In fulfilment of this curse your government is disregarding and nullifying the Fourteenth and Fifteenth Amendments. In fulfilment of this curse San Domingo bankers are thrown out of Pullman sleeping cars at St. Augustine. In fulfilment of this curse negroes came to a cruel end in the Congo Free State. In fulfilment of this curse black farmers in East Africa are evicted from their ancestral land by English descendants of Japeth.

The Methodists and Mormons and Kukluxers have invented a new false religion whose prime tenet is a taboo on wine. It is as blasphemous against the New Testament as against the Old.

In the New Dispensation God himself took on the form of man, to crate anew human happiness and human virtue by His precepts and His august example. He was not ignorant of the

---

country has deliberately undertaken a great social and economic experiment, noble in motive and far-reaching in purpose. It must be worked out constructively." [Neither Harding nor Coolidge had gone so far in their support for Prohibition.]
32. Elbert Henry Gary (1846-1927), chairman of the board of directors, U.S. Steel, 1903-1927); president American Iron and Steel Institute from its founding in 1909 to his death. Repeatedly expressed his belief in the beneficial effects of Prohibition, though he did believe light wine and beer should have been legalized. Member of the Conference Committee on Law and Order (which included John D. Rockefeller, Jr.) which met with Coolidge in 1924 to pledge support for the enforcement of the 18th Amendment and other laws.

luminous idea held by ascetic fanatics that drinking is a sin and that wine is a poison. Essenes[33] and neo-Pythagoreans[34] had spread this mirthless nonsense all over the Levant[35] at the beginning of our era.

The Lord's forerunner, John the Baptist, was a dry and the Lord took an early opportunity to rebuke John's fanaticism. John, the Baptist, He [God] tells us, was an abstainer, but the Son of Man came eating and drinking and men called him a drunkard. The first proof He gave of divine power was the miraculous making of wine and at the last supper He gave His disciples wine and ordered them to drink wine forever, in memory of Him.

In the sixth chapter of Revelation, the last book of the sacred canon, a voice from Heaven speaks, "with the sound of seven thunders," almost loud enough to reach the long, thick, hairy ears of the Methodist Committee. When that voice spake for the third horseman of the Apocalypse, it cried out, "Hurt not the wine."

The Bible is an epic of alcohol, a saga, that glorifies wine.

The Holy Grail was a wine cup, the Lord's emerald wine cup, that passed from Him to Joseph of Arimathea.[36] Christian knights no longer ride to seek the Grail. Our pure young Galahads have a new quest of the grail. They seduce a servitor into bringing them a chalice of champagne and then they earn a Judas reward by betraying their host to federal detectives.

"Wine was raised by the Founder of Christianity to a dignity of the highest religious import. It became well-nigh typical of Christianity and in a manner, its badge." The chief motive for "the Mohammedan prohibition of wine" [Not a direct quote.] was "the Prophet's antipathy to Christianity and his [a] desire to broaden the line of demarcation between his followers and those of Christ. To declare wine 'unclean,' and 'abomination' and 'the work of the devil' [To declare the social, the sacred liquor which had become well-nigh typical of Christianity, and in a manner its badge 'unclean'..."] was to set up for the faithful a counter-badge." (Westermarck, *The Origin and Development of the Moral Ideas*, II.345: Palgrave,

---

33. Religious sect flourishing in Judea in the second and first centuries B.C. Members rejected the sacrificial temple cult, practiced ceremonial purity, and refrained from eating meat.
34. Ascetic religious sect first appearing in the middle of the first century B.C., reviving the doctrine of numbers of the philosopher Pythagoras (582-507).
35. All the countries bordering the Mediterranean Sea from Greece east to Egypt.
36. He is described in the New Testament as having been the one to give the body of Jesus burial, and by Christian legend as the inheritor of the Holy Grail.

*Journey Through Central Eastern Arabia*, I. 428.).[37] It is true, of course, that Mohammed's prohibition has not produced uniform aridity in Islam. The laws forbidding wine, sometimes under the death penalty, "of the Moslem religion have proved as ineffective [have proved on the whole, as ineffective] as modern Christian experiments in the same direction. There is probably not a literature in the world so reeking of wine as that of the golden age of the highly religious Abassid Caliphate in Bagdad." (George F. Moore, History of Religions, II. 496.)[38] But Mabel Willebrandt[39] should be told that the Crusaders fought for a religion that held wine in reverence as its most sacred symbol and gave their lives to rescue the scene of the Last Supper, the last drinking together of the apostle, from the defiling grip of a nation of prohibitionists.

This insane superstition of forbidding wine is a flare-up from the embers of a great and ancient heresy that terrified the Church for a thousand years and which the Church thought it had stamped out at the tail end of the middle ages. Under the deadly pressure of Roman persecutions a few Christians, who had no scruples about wine, began to use water instead of wine at the Communion, because their pagan neighbors, when any group got together to drink wine in the morning, suspected the wine-drinkers of being Christians. The fiery martyr, Cyprian of Carthage,[40] condemned the practice. It seemed to him better that Christians should be torn in the arena than that they should insult the memory of their Lord with water. I am heartily of Cyprian's opinion. So that practice ended. But, soon after, arose the Gnostic heresies and Gnostic

---

37. Edward Westermarck, *The Origin and Development of the Moral Ideas* (London: Macmillan, 1908).
    William Giffford Palgrave, *Narrative of a Year's Journey Through Central and Eastern Arabia*, (London: Macmillan, 1865), pps. 428-9.
38. George Foot Moore, *History of Religions* (N.Y.: Scribner's, 1916-1919), Vol. II, p. 496.
39. Mabel Walker Willebrandt (1889-1963), lawyer, appointed U.S. assistant attorney-general by Harding in 1921, resigned in 1929. As such, had jurisdiction over all questions of policy, appeals,and directions to federal attorneys in taxation and prohibition cases. See Footnote 19 in "Tests for Leprosy."
40. (C.200-258), early Christian theologian and bishop of Carthage. In his remarkable letter LXIII, addressed to the bishop Caecilius, "our first extant extended study of the nature of the Eucharist," Cyprian cites scripture to show that wherever water alone is mentioned baptism is signified; but the communion cup must be mixed (i.e., neither wholly water nor wholly wine), symbolizing the union of Christian believers with Christ. The sense of the passage on which Martin draws is a bit different in the original text: "It may be that some feel apprehensive at our morning sacrifices that if they taste wine they may exhale the smell of the blood of Christ. That is the sort of thinking which causes our brethren to become reluctant to share even in Christ's sufferings in times of persecution, by thus learning in making their oblations to be ashamed of the blood that Christ has shed himself."

sects,[41] Manicheans,[42] in many forms that overran christendom. The Gnostics were milder than our Methodists. They left, ordinarily, some latitude to laymen, but held that a perfect Christian would abstain from wine and wedlock and from milk and meat and eggs and wealth, and, so far as possible, from all things nice. Among them, Hydroparastatae and Aquarii[43] went so far as to insist that even the communion service ought to be made disagreeable by cutting out wine. For this many of them were thoroughly racked and carefully burned. The Gnostics did not argue that either wine or wedlock or roast beef corrupted men or women; but they held that such luxuries draw our thoughts away from heaven. The Gnostics left their traces in orthodox creeds and many orthodox practices; multitudes of them became martyrs, after living lives of disgusting self-denial. They should chuckle in their graves, if they could be told that a government of a great free republic abases itself before a Church Board that plans, by and by, to take away from me, not only my Demon, Rum, but also my mild cigar.

I used to think Manicheans the supreme asses of our galactic universe. By they were abstainers, not prohibiters; and the silliest of them would not have ventured to impose a fantastic Gnostic asceticism on a modern nation. A suggestive point of likeness between the old Manichees and the new is their contemptuous treatment of the Bible. The old Manichees threw overboard so much of the Bible as they did not like. The Cerdonians, you will remember, led in this heresy.[44] Our new Manichees have begotten lately, a litter of bastard Bibles, expurgated, Bowdlerized,[45] and abridged, to suit their own morbidity. One, from Yale, cuts out

---

41. Gnosticism, a religious and philosophical movement, both Jewish and Christian, in its origins dating back to the Hellenistic era, held that salvation is obtained through knowledge rather than faith or good works. Not pronouncedly ascetic until it merged with Manicheism.
42. Members of a religious sect founded by the third century A.D. Persian, Mani, who understood the world in terms of a struggle between good and evil. Its elect were enjoined to a strict austerity, and rejected the use of wine as something evil.
43. The Hydroparastatae were a Manichean sect consisting chiefly of followers of Tatian, himself a follower of Justin the Martyr (c. 100-c.165), who rejected marriage, the use of animal food, and wine. The Aquarii, who rejected wine, were one of the two principal branches of the Hydroparastatae, the other being the Encratites, who rejected meat.
44. Followers of Cerdo, a second century teacher in Rome. His, and their, methods of exegesis eventually compelled the rejection of the Old Testament and the removal of what they understood as Jewish interpolations from the New Testament.
45. Thomas Bowdler (1754-1825). In 1818 this English editor published a severely expurgated version of Shakespeare, giving his name to those who would remove what they consider to be offensive passages from any book.

Noah's great invention.[46]

Remind your people that, in the light of the Bible story, the prohibition of wine, invented by calculating hypocrites and opinionated ascetics, is blasphemous. When you recommend the Bible as a moral guide you surely make no mental reservations. If, however, you think the Bible is all wrong in the matter of wine, it would be just to add to your recent official advice by a warning, point out out the errors on this point of the Old and the New Testament, God's mistakes. If, on the other hand, you are sincere in describing the Bible as the basis of our morals, your great office gives you a pulpit from which you can teach truth by the example of your own faith.

To fix his ethics in the minds of his people General Nogi,[47] the noblest exemplar of our time, made the great resignation, and for that Japan worships his memory. So you, with heroic abnegation, can resign your place, refusing to execute a statute that offends your conscience. You will thus imprint, unforgettably, on the minds of your people the value of the Bible as a moral guide and will distinguish yourself agreeably above several of your predecessors.

It is fine to see the office seek the man. It is finer to see the man forsake the office, for conscience's sake. If you do that, never more will it be said that office-holders never resign. My prophetic thought sees your statue, a Bible in the left hand, in the right hand, held high, Jeremiah's jolly cup of consolation. I see bus-loads of merry Bible classes, thronging to view the magnificent Coolidge Memorial. I see gloom driven from your Commonwealth, and wherever warm hearts and laughing eyes revel together in the

---

46. Noah Webster published what Noel Perrin, in *Dr. Bowdler's Legacy*, calls "the first and last avowed expurgation the Bible has ever had" at New Haven in 1833, to the approval of Yale President Day and most of the Yale faculty. Not the "last" however. The so-called "Prohibition Bible," *The Shorter Bible*, two vols. (N.Y.: Scribner's, 1925), was translated by Charles Foster Kent, Woolsey Professor of Biblical Literature at Yale, in collaboration with Professor C. T. Torry of Yale; H. A. Sherman, head of the religious department at Scribner's' Frederick Harris of the YMCA; and Ethel Cutler of the YWCA. Critics at the time complained that the word *wine* was deleted or had its meaning changed whenever the Bible used it approbatively but that all unfavorable references were retained, as in II Samuel 6: 19, where King David dealt out a cake of raisins instead of a flagon of wine. However, Torrey, in a *New York Times* letter column defending the work (May 3, 1925), cited several favorable references to wine in the translation.

47. Count Marasuke Nogi (1849-1912), Japanese general and hero of the Russo-Japanese War who committed hara-kiri together with his wife in observance of the death of Emperor Mutsuhito.

re-birth of freedom, I hear, in reiterated choruses, Here's to grand old Coolidge, drink him down.

Respectfully,<br>Newell Martin

Huntington, New York

ꕤ ꕤ ꕤ

Bermuda, February 29, 1928

# Tests for Leprosy

TO the Committee on Admissions of any Club in
    Arid America (America Deserta):

Sirs:

    This letter deals, not with the private affairs of any club, but with a question that concerns all clubs. I would like to have it read in every club. It may be of some use, although club life in America is extinct. You and I and many others still pay club dues, from force of habit. But we find no pleasure in clubs. I have begun to forget what clubs I belong to and where they are. I think I still belong to the Paleocrystic Club, of New York,[1] and to some other houses of gloom. I have already wearied the council of each of these clubs by urging that, as protest against misgovernment and barbarism, we should sell the club house and buy a modest home in Bermuda or Montreal. Better fifty hours a year of club life in a land of wine and freedom, than a cycle of club life that is based on ice-water.
    In the stately dining room of the Paleocrystic Club we used to choose, at leisure, from a long list of vintage wines. In the big parlor of the Paleocrystic Club, that looks out on Gramercy Park[2]

---

1. Of course, no such club. The OED defines *paleocrystic* as, "consisting of ancient ice, applied to parts of the polar seas."

(or Thirty-Seventh Street or Central Park; or some other street; I have forgotten which)[3] we used to enjoy social happiness, and form enduring friendships, with the incidental aid of an occasional cocktail and hot spiced rum and planter's punch and eue de vie de Dantzig [Danzig brandy] and mugs of ale. Now, by preference, on my way uptown, when I am in town, I avoid clubs and go to the morgue, in 26th Street,[4] and smoke my afternoon cigar in the presence of the quiet corpses and am not annoyed by frigid conversations or by offers of a sparkling glass of ginger ale.

There is no longer any rational motive for belonging to any American club. But men who are trampled on and are uneasily conscious of their degraded conditions and of the extinction of civilized society naturally huddle together, in whatever wretched shelter they call their own; and their oppressors sometimes enjoy looking in on them there. Candidates for your club, therefore, still present themselves.

In studying such candidates you find yourself beset by a new trouble. In the old times nobody ever dreamt of admitting men of the Carry Nation[5] type to any decent house or club. Now such men arrogantly rule the nation and put on the airs of a dominant aristocracy and intrude boldly into places from which, formerly, they would have been barred, because of their bad morals, bad manners and bad record.

I am expiring, slowly and agreeably,[6] on a balmy coral island, where freedom is not an empty name and where food and drink are under no superstitious clerical Taboos; but I have not lost my sympathy for the enslaved millions of the mainland. I suggest to you, therefore, a short way of ascertaining whether any candidate has about him or in his record anything intolerably loathsome that should shut him out from human society. The tests that I propose will be found especially useful in dealing with philanthropists, clergymen, policemen, publicists, politicians and statesmen.

---

2. Perhaps Martin refers to the Players' Club at No. 16 Gramercy Park South which was founded in 1888 by Edwin Booth primarily for members of the acting profession.

---

3. The Union League Club is at No. 38 East 37th Street; founded in 1863, and was known as a stronghold of Republican conservatism throughout the latter 19th century. The Metropolitan Club, 60th Street and Fifth Avenue was a center of late 19th-century exclusiveness.
4. Bellevue Hospital: A complex of buildings stretching from 26th to 30th Streets housing the New York City Morgue, which is itself located at 29th Street and First Avenue.
5. Carry Amelia Moore Nation (1846-1911), U. S. agitator for temperance. See Footnote 30, "Coolidge and the Bible."
6. Actually Martin lived (and wrote) for some 13 years after publication of this tract.

82    WETS AND DRYS

All serious committees of admission, of course, look with especial care, at this time, into the records of all clergymen that come before them. They often have the pleasure, also, of finding that a clerical candidate has a spotless character and is admissible. Some clergymen are lovers of Gascon wine [any wine from Gascony in southwest France]. Some clergymen, I am glad to say, are loose fellows that approve of serving wine at weddings. Some are like Empringham[7] and are free from the vices that so often flourish in the pulpit. But too many of our Protestant clergymen and some Catholic priests and a few rabbis have conspired to betray us, in their eagerness to control the state and to regulate our habits. The highly orthodox, like Bishop Manning[8] and the Reverend Doctor Straton and the Reverend Doctor Norris (The Texas clerical gunman),[9] and dissenters, like Norman Thomas,[10] and the utterly heterodox, like John Haynes Holmes,[11] have set up asceticism as a new religion and Volstead as the inspired author of a holy Twelfth Commandment. All clergymen, therefore, are suspect; even those

7. James Empringham (1875-19??), American temperance advocate, born in England. Rector St. Paul's Church, Syracuse 1906-1916; superintendent of the Anti-Saloon League of New York; national superintendent of the Episcopalian Church Temperance Society beginning 1916; vice-president of the Anti-Saloon League of America beginning 1917. In February, 1926, two years prior to publication of "Tests for Leprosy," the Episcopalian Church Temperance Society had issued a statement opposing Prohibition. In 1930, Empringham was unfrocked at his own request due to a conflict with his superior, Bishop Manning, over, among other things, his methods of conducting anti-Prohibition propaganda.
8. William Thomas Manning (1866-1949), rector of Trinity Church 1908-1921; American Episcopal Bishop of New York 1921-1946. Characterized Prohibition as "one of the greatest efforts toward moral and social betterment that has ever been made."
9. John Franklin Norris (1877-1952), pastor of the First Baptist Church, Ft. Worth, Texas, 1909-1952; simultaneously pastor, some 1,200 miles north, at the Temple Baptist Church in Detroit through 1951. Leader in fight for legislation against racetrack gambling, for Sunday closing laws, closing of pool halls, and Prohibition. His activities and statements, certainly pistolary, included preaching a sermon entitled, "The Ten Biggest Devils in Ft. Worth, Names Given," and of referring to a colleague publicly as "the Old Baboon." In 1926, Norris accused the Roman Catholic mayor of Ft. Worth of channeling city funds to the Roman Catholic Church, saying the mayor "wasn't fit to be manager of a hogpen." A friend of the mayor's threatened Norris first by phone, and then came to his office study. After a heated verbal exchange, Norris shot and killed him. The jury ruled it self-defense.
10. Norman Thomas (1884-1968), political leader and author; six times Socialist Party candidate for U.S. President. Socialist candidate for governor of New York in 1924, when he took a strong stand for the enforcement of Prohibition and denounced the hypocrisy of public officials entrusted with it.
11. John Haynes Holmes (1879-1964), American clergyman (nondenominational), minister 1909-1949 of the Community Church, New York City. Founder of both the National Association for the Advancement of Colored People (NAACP) and the American Civil Liberties Union (ACLU). Socialist and pacifist. Consistent and ardent supporter of Prohibition; preached sermons in its favor (once made the point that 3,000 years of legislation against murder had not eliminated it; hence seven years was too soon to expect results from Prohibition); stated in the latter 1930s that the effects of repeal were working themselves out "like maggots in rotten meat."

who are so liberal as to wish to join a club in which artists and professors of anthropology and other sons of Belial [Satan] are frequent. Any club that honors the memory of our dead liberty will request the nominator of a clergyman to give strong proof that his man is not one of freedom's assassins.

I hope that soon all committees of admission in clubs of any standing will demand similar assurances as to laymen. Consider, for instance, such august figures as Irving Fisher, John D. Rockefeller, Junior, and V. Everit Macy.[12] In old times, if any one of them had come before any committee that I know, the committee would have been dazzled by his splendor and would have admitted him eagerly, asking no questions. But if he came before such a committee now, he would be questioned closely as the evil he has done because we owe the prevalent dryness to those three men more than to any others. I hear a rumor that one of those three has repented; but what does the repentance of one murderer of happiness profit a nation in which innocent gaiety is dead?

I advise you to take note of the change that has come over American minds since the dark hour when these misguided philanthropists and their associates blighted America with the Eighteenth Amendment. Our new hatred of prohibiters grows wider and deeper and hotter. This change in feeling is like the change in thought that came about under the Fugitive Slave Law. That law was framed to enforce a clause which still stands forth as one of the conspicuous fossils in our constitution, and which, in its youth, was cherished as of sacred origin and was supported by multitudinous sermons. When Chief Justice Taney[13] was in his

---

12. Irving Fisher (1867-1947), political economist specially concerned with American national health, which he believed could be promoted by reducing alcoholic intake. Became president of the Committee of Sixty on National Prohibition in 1917.

　　　John D. Rockefeller, Jr. (1874-1960), a Baptist, strict teetotaler, and temperance advocate. Rockefeller initially gave Prohibition his full support, but became convinced by the mid 1920s that "the Eighteenth Amendment has not accomplished the objectives which its enactment sought to attain." He was one of several eminent Americans who issued statements supporting repeal in 1933. From 1917-1925 Rockefeller contributed some $174,000 to the Anti-Saloon League, making him its #1 contributor. V. Everit Macy was #2.

　　　Valentine Everit Macy (1871-1930), financier and philanthropist. Director of numerous corporations; member of both the Century and University Clubs. From 1917-1925, Macy contributed $126,500 to the Anti-Saloon League.

13. Roger Brooke Taney (1774-1864), Chief Justice of the U.S. Supreme Court 1836-1864. In the Dred Scott Case of 1857, Taney delivered the Court's opinion that a Negro "whose ancestors . . . were sold as slaves," however long he had resided in free territory, was not entitled to the rights of a Federal citizen and had no standing in court, and that the Missouri Compromise prohibiting slavery in the Louisiana Purchase north of 36' 10" was unconstitutional. [Ed. Note: We feel Martin would have cheered, had he been alive in 1954 for *Brown v. Board of Education of Topeka*.]

prime and the Dred Scott decision was still applauded by all law-abiding people, a man who helped a run-away slave could not hope to be invited to dinner in New York or to get into a good club. But a change came over northern society. When Taney was in his decline and Abraham Lincoln began to be ascendant, if any man helped a United States Marshal to take back a run-away slave, that man could not get into any good club anywhere north of Philadelphia. Such men were deemed ineligible for office; and such men because diligent, during the civil War, in effacing their own records and trying to persuade people that they had always been personal friends of John Brown of Ossawatomie.[14]

So is it now with us. It makes us bitter to see Mr. Buckner's[15] padlocks and to think about Mr. Lowman[16] and his reckless coast-guards, that fire on pleasure boats and trample over submarines, and to hear about Mr. Doran[17] and his poisons and to read about Mabel Willebrandt[18] and her armed spies. If any committee, now, should admit to a New York club that notorious marine, Smedley G. Butler,[19] all the desirable members of that club

---

14. John Brown (1800-1859), American abolitionist, who killed five proslavery men on the banks of the Pottawatamie River as a retaliation for the proslavery raid on Lawrence, Kansas, and was hanged at Harper's Ferry, West Virginia, after capturing the federal asenal there.
15. Emory G. Buckner (1877-1941), U.S. District Attorney South district of New York 1925-1927. In 1925, Buckner requested four lawyers to visit all-night restaurants and dance halls and attempt to buy liquor. The evidence obtained resulted in the padlocking of 14 such establishments.
16. Seymour Lowman (1868-1940), lawyer, businessman, and politician. Lt. Governor of New York 1925-1926. While assistant secretary of the U.S. Treasury, charged with prohibition enforcement. There had been numerous instances of Coast Guard ships firing on unarmed pleasure boats who responded slowly to signals; two of the most contemporary and best-known being the firing on the British schooner *Eastwood* off the Long Island coast, Feb. 15, 1926; and the yacht *Aloha* off Newport, Rhode Island, June 15, 1926. The latter led to a government investigation in which the Coast Guard denied firing in anything but emergencies. On December 17, 1927, the Coast Guard destroyer Paulding rammed the submarine S-4 off Provincetown, MA, causing the loss of 40 men, the S-4's entire crew.
17. James Maurice Doran (1885-1942), chief of the chemical and technical division of the Prohibition Bureau of the Bureau of Internal Revenue 1920-1927; U.S. commissioner on prohibition 1927-1930. The regulations of the Prohibition Bureau for denaturing industrial alcohol provided for, among other, the following agents: lavender, soft soap, oil of wintergreen, oil of peppermint, iodine, tobacco solution, sulphuric acid, carbolic acid, menthol crystals, acetone, brucine sulphate, camphor, bezine, pyridine, ether, kerosene, gasoline, mercuric acid, benzoin, formaldehyde, bichloride of mercury, and methyl (wood) alcohol.
18. Mabel Walker Willebrandt (1889-1963), lawyer, U.S. assistant attorney-general 1921-1929, with jurisdiction over all questions of policy, appeals, and directions to federal attorneys in taxation and prohibition cases. [See Footnote 39 in "Coolidge and the Bible."]
19. Smedley Darlington Butler (1881-1940), Marine officer who served in the Spanish-American War, Boxer Rebellion, and the 1915 Haitian uprising. In 1924-1927, Butler was director of public safety in Philadelphia under a reform administration, and won a national reputation for eliminating corruption in law enforcement.

would resign.

In future years our outraged and disorganized society will resort to an effective boycott against those who have conspired against its happiness. But, even now, the black-ball can make its small beginning in preparation for the boycott. Any club of slaves can express in private its secret disapproval of slave-drivers and slave-dealers. Therefore, I suggest a means by which each candidate can show his own chief virtues and can also inform you as to whether he has any disqualifying social leprosy. I am not so unpractical as to ask any man to join me in vowing to boycott the clergy and the Department of Justice and the Secretary of the Treasury and several hundred thousand sordid politicians and the rabid fanatics that vote to make us abstemious. Small groups of obscure persons of luxurious habits cannot yet boycott Kresge[20] and Henry Ford.[21] They cannot yet rebel against the Rockefellers. Benefactors, of great wealth, have taken the lead in committing a crime against civilization. They have thus become, again, "malefactors, of great wealth." With the careless signing of a few checks, by giving a little superfluous money, they have turned a nation from harmless self-indulgence to the misery of total abstinence. But, to try to boycott flood and hurricane, would be more profitable than trying to boycott unlimited wealth. Powers grotesquely diverse in their motives and character are irresistibly joined against us. Protestant churches, the State, the dominant political party, several of the few men who own most of the nation's money, and the opulent and unscrupulous speculators who reap the vast illicit profits of the liquor trade are united in spending money, in ignoring the Bill of Rights and in breaking laws, to enforce the dry law. The power of our oppressors is omnipotent, omniscient, and omnipresent and they tell us that it will be eternal. No boycott in our time can shake it. Ragged Irish peasants and hungry Chinese coolies have boycotted, from time to time, the British Empire, with success. But they are of firmer fibre than we docile Americans. Boycott and barricades and civil war may come in time, if our

---

20. Sebastian Spering Kresge (1867-1966), merchant, founder of S. S. Kresge Co., chain of five-and-dime stores, of which he was president 1907-1925, and chairman of the board 1913-1966. Founder of the Kresge Foundation. Active in Prohibition work and contributed extensively to it.
21. Henry Ford (1863-1947), lifelong supporter of Prohibition, which he viewed as both a barrier to urban intemperance and promoter of industrial efficiency. In 1918, ran as dry Republican candidate for U.S. senator from Michigan. Together with Rockefeller and Macy, one of the financial pillars of the Anti-Saloon League.

grandchildren are less patient than we; but not in our time. There is only one small beginning that we can make. There is one thing we can do. When, in our little social gatherings, we are grumbling together, before our cheerless hearths, if one of our oppressors asks to join us, we can assume an unfriendly expression. Even the meek fellaheen [Arabian peasant] and the servile Bengalees resist and resist to the death, rulers whom they choose to regard as oppressive; rulers who are gentle and mild compared with our oppressors. I do not ask any American to show such spirit or to forget on which side his bread is buttered. But I do hint that he can withold the glad hand.

It will lighten your labors, if your secretary will hand to each proposer of a candidate a list, naming a few of the governing societies that dominate America. I append such a list, Schedule A. It is not improbable that the proposer will then, usually, ask some member of the club the purpose of the list. Any man so questioned would then, probably, make, orally some such remarks as I suggest below in Schedule B.

P.S. The Century Dictionary justifies me in
saying that a Paleocrystic Club is a house
encumbered with ancient ice, the result of
the presence of water, in great quantities,
for long periods, under Arctic conditions.

## SCHEDULE A

A list of philanthropic societies.

The Watch & Ward Society of Boston.[22]

The Society for the Supression of Vice (this is the Anthony Comstock and John S. Sumner Society); No. 215 West 22nd St.[23]

---

22. The New England Watch and Ward Society was founded in 1878 by Anthony Comstock, and aimed at supressing all local traffic in matter appealing to a prurient interest; i.e., "banned in Boston." Responsible for the arrest of more than 3,000 persons and the destruction of some 160 tons of books and pictures.
23. Founded in New York City in 1873. Founders included John D. Rockefeller and J. P. Morgan. Its primary organizer, and lifelong secretary, was Anthony Comstock (1844-1915). Upon his death he was succeeded by John Saxton Sumner (1876-1971), who retired in 1950. Its primary objectives were displayed in its primary accomplishment, the U.S. "Comstock Law" excluding from the mails all matter "designed to incite lust." *Ulysses*, *Lady Chatterly's Lover*, James Branch Cabell's *Jurgen*, and Edmund Wilson's *Memoirs of Hectate County* were among the Society's more notable targets.

The Christian Fundamentals Association, for compelling the substituting of Moses for Darwin in schools.[24] Its President is Rev. Dr. W. B. Riley, pastor of the First Baptist Church of Minneapolis.

The Reverend Dr. Bowlby's Lord's Day Alliance (for the supression of Sunday gold and Sunday baseball).[25]

The Sabbath Association of Pittsburgh.[26]

The Committee of One Thousand, for the enforcement of various laws.[27]

The Anti-Saloon League.[28]

The Committee of the Methodist-Episcopal Church on Prohibition, Temperance and Public Morals.[29]

The Ku Klux Klan.[30]

---

24. The World's Christian Fundamentals Association was founded in Philadelphia in 1919 for the purpose of organizing American fundamentalism on a nationwide basis. William Belly Riley (1861-1947) was its executive secretary. The Association was responsible for securing William Jennings Bryan for the prosecution in the 1925 Scopes trial.

25. Founded c. 1900 for the purpose of organizing 23 Protestant denominations around the primary object of preserving Sunday as a day of rest. Harry Laity Bowlby (1874-1966) was its general secretary from 1913-1954. It still exists.

26. Founded in Pittsburgh in 1874; was a temperance organization emphasizing legal rather than political means (i.e., prohibition *eo ipso*) to attain its objectives.

27. The Citizen's Committee of One Thousand for Law Enforcement was founded in New York City in 1925 as an offshoot of the Committee of One Hundred, which was itself a temperance rather than a Prohibition organization. The Committee of One Thousand was nominally anti-prohibition, regarding it as having rather increased than reduced vice; however, it took the position of either complete enforcement or repeal — no middle ground — which in effect meant supporting Prohibition for the duration. The Committee also devoted its attention to the general issue of obedience to enacted legislation, taking a particularly strong stand on the issue of the corruption of legislative bodies by monied interests.

28. Founded by the Rev. H. H. Russell in Ohio in 1893; became national in 1895. Prior to Prohibition the League centered its attention on the destruction of the liquor traffic by legislation; then sought to achieve maintenance and enforcement of the Eighteenth Amendment. The League was accused during the '20s of contributing to the vice which Prohibition fostered, and rapidly lost ground during the latter part of the decade. By 1933, it was no longer a force in national politics. It became the Temperance League of America in 1948; and in 1950 merged with the National Temperance Movement to become the National Temperance League.

29. This Committee was founded in 1910 by Clarence True Wilson and Deets Pickett.

30. The Klan had been revived in Georgia in 1915. Though its policies were dry, probably its appearance in this list is Martin's way of saying all those other organizations are just as nasty as . . .

## SCHEDULE B

Any member of your club, questioned as to Schedule A, could say to the candidate's proposer something like this:

You have here a convenient way of giving the committee a portrait of your candidate. The candidate's backers can indicate, on the questionary, whether your man is a member of any of the societies listed in Schedule A and can tell the committee whether he has given money to any of them and whether he is in favour of any of the purposes of any of them, or has ever been employed as a spy or has employed a spy, in aid of any of them. The committee has not suggested that an active support of all of these societies will assure the committee's favor; or that coolness towards such groups of active reformers will prejudice the committee against the candidate; but, obviously, to know which of these societies your candidate does or does not favor will lighten the task of ascertaining whether he is the sort of man that ought to be eating locusts and wild honey in the wilderness, among the Wahabees; or whether, on the other hand, he would know how to behave in a group of sane men, who use the ordinary good and drink of civilised people; or whether he would be stimulating and congenial in a society of authors and artists; or whether he would be welcome in a club made up of graduates of European and American Universities.

## SCHEDULE C

An experienced diagnostician tells me that an efficient leprosy test of any candidate for admission to a club is to ask his proposer to answer these two questions:

Is your candidate a man that the Anti-Saloon League would declare to be satisfactory to it, if he were a candidate for office?

Has he ever received such approval?

# Letter to R. R. Bowker

*Richard Rodgers Bowker (1843-1933), publisher and economist, launched the English edition of* Harper's *in 1882; and in 1911 began publishing numerous book trade guides. He was acting president of the American Copyright League; vice-president of the Edison Electric Illumination Co. of New York from 1890-1899; member and officer of numerous free trade organizations. And author of books, ranging from economics to science to light verse.*

*Just three months prior to publication of this pamphlet, the U.S. Supreme Court, in Olmstead v. U.S. (277 US 438) — Taft, speaking for the majority — held that a wiretap did not violate Fourth or Fifth Amendment rights, drawing the parallel that the failure to produce subpoenaed books and papers was taken to affirm the evidence they would have proven if produced; i.e., such a court order was tantamount to compulsion. The wiretaps in question had supplied decisive evidence as to a large-scale bootlegging operation. (Holmes, Brandeis, and Butler dissented.)*

Huntington, September 4, 1928

R.R. Bowker, Esqr.
Glendale, Massachusetts

Dear Bowker:

You are eighty today. That is a serious matter. Do you realize that you have used up nearly four-fifths of the playtime allotted to you on this exciting little planet? Sober down and live carefully and be more serious, that your days may be long in the land where you have done so much for the happiness of others. You have had the fun, already, of enjoying the ruin of many disgusting statesmen and pernicious monarchs. In your time the Manchu Empress Dowager[1] and the last Emperor of the French[2] and the last Emperor of the Germans[3] have been dragged delightfully in the dust. You have also borne serenely some disappointments. In the

---

1. Tz'u or Tsu Hsi (1834-1908), dowager empress of the Ch'ing dynasty of China. Hostile to the West, she encouraged the Boxer uprising, and was forced by foreign troops to flee Peking and accept humiliating peace terms.
2. Napoleon III (1808-1873), deposed in 1870; went into exile in England in 1871.
3. Wilhelm II (1859-1941), abdicated in 1918, and fled to Holland.

auspicious year of 1848 which saw your birth Europe resounded with the crash of falling bastilles and the voice of patriots, on barricades, calling to their comrades to make their countries free, like high-souled America. Today the whole place is cluttered up with censors and dictators from Boston to Buda-Pesth, from Belgrade to Madrid. On the banks of the Merrimac and the Charles, in old times, Minute Men and Henry Thoreau and Crispus Attucks[4] lived or died or wrote for freedom and revolt. There, today, a tyranny that is bossed by Methodist parsons and Fundamentalists thinks it has a right to set its sneaking spy at any key-hole. And it has been adjudged, by a Republican Supreme Court, at the instance of a Republican Administration, that the foul ears of the Official Wire-Tappers of the Government may drink in, wherever the Government pleases, revelations of trade secrets and hidden sins. The deceased buccaneers of the Spanish Main must turn sick with envy in their graves when they hear of such golcondas [sources of great wealth] opened to enterprising officeholders in the name of temperance and public morals. In Washington, high on a throne of state, sits a woman[5] whose presence in the Department of Justice marks the descent of our nation into fanatical barbarism. I do not call her the Jezebel of the Department of Justice; but it is a matter of common knowledge and one that is regarded with servile indulgence that men quite as innocent as Naboth,[6] have been done to death by sons of Belial, appointed to enforce the Volstead Act. The admirers of this woman count already on the fast-approaching day when she can display her charms at the window of the best guest room in the President's Palace.

Preserve, my youthful friend, your splendid patience. Time will bring its slow revenge. I accept eagerly your invitation to fly to your camp-fire on September 4, 1948. It will be lawful, then, for me to bring to you a dozen jorums[7] of cold punch, the same that Mr.

4. (1723-1770), described as "the first black to die in the Revolutionary War." On March 5, 1770, he led a group from Dock St. to State St., Boston, where he was one of the five persons killed when the British opened fire.
5. Mabel Walker Willebrandt (1889-1963), lawyer, appointed U.S. assistant attorney-general by Harding in 1921, resigned in 1929. As attorney general, had jurisdiction over all questions of policy, appeals, and directions to federal attorneys in taxation and prohibition cases. See notes in "Coolidge and the Bible," and "Tests for Leprosy."
6. In I Kings 21, Naboth refuses to sell his vineyard to Ahab, the king of Israel, whereupon Ahab's wife, Jezebel, contrives slanders against Naboth and induces the people to stone him to death, giving Ahab possession. In II Kings 30, it is related that, immediately prior to her deposition and murder by Jehu, Jezebel "painted her eyes, and adorned her head, and looked out of the window."
7. A jorum is a large drinking bowl; generally, two jorums make one bottle.

Pickwick[8] had too much of, a dozen jorums of highly intoxicating Bermuda's milk punch.

Affectionately,<br>Newell Martin

🙵 🙵 🙵

## Aqueducts Are Unlawful

Under the Volstead Law, if you add five one-thousandths of a pint of alcohol to nine hundred and ninety-five one-thousandths of a pint of lemonade and then sell the drink, you may be sent to jail. But the Eighteenth Amendment goes farther than that. It forbids "the sale or transportation of intoxicating liquors...for beverage purposes". We could have drafted it in such form as to forbid only alcoholic liquors. But we wisely made it forbid all intoxicating liquors; those that carry alcohol and those that contain no alcohol. Alcohol is not the only intoxicant. Water, itself, if the courts follow conscientiously their established precedents, will be held to be an intoxicating liquor. Water is a liquor. "Liquor: A liquid or fluid substance, as water, milk, blood, sap, & c." (Century Dictionary.)[1] Water is intoxicating.

Usually, it neither cheers nor inebriates, but it is intoxicating to certain people at certain times. It must therefore take its shameful place as an unsalable beverage with beer and claret. Beer is as criminal as brandy. A glass of claret carries as much moral turpitude as a quart of whiskey. This is because Congress and the judges, inspired, have made it the law that a liquid is intoxicating if, under any circumstances, it can ever intoxicate.

At the last New York meetings of the American Association for the Advancement of Science the Association gave its highest honors to Dr. Oliver Kamm, the research director for Parke, Davis

---

8. In Chapter XIX of *The Pickwick Papers*, after too many glasses of cold punch, Mr. Pickwick "fell into the [wheel] barrow, and fast asleep, simultaneously."

1. Webster's Second College Edition: "Liquor: any liquid or juice."

& Company, for his paper entitled "Hormones of the Pituitary Gland", which the Association chose as the best of the 2,000 theses that were presented at these meetings. In that essay Dr. Kamm discussed water as an intoxicating liquor and showed when water is intoxicating.[2]

I quote from the "Science News-Letter" of October 13, 1928:

"Aqueous Intoxication

"Intoxication by water is declared possible
"by Dr. Oliver Kamm of Detroit. Whether
"water is a harmless beverage depends upon
"the amount imbibed and the cellular con-
"stitution of the imbiber. The four glasses
"a day recommended by one of the insur-
"ance companies * * * may be too heavy
"drinking for some people."[3]

All physicians know the disastrous consequences of administering water to excess or at the wrong time or to the wrong man. When a man is over-heated or is weakened by a long period of thirst, as often happens at sea or in the desert, care is taken to administer water only in small quantities. If it is given carelessly in excess, exhilaration, intoxication, and collapse may ensue. Intemperance in the use of water is a matter of daily experience. Such intemperance began early on our coasts. You will remember a gross instance in the journals of Bartholomew de Las Casas: "The Captain, Francisco de Soto, after three days' search, was found dying of thirst, and, on being brought on board and given water, he finished himself by drinking to excess."[4]

More recently Manila was mildly amused by the mishap of an abstinent official who had served for a year on an iceless islet,

---

2. Prize was awarded Oliver Kamm in January, 1929, for a paper discussing the role played by the alpha and beta hormones secreted by the pituitary gland in controlling the body's ability to retain water and hence function properly; e.g., put on or not put on weight, or repair injured tissue.
3. Quotation marks and line length in original Martin pamphlet.
4. Bartholomew de las Casas (1474-1566), Spanish missionary and historian of the Spanish New World conquests who worked for the abolition of Indian slavery and the betterment of the lot of all Indians. The incident is related in Vol. IV of his *Historias de las Indas*, called "the most valuable single account of the discovery of the New World." DeSoto (not to be confused with Hernando de Soto of Mississippi River fame) was among the survivors of an Indian attack, and the water apparently worked in conjunction with a

somewhere down by the Sulu Sea.[5] When the government boat came, for the annual inspection of his conduct, he went aboard and got ludicrously fuddled on simple ice-water.

Dr. Eugene Lyman Fiske, Medical Director of the Life Extension Institute, in discussing certain dangers of excess, says, as to water: "Animals have been known to get drunk on this [otherwise] highly beneficial beverage" (N.Y. Times, Apr. 9, 1929).[6]

It is clear, then, that the Constitution prohibits the sale and transportation of water for beverage purposes.

There is merit as well as inconvenience in this prohibition. It favors villages and farmers and forbids aqueducts, which, from the days of Nineveh[7] and Rome have fostered metropolitan luxury. It seems to be intended to break up the hypertrophied cities that are the curse of our century. Farmers and villagers can supply themselves from wells; and from cisterns of rain-water, as do the innocent inhabitants of Bermuda. Under a strict enforcement of this prohibition the privilege of living in the States would be reserved, in effect, to such law-abiding persons as can use their own wells or cisterns and to such others as would be content to drink the unfermented juice of oranges, apples, grapes and berries, and the milk of coconuts and quadrupeds. There are citizens who cannot afford to dig their own wells or build their own cisterns and do not like orange juice and must have their four glasses of water. Such persons may move out into Canada or Mexico. The sooner the better. We have already too many people, more than we can employ. We have too many that indulge in vice and revelry, too many whose self-indulgence resists the best efforts of church and state.

Congress, made up largely of water-drinkers, has chosen to neglect, thus far, this prohibition of water.

Neglect to pass an enforcing statute does not cancel a constitutional prohibition. No legal rights can be based on a violation of the Amendment. I shall dispute my water-rates. I admit that it is lawful for New York to use Catskill water for water-power and in certain other ways; but I hope that some tax-payer, inflamed by Civic Virtue, will sue, asking the Court to

---

5. Sea southwest of the Philippines, between the Philippines and Borneo.
6. Eugene Lyman Fisk (1867-1931), first director of the Life Extension Institute, founded 1913; author of numerous books promoting health and longevity. In the *Times* quotation, he was replying to an exercise and cold water enthusiast pointing out that all health measures are relative to person and circumstance.
7. Capital city of ancient Assyria on the Tigris River; reached its peak c. 8th century B.C.

padlock the Catskill Mountain reservoirs unless the city will stipulate not to sell water "for beverage purposes." The city's lawyers will attempt, of course, some defense by saying: " 'Liquor' has a broad meaning that includes water and a narrow meaning, as in the ancient sign-boards, 'wines, liquors and segars'. The Constitution uses 'liquor' in its narrow meaning." The Court will reply: "So has 'intoxicating' a broad meaning, anything that has five one-thousandths of an exhilarating element in it, and a narrow meaning, anything that actually makes you drunk. We judges have given 'intoxicating' its broad meaning. Therefore we must give 'liquor' its broad meaning. We can't take a phrase of two words, and give a broad construction to half of it and a narrow construction to the other half. If, at your request, we give a narrow meaning to 'liquor', then we must cut down 'intoxicating' to its narrower meaning; and then, where shall we get off?" No answer to this prohibition of aqueducts can be made except such answers as the Courts have already knocked out in dealing with claret and beer.

**NEWELL MARTIN.**

Huntington, August, 1930.

# On Drinking Alone By Moonlight

*Martin's father translated from Chinese to English two well-known poems about drinking. One is an ode written by Li-po in 720 A.D. (See footnote #12 in "The Yale Commencement.") Of this poem he noted, "This is an attempt to render the best known ode of China's favourite bard." The second is an anonymous work from the Book of Odes, B.C. 500. The note accompanying this short work explained: "This was printed some years ago in another paper, and it is now reprinted as a companion to the foregoing. It is specially suitable to these last days of the Chinese year."*

I. On Drinking Alone By Moonlight.

Here are flowers and here is wine,
But where's a friend with me to join
Hand to hand and heart to heart
In one full cup before we part?

Rather than to drink alone,
I'll make bold to ask the Moon
to condescend to lend her face
To grace the hour and the place.

Lo! she answers, and she brings
My shadow on her silver wings,
That makes three, and we shall be,
I ween, a merry company.

The modest mood declines the cup,
But shadow promptly takes it up;
And when I dance my shadow fleet
Keeps measure with my flying feet.

Yet though the moon declines to tipple,
She dances in yon shining ripple
And when I sing, my festive song
The echoes of the moon prolong.

Say, when shall we next meet together?
Surely not in cloudy weather:
For you, my boon companions dear,
Come only when the sky is clear.

                              W.A.P.M.
Pearl Grotto, 24th Aug., 1889.

II. - Adieu to the Year. -A Drinking Song
of the Old World.

The voice of the cricket is heard in the hall,
The leaves of the forest are withered and sere:
My spirits they droop at those chirrupping notes
So thoughtlessly sounding the knell of the years.

Yet why should we sigh at the change of a date,
When life's flowing on in a full steady tide;
Come, let us be merry with those that we love,
For pleasure in measure there's no one to chide.

W.A.P.M.

30th December, 1876.

# THREE

# WAR AND PEACE

Paper Umbrellas . . . . . . . . . . . . . .98

From Washington's Farewell . . . . . 107

This Is a Tract . . . . . . . . . . . . . . . 111

Letter to Major-General
    Robert Alexander . . . . . . . . . . 114

Letter to Molly,
    August 12, 1938 . . . . . . . . . . . 118

War List of an Ordinary,
    Harmless American Family . . . . 119

## Paper Umbrellas

To the Editor of *The New York Times*:[1]

The Kellogg pact, under which everybody promises not to try to overawe anybody and not to use an army or navy to coerce anybody is a paper umbrella. Paper umbrellas are quite all right until it rains.

The prognosis of the new treaties is borrowed from H. H. Munro, who said in 1911 that the Triple Alliance was a paper umbrella, all right as long as you didn't take it out in the rain. Munro printed this modest prophecy three years before von Bethmann-Hollweg[2] made his famous remark about the Treaty of 1839, three years before the Triple Alliance melted away in the storm of war.

In the last thirty years the rulers of great nations have done more harm than good by entering lightly into agreements as to war which they did not intend to keep. I write to remind you of a fat volume, prepared by learned and benevolent men, that contains many proofs of this. It is entitled "Judicial Settlement of International Disputes." It was published by Willams & Wilkins in the Summer of 1914. That was not the time to publish optimistic essays on world peace, and therefore nobody has ever regarded this book as anything but a collection of jests.

NEWELL MARTIN.

New York, Dec. 13, 1928.

*In the spring of 1927, Aristide Briand, the French foreign minister, suggested to the U.S. the signing of a bilateral nonaggression pact. The then U.S. Secretary of State, Frank B. Kellogg, embraced the concept, adding the stipulation that it be converted to a multilateral nonagression treaty.*

*Known as the Kellogg-Briand Pact, it was signed on August 27, 1928, by virtually all nations. While the Kellogg Pact renounced*

---

1. *The New York Times* December 19, 1928, p. 26.
2. Theobold von Bethmann-Hollweg (1856-1921), Chancellor of Germany 1907-1917, famously declared in 1914 that the Treaty of 1839, ending Belgian rebellion against Dutch rule and providing for the maintenance of Belgian neutrality by the three great European powers, was "a scrap of paper."

*war as a method of settling disputes, it did so under a variety of qualifications, and failed to provide for enforcement.*

*Martin printed three separate tracts headed "Paper Umbrellas:" the first dated December 9, 1928; the second Dec. 14; and a more comprehensive eight-page pamphlet dated December 29. The Dec. 9 tract is addressed, as a letter, to Henri Lambert of Charleroi, Belgium, in reaction to a letter of Lambert's which had appeared in* The Nation.

*Mr. Lambert was a Belgian glass manufacturer who wrote extensively during and after WWI on the need for all nations to share equally in trade and colonizing opportunities — the only means, as he saw it, for avoiding modern war. Lambert's letter stated that while "taken in itself, the mutual promise of the nations never again to make war on each other (although they have not been able to solve to their mutual satisfaction any of the grave questions which profoundly divide them) is the most flagrant childishness and stupidity to which diplomats, statesmen and princes have ever subscribed in the course of human history..." Yet his letter conceeded that the Kellogg-Briand Pact assured peace "for many years to come," since, as he saw it, the U.S. would not fail to aid any victims of aggression.*

*We reprint the so-called letters to Lambert; and the full text of the eight-page tract.*

Huntington, Long Island, New York
December 9, 1928

Henri Lambert, Esq.
Charleroi, Belgium

Dear Mr. Lambert:

Yesterday I wrote to you of the jocosity of American publicists. Even sober leaders of our bar, when they are writing eulogies of departed great men, have been known to indulge their ironic humor. This morning I read two books[3], each of which, oddly enough, culminates and perorates in an obituary of Harding, a recent American president. I myself was one of the multitude that voted for Harding. But even his partisans know that he was the crony and patron of Fall, Forbes, and Daugherty[4], whose repute has crossed

---

3. S. M. Meyer, Jr., says that Other Gomby was a constant reader, devouring as many as five books a day.
4. Senator Albert B. Fall (1861-1944), N.S. senator from New Mexico 1912-1921; U.S. Secretary of the Interior 1921-1923. In the latter position he controlled the leasing of mineral rights in the Teapot Dome naval oil reserves in Wyoming, was fined $100,000 for his part in the scandal of that name, and sentenced to one year in prison.

the Atlantic; and that Wayne B. Wheeler[5] was his Rasputin. One of these books is entitled "Law Reform" and is written by Henry W. Taft[6]. Law reform, in America, is always a joke. The other is the Pathway of Peace" and is written by Charles E. Hughes[7]. You will remember that it was Mr. Hughes who thought the path to peace lay in sinking the battleships of the only nation that desires to end war.

Mr. Hughes, in 1925, at page 306 of his book, says: "Harding gave his life for his country. He exhausted himself in service, a martyr to the interests of the people. He will ever be an exemplar."

Mr. Henry Taft says, in 1926, at page 264 of his book: "Mr. Harding fell a victim to the cruel exactions of the arduous office which he so honorably filled. Mr. Harding's life affords an example by which we loyal Americans may well guide our conduct."[8]

[No closing signature.]

---

Charles R. Forbes (1878-1952), WWI soldier, won Croix de Guerre. Personal friend of Harding; appointed by him as director of the Veterans' Bureau. After Forbes resigned inresigned in 1923, a senate investigation uncovered evidence of graft in connection with the location of hospitals and contracts for their construction, and Forbes served a term in Leavenworth.

Harry Micajah Daugherty (1860-1941): Lawyer and politician, appointed U.S. Attorney-General by Harding in March 1921. Repeatedly accused in congress of laxness in investigation of alleged wholesale profiteering and fraud connected with war contracts.

5. (1869-1927), lawyer and prohibitionist. Until 1917, general counsel to the Anti-Saloon League; subsequently its legislative superintendent. As president and Washington lobbyist of the Anti-Saloon League during Harding's presidency (1920-1923), and possessor of tenacious political roots in Harding's native state of Ohio, Wheeler came to exert considerable control over Harding's conduct in prohibition-related matters, from government appointments to detailed advice on the wording of public utterances. (Harding, as one historian puts it, was "not to act too dry in order to keep the country very dry," and in fact in both his senatorial and presidential campaigns Harding brilliantly straddled the prohibition fence.) Wheeler managed to get Harding, a mild lifelong drinker, to sign the pledge during his term as president.

6. Henry W. Taft (1859-1945; Yale '80): Brother of William Howard Taft. New York City lawyer; commissioner of education New York City 1896-1900. University Club member. Possessed a keen interest in law reform. Author Law Reform: Papers and Addresses by a Practicing Lawyer (N.Y.: Macmillan, 1926).

7. Charles Evans Hughes (1862-1948; L.L.D. Yale '15): U.S. Secretary of State 1921-1925; author The Pathway of Peace (N.Y.: Harper's, 1925) Quote (p. 307), accurately would read: "Warren G. Harding gave his life for his country....He exhausted himself in service, a martyr in fidelity to the interests of the people....If American life with all its possibilities of conflict and turmoil is to be worth living it must be lived in the spirit of brotherly understanding of which he will ever be an exemplar in high office."

Hughes initiated an arms-reduction conference held in Washington in 1921 at which he suggested that the U.S., Great Britain, and Japan should immediately abandon their capital ship-building programs and scrap enough of their existing ships to bring their respective naval strengths to a 5-5-3 ratio; this reduction to be followed by a ship-building moratorium of at least ten years. The program essentially was adopted, and the U.S. scrapped about forty vessels, including capital ships, in 1923.

8. The Taft quote comes from a public address made at White Sulphur Springs, Montana, in August, 1923. The second sentence reads in full: "Mr. Harding's life affords an example, an easily understood model, by which we loyal Americans, as units of the body politic may well guide our conduct."

## Paper Umbrellas[9]

*"The rights of each nation, at sea, under international law, are measured by the tonnage of that nation's navy."*

I ask the secretary of any Senator to whom this volume may be sent, to study, for his own profit, the three marked lines on page six of this book, before he drops it into the ashcan.

## Preface

Charles A. Beard, in the January *Harper's*[10] shows that Kuropatkin[11] suggested the Hague Peace Conferences and that his motives were those of the sportsmen that organized the late Arnold Rothstein's last card party.[12]

New York has a curious "Sullivan Law" which forbids peaceable citizens to carry revolvers and fails to disarm desperadoes. Kuropatkin desired a sort of International Sullivan Law under which opulent and peace-loving nations would reduce their armament while international burglars would secretly buy new weapons. In private life there is some protection against burglars. One seldom has to rely on a burglar's assurance that he has abandoned porch-climbing as an instrument of policy. True, a man of large means is often in danger from hungry men who are tempted to take aggressive measures of self-defense to protect their

---

9. Separate tract, not written in letter form.
10. Charles Austin Beard (1874-1948), American historian, professor 1904-1917 at Columbia University, author of numerous books, notably *An Economic Interpretation of the Constitution*. The article, "Bigger and Better Armaments" in the January, 1929, *Harper's* stated that the Bolshevik disclosure of the Tsarist archives showed that the Hague Peace conference in 1899 had been originated by Kuropatkin as a means of restoring the loss of Russia's power balance caused by new German armaments, notably artillery.
11. Alexi Nikolaevich Kuropatkin (1848-1925), Russian general, minister of war 1898-1905. Opposed the Russo-Japanese War of 1905-1905, but took command in Manchuria after its outbreak.
12. (1882-1928), professional gambler and racketeer. In the summer of 1928, Rothstein lost some $322,000 in a two-day poker game and failed to pay his IOU's. On November 4, he was called to a card game in the Central Park Hotel (New York City) where he was fatally wounded. George McManus, who had held the game of the preceding summer and by gambler's code was responsible for unpaid debts deriving therefrom, was tried for Rothstein's murder, acquitted for lack of evidence. The case remained unsolved. Rothstein was the original for Nathan Detroit in *Guys and Dolls*.

interiors from starvation; but, in private life prosperous persons, are made safe, more or less, by the police and by the simple-minded honesty of the poor. It is not so with nations. Nations, in dealing with each other, have no scruples, are bound by no law, and are held back by no police. A rich nation, so imperfectly armed that it carries no fairly sure knock-out punch is about as safe as a corpulent, well-dressed jeweler, alone, with a pocket full of diamonds and without a gun, on a dark night, in the thieves' quarter of a tough town.

*[The final letter re: Paper Umbrellas.]*

Dear Mr. Lambert:
My foregoing prognosis of the new treaties is, perhaps, less accurate than your mournful and prophetic appraisal of them, set forth in your recent letter, which was published in *L'Echo de la Bourse* and in *The New York Nation* of October 17. My thought as to those entertaining documents is taken from H. H. Munro, who used to write little romances, under the musical name of Saki. In his "Chronicles of Clovis," at page 97, Munro represents a certain Baroness as saying: "Elsa said something quite clever on Thursday about the Triple Alliance. Something about it being like a paper umbrella that was all right as long as you didn't take it out in the rain. It's not every one who could say that." In Munro's story, a certain Grafin then answers: "Every one has said it; at least, every one that I know." Munro printed this modest prophecy in 1911, three years before Von Bethmann-Hollweg made his famous remark about the Treaty of 1839, three years before the Triple Alliance melted away in the storm of war. Munro's prophecy came true. When war broke out, the Italian government looked at the map, observed the vulnerability of Italy's long coast line and remembered that Britannia rules the waves. She rules them discreetly and is liberal towards subordinate frequenters of the sea; but on her favorite domain, she has been, for a long time, irresistible. She is an easy boss, but she is the boss. With this in mind, Italy shrewdly announced that Germany was the aggressor and that, therefore, the solemn documents that created the Triple Alliance were n.g.

Until I read your letter I thought that the new treaties were meant only to divert us from thinking about our own misery and to add to the gaiety of nations. My excuse for so thinking is that American statesmen have an incurable tendency to make a joke even out of such horrors as an impending war. Before me, for instance, lies a fat volume entitled "Judicial Settlement of International Disputes." It was published by Williams & Wilkins, of Baltimore, amid roars of laughter, in the summer of 1914. I need not say to a Belgian that this was the wrong summer for sending out a joke-book of this sort. This book reports the meetings, in December, 1913, of the American Society for Judicial Settlement of International Disputes.[14] That humorous society had among its officers and directors, Joseph H. Choate, William H. Taft, Charles W. Eliot, John Hays Hammond and Simeon E. Baldwin. The book was edited by James Brown Scott.[15] I quote some of the jests.

Sam Elder,[16] a Boston wit, says in this book, at page 326, "The necessity which compelled the establishment of courts in communities is irresistibly forcing their establishment between nations. Such courts are no longer the dreams of philosophers and philanthropists. They are necessitated by the ever increasing accord of nations." I knew Sam Elder. He was a fellow of infinite jest; but he was never funnier than when, in 1914, he spoke of the "ever-increasing accord of nations." The learned Horace G. Macfarland[17] said, at page 307, "In times past nations thought to rise by the destruction of their neighbors. Now war for aggrandisement, war for so-called conquest, is unthinkable."

I began to doubt whether serious publicists, Macfarland, David Jayne Hill,[18] Choate, really held these meetings. It is easier to believe that they hired Mark Twain, F.P. Adams, Will Rogers, Robert Benchley, Robert E. Sherwood and Ring Lardner, six of our professional humorists, to write these speeches. Macfarland's joke was borrowed, at once, by Asquith, who said, early in 1914, that war between England and Germany was unthinkable. The best thought

---

14. From 1910-1917, excluding 1915, the American Society for the Judicial Settlement of International Disputes published a volume of the addresses given at its annual meeting.
15. Joseph H. Choate (1832–1917), L.L.D. Yale '02): American lawyer and diplomat; ambassador to Great Britain 1899-1905. Charles W. Eliot (1834-1926' L.L.D. Yale '70): American educator; president of Harvard 1869-1909. John Hays Hammond (1855-1936; L.L.D. Yale '25): American mining and electrical engineer; captured in the Jameson raid in South Africa; involved in defense projects. Simeon E. Baldwin (1840-1927; Yale '61): American juror; chief justice of the Connecticut Supreme Court 1907-1910 (and uncle of Martin's friend E.B. Whitney). James Scott Brown (1866-1931): American lawyer and educator; specialist in international law; trustee and secretary of the Carnegie Endowment for International Peace. See Section Ten — "The Climenole."
16. Samuel James Elder (1850-1918; Yale '73, where he won several literary awards),: American lawyer; expert on international law; president of the Massachusetts Peace Society; member of the board of trustees of the World's Peace Foundation.
17. Horace G. Macfarland (1872-1915), Lieutenant Commander, U.S. Navy; was retired in 1909, for physical disability, following which he studied and practiced law.
18. David Jayne Hill (1851-1932), American diplomat and historian; ambassador to Germany 1908-1911.

of diplomatists has been concentrated on unthinkable wars. Then came Hannis Taylor,[19] at page 230, discussing "the rule of international law" that "all agreements are necessarily made subject to the general understanding that they shall cease to be obligatory as soon as the conditions upon which they were executed are essentially altered." Taylor said he was quoting from Hall. The rule sounds to me more like Lewis Carroll. The meeting was opened, with a delicious pretense of gravity by Joseph Choate, whose wit has lighted up a lot of London dinners. "We are told," said Choate (pages 4, 5 and 6), "that there are certain reasons why some of the nations are not in favor of calling the Third Hague Conference as early as 1915." Pichon and Isvolsky[20] might have smiled if these words had been reported to them. There was no Third Conference at The Hague in 1915. The arguments of 1915 were exchanged with heavy guns, *ultima rationes regum*. Then Mr. Choate took up, lightly, the Declaration of London,[21] and other historical curiosities. Thousands of pages have been written about the Declaration of London. College boys are asked foolish questions about it, in examination papers. To that extent it has affected the world's affairs. "The Declaration of London," said Choate, "laid down what naval powers regarded as rules that should be acceptable to all nations for the conduct of naval warfare." Choate then proceeded to advise his auditors as to the law that governs aerial warfare. "the first Conference in 1899," said he, "voted that the launching of projectiles from dirigible balloons or other similar vehicles...should be unlawful until the adjournment of the Third Conference. The Second Conference continued that prohibition." So, I learn from this volume that, in 1914, it was in the quaint archaic language of 1899, "unlawful to launch projectiles from dirigible balloons or other similar vehicles." It was quite unlawful for Guynemer and Immelman,[22] in "similar vehicles" to drive miraculously through the sky, bearing death on their fearless wings.

Not one of the saturnine Americans that listened to Joe Choate did so much as wink when he went on to describe the swift

19. (1851-1922), lawyer and economist; expert on the English Constitution and international law.
20. Stephan Pichon and Alexander Izvolsky, respectively French foreign minister and Russian ambassador to France.
21. Delegates of ten naval powers convened in the London Naval Conference of 1908-1909, to codify the principles of international maritime law in regard to prize cases (legality of capture at sea during wartime). The opposition of the House of Lords in 1911, prevented British ratification of the "Declaration of London," and the treaty never went into effect, though it is sometimes said to have influenced international law.
22. Georges Guynemer and Franz Immelmann, French and German WWI air aces.

and gratifying growth of international law, in these words: "At the Second Hague Conference twenty-one nations were in favor of the establishment of the rule that private property should be just as safe from the ravages of war upon the sea as upon the land."

The war confirmed this agreement of twenty-one nations by wiping out the obsolete notion that private property should be any safer on land than at sea. America sequestrated, on land, the private property of German merchants that had been made inviolable by special treaty.

And feeble neutrals learned that there is no law that makes them safe on either sea or land. The United States and England seized at sea and in port, every desirable ship of the neutral Dutch.[23] We made it clear to the Dutch that the rights of each nation, at sea, under international law, are measured by the tonnage of its navy. "This is piracy," said the Dutch. "These are good ships," we answered, "and it would be absurd to buy them at war prices. So we take them, under the law of angary." "What is angary?" asked the Dutch. "You will find it described," said we, "by your own Grotius. When the couriers of a Persian satrap took for public use the property of any Persian subject who did not have a pull at court, that was angary."[24]

No patriot would condemn those seizures. But all of us patriots deplore them, because, while they may have produced some small private profits, they were not needed for the winning of the war. They seemed to put us in the position of a gentleman who, holding already four aces, draws from his sleeve a superfluous fifth ace. I mention these unimportant seizures to show that even virtuous nations will lapse from virtue if effectively tempted. Not long ago we, the Christian Powers, under trivial inducement, raided Russian legations and consulates, particularly in China; where, in 1900, we demonstrated the sanctity of envoys, at the expense of the Chinese.

*[Editor's note: The advances of the Kuomintang (name for the Chinese National People's Party, then a precarious alliance of communist forces with Chiang Kai-shek's nationalists which was to fracture in a few months) in 1926, and early 1927, had been*

---

23. In the "preface," Mr. Martin requested the "secretary of any Senator to whom this volume may be sent, to study, for his own profit, the three marked lines ... before he drops it in the ashcan." It is the following lines which were so marked by the silhouette of a cuffed hand with a pointing index finger.

24. The OED defines "angary" as "the right of a belligerent to use and destroy neutral property."

*accompanied by widespread anti-foreign outbreaks and a number of actual atrocities. The Western powers viewed these events as communist-inspired; and when 50 soldiers of the nationalist warlord Chang Tsu-lin raided the Russian embassy in Peking on April 6, 1927, the Dutch minister who headed the diplomatic corps and was effectively in charge of the common legation grounds gave them permission for what he later called a "limited search."*

*Partly burned documents captured in the raid revealed a Moscow plot for the massacre of foreigners in China as a means of bringing about Western intervention that would in turn lead to world revolution. Moscow denounced the papers as counterfeit, and characterized the raid as an attempt by Great Britain to stampede public opinion in Britain, the U.S., and Japan into thinking of the Chinese communists and nationalists as plotting against the lives of foreign nationals in China.*

*(Russia, scholars agree, was in no position to cause all the anti-foreign rioting, but unquestionably she was engaged in serious revolutionary adventurism in China in the person of her agent Borodin, who was forced to flee later in 1927.)*

*On May 12, 1927, a force of some 150 London police raided the headquarters of the Soviet trade delegation and the London office of Arcos, Ltd., the trading organization of all the Russian cooperatives in Great Britain. The documents seized, which included evidence of a plot to purchase arms in Ireland for the Canton communists with a view to implicating Britain, led to the expulsion of the Soviet diplomatic corps.*

*The 1900 reference is of course to the Boxer Rebellion when the foreign legations at Tientsin and Peking were besieged.]*

Paper barricades will not shield non-combatants against the flame of the next war. It will be one of the most interesting features of the next war that it will slaughter large numbers of non-combatants and will set in operation again the salutary law of the extermination of the unfit.

I must remind you that the great war, which America entered, "to make an end of war," failed to achieve our benevolent aim, because in that war, only young men were killed. The non-combatants and the old women were left alive and more potent than ever. People of that sort, in times of excitement, become unduly bloodthirsty and uncompromising. It is people of that sort that make wars. The next war will be different. Our canal will be blocked and our navy sunk shortly before a formal declaration of war; and flying "vehicles" will then bombard our towns. In such a war many of the young and vigorous will escape, but few of the aged will survive. It was so, also, in the old-fashioned wars of Jenghiz Khan. The strong and nimble often got away to the woods and hills. The opinionated old men and the irascible old women were ridden down and put to the sword. Their empty skulls were then piled on garbage dumps, in pyramids. For that reason, the campaigns of Jenghiz were followed by an era of vivacity and enlightenment. I beg you, therefore, not to advise any precautions that may tend to postpone the next war.

ᵹ ᵹ ᵹ

# From Washington's Farewell, 1796

*George Washington's Farewell Address was submitted to the Cabinet September 15, 1796, and appeared in Claypoole's* Daily Advertiser *on September 19, at Washington's own request, "as proper to communicate to the people of the United States."*

*Newell Martin's excerpt appeared in pamphlet form (4.5" X 7.5"). We have noted in brackets minor differences between Martin's version and that supplied in the authoritative,* The Writings of George Washington, *Vol. 35 (Washington, D.C.: Government Printing Office, 1940), pp. 214-238.*

*David C. Claypoole, in his contemporary account of the publication of George Washington's Farewell Address, wrote, "After the proof sheet had been carefully compared with the copy, and corrected by myself, I carried two different Revises, to be examined by the President; who made but few alterations from the original, except in the punctuation, in which he was very minute." As for Martin, he made liberal use of the comma, and sprinkled them through Washington's text* ad libitum. *Text in* **bold type** *appears in that format in Martin's pamphlet.*

"* * * Cherish public credit. One method of preserving it is to use it as sparingly as possible; avoiding occasions of expense by cultivating peace, but remembering also that timely disbursements to prepare for danger frequently prevent much greater disbursements to repel it; avoiding, likewise, the accumulation of debt, not only by shunning occasions of expense, but by vigorous exertions in time of peace to discharge the debts which unavoidable wars may have occasioned; not ungenerously throwing upon posterity the burden which we ourselves ought to bear. * * * Observe good faith and justice towards all nations;[.] c[C]ultivate peace and harmony withal;[with all.] r[R]eligion and morality enjoin this conduct, and can it be that good policy does not equally enjoin it? It will be worthy of a free, enlightened and at no distant period, a great nation, to give to mankind the magnanimous and **too novel example of a people always guided by an exalted justice and benevolence.** * * * In the execution of such a plan, nothing is more essential than that **permanent, inveterate antipathies against particular nations and passionate attachments for others should be excluded;** and that in place of them, **just and amicable feelings towards all** should be cultivated. The nation which indulges towards another an habitual hatred or an habitual fondness, is, in some degree, a slave. * * * The Government sometimes participates in the national propensity and adopts, through passion, what reason would reject,[;] at other times it makes the animosity of the nation subservient to projects of hostility instigated by pride, ambition and other sinister and pernicious motives. The peace often, sometimes, perhaps, the liberty, of nations, has been the victim. [paragraph in original] So, likewise, a passionate attachment of one nation to another produces a variety of evils. Sympathy for the favorite nation, facilitating the illusion of an imaginary common interest, [in cases where no real common interest] exists, and, infusing into one the enmities of the other, betrays the former into a participation in the quarrels and wars of the latter, without adequate inducement or justification. It leads also to concessions to the favorite nation of privileges denied to others, which is apt doubly to injure the nation making the concessions, by unnecessarily parting with what ought to have been retained, and by exciting jealousy, ill-will, and a disposition to retaliate, in the parties from whom equal privileges are withheld: and it gives to ambitious, corrupt or **deluded citizens** (who devote themselves to the favorite nation) facility **to betray or sacrifice the interest[s] of their own country, without odium; sometimes even with popularity; gilding with the appearance[s] of** * * * **a laudable zeal for public good,** the base or **foolish compliances** of ambition [, corruption,] or **infatuation.**

[paragraph in original] As avenues to foreign influence, in innumerable ways, such attachments are particularly alarming to the truly enlightened and independent patriot. How many **opportunities** do they afford to tamper with domestic factions, to practice the art[s] of seduction, to mislead public opinion, **to influence or awe the public councils.[!]** * * *

**Against the insidious wiles of foreign influence (I conjure you to believe me, fellow citizens) the jealousy of a free people ought to be constantly**[italicized in original] **awake, since history and experience prove that foreign influence is one of the most baneful foes of republican government.** But that jealousy, to be useful, must be impartial; else it becomes the instrument of the very influence to be avoided, instead of a defense against it. Excessive partiality for one foreign nation and excessive dislike for another, cause those whom they actuate to see danger only on one side and serve to veil, and even second, the acts of influence on the other. Real patriots, who may resist the intrigues of the favorite, are liable to become suspected, and odious; while its tools and dupes usurp the applause and confidence of the people, to surrender their interests.

**The great rule of conduct for us, in regard to foreign nations, is**, in extending our commercial relations, **to have with them as little *political* [italicized by Washington] connection as possible.** * * *

**Europe has a set of primary interests, which to us have none, or a very remote relation. Hence, she must be engaged in frequent controversies, the causes of which are essentially foreign to our concerns. Hence, therefore, it must be unwise in us to implicate ourselves, by artificial ties, in the ordinary vicissitudes of her politics, or the ordinary combinations and collisions of her friendships or enmities.**

Our detached and distant situation invites and enables us to pursue a different course;[.] If we remain one people, under an efficient Government, the period is not far off when we may defy material injury from external announce; when we may take such an attitude as will cause the neutrality we may at any time resolve upon, to be scrupulously respected; * * * when **we may choose peace or war, as our interest, guided by [our] justice, shall** counsel.

**Why forego the advantages of so peculiar a situation;[?]** * * * why [Why], by interweaving our destiny with that of any part of Europe, entangle our peace and prosperity in the toils of European ambition, **rivalship, interest, humor or caprice.[?]** [paragraph in original] It is our true policy to steer clear of permanent alliances with any portion of the foreign world. * * * **Taking care always to keep ourselves, by suitable establishments, on a respectable** [respectably] **defensive posture, we may safely trust to temporary alliances for extraordinary emergencies.** * * * Constantly keeping in view, that it is folly in one nation to look for disinterested favors from another; **that** it must pay, with a portion of its independence, **for whatever it may accept under that character.** * * * There can be no greater error than to expect or calculate upon real favors from nation to nation. * * *

In offering to you, my countrymen, these counsels of an old and affectionate friend, I dare not hope they will make the strong and lasting impression I could wish; that they will * * * prevent our nation from running the course which has hitherto marked the destiny of nations; but if I may even flatter myself that they may be productive of * * * some occasional good; that they may now and then recur * * * to warn against the mischiefs of foreign intrigues [intrigue], to guard against the impostures of pretended patriotism; this hope will be a full recompense. * * *

With me, a predominant motive has been * * * to gain time to our country * * * [1] to give it * * * the command of its own fortunes."

ta ta ta

---

1. Original text: "The inducements of interest for observing that conduct will best be referred to your own reflections and experience. With me, a predominant motive has been to endeavour to gain time to our country to settle and mature its yet recent institutions, and to progress without interruption, to that degree of strength and consistency, which is necessary to give it, humanly speaking, the command of its own fortunes." [In other words, in its mere youth the America of 1796 had an additional motive for avoiding foreign involvement.]

# This Is a Tract

January 1, 1939.[1]

This is a tract[2] sent by Newell Martin from
West Main Street, Route Three,
Huntington, Long Island, New York.

Forgive me for sending this tract. It calls for no answer. I am anxious to remind a few thoughtful readers of some obvious dangers and difficulties.

The more Americans give thought to the possible darkness of their future the more likely are we to enjoy many happy new year days. Our nation has the sort of protection that is given by distance and by encircling seas. We are tempted to believe that we can be frugal in preparing our defenses because we have oceans about us. For five hundred years English statesmen thought they could practice that sort of frugality. But Englishmen have begun to wish that their statesmen had never learned to put so much faith in the protection given by large bodies of water. In England "every schoolboy"[3] used to be taught to describe England's safety by reciting from the Second Act of *King Richard II* lines which are known, even in America, to "every schoolboy."

This scepter'd isle,...
T[t]his fortress built by nature for herself,
... This little world,
This precious stone set in the silver sea,
Which serves it in the office of a wall
Or as a moat defensive to a house,
Against the envy of less happier lands.

Today many Englishmen are inclined to think that their rulers have forgotten too often that it is the duty of English statesmen to make sure, so far as human prudence can make sure, that Englishmen shall not be ruined by any enemy using any new

---

1. At this date, Other Gomby was bedridden with arthritis.
2. Ten pages, stapled, double-spaced, 6.25" X 3.50."
3. English historian and author Thomas Babington Macaulay (1800-1859) was fond of beginning an allusion with, "As every schoolboy knows..."

invention.
That duty has been tragically neglected.

England, bound in with the triumphant sea
Whose rocky shore beats back the envious siege
Of watery Neptune, is now bound [in] with shame.

The English are taxing themselves now to save the empire and to atone for the mistaken frugality of yesterday. They may find that they waked up too late. The lesson offered by England's misfortune should not be disregarded by Americans.[4]

I think I am not guilty of exaggeration when I say that most of us Americans believe that the United States should be so equipped with army and navy and flying machines as to be able to resist any combination of enemies; not any probable combination, but any combination.

Are any of us content to have the fate of our grandchildren left to probabilities?

America needs a navy that can meet the four corners of the world in arms. It needs such a navy in the Atlantic and such a navy in the Pacific. The man who denies this may be wiser than you or I and he may be right. He may be advising a wise economy. But he must remember that what we risk, in the next war, is the ruin of our descendants. He proposes to stake their future on the safety of a single delicate and remote piece of machinery, our Panama Canal.

What limitations should we put on our expenditure for defense? We can put that question in another way. What will happen if our defenses fail? That is a question easy to answer.

Two thousand million years have passed since life began on this agreeable planet. Our predecessors, driven by harsh necessity, did their best to make the most of their chances. Some of our ancestors achieved an astonishing change in their condition. By almost imperceptible slow steps they got out of the sea and became land animals. That was the first of the two greatest steps in our progress. Of late years men began to observe and envy certain glorious advantages enjoyed by birds. But philosophers used to assure us that we were hopelessly earth-bound. Suddenly, to our astonishment, men have leaped to the freedom of the upper air. Thus, in our own time, the second great step in our advance has been

---

[4]. "As every schoolboy should remember," Britain and France did not declare war with Germany until September 3, 1939.

WAR AND PEACE 113

achieved.

If Bacon, Darwin or Leibnitz[5] could be consulted he would give us his amazed congratulations. But he would warn us that this momentous development must bring not only unparalleled opportunities for advancement but also perils transcending all that the race has survived.

A fate worse than extinction threatens the peace. There is no precedent for flying and there is no precedent for the new perils of this hour.

The governments of Germany, Japan and Italy have joined in far-sighted plans for unscrupulous conquest.[6]

They begin by disabling, one by one, possible allies of any power that might be tempted, in the future, to resist these robber governments.

Many accurate volumes have been written about the benevolence, wisdom and charm of the people of Germany, who used to stand at the head of civilization; and about the benevolence, wisdom and charm of Italians and Japanese. But these three peoples have fallen into the hands of ruffians.

The alliance of the Three Powers is a sinister portent. Sometimes they are called the Totalitarian Powers; and not without reason, for in astronomy, "totality" is defined as "the time of total obscuration."

Consider the possibility of a great war in which on one side will stand the three totalitarian nations, with England, France, Russia, and our United States against them. Or, rather, imagine, as more probable, a war in which only two of the civilized governments have the courage or the prudence to fight against the three totalitarian powers. I can imagine our States and Russia uniting against three totalitarians; and I can imagine France and England afraid to join in such a war. They might remember General Boulanger.[7] He has been quoted as saying that one may calculate

---

5. Francis Bacon (1561-1626), English statesman and philosopher; first major thinker to propound the use of knowledge to advance man's earthly estate.
    Charles Robert Darwin (1809-1882), English naturalist, cheering on the fittest emerging from water to land.
    Gottfried Wilhelm, Baron von Leibniz (Leibnitz) (1646-1714), German philosopher and mathematician, essentially formulated the ontological basis of modern physics.
6. Reader is reminded that this prescient statement preceded by just 1,073 days the December 7, 1941, attack on United States naval forces at Pearl Harbor by Japanese "flying machines."
7. Georges Boulanger (1837-1891), French minister of war 1886-1887; leader of the reactionary nationalist party called Boulangism.

the profits of war against a small nation but that no man can predict the incidents and results of a great war.

Let us suppose that the three totalitarian powers win in a war against us. It is not inconceivable that they might win, in such a war; and it concerns us to consider the results of such a victory. What nations after such a victory could stand against the victorious and unscrupulous three? What then would the three decree, in their peace terms? Let us consider one point.

The victors would announce that in the future all flying would be reserved to trusted soldiers of the three. Nobody of any other nation would ever be allowed to fly, in war or trade or for pleasure. This would give to three groups of tyrants control of all the world's war, commerce, food, work, play and education. This would mark a division of the human race into Air Men nations and Ground Men nations. The people of nations forbidden to fly would undergo degradation and enslavement. Their women would be used to breed slaves and robots.

The low-minded chiefs of the Totalitarian Three would regard such a result as a desirable war prize. But Russians, French, Americans and English do not need to create any such unequal conditions for their own benefit.

You and I believe that all wisdom and all invention and all progress should be used, in the long run, for the good of the whole race. You and I believe that it is the duty of the human race, no matter how much hatred and cruelty prevail, to see to it that all men have a chance to advance in happiness, wisdom and power. But three maleficent governments ardently desire the ruin and enslavement of such nations as they have marked down to be their victims.

# Letter to Major-General Robert Alexander

*The General was a friend of Martin's. Other Gomby's granddaughter, Molly, received (and preserved) a typed carbon copy of a letter her grandfather had written to the general on April 9, 1937, which included notes to her scribbled in all four margins and on the overside. Seems Molly's picture had appeared twice in the April 1, 1937, issue of* Vogue Magazine, *and Martin had sent a copy of the magazine to the general suggesting that he "cut her out and paste her 2 pictures on the wall of your garage."*

*Alexander (1863-1941) fought against the Sioux, fought in Puerto Rico in the Spanish-American War, commanded a regiment in the Mexican Border War of 1916, and was the Commander of the 63rd Infantry Brigade in WWI which subsequently became the 77th Division. He was known as "the private's general," both for his solicitude for his men and his frequent visits to them in the front line, often at considerable risk from enemy fire. Received, for his WWI service, the Distinguished Service Cross, Croix de Guerre with two citations, and the Legion of Honor.*

*Alexander characterized the soldiers of the 77th them as: "these backwoodsmen of the Bronx, the Bowery, and Hester Street." Further, "It was currently said that there were forty-three languages and dialects among the men, and there were quite as many shades of religious belief and disbelief. Besides Americans of English-speaking lineage there were large numbers of Hebrews with the Italians a close second. There were those of German, Polish, Austrian and Russian origins and probably every race on the globe was represented except the Negro. We even had a number of Chinese, born in America and consequently citizens." Newell Martin's son, Grinnell served in the 77th Division.*

*The quotations are taken (pp. 107-108) from the Major General's* Memories of the Great War *(N.Y.: Macmillan, 1931), in which Alexander consistently praises the bravery of the men under his command, but is extremely critical of America's lack of military preparedness, the character and quality of American training, and the caliber of some army leadership.*

*Martin's printed tract contained a notation at the top in his own handwriting: "Letter sent by N.M. to Major General Alexander. Text follows.*

           Huntington
           Long Island, N.Y.
           January 31, 1936

I esteem your words, sent to the British Minister at

---

1. Eton and Oxford-educated Eugene Millington-Drake (1889-1972) was the British minister at Montevideo 1934-1941. Extremely popular (the football stadium was used for

Montevideo, to be filed away at Eton[1]. Your book and the true words you have inscribed at the head of it will be buried in a library. Nothing like a library, for burial purposes. Eratosthenes knew that the world is round and about how much it weighs[2]; and his facts were buried in libraries for two thousand years. Pepys' diary was buried for centuries[3]. You have written: 'However completely either industry or war may be mechanized the preponderant factor will always remain the human element, in war or peace. The qualities of courage and determination still remain; and will always so remain; as essential as they were when Caesar sought for them among his primipili [The senior centurions of a legion.]'. Edward VIII, dwelling in precarious comfort at Windsor, will find leisure sometimes to stroll over to Eton[4] and dip into the 1000 volumes among which your reminiscences will be preserved. I hope he will pick up your book, and find your statement. Your statement is true because men 'determined to be free' will always be willing to spend enough money on the equipment of armies and navies to make their courage effective. The most notable recent examples of this truth

---

his farewell ceremony), he did much to encourage both British and national sports in Uruguay, right up to taking charge of the country's 1936 Olympic delegation. However, by a twist of history which would have pleased N.M., Millington-Drake has gone down to posterity as the diplomat whose 72-hour running battle of wits with his German counterpart in 1939 resulted in the expulsion of the *Graf Spee* from the Montevideo harbor, forcing its engagement with the Royal Navy and subsequent self-destruction.

    In a ceremony held at Eton on December 10, 1938, Millington-Drake gave his school a collection of 5,000 books on WWI that he had spent some 15 years acquiring. Housed in a special room adjoining School Hall, the collection was called the Hugh Mcnaghten Library, in memory of the 53 boys from Millington-Drake's Eton house, Mcnaghten's, who had died in the Great War, and eight other boys who had been his close friends and also perished. (One's house at Eton is called after one's tutor, that is, house-master; thus "Mcnaghten's" not only names the house but the period.) Some 80 percent of the books were autographed, including the contributions of Foch, Petain, Joffre, Hindenburg, Ludendorff, Pershing, Mussolini, Haig, Poincare, Clemenceau, Wells, Sassoon, Kipling, Balfour, and the German Crown Prince. A good number, like Alexander's, also carried inscriptions, ranging in tone and address from *Foch, Vaincre c'est avancer*, to the Crown Prince, *Audiatur et altera pars* ("May the other side too be heard"); to Wells, "Mr. Britling [i.e., diminutive of Briton], poor dear, is still seeing it through"; to Balfour, "As yet unread by yours sincerely, Balfour."

2.  Eratosthenes (c. 275–c.195 B.C.), Greek scholar who was head of the library at Alexandria. Predicated the spherical character of the earth, and calculated its circumference, weight, and inclination to the ecliptic with – given his available means – remarkable accuracy.

3.  Samuel Pepys (1633-1703); his diary was bequeathed, along with many of his other papers, to his old school, Magdalen College, Cambridge. It remained in the Magdalen library, unpublished, until 1825, some 122 years after his passing.

4.  Edward VIII, subsequently the Duke of Windsor, who had become king January 20, 1936, with the death of George V, would abdicate in December. Eton is situated almost under the walls of Windsor Castle, separated from it only by the Thames River.

are Russia and Japan. Those two nations, in the last twenty years, have insured their freedom by making almost unendurable sacrifices to equip their armies and navies. No nation that does less deserves to live. Each nation should be great and strong and well-armed, an impregnable fortress, to keep all its people free. Small nations should get together, in powerful groups, as our 48 states have done. And then, each federal government should be so armed that its citizens cannot be enslaved. I owe no allegiance to my own nation unless I can say:

'Come the three corners of the world in arms and we shall shock them.' (King John V:7).

It horrifies me to see liberty-loving nations like Holland, Switzerland and Norway, complacently leaving their people in danger, from year to year, hoping that chance, in some fashion, will take care of them in the next war. Our civil war was fought to establish the rule that our nation must be big and that nobody may whittle away any fragment of its frontiers or citadels. There, again, your maxim is true: Men who have a "determination" to be safe, will see to it that their nation is big enough to be safe. It grieves me to see how the planet is cluttered up with little nations and to see how they waste their time pretending to combine, from time to time, in a preposterous, unstable and fraudulent league of nations.[5] Our states, 149 years ago [Editor's note: U.S. Constitution was signed in 1787], showed how freemen, that have 'determination', will make the sacrifices of state pride that are needed to make a big and safe nation.

I hope posterity or somebody will upset the old-fashioned doctrine that we must have a helpless nation and strong states.

---

5. The League of Nations, founded in 1920, had revealed its impotence through its failure to deal with the Japanese in Manchuria, the 1934 Chaco War between Bolivia and Paraguay, and the Italian invasion of Ethiopia, as well as numerous lesser matters. Japan, Italy, and Germany, faced with the threat of censure or boycott, had simply ignored the League or resigned from it.

## Letter to Molly
Friday, Aug. 12, 1938[1]

To Miss Molly Meyer
Care of Schuyler M. Meyer, Esq.
Care of H. M. Paul, Esq.
Blue Mountain Lake, New York

Dear Molly
 Modern barbarism makes the world unsafe for everybody everywhere. The Japanese, to draw Moscow's attention, or, rather, to learn whether Moscow intends to resist aggression, drops [sic] high explosives on the Russians, for 3 hours. The Russians then bomb Japanese & Koreans & on Manchuquotes for 4 hours. The Japanese then abstain from further efforts in the north. During this war, diplomatic relations between Japan & Russia continue, unfriendly but undisturbed.[2] In these modern times it is the duty of every government, at any expense, to keep every city fort & war-ship prepared, at all times, against any & every possible attack. London is quite right in putting gas masks on its women & children.[3] I think every baby-wagon in Central Park should have hanging at its corners two gas-masks, one for the baby & one for the nurse. I have the lowest opinion of the English government & of Chamberlain;[4] but the English are better than most of the others. I think Russia, the United States of America, England & France should come together & say "We 4 have agreed to be the only owners of flying machines. You others can hire our fliers when you wish to fly." Forthwith there would be war.
 Better now than later. Then, after the war, there would be a

---
1. Handwritten on letterhead: "Turkey Lane, Huntington, Long Island, New York."
2. On August 12, a truce ended roughly a month's sporadic fighting between Japanese and Russian troops along the Manchukuoan-Siberian frontier. (Manchukuo — where lived Martin's "Manchuquotes" — was a Japanese puppet state comprising present Manchuria and Jehol provinces; restored to China after WWII.) Hostilities had been occasioned by the Russian fortification of the heights of Changkufeng immediately adjacent to the border. Had Japan not already been at war with China, open war with Russia probably would have broken out; but one reason diplomatic relations continued was the fact that by then the conduct of the Japanese army had little to do with Japan's civilian government.
3. The 1938 war scare resulted in Great Britain in the massive digging of bomb shelters and issuing of gas masks, some of the latter actually being carried on perambulators and baby-carriages.
4. Neville Chamberlain (1869-1940) became British prime minister in May, 1937. It was in the September following Martin's writing that he held the three conferences with Hitler that gave Germany the Sudetenland for the sake of "peace in our time."

lot of disagreement, among the survivors.

Affectionately

*Newell Martin*

⁂

# War List Of An Ordinary, Harmless American Family.
January, 1918.

*Accompanying the list, is a sheet in Martin's handwriting stating: "This war list of the fighting Grinnells will remind you of Artemas Ward — [pseudonym of Charles Farrar Browne (1834-1867) the U.S. humorist] — who said that he had urged all his wife's relatives to join the army."*

George Grinnell, Mrs. Martin's paternal grandfather, was a peaceful Massachusetts man.
Of his great-grand-daughters, one is engaged to a soldier, and five are married to soldiers.
These soldiers are:
Renzo Brusati,[1] Major, Italian Artillery
    (married Sylvia Page)
Capt. Harry Sturges
    (married Violet Grinnell-Milne)[2]
Capt. Gilliat (married Muriel Grinnell-Milne)
Capt. Mann (married or engaged to Mary
    Hopkins daughter)
Another Captain, whose name I do not know
Capt. Ralph Speed (married Lucy Landon)

---

1. (1884-Dec. 29, 1918–victim of the post-WWI influenza epidemic), Italian count; educated at the Royal Italian Military Academy; military attaché at the Italian Embassy in London (1913-14). At the outbreak of the war he returned to Italy to command a group of batteries in the Italian Royal Horse Artillery, which he did for the war's entire duration, being twice wounded and decorated several times. His widow, Sylvia Page Brusati, daughter of Mrs. Martin's sister Helen - was remarried in 1923 to Theodore Lilley (Yale '10). Mrs. (Laura) Martin and Helen Page were daughters of George Grinnell's son, George Blake Grinnell.
2. A Harry Sturges (b. 1894), described as having left Harvard to go to war, made the front page of The New York Times in 1925 through having become at the age of thirty-one a director of the Erie Railroad Co.

His great-grandsons, of "draft age" (including those old enough to fight, but under 21) were 8 in number:

With the 6 officers above-named this makes 14 young men to be considered:

Of these, one is in an industry regarded by the government as of prime necessity for war purposes.

The other 7 are:
Lieut. Blythe Bogle, British Army, killed.
Lieut. Douglas Grinnell-Milne)   English aviators brought
Lieut. Duncan Grinnell-Milne )
    down in action. Both are prisoners
    of war in Germany.
Harold Morton Landon, First Lieutenant, in France.
Wm. G. Landon, in English Army[3]
Galloway Cheston, Aviator, U.S. Army, abroad.
Grinnell Martin, First Lieut. 304th Field Artillery.[4]

Thus, of 14 in whom George Grinnell, now in heaven, is particularly interested and who could fairly be regarded as suitable for the army:

|  |  |
|---|---|
| In industries, needed for war, | 1. |
| In army service, | 13. |
| In other occupations, | None. |

Of the soldiers:

|  |  |
|---|---|
| Major | 1. |
| Captains | 5. |
| Aviators | 3. |
| Lieutenants other than aviators, | 3. |
| Private, | 1. |
| Italian army, | 1. |
| British " | 9. |
| U.S. " | 3. |

---

3. Both Harold (Yale '11) and William were sons of Edward Hunter Landon (1851-1942; Yale '75), who married Mary Grinnell, daughter of George Grinnell's son William. Harold served in the 369th Infantry, receiving the Distinguished Service Cross for an action near Sechault on Sept. 29, 1918, in which he first carried a communique to a neighboring regiment through a heavy artillery barrage; then -- seeing the unit's officers had been greatly reduced by enemy fire -- led its first attack wave 1000 meters, securing its objective. In 1916 *The New York Times* had published a letter from Harold severely critical of persons recommending a mild or at least impartial treatment of Germany by the U.S. after the war (this was of course before U.S. entry). The senior Landon was on assignment in Paris with the American Red Cross from 1915-1918; William's and Harold's mother and two sisters were killed when a long-range German artillery shell struck the St. Gervaise church in Paris on March 29, 1918.

4. Newell Martin's only son.

Casualties:
    Killed, 1.
    Wounded 3 times, 1.
    Brought down
    within enemy lines,
    and taken prisoner, 2.
    Robbed
        of 700 lire, 1.

# FOUR

# BUSINESS AND BUSINESSMEN

Martin's Bank Balance ........ 124

A Deplorable Occurrence ....... 129

Spinach and Zweiback ........ 131

Bad News: A Letter to
   Frederick A. Stokes, Esq. ..... 135

## Martin's Bank Balance
[January 20, 1926]

The 10-page tract carries an "Index" instead of a title on the cover page, then has an "advertisement" on the title page. The following page contains the statement: "Form for a letter to your bank, asking what your balance is, if any. (This is a copy of a letter that served its purpose and it is therefore recommended as a labor-saving model)." This is followed by the text of a letter to one James. J. O'Shaughnessy followed by both a post script and a post post script.

O'Shaughnessy (1872-1945) became executive vice president of the Bank of Washington Heights in 1918; in 1927, it merged with the Bank of the Manhattan Co. Subsequently O'Shaughnessy became principal examiner of the New York State Banking Department. (See also "A Deplorable Occurrence.")

Martin is having more than a bit of fun with his banker and is discussing not only his bank balance but political knavery, greed, and exploitation. He recalls an incident in a convict camp in Florida: In June, 1923, Thomas W. Higginbotham, a convict whipping boss, was himself convicted of the murder of one Martin Tabert of Munich, North Dakota, early in 1921.

Tabert had been served a 90-day sentence by a Florida court for stealing a ride on a railroad. Tabert was then leased out by a county jail for labor in the town of Santa Clar's Camp of the Putnam Lumber Co. based in Wisconsin. (There were unproven allegations that a Florida county sheriff was collecting $20 under the counter for every convict delivered up for leased labor and was purposely scouring the railroads.)

There Tabert, became ill with malaria, and couldn't work hard enough to please his overseers. A witness testified that Tabert was beaten some 96 strokes with a seven-pound whip. Undoubtedly, Martin had read of the incident in The New York Times. After an extensive state investigation throughout April and May of 1923 led to the termination of all leasing of convict labor and a ban on whipping, The Times wrote "Why the county system [of leasing out convicts] was not done away with only certain employers of labor on a large scale and conniving politicians could explain."

# BUSINESS AND BUSINESSMEN 125

*Martin's advertisement:*

(The Daily Neech, co-operating with the New York University's School of Business, issues Forms of Letters, convenient models, adapted for all sorts of daily use -- e.g., we issue a Form for Letter to a grandchild, asking her not to marry a gentile and showing that it is better not to marry anybody; and a form for a letter to a philosopher, twelve years old, expressing concurrence with her views).

## INDEX
PAGE

Advertisement of labor-saving forms . . . . . . . . . . . 1
Florida's faults . . . . . . . . . . . . . . . . . . . . . . 3
Almendares . . . . . . . . . . . . . . . . . . . . . . . . 4
Brown girls . . . . . . . . . . . . . . . . . . . . . . . . 4
Water for external use . . . . . . . . . . . . . . . . . . 5
St. John . . . . . . . . . . . . . . . . . . . . . . . . . . 5
The Great Inagua . . . . . . . . . . . . . . . . . . . . 6
Grand Cayman . . . . . . . . . . . . . . . . . . . . . . 6
Innocent fantasies . . . . . . . . . . . . . . . . . . . . 5
Total abstinence . . . . . . . . . . . . . . . . . . . . . 5
Civic virtue in Jamaica . . . . . . . . . . . . . . . . . 6
Schedule of tonics . . . . . . . . . . . . . . . . . . . . 6
Wine measure . . . . . . . . . . . . . . . . . . . . . . 7

January 20, 1926.
**James J. O'Shaughnessy, Esq., Vice-President, Bank of Washington Heights.**

Dear O'Shaughnessy:
 1. Give my affectionate regards to John Whalen[1] and John Beals.[2] Beals may have a place as fine as Berolzhiemer's,[3] but I do

---

1. (1856-1927), lawyer and politician; one-time New York City Corporation Counsel; close friend of Richard Crocker, lord of Tamany Hall. Much eulogized for serving as president of the Bank of Washington Heights without pay.
2. John David Beals (1868-1928), one of the organizers of the Bank of Washington Heights in 1901. Was vice-president of the bank from 1901-1925 and became president in 1927. He was a director of Scott and Browne Co., manufacturing chemists; the Reid Ice Cream Co., which he helped to organize; the Seminole Fruit and Land Co.; and the Bronx Heights Development Co. For twenty-two years president of the Washington Heights Taxpayers Association, and senior member of the law firm of Beals and Nicholson. See "A Deplorable Occurrence."
3. Philip Berolzheimer (1867-1942), president of the New York City-based Eagle Pencil Co.; one-time New York City Chamberlain; president of the Park Board. Berolzheimer had a large estate on Little St. Simon Island off the Georgia coast, and newspapers had

not envy him. I cannot forget Florida's convict camps and Tabert and the Santa Clara lumber company. If the dark and secret places of a country are stained with fiendish cruelty, if its richest men encourage the committing of hideous crimes for a petty gain in profits, I cannot endure its sunny pleasure cities.

And, in Florida, one has the shame always with him of remembering that his wine has to be smuggled in, by gallant adventurers, at the risk of their lives, under cover of night.

A man spending his holidays in Florida is like one who would choose to spend his Saturday afternoons in the garden of a penitentiary or insane asylum.

2. In another envelope I enclose the affidavits you asked for. This I have done, in haste, being anxious to make my record good with the recording angel, because I am so near to the shining gates of the newest Jerusalem.[4] At those gates, Saint Peter, perhaps next summer, will say to me, "Did you ever hesitate to sign an affidavit to oblige a friend?" and I will answer, "No, sir", and he will say, "Well done, good and faithful friend. In our place are many mansions made without mortgages. Enter into the abode of the blessed, where everybody has a surplus and where depositors share equally with bankers in the profits of their deposits."

3. Do me a favor. Ask Pletz[5] to write up my account, as of the 23rd. I ask this because my five specialists are putting the last touches of repair to my shattered hulk, to have me ready to sail for the Spanish Main on February 3.

I long to leave the Land of the Dry and the Home of the Slave, to lie on the seashore, in the sun or just near enough to a palm grove to profit by its shade and be secure from falling coco nuts.

I have been thinking about the Casa Marina and the Almendares and the innocent pleasures of the American Jockey

carried accounts of a hunting party he had held there with big New York City politicos the preceding November, ferrying them from Savannah in his yacht.

---

4. Newell Martin was born September 17, 1854; died November 15, 1941. When this letter was written, he was 71; he lived until he was 87. Martin was not as near to Jerusalem as he would have led his bank vice-president to believe.
5. No public reference; possibly bank clerk.

Club of Havana.[6]

But I shall leave them for a hidden corner of the Caribbean where one goes down through a cave into a low cliff of coral rock, to firm golden sand. There he finds lovely brown girls diving into the surf and lunching, in the surf, on mangos.

A reef set with white and purple fronds of coral keeps out most of the sharks.

There I drift out into the sea water, of rainbow hues, that is softer than any silk, clearer than any crystal.

The water is an exquisite coolness and of a voluptuous warmth. One can swim in it for hours or, in it, one can float and fall asleep. One could rest in it forever, but for hunger and for having promised to go ashore, to play penny ante.[7]

If St. John [author, Book of Revelation] had known about that super-naturally enticing sea and its temperature, he would have promised it, as a supreme inducement, in his advertisement of Heaven. But St. John knew of no soft seas and tempting islands, west of the Hebrides, and it never occurred to him that bathing could be a pleasure.

4. In two days, from New York, I shall see the sun rising above the white foam that breaks on the long beaches of Great Inagua.[8] In six days I shall see him sink, in clouds of splendor, over the Grand Cayman.[9]

Ecstatic visions flit before me of total abstinence from ever drawing a sober breath; and visions of being put to bed every night by a courteous coal-black head-waiter, clothed in dignified spotless white linen.

I shall squander my happy hours in admiring, idly, the cheerful industry of broad-shouldered negresses, in Jamaica, freedom's island, where murders and hold-ups are unknown, where there is no Sullivan law,[10] no Sabbath law, no censor, no crime;

---

6. The Almendares is a river nearly circling Havana, Cuba, to the south, emptying into the sea at Chorerra. The American Jockey Club of Havana is (was) connected to the grandstand of the Havana racetrack. A tourist guidebook [perused by indefatigable Audette] written at that time reports gambling rooms and a good restaurant at the Club.
7. Generally refers to poker played with a penny at stake.
8. Island in the southwest Bahamas.
9. Largest and furthest west of the Cayman Islands, southwest of Cuba.
10. New York State law passed in 1911 under the sponsorship of Timothy D. "Big" Sullivan, and most rigorously enforced in New York City, making the carrying of concealed weapons a felony, requiring persons using revolvers and small arms to obtain licenses, and requiring registration by dealer of all persons buying revolvers and similar weapons.

where nobody ever locks a door, where young girls and old men are safe, where happiness is not enjoined, where no spy dogs our footsteps and no informer sneaks into our hotels and no padlocks offend our eyes.

5. I long for planters' punches and sunrise swizzles and Manhattan cocktails. I prefer Jamaica rum to synthetic gin. Magnums of Bollinger, jorums of Ruinart, jereboams and rehoboams of Ayala [three major French champagne houses], call to me and I must go.

Gratefully

NEWELL MARTIN

P.S. In the arithmetics of our youth was "wine measure" that came, just before "apothecary's measure". I quote it, from memory, perhaps erroneously: Two jorums make a bottle, two bottles make a magnum, two magnums make a jereboam, two jereboams make a rehoboam.[11]

P.P.S. I am taking with me, on the ship, the Almanach de Gotha. Since Americans have become, in it, so abundant, it is more amusing than ever. For instance, to insure his salvation, a certain Portuguese prince, who was given, in baptism, twenty-two names, was named after a saint, a missionary and two archangels. Now see what happened to him (page 34):

> Maison de Bragance-Saxe-Cobourg-et-Gotha. Pr. Roy.: Alphonse, Henri, Napoleon, Marie, Louis, Pierre d'Alcantara, Charles, Humbert, Amedee, Fernand, Antoine, Michel, Raphael, Gabriel, Gonzague, Xavier, Francios d'Assie, Jean. Auguste, Jules Volfand, Ignace, duc d'Oporto. m. 1917 a-Nevada Hayes, veuve d'en Ires noces de van Volkenburg, nee a Ohio; Etats-Unis, 1885.[12]

❧ ❧ ❧

---

11. Exactly correct.
12. The quotation from the 1921 *Almanach de Gotha* included, after "duc Oports ...m" d'Rome ...m" 26 Sept. 1917" "di...du banquier van Volkenburg."

# A Deplorable Occurrence

<u>Deplorable occurrence at the Bank of Washington Heights dinner -- a dinner of the bank's stockholders and staff, May 7, 1925.</u>[1]

The Chairman, James J. O'Shaughnessy, is delivering a eulogy on John D. Beals.[2]

[Martin.] Mr. Chairman, may I interrupt you. I rise to a point of order.

[The Chair.] I never heard of a point of order at a public or private dinner. You seem to be a point of disorder.

[Martin.] It is about this man Beals, you are praising. He's the only man on this board, that was not born in Ireland, or in Washington Heights, which was the same thing, till these foreigners came in. And I was sitting here, quiet, eating my dinner, up among the wax works, thinking how nice it is not to have to make a speech and not to have to think about anything, and it is little thinking I have heard this night, from anybody, and this Beals sits between me and Doctor Gates[3] and keeps interrupting me about the gold he makes in Florida, Bryanizing,[4] Kukluxing, Landlording, and Bootlegging. Four dirty jobs, I call it. "Olet" says I to him. But he never understood me, being brought up in a heretic college. He never heard of the good bishop and the "non olet" money.[5] "How much Miami land did O'Shaughnessy say I bought?" asks Beals.

"Eight thousand acres at $3 an acre." "The dam liar", says he, "it was eighteen square miles." "Dam", said he, like that, out loud, right before the holy clergy, Monsignor Lavelle[6] and the kind Father from St. Catherine's of Genoa,[7] I disremember his name, some Scotch name.

---

1. Both the underlining and the names in brackets in Martin's tract.
2. See previous essay, "Martin's Bank Balance."
3. Reverend Milo Hudson Gates (1864-1939), Episcopalian clergyman, vicar of the Chapel of the Intercession of Trinity parish, New York City, 1907-1930. Was prominently mentioned to fill vacancy of suffragan bishop of New York, but declined the honor in order to continue his work in Trinity parish.
4. That is, advocating Fundamentalist views resembling those of William Jennings Bryan.
5. *Non olet* means "it does not smell sweet."
6. Michael J. Lavelle (1856-1939), Catholic priest. Appointed rector of St. Patrick's Cathedral, New York City, in 1886; subsequently diocesan consultor, Archdiocese of New York. Became vicar general of New York in 1902.
7. St. Catherine's of Genoa was completed in 1911, at East 41st Street and Linden Avenue, Flatbush, Brooklyn. Its pastor in 1925 was Fr. Joseph Smith.

There's not much they cannot do at Saint Catherine's, taking Whalen,[8] that was a baseball sport, and a lawyer, and a banker, all three, and making a good Christian out of him. And here was Beals, going on and asking me how much did O'Shaughnessy say Beals was getting for his Florida land. Four thousand dollars an acre, says I. "The dam liar", says Beals.

"It is $8,000 an acre I am selling for, this day", says he. "Dam", said he, again, and him sitting next to Doctor Gates, the architect and bell-ringer who refused to be a bishop. A good man is Doctor Gates, if his father was born in Londonderry.[9] The Curse of Crummle[10] on the place. And it's little you could gain, Doctor Gates, by being a heretic bishop. You confirm a bunch of young girls and they go to Barnard College and grow up to be Huxleys[11] or worse and then you die, yourself, and go to some uncomfortable place. And this Beals used to be an honest milkman, selling his ice cream cones and Sealect milk. And I give him credit for that, for the clergy are right when they say water is a dismal drink, whether you get it out of a milk jug at breakfast or out of a Venetian goblet, at a bank banquet. Mr. Chairman, may I interrupt myself?

[The Chair.] The sooner the better.

[Martin.] It is not for want of more to say about Beals. But I want to say one word to these young people out in front. It is easy to have a happy time, aye, even on water, when all the girls are clever and all the boys are handsome.

[Many angry voices.] You've got your words mixed. It's the other way about. Sit down.

[Martin.] And well may I sit down, if I get my words mixed, and me drinking nothing but water, the night long.

[Sits down, and the eulogy proceeds.]

ta   ta   ta

---

8. John Whalen (1856-1927), vice-president and treasurer of the New York Giants baseball team. A leading Roman Catholic layman; was also president of the American Federation of Catholic Societies. Most of his large estate was left to the Roman Catholic Church, which successfully defended its interests throughout several years of litigation by Whalen's relations (a lifelong bachelor, he had none closer than cousins).

9. Londonderry, a maritime county in northern Ireland. In 1609, James I granted a charter for a settlement there by merchants from London, and, in consequence, its history has been largely Protestant. Londonderry town, or Derry, is only a little more than half Roman Catholic, and the countryside has a Protestant majority.

10. "Crummle" is Irish for Cromwell. Hence, "The Curse of Cromwell on you." That well-known Irish imprecation alludes to the Lord Protector's conduct in Ireland 1649-50, notably the slaughters at Drogheda and Wexford.

11. An allusion to Thomas Henry Huxley (1825-1895), English biologist, defender of Darwin, rationalist.

… BUSINESS AND BUSINESSMEN    131

# Spinach and Zweiback
[April 24, 1925]

*As beards figure so prominently in this satirical monograph, it is interesting to note that, in 1895, all but two of the members of Martin's Yale class ('75) wore beards and/or mustaches. Martin appears with sideburns and attached mustache in the alumni class notes of 1895, and all subsequent photographs show him with both beard and mustache.*

*George Hazen (1858-1934), to whom the tract (or monograph) is dedicated, was CEO of Crowell Publishing Co. and on the boards of directors of several New York financial concerns. Beard-wearing Charles Evans Hughes (1862-1948; Yale L.L.D. '15), to whom Martin explicitly states he did not dedicate the tract, was Governor of New York (1907-1910), an Associate Justice of the U.S. Supreme Court (1910-1916), U.S. Secretary of State 1921-1925, and Chief Justice of the Supreme Court 1930-1941. Hughes resigned as Secretary of State in March, 1925, just one month before publication of "Spinach and Zweiback."*

I thought of dedicating this monograph to Charles Evans Hughes,[1] as Samuel Johnson once dedicated something heavy to Chesterfield;[2] but as that might savor of sycophancy, I address and dedicate it to George H. Hazen, who was one of the inventors of "trade propaganda" and who is "on a diet," at the Roosevelt Hospital.

Multitudes of us American men and women, and above all, you and I, are "on a diet." Our food is weighed, measured and prescribed. The number and hours of our meals are ordered, like the stars in their courses, and at such times as are most irksome.

The glutton is given one meal a day and to him that is

---

1. "If there is a better promise than at any time since the war of recuperation and peace in Europe it is due to the voluntary contribution of American business men at a critical time. Perhaps the best service government can render is to let American expertness have a chance. It may be said without extravagence that a large part of the hope of the world is due to direct American endeavor in assisting economic revival, and there may be found in this chamber many of the peacemakers." Quotation from a speech given to The New York City Chamber of Commerce by Hughes in April 1925.
2. Actually what he dedicated was not his dictionary, but the plan for his dictionary. As Boswell put it: "I (Johnson) may hope, my Lord (Chesterfield), that since you, whose authority in our language is so generally acknowledged, have commissioned me to declare my own opinion, I shall be considered as exercising a kind of vicarious jurisdiction; and that the power which might have been denied to my own claim, will readily be allowed me as the delegate of your Lordship."

abstemious are given seven, that seem seventy times seven. Each meal must carry exactly so many vitamins, ptomaines, chromosomes, hormones, calories, bacilli. What we like is cut and what we dislike is put in. Our reluctance to follow our regimens is enhanced by our knowing that, for thousands of years, doctors practiced letting out blood, to save life; and that suddenly, they decided, instead, on transfusion, and now pour in blood, to save life. We fear, therefore, that, with the swift march of medical science, it will be found tomorrow that all these diets are wrong. Our sorrow's crown of sorrow is the fear that we are barking, at a great discomfort, up the wrong tree. The census does not report how many are under these dietetic torments. My guess is that we number a little more than sixty millions. Not one of us is given anything that is fit to eat. We detest the food that is set before us and we do not give thanks for it. We loathe the very name of every dish on our bill of fare. This hatred has had momentous consequences.

1. Ephraim Johnson's[3] imposing fortune was made by the Darwin Safety Razor.[4]

The name of that razor was suggested by this pregnant passage in the second volume of the "Descent of Man:" "In a warm climate such as our remote ancestors enjoyed, those of the pithecanthropi [pithecanthropus or Java Man] who developed a tendency to be hairless had an advantage in the struggle for existence. Thick mats of hair made a nest and breeding-place for germ-laden vermin. And a hairy ape, in pursuit of parasites, preoccupied with trying to look over his own shoulder and scratch his own back often became dangerously oblivious to the approach, from leeward, of a sabre-toothed tiger." Ephraim Johnson told me this story of his rise from poverty to wealth.[5]

"When Philip was King in Macedon beards were the ornaments of rich and poor and the mark of things so incongruous as wisdom and fashion. Olympias,[6] being a little loose, herself, was strict with her son. She insisted on his toiling, through tiresome long hours in the school room. In that school room Aristotle kept, always, before the boy's eyes, a bust of the bearded Socrates.

3. (1862-1937), a New York City architect.
4. What follows is not — should a gullible reader be drawn in to Martin's "story" —an actual quote from Darwin's speculations on the origin of human hairlessness in *The Descent of Man* (Pt. III, chapter XX.)
5. Most probably, the good architect Johnson knew little of this story until he was the recipient of this 6-page monograph.
6. According to Plutarch, Olympias was addicted to the Orphic rites, and had had commerce with some god in the form of a serpent.

"The boy learned to hate Socrates' beard as much as he hated the blackboard, and when he became Alexander the Great, he said, 'To hell with beards,' and set a fashion of shaving that became as world-wide as his other more celebrated conquests. But in seventeen hundred years, the pendulum swung back and the western world relapsed into the barbarism of beard-wearing. Advances in civilization are intermittent gleams of sun-shine.

"A westward tide of Mongols was set in motion when a rash of Persians, by way of insult, cut off the beards of the envoys of Genghis Khan. Byzantium fell before the whiskered Turk, whose solemn oath was 'By the beard of the Prophet'[7] and beards spread, like a blighting fungus, over the face of Europe.

"The Dark Ages set in, those recent centuries in which Europe and America have been over-shadowed by whiskers.

"Prince Albert, the good Prince Consort, arbiter of elegance and leader in morals, wore a beard; and so did D'Orsay,[8] all the Czars, all Grand Dukes, Du Maurier,[9] Edward VII, the Kings of Saxony, Bavaria and Belgium, Henry Cabot Lodge, the Emperor Frederick,[10] James Russell Lowell,[11] Hugh McBirney of Chicago,[12] and George V. Our pictures of Bible stories painted two thirds of the Trinity as wearing whiskers.

"The most hideous atrocities of our Civil War were the beards of our generals. The iron features of Grant were hidden by a mask of hair. On Stone Mountain Borglum[13] has carved Robert E. Lee's beard, eternal, colossal, sixty feet square. The whiskers of the first Cornelius Vanderbilt and of the first William H. Vanderbilt[14] were as conspicuous as their wealth.

"In the early days of the Darwin Safety Razor Company, therefore, there was no money in razors. Beards and whiskers were in the height of fashion. Our stock sank to a nadir of unsalability.

"In despair I counted up the remnant of our advertising fund.

---

7. Note: Mohammedans are forbidden to swear by any part of the prophet's body.
8. Count Alfred Guillaume Gabriel d'Orsay (1801-1852), French dandy and wit who married into English nobility, and resided in London from 1829-1849.
9. George du Maurier (1834-1896), English artist and novelist.
10. Emperor Frederick (1795-1861), Emperor of Prussia.
11. James Russell Lowell (1819-1896), American poet, author of The Bigelow Papers.
12. Hugh J. McBirney (1853-1926; Yale '75), captain of the football team. At the time of his death, assistant local manager of the National Lead Co. in Chicago.
13. Gutzen Borglum (1867-1941), also carved Washington, Jefferson, Lincoln, and Theodore Roosevelt on Mt. Rushmore.
14. Cornelius Vanderbilt (1794-1877) and William H. Vanderbilt (1821-1885), father and son, presidents of the New York Central Railroad Co.

I took the whole of it and spent it in bribes to newspaper reporters and vaudeville performers. At a low price I hired a few of them to refer to whiskers and beards as 'spinach.' A reporter or story teller would say, for instance, 'The felon's face was disfigured by a thick growth of spinach.' This vulgar word caught on and became popular slang and the sixty million Americans who were 'on a diet' and who were compelled to eat spinach and who could not bear to hear the stuff even mentioned, began to loathe beards, as a repulsive display of 'spinach.'

"Every man who was 'on a diet' was made sick, in the street or indoors, whenever he saw a beard. So every American found himself compelled to shave. Our stock went up, like a magic carpet."

2. I sat in a cool embrasure of the romantic old fort that overlooks the Bay of Lucia [Bay of Lucea in Jamaica]. My companion was the brilliant heir of the historic towers of Audly Middleditch, Major General, the Honorable sir John Fortescue-Shuttleworth, Bart.[15] When I first saw his name written thus, above mine, in the register of the Myrtle Bank Inn, I thought, "How comfortable it is to be an Englishman and write your name in hexameters with an abrupt Selah[16] at the end of it." At the Myrtle Bank he avoided me, because, quite properly, he disliked all Americans who were neither good-looking nor opulent; but, at Lucia, we came together by chance, and he made the best of it and was polite.

He talked politics inside politics. In the deep shade of the embrasure, watching the lazy sunlit waves break on the coral reef, he told me this story: "My uncle was fired from his Embassy at Washington by Grover Cleveland for advising an American of English birth to vote the Democratic ticket. The people at home secretly patted my uncle on the back, because, for more than fifty years, our government has been sympathetic with the Democratic party. But England desires at any cost, under either party to win and keep America's affections and to persuade Americans to hate the enemies of England. Edward VII was distressed because he observed that Germans were immensely esteemed and respected in America. In those days, if capitalists wanted to make a bank or an

15. The "General" would appear to be a fabrication; in any event quite unknown to Burke's Peerage or to Burke's Landed Gentry.
16. Selah: The OED indicates it may mean pause or rest. Frequently at the end of a verse in the Psalter.

insurance company popular in America, they called it "the German-American." Edward found a way to change all that with one word. He had observed that a sort of disgusting rusk was prescribed by doctors for people who were 'on a diet.' These people hated this beastly food, and they hated the name of it. It was called 'le biscuit hygienique' and biscuit d'enfer'. 'This will never do,' said the King. 'I have an entente with France and this food makes France unpopular.' He sent over a secret service fund, about two million, sterling, and by the discreet use of it he induced the doctors and the apothecaries, and the bakers of America to speak of these biscuits always as Zweiback. Within a year every diet list in America bore the name of Zweiback; and the word became, to dieters, so hateful, that they learned to hate, also, every other German word and every German person and thing. So fell the Hohenzollerns."[17]

NEWELL MARTIN.

Huntington, April 24, 1925

ta ta ta

# Bad News
## A Letter to Frederick A. Stokes, Esq.

*Although Other Gomby wrote job-hunting Molly on October 19, 1937, telling her he would not "draft a letter to an aged publisher" on her behalf, nevertheless, he did just that and sent a copy to Molly. First we reprint the handwritten letter to Molly, then the typewritten letter to Stokes.*

Huntington, N.Y.

Oct. 19, 1937

Miss Molly Meyer
  39 East 78th St.
  New York
  N.Y.
Dear Molly
    I am planning to draft a letter, (which I shall never send) to

---

17. Dynastic rulers of Prussia. Emperors of Germany beginning 1871.

an aged publisher, saying,
 "It is not right for me to ask you to see, at your office, any of my descendants.
 "Your doctor probably tells you to refuse to see any unemployed young people.
 "I am afflicted with a granddaughter who has recently immerged [sic] from Bryn Mawr. Some people there have made much of her and she showed, there, that she is diligent and has a good mind. I would be grateful if you would say that you would see her some time at your office.
 "I have told her that in all probability you made a resolution when you were 75, never to see, at your office, any unemployed person.
 I have told her also that Horace Greeley, once a noted American, said, "of all horned cattle, deliver me from college graduates."[1]

*h. M.*

Frederick A. Stokes, Esq.
443 Fourth Ave.
New York, N.Y.

Nov. 26, 1937

Dear Fred:

Before this, perhaps, my granddaughter, Molly Meyer, will have called on you. I am fond of Molly. She was born while I was in Hawaii or thereabouts. I had made all my plans for spending a few weeks on Mauna Loa[2] and Haleakala.[3] My wife, however, was so anxious to see Molly that she hurried me away from the islands before I could see those wonders.

I have told Molly much to hold her back from troubling you:--
1. "Your grandmother and I," said I to Molly, "have shown that we

---

1. Perhaps Martin had read *The Life of Horace Greeley* (Philadelphia: Potter, 1874), p. 466, by L.D. Ingersoll who attributes the following quote to A. J. Cummings: "You ask me if female reporters and correspondents are employed on the *Tribune* [later, the *Herald Tribune*]. They are. Miss Dunning writes the fashion reports; Miss Kate Field occasionally sends a letter; Miss Booth frequently vouchsafes a readable article; Miss L. G. Calhoun writes sparkling correspondence, and Olive Logan occasionally bubbles over from the Magazine into the Weekly Tribune. Year before last Mrs. Calhoun reported the grandest city balls, and her descriptions of the Arion and Liederkranz carnivals attracted great attention."
2. Volcano, south central Island of Hawaii
3. Dormant volcano, East Maui Island, Hawaiian Islands.

would rather see Molly than see the most majestic of mountain views, the most tremendous of volcanoes. But Mr. Stokes is different. He would rather see one volcano, any volcano, than any nice young girl.["]

2. Molly was beloved by the best people in Bryn Mawr and was diligent in college; and still is industrious. Molly has traveled, in Brittany, Montana, Germany, Denmark and many other places. Molly has 4 times as much polish and sense as I had when I came out of college. I have told her, however, that your reception room is constantly crowded and cluttered with young women of education, learning, beauty, wisdom, and polish; and that your secretaries are worn out with the labor of driving them off into outer darkness.

3. I have told Molly that another depression has struck this shuddering planet; and that, in bad times, men slowly learn to deny themselves necessaries. They turn away, reluctantly, from what they need; but always in alphabetical order, forsaking and forswearing

        First, books,
        Then, charity,
        and, after that,
        church,
        clothing,
        food,
        newspaper, &
        whisky.

4. I have read, with great interest, published reports of the commiseration publicly showered on you when you became 80. I have told Molly that, undoubtedly, your physicians, experts in gerontology, have told you that you may go to your office, daily, but that, in your office, you must leave to others all the disagreeable work, such as seeing unemployed young women.

To all this Molly has answered, in effect: "I agree with you. I know that Horace Greeley said 'Of all horned cattle, deliver me from college graduates, especially women graduates.' I know that there is no place in Germany for women looking for work and that there are few places for such women in America. But if a man 83 years old cannot arrange an interview, a harmless amicable interview, between his favorite granddaughter and his oldest friend, then my professors did not tell me half the story when they told me that the world is cold and overcrowded."

It would be delightful if you would say: "Molly, I remember your grandfather. I will not see you at the office, but I will see you once, or twice or three times, at lunch time. You may call, at such and such a time, and take me, in a cab, to lunch."

It occurs to me that I may venture even farther. From the time of my collapse, in April, for 6 or 7 months, I was shut up as it were, on this island [Long Island] and never saw New York. But this affair seems important. Would you be willing to let me call and could you be persuaded to go out with Molly and me; and then you, if you could endure her conversation, could appoint a day for further adverse criticism of her and of this world[?]

Affectionately,

*Newell Martin*

# FIVE

# HYPHEN-BEARERS

Hyphen-Bearers ............. 141

A Private Letter .............. 144

The Book of Revelation and
    The University Club .......... 153

Copy of a Letter to a Publisher .... 154

Armenoids .................. 159

Jews and Philistines ........... 165

Jews ....................... 172

# Hyphen-bearers

*Martin's article, "Hyphen-bearers," appeared in* The Century Magazine *(Vol. 93) in December, 1916, and carried his byline.*

With deep interest I have been studying an old Telephone Directory[1] to learn what sort of people make the greatness of New York. Our chauvinists should do the same, and learn something about the newest Americans. At every stage of our progress, narrow-minded people and crooked-minded people have had much to say against the latest arrivals. Some profound student of social movements has always stepped forward, with the air of a scientific discoverer, to say, "The immigrants of fifty years ago enriched the nation, but these new immigrants are undesirable." There are also, always, everywhere, ardent exclusionists and expulsionists. One well-known magazine[2] has hinted that some way should be found to induce German-Americans to go back to their old home after the war, and it is obvious that some of our prominent publicists are of the same opinion. In London, Herbert Samuel, a prosperous Hebrew, threatens to send back to Russia some thousands of less fortunate Hebrews.[3]

But, aware as I am of the shortcomings of our new competitors, I suspect that it is a fallacy to pretend that our immigration is falling off in quality. Study of the recondite sources of information that lie before me indicates that immigrants of late years are of better stock than we used to get.

It is true that in my grandfather's time there were among us descendants of patriots who had left England for lack of liberty, or who had been exiled from Ireland, or who had fled from Continental

---

1. Capitalization in original.
2. Unable to determine source.
3. Sir Herbert Samuel (1870-1963), liberal politician, administrator, first high commissioner for Palestine. As home secretary, which he had become the preceding January, Sir Herbert had proposed on August 23, 1916, that Jewish refugees from Russia of military age either be drafted into the British army or returned to their homeland. (Under tsarist law, such persons would have been regarded as traitors and either banished or imprisoned.) An estimated 25-30,000 persons would have been affected. Public outcry forced the reduction of the measure to an active recruiting campaign coupled with financial inducements. The measure must be viewed in the light of the universal draft of native Britons instituted earlier that year, the overwhelming losses on the Somme in July, and the fact that hardly a British family with a son of military age was not being called upon in some respect.

Europe to get away from the Inquisition or the Holy Alliance;[4] but we used to import great numbers of negro slaves and transported convicts. Now among the immigrants who come to us are descendants of the Italians, who built up the civil law, of the Jews, who founded all our religions, and of the Turks, who set Constantinople free from the effete Byzantines.

We used to be as insular as our English founders. In my college class there was not one student whose name indicated an ancestry from outside of the British Islands.[5] The New York Directory of 1850 was a slim, shabby little book, full of English names. But we have gloriously ceased to be provincial. I turn to the Telephone Directory for May, with its 850 pages and 350,000 addresses, and see that New York is no longer an English colony. I open it at random, and read two dozen names in succession, one from the head of each column, and find this:

Runkle, Ruskay, Russell, Russian Volunteer Fleet, Ruton, Ryan, Rybakoff, S.&S. Delicatessen, Saccoccio, Sackin, Safferstone and Salb, St. Andrew's Society, St. Vincent Ferrer Literary Society, Salinger, Salomon, Saltzseider, Samberg, Samson, Samuels, Sand, Sanders, Sanes. Only two of those names are English.

Turning now to the "Times," I find among the advertisements the official list of the dazzling boys and girls who took the highest marks this summer in graduating from the high schools of New York and its suburbs, and are qualified for college scholarships from the treasury of one hundred dollars a year.[6] There are more than three hundred of these marvels, five columns of these wonder-children, battalions of intellect. Louisa Viggeani[7] is the foremost of them all,

---

4. The "Holy Alliance" was a loose organization of most European sovereigns formed in Paris in 1815 by Alexander I of Russia, Francis I of Austria, and Frederick Wilhelm III of Prussia when negotiating the Second Peace of Paris after the final defeat of napoleon. Its ostensible object was the promotion of Christian principles in the affairs of nations, but it came to be regarded as a major force and symbol of conservative repression in central and eastern Europe.

5. Martin's 1875 class included Henry Moses Walradt, father Moses Walradt, whose ancestors came to America from the Palantinate (Bavaria) in the eighteenth century. However, Walradt's mother was a Prouty, and he himself held office in the Anglican and Congregational churches.

6. Page 16 of The New York Times, August 22, 1916, nearly filled with the list of New York State Regents' scholarship winners. All students over a certain grade average are eligible; and each county receives five times as many scholarships as it has assembly district. In 1916, roughly 1,300 students were eligible for 340 scholarships.

7. Louisa Viggeani was born in southern Italy. The family lived on west 95th Street, in those days a rough, but not rugged neighborhood. Her father, an educated man who worked in a New York City publishing house, kept to the downbeat location only in order that he might have the means to provide all five of his children with an advanced education. Louisa intended to become a teacher.

with the impressive mark of 95.99. The first girl after her has 94.92. Of course seven of the first ten are girls. Twenty of the first twenty-five are German-Americans, Hebrew-Americans, Irish-Americans, Italian-Americans. They have all risen to the dizzy height of a mark of over 90. Here are their names and of such is the kingdom of this world:

Louisa Viggeani
A. Greenberg
Melanie Rohrer
Ruth Harr
Elsie Hoerrel
Jacob Kabak
Bertha Shoenberg
S.B. Gishkind
Helen Meyer[8]
Victorine K. Mayer
J.S. Orliansky
C. H. Tobias
Lydia Felder
B. Mack
Hermina Schaff
F. M. Sommerfield
Ellen Ahern
A. F. A. Ziegler
Sam Saretsky
M. M. Polenski
     I turn to the second column of prize-winners and read:
Bertha Silberberg
Julia Keegan
Rose Sperber
Morris Bunsis
M. W. Feinberg
Mary B. Cowley
Nora Mulvey
Kathryn Noone
Susette Burns
Ada Isaacs
Herman Zazeele
Jonas Massims
Naum Shamroy
Marie Zadoorian
Ruth Biegeleisen

---

8. No relation.

Rebecca Shub
John Hanselman
Louis Holl
Sydney Heimer
F. H. Villaume
Florence Flynn
M. Skolnik
Sophie Sachatoff

  The Telephone Directory is itself a sort of prize-list. The submerged nine tenths do not hire telephones.
  And as to the school-list, every child on that list is one out of a thousand, a survivor from the competition of myriads.
  On that last list all but two are hyphen-bearers. Hebrew-Americans, German-Americans, French-Americans, Irish-Americans, Syro-Americans, Armenian-Americans. Among these boys and girls are governors and governesses, mayors and alderwomen, of the future. When you see an editorial about the "Inefficiency of the Melting-pot," or "America for the Americans," remember this list of honors and be glad that the stream of the elect has not ceased to flow westward.

❧ ❧ ❧

# A Private Letter
[November 3, 1920]

*In a 12-page pamphlet (3 1/2" wide and 6" long) written as a letter, and marked* <u>CONFIDENTIAL</u>, *and addressed to the "Chairman of the Committee on Improvement of the University Club," 1 West 54th Street, New York, Martin takes up the sensitive issue that no Jews are members.*
  *The University Club was founded in 1865, and is, according to its present librarian, "still very much in existence." There is no record of a "Committee on Improvements" in 1920, and again from the librarian — "no record that the Club has ever had a policy of discriminating against Jews." The University Club did begin admitting women in June, 1987. It's possible, of course, that a "Committee on Improvements" headed by someone named Henry \_\_\_\_\_, was formed in 1920; though our researcher thinks it possible that "the committee and its chairman are rhetorical fictions."*

*According to available testimony, during his lifetime, Martin was a member of four clubs: The Midday Club, The Adirondack Mountain Club; the Century Association; and the University Club. In 1939, he responded to a Yale University Alumni questionnaire asking him to "...name the principal business or institution with which he was connected..." by stating:*
      "No company
      "No business
      "No religions
      "No party
      "No office

ta ta ta

Dear Henry:

Our club is rich. Our house is beautiful. Few vistas in New York are more pleasing than the long view, east and west, that rewards him who enters our door. It is a delectable of gleaming marbles and stately monoliths. The men that wait on us are deft and thoughtful of our comfort. Our house-keeping is so nearly perfect that it gives an added pang to death, because in heaven, no Ennis, as yet is set to care for us. Our library is a palace of learning, an irresistible beguilement to books. Nevertheless, your committee has been appointed, because it seemed possible that some one might think of something that would better even our halycon estate. To my astonishment it has been my good luck to think of a vital improvement; one so obvious, however, and so near at hand, that many, perhaps, have forestalled me.

It delights me to lay it before your committee, who now have a chance to render a notable service to the club and do a little for civilization.

Throughout all these years, without deliberate intent, we have suffered a certain peculiar shame and discomfort. When a few college men set up our club, in the rude, uncultivated seventies, or thereabouts, few Jews went to American colleges, and so there happened to be no Jews in the group of founders. Thus, through inadvertence, our club grew up as a gentile club.

As we gained in numbers, there came in to us, of course, a few who, from early disadvantages or lack of modern education, or lack of foreign travel, or from some other mischance, cherished medieval prejudices. As a small group can keep anybody out, it became impossible to bring in Jews. Most of us feel keenly the shame we suffer on this account. We know that people point at us and say that we a gentile club. The men on the rubber neck wagons tell the rustics that we are an anti-semitic club; and the rustics gape at us, as at a pogrom or a black hundred [an anti-Jewish society in tsarist Russia].

Our club is out of touch, in this regard, with modern progress. It may be taken as an axiom that a gentile's fitness for social life is proportional to his access to Jewish society; and it is proof of this, that Rasputin and Nicholas II would have denied it.

When a question of semitic pride or anti-semitic envy comes up, a list of resplendent Jewish names, qualities, and achievements, leaps to the mind of any man, or a dozen lists, any one of which suggests the height and depth, the length and breadth, spanned by Jewish talent. One such illustrative list might remind us, for instance of the lofty philosophy of Baruch Spinoza and the practicality of Barney Baruch;[1] the supple grace of Pavlowa[2] and the rigid piety of Felix Adler;[3] the fist of Benny Leonard;[4] Rszeschewsky's chess;[5] Kreisler's violin; the munificence of Sir Moses Montefiore;[6] the massive legs of Horween;[7] the tragic art of Rachel and Bernhardt and the strategic art of Trotsky; the universal learning of Maimonides; and the acuteness, as to real estate, of Morgenthau.[8] Bischoffsheim[9] gives us lessons in gathering property and Marx teaches us how to scatter it, among communists; Bloch[10] is a leader of pacifists; but Sir John Monash[11] was the commander-in-chief of those Australian armies that yield

---

1. Bernard Mannes Baruch (1870-1965), agricultural and economics expert; chairman of the War Industries Board 1918-1919.
2. Anna Matveyevna Pavlova (1882-19310), one of the ranking dancers of the twentieth century.
3. Felix Adler (1851-1933), professor of ethics at Columbia (1920-1933); founder of the Ethical Culture Movement.
4. Benny Leonard (1896-1947), world's lightweight boxing champion 1917-1925.
5. Samuel Rzeschewski, child prodigy chess master in both Europe and America in the late 'teens-early 1920s.
6. Sir Moses Haim Montefiore (1784-1885), British philanthropist active in alleviating anti-Jewish discrimination and in preparing the way for Zionism.
7. Arnold Horween, captain of the 1920 Harvard football team; appointed Harvard head coach in 1926.
8. Henry Morgenthau, Sr. (1856-1946), American banker, diplomat, and philanthropist.
9. Louis Raphael Bischoffsheim (1800-1873), French banker and politician; involved in all the great European financial affairs of his time.
10. Ivan Stanislavovich Bloch (Blioch) (1836-1901), Russo-Polish financier, economist, and railway contractor, who in 1898 published a six-volume work, Budushaya Voina, advocating the settlement of international disputes by arbitration.
11. Sir John Monash (1865-1931), WWI commander of the Third Australian Division.

HYPHEN-BEARERS    147

to none in pride of military achievement.

Our club abounds in lawyers, but none of them are too good to associate with such as Sir George Jessel, Cremieux and Judah P. Benjamin;[12] and it has plenty of stock-brokers; but none of these are better than Mocatta [English] and Hallgarten [American], merchant princes, of the race that invented the art and mystery of stock-brokerage.

We are in the habit of being perhaps too obsequious to the English aristocracy, the only surviving aristocracy of the western world; but unlike London clubs, we would bar out Jews that are not far from leading that powerful aristocracy. Our committee would not be permitted to admit such men as Lord Beaconsfield [Benjamin Disraeli], Lord Rothschild, Lord Reading,[13] Primrose, the heir of the Earl of Rosebery [leader of the Liberal Imperialist division of the Liberal Party from 1895-1905], Lord Swaythling,[14] Sir Herbert Samuel,[15] or the Secretary of State for India.[16] We would shut out Siegfried Sassoon, a poet without illusions, and Sir Philip Sassoon, of Hythe, the most brilliant young figure, since Disraeli, that has dazzled the society of London.[17]

We discriminate even against half-Jews. If there were a second coming of the Lord and he wished to lecture in our dining room, he could not choose, a second time, to have a Jewess for his mother. Millerand (President of France from 1920-19243), Columbus (Christopher), Gambretta (French Premier 1881-1882), and Booth, Founder of the Salvation Army, also half-Jews, could not come into our company. Both Henry James (author) and Du Maurier (English artist and novelist) have hinted that any man surpassingly clever in the arts must have some Jew in his ancestry; but if any such man wishes to come to us, he must have his Jewish

---

12. Sir George Jessel (1824-1883), British lawyer; Master of the Rolls; head of the patent office.
   Isaac Adolph Cremieux (1796-1880), French minister of justice.
   Juday P. Benjamin (1811-1884), successively attorney-general, secretary of war, and secretary of state of the American Confederacy; subsequently practiced law in England.
13. Aufus Daniel Isaacs Reading (1860-1935), British attorney-general; subsequently lord chief justice and viceroy of India.
14. Samuel Montagu (1832-1911), banker and politician.
15. Sir Herbert Samuel (1870-1963), liberal politician; administrator; philanthropist; first high commissioner for Palestine.
16. Edwin Montagu (1879-1924), son of Samuel; secretary of state for India 1917-1922.
17. Sir Philip Sassoon (1888-1939), connoisseur of the arts; politician; twice under-secretary of state for art.

ancestor well hidden. We would exclude Ehrlich[18] and Epstein (British sculptor). Einstein may step over into the fourth dimension but he cannot cross our threshold. We would keep out Schiff, Otto H. Kahn, Warburg, Elsberg, Goldberg, Goldwater, Boas, Blumenthal, Speyer, Lehman, Flexner and Jacoby.[19]

By yielding to a prejudice that still flourishes in a degraded Hungary and in illiterate Poland but has no place in the best clubs, the best hotels, and the best society of London, we run the risk of declining into a sort of provincial second class.

An answer to my suggestion, commonly made in such cases, would be that, when Christ himself chose eleven Jews to be his comrades and supper companions, one of them was what is technically described in our Department of Justice as an "under-cover man"; to which the reply is that our club would gain by taking in the twelve apostles with all their drawbacks.

If the witty and delightful author of Ecclesiastes and St. Matthew, the divinely appointed transcriber of the Sermon on the Mount, should be sent back here, with letters of introduction from the Angel Gabriel to Bainbridge Colby[20] and me, and they desired to collaborate on a new gospel of goodwill toward all mankind and to use our library for the purpose, we cold not let them enter it.

Men who have studied at Tufts and men who have studied

---

18. Paul Ehrlich (1854-1915), German bacteriologist, winner of 1908 Nobel prize, discoverer of anti-syphilitic drugs.
19. Jacob Henry Schiff (1847-1920), American banker/philanthropist.
   Otto H. Kahn (1867-1934), banker, railroad magnate, chairman of the board of directors of the Metropolitan Opera.
   Paul Moritz Warburg (1868-1932), American banker; appointed in 1914 to the first Federal Reserve Board.
   Charles Albert Elsberg (1871-1948), American neurosurgeon.
   Louis Palatnik Goldberg (1888-1957), eminent N.Y. lawyer.
   Sigismund Shulz Goldwater (1837-1942), hospital administrator and consultant; director of Mt. Sinai Hospital, New York.
   Franz Boas (1858-1942), American anthropologist, Columbia University professor 1896-1936.
   George Blumenthal (1858-1941), American banker and philanthropist; major contributor to Mt. Sinai Hospital and the Museum of Modern Art.
   James Speyer (1861-1941), American banker and philanthropist.
   Allan Sigmund Lehman (1885-1952), general partner in the New York banking firm of Lehman and Bros.
   Abraham Flexner (1866-1959), American educator; founder of the Princeton Institute for Advanced Studies.
   George W. Jacoby (1856-1940), eminent New York City neurologist.
20. (1869-1950), lawyer and politician; appointed U.S. Secretary of State nine months previous to the publication of "A Private Letter;" member of the University Club.

under Hibben,[21] belong to our club in hundreds; but Peter, who was taught by the Lord, and Paul, who sat at the feet of Gamaliel,[22] would be blackballed.

Most of us have had the pleasure of belonging to clubs that have enjoyed the oriental courtesy and intellectual competency of Jews. In the City, Midday Club, a prominently successful and comfortable house, we had a waiting list so long that candidates, like Jacob, spent seven years in getting admitted; and there we recognized our Jewish members as our better element.

A way out of our embarrassment has occurred to me, and I make a present of it to your committee.

Let us negotiate with one or two of the chief Hebrew clubs, and let us persuade them to amalgamate with us. A handful might secede from our club; and several handfuls of men too proud to break bread with gentiles would secede from the Jewish clubs; but we would have the honor of shaking ourselves free from a vulgar form of superstition and prejudice.

Such details as kosher and oysters and bacon and Sunday and the Sabbath could be adjusted easily. Our club would become a club of civilized Jews and civilized Christians, and of such enlightened persons as are neither Jew nor Christian.

The absurdity of our present position admits of little delay. We call ourselves the University Club of New York. When we were founded New York was a provincial town. Since that time, it has profited by the zeal, exhibited through 3,000 years past, of those European conquerors and Chaldean kings and other bull-headed tools of fate, who scattered, over the West, a Bedouin tribe, that was singularly equipped with courage and all the talents, for milleniums of exile. Today, unbroken by oppression, children of Israel are among the first in all the competitions of art and commerce; and, unembittered by cruel wrong, children of Israel are among the first in charity and reform. Bringing with them some of their brightest and best, men and women of that great race have gathered, in unprecedented numbers, to adorn and enrich the city that we love. It has become the world's metropolis, in great degree through the brains, character, and industry of Jews. It is, already, the greatest Jewish city ever dreamed of. Its glorious pinnacles are the towers of the New Jerusalem.

21. John Grier Hibben (1861-1933), president of Princeton University 1912-1932,
22. The Rabbi Gamaliel, according to Jewish tradition, was the son of Simeon and grandson of Hillel.

On our imperial island are two great universities. Roughly, half the student in one, and all the students in the other, are Jews, and yet, in the presence of those universities, we have the assurance to call our club, which those Jewish students can never enter, THE University Club.

We would be glad to admit Howard Robbins, dean of the Cathedral of St. John the Divine; but St. John the Divine himself, the beloved disciple, is not eligible to our house.

In this Jewish metropolis, Jewish judges send us to jail, Jewish bankers multiply for us our millions, Jewish shopkeepers ordain for our daughters the shortness of their skirts, and Jewish editors manufacture, every morning the conservative opinions, and once a week the liberal opinions, which we fondly regard as the product of our own minds.

Yet, in their presence, we play at being Polish reactionaries, Prussian Junkers, Hungarian White Guards, Austrian Gottseidanks, Czarist tchinovniks [bureaucrats], and Spanish priests, and we bar out the sacred race which has given us all our holy prophets and most of our cleverest infidels.

It is now, more than ever, in all the centuries since a primeval man threw the first stone at his hairy neighbor, it is now, supremely, the time for those who dislike to see society slipping back into new Dark Ages, to break down artificial barriers and forswear artificial hatreds, and cherish everything that makes for peace among the races of mankind. I am confident that in our club you will find an almost unanimous feeling that it is in America's distinction and good fortune that, here, Jew and Gentile, side by side, move forward to the light, in a firm friendship, free from the blind prejudices that so deeply dishonor those who entertain them.

It never occurs to an Asiatic that it is the correct thing to dislike Hebrews. Hatred of Jews, like witch-hunting, is one of the many weeds planted and watered, in the middle ages, amid the ruins of civilization.

In a benighted Europe, sunk deep in ignorance and superstition, the curse of popular suspicion and envy that fell upon the Jews was the fit punishment and logical result of their selfishness and rashness in making themselves "one hundred per cent literate." In the valleys of the Vistula [river in Poland] and the Rhine, in many a hamlet where even the baron in his castle signed his name with a mark, every Jew could read, in the language of the country or in his own or in both, thus making himself an irresistible competitor. The baron and the village priest and the gentile shopkeeper, to hold their own, taught the unlettered Christians that these Jews, with their mysterious books, were practitioners of black magic and addicted to ritual murder and that their ancestors had crucified the Redeemer and that they inherited the guilt of their forefathers. Disraeli had shown that the third of those charges is untrue. The other three have never been believed in America, except by Watsons[23] and in the more barbarous regions of the South and in Darkest Detroit. As the direct progeny, however, of those maliciously implanted superstitions, we hear, even in America, anti-semitic parrot-phrases, uttered, often, by people that think it a mark of intelligence or fashion to import a bad habit from Europe. Like a boy who comes back from his boarding school with nothing learned but a few petty vices; like the Arabian who raided his enemy's tent and got nothing but the smallpox; we have acquired nothing out of the possessions of poor old vanquished Central Europe except her Judenhetze. A man sitting in Delmonico's or the Ritz, surrounded by polished Jews, will tell you gravely how bad it would be to let Jews into his ramshackle hotel on Podunk Beach. But you and your comrades, trained in library and laboratory, think for yourselves and have no inherited or imported prejudices.

In those parts of this town where life is most vivid, race barriers are already melting away. A warm-hearted New York gentile judge (you will recognize his style) said to me today, "Of all the men that I had known and loved and looked up to, only four have seemed to me to be perfect Christians and three of the four were Jews."

I know you will be pleased with my suggestion. Forgive my hurried letter. The idea seems so obvious that I dare not wait to put it in proper shape, for fear I may lose the credit of it. You will be eager to begin to ascertain the views of some of our companions as to the proposed remedy. We must hasten, or other clubs, in our own evil case, may steal a march on us. Forgive, also, my prolixity, in writing lists of eminent Jews. In some of the arts it would make for brevity to give a list of great gentiles and say "All other great men in this art were Jews."

Your associates will not say "almost thou persuades me to be

---

23. (1856-1922): publisher of the anti-Semitic Watson's Magazine; notable for agitating the guilt of Leo Frank, who was lynched in Atlanta in 1915, after having been convicted on the flimsiest evidence of the sexual assault and murder of a 14-year-old girl. Elected U.S. Senator from Georgia in 1920.

a Christian"; but they will say "you have persuaded us to act like Christians."

I have spent happy hours in Jewish clubs, where Hebrews have shown me their liberality and breadth of thought, and that hospitality for which their race is famous. Their hospitality has been inherited from the time when their fathers entertained angels unaware, and were familiarly visited in their desert camps by the Ancient of Days. But I lead so retired a life and am so out of good society that I can make no suggestion as to what Jews you should approach first. That is a problem for your energy and tact.

       Sincerely,
                 Newell Martin.

# The Book Of Revelation and The University Club
[August, 1926]

*Possibly this one-page tract contains the text of Martin's resignation letter to the University Club; if so, the statement, "Some of us may prefer to stay 'without'," has a double meaning. Martin was not a member of any church, though the son, grandson, and great-grandson of clergymen. Granddaughter Molly says that he often read and marked passages in the Bible (King James Version), and his many writings display familiarity with a wide variety of religious writings.*

The Book of Revelation, granted to St. John, in Patmos,[1] has had a greater influence on Christian thought and conduct than all the rest of the Bible. It is the climax of inspiration; and, when it closed the sacred canon, inspiration and revelation ceased. At least, so believe such of us as are orthodox, altho [sic] Mohammedans, Christian Scientists, Mormons and other infidels vehemently deny this article of our faith.

Chapter 21 describes, with mathematical precision, a place that is harder to get into than our University Club.

The home of 'the blessed that have part in the resurrection, 'the beloved city, the holy Jerusalem", lieth foursquare, twelve thousand furlongs wide and long.

It is borne up in, in interstellar space, by twelve magic foundation stones,[2] jasper, sapphire, chalcedony, emerald, sardonyx, sardius, chrysolyte, beryl, topaz, chrysoprasus, jacinth and amethyst.

On each of eleven of these miraculous supports is the name of a Jew that became a Christian.

And the twelve gates are of twelve pearls. Every several gate is of one pearl; and on every several gate is written the name of a Jew that never became a Christian (verse 12).

Written on the twelve gates are the names of the twelve tribes of the children of Israel. Yet, if a learned, lovable and just man has one of those twelve sacred and august names, if the surname that

---
1. Aegean island where St. John reportedly wrote the Book of Revelation, final book in the Christian *Bible*.
2. Properly, the foundations are adorned with these stones.

shows his descent from demigods is Levi or Benjamin,[3] he cannot enter the University Club. Some of us may not care to live in a city whose only inscriptions are of such despised origin, whose gates and foundations commemorate 23 Jews, and give us no assurance that within we shall not be compelled to associate with Hebrews. Some of us may prefer to stay "without" (Rev. 22; 15), "where are dogs, and sorcerers," and "murderers, and idolaters."[4]

        Newell Martin
        Huntington, N.Y.
        August, 1926.

# Copy of a Letter to a Publisher
August 10, 1924
*"...only the best get their names in print."*

*Apparently, the Immigration Act of 1924 was the inspiration for this three-page pamphlet. By the early 1920s Asiatic immigration to the United States had effectively been barred, and quotas adopted for Asian nations were in most cases created for the use not of native populations but of Caucasians born there.*

*In 1921, in an effort to restrict immigration from southern and eastern Europe, Congress enacted temporary immigration quotas proportionate to the number of foreign-born from each nation already resident in the U.S.; national origin being determined chiefly by name. These quotas actually reversed the percentages admitted from northern and western Europe as opposed to southern and eastern, reducing the latter by a factor of five.*

*Nonetheless, by 1924, total annual immigration had risen to some 700,000, and fresh measures were thought necessary. The 1924 Immigration Act, one of the most hotly-debated domestic political issues of that year, set up new quotas based on the percentage of foreign-born from each nation resident in the United States. This arrangement reduced the existing quotas for southern*

---

3. Two of the twelve tribes of Israel.
4. Rev. 22: 15 "For without are dogs, and sorcerers, and woremongers, and murderers, and idolaters, and whosoever loveth and maketh a lie."

*and eastern Europe by 87 percent while reducing that for nothern and western Europe by only 29 percent (e.g., Poland's quota was reduced from 30,977 to 5,982). The intent was clear, and, in fact, a group of 20 senators, opposed to the law, pointed out its transparent Nordic bias.*

*The Act provided furthermore that after July, 1927, the quota for each country should be a percentage of 150,000 proportionate to the total number of persons in the U.S. in 1920 of that national derivation.*

*While this pamphlet is nominally a "letter to a publisher," the publishing house is not identified, and the surname of the person to whom the letter was written is not given. But there are some clues, as the pamphlet lists three men to whom the publisher ("Dear George") is asked to show the letter: Lothrop Stoddard, Madison Grant, and Charley Gould.*

*Theodore Lothrop Stoddard (1883-1950); Harvard '05, M.A. '10, Ph.D. '14): author, one-time editor of* The Century Magazine. *Stoddard wrote some 22 popular books on world affairs, including* The New World of Islam; Master of Manhattan, the Life of Richard Crocker; *and* Europe and Our Money. *Stoddard was also the author of* Social Classes in Post-War Europe *(Scribner's, 1920);* The Rising Tide of Color Against White World Supremacy *(Scribner's, 1920);* Racial Realities in Europe *(Scribner's, 1922); and* Revolt Against Civilization: The Menace of the Underman *(Scribner's, 1922).*

*Madison Grant (1865-1937); Yale '87; L.L.B. Columbia '90): zoologist, hunter, and explorer of backwoods America. Private means enabled him to devote much of his life to scientific pursuits and conservation movements. He was, along with Martin's brother-in-law, George Bird Grinnell, one of the initiators and first president of the New York Zoological Society (familiarly known today as the Bronx Zoo); and president of the Bronx Parkway Commission 1907-1925. With Martin, he was a member of both the Century and University Clubs.*

*Grant wrote the introduction to Lothrop Stoddard's* The Rising Tide of Color Against White World Supremacy; *and was the author of* Passing of the Great Race; or the Racial Basis of European History *(Scribner's, 1922). And was co-author with Charles S. Davidson of* The Alien in our Midst *(Galton, 1930). He took the position that to share democratic ideals among a homogeneous population of Nordic blood is one thing, but that it would be racial suicide for the white race to mix its blood with, or entrust its ideals* to, men of other colors. Lothrop Stoddard had reached much the same conclusion, but on cultural and political rather than biological grounds.

Charles W. Gould (1849-1931; Yale '70), also a member of the University Club, was elected president of the Eugenics Research Association in 1924, and was the author of America: a Family Matter *(Scribner's, 1922),* is a study of race relations in the U.S. that emphasized the importance of Nordic supremacy. Letter follows:

(It is hoped that he will show it to Lothrop Stoddard, Madison Grant and Charley Gould.)

Ku Klux Korners:
County of Chadbands;[1]
State of Stigginses;[2] in a
Republic that is not without its Pecksniffs.[3]

November 10, 1924

Dear George:[4]
When the Trumbulls of Salem and the Minotts of Minott's Ledge[5] were on the Cambridge team Harvard was often as effective in football as she is in learning and libraries. But many years of a deplorable immigration of Alpine and Mediterranean adventurers have made our autumn Saturday afternoons unduly gloomy for us Anglo Saxons. In the last days of the football season we pay out, in gate-money, a sum greater than a Republican Campaign Fund, to

---

1. Rev. and Mrs. Chadband in Dickens' Bleak House are canting, self-seeking hypocrites engaged in blackmail of Sir Leiceister Deadlock.
2. Mr. Stiggins ("Stiggins" is Mrs. Sam Weller's pronunciation) in The Pickwick Papers. "Prim, red-nosed man, with a long thin countenance, and a semi-rattlesnake sort of eye — rather sharp but decidedly bad."
3. Seth Pecksniff and his daughters Mercy and Charity in Martin Chuzzlewit are paradigms of moral hypocrisy.
4. Most probably George H. Hazen (1858-1934), who was chairman of the board of Crowell Publishing Co. He was associated for some 30 years with the publishers of The Century Magazine, and was a member of the University Club; which is to say, had business and/or social connections with Stoddard, Grand, and Gould. See Section Four - "Spinach and Zweiback."
5. Walter Henry Trumbull (1893-1976; Harvard '15; All-America tackle '14) was co-captain of the team some have called Harvard's greatest.
Wayland Manning Minot (Harvard '11; All-American halfback '10).

watch the competitive activity of husky Irish and solid Slavs. And what would Cotton Mather say, to see Andover beaten by Holy Cross?[6] If Jonathan Edwards had seen old Nassau [Princeton] smeared by Notre Dame, he would have said, "This is hell."[7] Of the hundreds that risk life and limb throughout November to win money and glory for their colleges, only the best get their names in print. From the three football pages of last Sunday's paper I have copied a list of students that were conspicuous last Saturday.

Sincerely,
Newell Martin.

6. Cotton Mather (1663-1728), clergyman and author educated at Boston Latin and Harvard. Even if he had lived two hundred years after his actual dates, he would not have had to witness Holy Cross beating Andover, as Andover Theological Seminary (founded in the early 19th century) did not — and still does not — field a football team.
7. Jonathan Edwards (1703-1758), Presbyterian minister and theologian who was the third president of Princeton. The match-ups are hypothetical, grounded in the respective Jewish and Roman Catholic compositions of Holy Cross and Notre Dame. On the preceding Saturday (November 7, 1924) Holy Cross tied Lehigh 3-3; Princeton defeated Harvard 34-0; and Notre Dame beat Wisconsin 38-3.

## ETHNOLOGICAL SCHEDULE

Some of the American students who were advertised by name in the Sunday papers for their football labors of November 8, 1924:

Kirkleski
Chicknoski
Koppisch (Columbia's
  chief hero)
Ernst
Benkert
Hazel (Rutgers'
  great man)
Singer
Kruez (Pennsylvania)
Bender
Kiernan
Hanff
Brennan
Fuchs
Booz
Gebhard
Highberger
Schwartz
Slagle (Princeton)
Gilligan (Princeton)
Krisel
Jaeger
Politica
Sohst
Sieracki
Raht
Braunlich
Scheib
Kemmerer
Bullman
Weihl
Middlekauff

Fidelglotz
Krauss
Fivas
Rugge
Starobin
Rokusek
Zuppke (Illinois'
  Captain)
Grange (Illinois)

Oberlander (Dartmouth's
  hero)
Movradian
Finsterbusch
Gamache (Harvard)
Gehrke (Harvard)
Samborski (Harvard)
Zarakoff (Harvard)
Jawish
Minihan
Busch
Degassis
Metzger
Kaufman
Plansky
Alleld    (Cornell)
Rosenberg(Cornell)
Kernwein
Kline   (Yale)
Joss    (Yale)
Herzog  (Yale)
Garbisch (Army)

Postscript, November 12. My Wednesday newspaper, under two sets of glaring headlines, promises the return of Columbia's center and full-back, kept out of play, on Saturday, by injuries. Columbia's 26,000 students take heart again. Our two protagonists will come back to us — Kirchmeyer and Schimmetitsch.

Postscript, November 21. A great engineer has shown me a delightful lyric, to the same effect as this letter, printed in the "Boston News Bureau," by C. W. Barron, the Cohasset Bard.[8]

Mr. Sherwood, in the current Life, prints the names of an All-America Eleven [see reprint of page from Nov. 13, 1924, issue of *Life*.], distasteful to the K. K. K. This is another case of Adams and Leverrier; two or more scientific observers at one time, at different points, drawing the same inferences from the obvious.[9] Nothing could be more obvious than a thoughtful Jew, removing two nordic students from the five-yard line.

Postscript, November 22. Today Chicago wins the championship of the conference, playing to a tie against Wisconsin. Neither side can score, when Greek meets Greek, Hobscheid, Poldelik and Pokrass against Techmayer, Stroubel, Bieberstein and Polaski.

Postscript, November 23. Yesterday, Bucknell, winning from Rutgers made the corridors of the Football Hall of Fame rattle with the cacophonous names of her most distinguished students, Buchevelsky and Karmileququiz.

Nov. 29. Fordham's full-back is Zakszewski.

ta ta ta

# Armenoids
[Nov. 16, 1931]
*"We Armenoids invented the zero."*

*Reading* Up from the Ape, by Earnest A. Hooton (N.Y.: Macmillan, 1931; revised 1947) stirred Martin into writing the following 900-word pamphlet. To make his point, Martin selected from Hooton's work passages which make Hooton out to be

---

8. Clarence Walker Barron (1855-1928), established the *Boston News Bureau* in 1901, subsequently acquired control of Dow, Jones & Co. and the "Wall Street Journal," and in 1921 founded the financial weekly — *Barron's*.
9. John Couch Adams (1819-1992), and Urbain Jean Joseph Leverrier (1811-1877): English and French astronomers, independently calculated the position of the then unknown planet Neptune.

somewhat of a racist. Not really accurate. Most of Up from the Ape is devoted to placing man within the family of the primates, and to tracing his ancestry. Hooton, in the first edition (pp. 501-2) in an analysis of race, wrote:

> Unhappily it is true that the term [race] is oftenest in the mouths of those who are attempting on the basis of their supposed lineage to claim superiority for themselves and inferiority for all others assumed to belong to less favored races. Among American anthropologists, indeed, the reaction against the proclaimers of Nordic preeminence and Negro debasement has been so violent that 'race' has become a hissing and a byword. Anthropologists know that a 'pure race' is little more than a philosophical abstraction and that the greatest cultural achievements of humanity have been produced, almost invariably, by racially mixed peoples. Unfortunately many students of man have gone to the extreme of denying any significance to the hereditary physical complex of which race consists, maintaining that it is nothing more than a combination of bodily trivialities either produced by the vagaries of purposeless heredity, or 'faked' by levelling environmental agencies which tend to cast all men within an area in the same mold. In taking this view I think these students are guilty of emptying the baby out with the bath water.

*In his second edition (pp. 572 & 575), Hooton wrote:*

> If science obviously flies in the face of the facts and ignores or denies taxonomic differences, it merely delivers over the whole dangerous business of interpreting human group physical variation to the tender mercy of the layman, the charlatan, and the political exploiter....I have dragged out these racial methodological skeletons from the taxonomic closet because I do not want my readers to be fooled by cocksure reconstructions of racial history made by German anthropologists and others. My long and extensive experience in the fields both of skeletal raciology and of the racial classification of living peoples has made me very critical of my own efforts and

those of other anthropologists. If I have achieved neither competence nor confidence, I have, at any rate, acquired candor.

*Earnest Albert Hooton (1887-1954 B.A., Lawrence '07; M.A., Ph.D., University of Wisconsin; Rhodes scholar 1910-1911). His early studies were in Greek and Latin, but he became interested in anthropology while at Oxford and received a degree in it with distinction. He started his professional teaching career at Harvard as an instructor of anthropology in 1913, and rose to full professor by 1930, remaining at Harvard until his death. He was one of Harvard's most popular teachers. His focus was primarily on physical and constitutional anthropology, and African and European ethnology and archaeology. He developed new methods of racial analysis by application of statistics to metric and morphological data.*[1]

*Hooton's general view was that heredity was a more important factor than environment, that the race had shown no sign of improvement in the last 30,000 years, and that the present course of evolution was downgrade. Of mental differences between the races, he wrote (first ed., pp. 596-7):*

> Anthropologists have not yet reached the point of an agreement upon criteria of race which will enable psychologists to isolate with any degree of facility the racial types which are to be studied. Psychologists have not yet been able to develop mental tests which anthropologists are willing to trust as fair gauges of mental capacity. Neither group has yet perfected its technique of measurement. Until we know exactly how to distinguish a race and exactly what intelligence tests test, we shall have to hold in suspension the problem of racial mental differences.
> That such differences exist I have not the slightest doubt; that with our present methods they can be summarized quantitatively so that we are justified in assigning one race a position of superiority as

---

1. His other publications include *Apes, Men, and Morons* (1937); *Crime and Man* (1939); *Twilight of Man* (1939); *Why Men Behave Like Apes and Vice-Versa* (1940); *Man's Poor Relations* (1942); *Young Man, You Are Normal* (1945).

contrasted with another, I deny. I hold no brief for racial equality; I do affirm with conviction that it is unfair to apply the standard of our own environment and our own race (whatever that may be) to groups of people differing from us in hereditary mental and physical characteristics and, as a result of such alleged 'tests,' hastily to stigmatize certain races or certain national groups as mentally inferior.

*While the following passage from Hooton's first. edition (p. 566) was not appropriate for Martin's "Armenoids," it must have been pleasing for him to read — and surely must have been shared with his wife, Gomby, the sister of George Bird Grinnell, author of* The Indian of To-Day *(1900):*

I confess to a possible sentimental admiration for [the American Indian], to my mind the most magnificent physical specimen of savage known to the modern world. Intelligent, even spiritual, too proud to be adaptable, these Indians have been unable to bend the neck to the yoke of the conquering Europeans. They went down, fighting to the last for the country which was wrested from them by fraud, trickery, and the superior numbers and better implements of war developed by European civilization.[2]

*But it was Hooton's passages seeming to denigrate the Jew which so roused Martin's ire. Martin text follows:*

Professor Earnest A. Hooton, of Harvard, in "Up from the Ape," gives us almost the latest scientific opinions as to the primates and evolution and the various divisions of the deplorable human race. His is free from all prejudices. He says that anthropologists now divide mankind into 4 groups, Whites, Negroids, Mongoloids and Composites, and each group into races (Hooton, page 502); and

---

2. Research specialist and Vietnam war veteran, Gregory Audette, remarked, "Wish he had told that to my draft board," after locating the following statement about French-Canadians: "Of all the white stocks in the United States the French-Canadian group stands out as physically the least fit by virtue of a high percentage of tuberculosis, pleurisy, nervous and mental defects, defective eyesight and hearing, valvular and functional heart disorders, poor teeth, defective appendages, and small size." (p. 498) Hooton, at age 30, on the other hand, was rejected by the draft when he applied in WWI.

the Whites into Alpine, Armenoid, Nordic, Mediterranean and Ainu. Typical of the Armenoids are "most Armenians, Turks, and Syrians; many Persians and" many of the Ashkenazim.[3] "Armenoids are concentrated in the Near East, Asia Minor, Syria and Persia; common in Greece, Rumania and Bulgaria; and largely present in urban populations of Russia, Poland, Hungary, Austria, Czecho-Slovakia, Jugo-Slavia, Germany and the United States" (505).[4] ". . . The beaky, busy Armenoids emerge from their Levantine obscurity as soon as cities and civilizations arise. This race, characterized, above all, by its sugarloaf head form and its convex nose with fleshy depressed tip and flaring wings, has its center of distribution in the Anatolian and Iranian plateaus of Asia (535). Little is known of its origin or prehistoric beginnings. . . . If there were Armenoids in the Old Stone Age, I have no doubt that they monopolized the trade in mammoth wool and skin garments and were the principal dealers in necklaces of shells and teeth. . . . The so-called 'standard' of Ur, a panel of mosaic in shell and lapis lazuli" of "about 3500 B.C., shows figures representing the Sumerian army. Of the 48 persons represented on this plaque, the characteristic Armenoid nose and the high pointed Armenoid head are clearly depicted in at least 30. A statuette of a Sumerian ruler of the early part of the third millennium excellently delineates this most prominent" nose "and shows also the typical continuity of the slope of the nasal bridge with that of the forehead. . . . It is clear that the Armenoid type was represented among this ancient people" (the Sumerians, long before they were "overcome by the Babylonians" (536).[5] "Babylonian, Assyrian and Hittite monuments show . . . these bearded Armenoids in Anatolia[6] and Mesopotamia throughout historical antiquity. . . . The center of development of this race was in Asia Minor. . . It spread southward to Arabia and eastward at least as far as India. . . . Writing is generally supposed to have originated from the conventionalization of pictographs having a magic or religious significance. It would then be the invention of . . . priests. I should think it highly probable, however,

---

3. Jews who lived in the Rhineland valley and neighboring areas of France before migrating to the Slavic lands in the 11th-13th centuries.
4. The revised edition (1947), perhaps taking note of intervening events, has, "Concentrated in Turkey, Syria, Palestine; common in Iraq, Iran, Balkan countries, and in urban populations of eastern and central Europe" (p. 580).
5. In the revised edition, the Armenoids become a subrace rather than a race, and "nearly all of the 50 individuals" depicted on the standard of Ur are of the Armenoid type.
6. Land area occupied by Asiatic Turkey.

that the necessity of keeping accounts drove inventive Armenoids to a reduction of holy to commercial writ at some very early period. It was of more importance to reckon profit and loss in business than to record victories. Prayers may be rendered vocally but promissory notes ought to be put in black and white." [Professor Hooton does not intend to suggest that we find cuneiform bricks in the nature of negotiable paper, a modern invention]. The first Early Iron Age, Hallstatt period,[7] saw Armenoids passing from Asia Minor to Greece, Italy, the Balkans, &c. the Etruscans, largely Armenoid, came from Asia Minor to Italy about the 8th century B.C. "The dispersion of the Jews, especially the Ashkenazim Jews, carried a great deal of Armenoid blood into eastern and central Europe" (538).

"Big hooked noses[8] may not, of course, be an exclusive Armenoid feature. Yet this type of organ as displayed by Syrians, Turks, Armenians and many Jews is one of the most dominant, distinctive and persistent of racial features. This most highly evolved and selected nose adorns a racial type which has been sifted through thousands of years of natural and social selection in the area where civilization first began.

["]It is casually rather than causally associated with a positive genius for commerce and an infinite capacity for material and intellectual advancement even under the most exiguous environmental opportunities."

My comment on Professor Hooton's summary of scientific research is this:

In short, in this sublime ascent, from ape to man, the initial step was to drop the tree-climber's prehensile tail and the crowning step was to put on the throne-climber's Assyrian nose. The impoverished Bourbon parades a coat of arms to prove that his ancestors were ignorant crusaders.[9] The Jew needs no coat of arms. He carries on his front the imperial Assyrian nose that says: "We, the Hebrews, are as good as the best of the Armenoid race; and what race is more clever than we Armenoids? We Armenoids invented

---

7. Term for the early Iron Age in central Europe, c. 1,000-500 B.C.; name derived from a prehistoric village at Hallstatt in the Austrian mountains near Salzburg.
8. Hooton devotes ten pages to a discussion of the importance of noses in racial classification, beginning with, "An inquisitive and curious person is called 'nosey,' but intellectual curiosity to a great extent accounts for man's material and mental progress. Anatomically, the more highly evolved man is, the 'nosier' he looks." (p. 425 1st ed.; 525 2nd)
9. The French house of Bourbon traces its lineage to Louis IX (1214-1270), grandfather of Louis, premier Duc de Bourbon. Louis IX led the seventh crusade to the Holy Land in 1248-1250.

writing. We Armenoids invented the alphabet. We Armenoids sat on Sumerian thrones when Babylon was a village. We Armenoids invented the Arabic numerals. We Armenoids invented the zero."
 And if I were a Jew, I would say: "There could be little of our modern progress if the zero had not been invented. Moreover, it serves to describe briefly the brains of such persons of Nordic, Alpine and Mediterranean descent, as find a pious delight in persecuting Jews."
Newell Martin.
Huntington, Nov. 16, 1931

"The most distinctive ... nose among the white races is that often described by anthropologists as 'Armenoid' and known to lay Americans and Western Europeans as 'Jewish'. . . . This nose was found among the ancient Sumerians, Babylonians, Assyrians, Hittites and Persians." It is a feature of many among the "Syrians, Armenians, Jews, Greeks, Turks, and other Levantine peoples of today" (Hooton, 431).

ta ta ta

# Jews and Philistines
(A Sermon. Text: 1 Samuel 29:3)
[August, 1933]

*The date, August 1933, is important. On the preceding May 10, the first great organized Nazi book-burnings had taken place. They had been scheduled for most of the thirty or so German university towns, but bad weather caused Cologne, Heidelberg, and several others to postpone the events until the following week.*

*Corps of students made bonfires of literature, correspondence, pamphlets, and records purported to display the "un-German spirit." In Berlin, which may be taken as typical, some 160 titles were included, primarily but not exclusively Jewish, including the works of Freud, Emil Ludwig, Erich Maria Remarque, Thomas and Heinrich Mann, Feuchtwanger, Theodore Wolff (former editor of the* Tagblatt), *Alfred Kerr (former drama critic of the* Tagblatt), *Georg Bernhard (former editor of* Volkische Zeitung), *Marx, Engels, Lenin, Stalin, Jack London, and Helen Keller.*

*At the conclusion, Goebbels declared in a public speech that, "Jewish intellectualism is dead. National Socialism has hewn the way. The German folk soul can again express itself." (Correspondents described the Berlin crowd as "unenthusiastic.")*

*In addition, by August, 1933, Nazi persecution of the Jews already had included denial of government employment, expulsion from positions of responsibility and power, the closing of synagogues, imprisonment, torture, and murder. An estimated 50,000 Jews had fled Germany. The response abroad had included public and diplomatic protests, economic boycotts, and threats by many nations to boycott the scheduled 1936 Berlin Olympic Games.*

*Martin places the text for his "sermon" (I Sam. 29:3-10), taken from the King James translation, on the final page of this 6" X 3.5" pamphlet.*

"The greatest master of the Roman language" in *De Officiis*,[1] repeated "the teaching of the Greeks, that the difference between the right and the wrong use of power . . . is the difference between civilization and barbarism" (235, Rise of Modern Industry, Hammond).[2]

We learn from ancient myths that the crimes and follies of our raw prehistoric predecessors were not unlike those of our own day. Let me tell to you again an old Levantine story with which you may be familiar. But first I must remind you of two other famous myths which have nothing to do with Syria, but which are of a majestic antiquity, so that you may realize how tremendously far back this legend carries us.

First: Paris awarded a prize for beauty to Venus, against Juno and Minerva. Paris had been a foundling, suckled by a she-bear. In "Non-Aryan" mythology, she-bears are used, not as wet nurses, but to teach children deportment in meeting elderly bald-headed clergymen (2 Kings 2:21).[3] This, the first European beauty competition, led to the Trojan War.

---

1. Cicero's (106-43 B.C.) *De Officiis* (On Duty), his last work, is a set of moral dissertations ostensibly addressed to his son Marcus; e.g. III, 2: "To take away wrongfully, then, from another, and for one man to advance his own interest by the disadvantage of another man, is more contrary to nature than death, than poverty, than pain, than any other evils which can befall either our bodies or external circumstances."
2. The full quote from John Lawrence Le Breton Hammond's (1892-1949) *The Rise of Modern Industry* (N.Y.: Harcourt Brace, c. 1926) is "...the difference between the right and the wrong use of power, the use that disregarded and the use that respected the claims of others, is the difference between civilization and barbarism."
3. In 2 Kings 2:21, per the curse of Elisha, two she-bears eat 42 boys who have called him a baldhead.

Secondly: Only four centuries after Venus won the golden apple, a she-wolf suckled Romulus.[4] This is an early form of the Mowgli story which is a part of many mythologies. The wolf's kindness to her foundling resulted in (a) The Roman Empire, (b) the great Roman Catholic Church, which has succeeded to some of the of the power of that empire, and (c) the defeat of Al Smith by Hoover[5].

Thirdly: Venus won her prize about 1194 B.C.[6] The wolf adopted Romulus about 773 B.C.[7] Between these two events, about 1063 B.C., according to Archbishop Usher, 131 years after the judgment of Paris and 290 years before the birth of Romulus, the giant Goliath challenged King Saul to send a champion to meet him in single combat.[8] The Goliath legend is a "Non-Aryan" form of a myth that has many shapes in Aryan folk-lore. The Odyssey has Polyphemus and Ulysses,[9] the Veda has Indra and Vritra,[10] the Edda has Sigurd and Fafnir;[11] and an ancient Teutonic story tells how Cinderella's brother killed a giant Troll.[12] The story of Jack the Giant Killer "is found all over the world". (John Fiske, Myths 151).[13]

4. Romulus, son of Mars, was the mythical founder of Rome; together with his twin brother, Remus, was suckled by a she-wolf after his mother's husband, King Numitor, discovered their parentage and cast them into the wilderness.
5. In the 1928 contest for the presidency of the U.S., Smith's defeat was attributed to his Catholicism.
6. The Trojan War was dated 1193-1184 B.C. by Eratosthenes. (Modern archaeology puts the date back one century.) Martin gets his date for the judgment of Paris by merely subtracting a year.
7. The Romans fixed the date of the mythical founding of Rome by Romulus at 753 B.C. He is described as being "in early manhood" at the time.
8. Usher has David born in 1085 B.C., and anointed king in 1063, hence David's slaying of Goliath would have taken place around a decade earlier than Martin's date.
9. In Book IX of the *Odyssey*, Ulysses and his men, captured by the cyclops Polyphemos and destined to be his food, escape through Ulysses' stratagem of getting the cyclops drunk and blinding his single eye with a scorching-hot beam as he sleeps.
10. The Veda, the scripture of Hinduism and the classic of Sanscrit literature, describes how Indra, the god of light, tends a herd of golden cattle; when they are taken and hidden in a cavern by Vrita, a snake-like monster with three heads, Indra slays Vritra and recovers the herd.
11. In the Edda, the Icelandic collection of Norse myths, Sigurd rescues Brunhilde, who has been immured in a castle by the dragon Fafnir.
12. Boots, a brother of Cinderella, tricks a troll into cutting wood for him. Boots then challenges the troll to an eating-match, hiding his own food in a leather sack concealed under his shirt. When he cuts the sack open, in a display of his powers, the troll follows suit, cuts open his own stomach, and dies.
13. John Fiske, *Myths and Mythmakers* (Boston: J.R. Osgood, 1873). Actually Fiske writes (p. 151): "The myth of Jack and the Beanstalk is found all over the world; but the idea of a country above the sky, to which persons might gain access by climbing, is one which could hardly fail to occur to every barbarian." Fiske uses the four preceding items as instances of the mythical conflict of light and darkness.

Goliath was a short giant, only 9 feet 9 inches high.[14] The ancient Jews that wrote down the David and Goliath story for their children, though primitive and unpolished, were sufficiently sophisticated to know that in the nursery, the bigger the giant, the more positive is the child's tendency to rationalist skepticism. Saul offered what has become the standard fairy tale prize. "The man who killeth" this giant "the king will enrich him with great riches and will give him his daughter" (1 Samuel 17:25). This was 2513 years before an Alexandrian publisher put together the "Arabian Nights" used in our nurseries.[15] German book-burners should notice that this form of reward is of Non-Aryan origin.

David, who was working on his father's sheep ranch, was shrewder than the ordinary Nordic giant killer. Before he took any chances he made sure that the advertisement was genuine (1 Samuel 17:30).[16] He then "chose him 5 smooth stones out of the brook" and with one of them ended Goliath. David married the king's daughter, but later, as often happens in fairy tales, the king turned against the hero. David was driven to take service with a Philistine king.

David then learned that some prejudices now intensely active in Central Europe were prevalent among the Philistines. In David's time the best people of Europe used to tomahawk explorers. Europe has given up stone tomahawks; but Germans cling to the ancient pogrom habit. In some regions of the human mind neither evolution nor the advance of civilization can do much in so short a time as thirty centuries. The Jews and Philistines of David's time were barbarous. With the simple-minded frankness characteristic of Hindoo and Hebrew sacred narratives the record describes David as a murderous barbarian. His massacre of the Amalekites and other aborigines,[17] "who were of old the inhabitants of the land," is almost as shocking, to a modern mind, as the religious conversion

---

14. "Six cubits and a span": (Hence Goliath would have been somewhere baetween 9 feet 9 inches and 11 feet 9 inches tall.) Webster's *New World Dictionary* puts the cubit somewhere between 18 and 22 inches, based on length of an arm from end of middle finger to elbow.
15. While the early publishing history of the *Arabian Nights* is obscure, general agreement places the first comprehensive edition in Malmuk (Mameluke) Egypt by about the 15th century.
16. Where David asks the people a second time, "What shall be done to the man that killeth this Philistine, and taketh away the reproach from Israel?"
17. Described in I Samuel 27: 8-11. The Amalekites were a nomadic tribe that occupied part of Sinai and the wilderness between the southern hill-ranges of Palestine and the border of Egypt. They repeatedly attacked and were attacked by the Israelites. David is said to have "left neither man nor woman alive," after smiting them.

proceedings carried on against American pagans by such powerful malefactors as King Ferdinand and Queen Isabella.[18] David's retaining his affection for his son Absalom after Absalom had raped in public all of David's concubines[19] is one of the incidents that show that the Israelites of David's time were less modern in their behavior than some of the 18th century cannibals described by Captain James Cook.[20] Evolution moves in two ways. Some races go forward and some go back into degradation. The Jews have gone forward. But every one of the many modern nations that have sought a profit in the persecution of Jews has in that chosen to go backward and to adopt a habit that should have become as obsolete as cannibalism 2800 years ago. I wish to remind you also that a policy of driving out Jews or torturing Jews has been more than once, a precursor of ruin, either for the persecutor or for his nation. Do not forget the fate of Russian czars and nobles, the fall of Spain from wealth and power,[21] the disappearance of primeval Philistines. Prehistoric Philistines thought they were long-headed and up-to-date when they resolved that there should be no Jews in their army. They had the sagacity, foresight and breadth of mind of the modern Philistine. Drive out the Jews, make our nation safe for mediocrity.

Gath, in 1056 B.C., was an ambitious city. She dealt with Crete and Egypt and Mesopotamia. People used to say "Tell it not in Gath" (2 Samuel 1:20).[22] As one would say now, "don't publish it in Chicago". David, 2989 years ago, became a soldier of fortune, a condottiere, hired, with his 600 Hebrew fighting men by Achish, son of the King of Gath. David loved domestic ease. He had three wives. He would have been glad to retire, after completing his military career, to a modest suburban villa, over-looking Ashod[23] and the sea; a house with a comfortable harem and Cretan

---

18. Ferdinand II (1452-1516), King of Aragon (in Spain), King of Castile with Isabella (1451-1504). Historians differ in their views as to the amount of violence employed by the Spanish in the conversion of the Indians of South and Central America; some even suggest (e.g., the relevant chapters of *The Cambridge Modern History*) that the Indians readily turned to the church as a substitute for the ritual of which they had been deprived by the prior destruction of their culture.
19. Described in II Samuel 16:22. A political move intended to make it impossible for his followers to be also followers of David.
20. In the journal of Cooks' first voyage, the entry for Jan. 17, 1770, states: "They [the cannibals] gave us to understand that but a few days ago they had kill'd and eat a Boats crew of their enemies or strangers, for I believe that they look up all strangers as enemies."
21. Spain expelled the Jews in 1492, and was in decline within a century.
22. Gath was one of the five royal cities of the Philistines, and the native place of Goliath. The "it" not to be told is the news of the Philistine victory in which Saul and Jonathan were slain.
23. Like Gath, one of the five royal cities of the Philistines.

plumbing.[24] By faithful service he had endeared himself to his employer; but the princes of the Philistines adopted a strong pure-Philistine policy. They were infected with the prejudiced imagination that, in France, only 27 years ago, covered with infamy the forgers that prosecuted Dreyfus.[25] These Philistines warned Achish that David would not be loyal to him. Achish himself earnestly stood up for David, but in vain. the watchword of the Philistine princes was "**What do these Hebrews here?**" They insisted on the expulsion of the Jews. Achish reluctantly yielded and dismissed David and his troopers. After that Gath's history is short. Archaeologists find her mentioned in a list of conquered towns and in the reports of Egyptian provincial governors. There are today Hebrew archaeologists digging in Palestine. If one of them were commissioned by the Julius Rosenwald Fund[26] to explore the ruins of Gath he would be uncertain as to where that city stood three thousand years ago. Three thousand years hence, in 4933, the ruins of Berlin will be hard to find, but learned Jewish archaeologists will be searching for them. The versatile Jew whom Achish had hired and fired began a new career, making himself a king and writing hymns. His hymns are good and have sold well. One American publishing house reported, several years ago, that it had printed them in 83 languages and sent out 45 million copies. David and his son, Solomon, and other Jewish monarchs established the Hebrew religion. In the course of ages it became a monotheism and the Hebrew family became monogamous; changes which would have jolted young David. After ten centuries a new religion, less obviously monotheistic, arose, in the house of one of David's descendants. It was founded on David's hymns and other Hebrew sacred books, and added a New Testament, admitting Gentiles to the protection of a Trinity.

24. Excavations by Sir Arthur Evans from 1900-1905 at the Palace of Knossos (fl. 18th-14th centuries B.C.) in Crete had revealed skillfully-joined clay water-pipes, the most advanced plumbing of its time outside the Far East.
25. The Dreyfus case divided most of French society along politico-racial lines. In 1894, the Jewish French army officer, Alfred Dreyfus (1859-1935) was convicted of spying for the Germans and sentenced to life imprisonment on Devil's Island, largely on the basis of a secret file of evidence that could not be used in open court. Many of these documents subsequently were found to have been forged, chiefly by a Major Henry of French intelligence, who committed suicide after confessing. In 1906, Dreyfus finally was cleared of all charges, reinstated in the army, and awarded the Legion of Honor.
26. Julius Rosenwald (1862-1932), merchant, philanthropist, president of Sears and Roebuck, established the fund in 1917 with gifts totaling $20 million. The bulk of its benefactions were in the field of Negro welfare, but the fund also made extensive grants to health and medical services, libraries, and rural education.

Sixteen centuries after David left Gath a morbid Arab built up Islam, borrowing large chunks of dogma from Hebraism and Christianity and honoring David as a holy prophet. Two of these three religions rule half the world. All this might have been quite otherwise if the princes of the Philistines had permitted David the Jew to hold his place as a contented and prosperous officer of the Foreign Legion of their kingdom.

1 Samuel 29:3-10. "Then said the princes of the Philistines, **What do these Hebrews here?** And Achish said unto the princes of the Philistines, Is not this David, which hath been with me....these years and I have found no fault in him? .... and the princes of the Philistines said unto him, Make this fellow return that he may go again to his place. ...Then Achish called David and said unto him, Surely, as the Lord liveth, thou has been upright, and thy going out and they coming in with me in the host is good in my sight: for I have not found evil in thee:...nevertheless the lords favor thee not. Wherefore now return and go in peace. ...And David said unto Achish, But what have I done? And what hast thou found in thy servant so long as I have been with thee unto this day, that I may not go to fight against the enemies of my lord the king? And Achish answered and said to David, I know that thou art good in my sight, as an angel of God: not withstanding the princes of the Philistines have said, He shall not go up with us to the battle. Therefore now rise up early in the morning with thy master's servants that are come with thee; and as soon as ye be up early in the morning, and have light, depart."

Newell Martin, R.F.D. 3, Huntington, N.Y., August, 1933.

# Jews

*Molly saved this commentary with her letters from Other Gomby. Also included was the following undated, unsigned, handwritten letter, noting that it was to be "confidential:"*

Dear Molly
  I don't wish to give you a gloomy view of your family, but confidentially — I handed them a mind test, questions on Sheet A & places for answers on Sheet B. They wrote their answers on Sheet A, thus entitling themselves to 105 zeros.
  (Letter of Mark Twain to Joe Twichell)
  Vienna, Oct. 23, '97:...There is much politics agoing...- The advantage with the superior man, as usual - the superior man being the Jew every time and in all countries. Land, Joe, what chance would the Christian have in a country where there were 3 Jews to 10 Christians? Oh, not the shade of a shadow of a chance. The difference between the brain of the average Christian and that of the average Jew - certainly in Europe - is about the difference between a tadpole's and an Archbishop's. It's a marvelous race - by long odds the most marvelous that the world has produced, I suppose...Mark.
  (Mark Twain's Letters, 2,647)

*R. M.*

# SIX

# POVERTY AND WEALTH

Eugene Meyer, Jr., and the
   War Finance Corporation . . . . . . 174

The Siamese Royal Commission . . . . 180

The Farm Surplus . . . . . . . . . . . . 195

Harrington Extra . . . . . . . . . . . . . . 196

Warning Against Some of the
Effects of the Slump . . . . . . . . . . . 197

Letter to Molly, February 7, 1936 . . . 199

# Eugene Meyer, Jr., and the War Finance Corporation
[May 28, 1922]

*"I know nothing about finance,
...a little of history,
a good deal about slavery, and
all about farmers."*

*Eugene Meyer, Jr. (1875-1932; Yale '95), a financier and publisher, was appointed by President Wilson in 1918 to direct the War Finance Corporation, which was created by Congress to extend financial aid to industries necessary for prosecution of the war.*

*The Corporation suspended operations in May, 1920, but was revived by a special act of Congress early in 1921 over Wilson's veto. An April 1922, report to the President, following Meyer's survey of agricultural conditions in the West, proposed remedies for "certain defects in our agricultural credit system which are of a more fundamental nature [than can be dealt with merely by government loans], and which cannot be remedied by temporary measures."*

*Eugene Meyer specifically recommended:*

*(1) Enactment of legislation authorizing the organization of institutions to rediscount the paper of livestock loan companies, and the establishment of a system for the more adequate supervision and inspection of the stock furnishing security for the paper;*

*(2) Recognition of the need for orderly marketing of American agricultural products in a more gradual way, and adjustment of banking regulations to this end;*

*(3) Establishment of a rediscount facility to make it possible for cooperatives always to obtain adequate funds for their operation;*

*(4) Extension of the power of the Federal Reserve Banks to include the purchase at market value of eligible paper secured by non-perishable agricultural commodities, properly warehoused;*

*(5) Encouragement of state non-member banks to enter the Federal Reserve system, and reduction of the minimum capital required for such admission; and*

*(6) Amendment of the National Banking Act to permit a limited amount of branch banking within a limited radius of the parent institution. As Meyer stated, in summary: "The processes of*

*financing should adjust themselves to the natural processes of production and distribution rather than vice versa."*

*Pending implementation of these measures, Meyer further suggested extension until January 1, 1923, of the period during which the War Finance Co. would make loans to cooperatives and livestock loan companies unable to obtain financing at reasonable rates through other channels, and to banking institutions on agricultural and livestock paper where it appeared such loans would serve the public interest.*

*Newell Martin's farm, which had been in the family for several generations and on which he lived prior to moving to Huntington, Long Island, was in Milford, Connecticut, near the Housatonic River, about halfway between Bridgeport and New Haven.*

*This pamphlet was printed as a letter addressed to a then-prominent New York City dentist. In 1931, after heavy financial losses, Dr. Concklin committed suicide.*

Milford, Connecticut, May 28, 1922.

Dr. Edward F. Concklin
No. 44 East 64th St. New York City.

Dear Doctor Concklin:
You have made me your debtor by lending me the April Report, to the President, of Eugene Meyer, Jr., Managing Director of the War Finance Corporation.

It is clear, simple, exact, comprehensive, instructive. I hope the President has read this report and committed it to memory. When it came to me, in my farmhouse, I felt the joy that the brick-makers felt in Egypt when the runners went by, shouting, "Procession forms at the East Gate at sunrise. Orders of Moses and Aaron. Heavy marching equipment. Carry forty years' provisions." Professor Ogg's good fat book on American Government[1] is on my desk; 840 pages. Out of all that, two pages for the Reserve Bank System, one page for the Farm Land Banks, and twelve lines for the War Finance Corporation. It is as if Ogg had written on astronomy and had not mentioned the warmth of the sun. This report stirs up the depths of a farmer's soul. I know nothing about finance. But I know a little of history, a good deal about slavery, and all about

1. Frederick Austin Ogg and Perley Orman Ray, *Introduction to American Government* (N.Y.: Century, 1922).

farmers. In the city you may be a gambler or a toiler. The farmer must be both. His labor never ends, his sleep is short, he goes to bed late and rises by candle-light and he has against him every chance of the roulette wheel of rural life; drought, flood, cattle ticks, sheep-lice, weeds, hog-worms, tuberculosis, murrain, deforesters, sportsmen, rats, mice, selectmen, supervisors, bats, field-mice, assessors, tax-gatherers, cut-worms, caterpillars, wood-chucks, locusts, grasshoppers, horse-flies, fruit-flies, house-flies, forty kinds of the glander-garget, potato-bugs, black blight, brown blight, wheat-blight, weevils, borers, San Jose scale, scorching heat, killing frost. He must sell cheap and buy dear. Forestallers stand between him and the market when he must sell and usurers bar him out of the money-market when he must borrow. The village usurer, the village lawyer, the village banker, he must be their slave. It is an ancient wrong. Our fathers came here to get away from it. Zola tells, in "Germinal" what it is in France. "Main Street" tells what it is in Minnesota.[2] It was a cancerous evil in Ur of the Chaldees.[3] We farmers felt the thumb-screws of the usurer before history began. The authors of the Pentatench and of Job tried to protect us and they had stronger backing than even Mr. Meyer.

"They take away flocks and the feed thereof. They take the widow's ox for a pledge (Job 21. 2,3). "They take a pledge of the poor. They cause him to go naked and they take away the sheaf from the hungry" (Job 24. 9 and 10). "No man shall take the nether or the upper millstone to pledge. For he taketh a man's life to pledge" (Deuteronomy. 24. 6). "If thou take thy neighbor's raiment to pledge thou shalt deliver it unto him by that the sun goeth down. For that is his covering: Wherein shall he sleep; and it shall come to pass, when he crieth unto Me, that I will hear" (Exodus. 22.26]). "The rich ruleth over the poor and the borrower is servant to the lender" (Proverbs 22.7).

The Roman Republic rotted and became an empire when usurers foreclosed on the Roman farmers. "The cost of living increased. The income of many landowners diminished. The small farmers were forced to sell at prices ruinously low. Usury soon became the scourge of the countryside" (Ferrero. The Empire

---

2. Emile Zola's (1840-1902) *Germinal* (1885) paints a heavily realistic picture of agricultural conditions in 19th century France; and Sinclair Lewis's (1885-1951; Yale '07) *Main Street* (1920) touches incidentally on the town or banker versus farmer issue.

3. Recent (20th century) excavations indicate that Ur, in Mesopotamia, existed as far back as 4100-3500 B.C.

POVERTY AND WEALTH        177


Builders, 34, 35).[4] Dip, at random, into the history of any nation, and age, and, if it mentions farmers, you will find them getting the short end of it. The story will sound like a Kansas newspaper. I have no doubt that, when the paleolithic farmer went out against the sabre-toothed tiger he got no profit from the venture and that, before he set forth on his perilous enterprise, he had to borrow a stone hatchet from the village usurer and give him a chattel mortgage on his wife.

India was once a land of riches and splendor, but, for more than a century, her government has been content to keep order while money-lenders put the screws on the farmer and she has become a continent of pestilence and hunger. One of the causes of her appalling famines is that she has had no administrator like Meyer to set money in motion to save the harvests. "A week or two after harvest India's surplus wheat and rice have passed into the hands of dealers" (Macdonald, The Awakening of India).[5] "The opening of agricultural banks was advocated as far back as 1884, and was promptly rejected by the Secretary of State" (India's Debt to England, Laipat Rai, 260).[6] "Forty million Indians go through life with insufficient food" (MacDonald). "Destitution, accompanied by disease and debt, is the normal condition of the bulk of the people" (C[chirravori]. Y[yajaneswara]. Chintamini). The Indian Industrial Commission's Report says, on causes of famine: "The capital in the hands of the country traders has proved in-sufficient to finance the ordinary movements of crops. This is one cause of the high rates that the ryot [peasant] has to pay for the ready money which he needs to buy seeds and to meet the expenses of cultivation. A better market system and co-operative selling, are needed."[7]

---

4. Guglielmo Ferrero, *The Empire Builders*, Vol. I of *The Greatness and Decline of Rome* (London: Heinemann, 1907-09). An exact quote would read: "The cost of living increased....The income of many landowners diminished....Whenever the small or moderate landowners of a remote district of Italy grew more than they needed, they were forced [by the lack of transportation] to place it on the market at rates so cheap as to appear miraculous to the Romans, after the high prices and standards of the metropolis....Usury soon became the scourge of the Italian countryside." (pp. 34-5)

5. James Ramsey Macdonald, *The Awakening of India* (London:: Hodder and Stoughton, 1910), p. 165. The context blames the railways, which, facilitating transportation both into and out of famine-stricken regions, broaden markets and prevent local fluctuation of grain prices, thereby destroying capital and consequently the demand for labor. The subsequent quote is from p. 159 (and properly should begin, "Sir William Hunter said that...")

6. Lala Lajpat Rai, *India's Debt to England* (N.Y.: Viking, 1917), p. 260.

7. *Report of the Indian Industrial Commission 1916-1918*. The commission was appointed by the government of India in 1916 to study the possibilities of further industrial development in India and to submit recommendations for a permanent policy of industrial stimulation.

178    POVERTY AND WEALTH

Exodus says that the Lord said, "When he crieth out unto Me, I will hear." Yes, but what has He done about it? What has anybody done about it, until somebody like Sir Horace Plunkett[8] or Eugene Meyer, Jr. has come forward.

Mr. Meyer knows, though he is too discreet to say so, that, if farmers are to have any pleasure or profit they must have big farms, or the small farmers must co-operate. He reports how he has helped even the big farmers, whom the Land Banks cannot help, and the co-operators. He shows how he can help farmers to hold crops for a fair market and borrow money on fair terms. He does not spend money, he uses it. The typical government manger spends money like a river that runs into the salt sea; but Meyer uses money to irrigate farms, as it were, and then still has the money and its power unspent. He has even aided co-operative farmers simply by letting lenders know that, if they do not lend, he will. A sort of farmers' big brother, standing in the background, to intimidate oppressors. He has put the breath of life into country banks by putting new money into them and making them strong enough to do their proper duty; and yet he has not spent the money: it is still ours and still at work. For years we farmers and tax-payers have been reading with despair the interminable story of drunken spenders, childishly throwing our money into bottomless chasms. Now we see Meyer using our money to set us free: and, at the end of the fiscal year, he still has our money, in shining reservoirs, ready to stimulate prosperity with it, over and over again.

To enslave a farmer put him in a hold where he can sell to only one man and borrow from only one man. Meyer sees millions of farmers treading a downward path; and he has set his ambition, his public spirit, his wide and exact knowledge, his breadth of vision, his energy and industry, in the task of making farmers free. A nation's liberty depends on its having such men at work for it. Life is not worth living, wealth is not worth having, in a nation that has not such men.

But I am not yet hopeful. If you observe "signs of hope" about me, dear doctor, have my head examined by Catell's psychological corporation.[9] In every one of three thousand towns sits some

---

8. Sir Horace Curzon Plunkett (1854-1932), Irish statesman, M.P. for South County, Dublin; organized large-scale agricultural cooperatives in Ireland and assisted in establishing a government Department of Agriculture and Technical Instruction for Ireland. These became models for subsequent such developments in England, Scotland, and Wales.
9. James McKeen Cattell (1860-1944), onetime professor of psychology at Columbia,

cold-eyed, usurious spider, reading, with a frown, the April report of the War Finance Corporation. "Take this," he roars to his stenographer:

"Hon. Jeremiah Higgenbottom.
County Chairman.

Dear Jerry:
Telegraph Congressman What's His Name to choke out this Eugene Meyer, Jr. Dissolve his corporation, stop his appropriation, remove him, throttle him. How can I foreclose on a farmer or on a dead farmer's farm, when I have to bid against public money. What's the use of having money, if I have to bid against other men for the farmer's stuff."

True, the usurers and forestallers are out-numbered by the farmers. On every hillside sweats or shivers a drudging farmer, but only a few farmers have heard of Meyer: and farmers, like other men, have a tendency to vote for squanderers.

Why does Meyer give up his leisure and pleasure for the grinding labor of running the War Finance Corporation? To widen the foundations of civil liberty, to strengthen his country, to make us ready for the next war. Men of leisure improve the breed of race horses. Meyer improves the breed of men. Have you thought, on how many lakes and rivers he is driving steamships, how many thousands of square miles of fields he has planted, how many billions of potato bugs he has poisoned? He is what your ancestors used to call a "gentleman farmer," on a colossal scale. And, as for selfish motives, let me quote what has been said about Julius Caesar's love of toil:

"There was revealed to him the possession of a quality which is given to very few, even among superior spirits, that intense and unflagging delight of the mind in the work upon which it is engaged which seems to make the powers of soul and body, of intellect and

---

established his Psychological Corporation in 1921, a joint-stock company with branches in several states, the stock owned by twenty leading American psychologists. Income derived from the sale of special services was used to promote psychological research.

imagination, ever brighter and more vigorous, as fresh prospects of activity are opened out to their labors."[10]
Sincerely
Newell Martin.

ta ta ta

# The Siamese Royal Commission
[March, 1928]

*Thailand (Siam) in 1919-1920 suffered an extremely large trade deficit mainly due to the postwar rice boom-bust cycle. In addition, extravagant government spending created serious financial problems there throughout the twenties. Undoubtedly Martin's omnivorous reading brought to his attention the royal commissions which were appointed to recommend solutions to Thailand's economic problems. And in this 20-page pamphlet, Martin uses these commissions as a foil to discuss such favorite targets as the Volstead Act and anti-Semitism.*

*It's quite possible that this piece was written by Martin while vacationing in Bermuda. The Martins were frequent visitors to Bermuda, and the original tract states at the top of the first page: (Printed by the Royal Gazette, in Bermuda, March, 1928.) The* Royal Gazette, *a daily newspaper still extant, began publishing in 1828, and an original prospectus states:*

> *The pages of the* Royal Gazette *will never be profaned by the scandals of private malice, or the bitterness of private contentions, but will be devoted to extracts from the most approved literature of the day, and to the best original composition within the Colony.*

*It has not been possible to ascertain whether or not this article actually appeared in the* Royal Gazette, *or even whether the*

---

10. Possibly Martin-adapted from Plutarch: "Caesar was born to do great things, and had a passion after honour, and the many noble exploits he had done did not now serve as an inducement to him to sit still and reap the fruit of his past labours, but were incentives and encouragements to go on, and raised in him ideas of still greater actions, and a desire of new glory, as if the present were all spent. It was in fact a sort of emulous struggle with himself, as it had been with another, how he might outdo his past actions by his future." (Dryden trans., rev. Clough)

POVERTY AND WEALTH    181

*pamphlet was printed by the daily paper's presses.*

*What we can be sure of is that Martin himself was the author; the "Siamese Royal Commission" was his concoction; and its report on the "Discovery of the Causes of American Wealth" his invention. Martin's explanations of the causes required extensive research in order to make them clear to today's readers, but even without footnotes, there are chuckles aplenty.*

*As is usual though, one is not always sure when a fact is a fact or a Martin fabrication. We are sure, however, that Rama VI had died three years prvious; his successor Rama VII, who ruled 1925-35, apparently was unsuited to Martin's purposes, as he did not appoint such royal commissions. Added to the literary license Martin so frequently awards himself, is his clever use of the commission report form including a "translator's" preface (Martin depicting himself as translator) -- omitting two schedules, reprinting all sections of the report, and the including an appendix, followed by seven "notes."*

### Translator's Preface

This is a translation of the report made by the Siamese Royal Commission of 1928. This report was published in Siamese and in French, in the Bangkok Gazette, in January. Rama VI, King of Siam, K.C.B., G.C.S.I., G.C.V.O., is a liberal and politic prince.[1] He has sent to Europe several commissions of inquiry. Readers of the *Hibbert Journal*[2] have means of being sufficiently informed as to the opinions of Siamese sociologists that served on these commissions; and the names of such Siamese publicists as Prince Devawongse,[3] Chak Falong, and Phya Buri are not unfamiliar to those who love the delightful Far Southeast.[4] The Commission of

---

1. See note at end of essay.
2. *The Hibbert Journal* was a quarterly devoted to theology and philosophy published in Boston 1902-1968. A perusal of issues 1920-1928, confirmed the presence of articles both from and about the East, but eastern religion rather than sociology. Martin undoubtedly was placing the opinions of his Siamese sociologists on a par with the speculations of theology.
3. Varopakar Devawongse (1858-1923), was a statesman rather than a publicist; half-brother of Chulalongkorn or Rama V (1853-1910) who ruled 1868-1910 (Rama V was the monarch played by Yul Brynner). Devawongse was Siam's first foreign minister and architect of its independence; modernized the foreign ministry and did much to end foreign extraterritoriality.
4. While Prince Devawongse was real, and certainly "not unfamiliar," Greg Audette, our tireless researcher, says of Messrs. Falong and Buri that "dozens of sources, including not only historical and cultural studies, but bibliographies of publications on Thailand that must have included among them three or four thousand books and articles in nine languages have yielded no positive reference for either."

182     POVERTY AND WEALTH

1928 was directed to visit the United States and study the sources of America's happiness. Among those who served on that commission were Siamese barristers who had acquired reputation and experience not only at home but also at Rangoon, Singapore, Nakawn-Lampang[5] and Kwala-Lumpor;[6] and other notables; and two college professors (note 4). Sections one to four of the report show a tendency to undervalue the asceticism of American legislators. This error is frequent among foreigners. I have buried these four sections, therefore, in an appendix, where the reader can avoid them easily, and I print, first, those findings of the commission that will commend themselves to everybody as obviously correct.

**The Royal Commission's Discovery of the Causes of American Wealth**
(Sections 5 to 10 of its report to the King of Siam)

5. In the foregoing sections of our report, sections one to four, we have tried to make it clear to Your Majesty that Mr. Herbert Hoover,[7] the late Carry Nation[8] (see note 7) and other American economists are wrong in contending that the Volstead Law and the new American habit of total abstinence have been controlling factors in producing America's wealth. This commission, therefore, does not recommend to Your Majesty the enactment of a law forbidding wine in Siam. Little wine is used in Siam and such a law might stimulate the thirst of the Siamese. We give this advice, in spite of the fact that we find that in one respect the existence of a prohibition law in America has been economically beneficial. The ordinary American resents a law of this sort and longs to drink. He says he must show his hatred of the Anti-Saloon League.[9] He resents also the suggestion that under the law rich men may drink freely while poor men must abstain. To get his wine in spite of police, detectives

---

5. A city in northwest Thailand more commonly known as Lampang.
6. Kuala Lumpur, the capital of Malaysia.
7. Herbert Hoover (1874-1964), while U.S. Secretary of Commerce (1921-1929), credited Prohibition for "enormously increased efficiency in production," and stated in 1927 that "there can be no doubt that Prohibition is putting money in the American pocketbook." In his presidential acceptance speech in 1928, he declared, "Our country has deliberately undertaken a great social and economic experiment, noble in motive and far-reaching in purpose. It must be worked out constructively." Neither Presidents Harding nor Coolidge had gone so far in their support for Prohibition.
8. (1846-1911), American temperance agitator. Under the conviction of divine appointment, she began attacking saloons with an ax in 1900. See Section Two - "Coolidge and the Bible."
9. The Anti-Saloon League was founded by the Rev. H.H. Russell in Ohio in 1893; it was accused during the 1920's of contributing to the vice which Prohibition fostered, and rapidly lost influence during the latter part of the decade. See Section Two - "Tests for Leprosy."

POVERTY AND WEALTH 183

and coast-guards, he has to use ingenuity and energy. There can be little doubt that the efficiency of Americans is stimulated by the need they are under of exerting themselves to circumvent the Volstead Law; and, to the extent of that stimulation, the enforcement of the Volstead law must be regarded as one of the causes of American wealth.

6. The cause of American wealth must be something that America has and that poor countries have not. Our earliest observations led us to surmise, erroneously, that America's great wealth might be caused by the presence of the Mormon faith. Mormons are an American phenomenon. Although Mormon missionaries are active in Asia and elsewhere, there are no Mormons of importance outside of America. In America there are 400,000 Mormons.[10] They are prosperous. They all know how to read and write. They have great political influence, especially in the Republican party. They worship Brigham Young and Joe Smith[11] and they abstain from tobacco. But, as against these 400,000, there are about one hundred and nineteen millions of other Americans, many of whom have money and many of whom use tobacco and many of whom believe in gods that are quite different from Brigham Young and Joe Smith. We therefore do not recommend the adoption of Mormonism in Siam.

7. One contributory cause of American wealth is that the States have received, through immigration, the best Jews. Some of the most brilliant bankers, economists and ethnologists in America are Jews. Among them we sometimes heard the opinion expressed that Jews have more brains than other people. We need not come to a conclusion on that debatable question. It is admitted by everybody that Jews have brains and that three millions of them have used their brains to plant themselves in America; and, while it cannot be shown mathematically, there is no escape from the fact that American law and practice have set up a sifting process calculated to secure for America the cream of Jewry. An immigration law has been adopted,[12] one of the objects of which was

10. In 1928, the Mormon Church estimated its membership at 640,000; the Reformed Mormon Church stated positively a membership of another 103,174.
11. Joseph Smith (1805-1844), founder of Mormonism. Brigham Young (1801-1877), its leader after Smith was murdered by a mob.
12. The Immigration Act of 1924, one of the most hotly-debated domestic political issues of that year, set up new quotas based on the percentage of foreign-born from each nation resident in the U.S. in 1890. This arrangement reduced the existing quotas for southern and eastern Europe by 87% while reducing that for northern and western Europe by only 29%. See Section Five - "Copy of a Letter to a Publisher."

to keep out Jews. Under the curious quota system of that law, a preference is given to immigrants from Great Britain and some other regions which have never had enough Jews. In the face of this stringent discrimination against Jews from Poland, Russia, and Rumania,[13] if a Jew from one of those countries wishes to enter America he often has to use ingenuity and go through a costly and roundabout process. A commonplace or inefficient Jew will seldom try to overcome in such a case the difficulties that lie before him. If, for instance, I am a Rumanian Jew and wish to take advantage of American opportunities, my easiest course is to make my way laboriously to Mexico, and there to perfect myself in the Spanish language and disguise myself as a Mexican miner. By this process ultimately I find my way to Arizona and thence by slow stages to Chicago, where in the course of time I am sure to win a rich reward for being more intelligent than the ordinary Goyim.[14] Critics of our report may say: "This immigration law, however, is a recent thing." But the Jews believe that, for many years before the present immigration law was adopted, it was secretly understood, among American consuls, that they were expected to discriminate against Polish, Russian and Rumanian Jews in the matter of passports, and to contrive that, in a long line of applicants for passports and visas, the Jewish emigrant should find himself subject to peculiar delays and refusals. Such obstructions could not fail to operate as a part of the process that has enriched America by securing to her more than her share of Jews of efficiency, learning, acuteness, ambition, public spirit, love of liberty and genius.

We see no prospect, however, of devising means to entice many Jews into Siam. More than two thousand years ago the Jews began to leave Asia; and from that time, Asia has been at an increasing disadvantage in her competition with Europe.

8. Another contributory cause of American prosperity is the bad state of what are called the courts of justice. American lawyers, from Chief Justice Taft[15] downward, tell the American public that the criminal jurisprudence of America disgraces the nation. American lawyers also deplore the inefficiency and congestion of their civil courts and the expense and delay of their operations. It

13. Poland's quota was reduced from 30,977 to 5,982, Russia's from 24,405 to 2,248, and Romania's from 7,419 to 603.
14. Plural form for a gentile or non-Jew.
15. William Howard Taft (1857-1930), chief justice of the U.S. Supreme Court 1921-1930; instituted numerous practical measures for expediting litigation.

POVERTY AND WEALTH 185

is hardly necessary to remind Your Majesty of the wisdom of the Chinese Emperor, Kien Lung [Ch'ien Lung (1711-1799) who ruled from 1736-1796], shown in a decree which has recently been republished in Europe and America and is known to everybody.[16] Certain censors memorialized the Chinese emperor as to the corruption and inefficiency of the Chinese courts. The emperor Kien Lung in his rescript said: "The worse the courts are the better. Do nothing to make them safe or attractive for litigants. If my subjects learn by experience that a law suit is almost as injurious to the winner as to the loser my subjects will keep out of court. They will so conduct their affairs as to avoid law suits and they will seek to settle whatever disputes they may have by peaceful arbitration."

We find that the Americans have adopted the Chinese idea and that their wealth is in part owing to their having learned that it is better to submit to any sort of libel, slander, assault, trespass or oppression than to go to the expense and inconvenience of a suit. We annex to our report a schedule [not included] showing that in a recent case the justices of the Supreme Court were invited to read eighty-three pounds of printed testimony[17] and another schedule [not included] showing that in 1926 in felony trials the time spent by jurors and witnesses in court, including the time spent by them in hanging about the courts during the empanelling of juries and in other periods of waiting, considerably exceeded the periods of imprisonment allotted to felons under verdicts.

9. We must distinguish between causes of wealth that are merely contributory and two causes of wealth that we have found to be primary and fundamental. A characteristically American feature of American life is the ease, frequency and even frivolity with which the American elects to end the life of other Americans (See note 1 and note 2). Murder is an American habit. Americans are courteous, hospitable, tolerant and cheerful. Nevertheless, they murder on slight provocation, and often, it seems to us, needlessly, inexcusably, and unprofitably. Some American sociologists have

---

16. No actual decree can be found, but throughout the 1920's in the U.S. the settling of commercial disputes by arbitration was on the rise.

17. Possibly *Myers v. U.S.* (272 US 52), decided Oct. 25, 1926. The postmaster-general had removed a postmaster from office before the expiration of his four-year term; the law provided that a postmaster serve his full term "unless sooner removed and suspended according to law or by the President by and with the advice and consent of the senate." Since a fundamental delineation of administrative powers was involved (the dismissal was upheld), the case required tortuous reference to both documentation and precedent. The decision occupies about 40 pages.

maintained, in discussing this point with us, that the American believes that, in killing another American, he is doing him a favour, in removing him from a gloomy and wine-less desert, governed by Methodists. We are not convinced, however, that any large number of American murderers are altruists, even when they are men who believe that the heaven of American theology is a better place than this world. Further, most of the American murders are committed in "dry" regions where, we are told, almost everybody believes that "dryness" produces happiness and that government by Methodists is desirable. It is not, however, a part of our duty to report on the causes of the murder habit. We report only on its existence and its effects. Official statistics show that, in each million of population, the murders committed in America are nearly fifty times as numerous as those that take place in England, and twelve times as numerous as the Canadian murders.[18] They are infinitely more numerous than those in Latin America. Professor Sheppard, of Columbia University, in his monograph on Latin America, says: "In Latin America, except in times of war, murders, burglaries and hold-ups are unknown."[19] No country in Europe, Asia or Africa has any such percentage of murders as the States. We submit herewith a graph [not included] showing that the ascending line of murders per thousand closely follows the ascending line of increase in the American gold fund. We venture a hypothesis to explain how the murder habit operates to increase the nation's wealth. In London a man begins his day and carries on his work with a feeling that he is secure against being murdered. The statistics show that there is less danger of his being murdered in London that there is of his being killed by the accidental dropping of heavy objects from upper windows. In America, on the other hand, every citizen that watches the statistics must feel that his life is at risk. This feeling makes a man alert and polite. If I am an ordinary American and not one of those incurably addicted to meddling with other people I bear the murder risk clearly in mind and take pains to attend to my own affairs and not to hustle other people or bother them. This makes wealth. The Americans accordingly have a proverb that runs thus: "I got rich by minding my own business." We report therefore that this close resemblance in lines of increase in murders and of

---

18. Contemporary figures approximately twenty for England and six for Canada.
19. William Robert Shepherd (1871-1934) taught history at Columbia 1896-1934. *Latin America* (N.Y.: Henry Holt, 1914), p. 153: "Burglary is practically unknown, and highway robbery a very rare occurrence, outside of the republics in which grave political disturbances still exist." Murder is not discussed.

increment of gold may be regarded, although nothing in economics is exact or certain, as showing one of the causes of American prosperity. We do not however advise Your Majesty to take any steps to increase the murder rate in Siam. Murder, like the prohibition of wine, is so inconvenient and uncomfortable socially that it is better for a country to abstain from prosperity if it can be got only at the cost of an increased murder rate.

10. Another primary cause of American wealth is an American habit that is peculiarly and entirely American, a habit in which the conduct of Americans differs from the conduct of all other people. This habit, happily, we can recommend for adoption. Your Majesty will observe that we have traced a line in an annexed graph [not included], founded on government reports, showing that the rising line of American wealth is definitely accompanied by a rising line showing the imports of chicle. America surpasses all other nations in the use of chewing gum. One of the tallest and most magnificent buildings in Chicago, an object far more conspicuous in Chicago than the Statue of Liberty is in New York, is the Wrigley Tower.[20] True, in some countries outside of America, a beginning has been made in gum chewing but the money spent for chewing gum each year in America now exceeds the amount that the whole country devoted to colleges in 1870.[21] We therefore report that American wealth is due, in great measure, to the American use of chewing gum. For this also we venture a hypothesis. In the old times Americans were said to eat too fast and not to chew their food enough. Fletcher wrote volumes on this point.[22] If a man does not chew, he upsets his digestion. But we no longer hear from the doctors that Americans do not chew and do not digest. The new and general use in America of chewing gum stimulates the salivary glands and this improves the American digestion and American efficiency. The steady motion of the jaws, during, for instance, an eight hour day, has also the effect of stimulating the circulation of arterial blood about the head and this has an enlivening effect on

---

20. Characterized as a "Spanish Renaissance white terra-cotta skyscraper," the Wrigley Tower was built in 1921 by the chewing gum company of the same name. At thirty-two stories, it was for the next five years the highest building in Chicago.
21. Some $91,861,572 was spent on chewing gum in the U.S. in 1925; approximately $36.5 million on higher and technical education in the U.S. in 1870.
22. Horace Fletcher (1849-1919). Forced by ill health to retire when only 46 years old, he devised a system of dieting described as, "abandoning the habit of rapid eating and thoroughly masticating his food, chewing each mouthful until all taste is extracted from it, and being reduced to a fluid state it practically swallowed itself." He authored *Nature's Food Filter*; *Glutton or Epicure*; and *A.B.-Z of Our Own Nutrition*.

188    POVERTY AND WEALTH

the cerebral cortex and makes American thought swift, bold, comprehensive and efficient. We advise that Your Majesty and the Royal Court begin chewing Beeman's pepsin gum and Wrigley's chiclets. Then the practice of chewing gum will soon prevail throughout your kingdom. Thus, without making anybody uncomfortable, and by operating along the lines of least resistance and without any irritating new law, we shall restore Siam to her old place among the wealthy states. In making this suggestion we have not forgotten that many of your subjects chew betel-nut, a languid sort of chewing that never made anybody rich; and that our projected reform will ruin the betel-nut trade. Siam, however, is an honest nation; and, even in the cause of reform, Siam will refuse to resort to any confiscation, robbery, swindle, or other crime. The betel-nut farmers should have their losses made good from the royal treasury, through a small excise and import duty on chewing gum.

(At the end of the report were affixed seals, representing white elephants, done in wax, and the other usual Siamese signs of formality, and the signatures of Plodalong and Tritothink[23] and six other members of the Commission.)

## Appendix
### (Section 1 to 4 of the Commission's Report.)

1. Many Americans have access to so small and so uncertain a share of the nation's wealth that they do not attain to a Siamese standard of comfort. Four millions of "workers" are out of work.[24] This must mean that eight millions are in desperate need or in desperate fear. Moreover, it is not extravagant to believe that, of those more happily placed than these unfortunates, there are eight millions who live in anxiety lest they or their husbands or parents may lose their jobs and their share of the national prosperity. It is also true as to perhaps eight millions of negroes in the States, that no Siamese cooley should envy them. We are told of poverty even among the whites in some parts of the South. "Squalid towns and streets or wretched hovels and dilapidated cabins and huts throughout the country side. The common run of people in the South

---

23. "Plod along" and "Try to think": rare use of word puns by Martin.
24. Senator Robert Ferdinand Wagner (1877-1953), a staunch anti-Prohibitionist, had issued this figure March 5, 1928, to contradict a statement by Coolidge and Hoover that there currently existed no widespread unemployment in the U.S. Wagner's four-million-out-of-work figure was regarded as controversial at the time, his opponents viewing it as a political bid.

are poor." (Note five.) An Australian commission has reported that the working men of the North are worse off than the working men of Australia. (Note six.) If twenty millions of people are uncomfortable, the rest of the community must be unhappy witnessing their misery. How can a man sleep peacefully in a Pullman car if he has seen a black woman thrown out of it? How can a man dine in luxury if he sees a hungry man on the sidewalk? The statistician of this commission, however, insists that he has found no statistical proof that any great number of Americans allow the sufferings of others to make them uncomfortable. But we confess that we have found all questions as to happiness and prosperity in America, what they are and whence they arise, too complex for us. We shall report simply on some of the causes of American wealth.

2. American wealth, while not quite enough to surpass the dreams of avarice, has risen to a point that stupefies statisticians.

In 1840 the total annual production of gold and silver in the world was thirty million dollars. In recent years the annual production of gold alone has been, in round numbers, about four hundred million dollars.[25] The Americans have more of this gold, and in some respects, more comfort and luxury than other nations. They have no wine, however, and therefore their dinners have become dreary exercises in deglutition [swallowing down] and they have forgotten the existence of most of the mild social pleasures that form so great a part of European life. It is thought, however, that prosperous Americans do not feel the loss of social pleasure because they derive an intense voluptuous enjoyment from the contemplation of their balance sheets.

When we presented, in Washington, the decree defining our duties, influential Americans were amused by Your Majesty's preamble, reciting that "the first duty of a government is to study the happiness of its people." "How quaintly oriental," said the Americans. "The first duty of a government is to compel its people to be chaste and abstinent."

Herbert Hoover, Carry Nation, Viscount Astor,[26] Wayne B.

---

25. Figures correct; $30 million probably culled by Martin from McCulloch's 1840 *Dictionary*. (See Section Seven - "Extracts From a Diary.")
26. Waldorf Astor (1879-1952), second Viscount Astor, son of William Waldorf Astor (1848-1919), grandson of John Jacob Astor (1763-1848). The first Viscount Astor had settled in England in 1889. Waldorf Astor held political office in the British parliament, and had served on the British Liquor Control Board during WWI. In an article, "Why Prohibition Will Win," published in *Forum* magazine February 1927, he declared that while prohibition might be modified, the American people would never recommence the general use of intoxicants. "[Alcohol] takes the edge off efficiency, blunts ideals, and is always on the side of the flesh in its war against the spirit."

## 190    POVERTY AND WEALTH

Wheeler,[27] Judge Gary,[28] Irving Fisher,[29] and other sociologists say that America's wealth is caused "by prohibition." By inquiry in London we learn that Viscount Astor is regarded there as an international nuisance. In New York we learn that Messrs. Wheeler and Gary and Hoover had professional motives for expressing such opinions. We assume, however, that these and many others of the essayists who have propounded this declaration are sincere.

For brevity we shall use an Americanism and refer to people of their way of thinking as "Drys" and to their opponents as "Wets." It seems to us that the Drys are deluded.

3. Let us suppose, first, that the Drys mean that the States are rich because they have laws that forbid the use of wine, and let us assume, for the moment, in this part of our report, for the sake of argument, that these laws are ineffective. Abstaining from some luxury or convenience may in some cases have some effect, but there is proof that the existence of an ineffective law demanding abstinence in a nation that continues, in spite of the law, to refrain from abstinence, has no important economic consequences. All Mohammedan countries have had, until lately, stringent laws against the use of wine. In Russia vodka was forbidden in the last years of the last Nicholas and the first years of the first Bolshevik.[30] Arabia, Afghanistan, the old Barbary States,[31] the Egypt of Ismail, Turkey and latter-day Russia, under laws forbidding strong drink, have been picturesque, but they should not be reported to Your Majesty as samples of success in producing wealth. If Mr. Hoover will send a committee of congressmen to spend next winter in Biskra [city in northern Algeria] and Cairo, they will confirm us on this point.

(Translator's note: This is Siamese ignorance.

---

27. Wayne B. Wheeler (1869-1827), lawyer, prohibitionist, until 1917 general counsel to the Anti-Saloon League; subsequently its legislative superintendent. See Section Ten - "A 1922 Christmas Card."
28. Elbert Henry Gary (1846–1927), called "Judge" for having served two terms as a county judge in Illinois. Member, with John D. Rockefeller, Jr., of the Conference Committee on Law and Order; repeatedly expressed his belief in the beneficial effects of Prohibition.
29. Irving Fisher (1867-1947, political economist who promoted the reducing of alcohol intake as a health measure; became president of the Committee of Sixty on National Prohibition in 1917. See Section Two - "Coolidge and the Bible."
30. Nicholas II instituted prohibition in Russia at the outbreak of WWI; alcohol was reintroduced in January, 1923, as a state monopoly.
31. Respectively: Western Libya, Tunisia, Algeria, and Morocco, Bokhara (Bukhara in the west of the Uzbek Soviet Socialist Republic), Western Turkestan (the region comprising the Turkmen, Uzbek, Tadhzik, Kirghiz, and South Kazakh Soviet Socialist Republics).

No executive officer has power to send any congressmen to Africa.)

Your Commission finds, therefore, that the most casual survey of the subject tends to show that the mere enactment of a law against wine does not produce wealth.

4. It is clear, then, that such intelligent men as Mr. Fisher and Mr. Hoover must mean that American wealth is caused by the fact that Americans, either through obedience to the law or of their own volition abstain from wine. We do not know whether they do abstain from it or not. We shall assume, for convenience, in this section of our report, that abstention from strong drink is, in the United States, substantially complete and universal. Is such abstention a cause of national wealth? There is much proof that it is not. There are great populations outside of America that abstain from wine. In some cases this is through obedience to law. The most barbarous, fanatical, backward and dangerous region in the work today is the Hejaz.[32] Its king, Ibn Saoud Sheik who founded Saudi Arabia in 1924, forbids a lot of things. He forbids the shaving of a beard, under penalty of death. He forbids the wearing of a plug hat [man's high silk hat], or an English sun hat, or a brown derby. He forbids the drinking of wine, under penalty of death. Among his wahabees[33] this prohibition is enforced; but there has not been much wealth visible in the Hejaz, since Lawrence ceased from distributing there his large sums of American money.[34] In India there are nearly three hundred and twenty millions of people who do not drink. Among these are millions of Mohammedans who abstain from wine from religious motives, because they wish to obey the Koran. Millions in India abstain because they cannot afford wine. Among millions of Hindus the use of wine has never been usual and no important number of Hindus have ever shown an inclination towards wine. If wine-drinkers were as few in America as in India the prohibiters might justly announce that "prohibition" has made its work perfect and that abstinence has become complete.

---

32. Region in northwest Saudi Arabia, on the Gulf of Aqaba and the Red Sea.

33. Members of Wahabee or Wahabi, a puritanical reform movement in Islam dating from the 18th century that was adopted by the Saud tribe and thus became the official religion of Saudi Arabia with the triumph of Ibn Saud.

34. T.E. Lawrence (1888-1935) disbursed considerable sums to various Arab sheiks during WWI to further the cause of Arabic revolt against Turkey and hence British military purposes; most notably the 1,000 gold sovereigns he picked up at Aqaba early in 1918, and handed over to Said Ibn Hussein. As the gold was British, not American, perhaps Martin is implying that it was in effect freed for this use by American entrance into the war.

In Siam, Burmah and Indo-China the demon, rum, is a stranger. Nobody drinks there, in any degree that should concern an economist, except the Christian visitors. The three or four hundred millions of China do not drink. In old time,, in China, particularly in the golden age that was lit up by the genius of the poet Li Tai Po,[35] there was a good deal of wine-drinking and still more of talk about drinking; but, since China has fallen into poverty, nobody drinks, to any degree that a political economist would notice, anywhere in China, except at treaty ports. No economist, however, would set up the eight hundred millions in Asia that do not drink as examples of the efficient production of wealth. It would not seem to any American or even to any Siamese that Arabia, India or China is enviably prosperous. A Dry might say: "The people of America, one hundred and twenty millions of them, abstain from wine entirely. See how rich they are. Imitate them and abstain and get rich." A Wet might say: "Observe the myriads of Asia, eight hundred millions of them. They abstain from wine. See how poor they are. Avoid their example and drink freely and you may avoid their fate." We must, therefore, dismiss the fact that the Americans have a law forbidding wine and the fact that the Americans abstain from wine. Neither of these astonishing facts has much to do with the creation of American wealth.

(Translator's note: Here, again, the Siamese err, through ignorance. The Commission is wrong in thinking that Asia can teach any lesson in morals to American statesmen. Asia is inhabited by timid and sluggish orientals who discreetly abstain from costly liquors and who are temperate when they drink. The United States are inhabited by great numbers of nordics, who fiercely desire strong drink at any cost and drink to excess when they can get it. But when they have been entirely debarred from the object of their desire they concentrate their passions on labour and produce prodigious wealth.)

Note 1. Figures from one hundred and nineteen American cities for 1926 showed about one murder for each ten thousand people. New York City had 268 [sic] homicides in a year. But the New York murder rate is trivial compared with that of other

---

35. 772-846 A.D .classical Tang dynasty poet; best known in the West as the author of several of the texts set in German translation by Mahler in *Das Lied von der Erde* (e.g., #5, "The Drunkard in Springtime"). See Section — "On Drinking Alone by Moonlight."

important places. New York has not acquired the American murder habit with any degree of thoroughness. This confirms what some Drys have told us, that New York is the most un-American of American cities. The murder rate per one hundred thousand varied greatly in different cities. In New York it was 5.7; in Philadelphia 8.6; in Chicago 16.7; in St. Louis 18.6; in Memphis 42.4; in Birmingham 58.8 in Tamp 67.6; and in Jacksonville 75.9.[36] It has been suggested by one of the most accurate mathematical minds in America that the rate varies inversely in proportion to the number of Jews in each town and directly in proportion to the number of Methodists; but, as Siam is not blest with many Jews and has few Methodists, your commission has not thought it necessary to test the suggestion.

Note 2. (From a New York Daily) Buffalo, August 29. Murders in the United States average one thousand a month the year around, Oscar Hallam of St. Paul, chairman of the Criminal Law Section of the American Bar Association told the opening session of the convention. (Mr. Hallam's figures are exact. He proceeded to make some suggestions; but as the suggestions of the Criminal Law Section of the American Bar Association are usually medieval, your commission will not burden Your Majesty with them.)[37]

Note 3. The American Chicle Company is by no means the chief producer of gum. But even this comparatively modest concern reports that its net profits for the third quarter of 1927, after providing for interest, depreciation and income taxes, were $455,898, against $344,349 in the same period in 1926 [figures accurate].

Note 4. (By the translator.) Professors of economics Plodalong and Tritothink, in the University of Muang Tai, at Bangkok.[38]

Note 5. From page 354 of "Why the Negro is moving North,"

---

36. Accurate quotations of figures released in mid-1927 by Frederick L. Hoffman of the Prudential Life Insurance Co.; except that he gives a total of 340 rather than 268 homicides for New York City. The larger figure is in fact required for a rate of 5.7 per hundred thousand.
37. Oscar Hallam (1865-1945), head of the criminal law section of the American Bar Association. His statistic is correct. In his speech he primarily urged full publicity for every step of the legal process from detention to release; and the promptness, certainty, and adequacy of punishment and the finality of a just judgment. His other suggestions included the elimination of straw bail, shortening the time of appeal, increased punishment for crimes committed with a gun, and paroles only after judicial investigation and notice to both the trial judge and prosecutor.
38. No such university.

by Howard Snyder, Plain Talk,[39] New York, March, 1928.
Note 6. "There were 160 men applying for every one hundred jobs in January, 1927 [figures accurate]. The housing of American workers is not up to the standard of the workers' homes in Australia...America works longer hours than Australia." (The Nation, New York, February 8, 1928.)[40]
Note 7. (By the translator). The Siamese are wrong in classifying the late Carry Nation with Mr. Hoover as an economist. Mr. Herbert Hoover and the late Carry Nation have little in common except that both are tee- totalers, both are prohibitionists and both were among those who should be remembered for a long time, as the creators of the Eighteenth Amendment and the Volstead Law.

*Vajiravudh or Rama VI (1881-1925) ruled Siam from 1910-1925. His orders are respectively Knight Commander of the Order of the Bath; Knight Grand Commander of the Order of the Star of India; and Knight Grand Cross of the Royal Victorian Order. [Ronald Reagan on June 14, 1989, received from Great Britain the Knight Grand Cross of the Most Honorable Order of the Bath, or G.C.B.] Rama VI was educated, and spent much of his adolescence and early manhood, in England. He had received the GCVO at Edward's VII's coronation in 1901, and the K.C.B. in 1911. And, in truth, he did appoint royal commissions.*

*Consonant with Martin's characterization, the King made monogamy the only legal form of marriage, adopted the Gregorian calendar, introduced vaccination, and used the press and mass organizations to urge the populace to accept modern ideas of nationhood, of duty to the nation, and the virtues of hard work and thrift. He insisted, however, on the absolute character of the monarchy, and refused to share rule even with Siamese elder statesmen. And a good part of the government extravagance referred to above was on royal ceremony and public celebrations, including a crack unit of palace guards.*

᭞ ᭞ ᭞

---

39. *Plain Talk* was a monthly published in New York City 1927-1931.
40. *The Nation* was quoting from the report of an Australian industrial delegation to the United States.

# The Farm Surplus
# Daily Neech: Comic Section

N. Y. Times, Aug. 25, 1930, page 2, column 6:

The top of this column reports as to Frank Murphy, 80 years old. Unwilling to beg, he stood in front of 2 Charles Street and took off his shirt and tried to find bidders for it. At Bellevue Hospital "it was found that he had been so long without food that he is not expected to live."

N. Y. Times, Aug. 25, 1930, page 2, column 6:
The bottom of this column reports an economic conference at Cornell and an address by Dr. C. E. Ladd in which he shows which devices are prudent and which are wasteful in "the reduction of acreage as a means of solving the wheat surplus problem."

*[Editor's note: First paragraph is an accurate summary of the item which did appear in the Times. The economic conference was reported on elsewhere in the Times. The second International Conference of Agricultural Experts took place at Cornell from August 18-28, with some 300 in attendance. The issue of acreage reduction was discussed at the conference. On August 10, the Times carried a brief description and list of speakers, furnished by Dr. C. E. Ladd (Carl Edwin Ladd, 1888-1943), director of the agricultural extension service at Cornell. Ladd was not himself listed as one of the speakers.*

*Alexander Legge, the director of the Federal Farm Bureau, had called for a reduction of acreage as the most realistic remedy to the then-existing agricultural depression, and had been backed in this idea by several senators, but no legislative action had been taken.*

*Professor John D. Black of Harvard, speaking at the conference, had ridiculed the idea of curbing production as a means of solving the farm surplus problem. The only speakers for acreage reduction mentioned by the Times were E. G. Nourse of the Brookings Institute and Dr. O. E. Baker, senior agricultural economist of the Division of Land Economics in Washington. They predicted that a condition of population stability and increased productivity would -- by 1960 -- either require the removal of some agricultural lands from production or the discovery of new markets abroad.]*

❧ ❧ ❧

# Harrington Extra

October 31, 1931.

Daily Neech

Yale was founded, I think, at a cost of $2500.[1] Mr. H.G. Wells thinks that such money is wasted.[2] Whether he is right or wrong, I wish our Fathers had slipped a few words into the Constitution, preventing any exemption from taxation in favor of any school, college, library, church, temple, religion or sect.

A man and his wife, both out of work, slept in the open, in Bronx Park, for three or four months, begged their food.[3]

The Yale Alumni Weekly says that Yale, this year, is spending $100,000 for the improvement of the Sir John Harrington Department of the Yale Bowl.[4]

Not knowing whether to praise or deplore any of the acts described above in our new department, we offer a prize for the best editorial, of 100 words, in praise or blame of any one of them. The prize is a paid-up 27-year subscription to the Neech.

ᴊᴀ ᴊᴀ ᴊᴀ

---

1. The founding of Yale in 1701, and its continued survival, were made possible by various contributions of land, money, and books, including a 500 English pounds appropriation by the Connecticut General Assembly and an annual grant by that body of £120, commencing in 1715. Martin doubtless alludes to the 1718 gift by merchant Elihu Yale of merchandise valued at £562, the largest single donation Yale had received to that date; which act became, of course, eponymous.

2. In his 1934 autobiography Wells summarized his lifelong views of modern degree-giving institutions as antiquated in both method and subject matter, jerry-built, and focused on examination-passing. More particularly, in a 1924 essay, "Blinkers for Youth," he stated, "Schools and universities are surely the most paradoxical things in the whole preposterous spectacle of human life. They exist to prepare youth for a world of enormous changes, and their chief activity seems to be, at Oxford and Cambridge quite as much as at Harvard and Yale, to get youth apart from the world and conceal the forces of change from its curious and intelligent eyes."

3. No reference. Worth noting that the New York City emergency unemployment committee had received a total of $8.5 million from private and institutional donors the preceding year; and that in the first week of October, 1931, the city had opened a Central Registry Bureau for the Homeless. Working in conjunction with such institutions as the municipal lodging house, Salvation Army, and the Bowery YMCA, the Bureau had registered some 5,000 persons in its first week, all of them described as in good health.

4. The Financial Report of the Athletic Association, appearing in the Yale Alumni Weekly of October 16, had listed among the $270,611.93 spent that year on improvements to the Yale athletic facilities an expenditure of $14,852.06 for new toilet buildings for the Yale Bowl. Several millions spent over the preceding decade or so, including $4.3 million for a new gym, had given Yale easily the largest athletic plant of any university in the world.

Sir John Harrington (1561-1612), English miscellaneous writer. *The Metamorphosis of Ajax*, written in 1596, "is a discourse on privies and excretions, arrayed in an elaborate scheme of three parts....In the middle is the design for a modified privy, with working diagrams; around it are layers of explanation, apology, self-defense, and discussion of terms....His device involves a flushing system, drawing on a cistern, and an inner 'stool pot' emptied and sealed by a plunger-type stopper. An historian of sanitation,

# Warning Against Some of the Effects of the Slump

(Extract from Sir Walter Raleigh (1552-1618), his advice to his son).[1]

Take care of thy estate, which thou shalt ever preserve if thou observe three things: first, that thou know what thou hast, what everything is worth that thou hast, and to see that thou art not wasted by thy servants and officers. The second is, that thou never spend anything before thou have it; for borrowing is the canker and death of every man's estate. The third is, that thou suffer not thyself to be wounded for other men's faults, and scourged for other men's offences; which, is, the surety for another. ...Believe thy father in this, and print it in thy thought, that what virtue soever thou hast, be it never so manifold, if thou be poor withal, thou and thy qualities shall be despised. Besides, poverty is a shame amongst men, an imprisonment of the mind: thou shalt neither help thyself nor others...thou shalt be a burden and an eyesore to thy friends, every man will fear thy company; thou shalt be driven basely to beg and depend on others, to flatter unworthy men; let no vanity, therefore, or persuasion, draw thee to that worst of worldly miseries.

If thou be rich, it will give thee pleasure in health, comfort, in sickness, keep thy mind and body free, save thee from many perils, relieve thee in thy elder years, relieve the poor and thy honest friends, ands give means to thy posterity to live, and defend themselves and thine own fame...It is said in the Proverbs 'The poor is hated even by his own neighbor, but the rich have many friends'.

Reprinted by Newell Martin, R. F. D. 3, Huntington, N. Y., August, 1933. [*Martin continues.*]

I dreamed that Sir Walter Raleigh visited me. I said to him,

---

Earnest Saline, calls it 'the first crude valve water-closet'." D. H. Craig, *Sir John Harrington* (Boston: Twayne, 1985), p. 68. Kudos to Greg Audette for answering the trivia question: What is the origin of the word "john?"

1. From Chapter V of *Instructions to his son and to Posterity*, the first prose work Raleigh composed during his imprisonment in the Tower, 1607. Written "for young Wat's benefit before the boy went off to Oxford, an austere set of principles regimented into a morality that Walter had never observed himself and which young Wat wasted little time keeping." Robert Lacey, *Sir Walter Raleigh* (N.Y.: Athaneum, 1974), p. 343. Martin's quotes mostly accurate; some ellipses missing, but not vital to flow or understanding.

"A young man is now tempted to ruin himself by becoming a surety. That path to poverty is closed. Corporations now do that sort of thing, safely, for profit. And science has shown that labor may cease to be a curse and that poverty may lose its sting. Charles P. Steinmetz, wise in electricity,[2] and Lord Leverhulme, supreme in soap, say that four hours of labor in a day, or three hours, are enough."[3] "Oh, bright new world," said Sir Walter. "Glad I came back." "But," said I, "Church and state and merchant princes, the rulers of wealth, may combine to find a new way out of our trouble; some scheme to make rich men richer and to make over all the rest of us into something like the industrious Chinese cooley class." "That will be finer yet," said Sir Walter. "When I sailed beyond the Spanish Main, I learned how to run a ship. Wine in the cabin, cockroaches and salt pork in the forecastle."[4]

*  *  *

2. Charles Proteus Steinmetz (1865-1923), American electrical engineer best known for discovery of the law of hysterisis. Steinmetz predicted in 1923 that the widespread use of electricity would reduce the average working day to four hours by 2023, and the working year to 200 days. The resulting leisure would stimulate intellectual interests "in every conceivable direction." In the same communication, this famous scientist predicted that "cooperative human effort would solve most of the difficulties facing mankind," that the Slavs, with their collectivized social structure, would be "the dominant race of the future," and very likely there would be radio communication with Mars. The *Times* dissented editorially.

3. William Hesketh Lever, Viscount Leverhulme (1851-1925), head of the English firm of Lever Brothers, at the time of his death the largest manufacturers of soap in the world. His conduct toward his employees included establishing a factory village at Port Sunlight near Liverpool, where workers could live in brick cottages at nominal rents, and enjoy such benefits as a hospital, library, swimming pool, and gymnasium. In 1919 he attempted to introduce a six-hour working day (twelve for machines), but was defeated by a union leadership more interested in increased production. When he advocated the measure in lectures in the U.S. in November, 1919, the *Times*, as in the case of Steinmetz, dissented.

4. Actually, though Raleigh's ships undoubtedly reflected the usual living and eating arrangements of the time, in his 1595 small-boat expedition "beyond the Spanish main" some 400 miles up the Orinoco River in search of the legendary city of Manoa, he shared in extreme privations equally with his men.

# Letter to Molly
# February 7, 1936
[handwritten on letterhead]

*Scribbled at the top above date and greeting: Do not write to me, ever, except when you find yourself absolutely at leisure.*

Feb. 7 - 1936

Dear Molly

Your mother kindly lent us this agreeable picture.[1]

I am studying your essay on Bolshevism. My opinion is this: The richest land on earth was opened to our ancestors free. Further, they had the advantage of seeing vast communal communities of Americans living happily in Central America & South America, nevertheless we made such a hash of our opportunities that ten millions or 15 millions — nobody seems to know which number is right — are out of work. That is, they are in hell & would be happier dead.

This failure marks all of our statesmen, of both parties, as lobsters, that should be in some prison or asylum. Fine, our system, for rich, childless, bachelors. But any man, rich or poor, that has descendants should look on it with horror. For, obviously, a rich man will have in 100 years, usually, 250 descendants. Four of the 250 will be rich. Most of the 246 will be coolies or paupers; under our social system. Therefore I am a bolshevik. The prosperity of the 4 does not reconcile me to the misery of the 246. If you ever become a bolshevik, never tell anybody until after you are 80.

*Newell Martin*

---

1. Not preserved with letter.

# SEVEN

# PROGRESS and REGRESS

Wireless Activity . . . . . . . . . . . . . 202

Extracts From a Diary . . . . . . . . . . 207

Magauk! Magauk! . . . . . . . . . . . . 210

Condolence - 1932 . . . . . . . . . . . . 214

Letter to Molly, March 12, 1933 . . . . 214

Letter to Molly, December, 1934 . . . . 215

Grammar . . . . . . . . . . . . . . . . . . 218

# Wireless Activity
## On Friday, June 8, 1928

Charles Lamb and Thomas Love Peacock[1] were clerks in the India House. They were appointed because what they wrote, in their hours of leisure, amused the directors of the august East India Company. They had plenty of leisure, because ninety years ago, in 1838, ten years before R. R. Bowker[2] was born, mails from India to the India House were delivered in London only twice a year. Peacock, in 1839, arranged for mail steamers, through the Red Sea, a bold experiment, that led to the great Peninsular and Oriental Steamship service. My father's[3] letters, in 1854, six years after R.R. Bowker was born, used to go in Chinese junks from Mingpo to Shanghai and from Shanghai in sailing ships around the Cape of Good Hope to New York, usually a four months' journey We sometimes had adventures to write about. My earliest distinct recollection is of 1857. In that year I assisted, as a spectator, at the massacre of the piratical Portuguese at Ningpo.[4] I was three years old and in the arms of my Chinese nurse. She and I were terrified by the flash and boom of the Cantonese artillery and by the sight of Portuguese vainly seeking refuge in tombs near our house. To that I attribute the imbecile cowardice that I now exhibit in the presence of thunder and lightning.[5] I was saved from becoming a part of the massacre by the accidental and timely arrival of the French warship, Capricieuse, a sailing vessel. In Peking, in the sixties, the postage on each thin letter was 35 cents. My mother used to "cross"

---

1. Charles Lamb (1775-1834) English essayist. Entered the employ of the East India Co. as a clerk in 1792, long before the commencement of his literary career, and remained in that tedious position until ill-health released him with a pension in 1825. In a letter to Wordsworth of April 7, 1815, he complained, "I do not keep a holiday now once in ten times." Author of *Lamb's Tales of Shakespeare*, which, presumably, the Other Gomby grandchildren would have read.

Thomas Love Peacock (1785-1866), novelist, poet, official of the East India Company. Appointed to that position in 1819. (Few men would have been less likely than the directors of the East India Co. to hire or fire on the basis of an employee's spare-time literary accomplishments.) Peacock began to concern himself with steam navigation in 1829; but actually opposed the use of steamers on the Red Sea, presumably out of deference to the Company's geographical interests (might have made the Near East a commercial rival). In 1839-40, war steamers were constructed under his supervision that doubled the Cape.

2. See Section Two - "Letter To R.R. Bowker."
3. See Section Seventeen – "Appreciation of W.A.P. Martin."
4. See Section Fourteen - Peaks and People
5. Verified by Other Gomby's grandchildren.

her letters, thus writing two pages on one and making trouble for patient relatives.[6] In winter, letters to us from America were sent through Moscow, Nijni Novgorod and Tomsk. They crossed Siberia by sledge. From Kiakhta mounted couriers carried them across the Gobi desert.[7]

In 1928 R. R. Bowker became 80 years old. During his life the sending of messages across the ocean became a matter of minutes rather than months. On June 8, this became to me peculiarly obvious.

Early in June my daughter Helen [Mrs. Schuyler Merritt Meyer, Sr.] sailed for Beg Meil, in Finistere,[8] with about fifty-eight percent of my grandchildren.[9] I warned her. "No child", said I, "should ever travel. Children should be regarded as immovable, as chattels real, annexed to the freehold, like serfs, under the old czars." I read to her De Quincy's "Flight of the Kalmuck Tartars"[10] and reminded her that the discomforts of the Kalmuck mothers were increased by their taking with them their numerous children. "No," said Helen. "These children need polish and so does their accent. Nobody knows what they are talking about when they use the simplest French words, se battre, je m'en fiche, tete de chou.[11] I have bought my tickets and Dr. Hill, the distinguished pediatrist, has inoculated and vaccinated all four of the children, at great expense, against everything they could possibly die of. Bridget Donohue is to have a holiday in Ireland. She will nurse them, tend them, mend them, all the way to Cherbourg. Madame Moliere will spend the summer filling the children with idioms and irregular

---

6. The family has preserved such letters written to her family in her youth by Martin's mother-in-law which illustrate this practice. She wrote two texts at right angles to one another on same side of sheet of paper.
7. Nizhni-Novgorod is present day Gorky, situated some 200 miles east of Moscow. Tomsk is a city in west-central Siberia, some 1,700 miles east of Nizhni-Novgorod. Kiakhta (Kyakhta), is a city in the Buryat Soviet-Socialist Republic near the Soviet-Mongolian border some 900 miles east-southeast of Tomsk.
8. Finistere is a department in northwest France at the extreme tip of Normandy; Beg Meil is a resort in the small (c. 5000 pop) town of Fouesnant, with scattered villas, a sandy beach, and rocky coves; visited by Proust and Renaldo Hahn in 1896.
9. The four children of Helen Martin Meyer; other three were the children of Martin's son, Grinnell. See Section Nine - "From the Family Tree."
10. Thomas De Quincy (1785-1859), English essayist, published "Revolt of the Tartars, or flight of the Kalmuck Khan and his people from the Russian Territories to the Frontiers of China" in *Blackwood's Magazine*, July, 1837. It describes the 1771 flight of 600,000 Tartars some 2,000 miles along the route named, through hardships and military attacks that destroyed around two-thirds of their numbers. (G. Audette, researcher, notes that the essay occupies, in the edition of De Quincy he consulted, some 50 closely-printed pages, and sympathizes: "I trust daughter Helen's patience held out.")
11. "To fight, I don't give a damn, cabbagehead."

verbs."

On June 8 I came to town to sit alone in a box above first base and watch Bill Sherdel pitching for St. Louis.[12] In the evening I went to see the movies, the "Fall of Petrograd."[13] Such lonely and silent pleasures are all that are left for the deaf. At the ball field I saw fifty deaf mutes in the gallery. Some of them, I noticed, did not have the usual peanuts that are essential to baseball. Secretly I sent them some with a request that they give a cheer for Al Smith.[14] They gave the cheer, ardently, riotously, with their fingers.

Before I reached the Polo Grounds I called my wife on the telephone. She said something alarming which I heard imperfectly. She was trying to tell me that she had heard, at 10 a.m., that two of the children were ill with measles on the *Arabic* in mid-ocean. I am 74 and am not permitted to aid in warding off any doom or disaster. So I went on in my pursuit of senile pleasure. But the children's mother, and their intelligent father, in New York, knew how to use the miracles of science. Helen gave up all thought of Cherbourg, where the sick children would have perished on wind-swept tenders or in a comfortless quarantine. She called up Plymouth. Plymouth, by wireless, refused to admit any infectious Americans. If I had been there I would have said to Plymouth, "Three hundred and eight years ago ancestors of these children sailed from Southampton on the Mayflower. In New England they diligently spread measles, fatally, among the fierce Wampanoags and Pequods,[15] thus opening the country for rapid colonization and laying a foundation for American power and making it possible for America to help England in the recent war. The peace and power of England, therefore, rest on a basis of American measles. There should be added, to the royal coat of arms, a proper heraldic design, representing, as one of the supporters of the crown, measles rampant. Now we bring the

---

12. On June 8, leftie William H. "Wee Willie" Sherdel (1896-1968) pitched the Cardinals to an 8-3 victory over the N.Y. Giants, holding them to only eight hits. In that season, the best of his career, Wee Willie went on to lead St. Louis to the pennant; overall record 21-10.

13. Vsevolod Pudovkin's 1927 film, usually Englished as *The End of St. Petersburg*, one of the classics of the Russian silent era, had opened at New York City's Hammerstein Theater May 30, having been briefly refused a permit by the New York State Board of Censors.

14. Alfred Smith, then Governor of New York; hearty opponent of prohibition.

15. What is known as "The Great Plague of 1616-1617" -- apparently a combination of typhus and cholera -- had killed thousands of Indians along the Massachusetts coast some three years before the Pilgrims' arrival. (It was probably, but not certainly, brought to America by English fishermen or other visitors.) Squanto, whom the Pilgrims met within weeks of their arrival, was in fact the sole survivor therefrom of the Patuxet band of Wampanoags, saved by having been kidnapped and carried off to Europe.

measles back to you. You ought to welcome it, gratefully."

Plymouth would probably have answered: "Plymouth suffers from the malign activity of Viscount Astor and his wife. [16] They harass us with undesirable reforms and thwart our attempts at desirable reforms. We wish no more undesirable Americans."

The father of Molly and Bear[17] then fixed his eye on Antwerp and, by telephone, melted the hearts of powerful princes of the sea and of the State Department. Our State Department, when aroused, moves with the speed of light. If you don't believe me, ask Chiang Kai Shek, Feng Yu Hsiang, Yen Hsi Shan, Tanaka, Matsudaira.[18] The State Department cabled to the Consul General at Antwerp.[19] He, by tact and ingenuity, persuaded Belgium to

---

16. Waldorf Astor (1879-1952) and Nancy Witcher, Viscountess Astor (1879-1964). Waldorf Astor held political office in the British Parliament, and had served on the British Liquor Control board during WWI. In an article, "Why Prohibition will Win," published in *Forum* magazine February 1927, he declared that while prohibition might be modified, the American people would never recommence the general use of intoxicants. "[Alcohol] takes the edge off efficiency, blunts ideals, and is always on the side of the flesh in its war against the spirit." The Viscountess, a Christian Scientist, became first woman member of parliament in 1919; was a lifelong champion of women's causes and of temperance. Her first significant action in parliament was to introduce and carry through a bill raising the British minimum drinking age to 18.

17. The two oldest children; the ones with measles. Schuyler (Bear) remembers having to be carried off the ship still weak and sickly.

18. Feng Yu Hsiang, (usually Yu-hsiang) (1880 or 1882-1948), Northern Chinese warlord who joined forces with Chiang Kai-shek in 1927, and became vice-president of the executive Yuan (cabinet) of the Nationalist government and its second minister of war.

Yen Hsi Shan, (usually Hsi-shan) (1883-1960), Northern Chinese warlord broadly sympathetic with the Nationalists though not properly a member of their forces.

Tanaka Giichi (1863-1929), Japanese general and statesman, Japan's foreign minister and minister of colonization 1927-1929, who on three occasions dispatched troops to Shantung "for the protection of the Japanese residents."

Tsuneo Matsudaira (1887-1949), Japanese statesman, ambassador to the U.S. 1923-1928.

The Chinese Nationalists, based at Nanking, had mounted the second stage of the so-called "Northern Expedition" in April, 1928, with the aim of removing the Communist forces from the Peking area and bringing all China under Nationalist control. Both Feng Yu-hsiang and Yen Hsi-shan had collaborated with Chiang Kai-shek in the organization and leadership of this campaign. Japan dispatched troops to protect its interests in the region, and clashes between the Nationalist and Japanese forces inevitably occurred, the first and largest being at Tsinan-fu, capital of Shantung province. These in turn threatened the estimated 1700 U.S. nationals in the region, and to these threats the U.S. Department of State did indeed respond with alacrity, notably in a stiff note on May 20 to the Nanking and Peking governments protesting the slaying of two American missionaries, and its refusal in early June to remove U.S. forces from Tientsin after a Nationalist request that it do so. (For contemporary U.S. presence in China, See Section Three — "Paper Umbrellas." Whether by luck or circumspection, the Japanese didn't come under as much diplomatic fire as the Chinese Nationalists, but throughout the crisis the state department kept in close correspondence with the Japanese government through almost daily meetings with Matsudaira.

19. George S. Messersmith (1883-1961) had been U.S. consul general at Antwerp since 1925, though he was to leave within a month for the American consulate at Buenos Aires. Later assistant secretary of state, ambassador to Cuba, and ambassador to Mexico, one of the few American career diplomats to attain such high posts.

admit the undesirable Americans. By wireless he re-assured the anxious mother. Mr. Franklin,[20] by cable, asked the agent of the line in Antwerp to use all his powers. By wireless, also, Mr. Franklin spoke, at length, to the Captain of the *Arabic*, presumably about thus: "When measles attacks children at sea, the ancient custom of the ocean gives the captain the right or duty of throwing them overboard or marooning them on Fastnet Rock.[21] I ask you to disregard such precedents. And I don't wish Molly and Bear to sail the North Atlantic forever, like two little Flying Dutchmen.[22] Try to land them at Antwerp." By wireless and cable Madame Moliere was discovered somewhere in Brussels; and by wireless and cable she assured everybody that she would go to Antwerp and there co-operate with all principalities and powers. The mother and the suffering children were kindly cared for in the ship's spacious hospital, far down in the bowels of the boat, in the company of a scarlet fever patient and a few reforming drunkards. There is a legend, perhaps untrue, that Helen said, when she entered that austere cavern, "This is surely the whale's belly. How could Jonah endure it for three days," and that, thereupon, a sick child murmured, "Mummy, who was Jonah?" At Antwerp, after atrocious storms, the sufferers were met by the agent of the line and his eminent physician. In the consul General's own car the pestilent children were carried to the dependance [annex] of the Grand Hotel.

All these changes of arrangement, all these precautions and provisions, complex and unprecedented, were begun, agreed on and perfected, between 10 a.m. and 5 p.m. on June 8, mostly by wireless. I reached my home by the late train and crept quietly into my wife's room. She told me, in whispers, so as not to wake our guests, of these swift, incredible wireless wonders. Then I told her that on this same day the first assuring wireless message had been faintly heard from the Italians on the ice, off Svalbard, in the Arctic Ocean,[23] and

20. Evidently Philip Albright Small Franklin (1871-1939), president of the International Mercantile Marine Co. The *Arabic* was a cabin steamer of the IMMC's Red Star Line.
21. Fastnet Rock is a rocky islet with a lighthouse some four miles southwest of Cape Clear, the southern tip of Ireland. Formerly first point in Europe sighted by eastbound trans-Atlantic passengers.
22. Allusion to the legendary captain fated to wander the seas forever for having, in a storm, defied both heaven and hell to sink him or drive him from his course.
23. The ill-fated expedition in the airship Italia, led by Umberto Nobile, had passed over the North Pole on May 24. Radio contact had been lost in an arctic gale the day following. At 7 P.M. on June 8, the Cita di Milano, home ship for the expedition, had picked up the first transmissions from the crew of the downed airship, giving their location as some 20 miles north of Cape Leigh Smith on the island of Svalbard or Spitsbergen, which is itself some 500 miles north of the northern end of Norway.

that by wireless, we had learned, in the evening, that Kingsford-Smith had landed in Australia.[24] "When did he land?" asked she. "At 11.40 to-morrow morning."

≈ ≈ ≈

# Extracts From A Diary.
## KEPT IN AN EARTHLY PARADISE

(Myrtle Bank, Kingston, Jamaica, B.W.I.
January 13, 1930.)

Two hard-working farmers, a few miles from here, starved to death. Their crops went wrong.

Coal-passers in Kingston have been on strike for an 8-hour day. A big coal boat, the *Seeladden*, of Oslo, is moored under my window. From my luxurious hotel I can see something of the "grimy miseries of stevedores" who sweat in the deep holds of iron ships, under tropic heat.

Two ignorant terrified old women, whose houses and farms are worth less than $25, have appealed to their friends for help, because some red tape bureaucrat has notified them that their homes are forfeit for arrears of taxes.

Two clergymen have been appointed to high places in the school system.

Three men of Argyll and Sutherland Highlanders at Newcastle, a romantic post high up on a palmy mountain, have met a cruel fate. They were rude to a lance corporal, and then to a subaltern; and then they sang the "red flag."[1] Some critics of their conduct explain it by saying that Argyll Highlanders come from Whitechapel;[2] others by saying that they come from Glasgow. The "red flag" is dull stuff. Less inspiring than the Marseillaise. These three foolish songsters have been condemned to five years in prison.

---

24. Charles E. Kingsford-Smith (1897-1935), in the airplane *Southern Cross*, had made the first Hawaii-to-Australia flight June 2-June 8 with a crew of three.

1. *Die Rote Fahne*, the communist marching-song.
2. That is, are agents of the British government.

That is the end of them. In the American Army they might have been given fifteen years or fifty. A little common sense, in them or in their officers, might have saved these men from lifetimes of misery and failure.

This was a happy island, when half a million gentle pacifist Arawaks[3] led, here, an idyllic life, before they were discovered by the unscrupulous and cruel ruffian that is called Columbus. There were no clothes then in Jamaica. There was no poverty and no incurable hunger. There were no professing Christians, no prosperous clergymen, no ticks, no mongooses.[4] Not that I have anything to say about clergymen or mongooses. Some of my kindest friends are clergymen. I am merely mentioning statistical facts. Church and state have always made rather a hash of this mountainous island; though it is now too prosperous; as they have of some other places. The island is so rich that it could profitably support its government, which, by the way, is far better than that of the United States, and its mongooses, if birth control were taught in the Jamaica schools.

January 14, Charles P. Howland edits an Annual View of Planetary Mismanagement.[5] His annual is easy reading. But most annuals are dull. In Bermuda, however, in that quaint little library in Queen Street,[6] I found a year book that did not seem to me dull. That lovable library had abandoned its effort to keep up with commerce and its latest annual of world Trade was McCulloch's Dictionary of Commerce for 1840, Longmans, 1400 pages.[7] This was printed only fourteen years before I was born. McCulloch was reverenced in my time, as Babson is now.[8] McCulloch paints a vivid picture of the quiet world into which I was born. He says not one word about balloons, aeronautics, Montgolfier or flying.[9] His was a

---

3. A group of Indians in northeast Central America, who spread eastward as far as the Florida keys. The first Indians encountered by Columbus were Arawaks.
4. Apparently "persons of mixed blood."
5. Charles P. Howland (1869-1932; Yale '91), New York City lawyer, member of the board of aldermen of New York City. From 1928 through 1931 Howland supervised the publication of the annual *Survey of American Foreign Relations*, published by Yale University Press.
6. The Bermuda Government Library, Queen Street, Hamilton, Bermuda.
7. John Ramsay McCulloch (1789-1864), *A Dictionary, Practical, Theoretical, and Historical, of Commerce and Commercial Navigation*, first edition London: Longmans, 1832; went through numerous editions up to 1890.
8. Roger Ward Babson (1875-1967), American statistician who founded in 1904 the Babson Statistical Organization, publishers of business statistics.
9. Joseph Michel Montgolfier (1740-1810) and Jacques Etienne Montgolfier (1745-1799, brothers who invented the first practical balloon in France in 1783.

serious book for the guidance of merchants and investors. On his fine engraved map, there is no San Francisco, no California, no Los Angeles. The British boundary meets the Mexican at 11 degrees of north latitude, just above where now is Marin County.[10] A great river rises, in "Youtaw Lake" and a dotted line suggests the hypothesis that it empties into the Pacific at "Port San Francisco." The Nile has no sources. There is no Hong Kong, no Shanghai. "Owhywhee" is the chief of the "Sandwich Isles."[11]

McCulloch has not one word about petroleum or benzine or motor cars or electricity; but he has two and a half pages about "Rum, a well-known and highly esteemed spirituous liquor."

North Carolina was the chief gold-producing state of the United States.

McCulloch has thirteen pages on canals, but only two pages on railroads, half a page less than he gives to rum. He cautions investors against railroads, Thus:

"Railroad, tram or wagon-road, a species of road having tracks or ways formed of iron, stone, etc." "The railroad between Liverpool and Manchester is by far the greatest undertaking of this sort" On that road thirty-one miles have been done in an hour and a half [and sometimes less.]

"So wonderful a result has gone far to strike space and time out of the calculations of the traveller."

"Astonishing as is this railroad, we doubt much whether there be many more situations in the kingdom where it would be prudent to establish one." This road "led to the most extravagant speculations. It was supposed that the whole country would be forthwith intersected by railroads; that locomotive engines would be as common as stage coaches. Soberer and sounder views are now entertained."

ಶಿ ಶಿ ಶಿ

---

10. County in California immediately north of San Francisco Bay, reached today by the Golden Gate Bridge.
11. That is, Hawaii is the largest of the Hawaiian Islands.

# Magauk! Magauk!

A Christmas Card, 1932

*One in a series of annual Christmas messages printed in pamphlet form. The earliest of these is in Section Ten.*

I write in praise of Merry Christmas, as celebrated in Bermuda and British North Borneo; and in sorrow, as to the sombre Christmas of Huntington.

Thinking of Bermuda sets me to thinking about the great island of Celebes.[1] A geologist tells me that, many million years ago, Celebes and Madagascar were united by a continent that is now at the bottom of the Indian Ocean. Geologists know this because some of the animals of Madagascar are like some of the animals of Celebes and not like any other creatures. Now, therefore, a great geological fact shines in on me suddenly. Millions of years ago North Borneo and Bermuda must have been joined together by land that has sunk. I am of this opinion because the best inhabitants of Bermuda are different from everybody else except certain inhabitants of British North Borneo. The best people of Bermuda are exactly like the Muruts of North Borneo[2] and like nobody else. To describe the Muruts and therefore also the better Bermudians I quote from the recent observations in the Malay Archipelago of Enriquez, the anthropologist and zoologist, whose books about the butterflies and mountaineers of Burmah are well known to you and me.[3]

"The Muruts are a simple attractive people. The young women are" not the least agreeable feature of the landscape.[4] "The

---

1. The Celebes are an Indonesian island immediately southeast of the island of Borneo. Some two-thirds of the island of Borneo belongs to Indonesia; North Borneo, or Sabah, being one of its other three political units. Enriquez (see footnote #3), pp. 23-4, cites the English naturalist Alfred Russell Wallace (1823-1913) as concluding as early as 1869, on the basis of interspecial resemblances between fauna that Celebes, in contrast to Malaysia and Australia, "belonged to the lost continent of the Indian Ocean and that it was once joined to Africa." Apparently Martin substituted "Madagascar" for his own purposes.
2. According to the *Encyclopedia Britannica*, "the least numerous of the indigenous ethnic groups of Borneo, living mostly in the Sabah state, Malaysia, speaking a language called Murut." Originally they were headhunters living on hilltops for defense, but gradually were displaced into the interior.
3. Major Colin Metcalfe Dallas Enriquez (1884-1937), *Malaya: An Account of Its People, flora, and Fauna* (London: Hurst & Blackett, 1927). Other titles include *A Burmese Enchantment* (Calcutta: Thacker, 1916); *A Burmese Loneliness* (Calcutta: Thacker, 1918); *A Burmese Wonderland* (Calcutta: Thacker, 1922); and *A Burmese Arcady* (London: Lippincott, 1923).
4. The following omitted form Martin's text: "The women are pretty while young, but age quickly into repulsive old hags...."

PROGRESS AND REGRESS    211

Murut is perhaps the most likeable native of North Borneo. It is doubtful if any native of any country in the world is so easy to get on with as the Murut.[5] He is hospitable and good-humored and so honest that theft is almost unknown, except the occasional theft of someone else's wife.... There is a ritual for their worship, an important item being a gorgeous" administration of King Solomon's anodyne.* [Martin Note: I quote from the Bible, Proverbs, Chapter 1: 1. The Proverbs of Solomon, the Son of David, King of Israel; 2. To know wisdom and instruction; to perceive the words of understanding; 3. To receive the instruction of wisdom...and judgment...; 4. To give...to the young man knowledge and discretion." And I quote from Proverbs, Chapter 31: 6,7: "Give strong drink unto him...Let him drink and foget his poverty, and remember his misery no more."][6]

Devout Muruts recognize three distinct stages in the effect of their ceremonial on the worshippers: Magauk; Magauk Ke-pi-oh; and Magauk Ke-pi-pi-oh. (*Malaya*: by Major C. M. Enriquez, Hurst & Blackett, London, pp. 93&94).[7]

Glossary of the Murut ritual: Magauk: Lit up; joyfully illuminated.

Magauk Ke-pi-oh: Exhilarated to the point of being, in a high degree, gay, altruistic, optimistic, affectionate and adventurous; and especially daring in the use of polysyllabic words which, at this stage of the ceremonies, tend to come out in kaleidoscopic patterns.

Magauk Ke-pi-pi-oh: Blissfully unconscious, with the serene happiness of nirvana; calmly oblivious; forgetful of all pain and sorrow.

More people would have a Merry Christmas, as do the innocent inhabitants of Bermuda and British North Borneo, if more people would study self-control, self-denial and birth control and

---

5. The full original states: "Notwithstanding his little idiosyncrasies, the up-country Murut is perhaps the most likeable native of North Borneo." Here, Enriquez was quoting Owen Rutter (1889-1944), *British North Borneo; an Account of its History, Resources, and Native Tribes* (London: Constable, 1922). Further Rutter descriptions quoted by Enriquez, and not used by Martin: "They...are more or less naked except for a loin-cloth -- which, however, is often 50 feet long. Formerly they wore beaten bark....These people are frightfully dirty, and suffer from ulcers, sore eyes and skin diseases. There is much blindness among them....Venereal diseases, introduced by Dyak and Arab traders, have spread disastrously."
6. The original text is: "One of their most interesting superstitions, which seems to be peculiar to Borneo, is their veneration of certain porcelain jars of Chinese origin. There is a regular ritual for their worship, an important item being a gorgeous drunk."
7. To quote further from Enriquez: "'Muruts,' says Owen Rutter in his delightful book on British North Borneo, 'recognise three distinct stages in drunkenness -- *Magauk* being "drunk": *Magauk Kepioh* "blotto": and *Magauk ke-pi-pi-oh* "blind to the world."'"

would obey the inspired commandments of Solomon.* [See Martin note above.]

In Huntington on Long Island, too many people forget these virtues. Mr. William B. Trainer, the Town Clerk, has compiled this report on the vital statistics of Huntington in the year of disaster, 1932:

Marriages, 147
Deaths, 262
Babies born, 430
Dogs licensed, 3,000

In other words, this record of sin, misfortune and self-indulgence runs nearly thus:
Marriages, 147; 3 in every week.
Deaths, 262; 1 in every 33 hours.
Babies born, 430; 1 in every 20 hours.
Dogs licensed, 3,000; 10 on every weekday.

Note 1. Next year my Christmas Card for you will be complete, with a bibliography and index. This year I must be content with a glossary and notes. The definitions in my glossary are longer than those given by Enriquez.

Note 2. You cannot have a Merry Christmas because harvests have been abundant and science has been efficient all over the place.

Note 3. Nobody can expect a Happy New Year because our affairs have been regulated through most of the Twentieth Century by the chosen best of our educated men: Roosevelt, Morgan, Wilson, Taft,[8] Dawes, Young, Hughes, Coolidge,[9] Stimson,[10] Hoover.[11]

---

8. Roosevelt, Harvard '80.

John Pierpont Morgan (1867-1943; Harvard '89): financier; involved – like Dawes and Young – with the adjustment of the German war reparations.

Wilson, Princeton '79.

Taft, Yale '78.

9. Charles Gates Dawes (1865-1951; Marietta College '84): American financier and diplomat, vice president 1925-1929. Best remembered as author of the Dawes plan (1924) for solving the problems connected with the German war reparations.

Owen D. Young (1874-1962; St. Lawrence '94): American lawyer, corporate executive, and statesman.

Charles Evans Hughes (1862-1948; Brown '81): Chief Justice of the Supreme Court 1930-1941.

Coolidge, Amherst '95.

10. Henry Lewis Stimson (1867-1950; Yale '88): American lawyer and statesman, secretary of state 1929-1933. Possibly cited by Martin because of the so-called "Stimson Doctrine," which answered the Japanese Manchurian invasion of 1931, not with military or diplomatic opposition, but with mere non-recognition of Japanese rule.

Note 4. The three Murut words that I have given you or their English equivalents should be nearly all the vocabulary you will need in society until repeal.

Note 5. Professor Gregory, the other day, in Atlantic City, told the Association for the Advancement of Science that it is more than 100 million years since our ancestors were old Red Sandstone sharks. Through that vast stretch of time "the drama of terrestrial evolution" has been and "is motivated by . . . strife for food and for reproductive mates."[12] But in 1932 ten million out of work Americans[13] and twenty million other Americans whom they promised to feed, in all thirty millions of formidable Americans, have learned that artificial arrangements have been made to debar them from "strife for food and for reproductive mates." My remote ancestor was a ganoid shark. He weighed five hundred pounds, he could swim twenty knots an hour, he had five rows of teeth and he could digest rubber boots and horseshoes. He was not the sort of person that you could pacify with a Y. M. C. A. soup ticket. We have slowed down since his time and grown soft and meek; but not to the point of enduring with contentment the loss of all the privileges that kept our ancestors alive through a million millenniums on a dangerous planet.

ﺎ ﺎ ﺎ

---

11. Hoover, Stanford '95. In addition to many other failings, all listed did publicly favor or otherwise support prohibition.

12. William King Gregory (1876-1970), curator of the department of comparative anatomy and department of ichthyology, American Museum of Natural History; professor of vertebrate paleontology, Columbia; vice-president of section H (anthropology) of the American Association for the Advancement of Science. In a speech given at the Association's annual winter meeting, December 29, 1932 (which would indicate that "Magauk! Magauk!" appeared after, not before Christmas, 1932) and published in the January, 1933, issue of *Science* magazine, Gregory postulated as stage four of his 25-stage evolutionary ladder a "basal ganoid fish" or palaeoniscoid from the Old Red Sandstone or Devonian period. This creature combined "a generally shark-like body-form with the bony armor over the head and shoulder-girdle of the earlier typical fishes."

13. The American Federation of Labor estimated the preceding November that between nine and eleven millions out of a working population of some fifty millions lacked employment.

## Condolence - 1932 [1]

I use this mourning paper,[2] because: Three quarters of my life, the U.S., richest field in the world, has been ruled by the Republican Party - my party; & 9 million are out of work.[3] I mourn not to show that any man is dead; but, because so many rulers are asses, which is worse.

ൠ ൠ ൠ

## Letter to Molly, March 12, 1933

Dear Molly

Many of the most lovable people in the world are Negroes, Chinese & Japanese.

When I was a boy we were kept in fear by stories of Malay pirates & bloodthirsty Malay Kris-bearers,[1] murderous men that run amok with fatal sharp swords. Now Mrs. Lorillard Spencer[2] & everybody else tell us that nobody is more agreeable than the Malays of the Sulu Seas[3] & all the cruise ships regard all their days as wasted except those that they spend among the exquisite lovable Malay girls of Bali.[4] Study geography & keep your mind wide open.

The last time I was in Peiping I showed Gomby "Swinton's Universal History,"[5] used in a mission school. It had no history, in

1. Sent to all the grandchildren.
2. Paper with a black border.
3. Corresponds to American Federation of Labor figures for late spring-early summer, 1932.

---

1. A kris is a traditional Malay dagger with a wavy blade.
2. Mrs. Lorillard Spencer, (?-1948) Caroline Berryman), widow of New York City publisher Lorillard Spencer (1860-1912). While traveling around the world after the death of her husband, she became interested in the Moro Educational Foundation in the Phillipines and worked for it until the buildings were wrecked and she herself badly injured by a hurricane in 1932. Upon her subsequent return to the U.S. she edited the *Illustrated American*.
3. The Sulu Sea is southwest of the Phillipines, lying between it and Borneo.
4. Bali is an island in East Indonesia between Java and Lombok.
5. William Swinton (1833-1892), prolific author of primary-school texts, including *Outlines of the World's History, Ancient, Medieval and Modern, with Special Relation to the History of Civilization and Progress of Mankind*, 1st edition N.Y. 1874, last edition 1902.

it, of China or Japan.
"Julius Caesar" by John Buchan is a new book.[6] Buchan says: "Caesar drew the habitable earth into an empire. [...] He gave humanity order, peace." It would have been well if he had never lived. Because of him, in the long run, Christianity, the most hideous of religions, overran the western world. But, observe how wildly careless Buchan is as to facts. The Mayas & the Peruvians, more civilized than Europe, never heard of Caesar, nor did the Chinese & Japanese; of Caesar's time, or India or Cambodia. Three fifths of the world, of Caesar's time, never heard of Caesar. Whenever you hear a man's remarks or read a man's book, say to yourself "Is that so?"

Affectionately

*Newell Martin*

ta ta ta

# Letter to Molly, December 1934

*A handwritten note at the top of the letter says: "You may throw away this & the enclosures, without reading them." These were clippings from the December 17, 1934, issue of The New York Times: (a) a picture of a natural arch in Death Valley; (b) an article headlined: "DR. KEPPEL DOUBTS VALUE OF COLLEGE/ Carnegie Fund President Says Most Institutions Ignore the Student, Stress His Courses/PRAISES HARVARD, YALE/But Declares Higher Training in General Must change if It Is to Survive;" (c) an article headed: "PHYSICIAN BITTEN BY DEADLY SPIDER;" (d) another column headed: "SPEED CAMERA FINDS SECRET IN THE CLAM;" (e) a short article headlined: "Will Rogers runs Across An Honest Divorce Plea"; and (e) a paragraph headed: "Childs Frick Home Robbed."*

Dear Molly
  The head-line over Dr. Keppel's report seems hardly supported by the quotations that follow it. But a full reading of

---

6. John Buchan; First Baron Tweedsmuir (1875-1940), author of histories and thrillers (best known for *The Thirty-Nine Steps*), governor-general of Canada 1935-1940.

Keppel's report would show that he is plunged in gloom as to our colleges.[1] An American college gives, in most cases, a miraculously rich return on their investment to two small classes of students: (A) The small group who achieve high distinction in their work & (B) The small group who form life-long friendships with the 5 or 6 best men (or women) in the class.

President Angell's report[2] came from Yale today. He is in gloom - He casually comments on the starvation of alumni. "Thousands of embittered graduates of our colleges...after years of grinding sacrifice have found themselves walking the streets in search of any job that would give them food."[3] He speaks also of the ruined universities of Germany.

For everybody except the 2 small groups I have mentioned the ordinary college means waste. In our time in the Yale Scientific School & the Columbia School of Mines many acquired technical knowledge of great value. But most of my classmates wasted their time & money. *

Prof. Leuba[4] will be pleased to hear from Dr. Angell that "in the world outside indifference to religion colored at times with hostility & contempt is a ... common phenomenon." (49)

Angell has a whole band of professors of the history & philosophy & practice of religion. There you will see a degrading waste of money.

1. Frederick P. Keppel (1875-1943), president of the Carnegie Corporation 1923-1941, overseeing the disbursement of aid to colleges, libraries, research, and publications in order "to promote the advancement and diffusion of knowledge among the peoples of the United States."
2. James Rowland Angell (1869-1949), son of James Burrill Angell (1829-1916), who was president of the Universities of Vermont and Michigan. Angell, prior to being president of Yale 1921-1937, taught psychology at the University of Chicago 1894-1920, was dean 1911-1918 and acting president 1918-1919. In 1925, Martin caused a flurry of excitement, in an exchange of letters with Angell in *The New York Times* regarding prohibition and his 50th reunion. See Section Two - "The Yale Commencement."
3. The report was the annual one made by every Yale president. Actually Angell contrasted the gloomy picture of the current graduate with an even gloomier picture of an America deprived of its institutions of higher learning: "Sober second thought can only reinforce the conviction that, whatever their shortcomings and whatever transformations it may be expedient that they should undergo, in their essence the colleges and universities represent indispensable intellectual and spiritual values which our social order, if it is to endure at all, simply cannot afford to forego. The distressing fate which has overtaken many of the continental universities, ravaged of their independence and prostituted to the dictates of political expediency, may well serve us as a grim object lesson of the evils which may flow from violent social upheaval." What really worried him was that the "present tendency to excessive taxation of personal income...coupled with further assault by inheritance taxes upon large testamentary estates" endangered the primary sources of support for American colleges.
4. James Henry Leuba (1868-1940), Swiss-born psychologist. Professor of psychology at Bryn Mawr. See Section Eight - "Letter to Molly" of Oct. 18, 1934.

* As to wasting time & money; to be exact, the original error as to most of my classmates, was that of their parents in not drowning them when they were babes. On the other hand, as most of those useless babies grew up & are in heaven now nothing can be done about that.

*Newell Martin*

ᴥ ᴥ ᴥ

## Grammar

The Conquest of the Maya
J. Leslie Mitchell (Dutton) [1935]
'The data is[1] untrustworthy', (p. 25).

Time, Jan. 13, 1936, p. 35.
'Marian Anderson[2] managed to exhibit one of the richest contralto voices that has been heard in the U.S. for many a year.'

Time, Jan. 13, 1936, p. 28
Arthur Compton,[3] Nobel prize winner, of the University of Chicago, concluded that most of the cosmic rays were electric corpuscles.
'When all the data[4] was in his hands, he found overwhelming evidence for variation by latitude.'

New York Times, Jan. 13, 1936, p. 15
'Eide Norena,[5] Metropolitan Opera soprano ...appeared...at the Town Hall.....After each song there was an excited outburst of applause and sometimes a bravo.'[6]

Newell Martin, Huntington, New York

ﻰ ﻰ ﻰ

---

1. Data is plural form of datum; verb should be are.
2. The contralto Marian Anderson (b. 1902), was, of course, the pre-eminent black singer of her time. The plural "voices" calls for "have," not "has."
3. Arthur Compton (1892-1962) was a physicist and Nobel prize winner, world-famous for discoveries in the field of X- and cosmic rays.
4. 'When all the data were....
5. (1884-1968), Norwegian-born soprano who had a highly successful career at the Metropolitan Opera 1933-1938.
6. Problem with subject and verb. Corrected would read: "After each song there was an excited outburst of applause; sometimes a bravo."

# EIGHT

# GOD, BIBLE, AND HEREAFTER

Football and Prayer . . . . . . . . . . . . 220

Letters to Bear, 1935 & 1936 . . . . . . 223

Wrigley's Cathedral . . . . . . . . . . . . 227

Letters to Molly, 1933 & 1934 . . . . . . 228

Letter to "Ferncliff" . . . . . . . . . . . 234

# Football and Prayer
### New Year Card, 1933

Buy Mr. Hearst's Cosmopolitan for December, 1932, and read page 139. Football and religion and prayer have always been mixed up together. Important things, like war, marriage, love, death and football, cannot get out of the jurisdiction of the church. At page 139 I read this about the hero of a game (obviously with Notre Dame): "always he had offered a prayer before a game ... But today he could ask for only one thing: 'Please, God, don't let the kickoff come to me.'"

In Heaven, as in the office of the Rosenwald Fund,[1] there must be intermediate clerks and committees that act with the speed of thought, on all requests, before they go to the Chief.

I can imagine this football prayer going to some angelic clerk in the outer office of the Prayer Department. I dreamt, last night, that I interviewed this clerk.

"After this I'm going to cancel these football prayers," said the clerk to me in my dream. "The Chief was in here yesterday, grumbling about prayers. We had a bit of argument about prayer. I see you think I am lying. About arguing with the Chief. But he is as easy to talk to as Einstein. The bigger they are, the less they put on dignity. The Bedouins that wrote the Old Testament were used to Arab Sheiks and African Chiefs of little tribes, who had to be 'majestic.' So, in the Bible, they make the Chief 'majestic' and fond of praise. Andre Gide tells of a Chief in the French Congo who appoints a couple of orators to stand behind him and 'praise' him, off and on, all day long.[2] Both the Testaments, Old and New, are full of the importance of 'praising' the Chief. But that's enough about archaeology. I'm telling you what the Chief said yesterday. He said: 'These minor prayers were all very well when the Universe was the two easterly corners of the Mediterranean. I made no complaint then about watching the fall of sparrows. But the sparrows have become more numerous. And the place has

---

1. Julius Rosenwald (1862-1932). Established the Rosenwald Fund which, in 1928, had assets worth $40 million, and spent more than $20 million from his personal fortune, including the erecting of YMCA buildings for Negroes in some 21 cities. See Section Five — "Jews and Philistines."
2. André Gide (1869-1951): He tells in *Le retour du Tchad, suite du voyage au congo* (1928), translated as *Travels in the Congo* (N.Y.: Knopf, 1929), pp. 315-316, how the lamido of Bibemi has, not two, but a dozen "nobles or captives" to follow in his retinue and continually praise him. After describing their varying styles of delivery, Gide asks, "Is it possible that the lamido's ears are really gratified by them? But is it possible, either, that a God can take pleasure in prayers to order, or in the telling of beads and rosaries?"

expanded. I may be working now on something big, one hundred million light years from here and a boy in an Illinois college will ask me to butt in on a football game. I have to direct three thousand million universes, each made up of billions of giant spheres. And here, every autumn, come a bunch of prayers from a speck of dust called the world, asking me to deflect footballs.'[3]

'Your Majesty,' said I, 'Wayland Williams, in one of his novels, which accurately describe American society, represents a Yale sophomore, on a domestic tennis-court, as praying to you to direct his tennis-ball so that he may win.'

'I have directed smaller missiles than tennis-balls,' said the Chief. 'The bacilli that killed John Reed and Lenin, two of the most useful three statesmen of Europe,[4] were microscopic. And I have directed a lot of filterable viruses.'

'I remember,' said I, 'that you ordered the sun, a notoriously insignificant luminary, to stand still on Ajalon, so that Joshua and the Jews could rob the industrious Philistines of their savings.'[5]

'True,' answered the Chief. 'I did it and I shall never hear the last of it. In this modern age I have to be more serious.' He reached over to my desk and picked up two petitions which I had marked 'approved.' 'Here is a harmless lawyer,' said he, 78 years old, in Huntington. His head presents extensive bald areas. This prayer is from his nurse. Wonderful how nurses do not become callous. She prays that these places where the surgeon fastens his adhesive tape on the superannuated lawyer may become bald. The hairs hurt when the tape is pulled off. And here is a prayer from the nurse of a distinguished major general who is being tormented by distinguished surgeons in San Francisco. She prays that the frightful business of the dressing of his wounds may be less rough.[6] I would like to favor those good men. But I have not time even for them. I am trying, over on the other side of the constellation of Andromeda, to develop a new universe, in which you can have

---

3. Wayland Williams (1888-1945; Yale '10; University Club member; lived in New Haven) wrote four novels, all published by Martin's publisher-friend, Frederick A. Stokes. Incident most probably in *The Whirligig of Time* (1916).
4. Reed died of typhus; Lenin of a series of progressive cerebral strokes. Presumably, Martin's third statesman is Trotsky.
5. Actually, in Joshua 10:12-14, the sun stands still at Gibeon, royal city of the Hivites in Canaan, and the moon in the valley of Arjalon, an Amorite city. Joshua, in this instance, was not fighting the Philistines, but the kings of Jerusalem, Hebron, Jarmuth, Lachish, and Eglon, all cities of the Amorites. We are told that in each city Joshua "utterly destroyed each person in it, he left none remaining."
6. Major General Robert Alexander: See Section Three -- "Letter to Major-General Robert Alexander."

progress without pain. In another place, I am working on the evolution of a new sort of animals, of high intellectual power, combining the best qualities of the ant, the bee, the elephant and the penguin. Until I get a little more forward with those jobs, don't bother me about any sphere smaller than Betelgeuse.'" [7]

January 23. Mr. Luce in "Time," quotes "Yale Divine Halford Edward Luccock"[8] who says that the Buchmanites[9] are wrong in imagining a diety almost completely absorbed in sending down hourly directions to his favorites.

≈ ≈ ≈

## Letters to Bear, 1935 & 1936

*Handwritten. The word "Confidential" appears at the top of the page. "Bear" is the family nickname for Schuyler Merritt Meyer, Jr. He was a student at Phillips Exeter Academy at the time.*

1935

Dear Bear

Don't publish this in your paper. The progress of civilization & of evolution depend on the extirpation of the deplorable Romish faith. One of the worst things that ever happened to mankind was the smashing up, by the Church, with its Inquisition & its tortures, of the admirable civilizations of the Aztecs, Mayas & Incas.

I long for the success of the gallant Mexicans in trying to end the 400 year old tyranny of the Church.[1]

Amen.

*Newell Martin*

---

7. Betelgeuse is the star marking the eastern shoulder of Orion, the 11th most luminous in the night sky. Its diameter is 535 times that of the sun, making it larger than Jupiter's orbit.
8. *Time*, January 23, 1933; p. 32. Halford Edward Luccock (1885-1960) was a Methodist theologian, professor of homiletics at Yale 1928-1953, and author of some 33 books. *Time*, founded by Henry Luce in 1923, was quoting from a Luccock article in the magazine *World Tomorrow*.
9. Name for the nondenominational Moral Re-Armament Movement (originally called the Oxford Group) launched in 1921 at Oxford and Cambridge by the American evangelist Frank Buchman (1878-1961).

Dear Bear                                  January 1936

    Send no answer to this.
    Do not read this, except when you are at leisure. At your grandmother's suggestion, I write to congratulate you on your birthday.
    Me reversed:
    I am 81
    You are 18.

------

    It seems to me that I wrote once to Molly that when I am 81 she is 18. Something wrong there. But, never mind. Anybody over 81; or, in fact, anybody over 18, will observe, day by day, in every way, that something is wrong. (Confidentially - & I don't tell anybody - but, this is the most important thing on earth -- Don't mention it to any friend -- It would vex your school authorities -- To Hell with the Pope.)[2]

    Further, confidentially, I have for years loathed everything I have heard about Stearns, of Andover[3]. Hurrah for Exeter & Modern Science.

                              Sincerely

                              Newell Martin

---

1. Late in 1934 Mexico's socialist government had passed a law prohibiting religious education in Mexico's schools; a second bill passed about a year later declared all buildings used for public worship since 1917 the property of the state. These measure led to widespread religious conflicts resulting in numerous deaths, and charges of religious persecution, mainly by the Catholic Church.

---

2. This rallying-cry of Ireland's Protestant Ulstermen, in frequent use by Martin, gave vent to his extreme dissatisfaction with his unmarried daughter, Janet, who became a devout member of the Roman Catholic Church.
3. Alfred Earnest Stearns (1871-1949; Amherst '94; A.M. Yale '05; Litt. D.'s Dartmouth '12 and Williams '21; L.L.D. Harvard '28). Registrar of Phillips Academy, Andover, 1900-02, vice-president 1902-3; headmaster 1903-33. In addition to the above, Stearns was D.D. Andover Theological Seminary '00, and his career exhibited throughout a pronounced concern with what he viewed as the necessary religious component of education.

*The following letter was typewritten, but included a handwritten note saying: "Burn this. It is a translation of an illegible hand-written letter."*
December 16, 1936
S. M. Meyer, Jr., Esq., Yale College, New Haven, Conn.

Dear Schuyler:
I return, with thanks, the Gundelfinger tract.[4] Every college has its pathetic crank, its Mr. Screwloose. Some towns make pets of their cranks. San Francisco, for 20 years, made a pet of a crank who thought he was an emperor.[5]

Cranks abound. Most of the important religions were founded by cranks who differed by only a hair's breadth from Gundelfinger. All Germany was ruined when Hindenburg became dotty.[6] Ludendorff is so dotty that he worships the old gods of the

---

4. See Section Two - "The Yale Commencement" for Gundelfinger reference. Possibly what Schuyler had sent his grandfather was issue #16 of Gundelfinger's magazine *Interquadrangular*, published in 1936 and reprinting pieces from earlier issues. "The Truth About Rowan, Hopkins, and Fain" was inscribed on the cover.
5. "Joshua Abraham Norton attracted little attention when he arrived in San Francisco in 1849. He was a dignified, quiet, good-looking Jew and brought $40,000 with him. He engaged in some mercantile business, and in 1852 his capital had increased to $250,000. Then, between one of San Francisco's disastrous fires and an attempt to corner the rice market, his fortune was swept away. He disappeared for a time, no one knew where. When he returned it was evident that he had lost more than lucre. His tall imposing figure was clad in a shabby blue uniform, decorated, however, with heavy gold epaulets, and on his head was a general's cap with a heron's plume. In his buttonhole was a red carnation. He solemnly proclaimed himself Emperor of the United States of America, and his colossal dignity would have abashed the Emperor of all the Russias.

"San Francisco was delighted with him. Instead of treating him as a figure of fun, with ribald hoots or silent contempt, or committing him to an insane asylum, it accepted him at his own valuation and cheerfully paid him the tribute he demanded....No bill was ever laid beside his plate in any of the restaurants where he took his three meals daily--save by some stupid waiter, and then apologies by the management were profuse. No ticket was ever demanded of him at any theater or other place of amusement he deigned to honor with his presence. He never asked for money. He demanded it when he needed cash in his pocket....Cigar stands were honored to accommodate His Majesty; the stores gave him 'credit' for underwear, handkerchiefs, etc., and when his uniform attained its final degree of shabbiness he inserted a notice in the newspaper that Emperor Norton I needed a new one, and subscriptions were immediate. When one of his two beloved dogs died, he gave it a public funeral, and the attendance was large and properly demure....

"Emperor Norton I died in 1880 at the age of sixty-five and received one of San Francisco's historic funerals....More than 30,000 men formed the funeral procession out to the local cemetery of the Masons, and for many days San Francisco was as sad as that happy-go-lucky city ever could be....Myself, I have dark suspicion that he was the cleverest man in that generous but gullible City by the Golden Gate." Gertrude Atherton: *My Golden Gate* (N.Y.: Bobbs, Merrill, 1946), pp. 174-7.
6. Paul von Hindenburg (1847-1934), German field marshal; president of the Weimar Republic 1925-1934. Much of the ease with which Hitler was able to outmaneuver Hindenburg in the former's rise to power was due to the combination of passivity and mere gesture which was Hindenburg's only opposition. Old age and at least a touch of rank senility unquestionably played a major part.

Teutons after whom we name Wednesday and Thursday.[7] I know some bankers who are so dotty that they worship the old Chief God of Palestine, whose priests used to go up on a hill and make a big smoke. Out of the smoke they would come down---or one of them would---with commandments, neatly carved on stone. The Protestant Church has a copy of these. Their 7th commandment forbids adultery. The Catholic Church has a different copy. Their 7th commandment forbids theft. Some forger must have monkeyed with one of these copies. The Catholic church says its copy came from God and that the Protestant copy is a vulgar forgery. The Protestant Church says its copy came from God and that the Catholic copy is a vulgar forgery. I am a devout Protestant and two of my nearest relatives are devout Catholics. Nevertheless, we have the impudence to despise Gundelfinger for being goofy. The sure test of goofiness is that it is unendurably tedious. The Catholics and Buddhists have noticed this and, therefore, instead of long sermons discussing theology, they count beads and say Ave Maria Purissima[8] or O Mi To Fu.[9] Take up a volume of sermons preached by your great-great-great-grandfather, Dirck Cornelius Lansing. Try to read two pages aloud. Impossible. We have outlived that sort of goofiness. An editorial in *The Herald-Tribune*, however, says that religion has regained its ancient strength. It has thrown an infidel king into the discard, this week.[10] So, you will observe, even a discussion of Gundelfinger brings us back to "King Charles's head." But you modern boys never heard of King Charles's Head.[11]

*L. M.*

ta ta ta

7. Erich von Ludendorff (1865-1937), German general, chief of staff in WWII; participated in Hitler's Munich "beer-hall putsch" of 1923. With his second wife, Dr. Mathilde Ludendorff, he founded the Nazi Ayran cult and churned out much crank literature on the subject; was a significant figure in the Nazi revival of the old Teutonic gods 1934-5.
8. "Hail Mary, most pure"; i.e., a "Hail Mary."
9. "O lotus"; that is,... invocation of Chinese Buddhists.
10. The infidel is of course England's Edward VIII who left the throne and England to marry Wally Simpson, an American divorcee. Unquestionably there was a religious component involved in his abdication, as the Church of England does not recognize divorce and will not officiate at the marriage of divorced persons.
11. The constant obsession of the slightly-touched Mr. Dick, in Dickens' *David Copperfield.*

# Wrigley's Cathedral

August 12 1937
Miss Jane Fraser Martin
Maine, U.S.A.

Dear Jane
 I have three descendants in Montana & one in Munich, one in Oyster Bay, one in Huntington & one in Maine. On their way through Chicago Ardie & Jonnie sent me a picture of the vast building reared by Wrigley,[1] on the shores of the Great Lake, for the making & selling of Wrigley's Chewing Gum.
 If the great church of Rome, Saint Peter's, were set down beside Wrigley's vast Cathedral of the Triturating[2] Jaws, St. Peter's would look like a fine elegant dog-house.
 They say that a slow movement of the jaws produces contentment; & that, when one is chewing gum, he cannot say anything rash until he has parked his gum in some suitable place.
 If that is true, Wrigley's Cathedral has done more good than St. Peter's Cathedral.
 Further, St. Peter's Cathedral has been consecrated to the propagation of all sorts of fables about Saint Peter, who never saw Rome, & to the worship of a large group of bogus saints & to the publishing of the story of a lot of legendary & preposterous miracles. Wrigley, on the other hand, is said to be truthful in his advertisement of gum; at least as to the origin of the gum.

Affectionately

*Newell Martin*

ta ta ta

---

1. The Wrigley Tower is a Spanish Renaissance white terra-cotta skyscraper at 400 North Michigan Avenue on the north bank of the Chicago River. Thirty-two stories, built 1921, and for five years the highest building in Chicago.
2. Rubbing, crushing, grinding, pulverizing (Webster's).

# Letters To Molly, 1932-1934

*Martin wrote regularly to his oldest granddaughter, Molly, at her boarding school, St. Timothy's in Catonsville, Maryland, and continued writing to her almost weekly while she attended Bryn Mawr College. She preserved a great many of the letters, which often ended with the declaration, "To hell with the Pope."*

Dear Molly

You are right in saying that I have more knowledge than some laymen of the Old Testament and of the New. But I never gave much study to the Prophecies or to the Epistles. Moreover, unhappily, I think too much about Hebrew poetry and too little about the Bible's practical teaching, much of which comes to those who read between the lines. E.G., The Bible leaves us to infer how the Children of Israel in Egypt became powerful so swiftly. There were seven years of excessive harvests and then seven years of famine. In the years of rich harvests Joseph bought up cattle and wheat at the lowest prices and in the famine years sold them at a fabulous profit. Then he pouched the profits and set up his relatives on Easy Street. If I had remembered this I would have sold all I had in 1928. 'Search the Scriptures.'

Bible. When I was a small boy, I traveled with William C. Burns, the "Evangelist of North China."[1] He wore Chinese clothes and lived in Chinese style, on $200 a year, and gave his surplus to the poor. The first morning that I breakfasted with him, when we began our travels, in 1866, he said, before breakfast: 'First, the Scriptures.' I reached for my Bible, but he said, 'No, we will recite.' I can't remember what text I offered. It is quite possible that I said, thinking about some of the Chinese caravanserais:[2] 'Exodus. 8,17: Aaron stretched out his hand with his rod, and smote the dust, of the earth and it became lice ...All the dust of the land became lice.' 'Go on,' said Burns. I do not remember my second text. Quite likely I said: '2 Kings 4, 14: Gehazi answered, Verily (the Shumanite) hath

---

1. William Chalmers Burns (1815-1868), Scots-born Presbyterian minister to China, beginning 1846. Burns learned the language (made a Chinese translation of *Pilgrim's Progress*), adopted Chinese dress, and lived like a native, taking little with him on his travels but bibles and tracts, and trusting to the hospitality of the people. Described by the *Dictionary of National Biography* as "often annoyed, once arrested and imprisoned, but bore all with the greatest meekness;" and "universally regarded as one of the most devoted missionaries since apostolic times."
2. Inns in the East where caravans put up, usually arranged as large quadrangles around courtyards.

no child and her husband is old. And Elisha said, call her. And when he had called her, she stood in the door. And Elisha said, ...Thou shalt embrace a son.'³ But I remember my pain when Burns said, 'Go on, recite. One chapter will be enough.' With distress I confessed that I didn't know any whole chapter. Oddly enough, I remember exactly something we had for breakfast. It was smoked Ass's Cheek.⁴ I remember cautiously suggesting that the ass must have died a natural death. Burns rebuked my suspicion and unbelief and assured me that he knew and trusted the butcher and that the ass had probably suffered a broken leg before he passed out of industry.

In 1915, in Peking, I lived with my friend Ogilvie. He was in the habit of reciting, from memory, all the Epistles. In Shanghai, the last time I was there, I visited a missionary blind asylum. All the blind men could recite one or more of the gospels. Freyer, who ran the asylum was apologetic for this low standard of pious achievement.⁵

It is a great advantage, in these times, when anybody may land in a jail or a bookless poor-house, to be able to recite at least the Book of Genesis or all of Shakespeare's Henry 4. I advise you, forthwith, to read 2 Kings, chapters 4&5. The story of Gehazi is the most ancient classic of graft. The whole story is the best in the English language, beginning with the shrewd advice of the little Hebrew maid and Naaman's preference for Abana and Pharpar, rivers of Damascus,⁶ and culminating with the prophet's giving Naaman permission to bow down in the House of Rimmon.⁷ When Disraeli appointed bishops for the Church of England, he must have

---

3. Properly II Kings 4:14-16, and "Shumanite" should be "Shunammite." The woman is being rewarded for her repeated hospitality to Elisha on his travels, and Martin may have been alluding to Burns' own manner of living. It is later in this chapter that Elisha resurrects the woman's child from the dead.
4. Capitals, as well as all other configurations, in Martin original.
5. John Fryer (1839-1928), English-born educator who carried out extensive works in China 1863-1896, including founding schools, editing periodicals, and translating into Chinese over 100 books. Decorated by the Chinese government. Taught at the University of California 1896-1914, but apparently was still spending sufficient time in China to found the Institute for the Chinese Blind in Shanghai in 1911 and the Fryer School for the Chinese Deaf, also in Shanghai, in 1926; these were subsequently managed by his son, George B. Fryer.
6. The Hebrew maid suggested that Naaman might be cured of his leprosy by Elisha. On being advised by Elisha to bathe seven times in the River Jordan, Naaman rather angrily asks whether the Abana and Pharpar, rivers right there at hand, wouldn't do just as well.
7. See Section Two - "Coolidge and the Bible."

whispered to the Countess of Sheffield,[8] 'Elisha, the prophet, foresaw this day.'

When Karl Marx was 7 years old, his father, a Hebrew lawyer, became a Lutheran.[9] History does not say what the father said to his little son; but you and I know that he whispered to the child, 'Who am I that I should be prouder than the Commander of the Syrian army?'

Christopher Columbus[10] was a Jew who declared himself a Christian, to save his bacon. And, to make his piety conspicuous he introduced the practice of giving theological names to places that he discovered. This practice became universal in Spanish America. Columbus began with San Salvador; and now the two cities in America which are most notorious for conduct that Miss Fowler would deplore have Spanish theological names. One of them is Los Angeles whose full Spanish name, is, I think, The City of Our Lady and of all the Saints and of all the Angels.[11] The other is an Argentine town that is El Puerto de Santa Maria de Buenos Aires.[12] You and I are familiar with a river in the Far West that is called the Picketwire River; but we know that its real name in Spanish and in French is River of Purgatory.[13]

Affectionately

*Lewell Martin*

[*Post Script*] All statements of fact in this letter are true. The

---

8. No "Countess" in British peerage; perhaps Martin intended Mrs. Disraeli, Lady Beaconsfield.
9. Herschel (Heinrich after conversion) Marx (1782-1838). Karl Heninrich Marx (1818-1883). The elder Marx became a Lutheran in 1816, two years before birth of son, Karl. He never gave his reasons for conversion, and historians have been able to do no more than guess.
10. Christopher Columbus (1451?-1506). Columbus' origins remain notoriously obscure, in large part through his own efforts. As Martin goes on to say, we indeed do not know that he was a Jew, much less what he saved himself from by denying it. Isiah M. Kyserling in *Christopher Columbus and the Part of the Jews in the Spanish and Portuguese Discoveries* (4th ed., N.Y.: Hermon Press, 1968) does not even advance the hypothesis, but Salvador de Madariaga's *Christopher Columbus* (N.Y.: Macmillan, 1940) does rather deftly explain the anomalies and obscurities by suggesting that Columbus' parents were Spanish Jews who had moved to Genoa.
11. Los Angeles began life as El Pueblo de la Reyne de los Angeles, "The Town of the Queen of the Angels."
12. Named by Spanish sailors after their patron saint, El Puerto de Santa Maria del Buen Aire; i.e., a favoring wind.
13. River in southeast Colorado, tributary to the Arkansas. Named by early Spanish explorers El Rio de Las Animas Perdidas en Purgatorio, "the River of the Souls Lost in Purgatory." Later changed to Purgatoire River by French trappers, corrupted to Picketwire River by American cowmen. "Purgatoire" is still the name on the maps.

statement that Columbus was a Jew is historical hypothesis, disputed by many. No matter, he was a low scoundrel and vile brute, unworthy to be a Hebrew.

❦ ❦ ❦

Mar 16  1932

Dear Molly

I sent you a tract about one of your 4 great-great-grandfathers.[14] Read only the passages underlined with lead-pencil.

You need not keep it. I have other copies. I send it because I thought you might like to show it to Miss Fowler.

Indiana has an unenviable pre-eminence in cruelty to Indians & in certain other forms of crime, such as Kukluxery & Prohibition.

Because the parsons used to preach for 1 1/2 hours. After the first 10 minutes of any sermon, Satan begins to go about in the congregation & suggest various kinds of misconduct.

Your beautiful colley [collie] has been washed. Your dog Heather continues to be a model of courtesy. She should be a professor at Bryn Mawr.

Affectionately

*Lewell Martin*

❦ ❦ ❦

March 10, 1933

Dear Molly

Read my book on Prayer. The Lake Dwellers & your other ancestors believed that God would not send harvest & sunlight & health, unless reminded of it & asked for it. Perhaps you know some father of 4 children, whose wife had to say to him, every morning: "John, your children love you & honor you. But they need shoes & food. Please go & work on the railroad & earn some money for them."

If you know any father that has to be flattered & entreated & honored, every morning, before he will exert himself, or give, out of

---

14. "Memorandum as to Rev. William W. Martin," dated 1905. See Section Sixteen.

his abundance, to his own children, you will observe that he ought to be put in the hoosegow or the bughouse. But last week, a new president, a good man, wise & efficient, observed that a modern nation, of 120 millions, was in dire trouble. So, he crept into the nearest god-box, & got the priests to play the organ & sing hymns, to rouse the god's attention; & then for 15 minutes he said: "God, I fear you do not read the papers. See what has happened in Wall Street. We admire you. So please put an end to the sufferings you have thoughtlessly inflicted on us."[15]

Affectionately

*Newell Martin*

ю ю ю

March 14 1933

Dear Molly

You should leave the enclosed Church Calendar[16] lying carelessly on your table among your cosmetics. When Miss Fowler picks it up you should say, '["]Oh yes, Dean Gates baptized me.[17] The Chapel of the Intercession is the largest Episcopal Congregation East of the Mississippi. My great-grandfather Grinnell was active in it.[18] Always sat in the front seat in that synagogue. My grandfather, O. G. [Other Gomby] Martin was one of the founders of its new church, by Goodhue, famous architect.["][19] Fleming is now rector of famous Trinity.[20]

15. Just prior to his inauguration on March 4, 1933, Franklin Delano Roosevelt had attended a private service held at St. John's Episcopal Church, Washington, accompanied only by his wife and members of his cabinet and their guests. Robert Johnston, rector of St. John's, had offered prayers for the country and the new president. The texts actually petitioned for "heavenly gifts," citing grace, health, prosperity, longevity, humility, wisdom, and thankfulness in that order. "Bless our land with honorable industry, sound learning, and pure manners," was about as close as the Reverend came to Martin's citation.

16. The preserved copy of the program calendar for the Trinity Parish of the Chapel of the Intercession is dated March 12, 1933. Martin had ticked the Rector, the Reverend Frederic S. Fleming, D.D., and notice of the evening phone number for reaching "The Clergy." Also ticked notice of an upcoming (March 17th) radio broadcast from Liverpool, England of a Lenten Devotional Service.

17. See Section Four - "A Deplorable Occurrence."

18. George Blake Grinnell (1823-1891), New York merchant and financier, for many years vestryman of the Chapel of the Intercession. He was Gomby's (1860-1940) father; also father of George Bird Grinnell.

19. In Martin's letter to the Admissions Committee of the Century Association re: Pell William Foster, dated December 1, 1923, Martin says of Goodhue's work: "All...should know the exquisite interior, unsurpassed in America, of the Chapel of the Intercession, at Broadway and 155th Street." See Section Ten.

20. Frederic Sydney Fleming (1886-1956), vicar, Chapel of the Intercession, 1930-1932; rector 1932 until his retirement in 1951.

The clergy may be telephoned at 2 A.M. if you want to confess anything.

Affectionately

Lewell Martin

≈ ≈ ≈

October 18, 1934

Dear Molly:

You will find it profitable to drop into the college school library now and then. When there read one or two of the more thoughtful essays in the magazines that are a little out of date. For all serious study a magazine three months old is better than a magazine of this week. I advise you to read in the August Harper's, page 291, "Religious Beliefs["] by Professor Leuba.[21]

Yesterday I took out my winter overcoat: Only once had it been worn since March, 1934. To my surprise I found in the pocket a letter from your mother to you.

It is either 2 weeks old or 10 months old. I shall give it back to your mother.

When I was young I never forgot a letter. I never forgot anything.

I never had a fault. I never yielded to a temptation. I never neglected my studies.

I have suspected one man's life that I knew of to be darkened by forgetfulness of letters.

Affectionately

L. M.

---

21. James Henry Leuba (1868-1940), Swiss-born psychologist, studied at Leipzig, Halle, Heidelberg, and Paris. Professor of psychology at Bryn Mawr 1889-1933, subsequently professor emeritus. Author of *The Psychological Origin and Nature of Religion* (1909); the *Beliefs in God and Immortality* (1916); *The Pychology of Religious Mysticism* (1925); and *God or Man?–The Study of the Value of God to Man* (1933).

The *Harper's* article, "Religious Beliefs of American Scientists," summarized "statistical informations gathered in 1933 regarding the attitude of American men of science toward the two central beliefs of the Christian religion: a God influenced by worship, and immortality," comparing it with analogous statistics gathered in 1914 and a less extensive investigation of the same beliefs among college students. Leuba found a larger proportion of believers among "(1) the scientists who knew least about living matter, society, and the mind; (2) the less eminent men in every branch of science; (3) the scientists and students of twenty years ago; (4) the students in the lower college classes." The differences he ascribed to "superior knowledge, understanding, and experience" (as opposed to intellectual pride) as well as greater independence of character. He concluded that in the light of scientific findings, the churches would have to "organize themselves about ultimate conceptions that are not in contradiction with the best insight of the time."

# Letter to "Ferncliff"

*A handwritten note addressed to a partner in the law firm of Meyer,[1] Kidder, and Matz appeared at the top of the following typewritten letter: "Dear Mr. Kidder, I send you this paper, a copy of a letter that I have sent to a mausoleum company, that offers enticing graves."*

March 9, 1938.

"Ferncliff"
366 Madison Ave.
New York, N.Y.

Dear Sirs:

I thank you for your beautiful book, picturing an enticing permanent home. I am glad to see among your adherents Mr. Pendergast of the Title, Guarantee and Trust Company. I was the Number Two man of that company in 1886. I was, also, five years old[2] when Mr. Lincoln moved into the White House. So, you see, I shall soon be looking for a place of long-time safe-deposit. Don't send any sales-man. There will be the usual subdued rejoicing when I cease to cumber my family and some active young grandson will probably telephone to you as to an engraved and padlocked ash-can.

Sincerely,

*Newell Martin*

[*The following postscript is handwritten.*]
I am bitterly opposed to the oriental &, also Romish practice of spending money on tombs. It is a waste of money to feed old men & a waste of money to furnish dead men with monuments & other "Persicos Apparatus."[3]

❦ ❦ ❦

---

1. His son-in-law, Schuyler M. Meyer, Sr.
2. Actually, was aged six and one-half when Lincoln was inaugurated.
3. Horace, Carmina I. 38. 1. *Persicos odi...apparatus*: "I hate Persian trappings (or paraphernalia)".

# NINE
# FAMILY

From the Family Tree . . . . . . . . . . . 236

Autobiography . . . . . . . . . . . . . . . 237

Geneological Data . . . . . . . . . . . . . 239

Letters from Newell
   to His Brothers . . . . . . . . . . . . . 240

Letters to and About the Family . . . . 251

Letters to the Grandchildren . . . . . 257

Words That I Had With Molly . . . . . 266

Molly's Will . . . . . . . . . . . . . . . . . 270

Some Advice As to In-Laws . . . . . . . 272

Recommendation for Schuyler
   from Phelps . . . . . . . . . . . . . . . 274

Pleonasm or Crime . . . . . . . . . . . . 275

Recommendation for Molly
   to Stokes . . . . . . . . . . . . . . . . . 277

A Summing Up . . . . . . . . . . . . . . . 281

# From The Family Tree

Newell Martin (1854-1941) was the son of William Alexander Parsons Martin (1827-1916), who was the son of William Wilson Martin (1781-1850), who was the son of Jacob Martin (1749-?), who emigrated from County Antrim, Ireland, to Lancaster, Pennsylvania. Jacob Martin and his wife, Catherine Wilson (1752-?), moved to Kentucky in 1792.

Their son William, Newell Martin's grandfather, was ordained a Presbyterian minister c. 1812, and moved to Livonia, Indiana, in 1816. He married Susan Depew (1789-?), and they had ten children, W.A.P. Martin being the second son. W.A.P. Martin also studied for the Presbyterian ministry, and soon after his marriage to Jane VanZandt (?-1893), went to China as a missionary where they had, according to one record, two sons: Newell and Winfred Robert (1852-1915).

But family correspondence and college alumni records indicate that Newell had three brothers, not just one, all of them born in China. Pascal (1850-1882), like Newell and Robert, attended college in the United States. Of another brother, Claude (1856-?), little is known. It is possible, though no records have been found to substantiate the speculation, that both Pascal and Claude were adopted, and only Robert -- as he was always called -- and Newell were natural sons of W.A.P. and Jane Martin.

Pascal and Robert never married; and while Claude was married twice, it is not believed he had any children.

Newell married Laura Griswold Grinnell (1860-1940), and they had one son and two daughters: Grinnell, Helen, and Janet. Janet never married. Grinnell (1888-1972) married Myra Fraser (1899-1969) and they had three daughters -- Myra (1921- ), Mrs. William H. Mathers; Laura (1926- ), Mrs. Richard S. Koehne; and Jane (1924- ), Mrs. John I. Handy.

Newell's daughter Helen (1889-1971) married Schuyler Merritt Meyer (1885-1970) and they had three daughters: Molly (1915- ), Mrs. Cathal O'Connor (divorced); Janet (1921- ), Mrs. Howard Denison; Helen (1922- ), Mrs. Oliver Germann; and one son, Schuyler M. Meyer, Jr.(1918- ), who married Barbara Scott (1920-).

Newell Martin's wife, Laura, was the daughter of George Blake Grinnell (1823-1891) and Helen Lansing Grinnell (1827-1894); her grandfathers were George Grinnell (1786-1878) and Dirck Cornelius Lansing (1785-1857). Laura's sister, Helen

Jesup Grinnell (1856-?), married Newell Martin's law partner, William Drummond Page (1853-93), and they had three sons: Frank L.G. Page (1886-1959), Rutherford Page (1887-1912), and Donald Page (1893-1958); and two daughters, Sylvia Page (?-?), Countess Renzo Brusati, subsequently Mrs. Theodore Lilley; and Laura L.G. Page (?-1945), who never married. Of Laura's four brothers, George Bird Grinnell (1849-1938), Frank Grinnell (1853-1875), Morton Grinnell (1855-1905), and William Grinnell (1858-1920), only George Bird and Morton ever married, and neither had children.

Newell (Other Gomby) and Laura (Gomby) Martin's great-grandchildren are: Peter and David O'Connor; Schuyler, Molly, Aileen, Allen, and Scott Meyer; James and Geraldine Denison; Laurie, Helen, and Michael Germann.

And the great-great-grandchildren, as of 1993, are:[1] Erin and Peter O'Connor; Christopher and Jennifer (David) O'Connor; Charles John (Allen), Lawton Grinnell and Anna Catherine Meyer; and Carmen (Geraldine) Denison.

☙ ☙ ☙

# Autobiography

*Martin, learning that Molly's teacher had told her to write, "as an exercise in story-telling," her autobiography, wrote one for her. Noting at the top, "Molly can throw this away before or after reading it. Send no answer."*

Prelude

Mine is an old family. My grandfather, of the forty millionth generation, counting backwards to fifty million years ago, was a ganoid shark,[1] prowling through the Flores sea.[2] His bones lie in

---

1. When Schuyler M. Meyer, Jr., grandfather of Charles John Meyer, was asked to supply the names of Other Gomby's great-great-grandchildren, he did so, then queried: "Where was Planned Parenthood when all this started?!?"

---

1. See Section Seven — "Magauk! Magauk!"
2. The Flores Sea lies in the southwest Pacific, bounded on the north by Celebes and south by the Lesser Sunda Islands of Flores and Sumbawa.

his family vault, in the Old Red Sandstone. He had little sentiment; but even he might have shed a tear if he could have foreseen all the troubles of all his descendants.

Two tragedies, in our mournful family history, were brought about by horses; or, rather, by the absence of horses. Two of my remote grandparents used to live at Solutré, not far from Paris. They lived chiefly on the meat of wild horses. To Solutré came, by imperceptible degrees, the last but one of the Ice Ages. Northern France became colder and colder, and wild horses moved southward, seeking warmer climates. This was sixty thousand years ago.[3] My grandfather came back from his last hunt empty-handed. "There are no more horses", he said to grandmother. "The children must starve."

The latest of my long line of grandfathers was a man of infinite patience and industry.[4] Toiling with two famous New Englanders, Sidney Winslow[5] and George W. Brown,[6] and with an Englishman that was still more famous, Sir Samuel Hudson Lever,[7] he helped in the building of a wisely-constructed monopoly. It was a source of happiness to everybody that came in touch with it, delighting the manufacturers of harness, for horses, the dealers in harness, and the users of harness; and, so far as I know, the wearers of harness. Cowboys in Idaho, 'starving farmers in Kansas,' belted earls in Rotten Row,[8] Kalmuck Tartars in Sungaria,[9] paid, each his tiny

---

3. In 1922, excavations at the Roche de Solutre near Cluny in the Grosne Valley some 200 miles southeast of Paris had uncovered evidence of a prehistoric horse-hunting tribe: dated, *pace* Martin, c. 17,000-21,000 B.C.

4. Martin, himself? Or Molly's other grandfather, Charles Barnard Meyer (1846-1923), New York City lawyer born in Germany of American parents; graduate of Columbia Law School?

5. Sidney Wilmot Winslow (1854-1917), president of the United Shoe Machinery Co. in Beverly, Massachusetts, founded in 1899 by the consolidation of the Consolidated & McKay Lasting Machinery Co., the Goodyear Shoe Machinery Co., and the McKay Machinery Co. Leasing rather than selling its equipment, the consolidated company secured a virtual monopoly of shoe-manufacturing machinery in the United States by means of a "tying clause" forbidding anyone who leased their equipment from using the machinery of any competitor. Federal legislation made the "tying clause" illegal in 1918. [There seems to be no evidence the United Shoe Machinery Co. manufactured horse harness machinery.]

6. (1841-1928), vice-president of the United Shoe Co.

7. (1869-1947). British accountant; joined the New York firm of Barrow, Wade, Guthrie and Co. in the 1890's and subsequently became a partner. Returned to England in 1912, and after 1915 represented the British Treasury in the United States, and was director of several industrial concerns.

8. A sand track for riders in Hyde Park, London.

9. The Kalmucks are a branch of the Oirat Mongols inhabiting, among other regions, that around the Sungari River in northeast China. Their flight from Russia in the 18th century was described in the De Quincy essay previously mentioned by Martin. See Section Seven — "Wireless Activity."

tribute to a ninety-five percent perfect, absolutely beneficent monopoly. Suddenly, motor cars came in and horses became extinct. The demand for horse-harness expired. My grandfather came home and whispered, weakly, 'Our grandchildren must starve.' 'Never mind' said my grandmother. 'You wouldn't wish them to be peculiar. I'm told everybody will starve in the Twentieth Century.'

☙ ☙ ☙

## Genealogical Data
[May 16, 1938.]

*This typed sheet -- set up as shown -- was preserved by a member of the family; added information in brackets.*

Laura Grinnell Martin,
the elder
Nov. 12, 1859. [died July 20, 1940]
---------------------------
U. S. Constitution - Sept. 17, 1787.
Newell Martin - Sept. 17, 1854 [died Nov. 15, 1941]
L.G.G. & N.M. [married] Apr. 27, 1886.
-----------------------------
Grinnell Martin - Feb. 18, 1887 [died 1972]
--------------------------------
Laura - May 17, 1926.
Jane - Jan. 28, 1924.
Myra - July 23, 1921.
Myra, the mother of Myra
Aug. 15 [sic Aug. 21], 1899. [died 1969]
G.M. & M.T.F. [married] May 29, 1920.
------------------------------------
Helen Meyer - Apr. 2, 1889 [died 1971]
S. M. Meyer - Oct. 27, 1886 [died 1970]
H.M. & S.M.M. - [married] Sept. 19, 1914.

Molly - Dec. 14, 1915.
Schuyler, Jr. - Jan. 20, 1918.
Janet - April 19, 1921
Helen - June 21, 1922

## Letters From Newell to His Brothers [1]

Shanghai, Dec. 6th. 1862[2]

Dear Pascal.

The ship that is bringing our things has been out seven months, but has not arrived. We came in a steamer, and sent our things in a ship. I will give you a list of my lessons. Dictionary, Spelling, Geography, Bible Verses, history of the United States of America, and fractions. Claud send you his love and so do I. Mr. Gamble has some bohemian ware in his parlor. end

Your affectionate brother.

*N. M.*

Shanghai, Dec. 6th, 1862

Dear Robert

We have just heard the sad news of Uncle Steel's death. Sad for us, but good for him.

We have bought a stove. You thought that the winter here is just as warm as your summer, but the winter here is so cold that the port at Tientsin[3] is frozen up so that no vessels or steamers can

---

1. Excerpts used where text is either illegible or repetitive.
2. Newell then age eight.
3. Port for Peking.

get in.
We are now residing at Mr. Gambel's house. Mr. Gamble has a little pup. It's [sic] Mother is a tientsing dog.
Your affectionate brother,

*/L. M.*


Shanghai, March 6 1863
My Dear Brothers.
One day as Claud[e] and I were walking along with Ma we turned into Mr. Dato's store to buy something. I asked Ma if I might buy a toy dog, which was on a shelf, then Ma told me that I would not like to spend my money for such a thing. Just then one of the clerks took it off the shelf and gave it to me.
The other day as we were out shopping we went into Mr. Dato's store, one of the clerks told us that if Pa would let us have him, he would give us a large dog.
Claud[e] and I are much obliged to you for promising us the skates, we shall be very glad to have them at Tientsing....
One day not long ago, we went to the pagda [?]. And there we saw a foreign house about seven miles from the city. When the Rebels[4] were there they broke it open and the people of the neighboring village came and plundered it of everything of value....
Your affectionate brother,

*Newell Martin*


Peking, Oct. 24. 1863.[5]
My dear Brothers,
The carpenters are at work upon the house. We expect to move into it in two or three weeks.
A few days ago the paperhangers were at work upon Ma's and our own rooms. We are living in another part of the house, while the men are at work at the main part.

4. Taiping rebels. See Section Twelve. "English Merchants."
5. On plain paper on which someone (Newell?) had drawn lines.

When we came here Pa bought a dog; at another time Ma bought two doves. They are tame doves, and were brought up by the Chinese for eating. I made a cage for them, they seem to be very happy. They look so innocent and pretty that I think that we shall not eat any that are brought to market. Oct. 28. Tomorrow will be your birthday Pascal, and we are going to have a holiday in honor of it. I wish you many happy returns.

Your affectionate brother.

*Newell Martin*

Peking, December 31st. 1863.

My dear Brothers,

On Christmas Pa and Ma, with Claude and myself were invited to a Christmas party by Mrs. Williams and she had a fine Christmas tree. A great many gentlemen were there, and Gerty, the daughter of the United States Minister; and Willy and Stratly [?] Colling. I got a Chinese Coach, a monkey, a Mongolian upon a camel, and a calendar filled with envelopes. I had also a nice fur cap. Claude received a water cart, a little dog, a Chinese upon a pony, and a fur cap.... I have a fine dog whose name is Sport. Not long ago Ma had a bookcase made for us, which we now have filled with books. Perhaps you would like to have a list of my studies. They are Geography, History, Spelling, Reading, Dictionary, Bible verse and Hymns. I am also reading the History of England.

There are a great many camels in Peking.

The people in the north of China do not sleep upon beds, but on brick furnaces built up from the ground with little cellars under them. There is a little trap door in the floor by which to put in the coal and kindle the fire. Many of the people are burnt, and some are suffocated while sleeping. The people do not use wooden floors but pave the ground with large square bricks and tiles.

The seven foreign children of Peking are invited by Mr. Burdon to meet at his house on New Year's Day. We are to have a grand romp to begin at 3 o'clock, then tea at five. Write to me and tell me all about your plays and studies.

Your affectionate Brother

*Newell Martin*

Masters P. and R. Martin.
Peking. Nov. 23rd. [1865]

My dear Brothers,
 I beg your pardon for my long silence, but the truth is, that whenever I sat down to write to you I gave up in despair, making mistakes both in grammar and spelling, but now am going to try in real earnest.
 I have often wished that I could have seen Heartsville when the rest of you (and us) went. I often ask Claude about it, but his reports are so different from those of Papa and Mama that I do not much trust them.
 I often look forward to the time when I shall join you at Heartsville.
 This city is not at all like Philadelphia. There are no fine streets, horsecars, and carriages. The streets are cut up by carriages and carts: we call them all carts without distinction, for they have no springs and it is a wonder our heads are not broken. As there are no lampposts, everybody has to carry his own lantern. As to restaurants there are none, and the cooking establishments are built in the middle of the street so that the carts have to turn out for them. Everybody here is quite poor and very eager to offer themselves for baptism thinking they will get chow-chow. Papa has baptized only two, who did not come for chow-chow. He has a school of sixteen boys, one of whom is a Christian. By the way, I forgot to tell you the policemen in winter dress in sheepskins and sleep in our commodius gateways. I believe that if thieves entered the house it would be empty by the time the policemen were awake. I believe that my dog Sport is the best policeman in the city. Just now she has four pups....
 Apropos to the subject of policemen; one afternoon Papa was returning home, when suddenly he came upon a number of men fighting terribly with cudgels as thick as his arm. Upon calling for the police he was informed that a number of them were among the lookerson. When he inquired for the higher authorities they dragged the warriors to the guardhouse.
                              Your affectionate brother,
                                  Newell Martin

*Noted on top of letter, "Received April 18th 1866."*

Peking, January 15/66

My dear brother Pascal,

In your last letter you asked how the Chinese send their letters, and I am now prepared to answer the question. They have a system of stamps, but the letters are either prepaid or paid for by the receiver. There are two mails[,] the official and mercantile. Nothing but dispatches and the letters of those in official employ are sent by the former. Relays of horses are kept on the route for the swifter transmission of news, so that news of a rebellion could pass from one end of the empire to another in ten days. The mercantile mail travel much more slowly and reaches but few parts of the country. Therefore though it is open to all classes when you wish to send to a remote place unknown to the world, your letter might lie years before you would meet with some one going to the place to which you wish to send. The English have established postal communication by which foreigners send but they only send letters to the ports. We send you by this mail several English stamps used in China but to understand some of them you must know that a candareen is the tenth of a mace which is the tenth of a tael. The two former are not coined. A tael is about equal to one dollar, thirty-six cents.

We have sold our pony, but have fine times skating. I use the pair of skates which you gave me. Some gentleman has lately discovered that they are after the Dutch pattern. But that deficiency, if it be any, is fully compensated for by the fact that you gave them to me.

Your affectionate brother

*Newell Martin*


Peking, July [January?][6] 16th 1866

My dear Robert,

We have recently had news from Uncle Samuel in Texas. Grandma enclosed a letter to us, which she had received from him. She said that it was well for me to write to you, at which I was pricked in my heart, not having written for a long time. We had a merry time at Christmas. The Christmas tree was given by Mrs. Williams. My presents consisted of a very pretty series of

---

6. Previous letter and this on same two sheets of lined paper.

lithographic "Views of Bible Lands," a picture Maclay "Life in China," "Biblical Geography," and a large journal book. Claude received "Views of Hereford," a picture, "Uncle Paul's Stories" and a pair of boots. He also received "Dick and His Friend Fido," and a beautiful pen from Mama. In your next letter please give me a list of your studies. I expect to commence Latin as soon as Papa will have time to teach me which will be when he has resigned his place in the school of interpreters. I have recently read the "Schonberg Cotta Family," "Mary Bunyan," "Faith and Victory," "History of Egypt" and "the Dutch Republic."

Your affectionate brother

*Newell Martin*

*Martin's father, writing to his son Robert on January 4, 1868, said of Newell, then age 14: "Newell is away at the hills -- 15 miles -- with Walter Burlingame,[7] seeking flowers, minerals and health. He, N., is a fine boy. You would love him, and be proud of him, if you could have him with you. So gentle and polite, so intellectual, and yet so modest, he is as nearly faultless, as an impulsive boy could be expected to be. But he is, I am sorry to say, not robust or vigorous in body.[8] Someday, I hope you will have the pleasure of helping him forward in his studies."*

Peking, Nov. 4, 1867

My dear Robert.

How I wish we could be with you running and climbing trees, and tossing hay.

Here, for exercise, we play tricks on the parallels, turn somersets on the horizontal, and swing dumb-bells. For a run we go onto the wall where we can run for miles without turning a corner. The city wall, about sixty feet high, is a fine place for a view. Looking toward the city, you see the yellow and green tiled roofs of the palaces of the emperor and nobles.

Rising by their side, is seen the noble Imperial or as the Chinese unpoetically call it, Coal Hill.

All around them stretches the vast city from wall to wall whose innumerable trees, though serving to hide countless

---

7. Son of Anson Burlingame. See Section Seven — "Letter to Myra of Oct. 30, 1938; and Section Sixteen — "Appreciation of W.A.P. Marton."
8. Newell, who died when he was 87, lived the longest of W.A.P. Martin's four sons. Robert died at age 63; Pascal at age 32; and Claude presumably before the age of 30.

deformities, cannot keep from us the buzz and whirr and roar and even unclean odours of a million and a half of people with scarce a single sanitary regulation.

Turning to the north, and west, we behold the northern and western hills, both spurs of the Atari range.

In the former runs the indistinct link of the Great Wall, on the farther, when neither the clouds are too dark, or the sun too bright, are revealed the picturesque temples to which in summer, we flee from these dusty streets and close courts....

But now that you have been with us on the wall, and at our sports, I will take you to my studies. It is true they cannot boast much. As to Latin, my favorite study, I am nearly through the reader, and will be in Caesar next week. I study two pages a day. Next in importance is my history which I study in Lymans Historical Chart. Then comes arithmetic (Greenleaf's in which I am rather behindhand), and then writing. My lessons are few and short, but I try to make up for it by reading out of hours. Natural history is my <u>forte</u> or hobby, call it which you will, and the microscopical branch I am particularly devoted to. Not long ago Aunt Jennie sent me a book on the latter subject, and materials for mounting objects. Some of them have been used, I believe well and worthily by

Your affectionate brother,<br>N.A. Martin.

*Several letters from Newell to Robert, written while Newell was at Yale, deal with financial concerns.*

New Haven, March 20, '74

My dear Robert,

I did not wish to answer your last letter but one till I could send ten dollars. It is a paltry sum but I owe already twice what I have, & feel that I sin almost as much in sending the amount as I would in paying it to some New Haven land-shark.[9] I send a money order for $10 in an accompanying envelope and hope it will reach you in time to relieve your difficulties, in part at least. I can imagine the painful position you have been in since I have hardly once been out of debt since Mother left me alone. I am economical but without a large allowance it is impossible to make close connections between my needs and the arrival of such supplies. I say this merely to

---

9. Landlord? Loan shark?

unburden my soul, not to make you feel under any obligations to me for the trivial and tardy assistance. I expect another remittance before the 1st. of April, but do not know whether it will be large enough even to pay my term-bill. Though you may not need it by that time, I will, if it is in any way possible, lend you a part of the money, and will not be mean enough to think of taking interest. It belongs properly to one son as much as another. I hope you will forgive me for being almost as poorly supplied as yourself. I think I did not tell you that Claude had at last taken the practical turn which we have hoped for so long in vain. He is with a wholesale & retail boot and leather firm in a responsible situation, and gives out that he is over 20. Mr. & Mrs. Smith say they could not think of passing through New York without seeing you. Give my love to Aunt Anne and to Laura & to Aunt Jennie & Lillie if you find your way in safety to [either the letter "G" or "Y"]. I have been invited for the holidays to W. Phila. & I hope there will be money enough to put me through, & pay my debts & start you on the path to comfort.
      Your aff. brother.
      *Newell Martin*

               New Haven, June '75
 P.S. You know that Mr. Jackson has deposited your money in a savings-bank & that you may draw from it whenever & whatever you please.

Dear Robert,
 Your last note, received an age ago, hinted at your fear that I might be in some silly fit of anger against you. You spoke of your lonely situation and must have felt doubly lonely when my answers failed to come...
 It is six months since I have written to Pascal, and have just now allowed six weeks to pass without writing to Father & Mother.
 I have just sent an epistle of great length, but it will not cover a multitude of sins, sins of omission for which there is no excuse comprehensible to any one but the wretched sinner. There is no telling what heavy penalty Father in his wrath will lay upon me, and in the happy interval I will try to forget my forebodings in the Adirondacks, where I will fish and walk with some choice spirit, apart from the little faction of the gay woman-world that finds its way into the wilderness. Even they bow down to the graven image

and think a senior neutral too "thin" to flirt with, and a nobody even in the woods where people are generally measured by very correct and simple standards.

If I had put two days' work on a dull and commonplace Lit. article four months ago I would now wear a Bones pin,[10] but I have committed neither the former folly nor the latter extravagance....

I have just come home from a party. Though I neither dance nor wear a dress suit, I ordinarily come back in a state of pleasurable excitement which makes writing impossible. But tonight I have been to the first large party since Senior pins appeared on Junior beasts. To be left out of this folly and secret mummery never disturbed me till now but tonight I fared worse than a negro would at a Fifth Ave. ball. Don't be distressed at this outburst, but write & tell me whether to send Smith's Greece which is the only one of the books on hand.

Tell me your future course, and if you are released in time and my chum goes soon enough I will try to entertain you here till the rooms are closed. I could do well by you and you could either study or loaf to heart's content. I got along very well as regards the article and feel ashamed of having troubled you.

Your affectionate & regretful brother

*Newell Martin*

New York, March 20. '76.
My dear Pascal,[11]

I sent you a photograph of Claude & take the liberty of asking you to send it on to Mother, after you have studied it long enough to see how the child has changed.... Mother has doubtless told you the news about Claude, so that even if I drop asleep, or die of suffocation, you will not lose much. I suppose you remember the two Chapmans who were in your class, & one of whom graduated. Claude has married their sister Emily, a very pretty girl who never before did anything that was not sensible. She is an accomplished musician, having held the place in the Centre Church choir which was formerly filled by Miss Sanford. She is full of pluck & has an affection for Claude which will not die except under very heavy pressure. It looks as if the little enthusiasts were going to have a hard time. My intention is that Father shall not be burdened with

---

10. Skull and Bones, secret Yale Society.
11. Excerpts only from a long eight-page letter.

my support after next summer;[12] this will leave him free to save something &, perhaps, do something for Claude.... We have a charming little sister-in-law, & ought to be very grateful to Claude for having fallen in love with her, instead of some old hag whom he might have inflicted upon us.... Their dove-cote is in a nice boarding house in B'lyn.... Their whole board-bill is $10 a week for two; but they live on the 6th floor & the dining room is in the basement, so that our young lovers need not go to the mountains for their climbing.... I have the highest hopes of Claude, with whose early education you & I had so much trouble. Claude is now tramping all over N.Y., looking for house-painting, graining, furniture-decoration, sign-painting, anything, but the times are as hard as the 10 commandments & there is not much hope...

My pleasantest friends here are the Burlingames, though I have only seen them three or four times this term.... Ned Burlingame is a very heavy literary man working with Bryant & Gayon, the new history, which is to be a beautiful thing. He gave me a pronunciation list, of 92 words...which is enough to scare the stoutest heart. He missed 28. I, 55, & a number of my friends about 60. I don't hear anything of China in the Centennial, but I suppose it will be there soon. the Japanese are making quite a stir at Phila. My old pupil, Kodama, has got himself put on the commission. I wish you were to come with the Chinese Commission. With the sincerest regards. Your brother & former chum,
Newell Martin.

July 7. 1876.
[Dear Pascal]
I have told Claude to apply to you for the "average" of his allowance, if it is in arrears, & for $15.00 on each Monday, till further notice from me, which will doubtless come soon. I do not like to give you this great trouble, but am compelled to do so for a little while... I earnestly hope to see you in Keene Flats,[13] for which place I leave on the 13th. Please write as soon as you can & tell me what money you have paid Claude & at what times.
Yours affec.
Newell Martin

12. Newell then at Columbia Law School.
13. In the Adirondack Mountains. See map in Section Fourteen.

Mrs. W. A. P. Martin wrote Pascal a letter datelined New York, July 26th, 1880, which stated, in part: "Poor Newell looked thin and worn, and hardly has a moment he can call his own. For three years he has had only one week's holiday. He works all day and half the night. He is managing clerk for a professional lawyer in Cedar St., Henry A. Root by name.[14] Newell considers his a life or death struggle and is working with all his might in the hope of retaining his place and making himself so useful to his penurial master that he will give him 900 dollars a year. He now receives 50 dollars per month but is docked if he does not succeed in doing so well for his chief as he thinks he should. Yesterday being Sunday, N. dined with us and spent part of the afternoon. His "combination club" is broken up for the summer and he eats at his old place and sleeps in the house of his friend Mr. L. Smith, whose family are [sic] out of town."

University Club, Madison Square. Aug. 3, 1889.
Dear Robert
I have answered this note but I told Prof. Packard that I would send it to you: so you had better send an answer to Princeton.

Lake Forest is a pretty strong institution & good men have found their opportunity there. My charming babies[15] are in Milford & I am as usual working for haresis.[16]

Your brother

Newell Martin

### Western Union Telegraph Company

New York April 24th 1893
Prof. W. R. Martin, Northam Trinity College
I have received a cable message from Peking announcing the death of our Mother [stop] I shall be grateful if you can find time to come to town [stop] if you prefer you can go to some Hotel and send word to me to come to you [stop] perhaps you would find the Imperial the most convenient or shall I come to Hartford [stop]

Newell Martin

ঞ ঞ ঞ

---

14. *Yale Obituary Record* states that Martin went into partnership with Root 1881-85, then with C.R. Smith in 1890.
15. No reference.
16. Greek for "good pleasure, favor."

FAMILY 251

# Letters To and About the Family

Oct. 30. Sunday. 1938

Dear Myra

Grinnell will say: "12 cents a day,[1] about what some people pay for medical insurance, that is what these old people pay, to let us know that the old people are still about & that our children are beautiful & well & that they are playing with the also-beautiful little Brewers.[2] Now if any of these people, old or young, fell ill, we would hear by telegram. Twelve cents wasted". But we love to use this modern machinery. Civilization is on the skids & pretty soon we will say "Back in 1938 we had civilization & air-mail". So my wife & I rush to enjoy civilization, while the civilization is good. Mrs. Martin is already forbidden all travel. I wish to go to Washington, for a farewell. But can I? Is it too late?

-----------

In Peking we used to pay 35 cents for each letter & an ordinary letter & its answer took nearly five months. We could pay for mail, by pony riders, through Kiakta & Siberia. That cost money & saved time. It was by pony mail to Peking that we heard through Mr. Burlingame[3] of Lincoln's death.

Affectionately

*Newell Martin*

---

1. Note on the envelope containing the following letter stated it had been sent by air mail at cost of $.12
2. Effie, Ann, Michael, and George F., the children of George E. Brewer, Jr. (1900-1968; Yale '22). Brewer taught English at Yale, and was the author of the play *Dark Victory* produced on Broadway in 1934 with Tallulah Bankhead, and made into a movie starring Bette Davis some five years later. Brewer also had another play, *Tide Rising*, produced on Broadway in 1936. He headed the OSS (Office of Strategic Services) mission to Sweden during WWII, and in his later years was a founder and mover in conservation matters and wrote extensively on them. Ann Brewer, his wife, was a daughter of George Corning Fraser (See Section Ten - "On Behalf of George Corning Fraser"), as was Myra Fraser Martin, hence Grinnell Martin's sister-in-law.
3. Anson Burlingame (1820-1870; University of Michigan '41; Harvard Law School '46), congressman and diplomat was appointed Ambassador to China in 1860 by President Lincoln. His son, Edward Livermore Burlingame (1848-1922; Ph.D. Heidelberg '69), served as his father's secretary in China, and subsequently accompanied his father through Europe when Burlingame was named Ambassador Extraordinary to China. After his father's death in 1870 served as a literary adviser for the publisher, Charles Scribner's Sons. See Section Sixteen — "An Appreciation of W.A.P. Martin."

*Typewritten and dated, Monday - October 31, 1938. Sent to Hotel Davenport, Spokane, Washington.*

Dear Myra:
The only bright point about current political news is that we shall not have to charge our minds, any longer, with the difficulty of knowing how to spell Czechoslovakia.
We have had the great privilege of seeing your children and three Brewer children.
When I saw at your house these six delightful people I said to myself: "How shocking it is when such agreeable young people are growing up that the world has become unsafe for everybody, everywhere."

Affectionately,

*Newell Martin*

Dec. 25, 1938

Dear Myra
For my poor dear wife, who has had a rough time, month after month, I write to thank you for your thoughtfulness & your delightful Christmas gift, a year of Punch.
There is no reading on earth, so soothing for the aged as Punch.
There is no statesman that is more agreeable than A.P. Herbert in Punch.[4]
And only yesterday my wife called me, across the room, three times, to sympathize with her, in her laughter, caused by pictures in your gift.

Affectionately

*Newell Martin*

[Postscript] There is nothing so comfortably & continuously agreeable as Punch's pictures.

*Martin sent a legal-size envelope to his daughter-in-law, enclosing a letter to her and separate letters in their own unsealed envelopes to his granddaughters; all handwritten.*

---

4. Alan Patrick Herbert (1870-1971) had a degree in jurisprudence from Oxford, but never practiced law; joined the staff of *Punch* in 1924, having been writing for it since 1910. Published more than fifty books.

Dear Myra

May I ask you to read the enclosed letters. If you disapprove of anything in any of them, send back the rejected letter & I will correct it. Please hand to your descendants those that are not disapproved.

Say to your descendants:

It is all very well for octogenarians to write letters that look as if they had been laboriously constructed in a pig-stye or under bombardment. But a woman must always write a neat letter. Her letter must look graceful & dignified. And she must never write anything that would sound wrong if read in court or on the radio or on the front page of the Herald-Tribune.

The rules for septuagenarians are not so strict. And as to octogenarians, there are no rules. Octogenarians are not classed as human beings. We treat them gently, as if they had escaped from the cemetery or been dug up; but we avoid them & we do not require from them even silence. Don't forget, children, the finest utterance in the English language.

*L. M.*

[*Postscript*] the finest words in our language were addressed to an octogenarian gaffer: "All we want of you is silence & dam little of that." Caesar, Cicero, Bonaparte never said anything neater.

Huntington, January 24, 1939 A.D.

Dear Myra [*Miss Myra Tutt Martin, then 18-years old.*]

Every child ought to have 1 copy of every book ever published by any of her kindred; & above all she should have a copy of every book written by any of her ancestors. But we shall be lucky if each of our descendants has a single volume to represent ancestral industry. Consider this pedigree:

Myra Martin
Grinnell Martin [father]
Laura Martin [Gomby, grandmother]
Helen Lansing Grinnell [great-grandmother]
Dirck C. Lansing [great, great-grandfather]

Before me is a book of "Sermons on Important Subjects" published by your great great grandfather
Dirck Cornelius Lansing in 1825, 114 years ago.

I have also a sermon, commemorative of Dr. Lansing, preached by Joseph P. Thompson, himself a famous divine, in 1857, when I was three.[5]

Your g.g.g.f. was sometimes called the Last of the Patroons.[6]

Affectionately

*Lowell Martin*


Huntington, January 24, 1939. (A. D.)

Dear Jane [*Miss Jane Fraser Martin; then 15-years old.*]

Your great great grandfather, Dirck Cornelius Lansing entered Yale in September, 1800. He was 15. He graduated when he was 19. In his class was John C. Calhoun, famous, in his time, as one of those that caused our Civil War. Lansing was a youth of "high spirit", "vivacity", "heartiness of soul," and "popularity."

"Sprung from an ancient, honorable and wealthy family -- his grandfather being patroon XXX of a large manor near Troy, he was inclined to seek his associates among the aristocratic & the gay." "He was born at Lansingburgh, March 3, 1785." (page 15, of Thompson's Memorial)

"Being of a Dutch family, he had not used the English language until he was a large boy." (Same book, p.19)

He lived to be 72.

Affectionately

*Lowell Martin*


---

5. See Section Sixteen - Dirck C. Lansing, D.D.
6. Abraham Jacob Lansing (1720-91), who purchased a tract of land in Rensselaer County, N.Y., in 1763 and divided it into lots in 1771, thus becoming patroon of Lansingburg. A patroon is of course one granted a landed estate and certain manorial privileges under the old Dutch government of New York.

Wednesday Sept. 20 1939
Dear Myra
1. With fear I write. My nurse says, ["]Exercise the lame hands.["] But my conscience says, Tire your hand & tomorrow both hands will be gone.
2. This morning I received an anonymous letter. My first impulse, with an anonymous letter is to leave it unread. My second, to send it back to the writer. Helen says that you know more about most things than most people. So, here goes.
The anonymous sender of a gorgeous metrical birthday card said "From a lady who loves you still always."
I made a long list of such ladies, but Helen shook her head. "It is not any of those." So, if you meet any "lady who loves me" will you thank her earnestly for remembering that I am 85.
3. Helen says that you are chiefly the agent in my wife's giving me, last Xmas, Jonah[7]. I have been reading it again, with great interest. An agreeable & witty & timely book.
4. I thank Grinnell for his thoughtful & beneficent telegram.
5. I thank you & Grinnell for Billy Phelps's book.[8] I have read much of it.
It is peculiarly precious to me, because Billy Phelps was a student under my brother Robert, in the Hartford High School. He gives 2 pages of most just appreciation to Robert. Page 102. He justly records W.R. Martin as "one of the most learned men." 104, 235.[9]
In 1871, 68 years ago, Billy Phelps's brother & I used to be in the same class. Billy's brother esteemed me because I used to get good marks.[10]
I never "pick up" Billy's book. But I often lift it, laboriously,

---

7. Robert Nathan (1894-1985), *Jonah* (N.Y.: Knopf, 1925; reissued 1934), novel based on the Biblical story, seriocomic in an Anatole Francian or Martinish vein. Nathan's name will recall for most readers *A Portrait of Jennie* (1941).
8. *Autobiography With Letters* (N.Y.: Oxford University Press, 1939).
9. See Section Seventeen - "Teaching" by Professor William Lyon Phelps.
10. The Rev. Dryden William Phelps (1854-1931). Entered Yale 1871, but after a year there accompanied his family to Providence and became a student at Brown, graduating in 1877. B.D. Yale '92; pastorates at Wilmington, Vt. and Mystic, Conn. Possibly the esteem was mutual. Phelps's *An Autobiography With Letters* states: "Dryden William...was entirely different from my brother Arthur and me, for he hated all games, never learned to swim or even to whistle, never fired a gun or a pistol; but had an accomplishment in which he excelled anyone I have ever seen or heard of. He could definitely remember something that had happened every day of his life after the age of five. For example: in the year let us say 1890, if you asked him 'What did you do February 17, 1868?' he could tell you within three minutes."

using 2 crippled hands.[11] I often happen on some interesting chapter that is hard to leave: something about the Whitneys[12], to whom Laura & I are devoted or Arthur Hadley, my companion in swimming. Phelps justly records William Dwight Whitney[13], with whom I used to camp, as the most learned man in the world. The English used to insist that Lord Acton[14] & the famous Gooch[15] were the most learned. Whitney surpassed them.

It is delightful to be treated so kindly & remembered so thoughtfully. Such kindness should carry me smoothly through the next ten years.

Affectionately

*Lewell Martin*

Oc. 23  1939

Dear Myra

Helen has written to you, doubtless, showing that nothing has happened here to discredit the 10th verse of the 90th Psalm.[16] My hands are twisted, but one finger & thumb are all I need.

I am cut off from dictionaries & big books --- but we have with us, always, Haldeman-Julius.[17] I am deeply interested in the talk of "6 man foot-ball" -- a game which may do away with the horrors & perils of American foot-ball.

---

11. Martin's grandson, Schuyler M. Meyer, Jr., reports that he and other family members would rip the backs off books, and tear them into sections, to accommodate Other Gomby's hands crippled by arthritis.
12. See Section Ten - "The Climenole."
13. See Section Two - "The Yale Commencement."
14. See Section One - "The Duty of Rebellion." Acton received a highly variegated schooling in England, Paris, and Germany; had a personal library of 59,000 volumes.

15. George Peabody Gooch (1873-1968), historian. Effectively, though not officially, Acton's pupil. Entered King's College, London, age 15; subsequently studied at Trinity College, Cambridge; Berlin, and Paris. Editor of *The Contemporary Review* 1911-60, author numerous authoritative studies on history and historiography, editor of *British Documents on the Origin of the War* (13 vols., 1926-38).
16. "The days of our years are three-score years and ten; and if by reason of strength they be fourscore years, yet is their strength labour and sorrow; for it is soon cut off, and we fly away."
17. Emanuel Haldeman-Julius: (1889-1951) Author and publisher; wrote books of a rationalistic or iconoclastic bent; published the "Little Blue Books," a series of thousands of titles in a 3.5" X 5" format that got him dubbed the "Henry Ford of Publishing." Martin was probably speaking of Haldeman-Julius' own *A Book of Problems, Puzzles, and Brain-Teasers* (Girard, Kansas: Haldeman-Julius, 1939).

I cannot believe that American fathers are so feeble-minded that they enjoy seeing their sons run the risk of concussion of the brain. Tell Grinnell that his mother's good spirits hold up, wonderfully; through the larger part of each day.
                              Affectionately
                              Newell Martin


*[Editor's note: The first game of six-man football was played by a high school in September 1934; one year later six-man football was being played in one of every 120 high schools in the nation; five years later in one of ten. (It was played at Galway Union Free School, Galway, New York, and in 1940, editor Cynthia Parsons was quarterback of the team, playing with five boys and competing against all-boy teams throughout Saratoga County.) The game gradually faded away over the next decade as it never caught on at the college level, and high school players who knew only six-man football were at a great disadvantage competing for a place on a college team. Touchdowns count for six points, safeties two, field goals four; two points for a successful after-touchdown kick between the uprights, one for an analogous pass or run into the end-zone. The offensive team must make a clear pass before the ball crosses the line of scrimmage. No mass assaults or heavy-cleated shoes are permitted. All players are eligible pass receivers.]*

ʦ ʦ ʦ

# Letters to the Grandchildren

October 17, 1935

Dear Myra

Last Sunday was a memorable day of happiness for my wife & me, because your three memorable & highly educated children[1]

---
1. Myra, Jane and Laura.

258  FAMILY

were here with Grinnell. Knowing that many of my ancestors, during the last ten million years, lacked polish, I am always profoundly impressed by the grace & kindness & exquisite politeness of your daughters.

Their deferential & affectionate demeanor sheds glory on the planet that they live in & makes me reluctant to leave the place.

Affectionately

*Lewell Martin*

[*Postscript*] Mrs. Martin and I are thinking, all the time, about you & your father & your mother, and desiring more earnestly than I can tell, the welfare of you three.

December 28, 1936

Dear Laura:
Dear Jane:[2]

I found two Xmas stockings hung in my honor filled with Xmas gifts, all of great splendor and convenience. First: I found a box marked

Xmas Joys
for
Grandfather[3]

My idea of Xmas Joys is to have you with me at Xmas. But I opened the box and found it filled with beautiful rubber bands. Rubber bands are a mark of affection: Affection that lasts a long time, but must not be put under any strain that is unduly heavy. In the beautiful words of the Persian poet, Hafiz:[4]

To make you love as I love you
These rubber bands should hold you true.

I fell ill at Xmas;[5] and in the rush of the holidays, my nurses mixed up the contents of the two socklets. So, in this letter of thanks, I may mix them up.

---

2. Laura, age ten; Jane, age twelve.
3. The children of Martin's son, Grinnell, called him "grandfather;" the children of his daughter Helen called him "Other Gomby."
4. (d. 1389?) Teacher of the Koran, whose numerous poems on love and drinking are interpreted allegorically by Moslems.
5. As arthritis advanced, crippling Martin's hands, many of his letters, as was this one, were typed rather than handwritten.

Gratitude to Granddaughters:

A. For 600 matches, from Jane, marked M. M for month, meaning that these will light my cigarettes for a month.

B. For 600 matches, from Laura, marked M. M for month, meaning that these will light my cigarettes for a month.

C. Black shoe-strings, from Jane; so that I may put on shoes and walk with her to the 8 houses.

D. Brown shoe-strings, from Laura; so that I may put on shoes and walk with her to the 8 houses.

E. A lead pencil, from Jane, and a lead pencil from Laura. I shall use those pencils to write, in 1937, often, long statements in praise of my dear grandchildren.

Gratefully,

*Newell Martin*

July 15, 1937.

Dear Jane:

Your father and your sister Myra came to our house last night so that Myra might bid us goodbye. They were in the highest degree polite and kind. Now that little Myra is gone and is going to have a happy and immensely instructive journey[6] I feel free to tell you, in confidence, that I make it a rule to avoid Germany. This is a secret. Don't mention this to anybody except your parents. My reason is this: Twenty-five years ago Germany was the most civilized nation in the world. But Germany has fallen into the hands of a gang of robbers and murderers. Her wisest men have been driven from their homes and their colleges. Therefore, I stay away from Germany until freedom and learning are restored. The two most precious things in the world are civil liberty and learning.

Affectionately

*Newell Martin*

[*Postscript*] When you write to Myra don't mention any of the things I have spoken of in this letter. My advice would be to send your letter to Myra through your parents.

---

6. A trip to Europe, as per the August 19, 1937, letter to her.

                                                    July 18, 1937
Dear Jane
    I have written to you, already, about civil liberty & the advancement of learning.[7]
    I may, however, take steps to abolish, suppress & burn that letter.
    The advancement of learning is not a proper subject for July. And who would talk about civil liberty to a kitten or a rose-bud?
    True, the other young girls at your camp might say that you are not in the same class as kittens or rose-buds. But I say that you are. I am glad to see you, always. Also, I am glad to see kittens, always. The grace & wit & sparkle of a kitten are among the wonders of this world. And young girls, unselfish, thoughtful of others, studious; such young girls are among the wonders of the world. Consider me & your grandmother, my good old patient wife. We could travel & spend our time looking at the Pacific Ocean & the Pyramid of Khufu. But we disregard those two important objects & prefer to stay where we can see you & talk to you about the Advancement of Learning.
                                    Affectionately
                                    *Newell Martin*

*The following letter was saved in an envelope addressed by hand to Miss Jane Fraser Martin, High Fields Camp, East Union, Maine. The date of the cancellation was July 19, 1937. A single sheet of paper was enclosed with the following message:*

   Don't write to me
   unless & until it rains.
   Never write to a grand-parent
   except when you would
   rather write than eat.

                                    July 26, 1937.
Dear Jane:
    Last Saturday your mother invited us to your country house in Cove Neck, Oyster Bay, Long Island, to witness the wedding of

---

7. Allusion to Francis Bacon, Baron Verulam, Viscount St. Albans (1561-1626), specifically the first volume in his complete works, advocating the endeavor named through the division of knowledge into various discrete categories, each restricted to its appropriate subject-matter.

Archie[8] and Dickey. Fifty people were scattered about, over the extensive and beautiful seaside lawns, in picturesque and agreeable groups. Two pipers marched, once in every ten minutes, from the shore to the front of the house. They wore the Stuart tartan and suitable memoranda of the Fraser tartan. The execution took place at the little gate of your mother's special own garden. The parson seemed sympathetic and said nothing about its being now too late to reconsider. The pipers played the Pibroch of Donald Dhu and Farewell to Lochaber and 50 other plaintive laments. Your little sister and the large dog were conspicuous in adding to the publicity, solemnity and legality of the ceremony. Little tables stood about at which we, the guests, were seated, in what seemed to me multitudes. Troops of waiters plied us with chickens, lobsters, ices and champagnes. Gomby took great pleasure in observing the efficiency and hospitality of your parents. I am writing a statement of all these historical facts to Myra.

*Newell Martin*

Thursday, August 19, 1937

Dear Myra,

I am grateful for your letter dated July 11, containing and setting forth all the most important news of Central Europe. Empires may rise and fall, Japanese may rage and bombard, but it does not stir my aged mind.

Everything you do and say, however, does interest me.

In going to see pictures, however, I venture this advice. Don't try to see too many, or too many at once. Go, for instance, every day, to see the Venus of Milo, and sit down before her, for half an hour. Do this six days in succession. Then, for four days, do the same thing with the Winged Victory of Samothrace. Then, three days with the Sistine Madonna.[9] And so on.

If you happen not to be in Paris or Dresden, choose the painter that moves you most deeply and study him, for half an hour, for each of six days. You catch the idea. Avoid weariness.

Beware of a multiplicity of impressions.

---

8. Archie Bogle
9. The first two in the Louvre, Paris; Raphael's Sistine Madonna was in Dresden at the time of writing, but was removed to Russia after WWII.

In the Adirondacks, at first, don't try to climb 24 different mountains. Make a study, first, of one big mountain. Become at home with each of its glens and brooks.

Your favorite clergyman will tell you about the rock in the desert of Horeb. Moses touched it, with his divining rod, and cheap and abundant streams of water gushed out, for the benefit of the Israelites.[10] Likewise, you touch me, with your agreeable and nice letter and vast masses of cheap and abundant advice gush forth.

Affectionately,

*Lewell Martin*

*On top of a carbon of this letter, Martin has written: "not for Little Myra. Do not send this to Little Myra. It refers to politics. But let Jane have hers."*

Friday, August 20, 1937

Dear Jane

Here is another experiment in writing multifold letters to multitudinous descendants.

My case reminds me of the Mahometan salutation: The Mahometan does not say, Merry Christmas or Happy New Year. He says: May you live a hundred years and have a thousand grandsons. I have lived nearly 100 years and have 6 granddaughters--much better than having 1,000 grandsons.

As you know, on September 17, there will be fireworks and cannon, all over the 48 states and Alaska and Porto [sic] Rico----but no; I will not be like the school-boy from Connecticut who wrote to his mother "I would rather be in Connecticut than in any other place. I would rather be in Connecticut than in Oregon, Washington.." and so he went on, listing the states -- the 47 other states.

Myra, in her last letter to me, listed and described 4 faults that some girls have. Then she added, quite justly, "I have none of these faults." I had written to Myra, praising the Bolsheviki for converting a number of cathedrals into horsebarns.[11] Myra reproved me by saying that she had been in a Bavarian cathedral and that she disapproved of certain people who talked loud in the cathedral. My excuse to Myra is that I was talking about cathedrals of the Greek Church. Myra will surely agree with me that it is fine to have cathedrals of the Greek Church converted into horsebarns.

---

10. Exodus 17:1-7. Horeb: another name for Mt. Sinai.
11. The overwhelming bulk of Russia's cathedrals had in fact been closed – sometimes turned to other uses, primarily storage – in the anti-religious campaign of 1929-1930.

Beware, all of you, of the Greek Church.
You will ask, why cannons and brass bands on September 17? I will not try to conceal from you that Sept. 17 is my birthday. On Sept. 17 I shall be 83. I earnestly beg you and all of you to give me no gifts. Nothing but postal cards. Something like the amazing Dionne pictures that Molly sent me from Canada.[12]

Affectionately,

Newell Martin

[*Postscript*] And, on September 17, 1937, the Constitution will be 150 years old. It needs to be doctored, thoroughly.

[*Post postscript*] Dear Myra I refuse to celebrate, on Sept. 17. No other document since Cadmus[13] has cost so much suffering as our Constitution. It is in need of amendment, through amendment.

N. M.

September 27, 1937.

Dear Jane:
I thank you again for observing twice that I am 83. I thank you valued Jane, for giving me a beautiful negress who dances. I find her a great comfort, in my latter days. I have left word that, when I am cremated, she is to be cremated also, in the Chinese manner, so that she may accompany me to the spirit world.

Affectionately

Newell Martin

January 26, 1938.

Dear Laura:
I went to California in 1868. That is the first time I visited that rich, fertile and beautiful state. I crossed the Pacific Ocean, early in 1868 and, at that time, no railway across the continent had

---

12. Of the Dionne quintuplets (Annette, Emelie, Yvonne, Cecile, Marie) born to Olivia Dionne at Callendar, Ontario, May 28, 1934. In 1935 the Ontario government made them wards of the province.
13. Iin Greek legend, the founder of Thebes and the inventor of the alphabet.

been finished. The first trans-continental railway was finished later in the year. Seventy years ago, I was in San Francisco.
Observe these historical dates:
1854. Newell Martin, grandfather of Laura Grinnell Martin, was born, in China.
1868. N.M. arrived in San Francisco. Later in this year, the first railway was finished, across the continent.[14]
1938. Laura Grinnell Martin crossed the continent, for the first time, in her experience.

If you happen to go to La Jolla, while you are in California, go to see Major General Robert Alexander.[15] He and your father used to be comrades, in the Great War, in France, in 1918. I will not, in this place, detain you with any statements as to the horrors of war. A great war combines in itself and repeats all the other forms of calamity.

Affectionately,

*Newell Martin*

26 Dec. 1938

Dear Grinnell

I thank you and Myra for your thoughtfulness & kindness in giving me, for a part of our unusually happy Christmas celebration, Geoffrey Garratt's "Shadow of the Swastika".[16] It has been said that a man should never read books that he already believes in; that he should keep an open mind & always read the enemy's story.

Tonight, however, I shall make a deviation from that rule and read Garratt's appalling story.

Gratefully

*Newell Martin*

---

14. Was actually not completed until May 10, 1869.
15. See Section Three - "Letter to Major-General Robert Alexander."
16. Geoffrey Garratt (1888-1942), *The Shadow of the Swastika* (London: Hamilton, 1938) analyzes the attractions of Hitler's and Mussolini's governments for their respective populations; discusses the conduct of various European powers vis-a-vis the Spanish Civil War and the Italian invasion of Abyssinia, and the appeal for the British public of what he, following E.M. Forester, calls "Fabio-Fascism," with its policies of isolationism, an expanded bureaucracy, and restrictions on freedom of speech and of the press.

December 26 1938

Dear Myra

My wife is deeply touched by your kindness & thoughtfulness & the great trouble you have taken to give her a happy Christmas, with such thoughtful & unusual & unprecedented gifts from you & your children.

Affectionately

Lewell Martin

*Following letter handwritten in entirety.*

Dec. 26 1938

Dear Grinnell

Your mother is weak, but otherwise is far better than we had any right to expect.

Your father is weak, but otherwise is far better that we had any right to expect.

I ought to put off all writing for a few days & then should write, separately, with my pen, to each one for each gift or endowment. There used to be a legend at Yale that the president of Harvard never sent a holographic [handwritten] letter of thanks for a gift of less than a million.

Your mother has found strength to speak on the telephone to your daughter Myra. Your mother was delighted to speak with Myra. We have spent the morning rejoicing over the precious stone statues of Confucius & Mencius[17] that came to us yesterday from Myra & you by way of Helen's Christmas tree.

Your mother thanks Myra & you for these dignified & precious objects.

Your mother also thanks (A) Myra Martin, daughter of Grinnell Martin, for 7 volumes of needles, threads & articles of daily use, of the sort that little Myra's ancestresses have used for a million years, to keep in order the garments of their husbands & children.

(B) Jane Martin, for a pin cushion of beauty & splendor, supported by 8 gnomes. Never before have I seen a pin-cushion so compact & quaint & beautiful.

(C) Little Laura Martin for a Japanese brown thrush, of ivory, resting on a Japanese base. So tiny a bird & so perfect -- the

---

17. Meng-tse (372?-289? B.C.), Confucian philosopher.

very bird, I doubt not, that visited your mother in the Gulf of Pechili.
Gratefully

*Lowell Martin*

*Also handwritten.*

May 27, 1939

Dear Myra
    Our maid, Madge Evans, called you on the telephone the other day. You gave her the information she desired & then instead of saying goodbye in the usual manner, you said "Give my love to Mr. Martin." For this benevolent thoughtfulness I thank you. I have reached a barren pinnacle of old age where kind messages are few & where few survive that remember me. I remember now that once, 50 or 60 years ago, somebody having sent me a regret, I said "nobody loves me"; whereupon Fred Davis, of Yale '77,[18] a famous foot-ball man of his time, said "why should they?" His answer was ungrammatical but instructive,
Affectionately

*Lowell Martin*

ta ta ta

# Words That I Had With Molly
[September, 1923]

*The Martins were living on a working farm in Milford, Connecticut, at this period, and had not yet moved to Huntington, Long Island. Molly often spent time with her grandparents, and apparently spent Christmas 1923 (when just eight years old) with Gomby and Other Gomby. Martin printed Molly's Christmas letter to her father, complete with original spelling and punctuation; also printed an essay he titled, "Words That I Had With Molly."*
My Dear Father.
    I hope you are well and I hope you are very happy. And I hope you had a very merry Christmas and New Year. I did Father Dear.

---

18. See Section Fourteen - "Six Summits. " Davis actually played football only in his senior year, and to no great effect as far as the Yale athletic records are concerned.

I love you very much Father Dear. How are Margaret and Mary and Annie and Katie and Janet [sister] and Helen [sister] and Mummy Dear, and your-self Father Dear. Give my love to Mummy and Janet and Helen and Margaret and Annie and Katie and Mary Father Dear. There were some boy's and girl's skating on the pounds yestoday, and Bear [five-year old brother] told them they could not, But Josephine told them they could.

Father Dear, I hope you all are very well, even Mummy and Margaret and Katie and Mary and Annie. Dear Father.
Devotedly Molly Meyer.<br>January 3, 1924.

Molly floated into my bedroom this morning without knocking. Although I have often given her a rough line of talk for such impulsiveness, she wastes no time on ceremoniousness.

This morning she chooses to walk on the tips of her toes. She often does that. It is one of the habits that distinguish her from pedestrian mortals. "I ken the manner of his gait," says Ulysses, of Diomed, "He rises on the toe: that spirit of his, In aspiration lifts him from the earth" (T. & C. r, 5).[1] Swinburne, in his youth[2] Molly, and Diomed; I cannot, at this moment, remember any others that have had this gait.

She seats herself on my bed, without leave, and puts her elbows on my bed-table, disordering, thus, my manuscripts, which I have been preparing, painfully, for rejection by the Century Company. She rests her smooth chin on her gentle hands and regards me, calmly, with untroubled blue eyes. Obviously, she will keep her charm, even in old age, that is already rushing toward her, though she does not know it; and she conducts herself, now, in ways that, in 1934, will cause bank robberies, murders, sonnets.

"Other Gomby", she begins, "your bottle is broken." Certain words and names are in use, between her and me, that might sound, to a bystander, unintelligent. For this there is high precedent. "The big bottle, Other Gomby," she continues, "The red bottle, with the long words on it. I took it up, to read the bottle, and Bear joggled my elbow."

---

1. Shakespeare's *Troilus and Cressida* IV. v. 14-16.
2. Edmund Gosse, in *The Life of Algernon Charles Swinburne*, quotes the recollections of Donald Crawford: "[Swinburne] walked delicately, like Agag, with a mounting gait, as if picking his steps."

"Molly, your love of reading deserves praise. Read, in every moment that you can spare from the more serious business of life. Clutter up your mind with books, good and bad. Read Munchausen,[3] Mannix,[4] Psalmanazar,[5] de Rougemont's[6] Ossendowski.[7] But some things, such as other men's letters, are not for general reading. Nobody reads anybody's medicine bottle. It is not done. And, remember, after this, kindly carry on your sports and studies in your own tub-room.

I deplore your fondness for taking your baths in my dressing-room. When you have been there the place looks like a West Kenia [Kenya] water-hole, one that has been used as a wallow by forty seven wild African elephants. I have, or had, four big medicine bottles, for four kinds of medicine, to be taken four times a day, some inside and some outside. It will be Thursday before a new bottle can come from New York and I shall suffer tortures. Tortures, like them tortures that William J. Burns[8] puts on Bolsheviks to make us confess to plots of his imagining. Those four bottles are the bodyguards that stand between me and the King of Terrors."

"Other Gomby, who is the King of Terrors?"

"My nearest and dearest friend. He haunts the door-step, urgently calling me to Nirvana, the land of delights, where grandchildren cease from troubling. To humor the unscientific, unphilosophic, paleolithic prejudices of my family, I stand him off, by turning my dressing-room into a chemical laboratory, an apothecary's laboratory."

3. The Baron, Karl Friedrich Hieronymus Von Munchausen (1720-1797), German soldier and adventurer known for his exaggerated tales.
4. In 1913, William Francis Mannix, an American journalist, published as authentic the fictitious memoirs of an actual Chinese statesman, Li Hung Chang, which Mannix had written to pass the time in a Honolulu jail.
5. George Psalmanazar (1679-1763), Presumed to be a Frenchman; masqueraded as an inhabitant of Formosa [Taiwan], and published extensive descriptions of that island.
6. Louis de Rougemont was actually a Swiss named Grin, who published in 1898 an account of 30 years spent among "the cannibals of Australia."
7. In 1922, Ferdynand Antoni Ossendowski, an emigre Russian nobleman, published *Beasts, Men and Gods*, a largely fictitious account of his experiences in Tibet while fleeing Bolshevik rule.
8. William John Burns (1891-1932), organizer and head of the William J. Burns National Detective Agency. Director (1921-1924) of the Bureau of Investigations of the U.S. Department of Justice, when he became notorious as a persecutor of radicals and radical organizations; typical allegations were that a miners' strike was "Moscow-inspired," and that the Third International sought the overthrow of the American Federation of Labor. Resigned following a senate investigation into his harassment of officials and witnesses involved in the investigation of Harry Daugherty, and was succeeded by J. Edgar Hoover.

"Other Gomby, what's a laboratory?"

"A place where one converts the simple into the complex, or the complex into the simple, the impure into the pure, the useless into the useful, the ugly into the beautiful. In laboratories the disciples of Madame Curie turn forty thousand tons of carnotite or pitchblende or something, into four grains of radium. But I use my dressing-room for the converse of this process, to delay the miraculous transmutation by which this gaunt body and this bony skull will cease to be a source of pain and expense. Wouldn't you like to see me transformed, in one glorious moment, into a beautiful, invisible spirit, free from fault and error? I know you would. That is why you busted my bottle. You are not to be forgiven. I shall make a revocatory codicil, to your disadvantage."

"Other Gomby, what's a codicil?"

"It is something formidable that rises up out of a man's grave, to terrify his descendants and enrich discreet old gentlemen, learned in the law. Sometimes it is witnessed by a housemaid and a hired man, as if it were a rural spectre."

"Other Gomby, what's a spectre?"

"You will know, Molly, when you hear my codicil. It will make a grewsome sound, like this:

'So much of my savings and estate, real, personal and mixed, as would pass, but for this codicil, to Molly Meyer, is hereby given to the hereinafter named four corporations, to be divided among them, share and share alike, that is, to the Margaret Sanger Birth Control Society, the Kiyo Midzu Temple,[9] of Kyoto, the Happy Despatch society of Nara,[10] and the Society for the Prevention of Cruelty to Old Men."

*  *  *

---

9. Usually "Kiyomizu," a Kyoto landmark — a famous temple built in 798 A.D., dedicated to the eleven-headed Kannon.
10. The Great Hall at Nara, Japan, a center of Buddhist worship, holds the famous 53' high gold Buddha dating in part from the 9th century A.D.; the religious society takes its name from the news of the discovery on a Japanese nobleman's estate of sufficient deposits of gold to make the statue possible.

# Molly's Will[11]
[January, 1927]

Molly's teachers told her to stay away from school, because of a scarlet fever alarm. We did not think her in danger but Molly seems to have taken the alarm more seriously. After much study she asked her brother and a nurse to witness a paper which she sealed with wax. She put it in an envelope and asked her father to keep it in his office. We do not know of anybody[12] that ever told her about wills or witnesses or the safe deposit of documents. Without her knowledge I borrowed and copied her "paper writing", which shows her to be "of sound and disposing mind and memory". The paper and its solemnities are the result of her own ceaseless search for information and her thoughtful use of such knowledge as she acquires.

Newell Martin
Huntington, January, 1927.

### MY WILL[13]

In case I dye with scarlit fever I will
leave my things to
To Father I leave my 100 dollars, and
pictures to do what he likes with.
To Mummy I leave all my jewelry (and
horse[14] if I get it).
To Bear I leave all my books.
To Jonny[15] I leave heather[16] and Roberta.[17]
To Ardee[18] I leave David[19] and George.[20]

---

11. Molly, today Mrs. M. M. O'Connor, former librarian, Dartmouth College, Hanover, NH, says of Other Gomby, "When, in a college English course, I was asked to write an autobiography, I remember saying that my grandfather had been the greatest single influence on my life." Molly was 12 years old when she made out her will. Martin in fact had Molly's will printed.
12. Editor's note: Both Molly's father and grandfather were lawyers.
13. Title in original.
14. Molly O'Connor, on December 8, 1988, recalling the request for a horse, stated firmly, "I did not get the horse!"
15. Molly's younger sister, Janet, called Jonnie.
16. Molly's dog.
17. A doll named Roberta was given to Molly on her 8th birthday. The same doll had been given to Molly's mother on her 8th birthday, by Uncle Robert, Uncle Gomby's brother.
18. Molly's sister, Helen, known as Ardee.
19. Molly's dog, David, Heather's puppy.
20. Molly: "I don't remember George."

To Josephine I leave my clothes and holy things.[21]
To Anne[22] I leave Patricia[23] and my handkerchiefs.
To Nina[24] I leave my pincushions.
To Lida[25] I leave my petit poins.
To Harriet[26] I leave all my pretty boxes and other pretty things.
You may divide the rest of my things to Grandma Gomby[27] (Anty[28] my bicicle).

[signed] MOLLY MEYER.
Witnesses:
S. M. Meyer[29]
Margaret Sexton.[30]
[Seal][31]

ᶫᵉ ᶫᵉ ᶫᵉ

21. Josephine, daughter of the woman who helped Gomby and Other Gomby, was to be the recipient of a prayer book and hymnal.
22. Anne Earle, a friend.
23. Another friend.
24. Nina Vitale, a friend.
25. Lidia Vitale, a friend.
26. Some needlepoint for Harriet McPherson, a friend.
27. Gomby, Molly's grandmother, George Bird Grinnell's sister.
28. Aunt Janet, Molly's mother's sister, called Auntie.
29. Schuyler Merritt Meyer, Jr., Molly's brother, former President of the Edwin Gould Foundation for Children and founder of the George Bird Grinnell American Indian Children's Education Foundation.
30. Ms. Sexton was Jonnie's and Ardie's nurse.
31. The seal is no longer in the family, but Molly remembers that it was made with sealing wax.

## Some Advice As To In-Laws
April 18, 1925

*Return address: Highland Pines Inn, Southern Pines, N.C.*
*Letter is addressed to William Dwight Whitney, Esq. and Schuyler M. Meyer, Esq.* [1]

Dear Bill:
Dear Schuyler:
 Neither of you is to answer this letter of advice, which is confidential.
 Each of you has or will have a father-in-law and a mother-in-law.[2] Each of you is learned in the law and seeks to guide himself, in dealing with his relatives, by the highest precedents. No one knows better than you that the law as written is something entirely different from the law as practiced, and that, to know the law, what one really needs is to know what has been done. To say, "It is not done," is equal to saying, "It is not the law." To a superficial reader of the law it would seem that there is no distinction in vital rights between (1) rich and poor, (2) black and white, (3) fathers-in-law and mothers-in-law. He would be grotesquely mistaken. I have been an expert in the law of domestic relations and it gives me pleasure to advise you as to the third of the classes of cases mentioned above.
 For centuries it has been customary to talk as if fathers-in-law were not objectionable and as if mothers-in-law were noxious. You know the ancient lines:
 You take the axe and I'll take the saw,
 And we'll cut off the head of my mother-in-law.
 The law has observed that this state of popular feeling creates a peril from which the mothers of married daughters should receive special protection. The law has, therefore, wisely decreed that a father-in-law must take his chances but that a mother-in-law must not be murdered. A father-in-law, therefore, should conduct himself with care if he proposes to be disagreeable to his son-in-law.
 In Danville,[3] the other day, a son-in-law visited his wife's

---

1. William Dwight Whitney (1899-1973; Yale '20), eldest son of Edward B. Whitney (1857-1911; Yale '78; Columbia Law School '80). Bill Whitney was an eminent New York City and Washington lawyer. Schuyler Merritt Meyer (1885-1970; Yale '07), New York City lawyer, member New York State Assembly 1914-17, New York State Senate 1920-21. Married Martin's daughter Helen in 1914.
2. Gomby, of course, was Schuyler's mother-in-law, and Other Gomby his father-in-law. Bill Whitney's first marriage to a Dorothea Ludington ended in divorce in 1936; in 1939 he married the English actress Adrienne Allen, who had just divorced actor Raymond Massey. The first Mrs. Whitney then married Massey the same year.
3. C. Parsons thinks reference might be to Danville, Vermont, where some of Martin's relatives had settled; G. Audette thinks more likely a small mountain town in Virginia or Kentucky, since Martin was in North Carolina, hence more likely to have known of such events occurring in the South.

father and shot him dead. The shooter's wife testified in his behalf. An ignorant judge might have charged the jury thus: "The son-in-law carried a gun when he went to visit his father-in-law, who had already told him that he never wanted to see him. The father-in-law, instead of welcoming the youth with any fatted or other calf, approached him in a threatening way with a 'rock' and told him to leave. Drawing a gun or a knife or a sand bag may be a threatening gesture, but, in the South, threatening a man with a rock if very much like tapping him on the wrist with a feather." In vain did the prosecutor tell the jury that the dead man, a dentist named Keen, was "prominent" and a relative of Lady Astor's.[4] The result was not affected by the fact that the jury felt, as I do, that Lady Astor and most of her relatives are superfluous. The jury kept their eyes clearly on the main issue and, because fathers-in-law are ferae naturae,[5] in ten minutes, brought in a verdict of "not guilty."

In Atlanta, Ida Hughes shot her mother-in-law, who had already made Ida's life unendurable, "as the old woman was rummaging through a trunk in the daughter-in-law's home in search for clothing she claimed was her own." The jury knew the unwritten law. Ida was convicted of murder and sentenced to execution and will be imprisoned for life.[6] These two precedents indicate, accurately, the practical view taken by the law.

A woman in Tennessee, has just begun to serve a life sentence for undue thoroughness, in killing both her father-in-law and mother-in-law. If she had consulted an intelligent lawyer before hand [sic], he would have said, "Shoot the old man and let the old woman live."

Last Sunday, near Pilot Mountain,[7] Case Jester was killed by his son-in-law. The son-in-law broke the old man's head with his gun. It is known that the son-in-law will not suffer any annoyance for thus ending a domestic disagreement.

Newell Martin

---

4. Nancy Witcher, Viscountess Astor (1879-1964). Became first woman Member of Parliament in 1919; was a lifelong champion of women's causes and of temperance. A member of the Christian Science Church, which advocates abstinence from both alcohol and tobacco. Her first significant action in Parliament was to introduce and carry through a bill raising the British minimum drinking age to 18.
5. Latin: "of a wild nature."
6. The incident occurred as described in December, 1923; the mother-in-law was in fact under the protection of two police officers at the time. Sentence was lightened in view of the fact that Ida was held to have been in a state of violent mental perturbation. Her husband, Frank, also was indicted but was not convicted.
7. About 60 miles northwest of Southern Pines, NC.

# Recommendation for Schuyler M. Meyer, Jr. from Phelps

*Professor William Lyon Phelps' recommendation, according to the postcard he sent Martin, read in part, "I know the boy's father as well as his grandfather & love them both." In his 1939 autobiography he wrote a stirring tribute to Martin's brother, Winfred Robert. See "Pleonasm or Crime?"; and Section Seventeen — "Phelps Tribute to W.R. Martin."*

February 15, 1937.

Dear Bill:

I have one grandson, a freshman at Yale, Schuyler M. Meyer, Junior. He earnestly desires to be admitted to Pierson College. His mother asked me to write a letter to some powerful person in New Haven, asking such a person to use his power in granting this favor or in persuading some other potentate to grant to this young man this favor. I tried to beg off from asking this boon. I said "This would have been easy when Arthur Hadley[1] was president and when I knew troops of people at New Haven. But I am 82 and have outlived everybody that knew me." But the whole family frowned on me and condemned me, fiercely, and said "You must appeal to somebody; even to somebody that despises you or to somebody that hates you or to somebody that does not know you. Surely, there is somebody that has forgotten you. Appeal to him. If you love your grandson, at least do that." So I appeal to you. My grandson was prepared at Exeter. He is diligent and friendly and easy to live with and his manners are good and his morals and conduct are, I am sure, far better than mine ever were. I have no right to ask for anything. I enclose a form of letter which indicated what I think you have a right to say. If you sign that, it will be all I ought to ask. (All the trouble in Europe is caused by old people who wish this and that for their grandchildren.)

Affectionately,

*Newell Martin*

Dear Newell:

You have no right to ask me for anything. Moreover, no man

has a right to ask me for anything. I have retired. I am told that in old Japan men used to retire at 45. Inkyo was the word for it. If a man asked a retired Samurai to exert himself or to stir about or to grant favors, the petitioner was loathed as a contriver of atrocities. I am Emeritus. Millions of Americans know that, if you do not. Emeritus means that I have fought the good fight and have done with labor. The rest of my days I can spend in high thought and delightful studies. I do not have to grant favors or exert myself. No man should ask me to consider the merits of any freshman or to promote the welfare of any freshman or to admit any freshman to any paradise or to say or write anything for anybody. No man should ask me to lift a finger, or my voice, or my pen, or even an eyebrow, for anybody be he freshman or philosopher. I have published books, for your enlightenment, and you have read them; but that does not justify you in interrupting my contented study of other men's books. Nothing justifies you in appealing to me to do something to increase the happiness of your descendants.

Yours Contemptuously and Indignantly,<br>
Wm. Lyon Phelps,<br>
An Instructor in English.

ta ta ta

## Pleonasm Or Crime?
[July 20, 1927]

*Granddaughter Molly and Professor Phelps stand convicted of either a redundant construction or a violation of the 18th Amendment. But we suspect Martin put the Usher's and other cereal on the table himself, after first removing the fruit.*

Six of my granddaughters breakfast with me, every Wednesday. After breakfast we have family worship, worshipping with readings, Fowler's Usage,[1] Professor William Lyon Phelps[2]

---

1. *Dictionary of Modern English Usage* (1926) by lexicographer Henry Watson Fowler (1858-1933).
2. William Lyon Phelps (1865-1943; Yale '87; Ph.D '91): Scholar and educator, taught English at Yale 1892-1933. Introduced the study of contemporary literature to America. Yale's most popular teacher, America's most popular literary oracle.

and the Society for Pure English.[3] This morning little Duodecima[4] came late, when everybody else was busy with waffles, karo, popovers, muffins, buckwheat cakes and other food. "Hurry Mary," she shouted, "Hurry with my cereal." "Is it in vain," said I, "that I spend my last days in trying to purify your English? Everything on this table is a cereal, except the coffee, the cream, the maple syrup, the herrings, the bacon and eggs and the marmalade. The Usher's Vatted Glenlivat[5] is a cereal and so is the toast. When you mean porridge, say porridge."[6] This afternoon Duodecima came to me, with triumph in her eye and a Scribner's Magazine of last autumn in her hand. "Other Gomby, you have slipped a cog. Here, Dr. Archibald Marshall[7] says that the ideal breakfast begins with 'Cereal and Toast' and Dr. William Lyon Phelps, on the same page, also talks about 'Cereal and Toast'."[8] "No, my dear," said I, "when Billy Phelps says that he begins his breakfast with cereal and toast, he means whisky and toast."

*Martin sent the following grammar exercise to Phelps:*

A TEST FOR STENOGRAPHERS.

Vincent de Wierzbicki[9] put to me this problem in grammar: The drawing-rooms of the princesses of Egypt were as

---

3. The Society for Pure English was organized in 1913 by English poet Robert Bridges (1844-1930), who became in that year the British poet-laureate; after poetry, the Society was thenceforth Bridges' chief public interest. Its members included G. B. Shaw, H.C.K. Wyld, Henry Bradley, Sir Walter Raleigh, Dame Rose Macaulay, Lord David Cecil, Lady Cynthia Asquith, Logan Pearsall Smith, and I.A. Richards. The Society regularly issued tracts proposing standardizations, alterations, clarifications of English usage. It passed out of existence during WWII.

4. Twelve-year-old Molly.

5. A premium single-malt scotch from the famed Glenlivet region. [Researcher's note: "Would have required a very classy bootlegger to be present on anyone's breakfast table in 1927."]

6. The OED does not give equivalence to cereal/porridge; American dictionaries do.

7. Archibald Marshall (1866-1934), prolific minor British novelist. (Honorary Litt.D. from Yale)

8. Actually the January, 1927, issue, p. 98. Phelps had a regular Scribner's column, "As I Like It," in which he discussed chiefly new books and other literary matters, but also just about whatever suited. The preceding October column, Phelps had quoted a letter from one Robert Hyde complaining of his inability to find both fruit and cereal among the vast number of combinations on American club breakfast menus, and that column had caused an overwhelming readers' response — some 3,700 letters. When he returned to the subject in his January column, Phelps again spoke only of "fruit and cereal"; then went on to quote a passage on breakfasts from Archibald Marshall's recent novel *The Allbright Family* (1926). The one sentence Martin might have been using comes from that quote, " 'In the manner of cereals, hot breadstuffs, fruit, abundance of cream, and, it may be added, in the excellence of their coffee, the American leave us beat, and cannot be complained of if they prefer their breakfasts to ours'."

9. Vincent de Wierzbicki (1869-1935), French count and statesman attached to the French High Commission in Washington, D.C. during WWI; lecturer on literary, musical, and artistic subjects.

familiar with the miracles of Moses as the Athens of Pericles was with the beauty of Venus or as the Court of St. James is with the philosophy of Bergson.

The pupil is asked to change the sentence, as follows, using the possessive case, and filling in the blanks:"

Egypt's ... drawing-rooms were as familiar with ... miracles as ... Athens was with ... beauty or as is St. ... Court with Bergson's philosophy.

I, in these wilds, would write it thus: "Egypt's princesses' drawing-rooms were as familiar with Moses' miracles as Pericle's Athens was with the Venus's beauty or as is St. James's Court with Bergson's philosophy."

I showed this puzzle to Mrs. Benjamin Walworth Arnold [wife of an Albany industrialist; nee Elizabeth van Rensselaer], and she answered thus:

"I am not at all cultured or wise, I have never yet taken a prize: And as for my S's, They're nothing but guesses; Ask some one who lisps to advise."

*[Phelps appended: "I do not agree with Mr. Martin's punctuation. I invariably write Pericles's, Moses's, etc."]*

Newell Martin.

ta ta ta

# Recommendation for Molly to Stokes
[Oct. 19, 1937]

Dear Molly

I am planning to draft a letter, (which I shall never send) to an aged publisher,[1] saying,

"It is not right for me to ask you to see, at your office, any of my descendants.

"Your doctor probably tells you to refuse to see any unemployed young people.

"I am afflicted with a granddaughter who has recently

---

1. Frederick A. Stokes. See Section Ten - "A 1922 Christmas Card."

immerged [*sic*] from Bryn Mawr. Some people there have made much of her and she showed, there, that she is diligent and has a good mind. I would be grateful if you would say that you would see her some time at your office.

"I have told her that in all probability you made a resolution when you were 75, never to see, at your office, any unemployed person. I have told her also that Horace Greeley, once a noted American, said, "of all horned cattle, deliver me from college graduates."[2]

*h. m.*

*What follows is a two-page typed letter addressed to Frederick A. Stokes, Esq. with a note in the left corner in Martin's handwriting: "This is a copy of a letter that has been mailed." And a further note, "This copy is to be sent to Molly Meyer 39 E 78."*

November 26, 1937.

Dear Fred:

Before this, perhaps, my granddaughter, Molly Meyer, will have called on you. I am fond of Molly. She was born while I was in Hawaii or thereabouts. I had made all my plans for spending a few weeks on Mauna Loa[3] and Haleakala.[4] My wife, however, was so anxious to see Molly that she hurried me away from the islands before I could see those wonders.

I have told Molly much to hold her back from troubling you:--

1. "Your grandmother and I," said I to Molly, "have shown that we would rather see Molly than see the most majestic of mountain views, the most tremendous of volcanoes. But Mr. Stokes is different. He would rather see one volcano, any volcano, than any nice young girl.["]

2. Molly was beloved by the best people in Bryn Mawr and was diligent in college; and still is industrious. Molly has traveled,

---

2. "You ask me if female reporters and correspondents are employed on the Tribune. They are. Miss Dunning writes the fashion reports; Miss Kate Field occasionally sends a letter; Miss Booth frequently vouchsafes a readable article; Miss L. G. Calhoun writes sparkling correspondence, and Olive Logan occasionally bubbles over from the Magazine into the Weekly Tribune. Year before last Mrs. Calhoun reported the grandest city balls, and her descriptions of the Arion and Liederkranz carnivals attracted great attention." A.J. Cummings, quoted by L.D. Ingersoll in *The Life of Horace Greeley* (Philadelphia: Potter, 1874).
3. Volcano, south central Island of Hawaii
4. Dormant volcano, East Maui Island, Hawaiian Islands.

in Brittany, Montana, Germany, Denmark and many other places. Molly has 4 times as much polish and sense as I had when I came out of college. I have told her, however, that your reception room is constantly crowded and cluttered with young women of education, learning, beauty, wisdom, and polish; and that your secretaries are worn out with the labor of driving them off into outer darkness.

3. I have told Molly that another depression has struck this shuddering planet; and that, in bad times, men slowly learn to deny themselves necessaries. They turn away, reluctantly, from what they need; but always in alphabetical order, forsaking and forswearing

First, books,
Then, charity,
and, after that,
church,
clothing,
food,
newspaper, &
whisky.

4. I have read, with great interest, published reports of the commiseration publicly showered on you when you became 80. I have told Molly that, undoubtedly, your physicians, experts in gerontology, have told you that you may go to your office, daily, but that, in your office, you must leave to others all the disagreeable work, such as seeing unemployed young women.

To all this Molly has answered, in effect: "I agree with you. I know that Horace Greeley said 'Of all horned cattle, deliver me from college graduates, -especially women graduates.' I know that there is no place in Germany for women looking for work and that there are few places for such women in America. But if a man 83 years old cannot arrange an interview, a harmless amicable interview, between his favorite granddaughter and his oldest friend, then my professors did not tell me half the story when they told me that the world is cold and overcrowded."

It would be delightful if you would say: "Molly, I remember your grandfather. I will not see you at the office, but I will see you once, or twice or three times, at lunch time. You may call, at such and such a time, and take me, in a cab, to lunch."

It occurs to me that I may venture even farther. From the time of my collapse, in April, for 6 or 7 months, I was shut up as it were, on this island and never saw New York. But this affair seems important. Would you be willing to let me call and could you be persuaded to go out with Molly and me; and then you, if you could endure her conversation, could appoint a day for further adverse criticism of her and of this world.

Affectionately,

*Newell Martin*

*A second letter was written to Molly apropos a visit to another publisher and Martin friend; we quote a portion.*
Dear Molly,

3. With heroic enterprise you went to see a publisher, one Shuster.[5] I hear that he said to you something like this: "My office is over run with intelligent, highly educated women. I advise you to go into the book business, on your own account. You will then learn, from experience, how hard it is to tell nice young women that you have no place for them in your office."

You should have run your eye over some of Shuster's writings before you went to see him.

Remember this: Most publishers have been authors. They never refer to their own books.

But, in some mysterious way, an author always knows it, if his visitor never heard of the author's books.

If I ever give you a letter to a publisher, remember this & glance over some of his books, before you go to him.

*N. M.*

≈ ≈ ≈

---

5. See Section Ten - "As to W. Morgan Shuster." He wrote but one book, *The Strangling of Persia*.

# A Summing Up

*[Editor's Note: Also included with Molly's papers is the following undated typewritten comment by Martin.]*

No observer more accurate, no reporter more conscientious than Maugham. When he tells about life and Englishmen he is sure; cocksure. The Summing Up - W. Somerset Maugham - Doubleday - Page 139.

"Anthony and Cleopatra has always been the least popular of Shakespeare's greater plays. Audiences have felt that it was contemptible to throw away an empire for a woman's sake. Indeed it it were not founded on an accepted legend they would be unanimous in asserting that such a thing was incredible."

Perhaps it was on the very day on which Maugham was writing these sensible words that Edward VIII abandoned the greatest empire the world has yet seen, for his love of a young woman from Baltimore.

The Summing Up - W. Somerset Maugham - Doubleday - Page 288.

"If I found life intolerable, I think I should not lack the courage to quit a stage on which I could no longer play my part to my own satisfaction. I wonder why so many people turn with horror from the thought of suicide. To speak of it as cowardly is nonsense. I can only approve the man who makes an end of himself of his own will when life has nothing to offer him but pain and misfortune. Did not Pliny say that the power of dying when you please is the best thing that God has given to man?"[1]

Publishing such remarks is probably a breach of the law of several states.

Caveat; Doubleday.

ݢ ݢ ݢ

---

1. Full sentence reads: "Did not Pliny say that the power of dying when you please is the best thing that God has given to man amid all the suffering of life?"

# TEN

# FRIENDS

A 1922 Christmas Card .......... 284

Facts, as to Dr. A.T. Osgood ....... 289

Seconder's Letter for
    Pell W. Foster .............. 295

On Behalf of
    George Corning Fraser ....... 297

As to W. Morgan Shuster ......... 304

Memorial of
    Charles Robinson Smith ...... 309

The Climenole ................ 313

# A 1922 Christmas Card

*Virgil guides yet another wayfarer through Hell and Purgatory. Martin presumably never having encountered his Beatrice, Heaven is only envisaged, but the vision leaves no doubt that the elect will include several of Martin's friends, and one in particular. Frederick A. Stokes[1] (1857-1939; Yale '79), briefly studied law, then entered Dodd, Mead & Company, subsequently forming his own publishing house bearing his name. During his tenure as head of the firm, he published the works of such famous authors as H.G. Wells, Stephen Crane, Robert E. Peary, John Masefield, General John Joseph Pershing, James Branch Cabell, and W. W. Jacobs. His firm was the first in the United States to publish the writings of Maria Montessori, and specialized in childrens' and educational works.*

*At one time Stokes was chairman of the American Publishers Copyright League. He deprecated book clubs as economically unsound and detrimental to the welfare of established bookselling outlets.*

*Stokes was president of the American Publishers Association from 1911-14, and first acting president of the National Association of Book Publishers. Family members are not sure, but believe that Other Gomby's pamphlets may have been printed courtesy Fred Stokes. Just a year out of Yale, Stokes authored and had published* College Tramps, *subtitled: "A Narrative of a Party of Several Yale Students During a Summer Vacation in Europe with Knapsack and Alpenstock and the Incidents of a Voyage to Rotterdam and Return, Taken in the Steerage" (N.Y.: W.W. Carleton, 1880).*

*Like Martin, Stokes was a member of the Century and University Clubs in New York City.*

*"A 1922 Christmas Card" is a six-page booklet (5" X 7") and contains both text and an appendix.*

To commemorate the winter solstice and to celebrate, in our sober, modern way, the Saturnalia,[2] I send you wishes for a Cheerful Christmas and a Comparatively Harmless New Year: and also this innocent fantasy. Christmas is a day for thanksgiving and praise.

---

1. See Section Nine - "Recommendation for Molly to Stokes."
2. The Roman festival of Saturn, held in December, was, according to the OED "observed as a time of general unrestrained merrymaking, extending even to the slaves."

Both are herein set forth, as to one of our friends, whose behavior is such that it reminds me of Kon Fu Tze's [Confucius'] picture of the Superior Man. The stationers, for Christmas cards, sell lithographs of spotless snow scenes. For a Christmas card, accordingly, I write of a man whose conduct is as spotless as his bald head.

Virgil, the other day, was so kind as to take me on a personally conducted tour, through Sheol [hell]. He was grumpy. "Any prosaic modern tourist," said he, "is a come-down for me. I used to be courier for Milton and Dante.[3] Dante gave me good advertising. The whole job is a come-down. Hell, heaven and purgatory are not what they used to be. To quote one of your philosophers, they never were. From the first, they were disorderly, theological, illogical. Of course, because they were hastily constructed by Alexandrian priests, at the request of Roman capitalists, slave-owners, who saw a profit in offering, to their credulous thralls, rewards and punishments in the next world instead of better food in this world. The poets improved these places a little. But now this region has yielded to the spirit of the time and been standardized. Let's begin with the Accountancy Department." Virgil then led me, over a bleak, granite ridge, to a vast plain, covered, to the horizon, with dreary gray office buildings. "Guess what this is," said he. "The hell," said I, "for people who lived in Brooklyn. Or perhaps it is their heaven." "No, this is purgatory. The Chief Recording Angel got his job, as a sinecure, through influence, before the Fall of Man. Later, he got tired of recording crime and cruelty and persuaded Jahveh to drown the human race. That scheme miscarried and the Recording Angel's task became unendurably burdensome. He offered fat bribes to various devils in hell to change places with him, but in vain. Then he went again to Jahveh and said: 'All these people in purgatory are idle, wasting the centuries. Lend them to me." That worked. He set up this book-keeping department and now the Purgatorians do the recording." We entered one of the enormous structures. Through a multitude of pipes, small carriers, like those used in pneumatic tubes,[4] poured into the shop in ceaseless streams. In each was the story of some kind act or some fault. Thousands of Purgatorians were at work receiving, classifying, computing, filing, and making

---

3. Virgil, in the *Inferno*, and most of *Purgatorio*, appears as Dante's guide, but Martin, once again using a self-awarded literary license, stretches the point for *Paradise Lost*, perhaps leaning on the Virgilian character of the songs and discources in Bk. II, 11.547.69.

4. Before the days of electronic message delivery, to move paper through stores (from sales counter to business office) and businesses (between departments on different floors of the same building), air-driven packets were shot through connecting pipes or tubes.

entries. The walls shook with the clatter and din of machines, adding machines, billing machines, charging machines, multiplying machines, computing machines, machines for subtracting and for striking balances. In myriads of huge, loose-leaf ledgers were inscribed the results, debits in black, credits in gold. Numberless receivers that had come in too fast for the workers, lay in heaps. Virgil explained that such confusion did no harm. "We have time to burn", said he, "Millions of years. Everything will be duly entered. And there is a premium for making note of golden deeds. Any Purgatorian that has made note of six good deeds is released at once to Paradise. This lets out half a dozen every year. There is fearful competition, log-rolling intrigue, for the privilege of working on a good man's ledger." Virgil showed me a worker, who, by tremendous effort, had got a place on Deb's ledger,[5] and had then been shoved back by the pressure of the crowd, and there he was, working on Daugherty's ledger and looking sick.[6] "See those monuments of evil", said my guide, pointing to Wayne B. Wheeler's book[7] and to those of Prohibitor Anderson and Pussyfoot Johnson,[8] and then to the book-stands that bore the names of Stiggins and Stolypin.[9] Huge piles of sombre ledgers, the open pages night-black with sins. Somewhere between Stiggins and Stolypin, on a golden stand, lay a golden ledger. Nobody was working on it. From its open pages blazed a blinding radiance. Virgil explained why no more entries were permitted in that book. "It is Fred Stokes's book. Good deeds used to come in for it, so fast, that too many Purgatorians got

---

5. Eugene V. Debs (1855-1926), American socialist leader who ran five times for president; was an advocate of industrial unionism and pacifism. Imprisoned in 1895 for violating a strike injunction at Pullman, Illinois, and again imprisoned in 1918 under the Espionage Act.
6. Harry Micajah Daugherty (1860-1941), lawyer and politician, appointed U.S. Attorney-General by Harding in March, 1921. Repeatedly accused in Congress of laxness in investigation of alleged wholesale profiteering and fraud connected with war contracts. At Christmas time, 1922, Daugherty was under investigation by the House Judiciary Committee. Was cleared the following month, but finally resigned at the request of Coolidge in March, 1924.
7. Wayne B. Wheeler (1869-1927), another lawyer and prohibitionist. Until 1917, was general counsel to the Anti-Saloon League; subsequently its legislative superintendent.
8. William Hamilton Anderson (1874-1959), New York State superintendent of the Anti-Saloon League. Convicted of and served a term for forgery in connection with League funds.
   William Eugene Johnson (1862-1945), known as the "Good Templar from Nebraska," spy and agent provocateur for the Anti-Saloon League.
9. Mr. Stiggins of *The Pickwick Papers* was, according to novelist Dickens, a "prim, red-nosed man, with a long thin countenance, and a semi-rattlesnake sort of eye — rather sharp but decidedly bad."
   Pyotr Arkadievich Stolypin (1862-1911), Russian premier 1906-1911, noted for ruthless suppression of opposition; was assassinated in Kiev.

released from labor; and St. Peter sent down a final memorandum, on a gold card, which was nailed to Stokes's ledger." I copied it. Here it is:

> Memorandum, sealed with the Fisherman's Ring: There is no sense in making any more entries in this book. They are all alike. I can't see why Stokes wishes to stay on an unworthy planet, wasting good deeds on mankind. As soon as he gets tired of his altruism, let no angel forget that this candidate is to be brought through my gate, in a special car, without any questionary or delay. I have reserved for him, Suite A, the south west corner of the second floor of Abraham's Bosom. He will find there music rooms, exactly four thousand books, lucidly indexed, vintage wines, sunny balconies, fragrant with orchids, roses and ferns, marble swimming baths, halos made to fit his shiny head, his favorite pipe, Small Olivaceous Fly-catchers,[10] Chinese servants, and every other appliance of Paradise.

Fastened to the card was a platinum sheath, set with an inscription in sapphires, which read thus: "Secret Orders for the Guardian Angel of the Inner Circle of the Elect."

A copy of those orders will be found in the Appendix.

### Appendix to the Stokes Christmas Card
*(The Secret Orders of St. Peter)*

At the first dinner, in the land of Great Rewards, Mr. Stokes' guests will be:

Will Carey,[11] Mark Twain,[12] Bill Law,[13] Simeon Ford,[14] David Haight,[15] and Barton Hepburn.[16]

---

10. While the small olivaceous flycatcher is a bird fairly common at lower elevations in the southwestern U.S., Martin may be referring, instead, to diminutive, olive-skinned, serving maidens.
11. Most probably William J. Carey (1869-1947), lawyer in New York City for a half-century.
12. Mark Twain (1835-1910). No reference connecting Twain to Stokes has been located.
13. William H. Law (1856-1915; Yale '78), lawyer and politician; onetime assistant tax collector for New York; represented New Haven in Connecticut State Legislature. Member, with Martin and Stokes, of the University Club.
14. Simeon Ford (1855-1933), manager, and subsequently proprietor, of the 700-room Grand Union Hotel in New York; retired in 1914. Described in the *National Cyclopedia of American Biography* as displaying "a pleasing personality, genial hospitality and scholarly mind, and a native bent for wit and humor. He attained national fame as an after-dinner speaker."

Perhaps Arthur Jackson[17] will come to us in time to be there. I have given orders that when Arthur crosses the Styx, he is to have no purgatory. He has suffered, on earth, enough injustice. Bill McElroy,[18] whose game has improved, will be there. There will also be a general, a judge and an admiral, of high repute in heaven. Not that we ever play eight in Heaven; or any greater number [i.e., any game requiring eight or more players]. Heaven, thank heaven, is not the Manhattan Club.[19]

But some of the others will wish to drop out, from time to time, for an hour, to enjoy the view. Penny ante, with the right men, is supernal bliss; but it is greater bliss, sometimes, to lean over the battlements of heaven and watch the torments of those who are roasting in hell: Sabbatarians, and Comstockers[20] and Torturers and Federal Detectives and Agents Provocateurs and Prohibitionists, and Jew-baiters, and also those who play too slowly. I remember that one of those slow players was playing, once, with some Americans, at the Hotel Adlon.[21] He was selfishly delaying the game, chiefly by verbosity and vacillation. There were 8,000 marks in the pot. He fussed about, keeping everybody waiting: and, before he got his bet made, the mark had gone down 300 points. Looking down into hell, the glorified saints will see there, also, all them that are noisy, and them that play too fast and them that despise the minor rules; among them, I grieve to say, my dear old friend Doc. Boz:[22] and them that speak out of turn and them that play with the joker and them that ask for one round more and them that insist on deuces wild.

ta ta ta

---

15. Dr. David L. Haight (1839-1918; Yale '60), member of the U.S. Sanitary Commission in 1862, and assistant surgeon at Douglas Hospital, Washington, DC, throughout the Civil War. He lived at the University Club from the time it was built until his death.
16. Alonzo Barton Hepburn (1846-1922), banker and philanthropist; president of the Chase-Manhattan Bank in 1904; was advisor to or member of numerous federal and state banking commissions. Of him the *National Cyclopedia of American Biography* says: "...sincere, gentle, modest, democratic and sympathetic; possessed a keen sense of humor and was straightforward and inflexibly honest in all his dealings."

---

17. Arthur Cornelius Jackson (1865-1941; Harvard '88), New York architect; member University Club. Did important work on the plans for the New York City Public Library.
18. Probably Dr. William H. McElroy (c. 1840-1918), onetime prominent newspaperman in New York and Albany; subsequently lecturer on literary, educational, and other topics.
19. Founded 1865, same year as the University Club. Prominent in the latter nineteenth century as headquarters of Democratic leaders. Birthplace of the Manhattan cocktail.
20. Followers of Anthony Comstock (1844-1915), American moral crusader; organizer of New York Society for the Suppression of Vice.
21. Famous Munich hotel (model for the Grand Hotel in the 1932 film of that title); reference is to the severe German inflation of the early '20s.
22. Dr. Nathan G. Bozeman (1856-1916; Yale's Sheffield Science School '82), like his father, Dr. Nathan Bozeman (1825-1905) an eminent New York gynecologist.

# Facts, as to Dr. A.T. Osgood[1]
[January 3, 1925]

*This pamphlet and the three which immediately follow were used to support applications for membership in the Century Association for four of Martin's friends: Alfred Osgood (19 years his junior), Pell Foster (8 years his junior), George Fraser (18 years his junior), and Morgan Shuster, (23 years his junior).*

*The Century Association was founded in 1847. Its charter states: "[The Association] shall be composed of [male][2] authors, artists, and amateurs of letters and the fine arts, residents of the city of New York and vicinity. Its objects shall be the cultivation of a taste for letters and the fine arts, and social enjoyment."*

*The Association occupied various New York City locations during the 19th century, but moved in 1901, to its permanent location on 43rd Street just off 5th Avenue.*

*Martin had become a member in 1900. These pieces clearly served as much to demonstrate his "cultivation of a taste for letters" as to recommend his friends.*

Dear Sirs:

Osgood is the sort of man that one would be glad to be marooned with, on a desert island, or in a wineless and therefore arid club. I desire his admission more earnestly than I ever desired anything else in connection with any club, more even, than I desire Romanee Conti and St. Marceux.[3]

I have been told that more good talk is heard in the Century than anywhere else between the Seine and the Chicago Drainage Canal. Someone may say, "You are urging us to admit into this enticing circle of conversation a man whose life has been spent on

---

1. Alfred Townsend Osgood (1873-1959; Yale '95), head of the department of urology at Bellevue Medical Center; professor of urology at New York University Medical School 1912-1936.
2. Excerpts from an article in the Sunday *New York Times* of November 27, 1988, some 141 years after the founding of the Association: "The current bulletin of the Century Association lists the first 20 women proposed for membership after the venerable club lost its long battle to keep them out... Now that the Century's doors have been opened to women, insiders say all but the most recalcitrant opponents in the about 1,900-member club are resigned to the prospect." [*Editor's note: We're sure that Martin, had he been a member in 1988, would have written a pamphlet, or possibly reissued "Wine and Women." See Section Two.*]
3. Romanee Conti: Cote d'Or burgundy, one of the most famous and exclusive of all wines, "with millionaires eager for every drop." St. Marceaux: Reims champagne. Now grouped under Chattelier.

subjects that cannot be mentioned in polite society." To this I answer: First: Osgood has pursued many humane studies outside of his specialty; and Secondly: The rules as to what we may be frank about are quaintly arbitrary. In a society in which some archaic persons, from unfathomable motives, still say "retire" instead of "go to bed", one acquires merit if he can be eloquent about chromosomes; and, even at dinners, a man in search of sympathy, may go far, without rebuke, in telling about the faults and prospects of his prostate gland.

Osgood is a good doctor. To me, a lawyer, standing in ignorant awe before modern science, a good doctor seems eligible to any group of artists and philosophers. A good doctor has to know much of many arts and sciences, and is apt to be particularly adept in the art of social intercourse. I myself would rather be here[4] when there are ten good doctors at the fireside than even when it is crowded with lyric poets. A lawyer naturally looks up to a doctor as to one who moves in a higher, purer air, a loftier ethic. The doctors surpass us in morals as well as manners. Consider the lawyers of this town. They heal not, neither do they cure. Yet not Solomon in all his glory had the income of one of these. When we lawyers teach law students, we fill our lectures with medieval bunk, and we seldom tell the students anything useful about the paths, crooked or straight, that led us up to wealth. We lawyers are smothering the American Commonwealth under a mattress of two million laws, on which we grow fat. Forty-nine bicameral gangs of lawyers perpetually make new laws. But the doctors use their scanty leisure in trying to teach all they know, to students, by lectures, clinics and books. When an old pestilence or a new one tends to enrich the doctors, the doctors search unceasingly to extirpate this source of profit. And the doctor's brightest dream is of a millennium in which all disease will be rooted out and little left for doctors to live on.

Osgood is a lecturer, fortunate above ordinary lecturers in the attentiveness of his students. Ordinarily, the more a lecturer on science unfolds the mysteries of Nature, the more his students fold their hands in slumber. But when Osgood lectures, he never lectures in vain. The human mind is constituted that it is alert whenever it is told anything about the domain that Osgood deals with in his lectures.

Osgood is a specialist, in a region that means much to philosophers, psychologists and men of imagination. Osgood is like

---

4. Presumably at the Century Association.

Stefansson.[5] In a dark and perilous tract of the Arctic Zone, where other explorers had already made their fame by brilliant adventure, Stefansson made himself at home, through skill and common good sense and power of thought. So Osgood has made himself a safe and honored guide in a much more perilous zone, in that important tract which the doctors call the G-U Tract.[6]

Osgood's education was begun and carried far by a father who was renowned for learning and for his mastery of many languages.[7] But, beyond what is known to most cultivated men, Osgood knows little of painting, except painting with iodine; and nothing of sculpture, except such carving as he himself does on the redundant figures of opulent elderly gentlemen. But his studies should make him more acceptable than if he were a dilettante. He is appropriate in the company of men whose thoughts are bent on works of imagination; for his specialty has made him a deep student of the scientific aspects of sex; and sex has to do with the origin of half our art and literature. I do not believe Freud when he maintains that even religion is nothing but the sublimation of thoughts of sex. Half our painting and writing will cease and the Century Club will close when the cold day comes that is foretold by J.B.S. Holdane;[8] the day when chemists and biologists, in laboratories, will see to the maintenance of the race; when sex will be as far away from our daily life as the central power house is from the electric light of this room. Then no Augustus Thomas[9] will write happy endings for his plays, no Robert Chambers will multiply romances.[10] Then the circulating libraries will have no trade except in the few , like Defoe and Stevenson and Jesse Lynch Williams,[11] who have known how to

---

5. Vilhjamur Stefansson (1879-1962), explorer of Arctic North America and Greenland.
6. Gastrourinary tract.
7. Howard Osgood (1831-1911; Harvard '58; M.A. '61; L.L.D. Princeton '94), Baptist theologian. Professor of Hebrew and church history at Crozer Theological Seminary 1868-1874; professor of Hebrew at Rochester Theological Seminary 1876-1901. Master of Hebrew, Greek, Latin, German, French, Sanskrit, and other ancient tongues.
8. John Burdon Sanderson Haldane (1892-1964), geneticist, biometrician, and popularizer of science. But cannot find any writings or statements by Haldene on "universal cold" or "universal entropy." Possibly Martin meant Arthur Stanley Eddington (1882-1944): physicist, and another popularizer of science, who wrote much on the subject.
9. Augustus Thomas (1879-1934), American playwright, author of staple 19th century popular stage pieces. Century Club member.
10. Robert Chambers (1865-1933), author and illustrator. More than 60 titles by 1930, including short fiction, historical adventure, sociological novels, verse, plays and children's books of the outdoors. He was a governor of the Century Club.
11. Jesse Lynch Williams (1871-1929; Princeton '92), prolific and versatile writer for more than 30 years; journalist for various New York City papers. Virtually all his stories, novels, and plays are full of women (e.g. "My Lost Duchess," "Remating Time," "They Still Fall in Love," "She Knew She was Right," "Why Marry?"), hence Martin must be speaking ironically.

write stories that hold our interest without having girls in them. A man with whom sex is a matter of science should be welcomed by men to whom sex is a source of art.

This Club is a home of diplomatists, statesmen and sages. Osgood, among such men, should be as much in his element as a trained nurse in hers, at the Sloane Maternity Hospital, because he is one of the specialists who qualify men for the final step, the highest grade in political power. In reading oriental history, you have noticed how inevitably power in Asiatic dynasties, Sassanids, Abbassides, Fatimides, Seljuks, Moguls, Mings, Tsings, tended to drift into the hands of eunuchs.[12] By a quaint historical parallel which has escaped the attention of publicists, in the West, under modern conditions, political power and economic power have tended to drift into the hands of old men who have been emasculated, having been deprived by modern skill of their prostate glands. In the little group of aged men, elder statesmen, who in 1919, held the world in their hands and made the Treaty of Versailles, the prostate gland was conspicuous by its absence. It is doubtful whether the Supreme Court, sacred palladium of our property, had, in 1924, any prostate gland whatever.[13] Among us, often, a quite ordinary man is thought to be worthy to give authoritative advice on peace or war or to be chairman of a board of directors, if he has become old and has graduated, without his prostate gland, from the operating table of some such surgeon as Osgood.

Osgood is no mean author. He has achieved the delightful distinction of making monographs that summarize with singular efficiency and completeness, the state of science in the field they

---

12. Sassanids: Last dynasty of native rulers to reign in Persia, c. 226–640 A.D.
*Abassides:* Line of Arabic rulers descended from Abbas, uncle of Mohammed, holding the caliphate from 749-1258.
Fatimedes: Family laying claim to the caliphate on the basis of alleged descent from Fatima, daughter of Mohammed; at one time ruled extensive territories in the East & South Mediterranean.
Seljuks: Subgroup of Turks who originally appeared in Iran in 10th century, becoming rulers of extensive territories (and occasioning the Crusades) by a victory over the Byzantine emperor at Manzikert in 1071.
Moguls: Moslem empire of India (1526-1857).
Mings: Dynasty of china (1368-1644).
Tsings: Ch'ing or Manchu Dynasty of China 1644-1912.
13. Allusion is quite probably to *Hester vs. U.S.*, a moonshine case decided by the Supreme Court in May, 1924, in which the Court found that the right of the government to secure convictions on the basis of evidence found on the defendant's premises but at some distance from his dwelling did not violate fourth Amendment guarantees against unreasonable search and seizure.

deal with. These monographs are no less literature from the fact that they are highly technical and for professional use and that they appear, not in separate bindings, but in surgical and medical encyclopedias and in the transactions of learned societies. Willard Gibbs' immortal work first came out in the proceedings of an obscure association in Connecticut.[14] Doctor Driver on Genesis, first came out in the Britannica.[15] I have read recently, the whole of one of Osgood's monographs, not without difficulty, as it is not written for the vulgar public. It deals with the obstructions and other horrors that befall a certain small obscure channel of the G-U Tract. And not all the prose and poetry ever written about the long and often tragic history of Hiddekel[16] and Euphrates, rivers of Paradise, have told me any such tale of grief and pain and terror. This small book, if it were distributed, in sufficient numbers, and at the right time and among the right people, would change the fate of society, as no man's book has ever changed it. If it could be read by all schoolgirls, surely girls would resolve never to have any female descendants.

Discreetly used, long ago, this one of Osgood's concise and learned little books would have materially affected and improved the course of history. On January 2, 4004 B.C., according to Archbishop Ussher[17] and the Reverend Straton,[18] Adam went to sleep , an optimist and a conservative, assured on high authority that the world was complete, and, like our constitution, in no need of amendment. He awoke with the dawn to see somebody that was better and more beautiful than Adam, a new woman, creation's ultimate achievement. In a moment, he revised his judgment as to his own place in the world, and changed his plans, with deplorable results. According to Milton, when the beasts came to Adam to be

14. Between 1871 and 1878, Josiah Willard Gibbs (1839-1903), professor of mathematical physics at Yale, produced three papers, perhaps the greatest achievement of his career, and in bulk approximately 1/3 of his published writing: (1)"Graphical Methods in the Thermodynamics of Fluids," (2)"A Method of Geometrical Representation of the Thermodynamic Properties of Substances by Means of Surfaces," and (3)"On the Equilibrium of Heterogeneous Substances." All were published in the *Transactions of the Connecticut Academy*.
15. Samuel Rolles Driver (1826-1914), English scholar, Regius professor of Hebrew and canon of Christ Church Cathedral at Oxford from 1883 to his death. His Genesis commentary appeared in 1904; his article "Adam" in the 9th (1878) edition of the *Encyclopedia Britannica*. See Section Two - "Coolidge and the Bible."
16. Biblical name for the Tigris River.
17. James Ussher (1581-1656), Calvinist theologian, chancellor of St. Patrick's Cathedral, Dublin, bishop of Meath, archbishop of Armagh, calculated from the Biblical genealogies a biblical chronology long accepted as authoritative.
18. John Roach Straton (1875-1929), pastor of the Calvary Baptist Church in New York City, which in 1923, acquired the first church radio station in the U.S. Trustee of the Anti-Saloon League and the Lord's Day Alliance. Fundamentalist.

named, they came, two by two, respectable and monogamous, and Adam, with profuse apologies, reminded the Creator that Adam was the only living celibate. Our ancestor thought that, although there were no clocks to watch, in the week-end hurry, something might have been forgotten. Be that as it may, I find nothing in Genesis to make me doubt Milton's statement that, the day before, Raphael walked with Adam in the Garden, arguing with him as to Presbyterian theology, and making predictions.[19] To that powerful seraph, limitations of time and space were as nothing. If the seraph had not been preoccupied with politics and with Lucifer's defeated attempt to set up an aristocracy, he would have been thinking about our welfare. It would have been easy for him, the best-informed of the angelic host, to cast his eye forward down the short corridor of human time and foresee everything. He would have said to himself, "Six thousand years hence, Osgood will write a compact book showing what perils attend the lives of the best of women. Adam is only two days old and is too young to marry. He is not fit to be entrusted with the welfare of a multitude of nice women. I will show him what tortures he will bring upon other people. I will throw a scare into him. I will translate to him Osgood's impressive monograph." If Raphael had done this, Adam certainly would have laid aside his boyish plan of founding a family. Then this would have been a wild and beautiful world, without women, and without clubs, sanctuaries in which men take refuge from women. It would also have been free from prolix, importunate letters.

Sincerely,

*Newell Martin*

※ ※ ※

---

19. Raphael tells the story of Satan's rebellion, and describes the order and history of creation in Books V-VIII of *Paradise Lost*, not walking in the garden but apparently seated at the table after dinner. He makes no predictions other than to point out that the weal and woe of all Adam's sons are in his hands. At the conclusion of the discussion (end Book VIII) Adam describes to Raphael the naming of the animals and his, Adam's, plea for what Milton calls union or communion, which therefore cannot have taken place the day following; i.e., a Raphaelian disclosure of Osgood's monograph would have come too late in any case. (Note from GA: "Eve, of course, had served dinner.")

# Seconder's Letter for Pell W. Foster[1]

December 1, 1923
To Edwin S. Jarrett, Esq.,[2] as a member of
the Committee on Admissions of the Century Association

Dear Jarrett

Molitor,[3] who has been trained to scientific accuracy, says, in his proposing letter, that Foster has an international reputation as an engineer. That is no exaggeration.

Molitor does not mean that Foster's solid reputation is like the fame of Pupin[4] and Baekeland:[5] but he does not mean that Foster is known, to men conversant with this branch of engineering, at home and abroad, for his admirable mind and for having done his full share of the world's work. His superheaters, over all the seas, have speeded up ships loaded with depth-bombs, missionaries, rum, standard oil and other necessaries.

Africa's sunny fountains are improved by his hydraulic devices.

In remote regions I myself have been drinking heavily, off and on, for many years, pure water raised by Foster's pumps.

The spicy breezes that blow over certain tropic cities would be quite vile, but for Foster's incinerators, which are "destructors", monstrous furnaces, so craftily designed that in fifty minutes one of them will transmute the sweepings of fifty streets into blue flame, gray ashes and white electric light.

---

1. Pell William Foster (1862-1947; Columbia '83), vice-chairman of the board of Foster Wheeler Co., NYC manufacturers; later director of U. S. Steel. Admitted to the Century Association.
2. Edwin Seton Jarrett (1862-1938), civil engineer; president of Jarrett-Chambers Co. 1914-1928; executive vice-president, later acting president of Rensselaer Polytechnical Institute 1935-1937.
3. Frederick Albert Molitor (1869-1938), civil engineer. Chief engineer in charge of construction of the Long Island Railroad (1895), subsequently chief engineer of the Choctaw, Oklahoma and Gulf Railroad. In private practice in New York City 1908-1933. Member Century Association.
4. Michael Idvorsky Pupin (1858-1935), American physicist and inventor, born in Yugoslavia. Associated with Columbia University. Famed for research in X-rays and invention of many electrical devices used in telegraphy and telephony. Member Century Association.
5. Lee Hendrick Baekeland (1863-1944), American chemist born in Belgium. Invented and manufactured photographic paper; invented Bakelite. Member Century Association.

Some, of your committee, may be old enough to remember how that fine old Centurion, Colonel Waring,[6] acquired merit by his masterly street cleaning and his part in reducing our death rate.

This is the sort of honor that Foster has earned. The Incinerator is civilization's housemaid.

Exploits in the destruction of rubbish should appeal strongly to a club that is full of critics. We have not enough destructors. How often one observes the need of an incinerator, in certain art galleries, or in the public library, or when one glances over a volume of presidential messages, of the adverse party.

It is not irrelevant to tell you that Foster is one of the twenty vestrymen who are charged with the great responsibilities of Trinity Church.[7]

That vestry is the best club in our town, not excepting the Century. Nobody is admitted there, until he has been tested to make sure that he is companionable, as well as discreet, capable, and devoted.

You justly welcome, as amateurs, men who aid, with their money or their influence, or their counsel, in the creation of works of art.

Foster is an amateur of that sort.

All the members of your committee, even those who have seldom seen the inside of any house of worship, should know the exquisite interior, unsurpassed in America, of the Chapel of the Intercession, at Broadway and 155th Street.[8]

The great chapel is the most distinguished of Trinity's Ten Churches. It and its beautiful attendant buildings are a delight to the eye and an inspiration for the soul. It is the ripe result of lives of artistic effort.

Its vicar, Dr. Milo H. Gates,[9] who is a high priest of beautiful church architecture, has consecrated to it I do not know how many years of creative design and aesthetic study.

6. George E. Waring (1833-1898), sanitary engineer. Colonel 4th Missouri Cavalry in Civil War. Began devoting himself to sanitary engineering in 1877; designed and executed sewerage systems in several major American cities. Commissioner of street cleaning in New York City 1895-1898. Member Century Association.
7. Located at Broadway and Wall Street, was the first Protestant Episcopal church in the United States, established by grant of Queen Anne in 1705. Parent of seven subsidiary chapels in New York, including St. Paul's Chapel and the Chapel of the Intercession.
8. The Chapel of the Intercession was completed in 1915. "With its chaste structural lines and the majestic height of its columns and ceiling, [the chapel] seems of cathedral stature," as one New York City guidebook enthuses.
9. Reverend Milo Hudson Gates (1864-1939), Episcopalian clergyman, vicar of the Chapel of the Intercession Trinity Parish, New York City, 1907-1930. Gates studied

Bertram G. Goodhue was its architect.[10]

Such an achievement depends for its success on the group of amateurs of art, lovers of architecture, who, in such a church, obey the artist and back him up and carry out his wishes and intelligently aid his artistic judgment and consult with him and direct the funds that are essential to his expressing his thought. Men that have thus served are efficient amateurs. Foster, who is one of the chief laymen of that church, is one of the group that thus served Goodhue and Gates and art.

For forty years I have been one of Foster's companions, in virtue and in vice, in business and in sport, in all parts of this island, from the Battery to Macomb's Dam bridge[11] (whose sacred name commemorates one of Foster's ancestors), and in forest camps and at sea and in canoes on rapid rivers; and he has persuaded me that he is always the sort of man that Centurions like to have about them.

Most sincerely

Newell Martin

❧ ❧ ❧

# On Behalf of George Corning Fraser

*George Corning Fraser (1872-1935; Princeton '93; L.L.B.. George Washington '95) and Martin were related through the marriage of Martin's son, Grinnell, to Fraser's daughter, Myra. A lawyer by training and profession and an amateur geologist of considerable ability, Fraser first practiced law in Washington from 1895-1901; then from 1901 to his death in New York City as a*

---

church architecture extensively in Europe, and not only supervised the construction of the Chapel of the Intercession, but planned, designed, and built St. Stephen's Church in Cohasset, Mass., and established the carillon in its steeple. He also designed several other Episcopal churches, and was advisor on the construction of some 800. Did much, as well, to familiarize Americans with carillon music.

10. Bertram Grosvenor Goodhue (1869-1924), American architect noted for an individual style in ecclesiastical design; "Gothic in form but modern in spirit." His ashes are interred in a memorial wall tomb of the Chapel of the Intercession. Member Century Association.

11. Spans Harlem River in North Manhattan at 161st Street and River Avenue, on site of a dam erected in 1813 by Robert Macomb, who operated a mill. The dam was torn down in 1838 by New York City citizens demanding free passage of the river.

*member of Fraser, Speir, Meyer and Kidder, the firm established by Martin's son-in-law, Schuyler Merritt Meyer. Fraser was a director of the Tri-Continental Co. and Woodlawn Cemetery. And was admitted to the Century Association in 1923.*

*The printed five-page pamphlet (5" X 8") bore the following note, underlined and in bold type:* **CONFIDENTIAL: Edition Limited to One Copy; Printed to Save Jarrett's Time.**

November 4, 1922.

Dear Jarrett:

Everybody is sorry, always, for the anxious candidates who are pilloried on the list that you hang in the hall of our club.

They seem like immigrants, from Philistia, eagerly seeking your permission to enter our prosperous commonwealth. You might write, at the head of that list, "Detained for examination on our Ellis Island."[1] On behalf of one of those candidates, in whom I am most deeply interested, I venture to submit an inadequate and unauthorized portrait, of him, as he seems to me.

George Fraser is such a man as one delights to meet in a club or a forest camp or in any other comfortable place. He is free from all those dreary faults that so often make tiresome bores out of successful and prosperous men.

He is wise and prudent and judicious, a man of almost infallible judgment; but he is modest, sympathetic, entertaining and companionable. He is a man of learning and a man of the world, but he is quite unconscious of his accomplishments. He has a talent for friendship and a habit of doing good, by stealth, to them that need help.

When our country was at war, he labored earnestly, in Washington, in the government's railway law department, at much cost to himself, without spurs or shoulder straps, without glory and without pay, and with no reward but the consciousness of having done his duty.

Fraser's father, who died about thirty years ago, was a member of the Century [1892-1896] and a lover of the club. A place in the Century is more to be desired than rubies and is more precious, to a right-minded man, than any ordinary earthly glory or happiness, and, therefore, cannot be acquired by inheritance. But, other things being equal, you are inclined to be kind to the sons of

---

1. Island in Upper New York City Bay, one mile southwest of the tip of Manhattan. From 1892 to 1943, the principal reception center for immigrants to the U.S.

our former comrades. For instance, you will rejoice, by and by, in admitting the sons of Edward B. Whitney[2] and Willard Straight.[3] Some of the intellectual aristocrats of the year 2050 will say, "We have been Centurions for five generations." I shall be grateful indeed if you can begin such a chain of honor for the Frasers.[4]

It is a matter of public record, also, that Fraser pays dues to the Metropolitan Club of Washington, the University, the City Midday, and eight other clubs.[5] This is mentioned merely to show that eleven committees of admission have approved of him and his family, and that he has had a preliminary club training that tends to fit him for admission to your society.

Fraser's chief fault is that he is a lawyer and of an enviable position in his profession. But he is not obtrusively a lawyer; and one can associate with him for days, without hearing of this blemish. He does not advertise his office or his efficiency, either in public or in private.

Perhaps you will say to me, "Fraser may be the most lovable of lawyers; but is he an amateur?" "Amateur" is an unpleasant, though necessary, word; and a man must hate to hear himself publicly described as an amateur. But Fraser is an amateur in two arts; the art of geology and the art of education.

You are justified, by a long line of your own precedents, in regarding these two sciences as arts, for the purposes of your committee. I am told that you are not bound, as to amateurs, by any rigid rule, so long as you follow a general policy that will keep our club from becoming a mere habitat of such competitive persons as desire membership in it chiefly as a mark of success.

2. As proof of Martin's prescience, William Dwight Whitney, (1899-1973), an eminent New York City and Washington lawyer, eldest son of Edward B. Whitney, did in fact become a Century Association member in 1939.
3. Willard Straight (1880-1918), American diplomat. His parents were missionaries to Japan and China; he accompanied them there and learned the languages "like a native." From 1901-1904, he served in Robert Hart's Chinese Imperial Maritime Customs Service at Nanking and Peking. Was consul general at Mukden (Shenyang) from 1906-1908; acting chief of the Division of Far Eastern Affairs 1908-1909; representative in China of the American Group (banks) from 1909-1912. During WWI was in charge of organizing the overseas administration for the War Risk Insurance Bureau. Had two sons, neither members of the Century Association. Whitney Willard (1912- ?) and Michael (1916- ?). Member Century Association from 1914-1918. (Straight married Dorothy Whitney, daughter of the well-known financier and secretary of the navy William C. Whitney. Dorothy and the Edward B. Whitney mentioned above had a common ancestor at eight generations removed.)
4. First generation: George S. Fraser, member 1892-1896. Second generation: George Corning Fraser, made a member in 1923. Third generation: George C. Fraser II (1897-1974; Princeton '20) became a member in 1937. Fourth generation: George C. Fraser III and Thomas T. Fraser, who did not become Century Association members.
5. Among them, the Princeton, Grolier, and Morris County Golf.

It has become your custom to disregard the vague and worn out boundaries that used to lie between science and art. You now welcome lovers of systematic and liberal knowledge and lovers of the beauties and mysteries of nature almost as warmly as those who love especially the beauty that is wrought by men's hands.

It is true that, in the far off days when the Century was founded, it was meant to be a club in which painters and writers and sculptors could meet, in a sacred fellowship, to drink hot spiced rum; and in which we would admit, also, a few amateurs, who knew how to praise our paintings and carvings. But we have widened the circle of the arts that make their devotees admissible; and you admit as artists, men who excel in managing universities, in controlling political conventions, in commanding navies, and in engineering, architecture, preaching, surgery, astronomy, physics, botany and geology. Your committee hold that, in the scientific and constructive use of imagination and observation and in trained skills of brain, eye and hand, a Jacoby[6] or a Pupin[7] is a true artist.

Geology is an art that is, peculiarly, a province for amateurs. The science of geology was founded by amateurs. The Piltdown man[8] and the Magdalenian cave pictures[9] were discovered by amateurs. Fraser has, himself, developed an original solution of one of the difficult problems of geology.[10]

Scrope[11] and Lyell[12] were amateurs and one of them was a lawyer.

---

6. Harold Jacoby (1865-1932), astronomer; member Columbia faculty 1888-1929, director of the Columbia observatory 1906-1929. Popularizer; wrote books giving plain explanations of Einstein's theories. Century Association member 1892-1932.

7. Michael Idvorsky Pupin (1858-1935), American physicist and inventor, born in Yugoslavia. Associated with Columbia University. Famed for research in X-rays and invention of many electrical devices used in telegraphy and telephony. Century Association member 1910-1935.

8. The so-called Piltdown man's fossilized remains were found at Piltdown in England in 1912, and exposed as a hoax in 1953, some 31 years after Martin published this pamphlet. Charles Dawson, a Sussex solicitor and amateur geologist, who discovered the remains, is one of the prime suspects.

9. "Magdalenian" is a generic term embracing the final Paleolithic tool industry of the Pleistocene in western Europe, approximately 17,000-9500 B.C.; the name is derived from the site of La Madeleine in southwest France. The most famous Magdelenian cave pictures are those at Lascaux, discovered in 1940. Martin alludes here to the ones at Altamira in northern Spain, discovered by a hunter in 1868, but introduced to the world by the Spanish nobleman and amateur of geology Don Marcelino de Sautola, who visited them in 1875.

10. Unable to find a reference for this statement.

11. George Julius Scrope (1797-1876), British politician and geologist. Early authority on vulcanism; Member of Parliament 1833-1868; published a work on political economy in addition to his geological treatises.

12. Sir Charles Lyell (1797-1875), British geologist, advocate of the theory of uniformitarianism; i.e., that geologic forces operative in the past were wholly consistent with those of the present. Studied for the law at Lincoln's Inn and practiced briefly in the 1820's. Scrope and Lyell were among the founders of their profession.

Sir William Van Horne,[13] for fourteen years one of us, was a noble amateur of geology.

Fraser is a skilled amateur of geology. I have it from a professional geologist of rank that he has never met a more efficient geological amateur than Fraser. Fraser devotes his holidays to this art and seems to long for the time when he can give up all professional duty and turn entirely to science.

Education is an art, within the spirit of the rules that guide your committee. The presence among us, of troops of college presidents and professors proves this. Fraser has been diligent, under Princeton guidance, in the art of education.

None of you like a blatant alumnus, a "professional Princeton man", a man who has himself photographed as reclining in the bosom of his alma mater. Fraser is not such a man. He tries to serve his college secretly; but I venture to say, here, privately, what he would forbid if he knew of it.

In the art of education, Fraser has always been a devoted aid to Princeton College, one of that group of ardent, indefatigable graduates, without whom the Faculty's laborious lot would be hard indeed. Fraser, himself, would angrily and modestly disclaim this praise and would say: "I have done nothing but carry on correspondence with agreeable professors and trustees and convey spectators to college contests and enjoy the pleasures with which the college rewards her visitors." But there are Princeton men who can testify that, in serving his college, he has been unfailingly useful, and as quiet as a mole, in such instances as these:

Having been, in college. a "business manager" in athletics, he kept up his helpful interest in the work of such managers through a long series of college generations. He was among the founders and builders of the Cottage Club.[14] He had a discreet, influential, and

---

13. Sir William Cornelius Van Horne (1843-1915), railway executive; president of the Southern Minnesota Railway 1874-1877; general manager of the Chicago, Milwaukee, and St. Paul Railway 1882-1888, president 1888-1899; chairman of the board 1899-1910 of the Canadian Pacific Railway, which he had been in charge of constructing from 1881-1886. He also was in charge of constructing the Cuban Railway from 1900-1902. Had a lifelong interest in paleontology and a large collection of fossils. Century Association member 1904-1915.

14. Second-oldest of the famous Princeton eating clubs, founded 1887, which would mean that Fraser would have been no more than near the starting-point. Characterizing the various clubs in *This Side of Paradise*, F. Scott Fitzgerald described the members of the Cottage as, "an impressive melange of brilliant adventurers and well-dressed philanderers." The clubs have remained a source of contention, many — such as Princeton president Woodrow Wilson — viewing them as an agency for separating the social from the intellectual lives of the undergraduates and divisive among themselves.

peacemaking part in the ancient Princeton war between those who loved college clubs and those who hated them. He served for years as a member of the graduate council. He was useful as a helper and adviser of the builder of an important laboratory for mechanical and physical study and research. He helped in setting up a very practical sub-department in economics. When Palmer gave Princeton her stadium,[15] Palmer chose Fraser to be his adviser and aid; in which connection we may remember that, ever since the time of Herodes Atticus,[16] it has been obvious that the creating of a stadium requires thought and toil, as well as money. When Princeton has been in travail because too many men clamor for admittance to the college and for the services of her professors, because her professors are underpaid and overworked, because the demand for learning is too great and the price of learning is too low, supply and demand, both, seemingly, being excessive: in this dilemma, Fraser has done his part as one of the group that aid the Faculty and agree with them.

In these and in a hundred other ways Fraser has been a successful and useful amateur of the art of college life and college teaching and has rendered public service.

Princeton affairs are well known to members of your committee. Some one of them may say: "How is this? I never thought of Fraser as an artist in education, like Bill Roper[17] or Max Farrand."[18] That is exactly what I urge. In education he is not an artist. He is an amateur. The artists are those who sweat and suffer in the dust of the arena. The amateurs are the men, out of uniform, on the side lines.

Our club tends, inevitably, to become a museum of celebrities; but its primary aim is to be a resort of boon companions, rather than a place pervaded by chilly eminence and frosty virtue. Fraser has

---

15. Palmer Stadium, completed in 1914, at the cost of $300,000, was given by industrialist (president New Jersey Zinc Co.) and Princeton resident Edgar Palmer '03.
16. Herodes Atticus (c. 101-177 A.D.), orator and writer who became consul in 143; directed the construction of numerous buildings throughout Greece, notably the Odeum of Herodes Atticus at Athens.
17. William W. Roper (1880-1933; Princeton '02), Princeton football coach 1906-1908, 1910-1911, 1919-1929, and a practicing lawyer. Author of *Winning Football* (1921) *and Football — Today and Tomorrow* (1926).
18. Max Farrand (1869-1945; Princeton '91, Ph.D. '96), taught history at Wesleyan 1896-1901, Cornell 1905-1906, Stanford 1907-1908, Yale 1908-1925. Director of the general division of education of the Commonwealth Fund 1925-1927; later director of the Huntington Library. Century Association member beginning 1910.

the proper degree of virtue and a comfortable degree of eminence, but he is not frosty.

You would admit Rosebery[19] rather than gloomy Kitchener,[20] George Ade[21] rather than John S. Sumner.[22] Yet it may be said that, in our library, I could not throw an inkstand in any direction, without hitting a bishop, or the president of some pious corporation. Our club has already become a favorite prowling place of the princes of the church. If the ghost of Laurence Sterne[23] is in the way of hovering, as he should, about our fireplace, he has heard much to enlarge even his knowledge of dogmatic theology.

I pray you, therefore, to discriminate a little, now and then, in favor of those who are not prohibitionists or Sabbatarians, in favor of those who are pre-eminently sociable; lest we become a club in which Cotton Mather[24] would be more at home than Robert Louis Stevenson.[25]

Fraser is, I must confess, utterly respectable. I have known him for thirty years and I know and love his immensely popular family and his cousins and his uncles and his grandchildren; and they are all respectable; but, in spite of that, Fraser's heart is on the side of those who think we should be careful not to trample out any of the beauty and joy of life.

Although he is a pillar of a church, I have forgotten which, he longs for the lawful return of punch-bowls and vintage wines, and he believes in Sunday sports and he is convinced of the inspired origin of the Second Chapter of the Epistle to the Colossians.[26]

Most Sincerely,
Newell Martin

---

19. Archibald Philip Primrose, fifth Earl of Rosebery (1847-1929), leader of the Liberal Imperialist division of the Liberal Party 1895-1905. Described in the *Dictionary of National Biography*, in part, as "a born talker, varied, witty, and informed, master of ironic banter and humor, passing easily from light to shade, from gaiety to earnestness and appearing always to give his best."
20. Horatio Herbert Kitchener (1850-1916), British field marshal and imperial administrator. Conquered the Sudan after the Mahdi uprising, commander-in-chief during the Boer War, secretary of state for war from the start of WWI.
21. George Ade (1866-1944), prolific humorous, American author and journalist, best known for his *Fables in Slang* (1900).
22. John Saxton Sumner (1876-1971), New York City lawyer, secretary, following Anthony Comstock, of the Society for the Suppression of Vice 1915-1950.
23. Laurence Sterne (1713-1768), British clergyman best-known as the author of that archetype of literary whimsy, *The Life and Opinions of Tristram Shandy*.
24. Cotton Mather (1663-1728), Puritan clergyman and author notable for his participation in the Salem witch trials.
25. Robert Louis Stevenson (1850-1894), British novelist, poet, and essayist whose works were characterized by fantasy, whimsy, and romance.
26. Wherein Paul instructs the Colossians to beware of gnostic and ascetic philosophies, as verse 16, "Therefore let no one pass judgment on you in questions of food and drink or with regard to a festival or a new moon or a sabbath." And in verses 20-21, "Why do you submit to regulations, Do not handle, Do not taste, Do not touch?"

# As to
# W. Morgan Shuster

*This six-page pamphlet is undated (we make it 1928), and notes that its printing took place in Bermuda, as did the tract on "The Siamese Royal Commission" (see Section Six). We've been unable to find any evidence that the pamphlet was ever sent to the Century Association. We do know that W. Morgan Shuster was never a member of the Century Association.*

*William Morgan Shuster (1877-1960) was a government official and publishing executive. In 1916, he became president of the Century Co., and subsequent mergers made him president of the D. Appleton-Century Co. and of Appleton-Century-Crofts.*

*In 1910, the Persian government, on the verge of bankruptcy, appealed to President Taft for an able American to take charge of its exchequer, and Shuster was appointed on the basis of his accomplishments in the Cuban and Philippines customs services. Shuster also appears, in Section One — "Extracts from the 'Confessions of a Timid Old Man'."*

*But Persia was caught between British and Russian interests, and Shuster returned to the United States in December, 1911, and wrote a book about the experience.[1] When the British government cooperated with the Russians, refusing both the loan of a Major C. B. Stokes to head up the Persian tax-collecting force and millions of English pounds to help stabilize the economy, the Persian Nationalist government collapsed in the face of an armed Russian intervention.*

*Shuster viewed the whole affair as part of Russia's historic drive toward warm-water ports, and saw British accession to the Russian demands as caused by the threat of a Russo-German alliance.*

To the Committee on Admissions of The Century Association

Sirs:
On the fourteenth day of the month Adar, in each year, the Feast of Purim[2] halts the stupendous trade of New York. The most modern bankers and artists of the metropolis then make holiday,

---

1. *The Strangling of Persia* (New York: Century, 1912).
2. The Jewish Feast of Purim, commemorating the deliverance of the Persian Jews from

drinking Pommery,[3] of the vintage of 1915, and other sacramental wines, and rejoicing, because Haman, two thousand four hundred years ago, was fired from his great office of Treasurer-General.[4] The world quickly forgets dead dynasties and fallen ministers, but it is not yet permitted to forget Haman's misuse of power. So notable is it to be Treasurer-General of Persia. The inspired writer of the Book of Esther has made the story of Haman's disaster an imperishable classic of romance. With dignified enjoyment he tells of the hanging of Haman and how Ahasuerus devoted one hundred and eighty days to showing "the riches of his glorious kingdom."[5] The drinking, says the Bible, at the seven days banquet that wound up this display of splendor was from golden flagons and was of "royal wine in abundance, according to the state of the King."

It has been the rare adventure of an American to supplement one of the historical books of the Old Testament. The story of Shuster is a post-script to the Book of Esther. Shuster succeeded, after twenty-four centuries, to the office that was wrested by Mordecai from Haman.[6] As Treasurer-General, Shuster administered the "riches of the glorious kingdom" of Persia.

The incident would have been more dramatic if Shuster had been of Mordecai's race; but I must admit that Shuster, the modern successor of Mordecai, is a Gentile by birth, faith and descent, and that no Esther or Vashti[7] was mixed up with his work.

You, members of the Committee on Admissions, have always had a cordial welcome for adventurers. You delight in such Americans as visit the North Pole or fill in, with new facts, the blank spaces of our maps. You remember gladly the fame of young Ward,

---

a massacre (Book of Esther, Chapters 3 & 9), is celebrated on the fourteenth day of Adar, the twelfth month in the Jewish calendar, corresponding to February-March in our Gregorian calendar.

3. Pommery and Greno, a dry French champagne.

4. Ahasuerus is the Jewish form of Xerxes. Haman, highest official of Ahasuerus, ordered the slaughter of the Israelites for Mordecai's refusal to bow down to him. Queen Esther, the adopted daughter of her cousin Mordecai, saved her people at the risk of her own life by going to the king without being called, a fatal offense. The Jews then "smote all their enemies with the sword, slaughtering and destroying them, and did as they pleased to those who hated them." (Esther 9:5)

5. The banquet Ahasuerus gave for "all his princes and servants" is described in Esther I:1-9.

6. Mordecai, who had warned Ahasuerus of a murder plot near the beginning of the book, succeeds to Haman's office.

7. Vashti refuses to come "before the king with her royal crown, to show the peoples and the princes her beauty" at the banquet which opens the Book of Esther, and is deposed by Ahasuerus. She is succeeded by Esther.

of Salem, who in China, created the "Ever Victorious Army";[8] and of Count Rumford;[9] and the European and African careers of Hoover and Hammond.[10] With pride you observe that we have now another band of adventurers whose deeds would have seemed to us incredible if they had been foretold thirty years ago. They have conducted memorable and perilous exploits in foreign politics and finance. Israel Smith, Jr. has shown how should be used the power that belonged to the Hapsburgs.

*[Editor's Note: Not "Israel," but Jeremiah Smith, Jr. (1870-1935), lawyer and statesman. Practiced in Boston beginning 1896; served with the American Expeditionary Forces in France in WWI, and on the American Missions to Negotiate Peace as counsel to the Department of the Treasury. Hungary, on the verge of bankruptcy in 1924, asked the League of Nations for a loan. Some $150 million was granted on the condition that the League appoint someone to oversee disbursements. Smith, given the job, became virtual dictator of Hungary; his work proved so brilliant that he was able to turn the entire Hungarian economy around within two years while expending only a portion of the loan. On departing Hungary in 1928, he refused the $100,000 offered for his services, declining to accept even an honorarium. Only ill-health prevented him from becoming secretary of the United States treasury in 1933.]*

---

8. Frederick Townsend Ward (1831-1862), adventurer. Fought in South America and the Crimea 1848-1853; in 1859 went to Shanghai and organized a force, primarily of mercenaries and conscripts, to oppose the Taiping rebels at a stipulated sum in gold per liberated city. This force was called the Chun Chen Chun, the "Ever-Victorious Army," and under Ward's leadership it very nearly proved so. A brilliant military career ended when Ward died at 31 from a gunshot wound sustained in an attack on Tse-Kzi near Ningpo.

9. Benjamin Thompson, Count Rumford (1753-1814), American-British scientist and administrator, Count of the Holy Roman Empire. Born in Massachusetts, went to England in 1776, later served as an administrator to the elector of Bavaria. Introduced social reforms in England and Ireland; reorganized the Bavarian army. Introduced new methods of heating and lighting and developed a scientific theory of heat.

10. Herbert Hoover organized and headed the Commission for the Relief of Belgium (CRB) 1914-1919, which distributed some $900 million in aid, the monies coming from both personal and institutional gifts and government subsidies. The CRB came to possess its own transportation and distribution systems, and indeed some of the characteristics of an independent government; its inflexible integrity and neutrality earned the respect of all belligerents. From 1919-1923, Hoover headed the American Relief Administration supervising $400 million worth of food and medical supplies in postwar Europe, most notably in Russia 1921-1923.

John Hays Hammond (1855-1936; Yale '76; L.L.D. '25), American mining and electrical engineer. Hammond was director of Cecil Rhodes mining interests in South Africa 1894-1895, where he was responsible for opening extensive new gold fields.

Both Hoover and Hammond were Century Association members.

S. Parker Gilbert[11] preaches frugality from the city in which the last of the Hohenzollerns [German emperors] used to utter balder-dash. Professor Kemmerer[12] has guided the successors of Sobieski [John III, ruler of Poland 1674-1696] and, at the other end of the world, South American republics. Sayre[13] has made, in Siam, an achievement in constructive diplomacy. In Japan, through war and peace, Denison[14] held the confidence of the Meiji emperor and of the Elder Statesmen. And Shuster, for many dangerous months, held power in the empire that was once the terror of the Pharaohs and that set bounds to Roman ambition. Shuster was one of the precursors in this world-wide flight of vigorous young Americans, who have written so bright a chapter in our history. Each of them has shown enterprise, judgment, financial skill and economic wisdom. Any people should be proud of having sent out such a group of brilliant and beneficent ambassadors, discreet, faultlessly efficient, devoted to their duty and thoughtful of the welfare of the people to whom they were commissioned.

This group of American financiers and advisers has known how to extract money for the state, not painlessly, but with the minimum of discomfort. Few tax collectors have been loved. Bonapart, indeed, collected enormous taxes; and, nevertheless, his people idolized him; and Mr. Mellon[15] seems to become popular in

---

11. Seymour Parker Gilbert (1892-1938), financier. First United States undersecretary of the treasury 1921-1923, appointed by Andrew Mellon. From 1924-1930 agent-general to receive and allocated WWI reparation payments to the Allies from Germany, and to stabilize the German currency under the Dawes plan. Gilbert earned the respect of the German government even though he was sometimes critical of its fiscal policies. Century Association member.

12. Edwin Walter Kemmerer (1875-1945), economist. Called the "money doctor;" financial advisor to numerous foreign governments including Mexico (1917), Guatemala (1919), Columbia (1923 & 1930), Chile (1925), South Africa (1924), Poland (1926), Equador and Bolivia (1926-1927), China (1929), and Peru (1931). Author of numerous books on economics. Century Association member.

13. Francis Bowes Sayre (1885-1972), lawyer, teacher, statesman. Advisor on foreign affairs in Siam 1926-1927, where he negotiated new political and commercial treaties with France, Great Britain, the Netherlands, Denmark, Spain, Portugal, Sweden, Norway, and Italy. From 1925-1934 represented Siam at the Hague court of permanent arbitration. In 1939 became Unites States high commissioner in the Philippines.

14. Henry Willard Denison (1846-1914), lawyer and statesman. Began his Japanese legal career in the Yokohama consular courts in 1868; from 1880-1914 an important advisor to the Japanese foreign ministry on treaty renegotiations and other matters. Represented Japan at the drafting of the Russo-Japanese peace treaty of 1905. Said to have been balanced in his views and highly popular with the Japanese; given the two highest Japanese decorations bestowed on any but princes of the blood.

"Meiji emperor" was the name for the regnate of Emperor Mutsuhito (1852-1912). The 1868 Meiji restoration overthrew the Tokugawa shogunate and returned full power to the emperor, leading to the supremacy of reform groups favoring Westernization.

15. Andrew Mellon (1855-1937), American financier, industrialist, public official. United States Secretary of the treasury 1921-1931, when he reduced the national debt.

proportion to the number of billions he takes from us. Shuster, in his comparatively minute, but infinitely difficult task, had similar good fortune. Shuster was appointed by the Persians to see that Persian taxes were used for Persia, and that the taxes were paid. Yet such is his personality that he acquired not only the calculating esteem that is given to an able officer, but, also, the almost superstitious love of the Persians. If, after all these years, he should land again on the southerly shore of the Caspian Sea, schools would declare a holiday, school-girls would strew roses, and torch-light processions would march, in his honor.

Shuster's path was not so protected as the path of Smith and Gilbert. Behind them stood all the victorious armies of the world. Shuster found Persia crushed in between two gigantic powers that chose to divide her wealth. Temptations were set before him. If he had not elected to be faithful to Persia, Russia and England could have shown him a way to easy wealth and agreeable honors like those earned by Sir Robert Hart and Stamford Raffles[16]; such honors as come to men that help kingdoms to widen their dominions. But Shuster, to all temptations, was utterly indifferent.

Persians, Cubans, Filipinos, men of the oldest civilizations, and of the newest, have tested Shuster, and to all of those he served he has endeared himself, by sound judgment and unshakable integrity and by being likable and easy to get on with.

I urge you to admit Shuster because there is nothing pretentious or stodgy about him. He is an entertaining and comfortable companion, always; whether he is standing by a band of devoted Persians who are to give their lives for freedom; or, as an editor, in rejecting, gently, one of my manuscripts; or, as a publisher, in reluctantly expurgating a text-book of biology, for use in Texas;[17] or is selling fifty thousand hymn-books; or is printing an essay by Bertrand Russell, to prove that hymn-books are bad for the mind.

I am grateful to Shuster for intellectual pleasures. I am grateful to him, also for many innocent pleasures, of a lower type, administered in the remote past, pleasures of the sort that are frowned on, now, by church and state. I cherish happy though

---

16. Sir Robert Hart (1835-1911), served in British administration of China, culminating in the post of inspector-general of the imperial maritime customs of Shanghai.

Sir Thomas Stanford Bingley Raffles (1781-1826), English East India administrator; largely responsible for the British purchase and occupation of Singapore, and governor there 1822-1824.

17. Allusion to the textbook review board, choosing texts for use in all Texas public schools, long notorious for its conservatism.

slightly confused memories of a Farewell to Wine that he celebrated, about 1920, on an islet in the Delaware. The stately punch bowl which then adorned that island was built and filled by him in conformity to a college song, now obsolete, that was taught to me by Noah Porter, President of Yale, in my far-off youth, when the Goddess of Liberty had not yet become a decayed gentlewoman. It runs thus:

"I wish I had a barrel of rum,
And sugar, three hundred pound,
The chapel bell to mix it in,
And the clapper to stir it around."

*Newell Martin*

(Huntington, New York)

P.S. If there is any error or impropriety in this letter, the blame should fall on me alone. As I am far from home, Shuster and his proposer and seconder do not know that this letter is written.

# Memorial Of Charles Robinson Smith
[1931]

*The 1931 Year Book of the Association of the Bar of the City of New York carried a memorial to one of its members — Charles Robinson Smith (1855-1930), even though he had retired from active practice of the law in 1907.*

*Smith was a classmate of Martin's both at Yale ('75) and at Columbia (L.L.B. '78), and in 1890 they formed a law partnership with the name Smith and Martin. Smith specialized in corporate law, and was active in the reorganization of a number of corporations following the panic of 1893-1894. One of these was the Martin Kalbfleisch Sons Co. which became the Martin Kalbfleisch Chemical Co., and subsequently part of the General Chemical Co. From 1899* to 1922, Smith was director and vice-president of the General Chemical Co., and subsequently its general counsel and associate general counsel.

Smith, who had a second home in Paris, was made Chevalier of the Legion of Honor in 1927. His second daughter, Gertrude Robinson Smith (1881-1963) had been made Chevalier of the Legion of Honor in 1916, for raising $70,000 to send surgical motor units to France and $100,000 for ice-making machinery for field hospitals. From 1934 to 1955, Ms. Smith was the founder and indefatigable force behind the Berkshire Music Festival in Berkshire, Massachusetts.

Charles Robinson Smith was said to display a great breadth of learning and marked intellectual curiosity, which extended to the writing of articles about Einstein's theory of relativity.

His New York club memberships included the City Midday, University, and Yale.

Apparently Martin reprinted the memorial to his former law partner in pamphlet form without identifying himself as the writer. Later, in a compilation of his papers, he had put his initials "N.M." flush right, at the close of the piece.

In 1929 Charles Robinson Smith celebrated his golden wedding with gay ceremonies, in the company of a great troop of affectionate friends. In the same year he commemorated his 50th anniversary of his admission to the bar. A few months later he attained to the 50th anniversary of his becoming a member of this Association. Cautious and conscientious, enterprising and generous, he had a strong will, studious habits, unrelenting industry, a restless scientific mind, skill in dealing with accounts, judgment in choosing advisers; indeed, most of the high qualities that, in our eulogies, we are in the habit of ascribing to our lost comrades. But he had no turn for oratory, no desire for court work, no love of controversy. He was skillful in reconciling differences and in foreseeing and guarding against difficulties.

When he was 20 he graduated at Yale where an 18th century curriculum did not prevent his imbibing the modern spirit of Andrew D. White[1] and John Stuart Mill. At Yale he excelled in

---

1. Andrew Dickson White (1832-1918; Yale '53), one of the founders, and first president of Cornell University (1867-1885). Wrote extensively on educational, historical, and political subjects, including *The Warfare of Science* (1876), a history of the interferences of theology with freedom of thought and investigation. One of the first educators to introduce the elective system.

mathematics and in the study of many authorities in political economy, most of them now exploded.

He passed without mental injury through another 18th century course of study, that used by the Columbia Law School, under Dwight,[2] at 8 Great Jones Street. In 1879, equipped with a fair working knowledge of Bracton and Fleta,[3] he went to the Tweed court house[4] to be sworn in as a lawyer. He went to it in a horse-car. In 1881 he began to earn $10 a week as a law clerk. Wall Street, then, was rather less than four stories high and was lit by gas. A new world, however, alive with electricity and chemistry, had begun to reveal itself. Smith made himself a part of the progressive forces of this new world.

He retired from general practice in 1907. Louis Dean Speir,[5] of Fraser, Speir & Meyer, one of our fellow members in this Association, is the only one of his former law-partners that is still active.

It is one of many examples that might be given, of Smith's efficiency in modern business, that, early in his career, he was the successful reorganizer of an important chemical company and that, in his latter years, he was one of the small group who were the directors of the Allied Chemical and Dye Corporation.

An example of his interest in statecraft is found in the letters about debts and reparations which he published in French journals. One may say without exaggeration that, when he wrote those lucid arguments, letters on such matters to the Debats and Figaro had already ceased to be a novelty.[6] But Smith's letters were received

---

2. Theodore William Dwight (1882-1892), lawyer and educator; organizer in 1858 of the Columbia Law School and for 14 years its only lecturer. Resigned in 1891 upon the introduction of the case system of teaching law then in vogue at Harvard.

3. Henry de Bracton (Bratton, Bretton) (?-1268), author of a comprehensive treatise on the law of England. *Fleta* is the title of a Latin textbook of English law, written c. 1290. Title may be derived from Fleet Street Prison, the work possibly having been written by one of the corrupt judges imprisoned by Edward I.

4. Familiar name for the Criminal Court Building back-to-back with New York City's Hall at Chambers Street and Broadway. Completed 1872, having taken nine years to construct. About three-fourths of its $12 million cost was diverted into the pockets of Boss William Marcy Tweed and his ring.

5. Louis Dean Speir (1869-1967), New York City lawyer who joined Smith and Martin in 1894. (The firm was successively Martin & Speir; Speir and Meyer; Fraser, Speir, Meyer, and Kidder; Speir and Kerbeck; then Speir, Kerbeck, and Stover.) Speir practiced law for some 66 years, not retiring until 1960.

6. It is the severest understatement to say that by the mid-20's, when Smith's articles appeared, the subject of France's war debt to the U.S. was no novelty to the columns of such publications as the *Journal des Debats* and *Le Figaro*. Smith took the position that, since the U.S. and the Allies had a common cause in making the world safe for democracy, the fifteen months in which the Allies fought unassisted in effect constituted repayment of most of the war debt; also that special considerations existed in the case of France both for her devastated condition and her aid in the Revolutionary War.

with admiring favor in Paris; and, than Frenchmen, there are no better judges of logic, style, and persuasiveness. He wore, with just pride, the decoration of the Legion of Honor; as does, also, one of his daughters, Gertrude Robinson Smith; an unusual coincident of compliment.

He delighted in the friendship, here, of such men as William H. Nichols[7] and Sanford H. Steele;[8] and felt himself honored by the friendship, in France, where he maintained one of his homes, of such men as Jusserand.[9]

For years his New York house, on Sunday afternoons, was a meeting place for men and women of wit and wisdom, addicted to music and the art of conversation; and was well known to many clever Frenchmen, whose custom it was to forget in his society the rigors of their American exile.

Smith died at his country house, in Stockbridge, on September 7, 1930. He was born at Buffalo on March 1, 1855. He followed the august example of Isaac Newton in being his father's only child. Like George Grote,[10] he was a banker's son [of Edwin Smith of Buffalo, New York]. This double good luck was the auspicious beginning of a life of great good fortune, usefulness and happiness.

*R. M.*

7. William Henry Nichols (1852-1930), manufacturing chemist; founded Nichols Chemical Co. of New York in 1890, which merged into the General Chemical Co. in 1899 and through subsequent mergers became the largest producer of heavy chemicals in the U.S. Director of other firms as well. Was described by one source as "well beloved by a large circle of friends for his gentle manliness, geniality, wit, human sympathy, and youthfulness."

8. Sanford Henry Steele (1847-1920), New York City lawyer specializing in corporation law. One of the founders of the General Chemical Co.; president 1899-1916, subsequently general counsel and director. Largely responsible for organizing the Allied Chemical Co. in 1920. University Club member.

9. Jean Jules Jusserand (1855-1932), French scholar and diplomat who as French ambassador to Washington 1902-1925 helped secure the entry of the United Stated into WWI. Had a wide range of intellectual interests which extended to writings on medieval English literature.

10. George Grote (1794-1871), British historian of Greece, son of banker George Grote (1762-1830).

# The Climenole

*This is a rather delightful light essay highlighting some Martin friends. As usual, Martin is engaged in considerable leg-pulling.*

*Today's family members recall no definition for the title of this essay. An Italian dictionary gives us "climeno," the botanical name of a species of climbing vetch; Greek mythology has "Climene," including an Amazon and a companion of Helen's on the way to Troy. But classical Greek has the noun "klima," meaning slope; and the verb "klinon," to cause to lean against or support. From these come the noun "klimaxs," a scaling ladder.*

Daily Neech, Sunday Supplement<br>Fiction and Short Story Section<br>October 31, 1925.

My wife[1] asked me to build for her a new house, a small one, on Long Island. I refused. "Of all the islands that blot the seven oceans," said I to her, "Long Island is the last island that I wish to live on. And it is written in the Gemara[2] that fools build houses and wise men live in them. I do not wish to build anywhere. I wish to go to San Diego and buy a house, cheap, from some foolish old man's executor. It has been the rule of my life never to build houses after I am seventy."

After the new house was built, my wife sent a truckman to the old house with directions to select some of my books and bring them in barrels. The truckman made his choice and sold the residue to papermakers. The few books that he chose to save were piled in a stable. Too weak, myself, to climb any barn stairs, or to wipe the dust from any books,[3] I advertised that I would like to employ, for six days, as librarian and secretary, a young man of high character, great learning, agreeable manners, infinite patience, tireless

---

1. Laura Griswold Grinnell Martin (1860-1940), daughter of George Blake Grinnell; sister of George Bird Grinnell.
2. Commentary on the Mishna, the canonic collection of Jewish law, the two comprising the Talmud.
3. Responding a year later to a Yale alumni questionnaire, Martin claimed his occupation was "resisting Volstead and all his works," and his recreation, "sitting at the feet of philosophers."

industry, and unusual bodily strength. Roger Whitney[4] was sent in answer to this advertisement. He met all its requirements. I made my bargain with him on the telephone. As soon as he got to my house he tried to change the bargain so as to make it less favorable to himself. From this I knew him to be a true Whitney.

Roger is, in one way, like Schuyler Meyer.[5] He uses short sentences and assumes that you have intelligence enough to fill in the elaborate conventional omitted clauses. Meyer, in the same way, sometimes neglects periphrasis [verbal circumlocution]. Helen Meyer[6] asked Schuyler Meyer the other day, whether he would play golf with her, and he said, "Yes, if I cannot get anybody else." We all knew that he meant that he would rather play golf with her than with anybody else, but that there were reasons why he should seek, that morning, to play with certain other people. On another day, dining with Myra Martin,[7] Schuyler said, "Is it only nine? I thought it was much later." We knew that he meant that he was surprised that he had condensed so much pleasure into so short a time. So, when we urged Roger to stay with us, after he had finished his Augean[8] job, Roger said, "I would like to very much if I had no other place to go to." We knew that me meant that it was a delight and a duty to go to his mother's farm and that nothing but such a combination of duty and pleasure would keep him from staying a little longer with us.

Roger used to work eighteen hours a day. This was rough on me because one of my motives in retaining him was to have somebody that would listen when I talked. My family, after fifty years of my remarks, have become slightly inattentive. I used to try to call Roger away from the hot garret to listen to me, just as Legree used to call Black Tom out of the cane field for the pleasure of giving pain.[9]

---

4. Roger S. Whitney (1903-1965; Yale '28), youngest of E.B. Whitney's (cf. footnote 20 below) four sons (one daughter). Practiced medicine in New Haven, moved to Colorado Springs sometime between 1936 and 1948; one of two members of a University of Iowa climbing expedition killed attempting to scale Iscina, a 19,000-ft. peak in the central Andes, according to the *New York Times* of July 24, 1965..

5. Schuyler Merritt Meyer (1885-1970; Yale '07), New York City lawyer, member N.Y. State Assembly 1914-1917; N.Y. State Senate 1920-1921. Martin's son-in-law (married to Helen Martin). Father of the philanthropist, Schuyler M. Meyer, Jr., author of the Introduction.

6. Newell Martin's daughter, Helen Martin Meyer (1889-1971), sister of Grinnell (1888-1972; Harvard '10), and Janet (?-?).

7. Schuyler's wife's brother's wife; Martin's daughter-in-law.

8. Hercules' fourth task, the cleaning of the Augean stables.

9. From *Uncle Tom's Cabin*.

We took Roger to play golf with a man who is in [Elihu] Root's firm and therefore a friend of Emory R. Buckner,[10] whom Roger so much admires. For convenience and to avoid litigation, I will call the man Mr. Harris. That is not his name. While we were waiting for Schuyler and Roger, I said to this man Harris: "It is a privilege to play with Roger Whitney. Roger is a philosopher himself and is descended from all sorts of philosophers. Among others, from the political philosopher, Roger Sherman,[11] who invented the Boss System. America has a unique Boss System; obviously, therefore, that is the cause of American's prosperity. Roger is also descended from Hassler,[12] who, like all Whitney ancestors, scorned money, but was willing to use enough to keep his scientific work in operation. Hassler once, for such reasons, asked to have his pay doubled; whereupon Andrew Jackson said: 'That will give you more than any of my Cabinet get.' Hassler answered, with the frankness of all Whitney ancestors: 'What of it? If I were not worth twice as much as a Cabinet minister I would not be fit to run the Coast Survey.'"[13]

"You know Roger's celebrated uncle," I continued, "J.D. Whitney, who was State Geologist of California.[14] His explorations covered the region that is bounded on the west by the oil wells that our Government virtuously gave to Doheney[15] and on the north by

---

10. Emory R. Buckner (1877-1941), U.S. District Attorney South District of New York City 1925-1927. Reference is facetiously unflattering. See Section Two — "Draft Not Used."
11. Roger Sherman (1721-1793), jurist and statesman. Led movement to form a city government in New Haven and held office there until his death; his position became "almost autocratic." Member of the Continental Congress 1774-1781; elected to the constitutional convention. See footnote 20 below regarding E.B. Whitney, whose mother was Elizabeth Baldwin, daughter of Connecticut governor Roger Sherman Baldwin (Yale '11), whose maternal grandfather was Roger Sherman.
12. Ferdinand Rudolph Hassler (1770-1843), American geodesist, born in Switzerland. Largely responsible for organizing the U.S. Coast and Geodetic Survey. E. B. Whitney married Josepha Newcomb, daughter of the well-known astronomer Simon Newcomb (1835-1909), who married Mary Caroline Hassler, daughter of Charles A. Hassler, son of F.R. Hassler.
13. A. Joseph Wraight and Elliott B. Roberts, in *The Coast and Geodetic Survey 1807-1957* (Washington, U.S. Department of Commerce, 1957), characterize Hassler as "irascible and intolerant" but extremely intelligent and conscientious in the performance of his duties.
14. Josiah Dwight Whitney (1819-1896), forty years service in the U.S. geological surveys; first Sturgis-Hooper professor of geology at Harvard (1865-1896). It was said of Mr. Whitney that "he never owned a share of mining stock, nor in any other way used his great opportunities to enrich himself by his discoveries."
15. Edward Lawrence Doheney (1856-1935), American oil magnate who founded the Pan-American Petroleum and Transport Co., which obtained under lease the rights to the Elk Hill naval reserve oil fields in California.

the oil wells that our Government wisely gave to Sinclair[16] and on the east by the Comstock lode.[17] Never in the history of pearls and diamonds and oil and gold, has any favorite of the Gods had any such chance to lay up riches with credit, and without reproach. But, compared with J.D. Whitney, St. Anthony[18] was a loose fellow, facile under temptation. Ignoring the temptations offered by mountain ranges filled with encaverned riches, of which he held the key, J. D. Whitney used to leave wealth untouched and used to spend his own money to print his reports.

If J.D. Whitney had been dropped by a roc[19] into a valley of diamonds, his report on the valley would have run thus: 'I did not bring away any of these interesting crystals. I thought it in line with the best professional ethics to leave all of them in situ for the use of the California Legislature and for the benefit of later visitors. I am now trying to find the nests of the roc so that the state government may domesticate young rocs and train them to collect jewels for the State treasury."

"This young fellow Roger Whitney"[20] I continued "is a son of Judge Whitney."

"I know" said Harris. "The Judge Whitney who gave us four years more of Grover. He was an anti-Tammany democrat, on

---

16. Harry Ford Sinclair (1876-1956), founder of the Sinclair Consolidated Oil Co. Sinclair's Hyva Co., a holding company, owned 25% of the stock of the Mammoth Oil Co., formed in 1922 to develop and operate under government lease the Teapot Dome naval oil reserve in Wyoming.

Doheney and Sinclair turned out to have bribed Senator Albert B. Fall, who controlled the leasing of mineral rights in the naval reserve fields, with some $400,000 in gifts and "loans." In 1929, Sen. Fall was fined $100,000 and sentenced to a year in prison. Sinclair received a short sentence for jury-tampering; Doheney escaped punishment.

17. World's richest known deposit of silver, situated in western Nevada on Mt. Davidson in the Virginia Range.

18. Egyptian hermit (c.251-356) whose conduct in the face of diabolic advances makes his name a byword for resistance to temptation.

19. Legendary (Arabia/Persia) bird of prey so enormous and strong it could carry away large animals. In "The Second Voyage of Sinbad," in *The Arabian Nights*, the sailor is carried by a roc to just such a valley.

20. Edward Baldwin Whitney (1857-1911; Yale'78; Columbia Law School '80), first assistant U.S. attorney-general under Grover Cleveland 1893-1897. As assistant attorney-general Baldwin took part in or prepared material for the income tax case, Debs' case, and others well-known. Became assistant corporation counsel of New York City under Tammany in 1901, but remained an independent in municipal politics, affirming himself a Democrat only at the national level. Drafted the tenement house law of 1901; had a share in defeating the so-called "railroad grab bill" of 1906; argued the "80-cent gas suit" before the U.S. Supreme Court, establishing legislative right to delegate rate-making powers to a commission; in this case, establishing low gas rates to householders. Along with Martin, a member of both the Century and University Clubs.

Manhattan Island. That means that he was unwilling to derive any profit from holding correct political opinions."

"Judge Whitney despised many things and many men," said I "and he believed in few things. He was devoted to civil liberty and free trade. Yet, with all his patriotism, he was the man that put the skids under our republic.

He planted the seed that will grow into a tree that will bust the pyramid of the American Empire. He fastened on us the Federal Income Tax."

"Don't you believe in the Income Tax?" said Harris. "All Christendom has learned to put its trust in taxes on income."

"True," said I, "but observe the working of the Federal Income Tax.

It siphons liquid wealth out of the rich communities and spreads it over the unprogressive and poor states. That process bleeds the rich states; and, at the last, the commonwealth will die of pernicious anemia. That is the way the Roman Empire fell. The wealth of the provinces was siphoned away into Rome and wasted there. After a few centuries, when Britain needed money to keep out the barbarians, when Mesopotamia needed money to keep up its irrigation canals, when North Africa needed money to hold back the sands of the desert, when Asia Minor needed money to drain marshes and suppress the malarial mosquito, no free capital was left, and the Empire went to pieces."

I went back to my scanty library and was delighted to find that Roger had arranged my books so that the most casual observer of their outsides would learn something. He had put, side by side, The History of Great American Fortunes and Esquemeling's Buccaneers.[21] He had put The Life of the Rev. Wm. G. Sumner under Religion,[22] and The History of the Opium Trade under Christian Missions, and the Rev. Dirk Cornelius Lansing's Sermons on Hell[23] next to Ellsworth Huntington's Climactic Changes.[24]

---

21. *History of the Great American Fortunes*, by Gustavus Myers, in three volumes, 1910. *Buccaneers of America*, by Alexandre Olivier Exquemelin (John Esquemelin), 1645?-1707).
22. *William Graham Sumner* by Harris E. Starr (N.Y., Holt, 1925). Sumner was a professor of sociology and economics, and an exponent of social Darwinism and of the view, expounded in his *Folkways*, that cultural differences are normatively decisive.
23. The Reverend Dirk Cornelius Lansing (1785-1857; Yale '04), Mrs. Martin's grandfather. Published in 1825, *Sermons on Important Subjects of Doctrine and Duty*. See Section Sixteen - "Dirck C. Lansing, D.D."
24. *Climactic changes: Their Nature and Causes*, by Ellsworth Huntington and Stephen Sargent Visher (New Haven, Yale University Press, 1922).

Then I went back to the Country Club and met Harris, and Harris, very unjustly, said, "Roger Whitney is one of those absent minded philosophers. He was anxious not to delay us. So, after driving off, he hurried away from the tee so as not to keep us waiting; and, behold, he had left all his clubs behind him."

"Roger Whitney," said I, "has better things in his mind than golf. And, at Christmas, I am going to give him a climenole."

# ELEVEN

# NEIGHBORHOODS

Letter to Molly January 1, 1936 . . . . 320

Not Even the Town Clerk Knows . . . 320

Harrisburg Analytical Laboratory . . 321

A 1935 New Year's Card . . . . . . . . . 324

# Letter to Molly, January 1, 1936

Miss Molly Meyer
Pembroke East
Bryn Mawr College
Bryn Mawr, Pa.

Dear Molly:
    I thank you earnestly for a necktie, labeled Pure Soie, to wear about my neck. I shall put it on daily, until 1940, when the America Fascists will begin to rage and imagine a vain thing. In that year a gang of Nazis from the militia barracks across the way, under Charlie Sherrill, will march into my house, without a warrant and will put a hempen cravat around my neck and string me up on the telegraph pole, in front of your house.
                              Gratefully,
                              Newell Martin

✤ ✤ ✤

# "Not even the Town Clerk knows..."

Huntington, Long Island, New York
Telephone, Huntington, 1484

    The Inhabitants of Huntington are divided, into an upper class, that sends hirelings for its letters, and a lower class, that receives its letters in rural free delivery tin boxes. To find my house, please drive westward, from Huntington, on West Main Street. Follow the straight street up the hill. Resist the temptation to turn away on any broad highway that curves to the right. Near where the asphalt ceases, and nearly opposite the camp ground of Troop C, you will find, on the north side of the road, a tin letter box, bearing my name. There turn to the north, on a narrow graveled lane, for about 300 feet. My house can be known thus: 1. It is built of bagasse, sugar cane refuse.[1] 2. It is finger printed, 2 feet from the ground, by the grimy hands of grandchildren. 3. It is the only house on the lane. West Main Street begins in a town that has many monogamous nordics, indigenous fundamentalists, prohibiters and kukluxers. As the street goes west, toward the Sin Belt of Long Island, which is infested with exotic hedonists, it changes; and somewhere, nobody knows where, it becomes Turkey Lane. Not even the Town Clerk knows whether I live in West Main Street or Turkey Lane.

*Newell Martin*

ね ね ね

# Harrisburg Analytical Laboratory
[September 6-20, 1926]

*Martin's four letters, a whimsical fabrication, were preceded by a note stating that they had been "published in the American Quarterly Review of Euthenics[2] and Archaeology, New York, October, 1926." The first letter is addressed to the Harrisburg Analytical Laboratory.*

Sirs:
After my bath, sometimes the water in the tub is clear, like an Adirondack brook, sometimes it is clear, except for soap, and at other times there is an inch of detritus, which makes the tub's contents look like bilge-water of a garbage-scow. I send samples for analysis.

Truly
MELANCTHON WITHERSPOON,[3]

---

1. Sugar cane refuse — "bagasse" — can be pressed and made into wallboard; however, our researcher suspects that here Mr. Martin is being facetious. See photograph of the house in question on Page ???
2. Webster defines euthenics as "a science that deals with development of human well-being by improvement of living conditions."
3. "Melancthon," from the Greek, is "black earth;" "Witherspoon" perhaps a reference to bile.

Huntington, Long Island, Sept. 6, 1926.

M. Witherspoon, Esq.,
Sir:
    All the samples of detritus show 90% of bituminous coal soot and 1% of snuff or rappee.[4]
    Some of the samples show 5% of face-powder and other show 5% of cigar ashes. We advise you to ask your village water-works to overhaul their screens and filters.
Faithfully<br>HARRISBURG ANALYTICAL LABORATORY.

Sept. 13, 1926.

HUNTINGTON WATER-WORKS.
Sirs:
    I enclose samples of detritus and report of analytic chemist.
M. WITHERSPOON.

MELANCTHON WITHERSPOON, Esq.,
Sir:
    The screens and filters of our water-works work well and the water we sell is of crystal purity.
    You will find, by experiment and further analysis, that the detritus in your bath that contains face-powder is deposited after you have been riding in the cars in which the Long Island [Rail] Road carries women to the New York shops. The Research Department of the Smithsonian Institute has shown that, in 20 years, 3 centimeters of face-powder will be deposited on the cushions of an ordinary commuters' passenger car.
    The cigar detritus, you will find, appears after you have been riding in a smoking car.
    The bituminous soot is from a railway engine. You must know that, often, at Jamaica, in Queens County, the Long Island Road is so unfortunate as to lose passenger cars, from their being hauled away, through a pardonable error of the drivers of the switching engines, who sometimes mistake passenger cars for coal cars.
    We have made special inquiry as to the snuff or rappee. We borrowed, from the Long Island Road, a cushion that formed part of the equipment of the car in which British officers rode, from Brooklyn to Huntington, to arrange for the Court Martial that tried the late Nathan Hale.[5]

---

4. Webster's: "A pungent snuff made from dark rank tobacco leaves."

An analysis of a piece cut from the cover of this cushion showed that these officers had spilled on it an appreciable fraction of their snuff.

Our finding these traces of the slovenly habits of a licentious soldiery will surprise nobody.

The most casual observer, in riding on the Long Island Road, is shocked by the obvious marks of the brutal carelessness of British and Hessian soldiers,[6] during the Revolutionary War, in their treatment of the company's rolling stock.

We sent a copy of our analysis to the Long Island Road. Upon receiving it the directors of that road, at a special meeting, Resolved, That such of their cushions as had not been cleaned since the deplorable Battle of Long Island,[7] should be sent for treatment to Barrett Nephews.[8]

Hoping that this will cause some diminution of the discomfort you have suffered, through no fault of ours, we remain
Faithfully
HUNTINGTON WATER WORKS.
Sept. 20, 1926.

ย ย ย

---

5. Nathan Hale (1755-1776; Yale '73), American Revolutionary officer and hero. On September 21, 1776, disguised as a Dutch school teacher, he went behind British enemy lines as a spy, was captured, and hanged the next day. Hale undoubtedly landed at Huntington Bay at the commencement of his spying mission, and a long-standing tradition located his capture there as well; in fact, in 1894 the Huntington residents erected a memorial column and fountain commemorating the event. (In a letter to granddaughter Molly, Nov. 18, 1932, Martin states, "Your mother has given me your room which, like the rest of your house, dates from the revolutionary war, when Nathan Hale and George Washington used to drink to excess here together.") However, the historian Henry Phelps Johnson in *Nathan Hale, 1776* (New Haven: Yale University Press, 1914), concluded that Hale was almost certainly captured while attempting to cross the picket lines in Manhattan, and subsequent scholarship has endorsed this conclusion. Moreover, Howe's headquarters were not in Brooklyn, but in Manhattan at Beekman Place (51st Street and First Avenue), and Hale was hanged at the Dove Tavern, present-day 66th Street and Third Avenue. Historians also agree that Hale was not court-martialled but condemned summarily by Gen. Howe on the basis of documents found on his person and his own confession.

6. England, lacking sufficient soldiers to prosecute the American rebellion, appealed for troops to the landgrave of Hesse-Kassel in Germany, whose first wife was the daughter of George III. Hesse-Kassel supplied some 17,000 soldiers, and the neighboring German principalities supplied another 12,000, who together constituted around one-third of the British forces fighting in America. "Hessian" became their generic name.

7. The battle took place on August 27, 1776; was a successful action in Brooklyn by British forces under the command of General Howe, initiating an attempt to seize New York State and thereby isolate New England from the remaining colonies.

8. Barrett Nephews & Co., "Old Staten Island Dyeing Establishment," with twenty-nine New York City branch offices.

# A 1935 New Year's Card

January 1, 1935. [9This is a New Year Card. To make sure that you will not think it is all prose, I explain, borrowing the words of J.O.P. Bland, that it is Verse and Worse.[10] The verse is to commemorate certain changes at the city's center. Five generations wore the tartan of their clan at 87 Park Avenue.[11] I know 3 respectable young girls, Models of Deportment, for whom that house was a beloved home. Jeannie Smith[12] and Charles Robinson Smith, in the far-off seventies,[13] used to adorn 91 Park Avenue. Adventurous builders have swept away 87 and 91. Where stood those happy homes,[14] multitudes, at 25 cents apiece, throng to study the 20th century ideal of a 7-room, 2-child house.[15]

The primal curse of Genesis 3:19, In the sweat of thy face shall thou eat thy bread, was put on man and not on woman. Husbands

---

9. Bracket here and after "hallowed spot," in Martin original.
10. John Otway Percy Bland (1863-19??): Author, using pseudonym "Tung Chi," of *Verse and Worse: Selections from the Writings of Tung Chi* (Shanghai: Oriental Press, 1902). Martin probably would have been most familiar with Bland as the author of several books on China and other eastern nations, of a political hue akin to Martin's own.
11. Presumably, though not certainly, the Frasers. See Section Ten - "On Behalf of George Corning Fraser." Simon Fraser, his 18th-century Scotish ancestor, appears in Section Twelve - "Scots."
12. Jeannie Porter Steele Smith (1858-1945): the wife of Charles Robinson Smith, and daughter of New York City banker William Porter Steele. Her widowed mother married Count Vincent de Wierzbicki. See Section Nine - Pleonasm or Crime. Jeannie lived with them in Poland 1866-1870. As a girl in Paris she met Dumas *pere*; and among the illuminati received by her at her New York and Paris homes were Emma Calve, Constant Coquelin, Gustave Mahler, Sarah Bernhardt, and Edith Wharton.
13. Smith (1855-1930; Yale '75; L.L. B. Columbia '78) had been Martin's law partner; married Jeannie Steele in April, 1879. See Section Ten - "Memorial of Charles Robinson Smith."
14. The land had been acquired in a bank foreclosure following the abandonment of a project to improve the site, formerly occupied by six old brownstone dwellings.
15. "America's Little House," built by the New York committee of Better Homes in America (BHA). The BHA had some 9,000 committees nationwide with intent to furnish helpful advice to private persons planning to construct a home either out of their own resources or with federal aid; the Little House was to be, as they put it, "an educational demonstration of values in house construction, interior decoration, and furnishing suited to the needs of the average homeowner with a moderate income." The ground had been broken by Mayor LaGuardia in a ceremony July 30, and construction, landscaping, decoration, and furnishing had been completed by the first week of November. The house, containing eight rooms, was in a Georgian style with furnishings to match, surrounded by a garden; the conveniences included sewing machine, electric washer, ironing mangle, air conditioning in the heating unit, a "housewife's planning desk," hardened surfaces for easy cleaning, mulberry carpet to conceal stains, and a baby's bed designed to be extended as baby grew. Construction costs were expected to vary nationally from $6,300 to $9,400, and the furnishings to cost around $2,000. The house was left standing for about a year.

have put off the worst of that curse on women, by making them do the housework. This Model House, in Park avenue, shows how women can get rid of some of the curse. Sir Walter Scott could have described my emotions on that hallowed spot.]

  Lines, On viewing the northeasterly corner of Park avenue and 39th street.[16]

> Breathes there a Model Child with soul so dead
> She seldom to herself hath said
> This is my own, my native corner?
> If such there be, do not unkindly scorn her.
> Ten thousand plunks, she's told,
> or at the most 11,
> Have built a Model Hut, deleting 91 and 87.

*Lewell Martin*

   ta ta ta

---

16. Takeoff on Sir Walter Scott's "Lay of the Last Minstrel." The image may have been inspired by the "Manhattan Girl Scout Minstrels," who, on December 20, had broadcast carols from a radio studio set up in the Model House garage, and then sung more carols on the front lawn.

# TWELVE

# CHARACTER

Scots . . . . . . . . . . . . . . . . . . . . 328
Rough Notes . . . . . . . . . . . . . . . . 332
English Merchants . . . . . . . . . . . . 334

# Scots
[April 1927]

I keep twenty frivolous books at my bed's head and copy from them what pleases me and send the stuff to people that already know all about it.

Being seventy-two years old, I turn for comfort to Horace Walpole.[1] In 1789 [on July 2] he wrote to Hannah More: "If I would live to seventy-two, ought I not to compound for the incumbrances of old age? And who has fewer? * * * Though my hands and feet are crippled, I can use both.[...] I am just infirm enough to enjoy all the prerogatives of old age and to plead them against anything that I have not a mind to do."

Walpole notes a painful incident in the family of one of my friends:[2] "You have heard that old Lovat's tragedy is over.[...][3] (There was) a squabble between (the Duke of Newcastle) and the Sheriff about holding up the head on the scaffold [,a custom that has been disused, and which the Sheriff would not comply with, as he had received no order in writing]."[4]

Walpole was a timid prophet. "My servants called me away to see a balloon. * * * I cheaply [chiefly] amused myself with the idea of the change that would be made in the world by the substitution of balloons to ships. (The ship news to go thus.) 'The good balloon Daedalus [,captain Wing-ate,] will fly in a few days for China. * * * The dread-naught from Mount Aetna arrived.' * * *[5] In those days * * * there will be fights in the air. * * * How posterity will laugh at us [one way or other]. If half a dozen break their necks and balloonism is exploded, we shall be called fools for having imagined it could be brought to use. If it should be turned to account, we shall be ridiculed for having doubted." (1784)[6]

"I have ever been averse to toleration of an intolerant

---

1. Horace Walpole (1717-1797), 4th Earl of Orford, son of statesman Robert Walpole, author, voluminous correspondent, and, incidentally, not Scottish in ancestry or upbringing.
2. Probably George Corning Fraser: See Section Ten - "On Behalf of George Corning Fraser."
3. Simon Fraser, 11th Baron Lovat, had, in his dotage, taken up arms in support of the Jacobite pretender Charles Edward Stuart (Bonnie Prince Charlie), whose abortive invasion was crushed at Culloden Moor in 1745.
4. From a letter sent by Horace Walpole to Henry Seymour Conway, April 16, 1747.
5. From a letter sent by Horace Walpole to Henry Seymour Conway, October 15, 1784.
6. From a letter sent by Horace Walpole to Sir Horace Mann, June 24, 1785.

religion."[7]

1778. Walpole left this message for Mussolini:

"Our empire is falling to pieces. We are relapsing to a little island. * * * When a kingdom is past doing anything, the few that are studious look into the memorials of past times. Nations, like private persons, seek lustre from their progenitors when they have no lustre" of their own ["and the farther they are from the dignity of their source"]."[8]

1769. One Smithson married the daughter of Algernon Seymour, Duke of Somerset and Earl of Northumberland, and assumed the surname of Percy and became, in 1766, Duke of Northumberland. Walpole ventures to remind us that, in the same family, just as Smithson became a Percy by marriage,[9] so centuries before, Joscelyn of Louvain, who was descended from Charlemagne, became a Percy by marriage.[10] It would have pleased Walpole if he could have forseen that, in the next century, a bastard of the same august line, bearing this same name of Smithson,[11] would make that name more illustrious than Percy by founding the Smithsonian Institution.

From Walpole I turn to Pepys.[12] Even so shrewd a man as Pepys can be mistaken in appraising real estate. We love Charles II for throwing out the Puritans and for keeping a gay harem and for enriching the Empire with Tangier, New York and Bombay.[13] Pepys thought that Tangier was precious, but he was bitterly disappointed in Bombay. "A poor place," said Pepys, "a poor little island." I do not remember whether Pepys thought any better of

---

7. From a letter sent by Horace Walpole to Sir Horace Mann, November 8, 1784.
8. From a letter to the Rev. William Cole, September 1, 1778.
9. Allusion here is to a letter from Horace Walpole to Rev. William Cole, June 26, 1769. Sir Hugh Smithson, "the handsomest man of his day," had, in 1766, married Elizabeth Seymour, and thereupon styled himself a Percy — a lineage running back to the Norman conquest, and one of the most illustrious of English families.
10. Agnes de Percy, daughter of the founder of the Percy line, William de Percy (c.1030-1096), married Jocelin of Louvaine, who did just as Smithson did.
11. James Smithson (1754-1829), who left the money for what became the Smithsonian Institution (founded in 1846), was Sir Hugh's natural son by a Mrs. Elizabeth Macie.
12. Samuel Pepys (1633-1703), English statesman, secretary to the admiralty 1672-1679 and 1684-1689, and diarist.
13. Charles II of England (1630-1685) reigned 1660-1685. In 1661, England acquired Tangiers and Bombay as part of the dowry of Queen Catherine of Portugal. Both places, however, had to be secured militarily. Expense caused England to abandon Tangiers in 1684, last year of Charles' reign. In 1664, the Dutch colony of New Amsterdam capitulated to an English expeditionary force, Charles having granted to his brother James, "all the land from the west side of the Connecticutte river to the East side of the De la Ware Bay."

Manhattan Island, a poor place, then, a poor little island.[14]

I have been told that the Scots are pertinacious; but not till today did I know that William Paterson,[15] who invented the Bank of England, dug the Panama Canal. It took him 200 years. At great cost in money, the finest colonists[16] that ever set sail in search of fortune founded his adventurous Darien, between Porto Bello and Cartagena,[17] to establish a free trade route to the Pacific, whereby to Britain would be secured "the keys of the universe, enabling their possessors to give laws to both oceans and to become the arbiters of a commercial world."[18] In 1701 Paterson recorded his conviction that a canal was practicable.

The jealousy and enmity of English merchants,[19] even more than the mosquitos, ruined Darien. It became, notoriously, the world's uttermost failure. The last ship that sailed from Darien with the last starving Scots, was the Rising Sun.[20] On that unhappy ship, eight or nine died every day and were thrown overboard. Disabled, she put in to Charleston; and there went to pieces in a hurricane. Jean Stobo had been one of her wretched company; but Jean was not drowned because Jean had gone ashore, before the

---

14. Though Pepys was one of the royal commissioners for Tangiers, on a visit there in 1683-1684, he recorded his first-hand impression that the place was a sink of corruption and England was well rid of it. The closest he ever came to enthusiasm for Tangiers was a diary entry for February 20, 1662, merely saying he was glad of the English possession "because now the Spaniard's designs of hindering our getting the place are frustrated."

 An entry for September 5, 1663, records "the inconsiderablenesse of the place of Bombain, if we had it."

 And one for September 29, 1664, mentions the conquest of New Amsterdam: "they say that we have beat them out of the New Netherlands too; so that we have been doing them mischief for a great while in several parts of the world, without publique knowledge or reason."

15. William Paterson (1658-1719), Scots-born, but English-nurtured; founder of the Bank of England.

16. According to Cundall (cf. note 24 below), p. 17, after describing 300 of the 1,200 Darien colonists as being of the best families in Scotland, and another 60 as military officers thrown out of employment by the peace of Ryswick, states, "Many of the remainder were, as in other enterprises of the kind, undesirables."

17. The Isthmus of Darien is the extreme eastern portion of the Isthmus of Panama; Portobello to its west being located just east of the Panama Canal, Cartagena in extreme northern Columbia to its east; the two latter being in the eighteenth century the largest settlements in the geographical neighborhood. The Scottish colonial project of Darien, chartered by the Scottish Parliament in 1695, made an attempt to establish a commercial port there in 1698-1699. It failed with great loss of life and money.

18. Paterson, quoted in Bishop's *The Panama Gateway* (cf. note 24 below), p. 38.

19. England saw in the Scottish venture a potentially serious rival. The subjects of James II were enjoined "at their utmost peril" from giving any aid to the settlers.

20. The *Rising Sun* departed Darien on April 16, 1700. According to Cundall, the sufferings of those aboard were "as bad as those on any of the slave ships on the 'middle passage.'"

CHARACTER 331

storm, to hear a sermon.[21]
Jean married a Scottish settler, James Bulloch.[22]
His son was Archibald Bulloch, of Georgia.
His son was James Bulloch.
His son was James Stephen Bulloch.
His daughter was Martha Bulloch.
In 1853 Martha married Theodore Roosevelt. Her son, Theodore, built the Panama Canal. Six generations and 200 years. Thus, but for the stubborn Scot, William Paterson, and the stoutness and pious habits of one of his Scottish emigrants, the Panama Canal would be as unfinished as is the Nicaragua Canal.[23] It would still be an affair of small men and interminable talk and endless argument.

Newell Martin.

Huntington, April, 1927.
Read, as to Darien, "The Darien Venture," by our old Jamaica friend, Frank Cundall, published by The Hispanic Society of America; and Joseph Bucklin Bishop's authoritative monographs on Roosevelt and on the Panama Canal.[24]

*Newell Martin*

≈ ≈ ≈

21. Jean's father, the Rev. Archibald Stobo, had, according to Cundall, gone ashore to preach a sermon requested by some Scottish residents of Charleston.
22. James Bulloch came from Scotland in 1715. Cundall records the following genealogy (pp. 99-100): Archibald Bulloch (c. 1730-1777), Governor of Georgia 1776-1777; James Bulloch, Captain of Georgia and Virginia troops in the Revolutionary War; and James Stephen Bulloch, U.S. Army major.
23. A canal through Nicaragua had been proposed in December, 1901, as an alternative to buying out the French Panama Canal Co., which held rights in the most desirable part of the isthmus and was asking $110 million for them. The French came down to $40 million after a bill for a Nicaraguan canal had already been passed by the U.S. House of Representatives, January 8, 1902, whereupon the Senate converted it into virtually a new measure.
24. Frank Cundall (1858-?), *The Darien Venture* (N.Y.: Trustees of the Hispanic Society of America, 1926).
   Joseph Bucklin Bishop (1847-1928), *Theodore Roosevelt and His Time*, 2 vols. (N.Y.: Scribner's, 1920); *The Panama Gateway* (N.Y.: Scribner's, 1913).

# Rough Notes
[June 1900]

| | | |
|---|---|---|
| Will you vote for McKinley? | 20 | (M)[1] |
| Do you wish for a better candidate than either McKinley or Bryan?[2] | 13 | |
| Are you an Expansionist? | 20 | (M) |
| Laodicean?[3] | 15 | |
| Contractionist? | 2 | |
| Anti-Kruger? | 22 | (M) |
| Pro-Kruger? | 10 | |
| Republican? | 22 | (M) |
| Mugwump?[4] | | |
| Democrat? | 6 | |

*Martin, secretary of his Yale class ('75), surveyed his classmates, one-third of whom responded, and circulated the information in a pamphlet. Tongue-in-cheek, he explained: "To ensure brevity, the committee has told the compiler that he must print at his own expense. This is mentioned, not to arouse gratitude, but to disarm critics. Binding will be extra."*

*The close of the nineteenth century marked something like the high tide of the United States' dalliance with imperialism. The conclusion of the war with Spain had left the country in possession of Cuba, Puerto Rico, and the Phillipines. John Hay had formulated the policy of the Open Door in China, and American troops had been among those dispatched to put down the Boxer Rebellion.[5] Territorial governments were being set up in Hawaii and Alaska, and a canal through the Isthmus of Panama was in the planning stage.*

*Neither presidential aspirant was wholly opposed to these developments. McKinley viewed the eventual United States' withdrawal from the former Spanish territories as tempered by the need of local populations to "attain that place of self-conscious respect*

---

1. Martin's vote.
2. William McKinley (1843-1901), Republican, 25th President of the United States, assassinated; William Jennings Bryan (1860-1925), Democrat (Populist candidate for the presidency 1896 & 1900). McKinley defeated Bryan by 271 to 176 electoral votes in 1896; it was assumed, at the time Martin circulated his questionnaire, that Bryan would challenge incumbent President McKinley.
3. Rev. 3:16 (lukewarm; neither hot nor cold)
4. Since 1884, term for a voter crossing party lines to support an opposition candidate.

*and self-reliant unity" befitting "an enlightened community for self-government." Republican opposition to U.S. occupation of these lands was largely economic in origin; and some Republican Congressmen sought to protect domestic suppliers from competition through what would effectively have been an internal tariff.*

*Bryan saw the issue of the war as whether the troops had "volunteered to break the yoke of Spain and nothing else," and favored the treaty annexing the Phillipines as the only grounds for fixing a concrete policy on the matter. The Democrats generally opposed the idea of a tariff, Bryan maintaining that an unequal tax for persons residing in territories acknowledged as part of the U.S. was the "baldest form of Imperialism," taxation without representation.*

*Thus the issue between the parties was strictly not colonialism vs. anti-colonialism, but more nearly a matter of colonial policy: whether, in the phrase of the time, the Constitution followed the flag. Imperialists and anti-imperialists could be found on either side, and motivated by differing concerns.*[5]

*Martin's questionnaire was evidently an attempt to sort out his classmates' positions, with Britain's most recent imperial adventure in South Africa, as a further point of reference.*[6]

*Not one to miss an opportunity to address a ready audience, Martin, in keeping with his duties, importuned his classmates: "Let me beg you, before it is too late, to remember that nothing helps a class secretary so much as promptness in sending him your obituaries."*[7]

ʲᵃ ʲᵃ ʲᵃ

---

5. McKinley again defeated Bryan, this time by one million popular votes, 292 to 155 electoral votes.
6. Paul Kruger (1825-1904), president of the Boer state in South Africa, 1893-1900.
7. Martin's own obituary appeared two months after his passing, in the Jan. 23, 1942, issue of the *Yale Alumni Magazine*.

# English Merchants
[May 10, 1927]

*"For English Merchants, a hundred million go hungry"*

Martin's "duty of rebellion" is evident in this strong piece. He ranges far and wide geographically and historically to recall atrocities and tortures he attributes to English (and other national) business interests which he claims put profit ahead of life itself.

Perhaps what triggered Martin's printing of "English Merchants" was the decision by Great Britain in early spring, 1927, to send 76 warships to China, which were joined by some 30 ships from the U.S., 49 from Japan, 10 from France, 4 from Italy, and 1 each from Spain, Portugal, and the Netherlands. They were sent to enforce demands for apologiies, reparations, and guarantees in connection with the Kuomintang advances in 1925-1926, which had been accompanied by atrocities against American, British, French, Italian, and Japanese nationals; also the violation of American, British, and Japanese consulates.

The jealousy and enmity of English Merchants ruined the adventurous Scots of the Darien Colony,[1] more than two hundred years ago. I mentioned this tragic incident to an irritable Asiatic who thinks the Pax Britannica is not beneficent, although he himself has enjoyed agreeable benefits from British commerce. He said a few words, in his hopeless Asiatic manner, which I translate thus:

"I remember Darien. English Merchants there wiped out a British colony, with the agony of hunger, disease, bankruptcy and death.["]

The very name of English Merchants makes me sick. It is one of the foul names of history. On the Judgment Day, it will delight me to see, brought up in accusation against English Merchants, multitudes of the women and children that they have brought to fatal misery in China, Africa, India, Persia, Germany, Russia. The ship Jesus,[2] beginning the great modern slave trade, sailed for English Merchants. Opium ships, for English Merchants, have

---

1. The Isthmus of Darien is the extreme eastern portion of the Isthmus of Panama. The Scottish colonial project of Darien, chartered in 1695, failed to establish a commercial port there. Nearby English settlers were enjoined by James II, "at their utmost peril," from giving any aid to the Scots, seen as serious commercial rivals. Cf. "Scots," footnote 17.
2. The *Jesus of Lubeck* was the principal ship of the second slaving voyage of the English captain John Hawkins, 1563.

CHARACTER     335

defiled the coasts of India and China. Rubber ships, for English Merchants, trafficked with the Putumayo[3] torturers and the Congo tyrants. For English Merchants, in East Africa and South Africa, whole tribes are stripped of their ancestral lands and made day laborers.
 The meek Egyptian fellaheen[4] have been driven, in our time, to revolt against English Merchants. In the nineteenth century the docile Hindoos[5] rose against them. The people of Boston have always been naturally submissive, complaisant, time-serving, slavish. Canons and cardinals tell them what they may read. Policemen club down the flower of their rich men's sons in front of their colleges. In the time of the American slave owners' aristocracy Boston's best people were 'dough faces.'[6] But English Merchants found a way, two hundred and fifty years ago, to sting into rebellion, even the servile Bostonese.
 For English Merchants, a hundred million go hungry every day in India. English Merchants put the damper on the French Revolution.[7] English Merchants in 1918, starved, by blockade, helpless, conquered nations.[8] English Merchants, some sixty years ago, smothered the Tae Ping rebellion,[9] at the cost of many millions of lives, and set back Chinese freedom by a hundred years. English

3. River rising in the Columbian Andes and flowing southeast to the Amazon, marking part of the boundary of Columbia with Ecuador and Peru. During the 19th-century wild-rubber boom, official inquiry revealed shocking working conditions in the area.
4. Arabic term for husbandman; i.e., peasant. Egyptian demands for complete independence from England, accompanied by widespread rioting and mob violence, began immediately after the WWI Armistice in 1918, culminating in the mid-1920s. Irreconcilable mutual demands prevented the conclusion of a treaty granting independence until 1936.
5. Reference to the Indian Mutiny of 1857-8, suppressed with great severity; incited, in part, by reports that British army rifle cartridges were greased with animal fat, abhorrent to both Moslems and Hindus.
6. Possible "doe-faced" was originally intended. The expression refers to northerners in favor of maintaining southern slavery; phrase attributed to John Randolph.
7. The French invasion of the Low Countries in February, 1793, caused England to declare war, both to protect its interests there and to exploit French weaknesses overseas. England forged an anti-French coalition with Austria, Prussia, Russia, Spain, and Holland, and only their disunity prevented an invasion of France. Their armies were finally repelled by massive French conscription.
8. The Allied military blockade continued throughout the period of the Versailles Treaty negotiations, November, 1918, through June, 1919, bringing much of Germany and Austria to the brink of starvation.
9. Usually called the Taiping Revolt. Was led by the visionary scholar Hung Hsiu-ch'uan against the Ch'ing dynasty of China, 1848-1865. Although he captured Nanking, the revolt was crushed with the help of Western aid, and in particular by an army led by the British general Charles George Gordon.

Merchants are now sending a great ship,[10] a carrier of air-planes, to bomb Chinese patriots back into torment and slavery.

Certain Christian merchants, engineers, teachers and missionaries, have made a noble record of self-sacrificing work in China,[11] But the Chinese have some excuse for believing that Christian missions and Christian commerce have brought China down to its present misery.

All our dealings with the Far East have been in violation of a wise policy of non-intercourse adopted by prudent Asiatics long ago. We Christians have three great wars in every century. The great wars of China, Korea and Japan used to break out about once in 200 years. This is because China, Korea and Japan, centuries ago, adopted the policy of having, in general no commercial intercourse with each other. They wisely chose, also, to have as little intercourse as possible with Christian nations. For our own profit we barbarously broke down this bar and forced China, Korea and Japan to trade with us.

When we see signs of an angry flood the proper course is to move out of the flooded district promptly and adjust the damages afterwards. So, we ought to say to the Chinese: "Our conduct in forcing ourselves upon you was indecent, unchristian and indiscreet. We shall now withdraw entirely. But, after we have withdrawn, we shall ask you to pay full damages to all our merchants, manufacturers and missionaries."

There is little hope that such a policy will be adopted. We have already forced Japan into a position where she has found it necessary, through the use of hired bandits, who call themselves Chinese Generals, to keep herself in control of the northeastern part of the Chinese empire, including Manchuria and Shantung.[12] She has resolved to use such territories until she has made herself rich enough and strong enough to defeat the United States. That process

---

10. Undoubtedly the HMS *Vindictive*, a heavy cruiser, modified to function as an aircraft carrier for operation is in the Baltic in 1919.
11. Notable among them Newell Martin's father, William Alexander Parsons Martin (1827-1916). The elder Martin went to China in 1850 to serve as a Presbyterian missionary, became in 1898 president of the Imperial University in Peking, and wrote several works in both Chinese and English. See Section Sixteen - "An Appreciation of W.A.P. Martin."
12. Employing Chinese warlords (and, in the 1930s, the last emperor of China, Henry P'u Yi) as cover, Japan had been making territorial incursions in northern China since 1915. No doubt she could hardly view the Western presence in Asia with detachment; but that it did not exercise compulsion would seem to have been shown by the fact that when the Japanese military began its program of open Manchurian conquest in 1931, it did so against the wishes of the Japanese government. See Section Thirteen - "Democracy's Crusaders."

will take a large part of a century.[13]

We have now begun to hear about prestige. Barnacles in our Foreign Office and "career men," who have been brought up in it, have formulated a policy of establishing American "prestige." I do not like to think that heaps of charming little Chinese children will be ripped open by shrapnel for American prestige.

Heaps of mangled girls and babies, in Amritsar,[14] have re-established English prestige in the Punjab. Heaps of mangled girls and babies, at Wan Hsien,[15] have restored English prestige on the Yang Tsze. It is now time to pull off a few massacres for American prestige.

When we make our campaign for prestige it will enrich many English Merchants. Our land forces in China are under the command of Smedley Butler,[16] who is something of a specialist in prestige. He has acquired prestige of several kinds for himself in Hayti, Philadelphia and California.

To keen observers it has become perceptible that the Chinese are not in love with Christian commerce or Christian missions in their present form; and that most of the Chinese think that Christians in their dealings with pagans, are swine and devils, and that the social and political systems of the Christians are undesirable and inconvenient. Such notions are in part the fruit of ignorance and prejudice and, in part, the result of painful experience. But, surely, in the 20th Century, every nation has a

13. Japan's attack on the U.S. came less than 15 years later, just 21 days after Newell Martin had died at the age of 87.
14. City in northwest Punjab, India; site of the April, 1919, Amritsar massacre in which hundreds of Indian nationalists were killed and thousands wounded by British forces. (Familiar to today's viewers of Lean's *Gandhi*.)
15. In September, 1926, a General Yang Sen seized two British steamers at the town of Wanhsien on the upper Yangtze river. He claimed the act was a reprisal for the willful swamping of two sampans, with extensive monetary loss, by one of the steamers a few days previously. (The British captain of that ship, on the other hand, maintained that the sampans had been swamped in the course of an unsuccessful boarding action by Yang Sen's forces.) Nevertheless, when two British gunboats tried unsuccessfully to retake the steamers, the action cost seven British lives and, according to British figures, 300 Chinese casualties. The Chinese representative at the League of Nations claimed the British had wantonly bombarded the town of Wanhsien, destroying "1,000" homes and killing "1,000" persons. The British claimed 300 Chinese casualties (and seven British dead.)
16. Smedley D. Butler (1881-1940): Commanded a regiment of marines in China in 1927-28. In San Diego, California, in 1926, Butler had charged a Colonel Alexander Williams of his command with intoxication and acts unbecoming an officer after accepting an invitation from Williams to a party in his hotel room. Williams went through a court martial, but was acquitted for lack of evidence. A *New York Times* editorial did some "tut-tutting" about Butler's conduct. See Section Two - "Petition to Bannard."

right to be besotted in its own ignorance and to make itself impermeable to beneficent altruistic Christian forces.

# THIRTEEN

# EAST AND WEST

**To A Few Friends
   and One or Two Foes** . . . . . . . . . . 340

**Democracy's Crusaders** . . . . . . . . . . 345

**Korean Christians** . . . . . . . . . . . . . 372

# To a Few Friends and One or Two Foes[1]
[Circa 1921]

*Ellen La Motte (see Section One - "Extracts From the 'Confessions of a Timid Old Man'."), published two books which brought forth the highest praise from Newell Martin. One, Peking Dust (N.Y.: Century, 1919) mixes vignettes of La Motte's experiences in Peking during 1916 and 1917 with political commentary. The other, Civilization (N.Y.: George H. Doran, 1919) is a collection of short stories thematically united by one or another aspect of the East-West confrontation. Professional reviews of the two books were generally favorable, qualified mainly by objections to occasional hasty or crude writing. The* Catholic World *said of* Civilization *that "while all its particulars might be right, it offered an inadequate view of the whole."*

*The following quotation from the introduction to* Peking Dust *provides a gauge for the tone of the book, and may help explain why Martin found La Motte congenial:*

> Two classes of books are written about China by two classes of people. There are books written by people who have spent the night in China, as it were, superficial and amusing, full of the tinkling of temple bells; and there are other books written by people who have spent years in China and who know it well -- ponderous books, full of absolute information, heavy and unreadable. Books of the first class get one nowhere. They are delightful and entertaining, but one feels their irresponsible authorship. Books of the second class get one nowhere, for one cannot read them; they are too didactic and dull. The only people who might read them do not read them, for they also are possessed of deep, fundamental knowledge of China, and their views agree in no slightest particular with the views set forth by the learned scholars and theorists.
> This book falls into neither of these two classes, except perhaps in the irresponsibility of its author. It is compounded of gossip -- the flying gossip of Peking.[2] Take it lightly; blow off such dust as may happen to stick

---

1. Not known to whom Martin sent LaMotte's *Peking Dust and Civilization.*
2. A sample of La Motte's "flying gossip" from pp. 47-49. "The head of a certain great corporation, out here seeking a concession from the Chinese Government, appeared before the Chinese officials one day and made his request. The officials, in their gorgeous robes, were all seated round a large table on which was spread a map of China. It was

to you. *For authentic information turn to the heavy volumes written by the acknowledged students of international politics.*

*Canterbury Chimes,"* one of the stories in Civilization, describes an Anglican bishop resident in China who is told by a Chinese youth that England encourages in China what she forbids at home, and that the church thereby profits. "Your salary, Sir -- as well as the salaries of the other priests of your established church, out here in this Colony -- comes from the established opium trade. Your Canterbury chimes ring out, every fifteen minutes, over the opium dens of the Crown!" The Bishop later discovers that a nephew, dispatched from England for unspecified disgrace and missed at the dock for having used a pseudonym on board, has died of the drug in an opium den. The last sentence in the story reads, " 'Thank God,' says the Bishop fervently, 'it was not my nephew'." (Historical exactitude compels us to note that at the first major meeting of the Anglo-American Society for the Suppression of the Opium Trade, held in England in 1881, the principle speakers were the Archbishop of Canterbury and Cardinal Manning, who condemned the trade as "opposed to international and Christian morality.") La Motte saw (pp.200-201) the European war as originating in a struggle for control of the Orient, which is probably to see too much; but was prescient enough (p. 229) to declare that "A revolution will offer the grand, final excuse for the 'protection' of China, by Europe." The following is Martin's text.

---

a wonderful large, map but all colored in different colors, some parts red, some blue, others yellow, and so on. Behind the chairs of the Chinese officials stood the representatives of the various European powers -- British, French, Russian, all of them. Our American laid his finger on that part of the map colored red.

"'I'll do the work here,' he said to the Chinese.

"'Excuse me,' interrupted a representative of a foreign government, 'you can't go there. That red part of China belongs to Great Britain.'

"'Very well. I'll go here,' said the American, indicating the blue part of the map.

"'Excuse me,' said another European gentleman, 'you can't do it there. That part of China belongs to Russia.'

"'Here, then,' continued the American, laying his finger on a green spot. 'This will do.'

"Another suave alert diplomatic gentleman stepped forth.

"'That,' he said regretfully, 'is French.'

"So it went all over the map. The Chinese officials sat silent, while one European representative after another stepped forward with his objections. Finally, in exasperation, the American turned to the silent Chinese and asked:

"'Where the hell is China?'" (pp.47-49)

I venture to send Ellen La Motte's 'Peking Dust' and her 'Civilization' (not to be confused with Duhamel's[3] or Buckle's).[4] Ellen La Motte is as free from bias as is Brooks Adams,[5] and as contemptuous of precedent as was Henry Adams.[6] She has seen the whole world, or as much of it as she has had time to see, and what she has seen has confirmed her belief in Ecclesiastes.[7] She has been sneered at because she is young; but so were Josephine Dodge Daskam Bacon,[8] and Francis Bacon, and Byron,[9] and Bonaparte.[10]

She is only a few years younger than Francis Bacon was when he took all knowledge for his province.[11]

Stodgy critics have called her frivolous. She is exactly as frivolous as Anatole France or Voltaire.[12] She turns her flashlight, for one illuminating moment, on old Asia; and we see such indecencies as have been practiced there since the days of Queen Esther[13] and the 31st Chapter of the Book of Numbers.[14]

---

3. Georges Duhamel (1884-1966). *Civilization 1914-17* (1918: translated 1919) is a collection of stories concerning the suffering Duhamel saw as a physician in an army camp. It won the Goncourt prize.
4. Henry Thomas Buckle (1821-1862). *History of Civilization in England* (Vol. I, 1857; vol. II, 1861), described by his entry in the *Dictionary of National Biography* as "the work of a brilliant amateur rather than a thorough student."
5. Brooks Adams (1848-1927), lawyer and author, youngest son of Charles Francis Adams. His *The Law of Civilization and Decay* (1896) attempted to solve major problems of civilization by applying scientific laws to the study of history. It has been described as the first American work to base the history of Western civilization systematically on economic evidence.
6. Henry Adams (1838-1918), author and editor, elder brother of Brooks. His *The Degradation of the Democratic Dogma* attempted to instruct historians in the importance for their study of current developments in physical science.
7. Perhaps Eccl. 8:14 "There is a vanity which is done upon the earth; that there be just men, unto whom it happeneth according to the work of the wicked; again, there be wicked men, to whom it happeneth according to the work of the righteous: I said that this also is vanity."
8. Ms. Bacon (1876-1961), at age 24, had her first writing success with *Smith College Stories*, and went on to publish 13 titles in the first decade of this century. In 1920 she authored the first *Girl Scout National Handbook*.
9. In 1812, at age 24, the sixth Lord Byron, George Gordon Noel Byron, had his first major literary success with *Childe Harold* in 1812.
10. Napoleon Bonaparte, at age 30, became first consul of France (1799).
11. This phrase appears in a 1592 letter to Lord Burghly in which Bacon also wrote: "I wax now somewhat ancient; one-and-thirty years is a great deal of sand in the hour-glass."
12. As Anatole France (1844-1924) in *Isle of the Penguins* or Voltaire (1694-1798) in *Candide*.
13. The Book of Esther details the attempted massacre of the Persian Jews. See Section Ten - "As to W. Morgan Shuster."
14. Describing the slaughter and pillage of the Midianites by the Israelites. "And they warred against the Midianites, as the Lord commanded Moses; and they slew all the males." (Num. 31:7)

We see, also, by her flashlight, in a dark alley, five old gentlemen in frock coats, kneeling on a throttled Chinese, and going through his pockets, while a priest stands by ready to give, to the victim, extreme unction.[15]

She has been persecuted for neglecting to whitewash embusqués;[16] but the real reason for persecuting her was that she will insist on talking against opium. If she continues to talk about it, she will end her days in some of the equatorial hells, Bilibid[17] or Devil's Island,[18] or the Andamans,[19] that she describes too vividly, and that we maintain, in the name of Jesus Christ and civilization. She tells, inter alia, of a holy bishop, supported by the opium trade;[20] the opium trade which has been one of the corner-stones of the policy of my two favorite empires, England and Japan.

For sixty years I have regarded myself as an expert in Asiatic politics,[21] and yet I do not know how you can learn more truth in one hour about the dark places of the Far East than in these two amusing little books, especially if you are open-minded and too honest to profit in politics of pocket by the misery of some far-off Chinese. That reminds me, by the way, of the famous French test of honesty. If, with perfect safety, by touching a button, you can kill a mandarin in China and thus make your fortune, would you consent to tuer le mandarin?[22] Rousseau, Balzac, thought it a fantastic, impossible case.[23] Frenchmen must have smiled when they saw Mr. Wilson, who has seldom underestimated his own virtue, put to this

---

15. According to La Motte's figures, 79% of China lay in the sphere of influence of one or another of five European powers: England 27.8%; Russia 42.3%; France 3.4%; Germany 1.3%; and Japan 4.3%. The United States "stands by."
16. That is, soldiers whose duties exempt them from drill or parade; hence slacker, dodger, or shirker of active service.
17. A Spanish-built prison at Manila in the Philippines, notorious in the nineteenth century for its harsh regimen, which included leg irons and torture.
18. One of the three Iles de Salut off the coast of French Guiana in South America. Site of a notoriously harsh French penal colony closed in 1951.
19. Islands in the Bay of Bengal, part of the union territories of India. Site of a British penal colony, established in part for rebels of the 1857 Sepoy Mutiny; abolished at the end of WWII, after having been occupied by the Japanese for three years.
20. The story "Canterbury Chimes," in *Civilization*.
21. That is, since the age of seven!
22. Allusion to a celebrated moral dilemma propounded by Vicomte Francois Rene de Chateaubriand (1768-1848) in *Le Genie du Christianisme*, I, 6, ii (1802), who qualifies the situation by proposing that the mandarin has no heirs, that he is burdened with illnesses and sorrows, that death is a good for him, that he asks for it himself, and has no more than an instant to live.
23. Balzac, in *Pere Goriot*, mistakenly attributes mandarin quandary to Rousseau (Goriot saying he is now on his 33rd mandarin); but Rousseau died in 1778, some 24 years before the dilemma was conceived.

very test. He touched the button to save his own political fortune, and extinguished the Shantung mandarins.[24]

Barring two misprints, 'Peking Dust' is free from error. Written in the dim antiquity of two years ago, it is still exactly true, except that, where Ellen La Motte says 'Europe' we must now amend her book to say 'Japan.'

Noah's curse has run out and Japhet will soon cease to dwell in the tents of Shem.[25]

In a stormy sunset, Europe's short day is drawing to its inevitable end. The day after tomorrow will be the day of huge homogeneous Asiatic[26] consolidations. Russia, Germany and Austria, fidei defensores, the strongholds of a worn out Christianity, the last firm fortresses of established churches, Greek, Protestant and Catholic, the three great Christian empires of the world, have suddenly gone down to ruin; and wise old heathen Japan has carefully and prudently entered into their vast Chinese possessions and has added to her own, their nefarious spheres of influence.

*   *   *

24. Japan, viewing the outbreak of WWI as an opportunity for territorial gains in China and elsewhere, entered the war on the Allied side. Early in 1915 she demanded some important political and economic concessions from the Chinese, including Germany's then-existing rights in Shantung, a province in northeast China. When the U.S. entered WWI in 1917, Wilson asked China to follow suit; and China, seeing America as the one friendly Western government, did so. When the Germans thereupon departed Shantung, Japan demanded the U.S. recognize (Japanese troops had already been landed.) special Japanese interests there. Wilson initially refused to do so, but the wartime demand for both merchant and naval vessels in the North Atlantic necessitated some kind of accommodation with a country capable of confining its strategic interests to the Pacific. Viscount Kikujiro Ishii and U.S. Secretary of State Robert Lansing negotiated an ambiguously-worded document which Japan was readily able to interpret as recognizing Japan's "special interests" in China, even though Wilson denied this. Japanese title to the German Shantung concessions already had been guaranteed by secret treaties with Britain, Italy, France, and Russia, and was confirmed by the Treaty of Versailles. China declined to sign, and concluded a separate peace treaty with Germany.
25. Allusion to Gen. 9:25-27, where Noah curses Ham, and through him Ham's son Canaan, for beholding his, Noah's, nakedness, which Shem and Japheth had been careful not to do. "And he said, Cursed be Canaan; a servant of servants shall he be unto his brethren. And he said, Blessed be the Lord God of Shem; and Canaan shall be his servant. God shall enlarge Japheth, and he shall dwell in the tents of Shem; and Canaan shall be his servant." The curse has sometimes been taken to refer to the subordination of the darker-skinned races.
26. "Fidei defensores," or "defenders of the faith." One of the titles of the monarchs of England (it appears on British coins). Martin may be alluding to the irony of the title having been awarded by Pope Leo X to Henry VIII for a Latin tract the latter had written on the Seven Sacraments, prior to Henry VIII's subsequent break with the Roman Catholic Church.

# Democracy's Crusaders in Shan-tung[1]

*"Democracy's Crusaders in Shan-tung" appeared in* The Century Magazine, *November, 1919, pp. 8-19. Martin's good friend, W. Morgan Shuster, was president of the Century Company at that time (see Section Ten - "As to W. Morgan Shuster.") A section on the issue's contributors -- who included James Branch Cabell, Agens Repplier, and George Moore — described Martin as a "distinguished New York lawyer, now retired from active practice, who for many years has devoted himself to studying political and social phenomena in Europe and the far East. Born in China, he is said to have spoken no English until four or five years of age. Perhaps that helps to explain his extraordinary knowledge and keen sympathy with the "sick man of the Orient." It is rare that scholarship like Mr. Martin's is found united with a fierce vigor of style. Because of its timeliness, as well as its wealth of information, this article on Shan-tung possesses unusual interest." The article was preceded by an italicized self-quotation taken from the text.]*

> *"The progressive partition of China went slowly because of the wealth at stake. It was sufficiently obvious that whatever outsider could annex China could rule the world. Russia hoped to get all of China for herself, but England, France, and Germany could not agree to that nor with one another. The survivors are at last ready to agree."*

In the Fourth Crusade, in 1202, the pious knights of France, England, and Italy, with such serfs as could be spared from the farms, set out to free the Holy Land. They were under the special blessing of Pope Innocent. We need not remember his number. He

---

1. For the general background to this piece, see note 24 in "To a Few Friends and One or Two Foes," explicating Wilson's conduct vis-a-vis Shantung.
    Wilson arrived at Versailles apparently determined to uphold the right to self-determination for China which had been part of the inducement offered for Chinese participation in WWI, only to be confronted by secret treaties made in 1915 and 1918 and co-signed by Japan, France, England, and Russia guaranteeing Japan's right postwar to the former German concessions in China. Japan threatened to withdraw from the Versailles conference unless these rights were upheld; and Wilson, viewing participation in the conference as naturally linked to participation in his pet project, the League of Nations, eventually gave way on every substantive issue. In 1922, the Japanese did withdraw from Shantung, though only with Chinese indemnification. Japanese forces returned in 1928, and from 1937-1945 occupied the whole of Shantung.

has been known for some time as the Innocent of the Fourth Crusade.[3] Unfamiliar with the practical side of crusading, he was easily maneuvered by Henry Dandolo[4] into a hole, or dilemma, where he had to admit himself a failure or connive at Dandolo's crimes. One of the declared objects of the Fourth Crusade was "the establishment of right everywhere."[5] In seven hundred years we have invented no new formula.

The crusaders dawdled too long in Dalmatia, setting Fiume "in order," a task still unfinished. Then, as now, French and Italians fell into deadly dispute about the occupying of Dalmatian cities.[6] Some of the knights began to hear that relatives, embusques,[7] at home, were making love to the wives, estates, or jobs of the absent heroes. Some had borrowed from the Jews for equipment; the interest was running against them. There was no cash to be had out of the Holy Sepulcher, and it looked as if they might get home with the Croix de Guerre just in time to be served with foreclosure papers. Some were sick with the various fevers that used to beset crusaders, and all of them were sick of sutler's pork.

Dandolo, Doge of Venice, more than eighty years old, but as cunning, unscrupulous, and obstinate as Satan, became their generalissimo. The Mohammedans of Damascus and Bagdad having sent him a huge cash bribe to induce him to divert the

---

3. Innocent III (1160 or 1161-1216), pope 1198-1216, acknowledged as one of the greatest of the medieval popes, remembered primarily for his attempt (largely successful) to establish the primacy of papal over secular rule.
4. Enrico Dandolo (c. 1108-1205), Doge of Venice 1192-1205.
5. John Godfrey in *The Unholy Crusade* (N.Y.: Oxford University Press, 1980), p.35, writes only that "Innocent formally published his plan for 'a sacred war against the Saracens, for the recovery of the Holy Land' in a general letter to the Western archbishops as early as August 1198."
6. Venice constructed a fairly magnificent fleet for the transportation of the crusaders to the Holy Land, for which the crusaders had contracted and finally proved unable to pay. Dandolo persuaded them to finance the ships by reconquering for Venice its former possession of Zara in Croatia (now Zadar in Yugoslavia), an important Adriatic seaport. Zara was indeed retaken, then sacked, the Venetians and the Frankish crusaders becoming involved in sometimes furious disputes over the division of the spoils which left many of them dead. The looting of a Christian and Catholic town by force committed to the liberation of the Holy Land violently angered the pope. He excommunicated the Venetians involved, who had remained unrepentant. Innocent also openly disfavored the diversion to Constantinople, and openly expressed his fury at the sacking of that city, though he did state his pleasure at the Eastern Church being placed under papal protection.

Fiume (Rijeka), Hungary's chief port prior to World War I located some 100 miles north of Zadar was, in 1919, seized by an Italian free corps under the poet Gabriele d'Annunzio, which skirmished with the French occupying force. Subsequently the 1920 Treaty of Rapallo made Fiume a free state; it was reoccupied by Italy in 1922.
7. Soldiers whose duties exempt them from drill or parade; hence slacker, dodger, shirker of active service.

Crusaders from their ideals, he told the chivalric knights of the wealth and weakness of Byzantium, and under his lead the Crusaders turned away forever from their holy quest and besieged, assaulted, captured, and sacked the metropolis of Christendom, Constantinople, then the City of Churches, and repaired their private fortunes, but not those of their serfs, and sold Christian girls to paynim Saracens.[8]

Venice carried off the lion's share — the British portion, so to speak — of the booty. Part of it was the four bronze horses which stand to-day in perpetuam rei memoriam ["In everlasting memory of the event"] above the portal of St. Mark's, one of Christ's premier churches.[9]

Other good things came in. Historians believe that Innocent and Fulc of Neuilly, the two great preachers of the crusade, were justly charged with profiteering and embezzlement.[10]

Chinese marvel at the Fourth Crusade, and ask whether the name of "Crusader" is not now an insult.

Italy and devout France regard Innocent, Fulc, and Dandolo as having written some of the brightest pages in Europe's annals, and worship their memory. Unpicturesque, unbarbarous countries like China and America have to content themselves with such drab heroes as Washington, Franklin, and Confucius. Michaud, a fervent admirer of these French and Italian miscreants, says that "the Cross was for them a sacred tie, which united all their interests. No one listened to those who persisted in raising scruples."[11] In hoc signo

---

8. The ostensible motive for the diversion of the Crusade was the restoration to the Byzantine throne of the prince Alexius, son of the deposed emperor Isaac II Angelus. Scholars disagree as to whether a "cash bribe" was involved, and recent historians do not even mention it. To the crusaders, desperately short of men and money, Alexius had promised in return an army of 10,000 and the maintenance of 500 knights in the Holy Land for the duration of his life. As Alexius probably knew, Byzantine wealth was by no means adequate to this commitment, and the sacking of Byzantium followed his reneging on his oath. Dandolo had sufficient motive in the restoration to the Eastern throne of an emperor beholden to the Venetians, and the restoration of Venetian trading supremacy in the Golden Horn.

9. A very great deal of St. Mark's artwork is in fact loot from Constantinople such legendary objects as: St. Mark's also acquired fragments of the Cross, a few drops of the Blood, a thorn from the Crown, a portion of the pillar across which Jesus was scourged, an arm of St. George, and a piece of John the Baptist's skull.

10. Fulk or Fulc of Neuilly (?-1202) was pastor of the parish of Neuilly, who abandoned a dissolute life and became an itinerant preacher after some sudden and pronounced religious experience. His passionate oratory did a great deal to make the Crusade a popular cause, and he did indeed collect large sums for the crusaders from his listeners. Although there were some contemporary allegations of diversions of monies by both Fulk and Innocent, they are not taken seriously by competent historians; e.g., Donald E. Queller, *The Fourth Crusade* (University of Pennsylvania Press, 1977), p. 45.

11. Joseph Francois Michaud (1767-1839), French historian. *History of the Crusades*, Vol. III, translated by W. Robson (N.Y.: Armstrong, no date), p. 62: "The cross of the

vinces ["Under this sign you shall conquer"] was the Crusader's battle cry, and when the helpless Catholics of Zara, huddled in terror behind their own holy cross, the Crusaders, thirsting for plunder, cut them down.[12]

We new crusaders run true to the form of the Fourth Crusade. Our "interests" are "united" by our high ideals. We do not "listen" to those who have "scruples."

For Mohammedan, Japanese, and Jewish reasons, we bear no uplifted cross; but we carry banners emblazoned with the golden words "Down with Autocracy," "Up with Republics," "No more Militarism," "Democracy," "Sanctity of Boundaries," "Nationality," "Self-determination," "Freedom of Weak Nations."

For some obscure advantage to our President and for some gigantic profit to England and France we have awarded Shan-tung to Japan.

We have sold to sword and whip, we have sold into perpetual slavery, China, our own brother in arms, whom we drew to our aid in war by our own pledges and promises. Ray Baker says that the President's sleep was broken by his anxiety about China.[13]

Our battle-cries prove to have been devised by our leaders with fraudulent intent. We know now what to expect from our partners and our rulers.

In international politics there is no morality, says Emil Reich of Paris.[14] Marquis Okuma[15] says:

---

pilgrims was, for the Venetians and French, a pledge of alliance, a sacred tie, which united all their interests, and made of them, in a manner, but one same nation. From [the time Dandolo himself took the cross] no one listened to those who spoke in the name of the Holy See, or persisted in raising scruples in the minds of the Crusaders."

12. The Zarans did hang crucifixes on their walls as an unavailing reminder that they were Christian subjects, and undeniably the city was severely pillaged. As to extensive bloodshed, Gibbon says, "Their lives were spared" and other historians concur. Apparently the city surrendered once resistance was seen to be futile.

13. Ray Stannard Baker (1870-1946), a journalist and author, was a friend of President Wilson, who appointed him director of the press bureau of the American Commission to Negotiate Peace in Paris, which led to his becoming historian of Wilson's role at Versailles. From Baker's *What Wilson Did at Paris* (N.Y.: Doubleday, 1919), p. 88: "Of all the important decisions at the Peace Conference none worried the President so much as that relating to the disposition of the Shantung peninsula – and none, finally, satisfied him less....He told me on one occasion that he had been unable to sleep on the previous night for thinking of it."

14. Emil Reich (1854-1910),, historian and lecturer; Hungarian-born, lived in Paris until 1893, and subsequently in England. Wrote *Success Among Nations* (1904) and *Imperialism* (1905).

15. Marquis Shigenobu Okuma (1838-1922), Japanese statesman who worked for parliamentary government and the strengthening of Japanese industry. Twice premier; in the second of these terms (1914-1916), Japan entered WWI and presented China with the Twenty-One Demands.

International relations are quite unlike those of individuals. Morality and sincerity do not govern diplomacy, which is guided by selfishness. It is the secret of diplomacy to forestall rivalry by every crafty means.

Nations, like thieves, do whatever will pay. Among private thieves, however, the Shan-tung award would be thought subversive of gang ethics. Hans, a lonely desperado, steals my valuables, including the key to my safe-deposit vault. Jimmy the Jap takes them from his corpse. The gang of which Jimmy and I are members meet to divide plunder. The gang awards the stolen treasure to Jimmy.

Befog the villainy as we may with talk of leases, concessions, treaties, the twenty-one demands,[16] economic reservations, and all the other smoke screens of diplomatic chicanery, that is the sum and essence of the deal. What France and England are to get is a secret. It may be that they do not intend to get from China as much as Japan will in coal, iron, copper, gold, petroleum, labor, and trade. Credat Judaeus.[17]

"Like wolves," wrote a Chinese viceroy, "the powers of Christendom close in about us." Three of the wolves, Romanoff, Hohenzollern, and Hapsburg,[18] have torn one another to pieces. They are dead dogs, no more to be thought about in Asia. Wise old Japan has carefully entered into their illimitable Asiatic possessions, and added to her own their nefarious spheres of influence. China is now bounded on the south and west by two insatiable imperial appetites, France and England, and on the north and east by the Japanese oligarchy, in desperate need, which must expand or sink into a decline.

Kiao-chau[19] is a city and district, and Tsing-tau[20] a port, both in Shan-tung, a province of thirty-odd millions. To China the loss

---

16. Demands made of China by Japan, agreed to by President Wilson, which included Japanese control over the German leasehold at Kiaochow (see note 19 below), control of Manchuria and Mongolia, exploitation of China's main coal deposits, denial of further territorial concessions to other powers, and the guidance if not control of China's military and domestic affairs.
17. Horace, *Credat Judaeus Apella*, "Let the Jew Apella believe it"; i.e., I won't. The Romans regarded the Jewish religion as credulous.
18. Respectively, ruling dynasty of Russia 1613-1917; ruling dynasty of Prussia, and of Germany 1871-1918; and ruling house of Austria 1282-1918.
19. Area of some 200 square miles in south Shantung province, leased by Germany in 1898.
20. Tsingtao or Ch'ingtao, capital of Kiaochow. Port on the Yellow Sea, leading naval depot and manufacturing center.

of these is what ours would be if the Paris partitioners had awarded to Liberia for her war services (she was one of the Allies) Chicago, Cook county, and the Illinois railroads. Our pain would not be lessened if the Liberians should kindly offer to limit themselves to the Lake Front and to share the railroads with us, particularly if they owned the police of the railway towns and he'ld Mississippi and Massachusetts, and had already got control, sometimes secretly, sometimes openly, of our finances, of our best iron mines and steel works, and of such of our cabinet and Congress as might be bribable. Japan, moreover, is one of the powers that. control China's tariffs and maritime customs and her salt gabel:

Few of us know Kirin[21] and Fu-chau.[22] One is far up toward the frigid north, and the other is down by the bamboos and camphor-trees; but both are rich, both are inhabited by Chinese republicans, both belong to China, and both are held by Japan. Shan-tung is between the two, a halfway-house of conquest. There the German robbers built their pirate town. There the Japanese have made permanent improvements, among them a yoshiwara[23] of fifty houses and a glorious Shinto temple.

Few Americans will deplore the sufferings of the Germans of the China missions, who with their wives and children were horribly packed into a sort of slave-ship and sent off through the Red Sea, where their Jehovah, despite frequent German prayers, performed no miracle for their relief.[24]

Few will deplore the yoshiwara. It is a dull tourist who does not prefer a yoshiwara to a Lutheran chapel. We have no houses of worship that can be frequented with such daily delight as the temples of Japan, and no houses of pleasure so beguiling as even those new houses in Tsing-tau. I myself prefer any Japanese, even geisha girls, to any Germans, even German missionaries. The Chinese do not. The Germans beat them with whips, but the Japanese scourge them with scorpions.

21. Chilin, province with capital city of same name immediately north of Korea.
22. Fuchou or Fouchow, port in southeast China roughly halfway between Shanghai and Hongkong, opposite Taiwan.
23. Old name for a district of Tokyo, location of the most famous of the government-regulated houses of prostitution; hence such a house.
24. In February and March of 1919 the Chinese government deported some 2,500 German nationals, who were returned to Europe on four British liners. In May the German government lodged a protest with Great Britain over the living conditions on the ships, which it claimed were so bad as to have caused numerous deaths. The British government gave an account, printed in the *London Times*, of what it said were all the deaths: a total of nine, all from normal causes.

My money still goes into the plate for China missions, but, while the music of the offertory thrills through the aisles, I wonder at the circuity of action which takes my Sunday money to build churches and hospitals in China and my income tax to maintain in China Shinto temples and yoshiwaras. If we did not pay our income taxes, those fifty enticing houses would be empty.

It is true that Shan-tung is China's Holy Land. Japanese roughs, rough with a Japanese perfection of technic, whose mission it is to stimulate "disorder," terrorize the region of the birth and burial of the placid Confucius, and harry the meek pilgrims that climb the fairy heights of Tai Shan, the sacred mountain.[25] But why complain? We left our Holy Sepulcher to infidels, and are now planning to intrust it to the descendants of Caiaphas.[26]

The new lords of Shan-tung will touch the Chinese in a more vital spot. The German robbers were strategists. Shan-tung lies athwart two great channels of Chinese commerce, the railroad from Shanghai to Peking, and the Grand Canal, which carries rice to the North.[27] Thus the Japanese "police" have a grip on China's windpipe and carotid artery.

The Japanese hold Port Arthur[28] and as much as they have had time to digest of Manchuria. Across the narrow entrance of the Gulf of Petchili,[29] the Chinese Mediterranean, they hold Shan-tung. These are two jaws closing on Peking, Tientsin, and northern China. The German pirates built their railway, now awarded by us to Japan, strategically, through Shan-tung, pointing westward toward Shen-si and Shansi.[30] These three provinces, with Chi-li and Manchuria, already in the invader's grip, hold deposits of coal and iron so rich that they will equip navies when the miner's pick is silent in Pennsylvania, and when young New-Yorkers are rickshaw coolies for Japanese gentlemen. This is not a fantastic prophecy. In Frankfort, Japanese push German barons off the sidewalk. It has

---

25. Peak in central Shantung province with many temples and monuments; from earliest times worshipped as the greatest of China's sacred mountains.
26. Acting high priest at the time of the trial of Jesus whose long term in office shows his relations with the Romans to have been obsequious and adroit. Apparently Martin's view of those Jews cooperating with the British in the contemporary establishment of a Jewish national home in Palestine.
27. The Yun Ho, at 1,200 miles, is China's longest canal and one of the longest in the world, extending from Peking to Ningpo, its entire central portion lying in Shantung province.
28. Also known as Lushunk'ou, city in Liaoning province in northern China, at the tip of the Liaotung peninsula.
29. Gulf of Pei Chihli (Bei Zhi), now called Po-hai. Arm of the Yellow Sea indenting the coast of northern China.
30. Respectively provinces in north central and northeast China.

been asserted that in Fiume, Chinese soldiers, under the orders of French officers, have shot down Italians.[31] If I had prophesied those things five years ago, you would have smiled. Above all, these northern provinces are the world's finest reservoir of labor.

Shan-tung is about one fifth of the field of campaign in the Japanese conquest of China. Shan-tung is the center of the attack. Manchuria and Fu-chau are the right and left flanks. With the Shan-tung attack pushed home, the conquest or partition of China will be completed with disastrous speed.

A voice from the grave, Mr. Taft, the Ben Gunn of the Republican party, says we exaggerate China's plight, and that Japan has promised to surrender Shan-tung.[32] That promise was made with the expectation that, through control by the associated governments of news and opinion, nobody would give any more thought to it than we gave to Japan's aggressions in Fu-chau. That promise could not come home to roost unless our Senate took it up. The powers counted on our Senate's becoming preoccupied with nearer difficulties, as it will be. Japan will use the disseisor's[33] best friend, time. She will so confuse our President, our editors, and us with concessions, withdrawals, reservations of economic interest, surrenders of political power, reservations of commercial interest, and distinctions between settlement and conquest, between soldiers and police, that, overburdened with our own sorrows, we shall leave it all to "experts," and finally Japan will take such steps as she desires, with Chinese "railway guards" and Chinese permits. She will give assurance of the "integrity" of China in the modern European fashion. She always assures beforehand the "integrity" of what she is about to swallow. It is her grace before meat.

England and Japan guaranteed the integrity of Korea. Then Hayashi[34] induced Lansdowne[35] to agree that Japan "is interested

---

31. In the last year and a half of WWI China sent some 250,000 laborers (no combatants) to the Western Front. In July, 1919, several soldiers from Annam; i.e., French Indo-China, were killed or wounded in clashes with Italian troops at Fiume. The French government in fact cited their nationality as evidence that the conflicts could not have arisen through personal anti-Italian sentiment.
32. William Howard Taft (1857-1930), former President of the U.S., overwhelmingly defeated by Wilson in 1912. Taft had toured the country in the spring and summer of 1919 giving speeches in support of the Versailles Treaty, the League of Nations, and Wilson's conduct generally. He had at least professed a belief in the Japanese promise to surrender Shantung. Ben Gunn, in Stevenson's *Treasure Island*, was the pirate marooned on the island by Captain Flint, and still alive there years later when Squire Trelawney came to seek the treasure.
33. One who dispossesses another of his land or other property.
34. Hayashi Tadesu (1850-1913), Japanese diplomat. As minister to Great Britain 1900-1906 helped to bring about the Anglo-Japanese Treaty of 1902. Later foreign

in a peculiar degree" in Korea. Then "disorders." Then military occupation.

The process of absorbing China is ludicrously and tragically the same. In the treaty between England and Japan in 1902 "the High Contracting Parties declare themselves to be entirely uninfluenced by any aggressive tendencies" in China and Korea.[36] In the Russo-Japanese agreement of 1907 "the High Contracting Parties recognize the territorial integrity" of China.[37] This was the prelude to concerted aggressions on China by both nations. "High contracting parties," says Anthony Trollope,[38] "do sometimes allow themselves a latitude which would be considered dishonest by contractors of a lower sort."

In 1908, in the Elihu Root and Takahira agreement, those humorists agreed that Japan and the United States are "determined" to support "the independence and integrity of China."[39]

The second move was in 1916, when Ishii induced Lansing to "recognize" Japan's "special interest" in China, a "region contiguous to" Japan's "possessions." The Lansing-Ishii agreement follows the rule of the thrifty farmer who said, "I'm not greedy, but I want what jines me."

The third, fourth and fifth moves, violation of neutrality, disorders, and military occupation, have been made almost simultaneously.

Shan-tung should be as free from Japan and Japanese as if no predatory German had ever landed on her coast. Short of that, Japan's withdrawals, promises, and compromises will deceive no

---

minister, in which post he concluded the Franco-Japanese Agreement of 1907 and the Russo-Japanese Agreement of 1907.
35. Henry Charles Keith Petty Fitzmaurice, 5th Marquis of Lansdowne (1845-1927), British statesman, foreign secretary 1900-1905.

---

36. Treaty provided for joint action in the event of encroachment by Russia in conjunction with any fourth power, and affirmed each other's special interests in China and Japan's special interest in Korea.
37. Treaty in which these powers agreed to respect each other's territorial integrity and to defend the maintenance of the status quo by peaceful means. Secret clauses delineated the spheres of influence of the two governments throughout northern Asia.
38. British novelist (1815-1882).
39. Elihu Root (1845-1937), American statesman, secretary of state 1905-1909. Takahira Kogoro (1854-1926), Japanese diplomat, minister to the U.S. 1900-1907; ambassador 1907-1909. The Takahira-Root agreement set forth the respective roles of the two countries in China and the Pacific, in effect insuring Japanese recognition of American priority in Hawaii and the Philippines and American recognition of Japan's position in Manchuria.

one who has watched France's acquisition of Morocco,[40] or who has seen how, after modest beginnings, small investments, the purchase of canal shares, and repeated denials of ambition and repeated promise to retire, England has become the owner of Egypt.[41]

The Chinese Government, lonely, starving, friendless, and helpless, may assent to twenty or thirty "demands," and may notify us that the Japanese in Shan-tung are heartily welcome. Jefferson Davis, in 1863, if he had thought it worth while, could have sent Lincoln a protest signed by half the blacks in the South against the misdirected zeal of the Abolitionists.

Avarice, ambition, fear of being forestalled by France and England, and the need of food, coal, and iron, and the very natural wish to get raw materials without paying for them, drive Japan to extend her "interests" on the mainland. It is suggested that this extension will pay her for her war services. For Japan, the joy of putting down autocracy and militarism should be reward enough. Her captured Pacific islands, indeed, are worth more than she spent on the war.[42]

A more altruistic pretext is offered by Japan and her accomplices: "China is in disorder; she cannot manage her own affairs; her officials have become too corrupt to be trusted with railroads and mines; bogus patriots set themselves up, like feudal chieftains, with armies, and obstruct commerce; no solid central authority exists."

China's disorders, weakness, and corruption are temporary diseases, traceable, in their present form and degree, to the malign activities of Europe and Japan. China during the larger part of some thousands of years has managed her affairs better than Europe has

---

40. Morocco's strategic position and economic importance excited an intense rivalry between the major European powers for control of the region throughout the middle and later 19th century. A formal settlement was reached at the Algeciras conference of 1906, assuring protection of German investments and giving France and Spain police authority. However, German military forces subsequently were dispatched more than once, ostensibly for the protection of German property during clashes between the French and the native population, notably at Agadir in 1911. Germany finally agreed to a French protectorate in return for French territories in the Congo.
41. The Turkish viceroy of Egypt, Ismail, bankrupted by his own policies, was forced to sell his share (some 44%) in the Suez Canal to Great Britain. When this measure proved insufficient a Commission for the Service of the Public Debt was formed, its members appointed by France, Britain, Austria, and Italy. Unrest caused by austerity measures and Ismail's unpopularity was put down by Britain in 1882. In effect a British government was established though never formally acknowledged.
42. In return for its participation in WWI, Japan received the Mariana, Caroline, and Marshall islands, all of them German territories since the latter 19th century. Wilson did not object.

managed hers, and can do it again if left to herself.

If I lock up and starve and drug an opulent relative, the time soon comes when I can persuade my accomplices that he has become unable to manage his estate, and that we should move in and take charge of his property, and, for the improvement of his mind, make him, in his own house, a scullion for us.

Pretext or no pretext, Japan is bent on making herself strong on the mainland, because she has no faith in the League of Nations.

To Asiatics all Europeans look alike. Few Asians lament the wreck of Europe. They see that the old concern is to be reorganized under a new name as a league. The chief bankrupts have the preferred stock, a majority of the directors, and most of the recently acquired real estate. The confiding old gentleman who was the largest creditor puts up all the new money. Japan sees, therefore, that she must be ready for the next break-up. She knows also that a committee is not more virtuous than its organizers or its members. She distrusts each of the new council. England, her old ally, sits at the head of the council. England's colonies, however, hate Japanese. Japan has seen England betray China to please Japan, and she fears that England may betray Japan to please somebody else. Iago's advice is well understood in Japan.[43]

France is second on the council. She is one of the three that stole Port Arthur from Japan.[44] In the Russo-Japanese War, particularly at Nosse-Be and Kamranh Bay, France broke her treaties with Japan.[45] These wrongs have not been forgotten, and do not inspire confidence. America sold her high ideals to Japan, and Japan fears that America may sell out again to some other customer. She thinks she cannot leave it to old foes and commercial rivals to say how much coal and iron she shall have. No requests of the league will relax her grip. To the league she will answer:

> We hold your covenants and awards, secret and open. Our Shan-tung is a *fait accompli*, beloved accomplices, like your Madagascar, Morocco, Egypt, and Ireland. We fought to set the world right, but it

---

43. *Othello* I, iii, "Put money in thy purse"; i.e., take measures to secure your future.
44. Japan captured Port Arthur in the Sino-Japanese War of 1895, but was immediately forced to relinquish it by the so-called Tripartite Intervention of Germany, France, and Russia, who were worried that the territorial reallocation would collapse the Manchu dynasty and throw China into chaos, to the detriment of their concessions there.
45. France harbored the Russian fleet on its journey to the Far East, most notably at Nossi-Be in the present Malagaysay Republic and Kamranh Bay in what is now Vietnam, thereby violating the neutrality provision in the Franco-Japanese Treaty on Trade and Navigation of 1896.

was understood that is was not the intent of any of us to redress any wrongs other than those perpetrated by our depraved enemies. Holland and China have shown that the world is not safe for weak nations.[46] We must be strong and we must grow great at China's expense. Will you leave Tientsin,[47] Hankow,[48] Wei-hai-wei,[49] Kwantung,[50] Kwangri,[51] Szechuen,[52] Tunnan,[53] the Yangtse Valley,[54] and Tibet?[55] We will leave China, in fact, if you Christians will do the same.

Japan, to carry forward her invasion, must break through a lofty barricade, built, perhaps not impregnably, of Mr. Wilson's words and American ideals.[56]

> Wilson demands, and the league is to insure the settlement of every question, whether of territory, 'of sovereignty, of economic arrangements [arrangement], or of political relationship, upon the basis of the full [free] acceptance of that settlement by the people immediately concerned, and not upon the

---

46. Holland succeeded in remaining neutral in WWI and was unaffected by it territorially. Martin presumably alludes to the Netherlands' history from 1794-1839, when it was successively occupied by the French, made a kingdom under Louis Bonaparte, annexed to France, joined with Belgium by the Congress of Vienna, rebelled against by that country, and forced to accede to Belgian independence by the European great powers in the Treaty of 1839. Or possibly he speaks of the bloody Spanish rule of the 17th and early 18th centuries.
47. City in Hopeh province, northern China at junction of the Grand Canal and Hai River; a leading port. Jointly occupied by French and British beginning 1858.
48. Hangchow, capital of Cekiang province, southeast China on East China Sea. Opened to foreign trade by the Treaty of Shimonsekei ending the 1895 Sino-Japanese War. Japan was in fact the primary foreign presence there.
49. Now Weihai, area of some 285 square miles in northeast Shantung province, British leasehold beginning 1898.
50. Now Liaoning, province in northeast China on the Pohai Bay, capital Mukden. Leased for 25 years by Russia in 1898, but the lease had in fact been taken over by Japan after the Russo-Japanese War.
51. Possible misprint for Kwangsi, province in southern China immediately north of present-day Vietnam, and formerly site of French concessions.
52. (Szechwan, Sichuan): province in southwest China, China's largest. The British and French held concessions there beginning latter 19th century.
53. Almost certainly a misprint for Yunnan, province in southern China bordering Burma and Laos on the west, Vietnam on the south; likewise former site of French concessions.
54. The valley of the Yangtze, Asia's longest river and navigable by ocean liners for some 1,000 miles, English concession since the 1860's.
55. Encouraged by Britain, Tibet had declared its independence from China in 1913. In 1918, Britain made twelve demands on the Chinese government for administrative and commercial rights in Tibet sufficiently extensive to amount to partial territorial control.
56. Quotation is from an address given by Wilson at Mt. Vernon, July 4, 1918, setting forth what he regarded as the "ends for which the associated peoples of the world are fighting."

basis of the material interests [interest] or advantage of any other nation.

Throwing open the last great gate of China before the Japanese is the most extensive violation of this rule that has ever been possible.

With pathetic zeal Presbyterians and Methodists are pouring out new millions in a "drive" for China missions, while Japanese soldiers stamp out Korean Christianity; while the mission board receive Viscount Uchida's congratulations of their "cordial and friendly spirit" and his advice that they "continue" their "moderate attitude" lest the "press of foreign countries rashly" "invite additional excitement," which might "seriously interfere with" "reforms";[57] and while Mr. Wilson extends the Japanese dominions so that Japanese torturers may cross over from Shan-tung and apply their skill to Chinese Christians. Chinese Christians deserve our thought, even if they have escaped the all-seeing eye of Mr. Wilson.

Many Chinese, it is true, are humorously agnostic as to the various gods of the Christians and as to their own. Chinese can be, however, fanatic devotees. Ancient and modern persecutions have proved their faith. An ever-increasing multitude of Chinese Christians follow the ideals of Chinese martyrs, whom in the Boxer War neither foment nor reward could shake. These Christians we sell to the only remaining pagan empire.

Nor should Chinese patriots be sold without some protest. Breathes there an American boy whose heart does not stir before the statues of Nathan Hale and the Minute-Man? Young hearts and old hearts beat with the same emotion, against an alien tyrant on the other side of this round world. China is a land of patriots -- patriots whom ruthless massacre and excruciating agonies devised by Oriental ingenuity have not put down.

Westward the star of empire takes its way -- the star of Japanese empire, the star to which Mr. Wilson has hitched his obedient wagon, and before it sinks a true democracy.

China has always had her kings and emperors. It has,

---

57. Uchida Kosai (1865-1936), diplomat and politician, foreign minister 1918-1923. Japan formally occupied Korea in 1910. Throughout the spring and early summer of 1919 there had been large-scale public protest against Japanese rule, in which Korean Christians had played a predominant role. These had been barbarically dealt with; e.g., between March 1 and April 11 some 361 Koreans had reliably been reported killed and 800 wounded (persons reporting these events were themselves often tortured by the Japanese police). In response to a protest by the Federal council of Churches of Christ in America, the Japanese government promised investigations and "administrative reforms," for which, as it put it, the time had not previously been "ripe." Uchida requested "the continuance of a sane and moderate attitude" on the part of the accusers. See "Japan's Attempt to Exterminate Korean Christians."

however, been the practice of her governments, ancient and modern, even under monarchs theoretically absolute, to act in substantial obedience to law, precedent, custom, and public opinion. In China there are no feudal lords, no caste, and, with small exceptions that do not affect the structure of society, there is no hereditary nobility. The poorest boy in China can rise to wealth and power. Until the withering hand of Europe fell on China, the machinery for finding talent among the poor and putting it on the path of ambition was singularly ingenious and effective.

The highest positions in the state have always been open to the humblest peasant.

Intellectual training is at the disposal of the poorest.

China has always been at the highest rung of the democratic ladder.

Local self-government, democratic equality of opportunity, and decentralization have always been the rule in China.

The secret of China's prolonged existence as a nation has been her democracy and freedom.

An imperial decree of 1122 B.C. ordered that in admitting students to examination for degrees no distinction should be made between high and low, rich and poor. The emperor's own son was sent to a common school.[58]

I do not find in the England of the twelfth century B.C. any such democratic ideas, or even in her subsequent history. There are only two great democracies, China and the United States. If each of these great democracies were independent and unhampered by the encroachments and alliances of selfish aliens, and if they were sympathetic with each other, and working together, without leagues and covenants, by the development of their own wealth and their own citizens and their own art, they would be impregnable.

Korea has shown that where the Japanese conquers a foreign country he abstracts with skill new riches from the land, but that under the cold tyranny of Japanese colonial officials men decay. Under them these Chinese democrats will become actually slaves and will decline in civilization. We bind the most democratic of democracies to a highly organized aristocracy, an oligarchy operating under the forms of autocracy.

The Japanese conquest is carefully arranged to fit in with the partitioning process begun by England and France before 1840, on

---

58. Mandarin China was indeed in some ways the home of the *carriere ouverte aux talents*. Whether that makes a democracy, of one blood with the United States, out of a country where no one ever voted for a person or a policy, let the reader judge.

the theory that China is "backward" and that it is for us to take her apart and enlighten her insides and abstract her valuables. It would have been better, if, instead, Chinese had been sent to put Europe together — Europe, in politics, is herself a "backward" continent. We have learned to think of the Indian peninsula, with its entanglements of races, languages, and religions, collectively, as India. It will tend to clearness of thought if we study in the same way the small disorderly peninsula of Europe. The inhabitants of Tahiti used to think about themselves as the "world." Europe has had a similar barbarous illusion. Most of our own statesmen, when small boys, were taught from Swinton's "History of Civilization and the World's Progress." That book is a literary curiosity. It contains no reference to Japan or China.[59]

The time is not so far distant when European wars will be known only to special students, as are now the wars of the fighting Cheyennes.[60] To them Europe's brilliant achievements in art and science will gleam as flashes in the darkness. Politically she will interest them chiefly as the mother hive of the American swarms and by reason of her raids on Asia.

In political evolution Europe is far behind the United States, China, and Japan. Europe, until recent times, has been torn by wars of religion. Such wars are unknown to us, and to Chinese and Japanese they seem absurd. Chinese and Japanese persecutions have been purely political in motive.

Europeans, in their old habitat, have shown no capacity to make any great combination in which the parts shall be friendly and equal. They do not know how to make a partnership, but they do know how to get a strangle-hold. They make short friendships and long hatreds and kaleidoscopic alliances, always for some temporary advantage. The small cities and states of ancient Greece, the Italian cities, the German principalities, the Balkan States, have exhibited, among the most brilliant and vigorous of Europeans, a weary succession of race wars and group wars. It is significant that to this day the history of the Peloponnesian War is the prime text-book[61]

---

59. William Swinton (1833-1892), prolific author of primary-school texts, including *Outlines of the World's History, Ancient, Medieval and Modern, with Special Relation to the History of Civilization and Progress of Mankind*, 1st edition N.Y. 1874; last edition 1902.
60. Martin's brother-in-law, George Bird Grinnell, was the author of *The Indians of Today* (1900), *The Fighting Cheyennes* (1915) and a definitive two-volume work, *The Cheyenne Indians* (1923).
61. By Thucydides (460?-400? B.C.), Athenian historian.

of the budding English statesman. Even Norway and Sweden,[62] even Belgium and Holland,[63] could not hold together.

It is an index of Europe's incapacity to cure race conflicts that, after mismanaging Ireland for four hundred years, the British colonized northern Ireland with Scotch,[64] as representatives of Ireland's conquerors, thus ingeniously infecting wretched Ireland with a new problem of conflicting religions and a new problem of conflicting races.

Has England learned anything from that object lesson or from the race conflicts that make Europe a museum of political disease? Wilson learned the lesson and preached it. What lure of ambition has led him not to practice it?

When we shout and fight for the "principle" of "nationality," I suppose we mean that men of one race should be free to make themselves into one nation. We ourselves, despite our blacks, are, as regards unity, a bright contrast to Europe; but China proper, the eighteen provinces, is the supreme example of the principle.

China, though herself a continent in area, has reached our ideal of coterminous race and nationality. China has no undigested Irish, Germans, blacks, or Jews. Like fossils that tell the geologic story, she has only a few picturesque traces of aborigines, Hakkas,[65] Lolos,[66] and wild mountaineers in Yunnan.[67] In India, the Black Jews of Malabar[68] are still Jews. The Jews of China are Chinese. Through war after war, through centuries of wise administration, by the Chinese genius for combination, and by art of the schoolmaster, she has made into one people all her tribes and nations. "The Han dynasty, B.C. 206, maintained nationalism against feudalism by the justice of its rule." Fur-clad trappers of the Yinesei head waters,[69] rude mountaineers of the Chinese

---

62. Norway was ceded to Sweden by Denmark in 1814; the countries remained a joint territory, though with separate constitutions, until 1905.
63. See note 46 above.
64. Scotch settlers were planted at Ulster during the reign of Elizabeth I, after three serious Irish rebellions in that period alone.
65. Strain of Chinese inhabiting Kuantung, Kuangsi, Kiangsi, and Fukien provinces, southern China.
66. (Lao-lao, Liao-liao). Native tribe of possible Indo-European descent occupying extensive parts of southwest China.
67. Chinese living in western and northwestern Yunnan province, immediately to the east of Tibet and Burma.
68. The Kala, subgroup of the Cochin Jews inhabiting the Malabar Coast of southern India. Until fairly recently they were rigidly divided by caste from the other subgroup of the Cochin Jews, the Gora, or White; likewise from most Hindu castes.
69. River some 2,500 miles long rising in extreme northwest Mongolia and flowing north through Siberia into the Kara Sea.

Himalayas, hardy sailors that brave the typhoons of the Southern seas, nomad herdsmen of the Northern plains, rice-planters and monkey-hunters of the tropic South, lumbermen of Yunnan, students of Ningpo,[70] silk-weavers of Soochow[71] — all are Chinese, believers in the philosophy of Confucius, reverent of age and learning, and schooled in that filial piety which is the foundation of China's social system. Yet they are still various in character and habits. A Chinese proverb says that customs change every ten miles.

Japan also achieved unity three hundred years ago; but China's unity has no parallel on a great scale except the glorious unity of these United States.

Despite recurrent famines and wars, China, alternately conquered and conquering, has maintained in each of many centuries an empire that might well be regarded as the greatest of its time. Even so late as the eighteenth century, when the statesman Kien Lung was emperor,[72] and the muttonhead George III was our king, China was richer and more formidable than any other state. Siam, Ryu Kyu, and Korea[73] were friendly and sent her tribute. Tropic Burma, rugged Nepal, and the chilly deserts of Turkestan heard the imperial thunder of her war-drums. Her three hundred millions of industrious and orderly people were free from opium and free from drunkenness, a paradisaic state to Europeans inconceivable. The splendor of this empire has faded, but the intrinsic unity of the people, despite all temporary discords, is still unbroken.

Some contend that by the Shan-tung award China loses nothing; that one of her provinces merely changes masters. The intrusion of the Germans, French, and English never drove the Chinese to despair. The Chinese knew them to be an ephemeral evil. Europe's brief day, indeed, may be already drawing to an end in a blood-red sunset. The Japanese, however, once planted in Shan-tung, are there forever. As Ulster is to Ireland, so will

---

70. Apparently an allusion to the Tianyise Library, on which the Imperial Library was modeled. The Tianyise was once China's finest library, housing some 73,000 volumes.
71. City some 50 miles east of Shanghai, officially called Wuhsien, in Kiangsu province; noted for cotton and silk manufacture.
72. Undoubtedly refers to Ch'ien Lung (1711-1799), who ruled China 1736-1796.
73. Ryukyu Islands, chain extending some 650 miles into the western Pacific between Taiwan and Kyushu in Japan, tributary to China in the 14th century. Siam was a tributary state of China by 1000 A.D.; Korea was made a vassal state of China early in the 17th century.

Shan-tung be to China; but where Ulster has tens of thousands, Shan-tung has millions.

Partitioned between France and England, each half of China might grow rich with railroads and factories, and then, with explosive force, the two nations would join, and the aliens would disappear. The importing, however, into China of Japanese, prolific, multitudinous, near at hand, means centuries of a new continental race war, another age-long struggle, the repetition on a giant scale of Norman against Saxon, French against Germans, Spanish against Dutch, Christian against Moor. It means the destruction of the unity of the Chinese and the downfall of the race, which is to-day perilously weakened by our having battered, poisoned, and undermined it for eighty years with every weapon of war and peace, with smugglers, diplomatists, and artillery, with opium and morphine.

The young men of America carried our flag to a splendid victory. The old men of Paris bemired it in diplomacy. Four men in Paris,[74] in the intervals between their more serious labors, pronounced the doom of the Chinese millions and of Chinese millions yet unborn. They plant with care the seeds, the dragon's teeth, of new war, eternal war. We went to war to set men free. These men enslave three hundred millions.

The old men of Paris, weary with a lifelong struggle for place, hardened by human suffering, by frequent disillusionment, their consciences seared by the habitual practice of diplomacy, have taught us new views.

One fifth of mankind, with blood and patience, has already lifted itself in its slow progress upward above the degrading afflictions of race conflict. Compared with the statesman who now plants in that nation a new race conflict, the distributor of typhus germs is a philanthropist.

The dissolution of the democracy of the East has been planned for many years, and was plotted with precision before the outbreak of the Great War. The crime of Paris is the latest in a long series of offenses. China is weak, unarmed, and backward in the use of modern machinery. This is the fruit of a process begun by England eighty years ago, in which we have all shared; in with the Romanoffs took the place of head devil, and in which Japan has now become the directing force.

---

74. Woodrow Wilson, Georges Clemenceau, David Lloyd George, and Vittorio Emmanuels Orlando.

The progressive partition of China went slowly because of the wealth at stake. It was sufficiently obvious that whatever outsider could annex China could rule the world. Russia hoped to get all of China for herself, but England, France, and Germany could not agree to that, nor with one another. The survivors are at last ready to agree.

Europe got the drop, to use the language of highwaymen, on China, through the happy chance of stumbling on steam.[75] That led to modern arms and to the means, still diverted by statesmen to other uses, to better the lot of all men. With our modern weapons we forced opium on China and poisoned her people. The Japanese continue the practice with morphine.[76] No modern improvement is neglected. We throttled Chinese patriots somewhat as if we had interfered in behalf of the Duke of Alva against the Dutch;[77] we caused civil wars to be prolonged, and cut down the strength of China with famine, sword, and disease. We crippled her finances, and imposed our own tariffs. Corruption follows impoverishment. It is not centuries since that an English king was in the pay of France.[78] The Romanoffs, experts in corruption, bought influence all the way up to the throne. They fomented the Boxer War.[79] To-day we take from every coolie in China some of his salt and rice to pay for this Romanoff crime.[80] The Japanese have inherited the place of the Romanoffs as purchasers of power and creators of disorder.

75. It wasn't just "happy chance," but the refusal of the Chinese government to adopt Western technology on the grounds it would necessarily be accompanied by general Westernization. For example, railways built by foreign concessionaires in China were actually purchased by the Chinese government and then disassembled.

76. Early in 1919 American newspapers had carried accounts published in the *North China Herald* the preceding December, detailing the Japanese introduction of morphine traffic into China, with the financial support of the Bank of Japan. The morphine was manufactured in Japan and transported via the Japanese postal service in China, which was immune to Chinese customs seizures. In the summer of 1919 there were reports that the Japanese had revived the opium trade, purchasing from the British in India.

77. Fernando Alvarez de Toledo, Duke of Alba or Alva (1508-1582), became regent in the Netherlands for Philip II in 1567, and created the so-called "Court of Blood" to deal with rebellion against Spanish rule. An estimated 18,000 were executed.

78. Allusion here to James II (1633-1701) and his son the pretender James Edward (1688-1766), maintained in exile by the French government after the Glorious Revolution of 1688.

79. In an attempt to gain an ice-free port more southerly than Vladivostok for the terminus of the transSiberian railway, Russia distributed some $5 million in bribes to Chinese officials in 1895-1896, including $1.5 million to Li Hung-chang (in vain, as it turned out). See Section Nine - "Words That I Had With Molly," and Section Sixteen - "An Appreciation of W.A.P. Martin." It was Chinese resentment over this kind of thing that led to the Boxer uprising.

80. Allusion the huge indemnities imposed on China by the foreign powers, including the United States, whose nationals had been killed and property destroyed in the course of the Boxer Rebellion.

The Japanese know how to make medicine of their great revenges. We cannot grudge them their secret rapture when they lay the whip across the Chinese back and know that each lash has a sting in it for arrogant America. For our abject submissiveness to Japan we have ourselves to blame. Our moneyed men, with that unerring instinct for making political blunders that has always marked the breed, sent Perry[81] to tear open the door of peaceful, cloistered Japan, and now she must arm herself; and some of us will be stepped on before she is done with it.

Japan's history shows that she has heretofore been led toward conquest, and has heretofore deliberately turned away from it. By the light of that history we may learn how Japan may be persuaded again toward peace. The Japanese, now the terror of the East, have been lovers of peace. In former times Japan sought conquest only to ward off conquerors. It is true that the soldier who brought unity to Japan laid plans for world-wide war. He said in 1577: "China, Korea, and Japan will be one. I shall do it all as easily as a man rolls up a piece of matting and carries it under his arm." In 1587 he said, "Invading the country of the great Ming, I will fill with the hoar-frost from my sword the whole sky over the four hundred provinces." To the viceroy of the Philippines he sent a message commanding him to leave the islands.[82]

But after him came Ieyasu,[83] the great shogun, whose sacred

---

81. Matthew Galbraith Perry (1794-1858), who, at the head of a U.S. fleet, secured naval and commercial treaties with Japan in 1853-1854.
82. Toyotomi Hideyoshi (1537-1598), warlord of humble origins who in 1591 completed the work of national unification begun by Oda Nobunaga; described as possessing an insatiable thirst for power. His unsuccessful invasions of Korea in 1592 and 1597 were viewed by Hideyoshi as a prelude to the invasion of China; in fact he planned to rule Japan, China, the Ryukyus, Taiwan, and the Philippines from a headquarters at Ningpo.
83. Tokugawa Ieyasu (1543-1616), founder of the Tokugawa shogunate. Became ruler of Japan after a victory over Ishida Mitsuwari, Hideyoshi's successor, in 1600. Virtually all his life was spent at war; and the *Kodansha Encyclopedia of Japan* regards him in rather dimmer light than Martin: "Many historians...have been beguiled into crediting him with the achievements of his subordinates or successors, and some have praised him for social and economic developments of which in fact he may well have been unaware, or in which he played no part." He certainly did not attempt foreign conquest, for which Hideyoishi and Mitsuwari had pretty well shown Japan's resources to be inadequate. (Ieyasu's victory over the latter was in fact made possible by the weakened condition of Mitsuwari's government following fresh attempts on Korea.) And he did send a secret envoy to Europe, one Nishi Soshin, a master of the tea ceremony, who meticulously studied Christianity for three years, going so far as to become a convert. Soshin's report on Europe's wars of religion and religious persecution caused Ieyasu to ban Christianity in Japan shortly before his death.

Ieyasu did, however, avidly seek foreign trade — though under strict control of the Japanese government — and offered inducements to the Portuguese, Spanish, English, and Dutch. He was bitterly disappointed at the failure of a decade-long attempt to establish regular commercial relations with Spain through the Philippines, and in fact ashes have lain for three hundred years under the solemn cryptomerias of Nikko. Like Washington, he had clearness of vision, freedom from prejudice, freedom from old ideas. He had notable powers of observation, reflection, and action. A man of less originality would have pursued the enticing path of conquest marked out by Hideyoshi. Japan would have made good the boasts of Hideyoshi and conquered China, then passing through one of her paroxysms of disorder and helplessness. Seeking all information, the shogun sent a secret envoy to Europe. The Europe of 1600 was a dove-cote to the Europe of 1919, yet the envoy's report filled him with horror. Thereupon, Japan, under his guidance, made her marvelous decision to turn away from all foreign adventure either of commerce or war, to hold no intercourse with Europe, to pursue the arts of peace, and to devote her energy to the welfare of her own people.

We have our Washington and Jefferson, who have warned us against the politics of Europe as the source of all evil. After a hundred years we have forgotten them; after three hundred years the Japanese have forgotten their great shogun.

We have been taught to detest ambitious conquerors, who add land to land, make slaves of free men, and rob nations of their riches. We cannot withold, then, our admiration of the great Japanese pacifist, the statesman, who resolved on a perpetual policy of non-interference. He gave his people solemn injunctions against ambition, and "employed scholars in constructing a solid framework of peace."

Two hundred and sixteen years of peace is a boon that neither God nor statesmen ever granted to any great modern nation but Japan. If the lesser Tokugawas,[84] rulers at Yedo[85] after Ieyasu, had followed his example, they could have enjoyed the peace he created, and at the same time, in their seclusion, could have moved forward step by step in the use of engines and steam and steel as fast as England, and been safe.

---

restrictions made all these efforts more or less unsuccessful.

　　　　Ieyasu's mausoleum is in the Toshogu shrine in Nikko, a town in central Honshu, some 75 miles north of Tokyo.

---

84. Shogunate 1603-1868, last and longest lived of Japan's three warrior governments (Kamakura 1192-1333; Muromachii 1338-1573).

85. Old name for Tokyo, in use from 1180-1868. Yedo was made a capital by Ieyasu's selection of the site for his court in the latter 17th century.

Before our Great War, Western nations had begun to prosper through the use of the scientific spirit, love of truth, and knowledge for its own sake. But to-day among us the scientific spirit is dead. Free research and the uncensored distribution of knowledge are no more. The lesser Tokugawas were like the small, modern Metternichs that now try to blind our souls.[86] The Tokugawas made no error in continuing to exclude Europeans, but they made the fatal error of excluding knowledge. They saved about two hundred dollars a year by not even hiring people to read the books that came once a year to Desima.[87] Perry's invasion and Japan's humiliating subjection to the powers were the retribution for this neglect, falling on them with the suddenness and horror of a thunderbolt from the blue sky.

By another of those swift, decisive, and complete changes of policy of which Japan alone seems capable, she changed the very foundations of her society, held fast to what she treasured of the old, and acquired quickly all the virtues and some of the vices of Europe. She has not only made herself one of the great powers, but she seems to have determined to become a great conqueror, flattening vassal nations. If she pursues this course, we may be sure that, with her fine Japanese hand, she will from time to time form all the combinations necessary, and with her military skill will win, and win cheaply, all the necessary battles. She has proceeded one by one against her enemies, and one by one, the nearest first, they have fallen in ruins, all the way from Fusan to Strasburg.[88] If she does not again become pacifist, the process of toppling over empires that trampled on her when she was weak may not stop at Strasburg. [*Editor's Note: Prescient conditional played out when Japan joined Germany in WWII.*]

She plays in steady good luck, because now she uses every weapon, and despises no knowledge, high or low. She studies the

---

86. Allusion to Clemens, Furst von Metternich (1773-1859), whose policies made him a byword for the suppression of liberal views.
87. (Deshima or Dejima): a small man-made island in Nagasaki harbor, now incorporated into the mainland. It was originally built by the Tokugawas to house Portuguese traders; after their expulsion in 1639 it housed the Dutch operation in Japan from 1641 to 1855. A strict ban on the importation of foreign books was relaxed in 1720, sparking a widespread interest among Japanese physicians and intelligentsia in what, according to the *Encyclopedia of Asian History*, were called "Dutch studies," transforming not only Japanese medicine and science, but art, military technology, and political and philosophical debate.
88. That is, from the extreme northeast border of China to the Alsace in Europe, demarcating the eastern and western limits of the collapsed or defeated regimes that were once Japan's opponents.

character of our elder statesmen, from Washington to Wilson, and of our younger patriots, from Nathan Hale to Hard-Boiled Smith.[89] She knows how to set Kodama against Kuropatkin,[90] Togo against Rojestvensky,[91] Ishii against Lansing,[92] and Saionji against Wilson.[93]

The solution does not lie in compressing a great race within narrow islands. Nor does the solution lie in helping them to enslave another great race, and to lift themselves, at the expense of a groaning world, into the possession of an empire like Great Britain or Russia.

The Romanoff Empire was a disease; the British Empire is an accident. Such empires carry in their hearts the seeds of ruin. Such empires are of evil example. The welfare of the world lies in Japan's turning away from following after them.

The remedy lies in persuading Japan to direct her energies towards eastern Siberia. Eastern Siberia is at this moment such a desert, in many respects, as was our famous "Great American Desert." China is like a rich thickly inhabited plain. Japan is like an overflowing mountain lake, ready to burst in an irresistible, destructive torrent over the rich inhabited plain. If the flood can be diverted and directed to the desert, peace and prosperity will follow. I pray that those who are of my way of thinking as to Russian policy will not oppose this remedy.

Fear and hatred of the Romanoffs has been with many of us all our days. We look with horror on Koltchak[94] and Sazonoff.[95] We

---

89. James Smith (1851-1927), Democratic boss of New Jersey, senator from New Jersey 1893-1899. He steamrollered Wilson into the Democratic N.J. gubernatorial nomination in 1910, seeing Wilson as naive and pliable, only to have Wilson ignore him once the former was in office.
90. Kodama Gentaro (1882-1906), army general, chief of general staff of the Manchurian Army in the Russo-Japanese War. Alexi Nikolevich Kuropatkin (1848-1925), commander of Russia's Manchurian Army in the Russo-Japanese War, whose poor leadership is often blamed for Russia's disastrous losses.
91. Togo Heihachiro (1848-1934), fleet admiral in the Japanese navy who led operations in the Russo-Japanese War. Under his command the Combined Fleet intercepted and destroyed the Russian Baltic Fleet at the Battle of Tusshima, May, 1905. Zinovii Petrovich Rozhdestvensky (1848-1909), commander of the Russian Fleet at Tsushima.
92. Viscount Kikujiro Ishii and U. S. Secretary of State Robert Lansing. See "To a Few Friends and One or Two Foes," note 24.
93. Saionji Kimmochi (1849-1940), statesman, prime minister 1906-1908, 1911-1912. Japanese plenipotentiary to the Paris Peace Conference.
94. Alexander Vasilievich Kolchak (1874-1920), Tsarist naval officer who headed the Manchurian White Russian armies in 1918-1919, and was recognized 1919-1920 by the Whites as ruler of Russia. Was summarily executed by the Bolsheviks after falling into their hands in early 1920.
95. Sergei Dimitrievich Sazonov (1861-1927), Russian statesman, minister of foreign affairs, whose views were reportedly relatively enlightened for the Russia of his day. At

deplore the temptations that led our Government to send men or munitions into Russia and Siberia.[96]

We regret, however, that some who are of our way of thinking in this regard have expressed the fear that the acquisition of land in eastern Siberia by Japan is a dismemberment of Russia and an interference in her affairs.

Eastern Siberia is no more a part of Russia than the Philippines are a part of our States. Russia's title to eastern Siberia, including Transbaikalia,[97] Kamchatka,[98] and those provinces which make the basins of the Amur[99] and Sungari,[100] is purely technical. Some of this land the czar got by bribery and coercion; other regions by the sending of an explorer with a flag to claim them. With all its wealth of minerals, forests, farm-land, and fisheries, the czar has never effectively used this territory. There has been but little effective settlement except in such towns as Vladivostok and the railway towns.[101] After all these years, the population is only four times as dense as that of the Sahar.[102] A traveler in the air will see only four times as many people in eastern Siberia as he sees when he crosses the Sahara. Most of the inhabitants are Japanese, Koreans, Chinese, Mongols, and Buriats.[103] Most of the immigrants are of the adventurous sort that could get along just as

---

the time of Martin's writing, however, the Bolsheviks had recently published documents purporting to show Sazonov's leading role in bringing on WWI.

96. Allusion to the 1918-1920 Allied interventions in the Baltic, the Ukraine, and eastern Siberia, beginning as efforts to protect and recover vital military stores loaned Russia and now desperately needed on the Western Front; also to assist the Czech Legion — which had served with Russia on the Eastern Front and was being shipped to the Western via Siberia and the United States. Under the influence of local commanders, however, the Allied forces engaged in large-scale anti-Bolshevik operations. United States participation in the interventions was decidedly secondary to the British, French, and Japanese.

97. Area to the east of Lake Baikal in southeast Siberia; includes what until recently was the Buryat Mongol in the Autonomous Soviet Socialist Republic (ASSR), Chita Region, and Khabarovsk Territory.

98. Peninsula in northeast Siberia separating the Sea of Okhost in the west from the Bering Sea and Pacific Ocean on the east.

99. River some 1,700 miles long in northeast Asia, some 1,100 miles of which actually compose the present Russo-Mongolian border.

100. River some 700 miles long arising in Kirin province, northeast China, flowing north to join the Amur some 500 miles from its mouth. The basin of the Amur and Sungari actually include a portion of extreme northeast modern China.

101. Vladivostok is, of course, the terminus of the transSiberian railway.

102. Yet, even in eastern Siberia, Russian settlers outnumbered the native populations by this time.

103. Buryat Mongols, herdsmen inhabiting the former Buryat ASSR in northwest Mongolia.

well with Japanese settlers as they ever did with the czar. The czar used to keep down Mongolian immigration by a sort of periodical pogrom.[104] Such acts forfeit title.

Our true course, our only honest course, is to propose that France, England, America, and Japan withdraw all coercion from China, and that she be left free to develop as she pleases her commerce and her manufactures. The Chinese are, as everybody knows, the most enterprising, the most honorable, and the cleverest of merchants. We can safely leave it to them to decide whether they will use junks or steamboats. We no longer would need to choose between Mr. John Hay's policy of the open door,[105] on the other side of which we always found a smiling Japanese, firmly seated, and Mr. Wilson's policy of the open purse, never open to China, but always open to anybody who would assure us that he could never pay.

It has always been as clear as a map that eastern Siberia is the "manifest destiny" of Japan. Similarly, it was clear to people of so diverse minds as Jefferson and Hamilton that the Mississippi Valley was marked out by nature as the manifest destiny of our own United States. Even if we had not found a happy chance for the Louisiana Purchase, no technical titles, no modest colonies like New Orleans and St. Louis, no weapons, and no diplomacy, could ever have kept our people from moving westward. So, also, when our people felt a desire actually to colonize Colorado and California, we could not be kept out by any technical claims in favor of a far-away political power — claims founded on discovery and military occupation, and not supported by civilization's use.

The time has gone by when bureaucrats, wrapped in red-tape, could sit behind their desks in Petrograd or London and dictate from motives of petty official profit that continental areas shall remain white upon the map, to the perpetuation of the misery of contiguous sweltering millions. Saghalin, an island bigger than two Denmarks, was kept for a convict settlement to please some small official speculator.[106]

---

104. Chinese rule being even less attractive than the Russian, the Mongols did often try to remove themselves from the former to the latter. When caught at the borders they were turned back; and even once inside they were frequently rounded up and returned. No evidence of pogroms in the usual sense, though treatment of native populations by individual Russians could be monstrous.
105. John Hay (1838-1905; Yale L.L.D. '01), secretary of state 1898-1905, in which office he devised, in 1899, the policy of the Open Door in China; i.e., equal commercial rights for all nations.
106. Sakahlin Island, some 590 by 140 miles; near the mainland of Asia between the

It ought to have been Japanese always. Japanese soldiers doubtless secretly occupy it to-day. I hope they do. Under the czar the north half of Saghalin was the worst place on earth. Under the Japanese it will support people of a high civilization and will produce wealth.

We have lately noticed how uneasy Italy is about the opposite shores of the Adriatic [i.e., Fiume]. It is absurd to ask a great modern power like Japan to be contented while the opposite shores of her narrow seas lie empty, waiting to be fortified by some hostile power. It is in the course of nature for the Sea of Okhotsk and the Sea of Japan to be Japanese lakes.

When swarming multitudes are waiting in Japan to enter on rich, vacant lands, an artificial policy of holding those lands idle in the hope that immigrants from Europe will at some remote period travel five thousand miles, over hundreds of miles of empty land, to settle on the shores of Okhotsk is a policy that cannot prosper.

Unimaginable evils come from the setting up of technical claims against the natural movements of the human race. Natural justice requires a bargain by which all of us intruders shall withdraw our guards and soldiers from China, and let the Japanese into eastern Siberia. Such a bargain can be made attractive to such investors, speculators, and bond-holders as have interests, or think they have, in China or Japan or eastern Siberia. Political objections could be easily handled. It is not unlikely that Japan would gladly give up her dreams of conquest and enter on an entirely new policy of colonization, like that which built up America.

Kamchatka and the southern parts of eastern Siberia are big enough and rich enough to support by themselves a power of the first class.

The Chinese, to save their great inheritance, the eighteen provinces, and their immediate dependencies, would gladly consent to see Japan in permanent possession of all the shores of the Japanese seas and of the lands that abut on those seas.

Even if the czar's title to eastern Siberia were such as to

---

Sea of Japan and the Sea of Okhotsk. The north portion was a Russian penal colony 1869-1906; some 30,000 prisoners were confined there at one time or another during this period, subject to forced labor, abuse, and corporal punishment. After the Russo-Japanese War the south half was ceded to Japan. White forces held the north half 1918-1920, and the Japanese did indeed occupy the whole island 1920-1925. A main reason for the establishment of the penal colony was the hope — finally defeated — of economic development, primarily through mining and forestry.

deserve consideration, and even if there was a population in eastern Siberia comparable to the French that were sold to us in the Louisiana Purchase, and even if a transfer of eastern Siberia involved an infraction of political principle, the transfer would be a small offense.

At the cost of temporary annoyance to a few it would create permanent benefits and security and peace for multitudes, like the numerous small, frequently salutary, crimes, by which we effected the expansion of the United States.

If Mr. Wilson were to commission me to write, for use in schools, a new Machiavelli, the first sentence would be, "Never commit for temporary profit any crime of permanent evil effect." Of two crimes, choose the little one.

It is a golden moment to induce France and England to give up their Chinese spheres of influence. Mr. Lansing even says that Mr. Balfour said that England is opposed to spheres of influence.[107]

Negotiations might be slightly embarrassed by the fact that Russian revolutionists in eastern Siberia are now the subject of punitive expeditions by Japanese generals, and that the prestige of America in the far East during the last few weeks has become about equivalent to that of the hairy Aino.[108] It is the duty of rulers to overcome difficulties or circumvent them, and not, at the first hint of opposition, to take cover in the shelter of some great crime.

European dominion of Asian peoples has here and there been beneficent. The French diverted the King of Annam from boiling his wives for lunch,[109] and the English stopped King Thebaw from roasting his wives in curry;[110] but there is grave doubt as to whether Burma is better off than it was.

In the nineteenth century we called ourselves Caucasians, and talked about the white man's burden, and firmly pretended to

---

107. Arthur James Balfour (1848-1930), British statesman, foreign secretary in latter part of WWI. Lansing had extensive personal contacts with Balfour during the latter's 1917 visit to the United States, one of them being the source of this remark. Balfour also told the House of Commons in 1917 that the U.S. was being frankly informed of all treaties between the Allies (see note 1 above).
108. The Ainu, aborigines inhabiting Hokkaido, Sakhalin, and the Kuriles. "Short, stocky, hairy, resembling Europeans more than Mongoloids."
109. The French seizure of control in Annam — the central portion of present-day Vietnam — in 1883-1885, put the old court of Hue out of business.
110. Thibaw or Theebaw (1858-1916) ruled Burma 1878-1885. His tyrannical character offered England an excuse for a takeover in 1885, the so-called Third Anglo-Burmese War, duration one week, thus giving the British a continuous coastline from Calcutta to Singapore. Of Thebaw's wife-roasting there is no evidence, but may be worth noting that relations had placed him on the throne after murdering ninety other potential aspirants.

believe that everybody would be improved by accepting our rulership. One of the many benefits resulting from the Great War and our great victory is that we have learned modesty. We have learned that we are not able to put our own houses in order, and that most of us are savages without even a veneer of morals. No Frenchman or Englishman any longer pretends that it will be for the benefit of any other human being to be ruled over by him any more than by Sir John Hawkins[111] or Leopold II.[112] If he now plans for conquest and mandatories, he says frankly it is because he needs the money.

In the nineteenth century we devised the partition of China, pretending that it was in the interest of progress. We now doubt whether peace or progress will ever again be our portion. Our highest ambition should be, the highest achievement of our statesmanship would be, to leave eastern Asia as happy as it was before it knew us. Our brightest Oriental dream should be of Japan and China, expanding each into its own vacant spaces, and growing rich as peaceably as the United States and Canada.

❧ ❧ ❧

# Japan's Attempt to Exterminate Korean Christians[1]
[1919]

*Japanese forces first occupied Korea during the Russo-Japanese War of 1904-1905, which was in fact chiefly occasioned by Japan's unwillingness to tolerate the expansion of Russian power southward from Manchuria into Korea, in her*

---

111. Sir John Hawkins (1532-1595), English captain, later treasurer and comptroller of the navy, who in his early career engaged in extensive slave-trading.
112. Leopold II (1835-1909), King of Belgium 1865-1909, and as such the outright owner under Belgian law of the Belgian Congo, from which wealth was extracted by the atrocious treatment of native populations.

---

1. Printed in booklet form on "Olde Style" vellum paper with a dark brown paper cover. Twenty-eight pages. Milford, Connecticut, listed as place of publication.

*historic drive for warm-water ports. The Rising Sun's motives, however, were hardly those of strict charity.*

*As one Japanese historian put it, Japan "must either die a saintly death in righteous starvation, or expand into the neighbor's back yard. Japan is not that much of a saint." Japan's population and limited territorial base (above all, limited mineral and agricultural lands) have historically made some form of colonialism virtually inevitable, and the economic, political, and military sophistication she had attained by the latter nineteenth century supplied all the requisite tools. Korea, not only much less developed and densely populated, but strategically the "arrow pointed at the heart of Japan," was — together with China's easternmost provinces — the obvious target.*

*The Portsmouth Naval Treaty ending the 1904-1905 war recognized Japan's "preponderating influence" in Korea. (There is reason to believe that President Roosevelt secretly informed the Japanese emissary that America would not object to outright Japanese annexation of Korea.) The ensuing difficulty was then quite candidly put by Japan's minister to Korea: "Japan is confronted by a most difficult problem — to maintain the fiction of Korean independence while practically establishing a protectorate, and yet to avoid assuming the responsibilities of a governing power."*

*The solution was thought to be straightforward Japanese direction of foreign affairs, in combination with a system of Japanese "advisors" to native internal administrators. It proved unworkable, given Korea's chaotic state, economic backwardness, and the resentment and sometimes outright opposition of her population.[2] Within less than two years, the power of the Korean government and in particular of the emperor, had become virtually signatory. When, in 1907, the emperor sent a delegation to The Hague to plead for Western intervention, the Japanese responded by forcing his abdication and replacing him with his more pliable son and heir.*

*The new emperor signed an agreement substantially transferring all Korean administration into Japanese hands; the treaty of August 22, 1910, annexing Korea to Japan, only formalized a loss of independence that had already taken place. Korea remained a Japanese colony until August 15, 1945, the end of World War II.*

---

2. Guerilla resistance was in fact organized in 1906, and reached a peak strength of 70,000 in 1908: in the face of massive Japanese reprisals, which included large-scale village-burnings. Statistics provide the whole sorry tale: 17,779 guerillas dead, 3,707 wounded; 136 Japanese soldiers dead, 2,777 wounded.

*Arguably, Korea at that time was the most backward of all the major civilizations on the Eastern Pacific rim, and a recent history taking an avowedly Korean point of view nonetheless concedes:*

> The thirty-six years of Japanese rule transformed the country: her political and judicial systems were modernized, her economy was transformed from that of an agrarian to one of a semi-industrial nature. The acreage of land under cultivation increased, her farm production rose, her railway mileage expanded, her industrial output increased, and her mining output grew vastly. Modern educational institutions which were established brought about an increase in the educated population, and the rate of illiteracy decreased. With economic development and the increase of the number of high school and college graduates, the middle class, which hardly existed in the past, emerged, the age-old social structure was overthrown, and the urban population grew.[3]

*The aim, however, was not Korea's well-being, but her complete transformation into a tool of Japanese policy. As Nahm explains:*

> [The Japanese] planned to assimilate the Koreans into Japanese culture and to construct a strong logistic base for Japan's continental expansionism. In order to achieve these objectives, the Japanese inaugurated many programs: the use of the Korean language was forbidden; and the Koreans were forced to abandon their traditional family and given names and adopt Japanese-style names....All the highest positions and those positions above the rank of clerk in both central and local governments were held by Japanese....[The Japanese] ordered all Korean political organisations to be dissolved and prohibited all meetings, debates, and public speeches by Koreans. All Korean and some Japanese newspapers were

---

3. Andrew C. Nahm, Korea: *Tradition and Transformation* (Elizabeth, N.J.: Hollym, 1988), pp. 258-9.

ordered to cease publication.....An increasing number of Japanese farmers were brought into Korea and were given free lands or were allowed to purchase a large amount of farmland at a low price. The Japanese population in Korea grew from 171,543 at the end of 1910 to 424,700 in 1925 and to 650,000 in 1939. In 1939 some 45,000 Japanese were engaged in agriculture as landowners. The amount of land owned by Japanese citizens increased from 217,150 acres in 1910, to 820,750 in 1923....All [Korean-owned] commercial and industrial companies [were required] to have Japanese either as co-investors or as managerial staff.[4]

*In addition, Japanese-Korean relations were permeated throughout by the racism Martin mentions, and which was so pronounced a feature of Japanese life during the years of the empire.*

*Woodrow Wilson's doctrine of national self-determination supplied both impetus and focus for Korean national resistance, and by late 1918 a number of independence movements had been organized.*

*The immediate occasion for the 1919 protests was the death of the Korean ex-emperor under circumstances which the Japanese government left undisclosed.[5] The funeral was scheduled for March 3 — eight days after his death — and the leaders of the most influential of the independence movements, the Ch'onogyo, decided on a symbolic action to take place in Seoul on March 1. One Ch'oe Nam-son wrote a declaration of independence, to which was appended three covenants emphasizing the movement's non-violent nature.*

*Some thirty-three "national representatives" signed both the declaration and a petition to be sent to the Japanese government, the United States government, and the Paris peace conference. Although thousands of copies of the declaration were printed, and many public readings took place, apparently the leaders had in mind no more than a public gesture confined largely to themselves. But Korean political tinder needed only a spark, and the announcement — coupled with one by a group of radicals who insisted that the ex-emperor had been assassinated — was sufficient to kindle the massive demonstrations described in Martin's 28-page pamphlet.[6]*

---

4. *Ibid.*, pp. 226-30.
5. There were rumors of both poisoning and suicide.

*Japan's response to what came to be known as the March First Movement was largely symbolic or at most tactical. In August Japan's emperor issued an imperial rescript stating that the government aimed at a reconciliation between the two countries, and henceforth its policies would be nondiscriminatory. Japan, the rescript stated, would no longer appoint only army generals as governors-general; it would respect Korean culture and customs, develop industry and education, and employ more Koreans in administration.*

*In a sense Japan was true to its word: the governor-general appointed that year was a retired admiral.[7] Certain benefits did follow for the Korean people. The pay scale for Korean and Japanese employees of the government was equalized; yet a monthly sixty-percent bonus was given only to the Japanese. A special ordinance allowed Koreans to be appointed to certain government positions as "special employees," and some 300 were. Political reforms gave Korean judges and prosecuting attorneys powers equal to those of Japanese. More than 54,000 persons in prison were paroled. Korean-language newspapers were permitted, although only under the strictest censorship. But probably the one serious and lasting consequence of the March demonstrations was to register Korean sentiment in Western eyes, and permanently to discredit Japanese rule.*

*Though dozens of nationalist organizations of all political hues were founded in Korea during the remaining twenty-five years of Japanese rule, they proved both ineffective and short-lived, being swiftly broken up either by internal dissent or by the Japanese police. Until Japan's defeat by the Allies in 1945, Korea remained a pawn in Japanese strategy, and an arena for the accumulation of Japanese wealth.*

*Perhaps Newell Martin would not have been surprised that it was not until August, 1990, that the Japanese government finally tendered formal apologies to Korea for its four decades of occupation.*

ے ے ے

---

6. In the final tally, some 1,200 Koreans were killed and 16,000 wounded. More than 19,000 Koreans were arrested, 2,656 of whom received prison terms. In contrast, six Japanese gendarmes, two Japanese policemen, and one Japanese civilian were killed, and some 130 wounded. Some 715 Korean houses were burned down, and 447 churches and schools destroyed.

7. Saito Makoto, who remained head of the Korean government until 1927; subsequently served as Japan's prime minister.

*Since Martin makes extensive use of a 25-cent pamphlet issued in August, 1919, by the Federal Council of the Churches of Christ in America (FCCCA), an introduction to this body seems appropriate. The Council was organized in 1908 as an executive body to act in matters for which individual churches were ill-equipped. By the year of Martin's writing, the Council included thirty-eight denominations, all of them Protestant. Each had four representatives, plus one additional for every 50,000 members. From the start, persons of opposing political convictions criticized the Council's goals as leftist; undeniably they have been very much this-worldly, which in 1919 meant support for the League of Nations, disarmament, and universal peace. In the year previous, in fact, the Council had set up a special Commission on International Justice and Goodwill to promote those ends; and perhaps some indication of the Council's subsequent history and overall tenor may be best supplied by a partial list of such commissions, which have included ones for Christian Unity, Church and Economic Life, Church and the Minority Peoples, Church and Race Relations, Church and Social Service, Goodwill Between Christians and Jews, International Cooperation, Just and Durable Peace, Marriage and the Home, Peace and Arbitration, Social Service, State and Local Federations, and Temperance. One admittedly disaffected commentator has gone so far as to say:*

> The history of the Federal Council of Churches is cluttered with committees and creations. They were created for every conceivable purpose, with duties and memberships that often overlapped and at times their chief effect is confusion for the serious student of the history of this organization. It is easy to get the impression that the leadership of the Council was convinced that the Kingdom of God would be achieved by creating a sufficient number of committees on [sic] the deliberations of which the Kingdom would be brought into being.[8]

*In 1950, the council was reconstituted as the National Council of Churches of Christ in America.*

*The Commission on Relations with the Orient was established in 1916 at one of the Council's quadrennial sessions, following a*

---
8. C. Gregg Singer, *The Unholy Alliance* (New Rochelle, N.Y.: Arlington, 1975), p. 48.

special conference on what the Council's contemporary historian calls "American-Japanese problems." Its declared purpose was "to bring Christian principles to bear on relations between America and Japan...and all countries from which immigrants are likely to come." That is, the Council was chiefly concerned with the fact that such immigration had effectively been terminated over the previous decade or so.

In 1913 several missionary organizations in Japan had expressed concern over the pertinent legislation and its effects on American-Japanese relations. Sidney Gulick[9] was dispatched to America, where he appeared before the FCCCA's Executive Committee; he subsequently toured the country, speaking to and conferring with various church bodies. In 1915 he returned to Japan bearing a letter of goodwill from the FCCCA.

The Churches of Christ in Japan viewed this as a most heartening development; it did at least result in the attendance of Japanese workingmen's delegations at several conferences of American labor unions, notably those of the American Federation of Labor and California Federation of Labor.

The FCCCA shortly expanded its area of concern to include China and Korea, and delegates from all three nations attended an FCCCA conference held by the Commission on Relations with the Orient. It seems undeniable that its report on the Korean situation was in large part motivated by concern for Japan's image, which concern also must explain its ostensible acceptance at face value of the Hara and Uchida cables.

That the reader may judge for himself the grounds for that acceptance and the justice of Martin's strictures, we reproduce here the forward to the FCCCA pamphlet, unabridged and without comment:

## FOREWORD
## IMPORTANT CABLE MESSAGES

Just as this pamphlet was about to go to press the following cable message was received from Hon. T. Hara, Premier of the Japanese Cabinet:

---

9. Sidney Gulick (1860-1945; A.B. Dartmouth '83; A.M. '86; D.D. '03; B.D. Union Theological Seminary '86; Hon. D.D. Yale '14). Ordained to the Congregational Ministry 1886. Headed American Board of Commissioners for Foreign Missions in Japan 1887-1913. Lecturer at Imperial University in Kyoto 1907-13; secretary of the FCCCA's Commission on International Justice and Goodwill 1914-34. Secretary of the National Commission on American-Japanese Relations 1921-34. Author numerous books and articles, mainly on American relations with the Far East.

"I desire to assure you that the report of abuses committed by agents of the Japanese Government in Korea has been engaging my most serious attention. I am fully prepared to look squarely at actual facts. As I have declared on various occasions, the regime of administration inaugurated in Korea at the time of the annexation, nearly ten years ago, calls for substantial modification to meet the altered conditions of things. Ever since the formation of the present Cabinet in September last, I have been occupied in working out the scheme of needed administrative reforms in Korea. A comprehensive plan of reorganization with this object in view has already been on the tapis. For obvious reasons it has not been possible to proceed at once to its formal adoption in the presence of the disturbances which have unfortunately broken out in various parts of the peninsula.

"In view, however, of the recent improvement in the situation, the contemplated reform can now be, in my estimation, safely introduced, and will be carried into effect as soon as the legal requirements of procedure to make them definite shall have been completed. Announcement of the plan in a more complete form shall be withheld for the present, but I trust that the fixed determination with which my colleagues and I have been endeavoring to promote the lasting welfare of our Korean kinsmen, and to insure a distinct betterment of conditions in the country will not be misunderstood or misconstrued."

The foregoing cablegram was received July 10th and came in answer to a cable sent him June 26, 1919, by the Commission on Relations with the Orient, as follows:

"Agitation regarding Chosen abuses

increasingly serious, endangering goodwill. Cannot withold facts. Urgently important you publish official statements that abuses have ceased and reasonable administrative reforms proceeding. Can you cable to this effect? Address Fedcil—Commission Relations Orient, Federal Council Churches."

At an earlier date, namely April 20, a cablegram regarding the Korean situation had been sent by Consul General Yada to Viscount Uchida, Minister of Foreign Affairs in Tokyo. In reply to that cablegram the following message was received by Mr. Yada and handed to this Commission on May 15, 1919:

"Premier Hara has for some time past been most deeply concerned in regard to the introduction of reforms into the governmental administration of Chosen. He is now in the midst of special investigations as to the best methods for the realization of these reforms, which might be seriously interfered with and made more difficult were the press of foreign countries rashly at this time to incite additional excitement.

"Therefore you are instructed to explain the situation as above stated to the members of the Federal Council Commission, conveying to them at the same time the appreciation on my part of their cordial and friendly spirit which has prompted them to take action in this present trouble. It is also the desire of the Premier that you should call their attention more especially to the gravity of the whole affair if it is not handled in a proper way, and ask for the continuance of their sane and moderate attitude."

These cable messages indicate the earnestness with which this Commission, the Consul General Yada and the Premier of Japan himself have been acting in

---

10. William I. Haven (1886-1928; A.B. Wesleyan '77; A.M. '81; D.D. '99; L.L.D.'21). Ordained to the Methodist Episcopalian ministry 1881; held pastorates in Boston area. One of the founders of the Epworth League. Member Board of Foreign Missions of M.E. Church 1899-1924; member various special commissions of FCCCA.

response to the appeals that have come from Korea.
There is every reason to believe that Premier Hara and his colleagues will exert their fullest power to rectify the wrongs and inaugurate a new era in Korea.

WM. I. HAVEN, Chairman,[10]
SIDNEY L. GULICK,
Secretary.

## JAPAN'S ATTEMPT TO EXTERMINATE KOREAN CHRISTIANS BY NEWELL MARTIN/

TABLE OF CONTENTS[11]

Page

Our Sources of Information . . . . . . . . . . . . . . 5
Praise of Japan . . . . . . . . . . . . . . . . . . . . . 7
Japanese Ambition . . . . . . . . . . . . . . . . . . . 9
Punctilious Observance of Treaties
    a Specialty of Japan . . . . . . . . . . . . . 9
Policemen's Fun . . . . . . . . . . . . . . . . . . . 10
Stamping Out Christians . . . . . . . . . . . . . . . 13
Machinery of Torture . . . . . . . . . . . . . . . . . 13
Story of the Pregnant Woman . . . . . . . . . . . 14
The Naked Widow and the Gay Lunch . . . . . . 14
Twelve Naked Methodist Women . . . . . . . . . 15
Story of a Young School-Girl . . . . . . . . . . . . 15
Kim's Torture . . . . . . . . . . . . . . . . . . . . . . 16
Chopping Up a Christian . . . . . . . . . . . . . . 16
Discouraging Christianity . . . . . . . . . . . . . . 17
Four Christian Students Scourged on the Cross . . 17
Massacre of Cheamni . . . . . . . . . . . . . . . . 17
Stench of Burning Flesh . . . . . . . . . . . . . . 18
Night Razzia on a Christian Village . . . . . . . . 18
Various Styles of Massacre . . . . . . . . . . . . . 18
Comforting a Christian's Mother . . . . . . . . . 19
Reverence for Gray Hairs . . . . . . . . . . . . . . 19
The Governor-General . . . . . . . . . . . . . . . 19
The Japanese Terrorize Korean Christians . . . . . 20
"Cordial" Messages to the Japanese Government . . 23
Hara's "Reforms" . . . . . . . . . . . . . . . . . . 23

---

11. As in the original pamphlet.

Nine Christian Boys. Read This Aloud at
    Family Prayers . . . . . . . 24
Suggestion for Diplomatic Action . . . . . . . . . . 25
Make No League With Hell . . . . . . . . . . . . . 25
John Milton's Prayer . . . . . . . . . . . . . . . . . 26
The American's Prayer . . . . . . . . . . . . . . . . 26
Faithful Death . . . . . . . . . . . . . . . . . . . . 27
Old Pagan is not Dead . . . . . . . . . . . . . . . . 28
A Christian's Vow . . . . . . . . . . . . . . . . . . 28

## TO ANY AMERICANS WHO ARE PREJUDICED AGAINST THE USE OF TORTURE AS A MEANS OF RELIGIOUS PERSUASION:

*For the Korean Christians no relief or remedy can be seen on this side of eternity. My prayer is that your hearts may be touched, so that none of those that hear me may consent to the sin of giving over Chinese Christians to the tormentors. If you had lived during the rise of the Dutch Republic, would you, for any political profit, great or small, have sold the Netherlands to the Spanish Inquisition? In those days of manly faith and honor what English statesman could have debated, even in his mind, the expediency of so dark a reason?*

In this letter is nothing new. In his "Mastery of the Far East,"[11] and in his short, clear article in "Asia" for September, Dr. Arthur Judson Brown[12] has told how Japan already intimidates and degrades the Shan-tung Christians and from a certain little brown pamphlet are taken the few examples of persecution in Korea here given.

---

11. *The Mastery of the Far East* (N.Y.: Scribner's, 1919), by Arthur Judson Brown, had appeared the preceding March. It focuses on Korea as the key point in the diplomatic and military mastery of the Eastern Pacific rim, but also discusses not only the whole range of power relations impinging thereon — i.e., China-Russia-Japan — but the general history and character of Japanese colonial rule throughout the region. "A Tenant in Shantung," in *Asia and the Americas* 19 (September, 1919), pp. 915-20, details Japan's overall aims and particular misdeeds there. As in Korea, the Shantung administrators saw the missionaries as a foreign presence bent on frustrating Japanese objectives, and systematically harassed and intimidated them. However, Brown reports no imprisonment or outright violence.
12. Arthur Judson Brown: (1856-1963: yes, one month past his 106th birthday!), clergyman and author. A.B. Wabash University '80; B.D. Lane Theological Seminary (later merged with McCormick Theological Seminary, where Newell Martin's father,

Nothing about Korea is here stated of my own knowledge. The Korean facts are all taken from that pamphlet in a letter dated July 9,[13] and that pamphlet (certain pages of which I shall refer to thus, "P. 30") is entitled "The Korean Situation: Authentic Accounts of Recent Events." The price is 25 cents. It was issued in August[14] by The Commission on Relations with the Orient of the Federal Council of the Church of Christ in America, 105 East 22nd Street, New York City. The foreword is signed by William I. Haven, Chairman, and Sidney L. Gulick, Secretary. The latter is widely known as a powerful propagandist for Japan. So much of the pamphlet as is written by him and Dr. Haven shows an intense desire that the laity keep quiet and not get excited, and a deplorable eagerness to persuade us that butter will not melt in the mouth of a Japanese torturer. The pamphlet is, obviously, issued reluctantly, under pressure of persistent inquiry from missionaries and other Christians.

The statements of fact in that pamphlet are not like tales of atrocity told by refugees, in places of safety, against a distant enemy. They are statements made in secret, in the hope of bringing some sort of hope or relief. Both victim and reporting missionary are still in the awful grip of the oppressor. Neither can hope to profit by falsehood or exaggeration.

All American missions, indeed, have many times been sternly warned, by their superiors that it will be worse for them if they mislead the home office by an exaggeration or show sympathy with any opposition to authority.

Published with reluctance by an advocate of the Japanese Government, the statements of fact tucked away in that pamphlet have more than the weight of charges against the Government. They are the unwilling confessions of its friends.

---

W.A.P. Martin, was class of 1849); numerous honorary degrees including D.D. Yale '13. Held several Presbyterian ministries; was appointed administrative secretary of the Presbyterian Board of the Foreign Missions in 1895 and held post until 1929 (and, as such, someone with whom Martin's father, W.A.P. Martin, had both professional and personal connections). Member, often chairman, of many of its special commissions. Officer in a wide variety of other missionary/charitable works, including first president of Save the Children Fund. President of the American Board of Governors of Cheloo University in China, and trustee and member of the executive committee of the Peking Union Metropolitan College. Author 16 books, including *Memoirs of a Centenarian* (1957).

---

"Little brown pamphlet": the 25-cent pamphlet issued July 12, 1919 by the Federal Council of the Churches of Christ in America (FCCCA) entitled, *The Korean Situation: Authentic Accounts of Recent Events12*. Typographical error in original: not "in," but "and."

13. Apparently an open letter from some missionary source in Korea.
14. Date of record: July 12, 1919.

The first five pages of that brown pamphlet make unintentionally a sinister and terrifying revelation of Japan's hidden hand in America.

The problem before Tokio was:

(1) to blast Korea with a sudden flame of persecution, so that no crop of Christian weeds would ever make head again;

(2) to terrify so profoundly all Koreans and Chinese that prudent men would know without ever being told again that in Japanese colonies faith in a crucified Saviour leads straight to a martyr's crown; to heavenly glory perhaps, but to certain earthly shame and ruin;

(3) to perfect this advertisement of her heathen power among her slaves before midsummer;

(4) and to keep America and Paris ignorant of the Korean horrors.

Japan achieved these seemingly incompatible triumphs with a skill beyond imagination. She began by choking off such voices as the *"Japan Chronicle,"* the most potent English newspaper in Japan, by a rigid perfection of censorship.[15] But how silence the angry, murmuring Christians of San Francisco and New York? How keep their murmurs from rising to a roar that might reach Paris over the heads of European censors?

Any American has cause for grave thought when he learns that all this was foreseen and provided for beforehand as carefully and completely as were the rawhides and hot irons that tore the flesh of faithful Christians.

Who knows by what magic or good luck or supernatural persuasiveness heathen Japan controls the time and manner of disseminating — no, of suppressing in a "publicity" department of our own Christian missions — the most important missionary news since Diocletion's day?[16] Hundreds of pages of facts had been brought through all the perils with speed and secrecy to the Presbyterian and Methodist mission boards. Published, those horrifying documents would have roused the most complacent priest of our city churches, the meanest deacon of us all, and the coldest of our politicians; and the persecutors would have been slowed up or inconvenienced; and Paris might have denied their prayer for added

---

15. *The Japan Chronicle* had published an article, "Nervousness About Korea," in early March, and promptly been shut down. The power of the Japanese government over publication was virtually unlimited, and so subject to the discretion or whim of local officials or even policemen that, for instance, the Foreign Ministry sometimes released news for publication and papers were suppressed for printing it.
16. Emperor of Rome 245-313, responsible for severe persecution of Christians.

power.[17] A machinery, however had been prepared beforehand, and according to plan, as the Japanese of Europe [Germans] used to say, the unsuspecting Presbyterians and Methodists poured their facts into the "publicity" department of a "commission" the secretary of which is Dr. Sidney L. Gulick, famous for his eulogies of Japan, many of them entirely just. Those facts were buried forever, then, in the office of a Japanophile enthusiast who was not less determined than Tokio to keep them from getting about among the Americans or getting to Paris. Dr. Gulick called in Japanese officials, who controlled and directed the obsequious whispers in which we Christians vented our fiery wrath. Month after month went by, and five months after the persecution broke out, Dr. Gulick's "publicity" department, under pressure, reluctantly printed that brown pamphlet. To kill all possible interest in it, he prefaced it with five pages of flattery of the Japanese Government and of advice to us to trust Apollyon to execute all necessary "reforms." Who wishes to read one single page of these atrocities when assured by Dr. Gulick in the "foreword" that a most efficient government is doing what we pray for and that the mission boards themselves are content? God will not be content, nor will the Christians of California.[18]

Perhaps you have not seen Japanese executioners. I have. July 6, 1919, was perhaps the very day on which Dr. Gulick was writing his misleading praise of Tokio. Months before that day Dr. Gulick had begun prostrating us in respectful telegrams before the Mikado's throne. On July 6, in the capital city of Korea, a muscular Japanese executioner strips to his task again. The sword-like rawhide whistles through the air, and falls with sickening force across the bare flesh of a Christian student. After ten cruel slashes, delivered with all his might, he is relieved by a second executioner for ten more cuts; and then comes a third, to give ten more.[19] On July 7, once more, three executioners drive the rawhide with full swing and force into the very place that was torn and gashed yesterday. The boy is again dragged back to his jail. If you were he, lying there, waiting for the next day's torture, would you not pray for death? Or would you, perhaps, curse the day you became a

---

17. In return for her participation on the Allied side in WWI, Japan demanded (and received) title to certain former German possessions in the Pacific, as well as the former German economic concessions in Shantung. See previous article, "Democracy's Crusaders." 18. California was, quite naturally, the home base of the Commission on Relations with the Orient, given its concern with Asiatic immigration.
19. *The New York Times* of August 18, 1919, cited an anonymous missionary source in Seoul as saying that "ninety strokes of the bamboo flail, thirty each on three successive days, is a frequent punishment. As a result of the beatings some of the prisoners have died."

Christian? Or, if you knew whose secret hand was guilty of your torments, would you not curse him?

A seventeenth century writer says that it is a sport to see a man on the rack for half an hour.[20] There are sadists that skin cats alive. But neither of these sports is so thrilling to amateurs of pain as the torment of the rawhide, and sadists gather where the police are torturing Christians.

On July 8 the boy is brought out for a third torment and at the first blow, as if the festering wounds were torn open by steel fingers, blood and pus and gobs of Christian flesh fly up and bespatter the locating [gloating?] bystanders. Thence young Christian goes to the American hospital or sometimes to his grave. He is but one of many; how many none will ever know.

The persecution has done its deadly work, and now the friends of the persecutors will ask us to trust and admire the new governor-general and his smooth words about gentleness and reform — the purring of the sated tiger.

I have no part in trade or politics or missions, but I have a powerful motive for beseeching your attention. Chinese is my native language, and I mourn over the all but hopeless enslavement of the land where I was born and which I have always loved. From childhood I have hated with an implacable hatred all those that trade in secrecy and all persecutors and torturers.

Newell Martin.
Milford, Connecticut,
September, 1919.

## JAPAN'S ATTEMPT TO EXTERMINATE KOREAN CHRISTIANS

Neither Italy nor the Aegean is so beautiful as Japan, nor is any people more lovable and admirable than the Japanese. Gentlest of men with their own children, fiercest to their foes, these indomitable islanders are aware from a calm observation of facts that they are above common human beings as Hebrews are above Hottentots, but that is no reason why common men should unduly smooth the path for their coming masters.

The Japanese have seen how a handful of Greeks under Alexander, and in their turn, a handful of British have risen to world dominion. The cold-blooded Japanese oligarchs think their own turn should come next. In the relentless pursuit of this

---

20. Unable to determine which writer.

unwholesome ambition Japanese politicians have set themselves to possess, enslave, and assimilate Korea and Shan-tung, the two keys of Asia.

To the Koreans, only fifteen years ago, they guaranteed independence.[21] To-day in Korea it may be death to speak the word. To the Koreans, nine years ago, they guaranteed freedom of religion. In Korea to-day to be a Christian is to be in deadly peril. To-day, in enslaving the Koreans, the Japanese recklessly degrade themselves and smirch the honor of their race.

Like forest fires in a season of drought, atrocities now break forth all over the world, and men become despairingly indifferent and wait wearily for the horrors to burn themselves out. But the Japanese atrocities in Korea demand our most intense attention, because: first, pagans are persecuting Christians; secondly, we are using our gigantic power to extend these persecutions to Shan-tung and the rest of northern China; thirdly, these are not war atrocities or civil-war atrocities, and these tales are not scandals invented by a feeble folk to discredit their tyrants, but are the horrors of religious persecution directed against peaceful Christians and unarmed women and children.

We begin to understand that in "opening" Japan we played the perilous part of the Rash Fisherman of the Arabian Nights. We unbottled the appalling Afreet[22] whose omnipotent form now towers to the stars and blackens all the eastern sky. But yesterday we were condescending to these islanders. To-day, under the dictation of Japanese, our huge nation turns to paths of shame. Imperious, on their tiny islands, they make cowards of us all.

If you are a Japanese policeman, you can have no end of fun with a Presbyterian school-girl. (P.47) Throw her down, kick her, here and there, hard; drag her to your police court. Beat her about the face and head and legs and back until she is all blood and tears and shrieks and convulsive sobs. Tell her to show her breasts. When she refuses, tear off her undershirt. Keep her four days, then take her to another prison. There strip her naked; have her "looked at by the men."[23] This is one of the mildest of the things done in Korea in March of this year, while the silent, inscrutable, secretive,

---

21. Such guarantees were given at the time of the original Japanese occupation at the start of the Russo-Japanese War.
22. Demon of Mohammedan mythology.
23. The beating was carried out by "twenty or more" policemen and was so severe "that at times I did not realize whether they were beating me or someone else." The prison treatment included not only exposure, but further torture: the binding and jerking of the girl's fingers; the forcing her to hold a heavy chair at arm's length for an hour. The charge was only participation in a demonstration.

thoroughly informed envoys of Japan, in Paris, were offering every diplomatic courtesy to our commissioners.

But for the calm confidence of those Japanese envoys in America's submissiveness to Japan that girl to-day would be like any New York maiden, securely studying her Bible lesson, and no harm would have come to her from the Japanese officials who, with greedy, lecherous eyes, watched her as she went by, all faith and hope and maiden modesty. The soldiers that gloated over her bare body are a part of the forces with which her [America's] own soldiers and engineers are affiliated to-day in northern Asia.[24]

In March, 1919, while we were praying daily that the Paris Conference might lay firm foundations for peace, righteousness, and freedom, the Japanese government secretly ordered its police in Korea to extirpate the Christian religion, which used to flourish there, and also the modern Korean religion, a sort of Sermon-on-the-Mount affair, whose creed begins with the fantastic proposition,

> Who waits on God,
> Will wield God's might.[25]

No non-pagan eye but that of the Recording Angel has ever seen that decree.

You can infer, however, with scientific accuracy, from the acts of Japanese soldiers and police, the orders of their Government, more exactly than you can infer from the movement of a man's hand the action of his brain.

From those actions we know that the Japanese Government had directed that the Korean people must be taught by terror that it pays to be a Buddhist, and that it does not pay to be a Christian or to follow the gentle Korean religion or to have dealings with American missionaries.

---

24. Referring to the contemporary Allied interventions in Siberia.
25. As described in a report from "A Britisher" appearing on pp. 108-21 of the FCCCA pamphlet: "The Japanese lay the chief blame [for the demonstrations] upon a sect called 'The Church of the Heavenly Way.' Their creed is a simple one of two lines, which, however, may not be as colorless as it looks: 'Who waits on God/Shall wield God's might; Who ne'er forgets/All things come right.'

"Forgets what? To the initiated this may hold more than a religious meaning. Be that as it may, it is worth nothing [noting] that this sect has been in existence, under this name, since annexation. Its membership exceeds a million. On three gala days enormous crowds gather in the capital and throughout the country, ostensibly to worship, but in reality to perpetuate the spirit of patriotism, and incidentally to provide the organization of a united effort when 'The Day' should arrive. The sect is avowedly politico-religious, and their prominence in the recent demonstrations is easily accounted for." (pp. 116-17)

The American missionaries had held utterly aloof from politics, but Christianity embarrassed the Japanese Government because it gave the Koreans an outlook from slavery, a window on the world.[26] You cannot be in the house of even an intensely neutral and cautious American missionary without stumbling on incendiary books like "Uncle Tom's Cabin," and Milton's, or John Bunyan's.[27]

Religious freedom in Korea is guaranteed by solemn treaties, but Tokio thinks it no longer necessary to wear any pretense about the sanctity of treaties or to make broad any phylacteries.[28]

Tokio found its opportunity to get rid of these irksome religions in the Korean Declaration of Independence of March 1. Never was so calm a declaration. As a result of skilful secrecy and combination, without a foreknowledge of missionary, priest, or police, all the people of Korea came forth on one day and peacefully declared themselves independent. Their sole object was to inform the Peace Conference of Paris that seventeen millions of Koreans desire to be free. (P. 22)

In this outpouring of unarmed multitudes who shouted "Mansay!" meaning "Hurrah!"[29] there was a natural pre-eminence of people with schooling. As a great number of those who have some education belonged to the two doomed religions, this gave the pagan persecutors their chance.

The Government resolved to strike terror forever into these Korean Christians, so that never again would they lift their meek faces from under the lash and cry out to mankind. They were to be taught that it does not pay to be mixed in the remotest way with Christians or Americans.

---

26. The missionary presence in Korea — preponderantly American and Protestant — dated back to 1885. It had been intent throughout not simply on religious conversion, but on the improvement of such matters as learning, health, sanitation, and living conditions generally. The concept of the inherent equality of souls had proved a very telling one among the Korean lower orders, and conversions had been massive. By the time of Martin's writing, practicing Christians comprised about a third of the Korean population. Although most Korean missionaries sedulously avoided any direct connection with politics, the Japanese government saw them as a hostile presence, in part simply for their connection with foreign nations, and in part because Christian ideas seemed to issue naturally in democracy. Ito had in fact declared that the missionary presence had seriously undermined the Japanese position.

27. Milton's *Areopagetica*, his impassioned defense of the freedom of the press, published in 1644; Bunyan's *Pilgrim's Progress*, published in 1678, first work of western literature (not counting the Bible) to be translated into Korean (1858).

28. Matt. 23:5 "But all their [scribes' and Pharisees'] works they do for to be seen of men: they make broad their phylacteries, and enlarge the borders of their garments."

29. "Mansay" (spelled "Mansei" throughout the FCCCA report) literally means "Ten Thousand Years": i.e., "Long Live Korea!"

Such of the declarants as were not shot down at once had gone peacefully home, to wait for Mr. Wilson's justice, now, they thought, thoroughly advised and aroused. To those homes went spies and gendarmes and police, and dragged the Christians away to torment, shame, and death.

In six weeks Korea was quiet with the stillness of death. Every Korean had learned that if he breathed a word about Americans or Mr. Wilson or freedom, he was to be classed with Christians and meet a Christian's doom.

The Christians were swept away like torn paper before a hurricane. We are told of 40,000 arrested and 6,000 killed in the Japanese fury.[30]

Not till the graves give up their dead will the numbers be known exactly. Those figures are probably low. The people of Korea are one sixth of those of the United States. It is doubtful whether even Japanese efficiency can strike utter terror into so great a population without killing at least one in every 2,000 and arresting six times as many. Some Japanese Torquemada[31] may offer to deny these figures. I will not argue with a murderer as to the number of his victims unless he permits me at least to inspect the cellar where he hides their skeletons. Will you, Prime Minister Hara of Japan,[32] invite an inhabitual commission to report, from sifted testimony, exact statistics as to how many women have been dishonored, how many maidens put to shame? And what can statistics tell us of the torments of Christians slowly done to death in heathen jails? Have the Japanese kept record with algometers[33] and registered the sum total of their torments?

When Torquemada ruled in Spain, what English Protestant would give statistics of his cruelties? When the Waldenses[34] went to the stake and the rack, centuries had to pass before the ledgers of the Inquisition were open to the historian. I offer only a few

---

30. The figures represent the upper limits of contemporary estimates, which had ranged as low, respectively, as 10,000 and 1,000.
31. Tomas de Torquemada (1420-98), Dominican monk who became inquisitor-general of Castile and Aragon in 1483 and founder of the Spanish Inquisition.
32. Hara Takashi (1856-1921), Japanese politician, prime minister 1918-1921. Baptized into the Catholic Church 1873. Began career as newspaper editor; entered foreign ministry 1882, where he held various posts including vice-minister 1895, and minister to Korea 1896-7. Was home minister 1906-8, 1911-12, 1913. Died by assassination.
33. Devices for keeping an exact tally.
34. Quasi-Protestant sect founded in early thirteenth century by Peter Valdo or Waldo, and condemned by the church as heretical in 1215. They were severely persecuted and for the most part exterminated.

examples of the different kinds of torture and massacre. You may infer the rest from the dumb terror that now binds all Korea and all Korean Christians.

In this persecution the resourceful Japanese use many different tortures for the body and, in addition, a torture for the mind that is a sadistic twentieth-century novelty in religious persecution.

"A Korean woman," writes a missionary, "would rather die than expose her naked body in ways not conformable to local custom. But it seems to be the common delight of official depravity just now to humiliate our Christian women by stripping them and beating them while naked." (P. 104)

Ingenious Japanese! Some Korean Christian might dare for himself sword or fire or Damien's [sic] bed of steel;[35] but let him think twice of his wife and daughters put to open shame.

The ordinary slaveholder used to be inclined to encourage modesty among his helots as increasing their market value; but the Japanese, in the systematic degradation of his new slaves, finds a profit in breaking down the personal dignity of wives and daughters. No chief of police would have ventured of his own accord to adopt such a system of organized indecency. It was obviously thought and and directed by the controlling brain at Tokio.

A government that rests on torture is a government of devils, unfit for even our time. But this Japanese Government plans carefully the violation of sanctities that lie at the base of civilized society. I remember no other modern government that has deliberately schemed to degrade the unhappy women who are its subjects. There is an unparalleled fiendishness in minds that can thus systematically befoul the purity and modesty of young girls. We might make league and alliance with an inhuman brute and put him in a council to rule over us; but we have some pride in our manhood, some reverence for womanhood, and we will not enter into covenant with a sadist.

Of those that were arrested, be they 40,000 or 4,000, or more or fewer, how can we sleep at night when we remember that every pang they suffered earned pleasure, profit, or reward for their tormentors? Of those that died, be they 6,000 or 600, or more or fewer, how many died an easy death? Those that died quickly were

---

35. The apparently demented regicide Robert Francois Damiens (1715-1757), whose attempt on the life of Louis XV actually resulted in nothing more than a slight stab wound. The tortures inflicted on him during the two months preceding his execution by quartering included being bound to a bed by metal rings around his trunk, his extremities being in turn bound to the rings by leather straps.

the lucky ones.

Japanese methods are precise and thorough. Christianity in Japan was stamped out utterly in the seventeenth century.[36] Then, if one Christian was found in any house, from four houses to the right of that house and from four houses to the left every man, woman, and child was taken, and died the death. Doubt not that in uprooting Korean Christianity to-day the Japanese use a similar perfection of method.

In the recent uprooting machinery, of course, was sometimes used. One man was squeezed in an upright press. Then a cord was tied firmly about one finger, and he was hoisted till his toes barely touched the floor. His two crimes were cheering in a procession and receiving a letter from a friend in America and withholding it (P. 45).[37]

In his case the Japanese applied an unnecessarily spectacular torture, so as to put another stumbling-block in John Hay's open door[38] by advertising to Koreans and Chinese that it is bad luck to receive letters from America.

The best modern tortures need no cumbrous machinery. The grewsome complexities so fashionable in medieval Europe were meant to save people from torture by frightening them beforehand.

The Japanese held wounded men in prison two days without water.[39] Think about that, quietly. They took out of our missionary hospitals men with gunshot wounds, and dragged them away to the horrors of the question (P. 44).[40]

---

36. Toyotomi Hideyoshi (see "Democracy's Crusaders in Shantung"), on July 25, 1587, issued an edict ordering all "foreign religious teachers" to leave Japan within twenty days under pain of death, because "they preach a law contrary to that of Japan" and "have even had the audacity to destroy temples devoted to our Kami and Hotoki." According to Brown (*op. cit.*, pp. 394-5), Japanese Christians "were persecuted without mercy — stripped of their possessions, burned, beheaded, crucified, thrown from cliffs, and subjected to every other form of torture and death that fanatical ingenuity could devise." By the mid-seventeenth century Christianity had been virtually obliterated in Japan. Hideyoshi's real motives do not seem to have been the proclaimed ones, and historians differ as to their nature. However, they were arguably those of the Japanese Shantung and Korea administrations; i.e., the simple objection to a powerful foreign influence.

37. The man had initially been imprisoned for participating in a demonstration, but merely released with a warning. He was tortured solely for refusing to disclose the contents of the letter.

38. John Milton Hay, (1838-1905), secretary of state 1898-1905, devised in 1899 the policy of the Open Door in China; i.e., equal commercial rights for all nations.

39. Such an incident was reported in the FCCCA pamphlet, p. 33. They were given a little rice, but no water. One man had to have his arm amputated at the shoulder because the absence of any medical treatment had permitted gangrene to set in.

40. Three men were thus treated; two, though, were left at the hospital due to a doctor's protests.

"Beating" is a weak word for a strong torment. Beating can easily be made the seventh hell of agony. With a club discreetly used, a Japanese can break the stoutest heart; he can in a few minutes drive the strongest to scream and beg for death. He can do the same thing with three feet of cord.

"Beating and torture," writes a missionary, "are the cardinal principles of Japanese police methods in Korea."

"It is usual for the arrested man to be cuffed and kicked by several policemen" (P. 16).

1. *The Story of the Pregnant Woman*[41] (P. 55). No machinery is needed to torture a pregnant woman. This woman had been a mission teacher, "very bright and intelligent." She was two months advanced in pregnancy. She had gone to the house of one "Pyo" to comfort the mother, who was distressed because her young daughter had been carried off by the Japanese police. "As she came out of the house several police and soldiers came into the yard. They knew she was the school-teacher and had been searching for her at the school.[...]They told her to[...]come with them. As she stood in front of the...police station, a policeman kicked her hard [*sic:* forcibly] from behind, and she fell forward into the room. As she lay, stunned, on the floor, a policeman put his foot on her head. Then he [*sic:* forcibly] raised her up and struck her many times over the head and face." He tore off her clothes, "meanwhile constantly kicking and striking her. He also beat her with a heavy stick and with a paddle. He tore off her underclothes and kicked her in the chest and beat her, accusing her of setting the minds of Korean children against Japan, and said that he intended to beat her to death."

"She tried to cover her nakedness with the underclothes that had been stripped from her," but they were torn away from her. "She tried to sit down, but was forced to rise by constant kicking and beating with a stick. She tried to turn away from the many men in the room, but was constantly forced to turn again so as to face the men. She tried to protect herself with her hands and arms, and one man twisted her arms behind her back and held them there while the beating and kicking continued. All parts of her body were beaten. She became benumbed and was losing consciousness of

---

41. As in most quoted material in Martin's writing, he often paraphrases; skips words or sections, sometimes using ellipses, sometimes not; frequently places material within single quotation marks for no apparent reason; and, from time to time, substitutes a synonym for a word or phrase. Corrections are made where needed to clarify meaning or to note significant departures from source; otherwise, original punctuation and phrasing remains.

pain. Her face swelled, and her body became discolored."

2. *The Story of the Widow Chung*, an attendant of [at] the Bible Institute (P. 54). She is thirty-one. She was taken into the office, and a policeman tore off her underclothes, and she protested. For this "they struck her in the face" till she was black and blue. She was beaten "systematically on the arms and legs with a paddle. The beating continued for some time. The police then stopped the beating and sat down to drink tea and eat Japanese cakes, meanwhile making fun of the woman sitting there naked. There were many men in the room." Nor was she the only woman there. The beaten mission-teacher woman was lying naked at the side of the room, while the tormentors rested and laughed and ate and drank.

3. *The Story of the Naked Methodist Women* (P. 50). Fifteen women, twelve of them Methodist and two of them Presbyterians, were held at the Pyengyang police station. One of them a girl of twenty-one, tells the story: "They stripped all the women naked in the presence of many men. They found nothing against me except that I had been on the street and had shouted 'Mansay.' [Mansei] They beat me. My arms were pulled tight behind my back and tied. They stuck me with the lighted end of their cigarettes. Some were stuck with hot irons. My offense was very little compared with those who made flags.[42]

"Some were beaten until they were unconscious. One young woman...resisted having her clothes taken off.[43] They tore off her clothing and beat her all the harder....After four days we were taken to the prison. Here we were packed in a room with men and women. One day an old man was beaten until he died. One of the Bible women was right next to him. She asked to be moved away from the corpse, but was denied....'They took our Bibles away and would not allow us to talk or pray.'...The jailers 'blasphemed the name of Christ,' and asked 'if there was not a man by the name of Saul who was put in prison.' They asked [us], most of all, as to what the foreigners had said, and were most vile and cruel to those who had been with the missionaries or who had taught in the mission schools. Some of the girls were so changed that they did not look like persons."

---

42. Continues "took part in the independence [sic], etc."
43. Ellipses omit, "who was just at the time of her monthly sickness"

4. *The Story of a Young Girl* (P. 47).[44] "Near the Dok Su Palace a Japanese policeman seized me from behind by my hair and I was thrown to the ground hard." "He kicked me several times." "At the entrance of the 'Chongo' [Chongno] police office twenty or more Japanese policemen who stood in line sneered and kicked me and struck me with their swords and struck me in the face many times. I became almost unconscious. My hands and legs were bleeding.

"I was led into a room and here they dragged me on the floor. They struck me in the face. They struck me with their swords. They flung me to one corner of the room. On coming to my senses I found myself in a room packed with young men and women. I saw some of them handled so brutally it almost broke my heart to see them beaten."

After some time "we were examined by a police officer, one by one. I was made to kneel with my legs bound [together]." Each question and answer was accompanied by "blows in the face." "I was ordered to expose my breasts." "They tied my fingers together and jerked them violently. This made me feel as if my fingers were being torn from my hand." She then tells of going to the cells. "As I made the first step down, my strength gave out and so I rolled down the whole length of the stairs.[45] I was obliged to crawl into a room. The policeman in charge [of the room] was very much amused to see me crawling into the room. He laughed loudly.... Then I prayed and seemed to see Jesus and was much comforted from on high. I spent five days in all at the police station. Then I was sent to the West Gate Penitentiary.

"There I was stripped naked and was looked at by the men."

5. *The Torturing of One Kim* (P. 51). Kim, a young[46] man of promise, a member of the Third City Church of Taiku, was heard by a friend in another cell "to cry out a number of times at the pain of the punishment inflicted on him in the jail." He was frequently beaten on the head with the key of the cell. After his release he suffered terrible pain in his head. "It seemed as if all one side of his head was gone." He died in ten days.

---

44. This is the Presbyterian schoolgirl mentioned previously.
45. As earlier reported, this young girl was forced to hold a chair in front of her for a long period, a torture which exhausted her.
46. The man is described as "the son of the Elder-Helper of the Third City Church," which position apparently was that of some kind of assistant to the church elders.

"The night he died he was protesting in his delirium that he was innocent and that his punishment was too severe. The doctor who attended him states that he died from blows on the head. The neck and the base of the skull were darkly discolored."

6. *Chopping of a Christian* (P. 43). "A young man was peacefully going home (he had, it is true, been shouting 'Mansay'), and was 'walking along a small street' when a policeman from behind threw him down and 'drew his sword and...hacked at him.' 'His skull was cut through so that the brain showed. This was done by three sword cuts in the same place.' The photograph showed ten sword-cuts. 'During the next day his little cousin, a mission school girl,' who was greatly attached to him 'stood watch over his body.'"[47]

7. *The Elder's Wife* (P. 34). On March 24 "soldiers looking for one of the elders" of a certain church, "took his wife, a bright looking woman of about thirty." "They stripped her of all her clothing and beat her without mercy" to make her tell where her husband was.

8. *Official Advice to Christians.* One missionary statement runs as follows:

"Wholesale arrest and beating of Christians simply because they are Christians.

"In some places the men and women of the village were called together. All those who admitted they were Christians were maltreated or arrested, and the others sent away. Wayfarers met by soldiers and gendarmes are asked whether they are Christians and beaten and abused on the admission of the fact." Korean Christians surviving"[48] are given all sorts of announcements by local police and gendarmes. They are told that Christianity is to be exterminated; that all Christians are to be shot, that meetings are to be forbidden."

"Throughout the country the police immediately[49] began to arrest pastors, elders and other church officers."

A Japanese vice-governor (the real executive of his province) "in a public meeting advised people to have nothing to do with

---

47. A Japanese policeman tried to prevent several passers-by who did their best to save the man from taking him to a foreign rather than a Japanese hospital.
48. Original reads, "Korean Christians remaining in the villages"; that is, who chose to stay even after being maltreated.
49. That is, immediately following the demonstration.

Christianity. Police officials are urging the same thing everywhere (P. 89).[50]

"Presbyterian and Methodist organizations are both obnoxious to the government."[51]

9. *Scourged on the Cross* (P. 67). Four young theological students who had taken no part in any demonstration "were found in the college dormitories by Japanese soldiers. Tied to a wooden cross they were given thirty-nine strokes with a paddle and told that, as Christ suffered on the cross, it was fitting that they should."

10. *The Massacre at Cheamni* (P. 74). The village of Cheamni lay only fifteen miles from the railroad by which all tourists used to travel on their way from New York to Peking and from Paris to Tokio.[52] Japanese soldiers were sent there in motor-cars.

"The gendarmes and soldiers marching into this village, summoned the men of the village to attend a meeting in the church, where, they were told, certain orders would be read to them."

The Japanese gathered in this way about twelve Christian men and about twenty-five of the Korean religion. As soon as the men had "been gathered together, the soldiers opened fire upon them through the open windows, after having surrounded the building. To complete their work, the surviving women of the village told the missionaries, the soldiery entered the building and bayoneted all the men whom the bullets had not killed, while two women who had approached the'building to learn the fate of their husbands were bayoneted and their bodies thrown among those of the men. Then kerosene was poured upon the dead and the bodies and the church building consumed by fire."

A missionary who saw the place the next day makes these notes: "Heaps of smoking ashes. Groups of women, children, and old men sitting on the hillside watching the ruins in dumb despair. Corpse horribly burned lying just outside of a building, which we learned later had been the church. This body was photographed where it lay. I questioned 'a villager' but fear and shock had numbed him. He held his head in his hand and said that everything he had

---

50. Actually from p. 88.
51. Original reads, "Presbyterian organization, with its self-government and unity, and Methodist organization, with its unity and its added relation to a foreign ecclesiastical body of great power are both obnoxious to the government."
52. The railroad is that running from Seoul to the port of Fusan (Pusan) on Korea's southeast coast.

and all the results of years of hard work had gone."

The missionary said, "How is it you are alive?" and he answered, "I am not a Christian."

These Christians were Methodists. "These people had lost everything, even their seeds for the coming year." Another man said that "his house had not been set fire because he was not a Christian."

The soldiers seem to have belonged to the 78th Regiment. The missionary says that at Cheamni "the odor of burnt flesh" about "the church was sickening."[53]

One of the men who accompanied the British consul to this place says:

"Whenever we started to talk to the natives" the "policemen would saunter up and the Korean would freeze up." "The number of Christian men killed is twelve, whose names were secured, in addition to which two women who went to find out what was happening to their husbands were killed, one a woman over forty and the other nineteen. These may have been the bodies we saw outside the church."

Cheamni is a type of one class of burnings and massacres. In that one district fifteen towns were burned.[54]

11. *A Night Massacre* (P. 80). A type of another kind of official burning is Soo Chon, where "the people were awakened by finding their houses on fire. As soon as they ran out they were struck with swords or bayonets or shot." A church and thirty houses were burned.

12. *Another Type of Massacre* (P. 33). Of massacres we find another type, exemplified in Marengsan [Maungsan], where fifty-six men [people] were summoned to the police station, locked in the police yard, and shot down by the police from the top of the wall.

The Koreans had heard, as a voice from heaven, the inspiring declarations of our President. It was their plan to march, utterly unarmed, and cheer for independence and their native land and to

---

53. These remarks submitted by a correspondent of *The Japan Advertiser*.
54. The FCCCA pamphlet, on pp. 72-4, reproduces from the *Japan Advertiser* an article describing Governor-General Hasegawa's admission that the village burnings had occurred. Hasegawa claimed that "the ones responsible had been punished, and strict orders had been sent throughout the peninsula forbidding further acts of this kind."

submit to any cruelty. Their whole aim was to tell the outer world of their woes. The outer world finds it profitable to be deaf to their cry, and hurries to put its obsequious neck under the conqueror's foot, and begs him to accept thirty million new slaves and pass on to fresh conquests. Resolved to use no violence, the Koreans kept themselves under firm control to a surprising degree. That was the case even where two women[55] were carried out from a police station, and the crowd of five hundred, that had gathered to protest, burst into sobs at the horror of their condition. That was the station where the police officer explained that, although it was not necessary to strip men or old women, girls and young women had to be stripped naked in the search for seditious papers (P. 56).

13. *The Story of a Brave Young Man* (P. 16). One young man, seeing the girl that he was engaged to in the hands of the police, went to her rescue. How many of us would have had that daring? Between him and that helpless girl stood all the armies of the League of Nations. What do you suppose was done to that young man in the dungeon where he lay when last heard of?[56]

14. *The Story of a Man's Mother* (P. 34). "The mother of one of the wounded men told a policeman that if her son died 'she would take revenge [on him]'."
The policeman went to her house and again stabbed her son who was lying on the floor wounded."[57]

15. *Respect for Gray Hairs* (P.32). At Suna Ub an old man went to the gendarme station to protest against the atrocities.[58] In the East reverence is paid to gray hairs, and old men can speak up where others fear to tread. "This man the gendarmes shot dead. His wife came in and, finding the body, sat down beside it wailing, as is the custom of Koreans. She was told to keep still, and not doing so she also was killed." The daughter who came to seek her aged parents was spared, being merely slashed with a sword.

---

55. These were the subjects of Martin's first two incidents, described as The Pregnant Woman and The Widow Chung. Some members of the crowd wanted to attack the police station and take revenge, but "Elder Han" managed to talk them out of it.
56. The "brave young man" was "set upon by several policemen and severely beaten. He was arrested and has not yet been released, having now been in custody about three weeks."
57. The man had been wounded by police firing into a demonstration.
58. Specifically, against keeping wounded men in prison without water for two days as Martin reported earlier.

This persecution throws light on the part which Japan will take in the League of Nations.

The Governor-General of Korea is close to the heads of the Japanese state and in the closest confidence of the court. What he says and what he does are in a high degree the voice and act of Tokio.

The great Ito was resident in Korea.[59] The powerful Terauchi was governor-general before he became prime minister,[60] preceding Hara, now prime minister.[61] Hasegawa succeeded Terauchi as governor-general.[62]

We may expect Hasegawa in a short time to rule over us as Japan's representative in the Council of the Big Five.[63]

This governor-general made a proclamation reminding the Koreans, with a view to letting them understand that there is no hope from any quarter, that Japan is, "one of the principal factors in the League of Nations." He exhorted Koreans "to participate in the great work of humanity and righteousness" of Japan "as one of the leading powers of the world" (P. 109).

Lovers of the League of Nations, which this governor-general describes so accurately, will be pleased to know what is done in this governor-general's house.

Pan Tun Nak, aged twenty-five, met with all the other people of his village at the end of March and without violence paraded the village, calling "Mansay." Gendarmes told them to go home. This they did, and that day there was no trouble. Five days later gendarmes went from house to house arresting people. Pak Tun Nak and many others were taken to the governor-general's and flogged. He received thirty strokes at 12 o'clock and thirty at 2 o'clock. He was taken to the missionary hospital (P. 41).

A government school-girl says: "On March 1, at two, we went to the French consulate and the American consulate and shouted 'Mansay.'[64] We pressed forward to the Governor-General's

---

59. Hirobumi Ito (1841-1909), outstanding figure in the modernization of Japan. Drafted the constitution of 1889; was prime minister 1892-6, 1898, and 1900-01. Responsible for the 1905 agreement making Korea a Japanese protectorate. Was first resident-general of Korea, 1905-09; his assassination was the pretext for annexation.
60. Terauchi Masatake (1852-1919). Japanese army leader; army minister 1902-12; first governor-general in Korea 1910-16; prime minister 1916-18.
61. See note 32 above.
62. Field Marshal Viscount Yoshimichi Hasegawa (1849-1924). Served with distinction in Chino-Japanese and Russo-Japanese wars; subsequently member of the Supreme War Council and Chief of the General Staff. Governor-general of Korea 1917-19.
63. Chief Allied negotiators at Versailles; the United States, Great Britain, France, Italy, and Japan.
64. She is described as actually having shouted in at least four different locations.

[Government General Offices], and there the Kotang Koan (high official) 'came out with his sword, beating all in his way. He struck me with his sword on the back, making a wound three inches long. The force of the blow threw me down, after which he stamped on my head with his foot' " (P. 82). [65]

Poor little lamb! Shouting her cry for freedom before France and England and before the august Governor-General who stands for the might of the League of Nations!

A peculiar gravity attends the Korean terrorizing. It has a two-fold object. It is to terrify the Koreans into silence; it is also to terrify Japan's new Chinese subjects into silence. When Japan moves in China, she wishes to hear no protests and to be bothered with no Christians. The prudent Chinese study the reports on Korea, and will hasten to avoid being mixed up in any way with Christians and Americans. The prestige of Christianity and of America is gone, and Hara is content. One would suppose that at the first offense the nearest missionary could go to the polished governor-general and through him and the polished Viscount Uchida[66] cable all the facts to New York and Paris. Nobody dares to mail even sealed letters from Korea about these crimes.

Japan controlled the mails and telegraphs. America, therefore, could hear nothing of these atrocities. America meekly waits for such news from Asia as Japan thinks wholesome for her weak mind. The Peace Conference was sitting, and we in our homes were invoking divine light and guidance for its counsels.

The facts about Korea were essential to aid our President in deciding whether he should award the thirty millions of Shan-tung to the cruel task-masters that hold the whip over the seventeen millions of Korea. If we had made any promise, it would be void because of the concealment of these material facts about the policy and conduct of the men to whom we awarded Shan-tung.

A missionary came to New York,[67] a messenger, as if we were back in the days of Erasmus.[68] Messengers with documents hidden

---

65. She was unconscious for about twenty minutes.
66. Uchida Kosai (1865-1936), diplomat and politician. Foreign minister 1911-12 and 1918-23, the latter time in three successive cabinets. Militant nationalist; advocate and promoter of Japanese power.
67. The Reverend A. E. Armstrong, Secretary of the Board of Foreign Missions of the Presbyterian Church of Canada, who was on the point of leaving the Far East after a ten-month tour when a cable from a Dr. Avison in Seoul asked him to visit Korea. He spent March 16-19 in Seoul collecting information.
68. Erasmus (1469-1536) carried out theological argument and polemic primarily through correspondence.

about their clothes, made their way out of Korea.

In a famous painting, "The Missionary's Story," a shabby priest tries to tell an absent-minded cardinal what the pagan wolves have done to the lambs of his flock.[69] I fear that some of the officers of the great mission boards were alarmed when they heard this Korean missionary's story lest the American people might hear what should fire the coldest heart. Who, with the smell of burning Christian flesh in his nostrils, could vote for Governor-General Hasegawa and his League of Nations?

The Commission on Relations with the Orient which operates as a brake on the mission boards has consistently followed the policy, in which it has been skilfully seconded by the press, of keeping everything quiet and keeping everybody cool.

There are indications that some of the hierarchy of our Protestant churches have been misled by Japanese diplomatists into believing that everything should be hushed up that may diminish the popular demand for a League of Nations and for a permanent alliance between our Government and that of Japan.

On April 16, 1919, the mission boards called a meeting of that commission of the sesquipedalian[70] name.

To two of such meetings "important Japanese were invited."[71] "Urgent and full cablegrams" were promptly sent to Japan by some of these "Japanese friends."

The commission sought by these "quiet and friendly methods" to exert influence. "It deemed it only fair and just to take up the matter first with the Japanese," "before giving to the daily press the rapidly accumulating matter from Korea."

Under pressure from anxious inquiring Christians, that commission scrambled together such papers as they could no longer withhold, and printed them in the little brown pamphlet of 125 pages referred to in the preface, entitled "The Korean Situation."[72]

That pamphlet begins by saying that "many exaggerations have been circulated."[73] It says that "there is good ground for belief

---

69. Unable to determine which famous painting.
70. Of many words or syllables.
71. Original reads, "...a group of important Japanese in New York City..." The commission held a dozen subsequent meetings.
72. The pamphlet states, "The Commission now feels that the time has come when the full and accurate information in its possession should be made available for the public."
73. Original reads: "In these days of excitement and political turmoil in many lands, we must accept with caution extreme statemments that are not capable of proof. Many exaggerations have been circulated. The facts described in the following pages speak for themselves." Apparently the intended meaning is that while there have been numerous contemporary exaggerations in such matters generally, the Commission's procedures have been sufficiently meticulous to make its findings authoritative.

that even before the uprising" — "uprising" is a strange word to describe the Koreans' peaceful protest — "the present cabinet" "was earnestly grappling with the problem of administrative reform in Korea" and that "there is every reason to believe that Premier Hara and his colleagues will exert their fullest power to rectify the wrongs and inaugurate a new era in Korea."[74]

The facts set forth here have been dug out of that pamphlet. You may rest assured, then, that these notes contain none of the "exaggerations" deplored by the Rev. Dr. Gulick.

How much effort has been made by the press and the commission to awaken and inform the public you may infer from the amount of information that you yourself had in regard to the Korean atrocities before reading these notes.

Viscount Uchida will smile and say, "You ask Americans to be more royalist than the king, to be more zealous against pagan cruelty than the mission boards." Let me remind you that there was once a mission board in London that derived revenue from the African slave-trade.[75]

Caesar's image and superscription go a long way with a mission board,[76] but when I hear of Christian maidens dishonored, Christian men with their finger-nails torn up by torturers, Christian women tormented to make them betray their husbands, I need no cautious clergyman or prudent prelate to tell me what to think or what to say.

The mission boards are made up of earnest, honest, able, learned men, devoted to spreading the gospel. In every board are

---

74. The Commission viewed the Japanese government as divided between "reactionary and militaristic forces on the one hand and liberal and progressive on the other," the 1919 cabinet being composed of the latter, but heir to its predecessors' policies; hence the Commission's belief about earlier grappling, halted only by "the turmoil." Hence, too, its belief that American public opinion could perform the greatest service, not by wholesale condemnation of Japan, but by distinguishing carefully between the two parties and encouraging "the new liberal policies and leaders that are now coming to the fore."

75. The Society for the Propagation of the Gospel in Foreign Parts, founded in London in 1701, was bequeathed the Codrington sugar plantation in Barbados in 1710; the plantation was worked by more than 300 slaves. (Thus, the revenue was derived not from the slave trade but from slave labor.) The anomaly did not go unnoticed. The Society attempted to justify itself by saying that the property was being held in trust for charitable purposes, and that the slaves were being treated with unusual humanity and given religious instruction, which was true if not perhaps vindicatory. Gradual emancipation began in 1830, but its completion was anticipated by the 1834 act of Parliament freeing all slaves in British dominions.

76. Matt. 22:19-21. "[Jesus said] Shew me the tribute money. And they brought unto him a penny. And he saith unto them, Whose is this image and superscription? They say unto him, Caesar's. Then saith he unto them, Render therefore unto Caesar the things which are Caesar's; and unto God the things that are God's."

ardent servants of God who plead with the board to make no bargain with such Japanese officials as are even now forcing morphine on Shan-tung[77] and always there is some unpractical zealot, like John Brown of Ossawatomie, who feels on his own back every lash that tears the flesh of a Christian slave.[78] But boards of directors bank and cool all apostolic fires. Six mission boards, acting through a commission, operate as a freezing mixture on righteous indignation. After ragged martyrs have told their tale, the chilly voice of Mr. Worldy Wiseman[79] advises pliancy and the conciliation of the powers of darkness.

On April 20 a cablegram was sent to Viscount Uchida, Minister of Foreign Affairs. We can infer from the answer that it was "cordial and friendly" and that the commission declared itself "moderate." The commission seems pleased with the answer they [sic] received. In that, Hara, while acknowledging the obsequious attitude of the commission, coldly threatens that any publicity, any excitement, and denunciation in the press, will "seriously interfere" with his "reforms." In other words, more torture, more massacre, unless you are silent under the whip. What Premier Hara means is: not one word from you Americans until we have carried our point at Paris and secured a free hand in China. When we Japanese have stamped out Korean Christianity we may, later, grant you some "reforms."[80]

The Premier Hara who said, in answer to the mission boards, that he was laboring on reforms is the same Hara who, on August 27, 1919, said: "Japan has no ambitious designs against China. The Ministry is urgently advocating closer friendly relations. The day will arrive when China will come to comprehend the sincerity of

---

77. See "Democracy's Crusaders."
78. John Brown (1800-59), American abolitionist, who killed five proslavery men on the banks of the Pottawatamie river as a retaliation for the proslavery raid on Lawrence, Kansas, and was hanged at Harper's Ferry, West Virginia, after capturing the federal arsenal there.
79. Mr. Worldy Wiseman, from *Pilgrim's Progress*.
80. See Introduction for complete texts of the Uchida and Hara telegrams. The following is courtesy of Mr. Dooley and Mr. Audette: "We make our lies be machinery; they [Easterners] tur-rn out theirs be hand. They imitate th' best iv our canned lies to deceive people that likes that kind, but f'r artists they have lies that appeals to a more refined taste. Sure I'd like to live among thim an' find out th' kind iv bouncers they tell each other. They must be gr-rand. I on'y know their export lies now—th' surplus lies they can't use at home. An' th' kind they sind out ar-re betther thin our best. Our lies is no more thin a conthradiction iv th' truth; their lies appeals to th' since iv honesty iv anny civilized man," (Finley Peter Dunne, *The World of Mr. Dooley*, selected and edited by Louis Filler [N.Y.: Collier, 1962], p. 175).

Japan."[81]

Korea and, I hope, some Americans already understand the sincerity of Japan.

On April 20 the "cordial and friendly" telegram was sent to Viscount Uchida, which elicited the information that "Premier Hara is now in the midst of special investigations [as to the best methods] for the realization of reforms" and his threat.

The Americans and the American press were humble and silent. Let me describe some of the activities of a liberal Japanese premier "in the midst of" plans for "reform."

On April 19,1919, Mowry, American missionary, innocent of any knowledge of the agitation, was sentenced to six months at hard labor.[82]

On April 24 a missionary writes, "Since the coming in of fresh troops and the inauguration of 'more severe' methods of repression as announced by the government, increasing numbers of reports come in regarding the violation of women by the soldiers." "The absence of this form of violence in the past" and "the sudden appearance of such reports coincident with the new order" — these things fit together. "The reports...come from trustworthy sources. Complaint made to the police in regard to this has been met by beating" (P. 85, 101).[83]

On April 26 a missionary writes [FCCCA, p. 82): "The Kwak San Church burned yesterday morning. Atrocious tortures of prisoners in Tyung Ta."[84]

On April 30 a missionary writes [FCCCA, p. 107] that Christian refugees "have no bedding, no clothes. The church at — better not give its name — was burned the other night."

Under date of May 25, [FCCCA, p. 107] thirty-five days after

---

81. On August 12, 1919, Hara said that "the length of time required for such arrangement [the return of Kiao-Chau—Shantung — to China] depends largely upon the attitude of China." However, on August 19, Viscount Kato of the foreign ministry announced that Japan "would maintain her special position in China by every means in her power."

82. Pp. 96-7 of the FCCCA pamphlet. Mowry had been arrested on April 4 for harboring men wanted by the police. Apparently he had actually done so, albeit unwittingly. (No public notification that the men were being sought by the police had been issued; moreover, Mowry had for years been allowing Korean friends – including some of these very men — to spend a few nights at his house.) The FCCCA pamphlet goes on to report that he was released on bail, pending appeal. The verdict was in fact upheld the following December, but sentence was reduced to a fine of 100 yen or one month in prison.

83. This missionary's report concludes with the statement that "in spite of Governor General Hasegawa's assurance on April 27 that the atrocities would stop...the burning of churches still continues." (FCCCA, p. 101)

84. Original reads, "The atrocious tortures of the prisoners in Tyungju are worthy of African savages and barbarians."

the "friendly and cordial" message, you will find a tragic report about nine Christian boys who were "beaten." Perhaps, besides being Christians, they had complained to the police about rapes. Let their case tell you what it means to be beaten, and I need not give more examples of Premier Hara's "reforms."

"Eleven Kangkei boys came here from_____. All the eleven were beaten ninety stripes — thirty each day for three days, May 16, 17 and 18. Nine came here May 22, and two more May 24.

"Tak Chank Kuk died about noon, May 23.

"Kim Myungha died this evening.

"Kim Hyungsun is very sick.

"Kim Chungsun and Song Taksam are able to walk but are badly broken.

"Kim Oosik seemed very doubtful but afterward improved.

"Kim Syungha reached here about an hour before his brother died. The first six who came into the hospital were in a dreadful fix, four days after beating. No dressing or anything had been done for them. Dr. Sharrocks just told me that he feels doubtful about some of the others since Myungha died. It is gangrene. One of these boys is a Chun Kyoin, and another is not a Christian, but the rest are all Christians.

"Mr. Lampe has photographs. The stripes were laid on to the buttocks and the flesh pounded into a pulp" (P. 125).[85]

"Ninety strokes of the bamboo flail, thirty each on three successive days is a frequent penalty."

Observe that after twenty-four hours the torn victim is given over again to the tormentors, and the flail falls exactly on the gaping wounds of yesterday. Now hear what the servants of hell were doing eighty days after our "cordial" telegram:

"Seoul, July 9, 1919. Yesterday we admitted — beaten cases, fifteen. Dr. Ludlow[86] has been treating cases which have come to us ever since early in March, but these fifteen students came straight from the West Gate Prison in Seoul, having received their last 30 blows in the morning. They expect 20 of their comrades to be released tomorrow — these beatings are given either with bamboo rods or rawhide and the blows are usually delivered on the

---

85. This statement, which concludes the FCCCA pamphlet, came from an anonymous missionary in Syenchun.
86. Working at (possibly in charge of) the Severance Hospital in Seoul. He was the doctor who protested the removal of the five wounded men as reported in note 40 above. This account was apparently taken from the open letter hypothesized in note 13 above.

buttocks.

"We have had cases, however, where the blows extend from the shoulders to the buttocks.

"In some cases, the men who do the beating are relieved after each tenth stroke."

I have nothing to say about Korean independence. I wish that in 1917 our President [Wilson] had asked the great powers, then in a frame of mind suited for virtuous resolves, to stipulate that China and Korea should be given such treatment as the American conscience can approve.

I wish our Secretary of State,[87] when the first messenger arrived from Korea, had conveyed to Japan in diplomatic language a statement of views and policy like this:

"I hear you are stamping out Christianity. That is old stuff, and will not go. America maintains that American missionaries can go anywhere in the world and preach their various gospels and set up hospitals and churches and make converts. No man anywhere in the world can interfere with them or their converts. You may threaten that my words will cause fresh sufferings to Korean Christians. Such threats also are old stuff. I require you to admit instantly to Korea commissioners to take account of facts and see that no such threats are carried out.

"You may retort that we have mobs and lynchings in America. That is true, but not in point.

"America is not in form a Christian nation, but to a great extent she is a nation of Christians. Many of these Christians are anxious not to be detected and exposed as hypocrites. If you show the slightest intention of carrying on in any respect a pagan persecution of Christians and Christianity, I shall instantly call on the governments of England and France to join with me in choking you, and shall ask them at once to lay aside all their crooked bargains with you.[88] If they decline, I shall report your refusal and their refusals to my people, and they will be guided in their dealings with other powers by the light that these refusals throw on governments that misrepresent their people."

---

87. Robert Lansing had, in fact, concluded the agreement with Japan giving it a free hand in Shantung. See "To a Few Friends and One or Two Foes." Both Dirck Cornelius Lansing and Robert Lansing were descendants of a Frederick Gerrit Lansing who came to New York from Holland in 1660; and hence Martin and the Secretary of State were at least some kind of cousins by marriage.

88. See the preface to "Democracy's Crusaders in Shan-tung."

It is your turn next, America. Japan is moving toward you by way of Korea and Shan-tung. With northern China enslaved and assimilated, Japan, with her speed and cunning, can smile at your measureless resources. When she chooses to move against you, some injudicious economizer will have disarmed you.

No nation can go unarmed while old Pagan gnashes his teeth, particularly when he sits in a high seat of the high council of the League of Nations. When she chooses to move against you she will embroil you in some new European quarrel, and you will have to face Japan and some European power at once.[89] Japan has a right to expect that at the critical moment our rulers will show themselves not infallible.

We can never make a greater blunder than alliance with Japan. We can never make a greater blunder than surrendering China to Japan. We have only one course to follow: cut loose at once from the League of Nations. Demand the withdrawal of America, France, Japan, and England from all illegitimate interference in China. Ask the Japanese Afreet to step out of China and confine himself to eastern Siberia.[90]

John Milton lifted up his voice and cried, "Avenge, O Lord, Thy slaughtered saints!"[91] The Lord has not avenged them to this day, and the Japanese know it. Milton and Hampden,[92] lovers of

---

89. Here Martin is remarkably prescient. As Gerhard L. Weinberg (*World in the Balance* [Hanover, N.H.: University Press of New England, 1981], pp. 88-93) analyses the Japan-Axis relationship in 1941, Germany sought a Japanese offensive against United States and British possessions in Southeast Asia in order to divert British forces, and American supplies, from the European theater; Japan, correspondingly, saw the European conflict as diminishing potential British and American resistance in that region. Each was worried that the opportunity might be let slip: in Germany's case, by a successful conclusion to the current U.S.-Japan negotiations; in Japan's by an Allied stalling for time in the Pacific until a successful conclusion of the war in Europe.

The wild card was Russia, which Japan's experience in Manchuria had led her to believe would successfully resist the German attack, and then be freed for her own offensive against depleted Japanese forces in Manchuria. Meanwhile, however, Russia's preoccupation in the west would enable Japan, with some skillful diplomatic work in Berlin, to obtain Axis cooperation while herself remaining neutral vis-a-vis Russia. Thus the time to attack was now.

In unilaterally declaring war on the U.S., Hitler of course contrived that embroilment himself; but behind the declaration was the fact that any Japanese war against Great Britain was naturally linked to a Japanese war against the U.S.

90. From "Democracy's Crusaders in Shan-tung," "The highest achievement of our statesmanship would be, to leave eastern Asia as happy as it was before it knew us. Our brightest Oriental dream should be of Japan and China, expanding each into its own vacant spaces, and growing rich as peaceably as the United States and Canada." Brown's *The Mastery of the Far East* develops a similar argument at some length.

91. Opening of the sonnet "On the late Massacher in Piemont," Milton's response to the slaughter of Waldenses in 1655 at Piedmont in Italy by Catholic forces under the command of the Marquis de Pianezza.

92. John Hampden (1594-1643), English statesman, cousin of Cromwell and popular hero of parliamentarianism. His arrest by Charles I in 1642 helped precipitate the Civil War.

God and liberty and honor, could waste their time on such invocations.

Listen to our modern form of prayer: "Lord God of Sabaoth, before whom lie Thy slaughtered saints, Thou does hear the long agony of tortured Christian women. Grant that there may be on earth the minimum of publicity, and no excitement, and that we may continue in our moderate attitude, and that we may still receive the congratulations of Viscount Uchida on our cordial and friendly spirit.

"Thou knowest, O Lord, that these inquisitors who are paid by Prime Minister Hara commit their deeds of cruelty against his wishes and in violation of his commands.

"Thou knowest, O Lord, that any public criticism will seriously interfere with the realization of the reforms with which Prime Minister Hara has been for some time past deeply concerned.

"Thou knowest, O Lord, and Prime Minister Hara knows, that during the several months in which he has been most deeply concerned in regard to the introduction of reforms in Korea, bodies of military have been talking more severe measures against Korean Christians which cannot be described in Church, and that the machinery of the Japanese government in Korea has been directed to the suppression of all practice and teaching of Christian religion; but thou knowest how unfaithful human servants are and with what helpless sorrow Prime Minister Hara has observed this disobedience of his orders.

"We pray Thee to open the ears of our people, so that they may aid the Christian powers in extending to China the dominion of Japan and the persecution of the Church.

"There now rises to heaven, as the incense of sacrifice, the smell of the burnt flesh of Korean Christians.

"Hasten, therefore, O Lord, the day on which we shall join the League of Nations and make firm alliance with the emperor and the various priesthoods, Buddhist and Shinto, of Japan; and above all, hasten the day on which the Japanese may enter into undisturbed possession of their promised land, Shan-tung, so that the smell of the burning flesh of Chinese Christians may float as incense to Thy throne. Amen."

John Bunyan, in the "Pilgrim's Progress," wrote a prophetic description of a Japanese police court and of the trial and execution of Christians in Korea.

"Then were these poor men brought before their examiners again and there charged as being guilty of the late hub bub.[...] So they beat them pitifully and hanged irons upon them ... for an example and a terror to others, lest any should further [interpolations] speak in their behalf or join themselves unto them. ...They were brought before their enemies and arraigned. Their indictment was ... that they were[...] disturbers.... that they had made commotions and divisions [in the town] and had won a party to their own most dangerous opinions in contempt of the law of the [their] Prince.

"Then Faithful began to answer:... 'As for disturbance, I make none, being myself a man of peace. The parties that were won to us were won by beholding our truth and innocence, and they are only turned from the worse to the better.'"

Testimony was given against Faithful.

In the course of his defence, Faithful said: "The Prince of this town, and all the rab[b]lement of his attendants ... are more fit for being in hell than in this town and country, and so the Lord have mercy upon me...."

Judgment was given against Faithful.

"Then they scourged him, then they buffeted him, then they lanced his flesh with knives and ... pricked him with their swords.... Thus came Faithful to his end."[93]

"At the end of the Valley of the Shadow of Death," says Bunyan, "lay blood, bones, ashes and mangled bodies of men.... I copied [espied] a little before me a cave where the giant Pagan dwelt in olden time, by whose power and tyranny the men whose bones, blood and ashes lay there, were cruelly put to death.... I have learned since that Pagan has been dead many a day."

John Bunyan wrote 244 [sic: 241] years ago. He thought, in his innocence, that pagan persecution of Christianity was at an end.

I can imagine Uchida and Hara and Hasegawa and Terauchi

---

93. This is Christian's and Faithful's trial in the town of Vanity.

smiling at this in the library of the Noblemen's Club.[94]

"Old Pagan is dead, is he?" says Terauchi. "We'll show them whether old Pagan is dead or not."

The Japanese Government invites us to enter into a permanent league in the face of George Washington's advice.[95] In that league the fiercest, most ambitious, and most formidable of its controlling members will be a heathen nation, drunk with ambition.

The world was backward enough in 1675, but even then we thought we were beyond pagan persecution. Now the pagans begin again, and we are their obedient acolytes and the familiars of their torture-chambers, and we hurry to give them fresh victims.

It is to believe that the powerful priests of the Missionary Coldstorage Commission say: "Hush! Let us be friendly with Old Pagan! Let us act so that he may realize reforms."

I have no prejudice against paganism. I love many pagan temples. Some of the religions of Japan are better than some of the religions that I see about me here. But let us use no tact with torturers. Let us hear of no policy of "cordiality and friendship" with any man in Asia that crucifies a Christian.

The pains and horrors of this persecution came to us here through secret messengers. The telegraph and wireless were closed by our own associates against the sending of these messages; and then the Government of Japan sends us word that we must not protest or publish. Yes, they threaten us. They say: "For a long time we have been planning reforms, but if you do not shut your mouths we will stop the reforms."

And this is the government that is to be one of the Big Five, who in the league are to dominate our own sublime free nation.

May my life cease and my hand wither before I consent by any voice or vote, public or private, to any such Japanese dominion!

ta ta ta

---

94. The *Rokumeikan*, later *Kozoku Kaikan* or Peers' Hall, quasi-British-style club built in Tokyo in 1883 near the site of the present-day Imperial Hotel as part of a general imitation of Western institutions. Torn down in 1941.
95. See Section Three - "From Washington's Farewell."

# FOURTEEN

# PEAKS AND PEOPLE

Modern Haste on the Hilltops ..... 414

Six Summits in One Day ......... 418

Great Adirondack Climbs ........ 430

Washing a Shirt on the Gothic ..... 433

Two Great Adirondack Guides ..... 437

Charlie Beede ............... 442

Helen Martin to Newell Martin .... 445

Letter to Myra After Reading
    "Camp Six" ............... 446

# Modern Haste on the Hill-tops

*While Martin also enjoyed climbing the mountains of Europe, it was the Adirondacks in upper New York State which held special meaning for him. First, we reprint the editor's introduction and text of the sixth installment of an "Historical Adirondack Character Series," which appeared in the January, 1932, issue of* High Spots, *the Adirondack Mountain Club magazine.[1] This is followed by Martin's own description of the one day's climbing record.*

Heretofore this series has told of Adirondackers who have lived in the past. This time we are happy to have one of our members, who distinguished himself by his diligence in climbing in the last quarter of the nineteenth century, both in the Adirondacks and elsewhere, speak for himself. Already we have become acquainted with him in "Peaks and People of the Adirondacks,"[2] and through the columns of High Spots. His record on August 5, 1894, of climbing six summits in one day, four of them trailless, which was the feature article in July, 1931, High Spots, stands out above all others. Mr. Martin, to many readers, is the outstanding climbing personality of Adirondack history. The years have not diminished Newell Martin's enthusiasm for the Adirondack Mountains, and at the age of seventy-eight he is an active member of the Adirondack Mountain Club. His interest is an inspiration to us.

BY RUTH V. RILEY

"Sir Robert Hart,[3] for more than twenty years had more

---

1. Volume IX, #1 (pp. 29-30). "Washing a Shirt on the Gothic," which follows "Two Great Adirondack Guides," appeared in the same issue (pp.20-21).
2. *Peaks and People of the Adirondacks*, (N.Y.; Doubleday, 1927), by Russell Mack Little Carson. Carson (1885-1961) was president of the Adirondack Club, president of the New York State School Boards Association, of the State Insurance Agents Association, the Glens Falls Saving and Loan Association, and the Glens Falls Board of Education. *Peaks and People of the Adirondacks* was his sole publication.
3. (1835-1911), Extended government service in British administration of China, culminating in the post of inspector-general of the imperial maritime customs at Shanghai, from which he resigned in 1906. Hart failed to anticipate the collapse of China in the war with Japan 1894-1895, but used every effort after its conclusion to induce the Chinese to introduce necessary reforms.

PEAKS AND PEOPLE    415

power than any European in the Far East and a fame like that of Rajah Brooke of Sarawak[4] and Sir Stamford Raffles of Singapore.[5]

"I have a letter from Sir Robert, written in 1894, the year that began the ending of all his greatness, in which he sent me 'his love' and reminded me that, when I was three years old, in Ningpo,[6] one of the most beautiful places in the world, I used to sit on his knee. This is the greatest height I have ever attained though I have been active in climbing mountains in various parts of the world. I was with him in a great adventure, that of the Ningpo Massacre. I quote from 'Sir Robert Hart: the Romance of a Great Career,' by Juliet Bredon. [Hart's niece.] Dutton 1909.

(p.40). "Rumors of Cantonese revenge (on a certain frequently piratical navy of Portuguese ships, called lorchas,[7] that had made themselves obnoxious on the China coast) began in the winter of 1856, when news came that all the foreigners in Ningpo would be massacred on a certain night...(I was one of these foreigners.)

(p.41). "The 26th of June, 1857, saw the vengeance consummated. With great bravery and determination the Cantonese" (themselves often piratical) "under Poo Liang Tai swept the Portuguese lorchas up the entire coast and into Ningpo. The fight began afloat and ashore." In the harbor fight between the Cantonese junks and the Portuguese lorches, the Portuguese were completely defeated. 'The [distracted] lorchamen ran wildly about hoping to escape the inevitable. Some of the poor wretches reached the British Consulate, alive or half alive, clamoring for shelter; but Mr. Meadows, then Consul, refused to let them in.' (For this refusal there were good reasons,[8] apart from the atrocious record of the Portuguese) 'and the unfortunate creatures frantically beat on the closed gates in vain...(42). The predicament of Meadows and young Hart, standing behind the barred gates of the Consulate, could have been little worse, mentally, than that of the wretches outside praying to them in the name of Heaven and the saints for shelter.'

---

4. Sir James Brooke (1803-1868), English Rajah of Sarawak on Borneo 1841-1863.
5. Sir Thomas Stanford Bingley Raffles (1781-1826), administrator in English East India. Lieutenant governor of Java 1811-1815; largely responsible for the British purchase and occupation of Singapore, and governor there 1822-1824.
6. City in East China, which then had a population of about 250,000.
7. The OED defines *lorcha* as "A light Chinese sailing vessel with the hull after a European model, but a Chinese rig, usually carrying guns."
8. Bredon describes Meadows as, "refusing to let them in, fearing to turn the riot from an anti-Portuguese disturbance into an anti-foreign outbreak."

"All were hunted down at last, dragged out of their hiding places in old Chinese graves among the paddy fields.' (our house stood among these graves) 'butchered where they stood [defending their lodging houses], or taken prisoners only to be put on one of their own lorchas, towed a little way up the river and slowly roasted to death........'

"The Cantonese stormed the Portuguese Consulate, pillaged and wrecked the building, and were just climbing on to the flat roof to haul down the flag when a stately white cloud appeared far down the river, serenely floating toward the disturbed city.'

"It was the French warship *Capricieuse*, under full sail. She had come straight from South America and put in at Ningpo after her long voyage, all unconscious of the terrible events passing there. Was ever an arrival more providential? I greatly doubt it; for had she not appeared in this miraculous fashion, who knows what would have come to the handful of white men" (and white babies) "left in that last outpost of civilization?"

My "miraculous" escape from Cantonese pirates made me believe that I had been preserved for some higher destiny; and I was right; for, in 1894, I set an example to the other Adirondack walkers of my time, by doing six hills in one day. That record stood undisturbed for thirty-six years and I used to cherish a hope that it would remain so through my time. A Chinese thus held an Adirondack record. But a Chinese had only "a Chinaman's chance" of holding anything valuable, if other people hear of it; and, when Carson[9] published this record, my dear young friends, Robert Marshall and George Marshall did nine peaks in one day.[10] This was an effortless stroll for Robert Marshall, who has shown great enterprise and endurance, in arduous scientific research and in mountain climbing, in summer and winter, above the Arctic Circle, in the Endicott Range, whose tremendous and perilous cliffs of ice and rock look out over uninhabited wastes and the Polar Ocean.[11]

---

9. Russell Mack Little Carson, author of *Peaks and People of the Adirondacks*.
10. Carson, in his preface to the Lowrie and Schenck letters (*High Spots* Vol. X, #1, January 1933), writes that on July 26, 1930, Robert and George Marshall climbed nine Adirondack peaks 4,000 ft. or over. See "Great Adirondack Climbs."
11. The Endicott (sometimes called Brooks or Arctic) Range extends from the Canadian border nearly to Kotzebue Sound in Alaska north of the Arctic Circle, dividing the Yukon waterhsed to the south from the Arctic Ocean watershed to the north. Robert Marshall was in the region during the summer of 1929, and again, from August, 1930, to September, 1931; his experiences are described in his book *Alaska Wilderness* (Berkeley; University of California Press, 1970; with an introduction by his brother George.)

PEAKS AND PEOPLE    417

Worse yet, on August 20, 1931, Professor Ernest S. Griffith of Syracuse University, did ten peaks in thirteen hours.[12] In the nineties, I used to go up on Whiteface[13] and show people my six peaks. Usually they said: "It sounds to us like a lie," and I would tell them it was my hope to go over the six peaks again on some August day, and then to go on over Colden and McIntyre.[14] I never even tried to do this. Advancing years tempted me to devote my leisure to physiological and ecological studies, specializing in the effects on the human system of Saint Marceaux,[15] Vouvray,[16] Bermuda Milk Punch,[17] and Myrtle Bank cocktails.[18]

On October 7, 1931, H. L. Malcolm [of Pompano, Florida] took up the ambition of my dreams and in thirteen hours and seven minutes, at surprising speed, covered eleven peaks. He added Colden and McIntyre to the Marcy range, and ascended and descended every desirable mountain top [all were more than 4,000 ft.] between the East Fork [East Branch] of the Ausable River and the Indian Pass [see map]. His achievement delights me. It proves that men are improving. It shows that modern botanists and learned professors can go now twice as fast and twice as far as ignorant primeval man, the sluggish, crawling pedestrian of the Nineteenth Century.

NEWELL MARTIN.

P.S. May I make a suggestion to these modern young men as to the only way of beating Malcolm's record? Go over the "Presidential Range," a bare ridge[19] which can be traversed at night, beginning at 1 A.M., with an electric torch. Then, by airplane, from

12. Both Carson in his preface to the Lowrie and Schenck letters, and the *New York Times* account give the date as August 21, 1931, and state that Prof. Griffith, a dean at Syracuse University, climbed ten Adirondack peaks 4,000 ft. or over in 13 hours.
13. The Adirondack mountain (4,872 ft.) immediately north of Lake Placid, and approximately 18 miles north of Mt. Marcy. Robert Marshall, in *The High Peaks of the Adirondacks*, describes the view from the top of Whiteface as "one of the broadest in the Adirondacks."
14. These two mountains would have taken Martin northwest of Mt. Marcy. Colden (4,713 ft.) is two miles northwest of Mt. Marcy, and McIntyre 3 1/2 miles northwest of Mt. Marcy. Actually "McIntyre" is a range of five mountains; but the highest, Algonquin Peak (5,112 ft.) is sometimes referred to as Mt. McIntyre.
15. Rheims champagne. Now grouped under Chattelier.
16. Mellow-sweet white wine from the Loire region; *Appellation d'Origine Controlee*.
17. To one glass milk add one tablespoon sugar, one egg, a jigger of rum, and serve over cracked ice.
18. May be Myrtle Bank Punch, presumably *specialte de la maison* of the Myrtle Bank Inn, Kingston, Jamaica. Make with one jigger of rum, juice one-half lime, six dashes grenadine, teaspoon sugar; shake over cracked ice; float maraschino liqueur on top.
19. The Presidential Range, so named because the individual peaks bear names of Presidents Washington, Adams, etc. Located in north central New Hampshire.

the Crawford House[21] to Keene Valley, arriving about sunrise; and then go over Professor Malcolm's course, on foot. Then you can say that you have done all the best White Mountains and all the best Adirondacks in one day.

*  *  *

## Six Summits in One Day

*Newell Martin's fame as a mountain climber, particularly among Adirondack Mountain advocates, continues through today. His "conquering" of six trailless, wooded peaks in less than 24 hours, on August 5, 1894, has been the subject of several essays, and included in several books on mountain climbing.*

*Carson, in Peaks and People of the Adirondacks, calls Martin "the most venturesome amateur climber of his day," and goes on to explain: "Martin climbed Gothics (4,738 ft.), Saddleback (4,530 ft.), Basin (4,825 ft.), Haystack (4,918 ft.), Skylight (4,920 ft.), and Marcy (5,344 ft.). His guides were Charlie Beede[1] and Wesley Lamb. This is probably the most remarkable one day's climbing ever done in the Adirondacks, and is a record that can never be equalled, for now there is a trail from Gothic to Panther Gorge, whereas Martin and his guides pushed through trail-less, unmarked forest."[2]*

*At the time of his six-summit ascent, Martin was 40 years old, and had been climbing in the Adirondacks since he was a teenager. A. A. Schenck,[3] who was at Princeton in 1869 with Newell Martin's brother, Pascal,[4] reports of meeting Newell and his brother on a*

---

21. Hotel at Crawford Notch, between Bretton Woods and North Conway, in the Presidential Range. Original structure built 1859; closed down in 1970's.

---

1. Aaron (Charlie's grandfather) and Phineas moved to Keene Valley sometime between 1806 and 1810. Phineas had three sons, Orrin, Alman, and Allen, and a daughter, Alma. Aaron had three sons, Smith, Edward, and David; Smith, guide and proprietor of the lodging-house, being much the most widely-known. Charlie was Smith's younger son.
2. The total distance traversed was 19 miles; total elevation climbed some 8,300 feet.
3. Archibald A. Schenck (1851-1946), Princeton '69, class valedictorian; civil engineer employed by New York Central and Union Pacific railroads.
4. Pascal Martin (1850-1882; Yale '72), born, like Newell, in Ningpo China; prepped for Princeton at Phillips Academy, Andover, Mass.; spent freshman year at Princeton; subsequently transferred to Yale. After Yale, he returned to China, and entered the Imperial Maritime Customs Service. See Section Nine - "Letters from Newell to His Brothers."

climbing expedition in the Adirondacks in 1871 (23 years prior to the six-summit feat).

Apparently Martin is credited — prior to his six-summit climb — with being the first Adirondack Club member to climb both Saddleback Mountain (4,515 feet) and Sawteeth (4,100 feet).

And while an undergraduate at Yale, Martin is credited with establishing steeple-climbing as an extracurricular activity. This "sport" got him in no little difficulty just prior to commencement in 1875. In the spring of his senior year, he climbed to the top of the highest steeple on the Yale campus and there placed some pantaloons. The result, as he explained in a publication compiled for his 20th reunion year: "I was not graduated quite so early as most of the class, my degree having been suspended three months for some trifle." In that same class book he categorized himself thusly: "I try to be a free trade, gold standard, states' rights , single tax, anti-income tax Republican. I favor municipal reform and civil service reform. I am against intercollegiate football."

Martin's pamphlet, privately printed in 1927, is almost an exact copy of the article he wrote for High Spots (Vol. 8, #3, July 1931). We've chosen to reprint the article from the magazine as it contains a bit more detail.

## SIX SUMMITS
By Newell Martin

Invitation and advice to one of my granddaughters.[5]

### INDEX

Pages
Beede, Charlie Beede's great merit. . . 8, 9, 10, 11
Champagne, infallible antidote to water. . . . . 7
Davis, Fred Davis's diligence . . . . . . . . . . 5
Isiah, the Prophet, his prophecy of
 the publication of this tome . . . . . . . . . . 2
Lamb, Wesley Lamb's great merit . . . . . 8, 9, 10
Marshall, intelligence and activity of
 Robert Marshall and George Marshall . . . . 3
Plutocrats, virtue engendered by plutocrats . . . 1

---

5. Molly Meyer O'Connor. Molly, oldest grandchild, when she was eight years old, along with the family cook, Mary McCousy, went climbing in the Adirondacks with Other Gomby. As Molly remembers that occasion today, she and the cook got lost and had to be rescued.

Professionals, more expert than pleasure-
  seekers ........................ 2
Romance, a product of the Cold Slough ..... 1
Russ, Charlie Russ's diligence .......... 5
Sermons, Walter Lowrie's sermons
  would irritate Ruskin ............. 2
Time-table for middle-aged pleasure-
  seekers ....................... 14

I find among my papers an ancient Adirondacks record, set forth in a letter written by me some time ago to one of my many granddaughters. There is nothing in that letter to interest anybody except such people as listen patiently to anything from anybody who talks about Shanty Brook[6] and Marcy Brook.[7] "Nothing is more monotonous than the woodland mountains of any of the ranges of eastern North America." (W.J. Stillman, *Autobiography*. Vol. I, page 175).[8] Nothing, except what I write about those mountains. Here is most of what I said in that frivolous letter:

Dear Molly:
  In 1935 I shall be 81 and you about 18.[9] A girl is seldom so happy as at 18, a man seldom so happy as at 81. He is then too old to be reproved when he babbles on his reminiscences.
  In 1935, therefore, you and I, who have done so much gentle mountaineering together, must visit Marcy[10] and listen to the music of Shanty Brook and drift over the smooth surface of the Cold Sloo.[11] There, if anywhere, the magic of an August moon and of lake and forest can tempt us to forget, for an hour, that this earth is the most dangerous and uncomfortable of the planets.
  Those romantic waters, in my time, were valued chiefly as the easiest path to the top of Mount Marcy and as the occasional haunt of Willard Gibbs, William James, William Dwight Whitney, Josiah

---

6. Joins Ausable River between Upper and Lower Ausable Lakes.
7.. Martin refers to the Marcy Brook running south from the foot of Mount Marcy to Cold Slough; not its counterpart running north from Mt. Marcy's further side.
8.. William James Stillman, *Autobiography* (N.Y.: Houghton Mifflin, 1901). Stillman was actually an enthusiast of the outdoors and the Adirondacks in particular.
9. Incorrect. Molly was 20; her brother, Bear was 18 that year.
10. Highest peak in the Adirondacks, located some 95 miles north of Albany.
11. Cold Slough, narrow extension running southwest from Upper Ausable Lake.

D. Whitney and other philosophers.[12] On the banks of the Ausable River,[13] I used to unfold to a great philosopher my childish faith in the improvability of mankind.

The philosophers are gone. The only important animals that now infest that wilderness are plutocrats. In those woods they are of the harmless kind. It is elsewhere that the venomous varieties of plutocrat abound, consorting with harpies of the Carry Nation[14] type, hunting in packs, like dingo dogs, and in committees, sometimes of fourteen, sometimes of more,[15] and spreading, all over the nation, morbid prejudice, chilly gloom and compulsory virtue.

In the Adirondacks, as in all mountains, you will be troubled with long stories of the far past. Obsolete old men will tell you how active they used to be. To them you may recite these verses:

"All ye inhabitants of the world, and dwellers on the earth, see ye, when he lifteth up an ensign on the mountains: and when he bloweth a trumpet, hear ye." [Isiah 18:3].

To prepare you for 1935 I submit some remarks on the ancient art of hill walking.

Walter Lowrie[16] once "did" five of the higher Adirondacks in one day. He afterwards became a real Alpine climber. He likes difficulties. For many years he has been trying to convert the City of Rome to Calvinism. Up-hill work. Ruskin would have had no praise for Lowrie's sermons and none for his mountaineering. Ruskin said that climbers are conceited.[17] Adirondack climbers,

---

12. See "Two Great Adirondack Guides"
13. Ausable River. Runs north through Keene Valley from Ausable Lakes.
14. Carry Nation (1846-1911), American temperance agitator. Under the conviction of divine appointment, she began attacking saloons with an ax in 1900. See Section Two - "Coolidge and the Bible."
15. "Committees...of fourteen, sometimes of more": Private anti-vice or prohibition groups in the late 19th-early 20th centuries often denominated themselves "Committees of..." and then a number, such as Five, Eleven, Fourteen, Fifteen, Fifty, and One Hundred Thousand. The Committees of Fourteen and Fifteen were active in New York City during that period; but perhaps the most famous was the Committee of Fifty, headed by Seth Low, president of Columbia University, and numbering among its members Charles W. Eliot, Carroll D. Wright, Francis G. Peabody, and Richard T. Ely.
16. (1868-1959; Princeton '90), Theologian, ordained to the Episcopalian ministry 1896, pastor at St. Paul's American Church in Rome 1907-1930, expert on Kierkegaard, author of 38 books. See "Great Adirondack Guides."
17. In the preface to the second (1865) edition of *Sesame and Lilies*, Ruskin states, "The real ground for reprehension of Alpine climbing is that, with less cause, it excites more vanity than any other athletic skill...Credit for practice in climbing can only be attained after success, which, though perhaps accidental and unmerited, must yet be attained at all risks, or the shame of defeat borne with no evidence of the difficulties involved." In *Our Fathers Have Told Us* (III, 29), he speaks of "the extreme vanity of the modern Englishman in making a momentary Stylites of himself on the top of a Horn or an Aiguille."

however, are seldom conceited. This is because the best of them are surpassed by the best Adirondack guides in woodcraft, speed and endurance. I have never known an amateur whose efforts could compare with the feats performed by such men as Charlie Beede and Wesley Lamb, in the course of their hunting, logging and trapping. Adirondack guides care little, it is true, for the making of "records." They gladly leave to amateurs the contriving and conduct of mountain competitions. They would look without envy on the achievement of that world-famous young American who was the first to do, in one day, the Jungfrau, the Monch and the Elger.[18] That is because the Adirondack guides have a short season and low pay and a hard life and are given no more for a great achievement than for an easy day. Contrariwise, in Switzerland and the Tyrol[19] and in what the new Caeser calls the Upper Adige,[20] a guide spurs his employer to effort because there the guide is paid in proportion to the toil and peril of his arduous day. He gets more for the Winckler Thurm[21] and the Mauvais Pas of the Little Zinne[22] than he gets for the Cinque Torri.[23] When he does three mountains in one day he is paid for three mountains.

Another thing that teaches modesty to a mild old walker of the Victorian era is the scientific thoroughness of the modern Appalachian. Robert Marshall and George Marshall of New York,[24] with Herbert Clark, their guide have trodden on forty-two different summits in the Adirondack Highlands that are more than four thousand feet high. In compiling that record they have been

---

18. The great triumvirate in The Bernese Alps, southwest Switzerland, respectively 13,653; 13,468; and 13,036 ft. The climb may be a comic invention of Mr. Martin. Neither *The New York Times* nor *The London Times*, nor the authoritative Alpine sources [searched to no avail by G. Audette] refer to this feat. It may have been a "stunt" climb, though, and therefore fall beneath the notice of serious writers about the sport.
19. Austrian Alps.
20. "The new Caeser" is Mussolini. The new provinces acquired by Italy in 1919 from the ruins of the Hapsburg Empire included the former South Tyrol, renamed the Alto Adige. Italy has retained these provinces to the present day.
21. The Winckler Thurm is the most difficult of the Vajolet Towers, a group of dolomites in the Eastern Alps, North Italy. First climbed by George Winckler in 1887.
22. The Kleine Zinne, smallest but most difficult of the Drei Zinne near Misurina in the Austrian Tyrol. The Mauvais Pas is a celebrated traverse on its south face.
23. Mass of enormous rocks near Cortina in the Austrian Tyrol; the highest tower is 7,760 ft. May be ascended by amateurs without a guide.
24. Robert Marshall (1901-1938), forester, graduated from N.Y. State College of Forestry in 1924, did post-graduate work at Harvard, entered U.S. Forestry Service in 1925. George (no dates, but was alive in 1970) graduated from Columbia in 1924. The two brothers were lifelong outdoorsmen, top-ranking amateur climbers and conservationists. With Herbert Clark (1870-sometime after 1938), whom Carson said was "the greatest mountain climber the writer has ever known," were the first to climb all 46 Adirondack peaks over 4,000 ft., 1919-1924.

intelligent, diligent and swift, through many bright summer weeks. But the speed of young Appalachians even, is only relative. Agnes Repplier,[25] in a recent essay, reminds us of the obvious fact that man is one of the slowest of animals. To find any beast that is slower, we have to go to creatures [such] as ant-eaters, sloths and barnacles. When a man speaks of going fast through the North Woods, over hills, he merely means that he is making, sometimes five miles, sometimes one mile, in an hour. Ruskin has expressed his disapproval of young men who hurry over beautiful mountains;[26] but he disapproved, also, of the railways that carry men to the foot of beautiful mountains.[27] On big mountains men must go fast, to make the ascent at all; and, on small mountains it is often worth while to go fast, and to climb several hills in one day, so as to produce, artificially, the excitement and pleasure of a long day of effort.

I have wasted many happy hours in idleness on hillsides. My first ascent of Mount Marcy was made in 1871. I have walked up Mount Marcy fifteen times. Many years ago, with two men famous in the Rocky Mountains and elsewhere, George Bird Grinnell[28] and Jack Monroe,[29] I made the first ascent of Mount Gould.[30] This was

---

25. Agnes Repplier (1858-1950; Yale Litt. D. '25), prolific American essayist.
26. In *Sesame and Lilies* (I, 35), Ruskin states, "the Alps themselves, which your own poets used to love so reverently, you look upon as soaped poles in a bear-garden, which you set yourselves to climb and slide down again with 'shrieks of delight'."
27. Ruskin's objections to railways were directed primarily at lines in areas noted chiefly for scenery; e.g., *Fors Clavigera* (Letter I), "I should like to destroy most of the railroads in England, and all the railroads in Wales."
28. George Bird Grinnell (1849-1938, Yale '70), Martin's brother-in-law, ethnologist, and author. Grinnell often lived with Indians, exerted influence on their behalf in the East, and was elected head chief of the Blackfeet Confederacy in early 1890's. Originated idea of Glacier National Park (est. 1910). Co-founder, with Theodore Roosevelt, of the Boone and Crockett Club.
29. John B. Monroe (n.d.). Positive identification has been difficult. James Willard Schultz, in *Blackfeet and Buffalo* (Norman: University of Oklahoma Press, 1962); first published 1907 as *My Life as an Indian*, tells how Monroe and William Jackson (one of the three scouts who warned Custer the day before Little Bighorn not to try the job with the forces at hand) came to live with Schultz on the Blackfoot reservation in 1886, describing Monroe as, "an experienced mountain man, hunter, and trapper." Grinnell joined the three that fall, and together they explored the region that subsequently became Glacier National Park. Schultz also speaks of Monroe as hunting in 1902 with Gifford Pinchot (Yale L.L.D. '25; Yale's first professor of forestry; then one of seven members of the National Forest Commission; subsequently governor of Pennsylvania) and Henry L. Stimson (then, like Martin, employed by Elihu Root's law firm; subsequently U.S. Secretary of State). A *New York Times* obituary of a J.B. Monroe (1857-1930), who was inolved in mining in northern Idaho, could refer to this Monroe. Schultz specifically rules out the coincidental name of one John B. Monroe, known first as "Little Wolf," and subsequently "Old Man" who was one of three sons of Hugh "Rising Wolf" Monroe (1798-1896), a famous pioneering figure who came to the Saskatchewan area in 1815 and married into the Blackfoot. Father and son were both Grinnell companions in this same region.
30. Mount Gould (9,541 ft.) in northeast center of present Glacier Park, itself located in Montana immediately south of the Canadian border.

years and years before the Glacier National Park was invented. I had then the thrill of scrambling around many awkward corners that no man, white or Indian, had ever seen before. We were out for twenty-five hours, and spent a night, in darkness, on a narrow ledge, with unscalable cliffs below us and above us. My last mountain climb was in 1909, when Archangelo Dibona and Anatonio Barberia Zuchin hauled me, with a rope, up the face of the Croda Da Lago.[31] In the seventies, Charley Russ,[32] Fred Davis[33] and I were the first to make in two days the "Old Round Trip" from St. Hubert's,[34] through the Ausable Ponds, over Marcy, to the Upper Works,[35] to John Brown's Grave[36] and back to St. Hubert's, by the Cascade Lakes.[37]

All those days were good. But the best walk I ever had, on any hills, came in 1894, when I was forty, an age at which one excels in diligence rather than speed. On that excursion my guides allowed me to lead so that I might have the pleasure of finding my way for myself through the woods. For many years I had made a study of going through the woods alone and without a guide. The Adirondack mountains are not great and the Adirondack forests are not vast; but in August, there are no other mountain forests that are so pleasant as those of the Adirondacks; and there is one best way to print their charm firmly on your memory. From a high point, take the bearings of some distant weather-beaten height and then dive into the woods and make your way to the goal at your best speed with no guide but your own woodcraft. Going fast, down hill, through a forest, you have to make quick decisions. New beauties of the forest, and new obstacles and even dangers of the mountain

---

31. Archangelo Dibona (1879-1956), guide in the Dolomites, northeast Italy. Led first ascent of the Lalidererwand in the Austrian Tyrol in 1911; participated in first ascent of south face of Meije, Dauphine Alps, southeast France, in 1912. A peak near the latter is named for him. The Croda Da Lago (8,813 ft.) is a much-favored peak in the Austrian Tyrol described as only slightly more difficult of ascent than the Cinque Torri.
32. Charles Trumbull Russ (1850-1899; Yale '75; Columbia Law School '78). Never practiced law. Died at age 29 of pneumonia, "leaving behind the record of a blameless life," as the *Yale Obituary Record* puts it. Classmate of Martin's at both Yale and Columbia.
33. Frederick Wendell Davis (1855-1917; Yale '77). Spent most of adult life in Hartford, Connecticut, employed as an auditor by manufacturing and insurance firms.
34. Inn at upper (southwest) end of Keene Valley, now home of Ausable Club.
35. Former iron works at upper end of Sanford Lake, some eight miles southwest of Mt. Marcy.
36. John Brown moulders on the land of his former farm in North Elba, some 10 miles north northwest of Mt. Marcy.
37. Two ponds some 8 1/2 miles east northeast of Mt. Marcy. The "Old Round Trip" would be some 40 linear, i.e., map, miles.

side, come before you, every moment, and are fixed, instantly, in your attentive mind. You must be alert and intent when going quickly down forested hills. As you run, you will come, for instance, to a long line of high, steep rock. You have to decide, in a moment, whether you will turn from your course, laboriously; and whether you will go to the left or to the right: and often you have a third choice. I have known such places where big trees grow from below in such a way that you can step directly off into a tree and scramble safely down through the branches. Again, few cliffs, big or little, are as steep as they look and you can often, safely, slide down the face of a high rock.

Often as you come suddenly to a windfall, you must decide, at once, whether to work through it or laboriously go around it. When you come to a fallen log, you must decide, without halting, whether to step on it or over it. Deep moss, before you, often calls for a quick decision as to whether it is on firm ground or hides a dangerous foot-trap. All the time, while you are running, walking, crawling or climbing, you must hold in your mind your main direction.

In my youth it seemed to me that no other forest could be so free from objectionable men, disagreeable insects, and unpleasant temperatures as the Adirondacks. I am still of that opinion. I have sat, entranced, by one of the three great places of the Japanese scene[38] and have suddenly realized, nevertheless, that I was longing to see again the broken sunlight falling through the thick leafage of great trees on the musical little waterfalls and brown transparent pools of an Adirondack brook.

Those Adirondack brooks are Rivers of Eden. Drink from every brook when you run or walk, through the Adirondacks. Such drinking will do you no harm if you are careful, after getting back to camp, to drink a quart of some sound vintage champagne.

It was my good fortune to climb, on that one day, in 1894, six high hills in the Higher Adirondacks. Those six hills are Gothic Mountain, Skylight and Marcy. Marcy, Haystack, Basin Mountain and Skylight are, in height, the first, third, fifth and seventh of the Adirondack Mountains. Gothic and Saddleback are the tenth and fourteenth. That walk is a languid stroll compared with some Alpine records that have been made by one of my descendants. It

---

38. The three finest views in Japan, known as the Sankei, are (1) the sea view from Matsushima, a small fishing town near Fukushima; (2) a view of the coast and wooded country from Ama-no-Hashidate near Kyoto; (3) the island of Miyajima on the Inland Sea between Kobe and Nagasaki.

has no athletic merit. But, through happy chance, it has become an Adirondack record.

There have been many men on those hills who could go faster and father than I but it never occurred to any of them, before 1894 to take those six summits at once.

The forests have been tamed. Modern boys and girls equal our old records and modern athletes easily surpass them. But for this they will not get due credit, because trails have been cut through all the woods, and paths cleared over all the summits traversed in that walk. From Gothic over Saddleback and Basin Mountain and Haystack, I went without a trail and without even a blazed line. Going through forest and through dwarf firs without a trail is harder than walking on a trail. Therefore, so much of this ancient record as was made in trackless woods stands by itself.

Some new man will traverse these six hills in better time and may add Dix[39] Peak or Mount McIntyre[40] to my list: but he will have a path already made for him.

"Gothic" is the mountain known (improperly) to the people of Lake Placid as "The Elephant." "St. Hubert's" is now the house of the Ausable Club. I was most fortunate in weather, and in having with me my old friends, Charley Beede and Wesley Lamb, guides of the highest quality, with whom in ancient times, I had spent many happy days, and who took a sympathetic interest in my competition with our enemy. Time. They were strong and speedy and good woodsmen. I knew the woods and did not need anyone to guide me, but I had to travel light. Wesley Lamb carried what we needed through the day and Charley Beede carried the things that would have been needed at night, if our enterprise had failed.

(End of my letter to Molly).

Thirty-six years ago I wrote the story of the walk described in that letter. The record set forth in that story has been made obsolete by Robert and George Marshall, who added the two Wolf Jaw mountains and Armstrong, making a one-day walk of nine hills.[41] See "High Spots" September, 1930, page 17. Nevertheless, here is my obsolete story and my obsolete time-table:

---

39. Adirondack mountain (4,842 ft.), some seven miles east southeast of Mt. Marcy.
40. Properly McIntyre Range: five Adirondack mountains some 3 1/2 miles northwest of Mt. Marcy. The highest, Algonquin Peak (5,112 ft.), is sometimes referred to as Mt. McIntyre. The two additional peaks would more than double the distance.
41. Upper Wolf Jaw (4,225 ft.), Lower Wolf Jaw (4,175 ft.),and Armstrong (4,455 ft.) are in a mountain chain located east northeast from Mt. Marcy.

1) Lv. St. Hubert's [Inn] at 6:50 A.M.
2) Reach north top of Gothic 9:15 A.M.
3) Reach top of Saddleback at 11 A.M.
4) Reach crest of Basin 12:10 P.M.
   (Rested for lunch 45 min.)
5) Reach top of Haystack 2:20 P.M.
   (Rested 30 minutes.)
6) Reach summit of Skylight at 5:00 P.M.
7) Reach top of Marcy at 5:45 P.M.
8) Arrive back at St. Hubert's 11:00 P.M.
   via Alderson Camp, Cold Slough Landing,
   and Left Lower Lake Boathouse.

Saint Hubert's Inn. Keene Heights, Essex County, New York, August 23, 1896. Suggestions as to how the six mountain walk should be made from Saint Hubert's.

On August 5, 1894, I left St. Hubert's, at 6:50 A.M., with Charlie Beede and Wesley Lamb. For several days we had been ready, some one of us rising early every morning to see if the day was of the right sort. The head waiter, also, rose early every morning to make sure of our having an early breakfast. A good breakfast was given us at the Inn before we started. We had caused a wagon from Jim Hall's (the boat house at the lower pond) to come down and wait for us in the woods, just inside of the Reserve. Lamb and I left the wagon and set out on the Gothic Trail at 7:10 A.M. Charlie Beede went on with the wagon and took with him blankets and enough food to make two meals for three men. By wagon to the Lower Lake and thence by boat and on foot, he went to the "Alderson Camp,"[42] on Marcy Brook, under Skylight. From the Alderson Camp, he went up Marcy alone. Then he went back to the "Alderson Camp" and waited there. Lamb and I, on the Gothic Trail, reached the falls on the brook at 7:20, the new slide at 8:15, and the north top of Gothic at 9:15. We had to go through scrub from the north top of Gothic to the most southerly top, which we reached, after some hard work, at 9:45. We reached the notch, between Gothic and Saddleback, at 10:15 and the top of Saddleback at 11. We reached the highest point of Basin Mountain and Haystack at 1:25 P. M., Little Haystack at 2:05 and the top of Haystack at 2:20. We left Haystack at 2:50 and reached the "Alderson Camp" at 4:20. I left the Camp immediately,

---

42. The Alderson Camp would seem to have been located either at site of Four Corners Camp beneath Mt. Marcy or just southwest of that, at the point of junction of the Haystack-Skylight trail and the Bartlett.

though I found that Charlie Beede had made a good bed for us and was getting supper. We decided to abandon the bed and most of the supper. I went on and reached the height of land in the Skylight Notch [between Skylight and Haystack Mountains] at 4:30 and the top of Skylight at 5:00. I turned, the moment I touched the summit of Skylight, and went to Marcy, whose top I reached at 5:45. I registered, with a brief statement of my walk, in the Appalachian Club's Register, though with some trouble, as it was growing cold. I left at 5:53. At the "Alderson Camp" I took a little coffee and some supper. The rest of our supplies we left with one of the the Twichell boys,[43] who happened to be going over the mountain. At 6:30 P.M., we broke camp and fled, reaching the Cold Slough Landing [At southwest end of Upper Ausable Lake] at 7:50 P.M. The guides rowed me from that landing to Charlie Beede's Camp, where we got a lantern. In the boat I took off my wet shoes and put on dry shoes. We left the boat house at the lower Lake at 10 P.M., and walked down to St. Hubert's, which we reached at 11 P. M. All of this was done on August 5, 1894. I had been traveling for more than 16 hours (including rests). None of us were very tired. None of us were stiff. But we all felt that we had done enough and went to bed without delay. The next morning I went to New York. But, before that, Charlie Beede rose early, went up to the Beaver Meadow and brought down a coat which I had left at the Brook Falls.

I make this memorandum from notes which I took during the walk.

Some suggestions may make this walk easier for others.

We found bad scrub on Gothic, after leaving the trail. The last time I was on Gothic, I found that the best way is to leave the extension of the trail where it looks towards March, after passing the Johns Brook slide of Gothic [rock slide on north face of Gothic, overlooking John Brook's Lodge] and before you turn off towards the Upper Pond. there find a little runway that drops below the ridge leading to the most southern top. By keeping a little below the ridge, you will find ferns and runways and fair going. We had clear cool weather. There is no trail from Gothic to the "Alderson Camp." Therefore, nobody should try this walk who has had no experience

---

43. One of the four sons (Edward, David, Burton, Joseph) of the Rev. Joseph H. Twichell (1838-1918; Yale '59) of Hartford, Conn., who summered regularly in the Adirondacks. Twichell was chaplain of the 71st Regiment, N.Y. Volunteers during the Civil War and a good friend of Mark Twain. (He appears several times in Twain's *Autobiography*.) One of the Twichell girls married the composer Charles Ives.

in walking without trails. Few should try it on a hot or rainy day. But so much of the walk is along hill tops and high ridges that it gives fine views and pays better than any other walk in the woods. We had the good luck to find no flies except a few on Marcy and Haystack. In making this walk before the end of August, it would be well to take tar and oil. We found plenty of water in the notches and some on top of Haystack. If one has much difficulty with scrub spruces or scrub balsam on any of these hills, and he is very likely to, he should drop quickly into the bigger timber or to a slide and then drift around to the next notch he is seeking. From Basin Mountain, follow runways, picking your way carefully on a line that points a little to the right of Little Haystack. Then go up to the bed of the brook that flows from the west side of Little Haystack. When you reach the level of the first big rocks on the west side of Little Haystack, go to them and you avoid all scrub.

I came down Haystack, on the side towards Marcy, by big rocks and slides and a brook. There is quite a "pitch off" here. I took a line for a point half-way between Skylight Notch and Marcy. Then, in Panther Gorge,[44] I turned to the left and made a straight line for the camp which the guides call the "Alderson Camp." It would have saved work, perhaps, to go down Haystack to the Bartlett trail and then to the Alderson Camp. One objection to that course is that one would be tempted, in many cases, on reaching Bartlett, to go to the pond, leaving the walk unfinished. I made a mistake in going up Skylight from the Notch without a trail. This made hard work for me. We had been told by somebody that the old Skylight Trail was "over-grown and hard to find. Therefore I went straight to the top without looking about for a trail. On my way down, however, I found a fair trail, running to the old notch camp. It had some blind places, especially at the start and finish. the trail to the Slough, from Marcy, was in good condition. We ate a good deal of maple sugar, and took care never to become uncomfortably hungry. I carried nothing.

≥ ≥ ≥

---

44. Panther Gorge, between Skylight and Marcy, is hundreds of feet deep. Marcy Brook leads out of it. William James describes a night spent in Panther Gorge in a letter to his wife written July 9, 1898.

# Great Adirondack Climbs

*The January, 1933, issue of* High Spots *carried an article by Russell M.L. Carson about a continuing rivalry by climbers attempting to best Martin's record regarding the number of peaks climbed in one day. He reprinted two letters from climbers well acquainted with the Martin record. The first was written by Walter Lowrie, a theologian; the second by Archibald A. Schenck, a civil engineer.*

Some one has just given me your letter entitled "Great Adirondack Climbs," dated Oct. 14th, and published in I do not know what paper (N.Y. *Herald-Tribune*) for only a clipping was sent me.

Because your letter reveals your continued interest in the history of climbing in the Adirondacks, I record here a climb which evidently ought not to be omitted when Mr. Martin's stunt is commemorated.

I have lived in Keene Valley since I was a boy and knew just what I could do and could not do. In the summer of 1892, two years after my graduation from Princeton, a classmate of mine spent a month with me. It was Malcolm McLaren, now professor at Princeton and head of the School of Electrical Engineering. He was the most tireless climber of my acquaintance, and after we had been climbing together steadily for a moth we were in such good form that the climb I here record was not at all a strain upon us. We were much more severely tried by another: from Jones Brook over Marcy, Colden, MacIntyre and down to the Iron works—all but the last stretch of it without a trail.

The notes which record the climb over the five peaks are in Keene Valley. I can from memory recall only that we started from my home in Keene Valley (near Phelp's Falls) at 5 a.m. and climbed in succession Marcy, Haystack, Basin, Saddle Back and Gothics, reaching the junction of the Gothic trail with the AuSable Pond road at about 7 p.m. and returning home from there by carriage.

It is, as you say, impossible to compare the difficulty of a climb without a trail with the climbs of today. The greatest effort was involved in traversing the zones near the summits where the dwarf balsams were so still that it was almost equally i\difficult to get under, over, or through them. I made a record that on Gothics it required 20 minutes of grueling labor to get from the peak nearest to Saddle Back up to the point where the trail stopped—whereas after the trail was made over the Range I could easily cover that distance in 3 minutes.

The authorities of the Adirondack Reserve were loath to have any trails enter their property which were not controlled by passing through the gate at St. Huberts. But because of several serious disasters to parties which tried without success to "do" the Range without a trail, the trail was made--and still climbers who were not fit continued to collapse with the effort. It was on the Range trail Prof. William James fatally strained his heart. The last disaster which prompted the making of the trail was that to the two Doctors Putnam, the owners of the Putnam Camp. They reached the summit of Gothics just at nightfall and miraculously contrived to get down the steep trail by lighting matches, but could not find the way from the River to the road, and so were out in the woods all night, and the elder brother was permanently prostrated by it.

This is for YOU, in my view of your interest in the history of climbing in the Adirondacks. The climb I here record does not seem a great one to me now. In the Alps I have made many climbs which involved far more effort and consumed far more time (from 2 a.m. till dark). Though I still have my home in Keene Valley, I have lived 27 years on the continent of Europe and consequently have spent most of my summers climbing in the Alps--yet never could boast that I was a great Alpine climber.

Very truly yours,
WALTER LOWRIE
Cedar Grove,
Princeton, N.J.

P.S. I am starting in a few days for China, incidentally with the hope of climbing the Five Sacred Mountains--or such of them as are not infested with brigands. Such climbs are befitting my age, for one can be CARRIED if necessary.

ᓚ ᓚ ᓚ

My old friend of Adirondack days, Newell Martin, has just sent me a copy of your splendid book, "Peaks and People of the Adirondacks." It is a wonderful combination of the graphic and the statistical. I first met Newell at the upper works at Hunter's in 1871. His brother Pascal was with him. I had met Pascal in college days at Princeton. They were sons of Dr. Martin, President of the Imperial College of Peking, China, an old friend of my father's. They had climbed Marcy in coming to Hunter's and urged me to return with them that way. We first went to Preston Ponds and built a log cabin on the north shore of the lower lake. Our trip down Marcy was in the dark. I went ahead with a candle picking out the trail. Then a night at the lake in a leaking shelter, in a hard rain, and foodless. The next year Newell's mother (he was very young)[1] put him in my charge financially and with two Jackson friends—we again visited the Adirondacks. In Indian Pass, Newell and I climbed the mountain on the left of the Pass, on its less precipitous side, leaving pieces of paper to enable us to find our footholds in descending.

We tackled Sanatoni in July, 1872, taking Dave Hunter with us. In going up the stream from Lake Henderson Hunter took a branch too far south and landed us on the top of the ridge too far south of the summit of the peak. We camped there that night and then fought our way the next morning through (mostly over) the thick low balsam to the peak, leaving our camp supplies in camp. The Jacksons were sons of wealthy people, luxuriously brought up and "soft." I did not think they could make the rough trip back to camp. I told all parties I would take a few drops of water trickling from the moss and follow the water flow to Lake Henderson, and sent Hunter and Newell back to camp to bring the outfit to the lake. When they left the Jacksons were in terror as lost in a wilderness. I determined to hold on to the tiny rivulet at all costs. In crossing a "deer mash" I got into the muddy gully many feet deep and crossed it without losing the stream. Reached Lake Henderson in the early afternoon. Sometime later Hunter and Newell appeared with all the outfit except the frying pan. That hung on Newell's back and twisted him and was cut loose. It now reposes somewhere there as evidence of our tramp.

At Avalanche Lake we climbed up a slide in a mountain (Colden) and left a nickel in the summit in 1872. The next day we climbed up McIntyre. Hunter started us up a slope with I was satisfied was not McIntyre. We soon reached the top and saw McIntyre and a steam coming from it. I told Hunter I would take that stream and go up the mountain. Newell and I reached the top first. Two Cincinnati men asked to accompany us from the lake to the mountain. In their fear of being lost they over-exerted themselves. One of them died a day or two later.

---

1. Martin was eighteen; Schenck, twenty-one.

Our party went out through Indian Pass, the Jacksons with great difficulty. I had to carry my own pack and one of theirs. A pouring rain came down, matches got wet. Just as we got through the pass, Newell lay down and vowed he would stay there all night, rain or no rain. (Three times I have had heavy men lie down in the wilderness in my 48 years of engineer-life and made it a rule to take only light wiry men like John Cheney.) I argued Newell to his feet, cached our outfit, reached shelter, and sent guides for the outfit. Am sorry to tell on Newell in his old age.

I was sent to Cheney's to recuperate after typhoid fever by my brother-in-law, Benj. Strong, Sr. (father of Benj. Strong, former Governor of Federal Reserve Bank of N.Y. and before that President of Bankers Trust Co.). Benj. Strong was a nephew of Archibald McIntyre, and left a son, Dr. Archibald McIntyre Strong, now living. John Cheney and my brother-in-law used to tell me how young Henderson was frightened stiff by the cry of a panther at night near camp, and the next morning fled from the wilderness.

Very truly,
A.A. SCHENCK
Princeton '69.

ta ta ta

# Washing a Shirt on the Gothic[1]
[January, 1932]

Russell M. L. Carson,
   Glens Falls, N.Y.
Dear Carson: --

Rock climbing is the best of sports. Good climbers complain, justly, that there is little chance for rock work in any Appalachian mountains and that the few cliffs and slides found in the Adirondacks from Indian Head to Indian Pass, are unpleasantly

---

1. Both the letter, written to Carson on August 20, 1896, and the article (a single paragraph) appeared in the January, 1932, issue (Vol. IX, No. 1) of *High Spots* (pp. 20-21), the official magazine of the Adirondack Mountain Club.
2. Indian Head (or Indian Face) is a rocky peak on the south side of the upper end of Lower Ausable Lake, some 5 1/2 miles east of Mt. Marcy. Indian Pass runs north from Henderson Lake approximately 7 miles west of Mt. Marcy. It is the "Old Round Trip" described in "Six Summits." These two features embrace the eastern and western borders of the central Adirondacks.

safe; and that, in the White Mountains, Tuckerman's Ravine[3] is the only place where you can get killed.

In 1896 I found some childish sport on the Gothic.[4] I send you my old notes of that walk. You will find it amusing to take those notes and follow our course, The white undershirt that we fastened on the face of the mountain, bleached by snow and rain, held its place for two seasons. In the morning, it would catch the sun, and be visible, as a speck of twinkling white, to tourists on the Upper [Ausable] Lake and they would ask "What is that shining jewel on the dark breast of the mountain?"

"Beede's," where these notes were written, is now the Club House of the Adirondack Mountain Reserve.[5]

--TITHONUS.[6]

On Thursday, Aug. 20, I went on the Gothic slide, the big curbing slide facing the Upper Pond -- not that on Pyramid Mountain. Went to white slide, facing the pond, that runs up near the south top. Crossed it about 150 ft. from top, lying down on our backs and pushing along with our elbows. Then went down about 150 ft. more. Below that there is a big piece of timber that crosses the slide. We[6] avoided that because too easy. We then crossed the narrow slide again. Down this we went north in the direction of the Pyramid. Here we fastened about 20 ft. of clothes line so as to use it in getting back if we should have trouble. Then we went down a short distance through grass and shrubs. Then we crossed a piece of slide again on bare rocks that was easy. This brought us on a band of grass and flowers growing in a crack, and very steep. Hathaway walked down here. I thought it more prudent to sit and slide down. Then we came to a jumping off place where the grass stopped. This checked us for a time but at the side of our line we found an overhanging rock and we easily got down by wedging our shoulders between the overhanging rock and the slippery surface of

---

3. A steep enfolded declivity on the east face of Mt. Washington descending some 1,400 feet in roughly one mile. Some 90 deaths have been recorded on Mt. Washington as of 1984, most due to its sudden bad weather — notoriously the worst in North America. Tuckerman's Ravine, snow-filled long after the winter season, offers the most formidable skiing challenge in the eastern U.S.

4. Adirondack mountain, 4738 ft., located some 3 1/2 miles east of Mt. Marcy. First of Martin's six summits.

5. Actually, notes must have been written at what was known as "Widow Beede's," the lodging-house built by Phineas Beede, c. 1877, located some one-half mile northeast of the original "Beede's," which burned in March, 1890. What stands today replacing "Beede's" is the building belonging to the Ausable Lake and Mountain Club, a wholly new structure.

6. Milford Hathaway (no data) accompanied Martin. His corroborating statement, dated August 20, 1896, appeared in the same issue of *High Spots*: "I have heard the foregoing memorandum read to me. The statements it makes about our walk on the Gothic are correct."

the slide. This brought us to the bottom. This whole place is very easy for people who don't mind standing in the middle of a cliff and looking down. Where we came down is 100 feet south of the exact middle of the cliff. The cliff has two faces that meet in the middle forming a sort of groin. We were then attracted by the appearance of the crack that goes up in the middle where the two faces of the cliff meet. We started up this place, having grass to help us at first. Then the grass gave out and we had to work up the crack, much of the way without any handhold. On our right rose one cheek of the cliff, bulging and overhanging. On the left the other cheek of the cliff sloped away very sharply without anything to stop us if we slipped. After the grass gave out, at first the crack was wide enough for us to work in our knees and push up that way. The crack was so straight up and down that we could not use it for handhold except in occasional places where we found roughnesses in the crack. Farther up the crack became so narrow that we could only get in a part of a foot; then so narrow that we could only get a part of the toe of a boot. We would first wedge in a toe of the right boot, straighten the leg and then wedge in the left toe above the right and so on. At last we got to the end of the crack and found that nothing showed above to help us except a small and very doubtful handhold on a bulging rock, so high up that one man could not reach it without standing on the other's shoulders. And if this could have been managed the first man could not have pulled up the second. Luckily, I saw a foothold projecting on the cliff to our left. By standing on my right foot and spreading myself against the rock and stretching my left leg I could just get my left toe on the foothold. It was disagreeable to do this, as there was no handhold and the only comfort to be had lay in pressing as close against the cliff as possible. I am used to high places but I found it well not to look down while making this traverse. As soon as I got my left foot firmly on the foothold I drew my right leg after me and soon found myself, with a little climbing, on a comfortable projection six inches wide on which I could stand against the cliff. Then Hathaway followed. He is some inches shorter than I but much stronger and more agile. Being shorter he found it extremely hard to carry his left toe to the foothold which I have spoken of, and ran a grave risk while trying to stretch over it. How he ever reached it I do not understand. I offered to steady him with the rope, but he declined, somewhat to my relief. He compassed the difficulty, at last, very handsomely, and our troubles were over. We worked up through the rest of the pass through some picturesque, but not very difficult places, and then worked our way down, southerly, over some curious ledges to the place where we had moored our clothes line. We found that we had become so familiar, in our short climb, with the particular sort of rock that makes the Gothic slide that we could walk across the strip of slide where our clothes line was stretched, without help from the line and without touching the rock with our hands more than once or twice. To show other explorers the best place to enter the slide we moored our clothes line to bushes and tied a shirt in the middle of it. The shirt can easily be seen from the point on the second knob of the Gothic where an extension of the trail was run towards the upper pond to a big rock which tourists visit to view the Gothic slide. The place where we went up the slide can be determined thus: — A stone rolled from that big rock on the second knob would stop in the big timber just 100 feet north of the foot of the trail up which we climbed; and the point where we began on the crack is exactly below the overhanging ledge at the top of the middle of the slide which is so conspicuous, from the upper pond, by the shadow it makes on the slide. The place is also marked by a lot of big steps just north of our place, that are cut in the face of the cliff. These steps are not attractive, though perhaps they might be managed with ropes and other appliances. They slope the wrong way. The way we went down is easy for people whose heads are all right. But if some of the grass should go it might become impossible. The place we went up is difficult, probably, for anybody; though anybody who has been up once would do it a second time more easily. Charlie Beede says that Verplanck Colvin[7] went from the Upper Pond to this place once with Stetson and Ed Phelps[8] to go up this place and gave it up. We would have given it up also, if we had first seen it from below, from which point it looks impossible. Going down and coming up took us an hour and a half. After getting up, we went over the most southern summit of the Gothic and down a little on the Johns Brook side of the mountain below the height of land of the ridge. There we found some ferny places and runways that led us easily back to the trail. It took two hours and four minutes in the morning to go from the

---

7. Verplanck Colvin (1847-1920), New York State park commissioner, first to advocate publicly the preservation of the Adirondacks as a state park; appointed in 1872 to investigate the feasibility of the Adirondacks as a state park. He carried out an extensive survey of the region 1872-1900, which Alfred L. Donaldson's authoritative *History of the Adirondacks* stated was "of uneven scientific value."

8. R. R. Stetson married Phineas Beede's daughter Alma, and until his death ran the lodging-house. Ed Phelps was the son of Orson Phelps, both were guides; Ed Phelps, working out of Keene Flats, was included in S. R. Stoddard's 1874 list of Adirondack guides.

road to the top; and coming down it took us an hour and a half, as we were tired, to reach the road. Both these times are much longer than are necessary. But people who are going to try this slide, which furnishes more entertainment than most places, ought not to hurry. My companion and guide was Milford Hathaway. He took much interest in the excursion and is in the highest degree competent to show the way on such walks.

--TITHONUS.[9]

⁂

# Two Great Adirondack Guides [1]

Huntington
Long Island, New York
December 14, 1935.

Miss Ruth Riley [Editor]
253 Main Street
Hudson Falls, New York.

Dear Miss Riley:--
You have written asking what notable animals I have seen in my 64 years of Adirondack adventure.

Let me tell you, then, about the worm's eye views that kind fate has granted to me of two famous philosophers. Chapters have been written about the last moose seen in Essex County, the laudable industry of our beavers, and the deplorable industry of our porcupines. But the quadrupeds of our forests are gentle and unobtrusive, and meeting with them is not an adventure. It is the higher animals in the North Woods, that have filled me with wonder. The modest mountains of our state are not lofty; and our delightful wilderness is not vast; but it has been fortunate beyond all other wildernesses in that it has harbored eminent scholars. I have seen there one historian, two theologians, a great philologist and a great

---

9. In Greek myth, Tithonus was son of Laomedon, king of Troy. Eos (Dawn) fell in love with him and obtained for him from Zeus the gift of immortality, but forgot to ask for eternal youth, so that he became "an old shriveled creature little more than a voice," according to the *Oxford Companion to Classical Literature*.

---

1. From *High Spots*, (Vol. 13 #1), January, 1936.

geologist: Francis Parkman,[2] Felix Adler,[3] Noah Porter,[4] William Dwight Whitney[5] and Josiah Dwight Whitney.[6] The best of these have been my companions in forest camps. But today I would like, if you will be patient, to indulge in senile reminiscences as to philosophers who have sanctified Adirondack trails with their footprints. Your forests, hardly less favored than the groves of Plato's Academy, have sheltered Emerson, William James and Josiah Willard Gibbs, the younger, usually spoken of as Willard Gibbs.[7] The greatest of these three is Gibbs. If you will turn to the "Education of Henry Adams," you will read that Adams learned from Langley that Gibbs is the greatest philosopher and one of the greatest physicists of all time.

*[Editor's Note: This statement requires considerable clarification. Samuel Pierpont Langley (1834-1906), American astronomer and aeronautics pioneer, was designer of the first successful (unmanned) heavier-than-air flying machine. The only coordinate reference to Langley and Gibbs in the 1974 critical edition of* The Education of Henry Adams *occurs at the end of Chapter XXIV, where Adams merely states, "The greatest of Americans, judged by his rank in science, Willard Gibbs, never came to Washington, and Adams never enjoyed a chance to meet him. After Gibbs, one of the most distinguished was Langley, of the Smithsonian, who was more accessible, to whom Adams had been much in the habit of turning whenever he wanted an outlet for his vast reservoirs of ignorance." In the first, privately-printed (1907) edition of the Education, Adams actually wrote "Wolcott Gibbs," and repeated the name further down in the same paragraph, having confused the Yale physicist with the more famous Harvard chemist. Adams went on to praise Wolcott Gibbs effusively at the start of Chapter XXXI. The first publicly-printed (1918) text incorporated revisions and corrections made by Adams in his copy of the book,*

2. Francis Parkman (1823-93), American historian, primarily of American West or frontier generally, American Northwest, and western Canada.
3. Felix Adler (1851-1933), American educator and social reformer; founder of the Ethical Culture Movement.
4. Noah Porter (1811-1892), American educator and philosopher; taught philosophy at Yale 1846-71; president of Yale 1871-86.
5. William Dwight Whitney (1827-1894), philologist, professor of Sanskrit, head of the Department of Modern Languages at Yale's Sheffield Scientific School.
6. Josiah Dwight Whitney (1819-1896), geologist and educator; forty years' service in U.S. geological surveys; first Sturgis-Hooper professor of geology at Harvard (1865-1896). Father of William Dwight Whitney. See Section Ten - "The Climinole."
7. Josiah Willard Gibbs (1839-1903), professor of mathematical physics; most famous for achievements in the field of thermodynamics.

which included altering the second but not the first reference to Wolcott Gibbs at the end of Chapter XXIV, and interpolating at the beginning of Chapter XXXI, "the more so because in his ignorance he confounded him with another great mind, his rival Willard Gibbs," after, "Wolcott stood on the same plane with the three or four greatest minds of the century." The baffled 1918 editors simply changed all mentions of Wolcott to Willard Gibbs, thereby misleading Martin. In any event, Adams never adverted to Willard Gibbs as a philosopher, though he did make a misconceived attempt to apply Gibbs' Rule of Phase to history in his 1909 tract of that title. However William H. Jordy does state in his Henry Adams: Scientific Historian that Adams probably learned of Willard Gibbs from Langley.]

Gibbs was one of four professors at Yale who were so kind as to be friends of mine rather than teachers. I greatly valued and reverenced Gibbs; but, in July, 1873, I did not know that Gibbs was great. Nor did I know that he was in Keene Flats, a lovely dale that is now called, unfortunately, Keene Valley. I was then on my way to the Upper Works, from a college boat race,[8] that had been won by a medieval hero, Bob Cook.[9]

I meant to spend a week in the woods and then to keep an appointment with Samuel Isham,[10] in Maine. A ramshackle wagon was carrying me and the mail to Smith Beede's.[11] Nothing was further from my mind than staying in Keene Flats. At nightfall we stopped for a moment at Seth Dibble's "Tahawus House," a rude mountain boarding house.[12] Dibble's lodgers came out to meet the mail wagon and hear from the outer world. I was glad and surprised

8. Martin, then an 18-year-old sophomore at Yale, was a spectator, as this was an intercollegiate race and Martin participated only in intramural rowing.
9. Robert J. Cook (1849-1922; Yale '76), captain of the Yale crew for four years; Yale head crew coach 1876-1898. Studied law immediately after graduating but practiced only briefly; during his period as Yale crew coach made his living as head of a small publishing firm. According at least to Yale sources, transparent referee error gave Harvard rather than Yale victory in a thirteen-college regatta, July 17-18, 1873. "Medieval" presumably alludes to the Yale crew's unprotesting acceptance of the decision.
10. Samuel Isham (1855-1914; Yale '75; L.L.B. Columbia Law School '80). Practiced law 1880-1885, but subsequently gave up law to pursue a successful career in painting, primarily portraiture.
11. Lodging-house run by the guide Smith Beede (1819-1891). Burned in 1890; St. Hubert's (Ausable Club) today is located on its site.
12. Tahawus is the Indian name for Mt. Marcy, highest (5,344) peak in the Adirondack Mountains. S. R. Stoddard, The Adirondacks (Albany: Weed, Parsons, 1874), states, "The Tahawus House is the largest in Keene Flats; a roomy comfortable looking structure, with a broad two storey piazza, and has accommodations for about forty visitors. Its proprietor, N[orman]. M. Dibble, seems to have learned the secret of success in that line, and has made his place very attractive in its clean, well ordered appearance; it is very much liked by former guests; teams are furnished for the pleasant drives north and south, and to meet parties at Westport when desired." The Tahawus House burned in 1908.

440    PEAKS AND PEOPLE

to see, among those lodgers, Willard Gibbs. I inquired as to his family and told him that I was on my way to Smith Beede's, the Upper Works and Maine. To my astonishment Gibbbs [sic] protested. "Stay with us. Stay here. You will be more comfortable here than at Smith Beede's. You will be lonely at Smith Beede's." Never before had anybody concerned himself much as to where I might go. I was flattered by the politeness of the professor. I followed Gibbs gladly into Seth Dibble's rude dining room. There were young women (now great-grandmothers), eager to hear about the boat race; young persons, who were ready to welcome anybody that was not a professor or philosopher. From that time, for years, the Adirondacks were my true home. Now, I see why Gibbs was so polite and insistent. In 1873 his powerful mind was at its highest tension, engaged in thoughts that will nourish smaller philosophers and suggest new inquiries, for centuries. Gibbs needed me to carry his sister's umbrella and to lead about, over the hills, the young women, who had been in the habit of interrupting his gigantic circles of thought with remarks about scenery and boat-races. I have, moreover, a suspicion that Gibbs took pleasure in observing my ignorance. A great philosopher would rather be attended by an ignorant boy than by some third-rate philosopher. And it is obvious now that Gibbs did not find us, boys and girls, unduly disturbing. He was like Sir William Rowan Hamilton[13] who built up [sic in] his mind a stately structure of quaternions while walking with his wife. Or Sir Isaac Newton, who cherished a dog, the celebrated Diamond. Or was it some other philosopher that owned that dog?[14] Gibbs found me as companionable as a dog and less disturbing than any more intelligent companion would have been. When I contemplate the sublime structures that have been reared on the foundations of his thought, I comfort myself with the remembrance that I never interrupted his reflections. Nor, in 1877— I think that was the year

---

13. Sir William Rowan Hamiliton (1805-1865), British mathematician, born in Dublin. Worked in optics and mechanics; noted for the discovery of quaternions, defined as "a complex number that is the sum of a real number and a vector; it depends on one real number and three imaginary units." P.L. Graves, in his monumental *Life of Sir William Rowan Hamilton* (London: Longmans, Green & Co., 1885), quotes a letter from Hamilton to his son, the Rev. Archibald Hamilton, August 5, 1865, concerning the moment of illumination: Hamilton tells how he was walking to a council meeting of the Royal Irish Academy, "and your mother was walking with me, along the Royal Canal, to which she had perhaps driven; and although she talked with me now and then, yet an undercurrent of thought was going on in my mind, which gave at last a result, whereof it is not too much to say that I felt at once the importance. An electric current seemed to close, and a spark flashed forth." (Vol. II, chap. 28, p. 434).
14. No, Diamond was Newton's.

— did I ever interrupt William James'[15] thought. In 1877 two groups dwelt together in Smith Beede's Old House, a little house at the head of Keene Valley. One was a group of dignified Harvard men, William James* and Putnam[16] and Bowditch.[17] In the other group were four people of Yale sympathies. Our fare was frugal. We lived on porridge and huckleberries and "Graham gems."[18] The three Harvard men were polite but haughty. We, on the other hand, were humble, frivolous and unpolished. Many years after, I realized that the philosopher, James, (we did not know, then, that he was a philosopher) was in fear that my companions, who loved the place, would try to buy it; and he and his friends had set their hearts on buying it for themselves and making it the world-famous "Putnam Camp."[19] Some of the inconvenient Yale group were agreeable and charming; and it was not without effort that William James and his companions resolved to be cold and forbidding. I can imagine the three scholars agreeing, reluctantly, to be reserved — "We must not be cordial, or some of these Yale people will buy the place." Plato, perhaps, felt anxious at times, lest some Athenian shopkeeper might buy the Groves of Academe. James and Gibbs are guides of the human race. Everybody, now, knows that Gibbs was great; and, for me, he acted as an Adirondack guide. But for him, I would have deserted the Adirondacks and gone far afield. But for him, long ago, I would have broken my neck on some cliff of the Caucasus or on some crumbling rock in the Selkirk Mountains.[20]

--NEWELL MARTIN.
--O--

15. William James (1842-1910), psychologist and philosopher; exponent of pragmatism. (See Martin's * footnote at end of this piece.)
16. Frederic Ward Putnam (1839-1915; Harvard '62), anthropologist; curator of Peabody Museum at Harvard 1875-1909, and simultaneously Peabody professor of American archaeology and anthropology.
17. Henry Pickering Bowditch (1840-1911), grandson of navigator Nathaniel Bowditch (1773-1838). Taught at Harvard 1871-82; known primarily for work in physiology and medical education.
18. Biscuits or muffins made with Graham (i.e., whole-wheat) flour.
19. From the Letters of William James, Vol. I, edited by Henry James (Boston: Atlantic Monthly Press, 1920), p. 195: "Where the Ausable Club's picturesque golf-course is now laid out, the fields of Smith Beede's farm then surrounded his primitive, white-painted hotel. Half a mile to the eastward, in a patch of rocky pasture beside Giant Brook, stood the original Beede farmhouse, and this Henry P. Bowditch, Charles and James Putnam, and William James had bought for a few hundred dollars (subject to Beede's cautious proviso in the deed that 'the purchasers are to keep no boarders'). They had adapted the little story [sic]-and-a-half dwelling to their own purposes and converted its surrounding sheds and pens into habitable shanties of the simplest kind. So they established a sort of camp, with the mountains for their climbing, the brook to bath in, and the primeval forest fragrant about them." (editorial interpolation for 1878) Freud and Jung once spent three days at what came to be called the Putnam Camp.
20. Range of Rocky Mountains in southeastern British Columbia.

\* S. C. S. Schiller, in his "Studies in Humanism," at page 352, says that great student of the human soul, William James, proclaimed the right of inclining the nicely-weighted equipoise of intellectual argumentation by throwing into the scales a will to believe whichever of the alternatives seemed most consonant with our emotional nature.[21]

# Beede
May, 1933

*The July issue of* High Spots carried an article by Martin honoring Charlie Beede, a beloved Adirondack Guide. The magazine reported that "Beede died on April 28, 1933, at his home on the east hillside at Keene Valley."

It grieves me to hear that my friend Charlie Beede has gone to the land where nobody needs a guide. There have been, in the delightful records of Adirondack sport, four generations of guides. In the first generation were such old-timers as Mitchell Sabattis,[1] Max Tredo, Levi Lamb,[2] John Cheney[3] and the famous Phelps.[4]. The third generation are now beginning to retire from hard work. The fourth generation are still active in camp and on the carry, and

---

21. S.C.S. Schiller, *Studies in Humanism* (London: Macmillan, 1912). Schiller alludes, of course, to a central doctrine of pragmatism.

---

1. In Alfred L. Donaldson's authoritative two-volume *History of the Adirondacks* (N.Y.: Century, 1921), he states, "It is impossible to say just when Mitchell Sabattis was born...I am inclined to place the date around 1801." (1801?-1906): Abenaki Indian guide, lived in and worked out of Long Lake, some eight-ten miles west of Mt. Marcy region.
2. Two of fifteen Keene Flats guides listed by S. R. Stoddard in *The Adirondacks* (Albany: Weed, Parsons & Co., 1874).
3. Born c. 1800 in New Hampshire; died 1877. May claim to be first Adirondacks guide; was guide for party led by state geologist Ebenezer Emmons on first ascent of Mt. Marcy in 1837.
4. Orson Schofield "Old Mountain" Phelps (1817-1905): Born in Vermont; settled at foot of Mt. Marcy in 1831, and devoted himself exclusively to mountain climbing, as opposed to hunting and trapping. Painted by Winslow Homer; subject of an article by Charles Dudley Warner in the May, 1878, *Atlantic*.

see campers by hundreds and thousands in the woods that Charlie and I used to revel in, when they were a lonely wilderness. Charlie Beede seemed to me to be the very best of the second generation. In the early seventies I had the honor of knowing him and camping with him and learning from him how to go through the forest without a trail. He then had the ardor of youth; and, in 1894, I found him still sympathetic, swift, untiring and ambitious for uphill achievement. He was a crafty fisherman. I have heard sportsmen, after working patiently up the length of a mountain brook, report wearily that there had not been a fish in that brook since 50 million years ago when our ancestors were ganoid[5] sharks. Then Charlie would slip away to that slandered brook and bring us a supper of trout so intelligent that they would not condescend to be caught by any but a master hand. He flourished in the fine old competitive days when an Adirondack guide, simply for the fun of excelling in his art, would take a cooking stove on his back over the Upper Pond carry or pack 100 pounds over the top of Marcy to the Upper Works.[6] Charlie was an axe-man of the first rank. There was no lumberjack in our woods that could excel him or that could stand longer than he on a rolling log in the rapids of a swift river. He loved the woods for their beauty and charm. You are perhaps wrong in calling our old friends "Great Guides."[7] They were, rather, guides who would have been great if storms and glaciers had not worn down the Adirondacks so that they were easy mountains and, for the trained woodsman, not perilous. It is great mountains that make the fame of great guides. For a Bennen[8] or Supersaxo[9] or Taugwalder[10] you must have Alpine heights and Alpine perils. But no guide that has won fame in the Caucasus or the Andes has been a better or braver man than Charlie Beede. He was an ardent sportsman, and a companion that inspired confidence and affection. When I first knew him no sentimental young woman had been permitted to

---

5. "Covered with polished bony plates."
6. A former iron works at upper end of Sanford Lake, some eight miles southwest of Mt. Marcy. See map.
7. "Great Adirondack Guides" was the name of the series of articles in the magazine *High Spots*, of which this was No. 3 in the series.
8. Johann Joseph Bennen (1824-1864), guide from upper Rhone valley; guided first ascent of the Weisshorn in southern Swiss Alps in 1860, and three unsuccessful attempts on the Matterhorn.
9. Ambros Supersaxo, nineteenth-century French guide; guided first ascent of Aiguille Blanche de Peuterey (13,482 ft.) in the Mont Blanc Range.
10. Peter Taugwalder, Sr., guide on first ascent of the Matterhorn in 1865.

change the name of his village.[11] Keene Valley was then Keene Flats, a lovable name. "Flats," because it was a narrow shelf of the mountains. Thus Eric the Red, in his time, named a continental ice-sheet Greenland. I know of another little valley, Saas-fe, in the Haut Valais,[12] that is barred off from the world by great heights, as was Keene Flats, and that is, like Keene Flats, the home of skillful, fearless and companionable mountaineers.

Robert Marshall is telling in his "Arctic Village" about a third hidden eyrie [aerie] of admirable mountain men like Keene Flats men, in Arctic Alaska.[13] Why is it that in such remote high-up hamlets you find men of character, agreeable, self-sacrificing and generous? Why do you find there no crime, and no sins except such as are harmless or even meritorious? Perhaps it is because extreme irregularities of the earth's surface disincline people to gross irregularities of conduct. Perhaps it is because the dwellers in such mountain hamlets do not flatten out their minds by submitting them every morning to the geological pressure of the numerous strata of a daily paper. They have leisure therefore for thought; and freedom to perfect their minds and manners.

Sincerely,<br>-NEWELL MARTIN

---

11. Whoever was responsible, of which sex, the change from Keene Flats to Keene Valley occurred c. 1890.
12. Described by one source as "an oasis in the Alps." It is a hamlet on a small secluded plateau located northeast of Zermatt, canton of Valais, Switzerland.
13. *Arctic Village* (New York: Literary Guild, 1933), a best-seller, describes the lives of whites and Eskimos at the head of the Koyukuk River north of the Arctic Circle in Alaska, "who have made for themselves the happiest civilization of which I have knowledge."

# Helen Martin[1] To Newell Martin
# Judith Is A Fictitious Name[2]

July 23, 1908.

This morning we did the Dent de Satarma[3] with Renzo[4] and the Life Saver. It is really a daisy good climb. Renzo went first (though he is really not as good as the Life Saver) and I came after him. It was perfectly easy for the first bit, with monstrous hand-and foot-holds.

Then there was a little sort of platform where I waited while Renzo climbed up over the hardest part and anchored himself at the top of it. When I tried it, though, I found it was ten times harder than it looked and I took a long time finding my way up.

Renzo, of course, all the time, kept the rope short but I didn't get any moral assistance, really and you can ask him if I did, though, of course, it would have been awfully mortifying if I had.

It was really hard, because the holds were so few and so worn down.

When I arrived where Renzo was, he climbed on to the top and I keep the rope short while the Life Saver came up.

Then I went up the easy way to the top and we waited in the most comfortable little place with a boulder for our foot stool, till the others arrived. There was just room on the summit for four and I do love these summits, dòn't you?

We stayed there a long time eating chocolate and enjoying the view. Renzo is like the boys in doing silly things for he tight-roped around the top of the summit and did all sorts of silly things while

---

1. Helen, older Martin daughter, was nineteen when she made this climb. No reference for "Judith" or "Life Saver."
2. Note in Martin's handwriting in right top corner: "Paste this in your life-book." Not pasted, but saved in a box of letters by Helen Martin Meyer's family.
3. To quote from *The Complete Mountaineer* (London: Methuen, 1908), by George D. Abraham: "It is usual for a first day's training at Arolla [in southern Switzerland] to walk down the valley, trudge up to the Lac Bleu, and climb the Dent de Satarma after picnicking in the adjacent pine forest. The ascent of this aggressive-looking pinnacle is short, but distinctly on the gymnastic side; and, if too much lunch is indulged in, its conquest is no easy matter. At one point near the top the situation is distinctly thrilling, because the hand- and foot-holds are scarcely large enough to ensure perfect safety, and the view down to the valley straight below is sensational. For some people the pleasures of such a climb can only be felt when they have reached the base again, for on the summit the climber is faced by the thought that the getting down again must prove difficult." (p. 383).
4. Renzo Brusati: see Section Three - "War List."

I was on the other end of the rope. Judith went down over the hard part first, with the Life Saver holding the rope, while I remained on the summit with Renzo.

After Judith had arrived safely at the platform, she unroped and sent the rope back to be attached to me, and I proceeded to make my way down, and it really was not easy.

Renzo came down next and we had the time of our lives watching from our comfortable position.

The Life Saver, then, being alone on top, doubled the rope over a jutting place and came down that way. It looked awfully difficult and he did it well.

He had to keep tight hold of the rope so it would not slip off. If it had, I hate to think of the result. xxxx

Here is something we found in the Alpine Journal:[5]

"They will dine on mule and marmot and mutton
    made of goats
They will taste the various horrors of
    Helvetian table d' hotes. xxxx
For a foot-hold or a hand-hold,
They will diligently grope
On the rocky, icy mountain
While we charitably hope
'Tis assistance only moral
That they're getting from the rope."

# Letter to Myra After Reading "Camp Six"

Thursday, August 19, 1937

Dear Myra

Here is an experiment. It will not amuse you. You do not need to read this at all. Throw it away, at this point.

---

5. *The Alpine Journal* is the original English-language mountaineering journal, published 1863-present. Quote is from F. W. Bourdillon, "Another Way of (Mountain) Love," (issue #180; [May, 1908] (p.150).

The experiment consists in trying to write to four persons at once. I am so old and weak that I can write only one letter a day, or, usually, one letter a week. Therefore, I make this experiment. I write one letter and then I hire the copying office, in town, to make four copies of it. Then I mail 4 copies of it, one to each of 4 women that, at the moment, I do love most admiringly.

I have been reading "Camp Six", the best of mountain books,[1] lent by Mrs. Grinnell Martin.[2] It tells how heroic Englishmen, aided by still more heroic Sherpas and Bhotans,[3] attainted amazing heights in trying to reach the top of Everest. To tell the story in round numbers, some of them came within 1,000 feet of the top.

Tell me if I remember this wrongly. I think Smythe, alone, achieved a height of 28,000 feet, through unspeakable danger, through ice and snow, and almost at the level where the air is too thin to support life. Let us hear no more scoffing at any Smith who spells his name Smythe. And remember this. In this little group of heroes that surpassed all previous achievements in climbing was another of the Smith tribe: do not forget Smijth-Windham.[4] He was one of the heroes that reached the highest camp on the roof of the world.

Affectionately,

Newell Martin

*** 

1. *Camp Six* (London: Hodder & Stoughton, 1937), by Francis Sydney Smythe (1900-49). Mountaineer Smythe took part in six Himalayan expeditions, including the Everest expeditions of '33, '36, and '38; and was the author of numerous books on climbing, relating both to his own experiences and the sport generally. He is described as weak and even asthmatic at low altitudes, but transformed into a new man at great heights. *Camp Six* is an account of the '33 Everest assault in which Smythe was the last member of the expedition to give up, reaching 28,000 feet, and outdistancing the next climber by some 400 vertical feet.
2. Myra's mother.
3. Nepal's famous Sherpa tribe has of course furnished guides and porters for all the important Himalayan climbs; Bhutan is an Indian protectorate in the eastern Himalayas between India and Tibet.
4. Lt. William R. Smijth-Windham (no dates), radio officer on the '33 and '36 Everest expeditions. Described as not properly a climber but nonetheless attaining remarkable heights.

# FIFTEEN

# SELECTED LETTERS

To Samuel R. Betts. Esqre. . . . . . . . . 450

To Myra . . . . . . . . . . . . . . . . . . 451

To Grinnell . . . . . . . . . . . . . . . . 457

To Laura . . . . . . . . . . . . . . . . . 458

To Molly . . . . . . . . . . . . . . . . . 459

To Janet . . . . . . . . . . . . . . . . . 471

Merry Christmas, 1935 . . . . . . . . . . 478

# To Samuel R. Betts, Esqre.
[June 9, 1930]

*After receiving an invitation from his Yale class of '75 secretary, Samuel Rossiter Betts, to attend their 55th reunion dinner, Martin wrote a brief two-paragraph letter explaining why he would not attend. He had it printed on one side of a small sheet (6" X 3.5"), perhaps for distribution to fellow classmates during the 1930 reunion.*

*Betts (1854-1930; Yale '75; L.L.B. Columbia '77), immediately joined his father's New York City law firm after graduating from Columbia; then, in 1887, went into partnership on his own, specializing in patent and trademark law. He retired in 1926. He was successively the director, secretary, vice-president, and president of the New York Institution for the Instruction of the Deaf and Dumb.*

*Betts was an alumni fund agent for his Yale class 1898-1930, and class secretary 1915-1930. Also was a member of committee on admissions of the University Club 1892-1901, hence was serving when Martin joined the Club in 1900.*

*Martin's letter to Betts was addressed to the Quinnipac Club in New Haven where Betts was either living or temporarily staying. The Quinnipac is a private — i.e., not Yale-connected — club founded in 1871, and still exists; has several dining facilities, health facilities, and overnight accommodations.*

Dear Sam:
 I thank you for your kind invitation to dine in New Haven, in commemoration of our being nearer to 80 than to 70; and of our having graduated in 1875, 55 years ago. I ought to save, for use at the 1935 reunion, the text that explains my absence from your banquet; but it is sufficiently appropriate now and circumstances beyond my control may prevent me from sending it to you five years hence.[1] I refer you to Second Samuel, Chapter 19, Verse 33:
 "And the king said unto Barzillai,[2] Come thou over with me, and I will feed thee.... And Barzillai said unto the king, 'How long have I to live, that I should go up with the king...? I am this day four score years old: and can I discern between good and evil? Can I taste what I eat or what I drink? Can I hear any more the voice of the men when they sing?... Wherefore then should I [thy servant] be yet a burden unto my lord the king? And why should the king

---

1. While Sam Betts died the following Dec. 13, Martin, though bed-ridden for several years, lived through his 66th reunion year (1941).
2. Barzillai was a wealthy Gileadite who showed hospitality to David when he fled from Absalom, and is here declining an invitation to end his days at court.

recompense me with such a reward? Let me, I pray thee, turn back again, that I may die in mine own city'."
           Gratefully
           *Newell Martin*

ta ta ta

## To Myra[1]

          Huntington, N.Y.
          November 1, 1935.
Dear Myra:
  I am grateful for the papers you sent me, about the drunkenness of Southern Methodists, in their hour of triumph and about the prevalence of sin among Baptists, and about the prevalence of Baptists in Southern penitentiaries.[2] The text printed at the head of the pious paper of the "Christian Church" that you sent me is "Second Timothy, 2,13".[3] For many years I have heard those words as a slogan shouted wherever certain kinds of peitists congregate. It is shouted, in chorus, as a welcome, as a battle cry, and as a farewell; and it is a shibboleth. As to jails, the Baptists say statistics are deceptive. The average convict, say the Baptists, is not ardently addicted to religion. But irreligious people have few friend and jailers, who are usually pious, love to hammer convicts that are heterodox. This is in violation of the Constitution. But no officials, of either party, ever respect the Constitution when they deal with poor people. When a Southerner goes to jail he declared himself a Baptist so that he may, in jail, flatter the Chaplain, who is usually either a Methodist or a Romanist, by pretending to be converted from Baptistry by the Chaplain.

          *N. M.*

ta ta ta

---

1. Myra, daughter of Myra, asked about her grandfather's relationship with her mother, his son Grinnell's wife, reports, "My mother adored him. She played endless hours of bridge with him. They wrote often to each other."
2. These particular papers not located.
3. "If we believe not, yet he abideth faithful: he cannot deny himself."

March 30 1938

Dear Myra

    My wife & I are deeply grateful to you for letting us have Jane with us.

    Tell little Laura & Mrs. Newcome that in Ella Maillart's agreeable & impressive book, "Forbidden Journey,"[4] which you gave to me, at page 44, is a photograph of a little wild Mongol prince, afflicted with chicken pox.[5]

    To suffer from chicken pox & from the thirstiness of the Tak La Ma Kun & the Gobi & other deserts, & from the icy beasts of Mongolia, all three at once;[6] that would make even Mrs. Newcome feel depressed.

                              Affectionately

                              Newell Martin

≈ ≈ ≈

4. Ella K. Maillert, *Forbidden Journey* (N.Y.: Henry Holt, 1937). China's Nanking government had placed Sinkiang Province (the Chinese name for Turkestan) off limits to travelers to conceal the absence of political authority there, and the book chronicles a journey Maillert undertook in defiance of authority to bring back a first-hand account of the region, unseen by any outsider for some four years.

5. Only photo of a Mongol child (opposite p. 26) appears to show a mild case of chicken pox, but according to the caption the markings on the face are actually tattoos intended to frustrate the evil spirits who cause this disease.

6. The Takla Makan is a desert in east Turkestan. The Mongol baby lived at Tungkuan, some 500 miles east, and probably didn't suffer much from the Takla Makan, nor from the Gobi Desert some 4-500 miles to his north. While Maillert doesn't mention "icy beasts," there are sandlice, mosquitoes, antelope, wild asses, and rumors of bears.

SELECTED LETTERS 453

*Following is a portion of a letter, undated, but probably sent on Oct. 17 or 18, 1939. It includes a sheet from* The Association of the Bar of the City of New York *listing the members of* The Special Committee on Round-Table Conferences, *and noting the "guest of the evening will be the Honorable Edward Lazansky."*[7]

Dear Myra
  Enclose a notice designed by 20 lawyers, all men of dignity & importance & tested character. 13 of them have modern names, such as Isidor Katz.[8]
  Bernard Hershkopf, Chairman
Nathaniel Phillips, vice-Chairman
-----Leo Guzik, Secretary
William S. Allen
Leonard Lovering Barrett
Chauncey Belknap
-----Leonard G. Bisco
Charles P. Blaney
-----Samuel L. Brennglass
-----Howard Henig
-----Isidor M. Katz
-----Joseph W. Kaufman
-----Caesar Nobiletti
Lawrason Riggs, Jr.
-----Max J. Rubin
-----Henry H. Salzberg
-----Joseph R. Shaughnessy
Alvin McK. Sylvester
-----Arthur Windels
-----Virginius Victor Zipris[9]

7. Edward Lazansky (1882-1955; Columbia '95; L.L.B. '97), lawyer and juror; U.S. Secretary of State 1911-12; N.Y. Supreme Court 1917-31; presiding justice New York's Appellate Division, Second Department 1931-42.

8. Martin placed a dash before Lazansky and 13 of what he called the "modern" names, referring to the other 7 as "primitive English names."
9. To identify the most prominent names on the list:
  Nathaniel Phillips: (1884-1970), leader of New York City bar; member of numerous government commissions at both the state and federal level; head of several bar associations.
  Chauncey Belknap, (1891-1984) secretary to Oliver Wendell Holmes, Jr.; served in 1st Division (as did researcher, Greg Audette, during the Vietnam War) WWI, where he was awarded the Legion of Honor; Princeton trustee; University and Century Club member.
  Joseph W. Kaufman, (1899-1981), counsel to state and federal government, including the New York Labor Relations Board, House of Representatives Small Business

Oc 31 - 1939

Dear Myra

My little bathroom is so small that when my nurse & I are in it, the room seems full of feet.

My nurse, a husky woman, trod heavily, yesterday, on my worse foot.

I surmise that, afterwards, in the kitchen, some talk like this went on:

Nurse: Where did he learn such language?

Mary, the cook: He was at sea 9 months. He was fond of the Mascarene Islands, where the Indian Ocean pirates used to have their harbors.[10]

Nurse: This was land talk, not sea talk.

Cook: Now I remember. In the Civil War, in the early sixties, he was in America, for 6 months.[11] He used to sit on his door-step & see the Army of the Potomac go by. He heard the Army Teamsters driving six-mule teams. He must have heard some harsh words. And why not use them? Most of the nurses I have known are much like Army Mules.

*Newell Martin*

ta ta ta

---

Administration, and Social Security Administration. Deputy chief counsel at the Nuremberg trials, and in 1948 chief prosecutor in the trial for wartime crimes of the head of Germany's Krupp firm.

Isidor Katz, (1902-70), general counsel to the United Textile Workers of America from its founding in 1939 to 1952; subsequently member New York City firm of Lieberman, Katz, and Aronson.

---

10. The islands of Reunion, Mauritius, and Rodriguez, located some 400-500 miles northeast of South Madagascar in the Indian Ocean. Together with the east coast of Madagascar, the Mascarenes were a stronghold of pirates — mainly English, French, and American — throughout the 17th century, most of them having fled there to escape British harassment in the Atlantic. These pirates were in fact largely eliminated by a British fleet in 1721.

11. Probably late spring-early fall, 1862, in the neighborhood of Philadelphia.

16. See Section Four — "A Deplorable Occurrence at the Bank of Washington Heights Dinner."

SELECTED LETTERS 455

*On November 3, 1939, Martin sent a Century Association pamphlet dated November 1939 (Vol. XII, No. 1) to "Mrs. Grinnell Martin," marking in the section titled, "Proposals for Membership," the names of George E. Brewer, Jr. proposed by William M. Ivins, Jr.[12] and Leonard Beacon.[13] He wrote in pencil on the cover: "Dear Myra: Talk to me sometime about the Century Club." NM [initials]*

[Robert Marshall[14]
[Fred Stokes,[14]    In November -- a month of
[Dean Gates[15]      final calamity
   Remind me to show you Bob Marshall's will, as reported in H.-T. this morning.[16]
------
   I was deeply moved by Dean Gates's death-bed letter.[17]
   When you are at your book-sellers you might ask whether you could buy for me for 25 cents Nicol's little book: -- See next slip.
   "Microbes by the Millions" by Hugh Nicol "in the popular Pelican series" "published at the fantastically low price of 25 cents" by the "English Penguin Books" *
   The last edition was 50000 --
* now on sale in N.Y.[18]


12. William M. Ivins, Jr. (1881-1961 Harvard '01; L.L.B. Columbia '07) Essentially founded the Metropolitan Museum of Art's print collection in 1916, and on his retirement as curator in 1946 had built it into one of the largest and most variegated print collections in the world. Century Association member 1919-death.
13. Leonard Beacon (1887-1954; Yale '09), poet and translator; author of some 20 books including a 1940 autobiography which won the Pulitzer Prize. Century Association member 1927-death.
14. See Section Ten -- "A 1922 Christmas Card." 15. See Section Ten -- "A 1922 Christmas Card."
15. See Section Four -- "A Deplorable Occurrence."
16. Marshall (see Section Fourteen - "Six Summits."), who died November 1, 1939, was unmarried and left an estate of some $20,000. He made one personal bequest to his lifelong Adirondacks guide Herbert Clark, and directed that the remainder be divided into equal portions to be held in trust by his brother George: one part "to preserve wilderness conditions in outdoor America" and educate Americans as to the necessity of such measures; one part to "safeguard and advance the cause of civil liberties"; and one part for education in economic conditions. (The figure $20,000 is taken from *The New York Times*. Marshall has been described elsewhere as a millionaire, whose wealth in fact made possible his wilderness activities, and the newspaper's sum may be a severe underestimate.)
17. Not available.
18. *Microbes by the Millions* (Harmondsworth, Middlesex: Penguin, 1939; 1940; 1945), by Hugh Nicol. A highly-popularized account of micro-organisms: their nature, varieties, manner of reproduction, dangers and uses both in medicine and in the home. Simple experiments are described. Says Mr. Nicol in his preface: "Specialists in English may be assured that I have tried not to offer hostages to Mr. A. P. Herbert, M.P., though I have started — or perhaps averted (it is yet uncertain) -- a new word war."

What slows up my reading is that I am so nearly paralyzed that I have great pains in handling even small books.
Can I get well?
Psalms 90 verse 10[19]

*Newell Martin*

ta ta ta

Dec. 1 1939

Dear Myra
I thank you for "Shanghai '37" by Vicki Baum[20] sent by you to me today. I shall begin it as soon as I have finished Prof. Hooton's "Twilight of Man" which I got from the library & I must return soon.[21]
I am deeply grateful.

Affectionately

*Newell Martin*

ta ta ta

---

19. "The days of our years are threescore years and ten; and if by reason of strength they be fourscore years, yet is their strength labour and sorrow; for it is soon cut off, and we fly away."
20. Baum (1888-1960) was best known for her novel *Grand Hotel*, scripted into the famous Hollywood movie of the same name. See Section Ten -- "A 1922 Christmas Card." *Shanghai '37* (N.Y.: Doubleday, 1939) is a fictional account of the lives of nine persons who died in an actual event, the dropping of a bomb by either a Chinese or Japanese airman on the Shanghai Hotel in the International Settlement at Shanghai. The book was something of a best-seller and was reprinted by the Book League of America the following year.
21. Ernest A. Hooton, *Twilight of Man* (N.Y.: Putnam's, 1939), takes a critical view of "the idea that we can remake man himself by infinite education and skillful readjustment of human institutions," and advocates that the results of inquiry into the human organism "be devoted to the very utilitarian problem of fitting each type of varying human organism to the cultural task for which it is best adapted and to the far more difficult and important problem of finding out how to breed better men," (p. 282). See Section Five — "Armenoids."

# To Grinnell

October 31, 1938

Dear Grinnell:
It is astonishing that so few people were killed in our storm. The noise of the hurricane itself was so great that I heard no crashing when our biggest tree, 60 feet high, went down in front of our house.[1]

I quote an item from the Yale Alumni Magazine of October 21, 1938, page 23, as to Byrnes, a graduate of the class of 1908, the class after Schuyler's: -- "Rollie Byrnes, whose summer residence was at Watch Hill, R.I., his wife and two daughters were victims of the storm. Rollie survived after being taken unconscious from the water, but Mrs. Byrnes and the girls were lost."

*H. M.*

᛫ ᛫ ᛫

---

1. Of the areas around New York City, Long Island suffered by far the most damage from the Hurricane of '38. The center of force came ashore some 100 miles east of the city at 3:30 P.M., September 21, and tracked directly north, meaning that Huntington lay right in its path. According to *The New York Times*: "The devastation exceeded anything ever before experienced there....Almost all of Long Island was plunged into darkness in the late afternoon. Along the shores the storm piled heavy seas over summer bungalows and highways. In the interior, for the whole length of the island, trees were uprooted and strewn over highways, live wires were down on all sides, streets and cellars were flooded from the unprecedented fall of rain, and communications and transport lines were completely disrupted." Some 54 of the 500 or so people killed by the hurricane were killed on Long Island.

# To Laura

Huntington, Sunday, January 24, 1939, Anno Domini

Dear Laura[1]

I am perhaps too careful in writing "New York, N.Y." It serves to remind me that the world is often governed with little wisdom.

Long ago a president named Cleveland appointed a postmaster-general named Key.[2]

This man Key suddenly announced that every letter must say, expressly, for what state it is destined. If it does not, back it goes for better direction. In vain the postmasters pleaded. "Thousands of letters are directed to 'Philadelphia' or to 'New York.'["] "No,["] said Key, one of the ultimate asses of Christendom. "It is not the duty of the post office to guess what state the letter-writer has in mind. Dump all letters that do not name a state."

Another man I dislike was [sic] John C. Calhoun.

He graduated at Yale in 1804 in the class of your great-great-grandfather, Dirck Cornelius Lansing. Calhoun was an ardent advocate of the right of secession. He thought the central government should be weak & the state governments strong & that every state should have a right to secede. Our Civil War went far, but, I think, not far enough, in strengthening the central government.

Affectionately

Newell Martin

🙵 🙵 🙵

1. Granddaughter Laura Grinnell Martin, daughter of Myra and Grinnell, then 13 years old.
2. David McKendree Key (1824-1900). Lieutenant-Colonel in Confederate Army. Appointed U.S. senator from Tennessee in 1875 to succeed Andrew Johnson; U.S. postmaster-general 1877-80, meaning he was a Hayes rather than Cleveland appointee. The directive was issued in the summer of 1879, and occasioned an entertaining letter from Mark Twain to the editor of the *Hartford Courant* (Twain was of course a Hartford resident). The letter in turn occasioned an almost equally entertaining reply from one Thomas B. Kirby, personal secretary to the postmaster-general, and was followed by yet another round of exchanges.

# To Molly

March 9, 1933

Molly. Tear up this & throw it in your ash can. Young girls that are free from superstition are not invited for dinners & dances. Any letter from me, especially if it says anything against Shamans & Devil Worship, tear it up.

Dear Molly
    I sent you my tract on the efficacy of prayer. Read it once a week, but do not let Miss Fowler or Miss Neely see it. When in church, with Miss Fowler, say to yourself, internally these words: "Primeval man, even before he ceased to be bored, learned to make a sort of shelter for himself. Thousands of years passed by before he learned to make, also, a stable for his horse, a kennel for his dog, & a sty for his pig. Then, at the campfire, spoke up the Old Man of the tribe & the Medicine Man, the shrewd fellows that did no work.
    'Your god, that sends the rain & ripens the corn, has no kennel, sty or other shelter. If you wish him not to wander away, you will build for him the biggest kind of hut & we will live in it with him & worship him. You must put a dozen young girls there, to do the housework, & no end of provisions.' Hence, cathedrals, nunneries, hymn-books & The Book of Common Prayer."

Affectionately

*Newell Martin*

⁂

*The following item from the United Press was clipped to the top of this letter. "LeBourget Airport, Paris. March 9. Eleven tons of gold in eight airplanes arrived from Amsterdam tonight. Three tons were dispatched by airplane immediately for the Bank of England in London."*

March 9, 1933

Dear Molly
    Mr. Winston Churchill, in "Amid These Storms" says, justly, that this prophecy, made by Tennyson, nearly a hundred years ago, when philosophers said that flying is impossible, is the

high-water-mark of sound foretelling.

W. Churchill is a pious goose in some ways, but he admits that Tennyson has put to shame those feeble-minded Hebrew prophets.

Tell Miss Fowler that it will delight her to read the chapter on Moses in Churchill's "Amid These Storms." (Between you & me it is ridiculous. He admires Gladstone's "Impregnable rock of Holy Scripture." Huxley punctured that book when I was a boy. Churchill, like most brilliant politicians, knows nothing about science & thinks that religions are important. He does not know that they are diseases, masquerading as remedies.)

Tell Miss Fowler to buy FOWLER'S "Modern English Usage" & to keep it where every girl can refer to it every hour. It should be entitled "What Every Well-Bred Girl Should Know Before She Speaks."

Affectionately

Newell Martin

ૐ ૐ ૐ

Turkey Lane
Huntington, N.Y.
April 21, 1932

Dear Molly

Jonnie's birthday party yesterday was an agreeable gathering. All the young women were entertaining & well-conducted. The superiority of women to men was proved again, as usual. There was no contention and no violence. There were no harsh words. Everybody was happy, polite & affectionate.

Eight boys or 11 boys, on the other hand, would have made a scene of horror & tumult, even if the Stowell boys had been absent. Tennis, jumping races & croquet were carried on with charming effect.

Croquet I have found dull usually, but these young ladies introduced a new feature, which you might try at St. Timothy's, & which should make croquet the most popular of outdoor sports. As 8 were playing, some of the girls, who were fairly clever gymnasts, while waiting for their turn, on the side-lines, did cart-wheels & summersets & stood on their heads. The effect, on a wide lawn, is picturesque & entertaining.

I thank you for taking the trouble to go to a speakeasy to collect for me anti-prohibition literature.

The other day, coming home in a cab with Harto, I picked up Josephine & a nice Jewish friend of hers who lives in Carley Avenue, & brought them both to their homes. Nice girls.

Jane Martin & Ardie Meyer lunched with us today. charming women.

Give my love to Miss Neely.

Affectionately,

*Newell Martin*

ᴥ ᴥ ᴥ

June, 1932 [What a year][1]
Dear Molly
Tell your teacher that you inherited your hand of write from me. Spare no effort to improve. Try to write like your mother or your sister, Jonny, or your Aunt Janet. Many a girl has written to some worthy young man, offering her affections, & been refused, on account of the gracelessness of her pen. Horace Greeley[2] & Rufus Choate[3] wrote bumly; but they never had to ask for favors. Nothing is so unseemly as an unladylike, unwomanly, handwriting.

Shakespeare had a bum hand of write, but it is doubted whether he wrote his own plays. Einstein, Willard Gibbs, Isaac Newton, Darwin & your grandmothers had a prepossessing hand of write.*

Affectionately

*Newell Martin*

* This phrase, you will remember, was John Silver's.[4]

ᴥ ᴥ ᴥ

1. No reference for Martin's bracketed comment; Molly 17 years old.
2. Horace Greeley (1811-1872), famous American newspaper editor, founder of the *Herald Tribune* in 1841.
3. Rufus Choate (1799-1859), lawyer, acknowledged head of the Massachusetts bar; state senator; U.S. House of Representatives 1831-1834; U.S. Senator 1841-1845. Greeley and Choate notorious for writing "bumly," the latter's "singular and celebrated" handwriting being some of the most hieroglyphic on record.
4. *Treasure Island*, Chapter XXIX. When the other mutineers try to depose Silver, he queries of the Black Spot and its accompanying message, "Your hand o'write, George?"

Telephone
Huntington 1484

Nov. 18, 1932

Dear Molly;

I have been reading a novel about an ancient castle where, at night, everything, in a ghostly manner, creaked and clanked. Your mother has given me your room[5] which, like the rest of your house, dates from the revolutionary war, when Nathan Hale and George Washington used to drink to excess here together.[6]

Nothing could be more terrifying than your ancient ramshackle room at midnight. The floor between the 2 beds creaks, spectrally. The curtains, all of which have broken ribs, rattle and groan, like the garrets of the haunted Dak Bungalow, in Kipling's story.[7] One knob is off the 4th bureau drawer, and the hole where the knob ought to be, stares at me gloomily, in the moonlight, like the eyes of a one-eyed ghost.

The window-frames rattle, like dry bones in the Valley of Golgotha [Calvary] and I have to block them with Bermuda wedges.[8]

I have no time to write to you because all my time is taken up with arthritis. I don't care who is president until they make a law for chloroforming us arthritics.

I care nothing for you or anybody, when my whole time and attention, as the lawyers say, is taken up with my own sufferings. I am going to give up the rest of my life to drink and self-indulgence as did the good men of the 18th Century.

Affectionately

Newell Martin

NM:HM[9]

ಜ ಜ ಜ

---

5. When the Martin's left their farm in Connecticut, they moved to a house in Huntington, Long Island, just across a small pond from Molly's family.
6. Not possible, Hale and Washington never having met. But there was a tavern at Huntington connected by hearsay with Hale's reputed (and disputed) capture there. See Section Eleven - "Harrisburg Analytical Laboratory."
7. In "My Own True Ghost Story" Rudyard Kipling has a rat running inside the ceiling cloth and a piece of loose window sash banging in the breeze create the illusion of a spectral billiard game. A dak route, in India, is one for post or transport by relay, and dak-bungalows are situated along it for travelers' convenience.
8. Possibly match folders brought back from Martin trips to Bermuda, (?)
9. Several of the letters are typed with penciled corrections in Martin's handwriting. Suspect at this date the initials "HM" are not those of a typist, but may stand for "himself," or for Helen Meyer. Although, as his arthritis worsened, some of his correspondence was, according to family members, typed by others.

March 11, 1933

Dear Molly

1. On Wednesday, at 1/40th of a cent per point, I lost 40 cents to your parents, at contract, not because they are so clever, but because nobody else will play with the aged so I become rusty & unskilful. Schopenhauer condemns cards as a waste of time.[10] When one gets to be 80 he realizes that nothing has been worthwhile or harmless except what seemed a waste of time.

2. Before the war one day I was with Fred Wells, (Judge Wells, who wrote that stirring tale of adventure, the Cruise of the Shanghai, & who was killed in Park Avenue.)[11]

I said "Fred, who is that playing backgammon with George Hazen?"[12] He said, "that is Von." I said "Von What?" And he said "Von Utassy. Everybody calls him Von." Vons were never numerous with us. Even Von Briesen,[13] Sol Stanwood Menken's father-in-law, used to be called Briesen.[14] But Vans were numerous. People like Van Brunt, Van Zandt & Van Tuyl[15] were often called Van. As to Von Utassy, I knew him well.[16]

10. Arthur Schopenhauer (1788-1860), *The World as Will and Idea* (1818), Vol. I, Section 57, "This need [of ordinary mankind] for exciting the will [as opposed to taking pleasure in pure knowledge] shows itself particularly in the invention of card-playing, which is in the truest sense an expression of the wretched side of humanity." (Translated by E.F.J. Payne [N.Y.: Dover, 1958], p. 314).

in pure knowledge] shows itself particularly in the invention of card-playing, which is in the truest sense an expression of the wretched side of humanity." (Translated by E.F.J. Payne [N.Y.: Dover, 1958], p. 314.)

11. Frederick DeWitt Wells (1874-1929), New York City lawyer, New York assemblyman 1906; judge New York municipal court 1908-1918, then returned to private practice. In 1924, with a crew of four, sailed a 47-foot ketch across the Atlantic via Norway, Iceland, Labrador, and Nova Scotia, per the Viking route; the voyage was described in the book Martin cites (N.Y.: Minton, Balch & Co., 1925). Wells, though not the *Shanghai*, survived shipwreck in a hurricane off Nova Scotia, only to be killed by an automobile in New York City.

12. See Section Four - "Spinach and Zweiback."

13. Arthur von Briesen (1843-1920), New York City lawyer, president New York City Legal Aid Society.

14. Sol Stanwood Menken (1870-1954), New York City lawyer active in the movement for municipal reform. Married in 1899 to Gretchen (?-1938), daughter of Arthur von Briesen.

15. Probably Charles H. Van Brunt (1835-1905), New York City lawyer and judge; justice of New York Supreme Court 1883-1905.

Probably Clarence Duncan Van Zandt (1853-1926), mayor of Rochester, New York 1922-1926. [*Note:* Martin's mother was a Van Zandt.]

Possibly George Casey Van Tuyl (1872-1938), Albany banker.

16. George d'Utassy (1870-1935), New York City publisher of, among others, *Cosmopolitan, Hearst's Magazine, Harper's Bazaar, Good Housekeeping*, and the *Illustrated Daily News*. Member University, Harvard, Rockaway clubs. According to his Times obit, George was the son of an Anton W. d'Utassy. A clipping from the *Herald Tribune* was enclosed with the letter, with the headline: quotes Babetta d'Utassy/And W. A. Castle 2d/To Wed on June 24."

The years rolled by & dynasties fell. One day I spoke to George about Von Utassy. "No, you must not say that," said George. "It is D'Utassy now." I used to be well acquainted with a young lawyer, Ellis Yates Samuel. One morning he laid on my desk a new card, Ellis S. Yates. You have a lot of Hebrews, Germans & negroes among your ancestors. But they are more than 1500 years back & no record reports them.

Affectionately

*Newell Martin*

ta ta ta

Jan 1934

Dear Molly

I send you the editorial.[17] Better keep it[18] to show to your nephews & your nieces, when you tell them that in your youth, you improved every hour.

We had a grand celebration, when Dean Gates christened you in Grace Church Chantry. Most of our dear friends were there; & most of them now are in hell or heaven. Sunday before last Gates preached in the Cathedral (A) against the habit young girls have of drinking at bars & (B) against birth control. Not that there is any connection between the 2 sins. Except that it is a sin to have babies & a mistake to take more than 1 drink at any 1 bar.

*Newell Martin*

### The Needs of Bryn Mawr

That small but distinguished institution of American learning, Bryn Mawr College, is about to embark on a campaign for a million-dollar fund. The sum seems ridiculously tiny, considering the vast gifts with which men's colleges have been enriched. But such is the plight of women's colleges generally. Bequests to them have been relatively few in number and limited in size.

There is all the more reason, therefore, why this Bryn Mawr effort should meet with a ready and

---

17. The Needs of Bryn Mawr," Jan. 6, 1934, *Herald Tribune*. Reprinted following this letter. Possibly written by Martin.
18. She did!

generous response from every friend of education. Here is a college, a pioneer in its field, which has held true to the highest standards through every shift of method and ideal. It has chosen to remain a small college, carefully limiting its enrollment upon a scholarly basis. To be accepted as a student at Bryn Mawr is a diploma in itself. It has stressed not less the maintenance of an able faculty and has counted among its professors ranking figures in the educational world.

The prospective campaign is directed primarily toward the securing of a new science building. The present structures have become grossly inadequate and the new plans are urgently needed upon every practical ground. More than that, as might be expected from such an institution of true learning, the new project is designed to unite all cognate subjects under one roof in pursuit of a new co-ordination of the natural sciences. The necessity for such development is obvious. As the old lines between physics and chemistry have broken down and such topics as bio-chemistry and geophysics have come to the fore, the borderlands between the older fields of research have become the most fruitful sources of study and discovery.

The maintenance of a graduate school has been a powerful factor in the success of Bryn Mawr in retaining both its ablest students and its most distinguished teachers. The new science building will be a powerful and inspiring aid to undergraduates and postgraduates alike. It should be not less a highly valuable experiment and object lesson for American education generally.

It is a privilege to record the progress of this outstanding college and to bespeak aid for its needs. Its students happen to be women, but its service is to the whole country, in developing brilliant students, wise teachers and women of intellect and leadership in every field. We are confident that the response to its forthcoming appeal will be instant and generous.

Aug. 3, 1936
Dear Molly

You and your sisters probably never heard of Ted Coy.[19] In this connection I may remark that the most famous of Yale oarsmen was Wilbur Bacon of the 1860's.

One of the members of his Yale crew was my dear friend Davis.[20]

The most famous of American oarsmen was Bob Cook. I gave him his first lesson in rowing.[21] He died, after a successful business career, which met with only one serious interruption. It was interrupted once, with a hatchet.[22] Ted Coy was the most famous of the Yale football players.[23] Walter Camp was the most famous of Yale football players.[24] Ted Coy flourished about 27 years ago. He was more or less idolized lionized. Even runners, in athletics, are idolized!

The H.T. [*Herald Tribune*], this morning, publishes a photograph of the finish of the 100 meters dash yesterday. You would think that, in any 100 meters dash of a group of world-famous athletes, all the racers would be close together. How can a man get far in front, in 10 seconds?[25]

But there was my admired negro, so far in front that

---

19. Edward H. Coy (1888-1936; Yale'10). Captain of his freshman football team; subsequently outstanding member of the the baseball, track, and football teams; captain of the latter his senior year. In later life involved in a wide variety of business concerns, including a stint as a Fuller Brush salesman during the first four years of the Depression.

20. Fred Davis ('77) was treasurer of his Class Boat Club in his sophomore year, and subsequently secretary; Newell Martin, during his sophomore year, was secretary and treasurer of his Class Boat Club. See Section Fourteen - "Six Summits."

21. Bob Cook entered Yale class of '75, as did Martin, spent the 1872-1873 college year in England, and joined the class of '76. Captained Yale crew all four of his college years. Cook brought to Yale the English varsity stroke universally employed by American crews for over a half-century; adapting it to the "physical limitations of American boys." That his first lessons in rowing should have come from Martin is worthy of note. Martin, on October 21, 1871, with his brother Pascal, Yale '72, won the double scull race in the Yale annual regatta in a time of 16' 43" decreased by handicap to 16' 18".

22. Unable to locate wielder of hatchet or circumstances related to this "interruption."

23. In 1907-1910.

24. Walter Camp: (1859-1925; Yale '80). Captain of his freshman baseball and football teams; subsequently outstanding varsity football player (1877-1880; captain junior and senior years); also rowed crew and represented Yale in tournament tennis. Later president of New Haven Clock Co.; author of books on bridge, football, and Yale; and Yale football coach for some 30 years, retiring in 1914.

25. A newspaper photograph dated August 3, 1936, does indeed show Jesse Owens setting the world record some four yards ahead of the second place winner. Jesse Owens (1913-1980), took the gold medal in the 100-meter dash in 10.3 seconds at the Berlin Olympics. He also took the gold in the 200-meter, broad jump, and relay.

spectators were falling asleep in their chairs before the second man came to the tape.

*h. M.*

ta ta ta

Huntington, L. I., N. Y., U.S.A.
August 14, 1936

Miss Molly Meyer
c/o Mrs. Schuyler M. Meyer
Bennett's Travel Bureau, Inc.
Copenhagen, Denmark

Dear Molly,
Deeply have I been impressed by what a man told me about an Italian, visiting France, who was accused, whether justly or not, I do not know, of some felony. He did not have much money and he did not speak French. At last, found guilty, he was imprisoned, and, later, sent to Devil's Island, off the Coast of Cayenne. He could not speak the language of his fellow-convicts, no conversation broke the tedium of his long days.

About him were sand-hills and sea-beaches. No forest, no groves, no flowers. In his ears, night and day, thundered, unceasing, the dull war of the surf.

'Tell me no more', said I to the narrator. 'Your story moves me deeply.'

That poor devil of a convict endured exactly what my granddaughters are suffering, today, at great expense, at the north end of Denmark. And none of them have ever been accused of any kind of felony.

Schuyler put a clause in the Dicks' lease to the effect that they were to keep the tennis court in order. They never play tennis; but their promise is sacred; so, at all hours, I see some toiling Dick, on her hands and knees, grubbing up weeds. I am sorely tempted to free the poor devils from their toil. I shall rush out and say: 'All Schuyler wanted was to escape expense and trouble. Let the weeds grow till Molly and Jonny come back.'

It delights me to hear how much happiness you have with the Benevolent Bodenhoffs; and of the fury of the Danish populace when Mrs. Bodenhoff, for your happiness, translates all the play, step by step, in a clear firm voice, into idiomatic English.

The next time the Danish populace expresses any displeasure

as to these translations, speak up and tell them that this is a gorgeous opportunity for them to improve their English.

The father of the Meyer children has been kind by letting us read their letters. But it makes me anxious when young girls write promptly. I fear it is a sign that they are not swimming and dancing sufficiently. Nothing sadder than to see a young girl, deserted by the human race, sitting down in front of the raging North Sea, to write to her grandfather.

Your Uncle Percy[26] sailed the Seven Seas in Mr. Merle-Smith's boat, the other day; and took Bear with him; and won the day's race; and was complimented, the next day, on his skillful seamanship, by the New York papers.[27]

The Seven Seas, you will remember, is a big boat and came in first in this year's Bermuda race.

Your precious box of Bryn Mawr accumulated learning, is in the second drawer of the taller bureau, in my bed-room. If I go to heaven before you come back, write or telegraph, reminding your grandmother to save those papers.

Your E.S.U. papers are in the same drawer.

It is lucky that you are not sailing about the European Coasts. In fact, you are not quite safe anywhere in or about Europe. Consider that poor devil of an English woman in her pleasure boat, somewhere near Biarritz, where your Aunt Jane used to live. She was bombarded by the Admiral Cervera for half an hour. Consider her husband, who was blown into Kingdom Come.

Your mother must have smiled, at this quaint exploit of the Admiral Cervera. After his death, as in his life, the name of Admiral Cervera is linked with nothing but blunder and disaster.[28]

Dr. Fleming, who used to adorn the Chapel of the Intercession (founded by me; don't sneer; Dean Gates says it was founded by

---

26. "Uncle Percy" (Percy Weeks) was the husband of Molly's father's sister and a consummate sailor.
27. On August 13, 1936, Van S. Merle-Smith's 12-meter sloop *Seven Seas* was the overall winner of the first leg of the New York Yacht Club competition, beating, among others, the America's Cup defender *Rainbow* captained by Harold S. Vanderbilt and taking the George E. Roosevelt's Cup.
28. On July 3, 1898, the Spanish Admiral, Pascual Cervera, in command of four armored cruisers and three destroyers led his squadron out of Santiago (Cuba) Harbor, there meeting an American fleet. The Americans suffered slight losses; Cervera's seven ships were all destroyed. As for the "poor English woman:" on August 9, 1936, retired British naval officer Captain Rupert Savile and his wife, sailing their yacht near Gijon in northern Spain were first bombarded by Loyalist shore batteries and then, when they moved out to sea, by the Rebel cruiser *Admiral Cervera*. After what Mrs. Savile described as some 50 shells, the Cervera finally scored a hit, killing the captain and seriously wounded his wife. The British government lodged a strong protest.

me),[29] now a great light of Trinity, has come out with an appeal to the clergy to stop preaching for two years.

'Silence, with these sermons', says he. 'They drive people out of the church.'

Dr. Fleming makes me smile. I could have told him all that, 60 years ago. Nobody ever offered to pay me $20,000 a year for saying that no sermon ever did anybody any good.

*Kewell Martin*

ta ta ta

Sept. 13, 1936

Dear Molly

Welcome to this ruined country, doomed to be the stamping ground of Fascists & Papists. I have in the high bureau in my bed-room, Dean Manning's letter to you, postmarked June 19, & a vast box of mss., belonging to you. I write this so that these papers may be found at once, if I die before you come here.

Welcome, indeed

*K. M.*

ta ta ta

Sept. 17, 1936[30]

Dear Molly

The Constitution was adopted, by the Convention,
Sept. 17, 1787.
That is regarded, not quite properly, as its birthday.
Today, therefore, it is 149 years old.
Next year there will be fireworks & speeches. Disregard the speeches.
When you become a statesman, never make a speech longer than the Gettysburg Address.

*K. M.*

P.S.  Welcome.

29. See Section Eight - "Letter to Molly, (March 14, 1933)."
30. Martin's birthdate, September 17, 1854.

*A clipping (a book review) from an unidentifiable newspaper accompanied this letter. Martin drew an arrow to the title of the book* Adele De Leeuw, A Place for Herself *(N.Y.: Macmillan, [?],) and wrote in the margin, "Dear Molly: I am thinking of buying this. If I do, I'll lend it to you." There is no evidence whether Martin bought or loaned the book.*

Second letter to<br>
Molly Meyer<br>
39 East 78th St.<br>
Oct. 19, 1937

Dear Molly,

1. "Silver and gold have I none," said the apostle, but I am always ready to give advice.

2. Never write down anything that is not absolutely legible. I note that your address is 39 East 78th St - & that your telephone number is Regent 4-2095. If this is wrong, let me know. If it is O.K., send no answer.[31] Your handwriting leaves me in doubt as to your address.

3. With heroic enterprise you went to see a publisher, one Shuster. I hear that he said to you something like this: "My office is over run with intelligent, highly educated women. I advise you to go into the book business, on your own account. You will then learn, from experience, how hard it is to tell nice young women that you have no place for them in your office."

You should have run your eye over some of Shuster's writings before you went to see him.[32]

Remember this: Most publishers have been authors. They never refer to their own books.

But, in some mysterious way, an author always knows it, if his visitor never heard of the author's books.

If I ever give you a letter to a publisher, remember this & glance over some of his books, before you go to him.

R. M.

ta ta ta

---

31. Three arrows placed in the margin pointing to "send no answer."
32. W. Morgan Shuster wrote but one book, *The Strangling of Persia*.

Sunday
Aug. 14, 1938

Dear Molly
 We were impressed by your goodness in going to see the girl who had been driven by calamity to Saranac.
 I shall sit with your mother this afternoon. I do not read aloud, usually.
 It is dangerous for a stuldbug [?] to use his throat much; just as it is dangerous for him to climb stairs. My average time for going up the stairs of this small house is two minutes. But I shall today, read to your mother *Pippa Passes*. I shall read slowly & your mother will say: "God's in his heaven." But 9 scientific men out of each ten say that this is quite incorrect. And the astronomers of the 20th Century have shown that there are hundreds of millions of universes, all of them free from any perceptible gods.
 "'All's well with the world.' All's well with some parts of the States. But 'the world' seems in a bad way."

Affectionately,

Newell Martin

≫ ≫ ≫

# To Janet

March 22, 1934
Thursday -
second day of Spring
Huntington, L.I., N.Y.

Mlle. Janet Martin[1]
Hotel Moderne, Parvis Saint Maurice, Lille (Nord), France[2]

Dear Janet:
 The 'criminal class', the 'gangsters', or 'organized crime', this week rubbed out Fred Goetz, the most successful of our younger

---

1. Granddaughter, born 1921.
2. Probably in Lille to visit the Palais des Beaux-Arts, famous for its collection of Flemish Renaissance paintings. The square (i.e., *parvis*) of St. Maurice's (14th-15th century) lies only three or four blocks away.

college graduates.[3] He was found in your favorite town, Cicero.[4] He lay in the street, perforated, like a colander. So many bullets had lodged in his body that the reporters got tired of counting them. He was thirty-four. At the University of Illinois, he was a 'star athlete', and an 'honor scholar'. Only once in his brilliant career has he been jailed.

You have read Hemingway's instructive story, 'The Killers'.[5] Goetz was the commander-in-chief of all the 'Killers'. He had risen to be head of the execution department of the associated gangsters of America. He and his henchmen executed the large group of gangsters who were massacred a few years ago in a Chicago garage.[6] I wish some newspaper would have enough enterprise to find what answers Goetz used to send to the questions sent out by his class secretary, as to his occupation, prosperity and income.[7] How many hundred people he executed, in his business career, we do not know-nor have we been told why he was deposed. All we know is that he was removed from his high office quietly and decisively. The "gangbusters" are efficient in removing associates who have become lax or too ambitious or in any way inconvenient. That makes me admire 'gangsters' more than legislators and clergymen and doctors and judges.

The offense for which Goetz had been jailed was rape, America's favorite sport. I advocate executing the nearest clergymen, the nearest lawyer and the nearest legislator in each case of rape. Then the suppression of prostitution would cease, and rape would be obsolete, as it is in civilized countries.

*   *   *

3. Fred C. Goetz (1897-1934), in classic gangster fashion, had received four shotgun blasts from a passing automobile in the Chicago suburb of Cicero two days previous. On him were found a $1000 bill and forged membership cards to a number of prestigious Chicago clubs; these were made out to "J. George Zeigler," under which alias Goetz had been receiving mail at a neighborhood bar. Goetz was wanted at the time not only for his involvement in the St. Valentine's massacre (cf. below) but for an alleged part in the killing of the gangster Frank Nash and four guards enroute to Leavenworth; also for bank robbery and attempted rape. He had served as a 2nd Lt. in the U.S. Army Air Force in WWI, and graduated with a good record from the University of Illinois in 1923.
4. Cicero, Illinois, western suburb of Chicago.
5. Hemingway's story first appeared in *Scribner's* in 1927, and was included in *Men Without Women* the following year.
6. The famous St. Valentine's Day Massacre, Feb. 14, 1929, in which Al Capone eliminated the most important members of the rival gang of George "Bugs" Moran. Goetz/Zeigler was Capone's chief deputy in this operation.
7. Martin was his Yale '75 class secretary for some twenty-five years. We do not know what appeared in the University of Illinois alumni material, but at the time of his death Goetz was living in a posh Chicago neighborhood under the name "George B. Seibert" (with a "Mrs. Seibert," who promptly disappeared). Other persons in the apartment building described Mr. Seibert as a cultured gentleman and loving husband, possessing studious tastes and a pronounced bent for landscape gardening.

3 April 1934

Dear Janet

The Newberry Diary,[8] written by a young woman of exactly my age has had a great run in Chicago. Julia Newberry cast a thoughtful eye on Seth Low,[9] Nourse,[10] Longworth,[11] the Fred Wards,[12] Ryerson (31, 50, 51, 81).[13] She records the declaration of war, France against Germany, July, 1870.[14]

I made no note of that in any diary. I was waiting in West Haven for Edward Whitney,[15] who was to swim with me. He was late in meeting me. He had waited to learn a little more about the declaration of war. Very old-fashioned. Hereafter, wars will be finished before they are declared.[16]

Julia stayed at Vevey; but not at our favorite Trois Couronnes.[17] She read "Jane Ayer"[18] and told of a city being 'under marshal law'. The Chicago Fire was in October, 1871.[19] It made little impression on us Yale freshmen, in October. In after years we gave more thought to it.

⁂

8. *Julia Newberry's Diary*, edited and with an introduction by Margaret Ayer Barnes and Janet Ayer Fairbank (Chicago: Norton, 1933). Newberry (1854-1876), a Chicago resident, began the diary in 1869 and ended it in October, 1871. She was sent east to school in 1870 and spent the following year in Europe.
9. Seth Low (1850-1916), Brooklyn-born political reformer, president of Columbia University 1889-1901, mayor New York City 1901-03, when he reformed the police and the city's schools, and reorganized its finances.
10. Henry Stedman Nourse (1832-1903; Harvard '53), civil engineer responsible for several important works including the Pennsylvania Railroad bridge across the Susquehanna; member Massachusetts legislature 1883-8; author of several books.
11. Nicholas Longworth (1844-1890; Harvard '66), judge; member Ohio Supreme court 1881-3; described as possessing a wide variety of interests including poetry, chemistry, woodcarving, photography.
12. Possibly Frederick Gamaliel Ward ( no dates), father of F. T. Ward. See Section Ten -- "As to W. Morgan Schuster."
13. Arthur Ryerson (1851-1912; Yale '71), lawyer practicing in Chicago; involved in important railroad litigation and advisor to a number of estates and charitable trusts. Died in the sinking of the *Titanic*. (The first of the four page numbers following "Ryerson" apparently should read "41."
14. Entry of July 17, 1870 reads: "France has declared war against Prussia, & the troops are on the march!"
15. See Section Ten -- "The Climenole."
16. Editor's Note: Martin died November 15, 1941, just 22 days before the Japanese strike at Pearl Harbor; unlike many Americans, he might not have been surprised.
17. Julia stayed at the Grand Hotel there in September, 1870, when she recorded Napoleon III's surrender at Sedan.
18. Martin error. Diary entry of Sept. 17, 1871, giving a list of favorite books includes "*Jane Eyre*, and all that Charlotte Bronte ever wrote."
19. Entry for Oct. 17, 1871: "Yes the whole North Side is in ashes, & every memory connected with my home is gone, every association, every link; never never to be again, irreparably & irrevocably gone. No one ever loved their home more than I did mine; I loved every angle in the house, every carpet, every table, every picture on the walls, every

474   SELECTED LETTERS

6 April, 1934
Huntington, New York.

To
Miss Margaret D. Whitney, New Haven, Connecticut[20]
Miss Janet Martin, Lille (Nord), France
Mrs. Grinnell Martin, City of Mexico, Mexico

I have drafted fragments of letters to each of you; but I am infirm today and the scraps I have written look ragged. So I have written them out with my own hand and consolidate them all in one letter and have it copied and send it to each of you. You don't need to read any of it. It is sent only to remind you that I am grateful to each of you and would lay aside my pencil and write with pen if I were a bright active young sexagenarian. I am grateful to Margaret for telling me how Simon has gone to Washington, to confer with many hopeful sans-culottes.[21] I am grateful to Myra for writing from the ship when she should have been drinking and dancing. I have been studying Grace line advertisements in Time. I infer from them that, in the Caribbean, only colored girls wear any covering over their legs.[22] I am grateful to Janet for political news and for gloomy facts as to Northern France. If the Church and the Fascists get control of France[23] I shall insist on leaving this world. There

---

book in the library, the stairs, the basement, the garret. When the house was rebuilt Papa's room was left untouched, & it was so exactly as it has always been, that his presence seemed to be there; it was sacred, & that is gone! And then my studio, my beautiful studio, & the private staircase, & my room that I have looked forward to furnishing myself in pink & grey." The fire destroyed her previous diaries.

20. Martin's pen pal, sister of his good friend E. B. Whitney. See Section One – "Letters to Molly, April 18, 1936."
21. Simon Whitney (1904-82; Yale '25; Ph.D. '31), (Margaret Whitney's nephew.) economist, author, teacher; director of the Bureau of Economics of the Federal Trade Commission 1956-61; taught economics at New York University 1948-71 and elsewhere — including Harvard and Barnard — at various times; author of several books on the subject.  Most probably in Washington to confer with the National League of Women Voters regarding their election-year program aimed at the improvement of service by government personnel, the elimination of "wholesale" party patronage, and the reorganization of the country's "antiquated" tax system so as to provide monies for essential services in spite of diminished tax revenues.
22. Indefectible Gregory Audette reports, "Actually, two of the nine women in that season's Grace Line advertisement were wearing pants, surely anyhow the less usual costume at the side of a shipboard pool."
23. Cumulative discontent caused by the Depression, an unbalanced budget, high taxation, and fear of the Nazi menace, and fanned into flame by the Stavisky financial scandal, led to widespread rioting in France during late January-early February, 1934, culminating in the bloody Paris riot of February 7 that left 21 dead and 2,400 seriously

are only three or four comfortable corners left on the whole planet. Jalisco[24] or Kashmir,[25] there's where my wife and I shall wind up. We can live in a house-boat on the lake, in Kashmir, at two rupees a day.

I wrote to Janet about a new feature of our twentieth century life, crimes of violence committed for money by college men. Here are more. Two students of the Brooklyn University were convicted of a holdup, at a filling station, that paid them $18. In Massachusetts, two students of the M.I.T. were found guilty of highway robbery. They were members of a large, well-organized gang. This year recent graduates of Harvard and other colleges have been found guilty of robbery with violence.

I don't blame any of these young men. They are spotless innocents compared with the ruling class.

I studied under Burgess, a teacher of political science,[26] at Columbia, fifty-eight years ago. He retired to Newport. During the War, I had some friendly correspondence with him. He was a wise man. Wise men should never have children. The children may go wrong. It is all right for foolish people to have children, because the children may turn out wiser than their parents and may improve

---

wounded. These had caused the resignation of French Premier Edward Daladier and the formation of a new government. A general fear among the French working classes that the new government was authoritarian or proto-Fascist in character led in turn to a one-day nationwide strike. The actual French Fascist Party, led by Marcel Bucard, placed a very minor role in these events, vastly less than that of the French Communists and Socialists.

24. Mexican state, capital Guadalajara, bordering the Pacific Ocean.
25. Lake region between Afghanistan and Tibet in Southeast Asia, famous for houseboating and superb scenery.
26. John William Burgess (1844-1931). Fought in Civil War 1863-4, studied law and practiced briefly, then pursued historical studies in Germany. Accepted chair of history, political science, and international law at columbia University in 1876; founded and was first dean of the Columbia School of Political Science, a post he held until 1912.

His Civil War experience led him to dedicate his life to the substitution of international arbitration for war; he also had close ties with Germany in consequence not only of his graduate studies but of having been a visiting lecturer at various German and Austrian universities in 1914-15; he had in fact become a personal friend of Wilhelm II. In a letter to the *New York Times* (October, 1934), Burgess stated that the American conception of the Kaiser was "a monumental caricature of biographical literature," and in the following year or two strove — as he put it — to "preserve American neutrality" by writing books and articles presenting the German view. But after his name appeared on a list — made public by the FBI early in 1918 — of 33 Americans reported as important to the German government, for being at least potentially friendly to its cause, he immediately issued a repudiation stating that, "When relations with Germany became strained I followed my own country and had nothing further to say." (Burgess was #6 on the list; #1 was fellow Columbia professor W. R. Shepherd. See Section Six — "The Siamese Royal Commission.")

the family fortunes. Burgess was persecuted, in the war, but, at last, died, old and somewhat honored. Then his widow died. Her funeral procession, on its way to a New Jersey graveyard was halted, while a writ of ne exeat or something of that sort was served on her son, who was charged with neglecting his wife and child.[27] Moral: People free from superstition should have their remains burned and should not have funeral processions.

My granddaughter Janet excels in such studies and exercises as require a good brain and good legs. Unhappily, in the school gymnasium, a gymnastic instructor rashly permitted Janet to do certain stunts that brought on housemaid's knee. I have always thought that ailment should be called Nun's Knee, because it is often caused by excessive kneeling on stone floors. In Janet's case the ailment came on violently because Janet has had little practice in kneeling. After long costly and troublesome treatment Janet is now beginning to recover from Nun's Knee.

Florence Allen,[28] the Ohio judge, has been appointed by Roosevelt to the Circuit Court of Appeals. This is the highest post reached by an American woman. The only higher law office in the Federal service is a place on the Supreme Court bench. In New York (in compelling people to be chaste)[29] and in Washington (in compelling people to be dry)[30] women have shown that they can be quite as disagreeable and incompetent as men.

All the ivy leaves on our house have been killed by cold. But perhaps the roots of the vines will live. My grandfather[31] would have said; "This is a judgment on you. You have tempted providence by boasting that your ivy has climbed up over the top of Janet's

---

27. Ruth Payne Burgess (?-1934), a noted portrait painter and etcher, had died the preceding March 11. At her funeral on March 14, her son Elisha Payne Jewett Burgess was arrested as the procession was leaving Columbia's St. Paul's chapel by a warrant officer who had been seeking him for a year in connection with the non-support of a wife and ten-year-old daughter. Burgess was paroled in court until March 23, whereupon the funeral proceeded. Everything may have worked out, however, since he received $100,000 in his mother's will. *Ne exeat: Ne exeat provincia*, legal writ to prevent a debtor from leaving the jurisdiction of a court.
28. Florence Allen (1884-1966; A.B. Salt Lake College '04; L.L.B. New York University '13). Admitted to the Ohio bar 1913, became a judge in that state 1920, and was elected to the Ohio Supreme court 1922. She remained a member of the U.S. Sixth Circuit Court of Appeals until 1959; was most famous for a decision defending the right of the TVA to sell power at rates undercutting private competitors. Ardent defender of women's suffrage; author of three books, including a volume of memoirs.
29. Probably Mary M.K. (Mrs. Vladimir) Simkovitch (1867-1951), leader in New York City settlement work; and head of Greenwich (settlement) House, 1902-46; strong opponent of prostitution.
30. Probably Mabel Willebrandt. See Section Two – "Petition to Bannard."
31. See Section Sixteen – "Memorandum as to Reverend W.W. Martin."

chimney." It would surprise my grandfather if he could know what is expected of the new two hundred inch glass that Mr. Houghton is trying to cast, at Corning.[32] It is expected to tell us about universes which are far away; distant from us nine hundred million light years.

Governor Lehman has tried to diminish the law's delays.[33] Three years, four, five, or six, it takes, to give relief; and then, perhaps a miscarriage. This tells in favor of the rich. If I run over a laborer, I can wait six years for a judgment, while he starves. English barons complained about this sort of thing, in 1215. The King and the big barons used to delay the relief demanded by the little barons. It is ridiculous not to strike at the root of the evil. Disfranchise the lawyers. In China, in her golden age; and in Russia, in her golden age, lawyers were deprived of power.[34]

*Kewell Martin*

ta ta ta

---

32. The Mt. Palomar telescope, proposed and funded in 1928, was currently undergoing construction, and was completed in 1948. Alanson Bigelow Houghton (1863-1941), owner and proprietor of the Corning Glass Works, had served in the U.S. House of Representatives 1918-22 and been this country's first post-war ambassador to Germany 1922-28, but had returned to the management of the factory the year following.

33. Herbert H. Lehman (1873-1963), Democratic governor of New York 1932-42, U.S. senator 1949-57. In a special message to the legislature on March 7, 1934, he had suggested both temporary and permanent measures to speed up the judicial processes and render them less costly to the poor. The message actually called for no case to be delayed longer than four years.

34. Law in imperial China and tsarist Russia was a function of a combined executive and judiciary: there were to some extent codes of legal penalties, likewise rules for taking evidence and conducting legal proceedings generally; but a lawyer would have been merely someone expert in these, whose advice might be sought, not the one on whose adversarial competence a case might hang.

## 1935 Merry Christmas

*Martin's message was handwritten in dark black ink on the back of a panel cut from a carton of Chesterfield Cigarettes picturing a woman in white fur driving a reindeer pulling a sleigh with the words "Merry Christmas" and "Happy New Year" prominently displayed.*

This is from a communist, whose favorite author is Veblen[1] & who disapproves of "conspicuous waste" & also of any expenditure of money that does not increase human happiness; & who values Christmas as an ancient holiday invented by our forefathers, many centuries ago, far back in B.C., when they made the wondrous discovery of the Winter Solstice.[2]

ta ta ta

---

1. Thorstein (Bunde) Veblen (1857-1929; Ph.D. Yale '84), U.S. political economist and social scientist who is best-known for his theory of "conspicuous consumption"; i.e., that people are more interested in the status conferred by their purchases than in their utilitarian value.
2. The time in the Northern Hemisphere when the sun is farthest south of the equator; December 21 or 22.

# SIXTEEN

# APPENDIX

An Appreciation of W.A.P. Martin . . . 480

Relations . . . . . . . . . . . . . . . . . . 490

Phelps' Tribute to W.R. Martin . . . . . 494

Memorandum as to
    Reverend W.W. Martin . . . . . . . . 499

Dirck C. Lansing, D.D. . . . . . . . . . . 504

# An Appreciation of Dr. W.A.P. Martin[1]

By Hon. John W. Foster, '55 [2]
Secretary of State under President Harrison

When the cable from Peking, China, announced to the world the death on December, 18 last of William Alexander Parsons Martin, of the class of 1846, it recorded the end of the career, in his ninetieth year, of the greatest alumnus of Indiana University.

The University has produced many statesmen, clergymen, lawyers, instructors, authors, scholars, and soldiers, who have served well their generation and added luster to their Alma Mater; but a brief review of the life of Dr. Martin will show that no other of our graduates has combined all of these qualities, nor have few of them served their fellow-men with such distinction and usefulness.

Dr. Martin was born in Livonia, Washington County, Indiana, on April 10, 1827, and graduated from Indiana University in the class of 1846. His career in life was early chosen, as he had decided before graduation to follow the profession of his father, who was one of the first Presbyterian preachers in the territory of Indiana.[3] With a devotion to the Master and a heroism which cannot be too highly praised, he had asked to be sent as a missionary to China. Volunteering for the mission work in the Celestial Empire today is a very different thing from what it was seventy years ago. Then that great country was practically closed to foreigners. A few ports in the south had been opened to trade by the British cannon, but intercourse with the interior was forbidden, and foreigners were regarded with intense hatred. A few missionaries had reached the ports, but they had not secured a single Chinese communicant. When I was a student at the University ten years later, there was a legend amongst us that young Martin had won the heart of one of

---

1. Father of Newell Martin; the essay appeared in the *Indiana University Alumni Quarterly*, April, 1917 (Vol. IV, No.2).
2. John W. Foster (1836-Nov. 15, 1917, Indiana State '55; studied law at Harvard one year; L.L.D.'s Princeton '95, Wabash '95, Yale '96, University of Dakota '07), soldier and diplomat; Major 25th Indiana Volunteers; fought at Fort Donaldson, Shiloh, and other famous battles; rose to brevet colonel by end of Civil War. Appointed minister to Mexico by Grant 1873; minister to Russia 1880, Spain 1883. In 1890 became special agent to state department to assist in negotiations of reciprocity treaties. Secretary of State 1892-3; thereafter served on various special ambassadorships. Author four books on diplomacy.
3. See in this section "Memorandum as to Reverend W.W. Martin."

APPENDIX 481

the attractive daughters of our President, but that Dr. Wylie[4] refused to allow him to take her to that barbarian country so far away from home.

After a three years' preparation at the McCormick Theological Seminary,[5] then located at New Albany, at the age of twenty-two he, with his young wife,[6] sailed for his field of labor in a small sailing vessel, which was nearly five months in making the tedious journey around the Cape to its destination at Ningpo, a port in the south some distance below Shanghai. Here he spent several years devoted, with that assiduity which always marked his work, to the study of that most difficult of languages with its many dialects.

While thus engaged the second Opium War[7] waged by Great Britain against China occurred, and the American minister, Mr. Reid,[8] with the European representatives went to Tientsin, at the close of the war, to negotiate treaties with China. He had already engaged the services of Dr. S. Wells Williams,[9] a missionary of the American Board of Missions, who had played so important a part with Commodore Perry in the Japanese negotiations; but he also secured the services of Dr. Martin because of his intimate mastery of the Chinese language and the Mandarin dialect, who also accommodated the minister as interpreter and adviser. Through

---

4. Andrew Wylie (1789-1851), first president of Indiana College 1829-1851). (Name was changed to University 1838; became the state university 1852.) Wylie himself converted from the Presbyterian to Episcopalian church in 1841. Sources say nothing about his daughters beyond the fact that he had some.
5. Founded at Hanover, Indiana 1830, as part of Hanover College; moved to New Albany 1840; to Chicago 1859 as result of bequest by inventor and manufacturer Cyrus McCormick (1809-84). Renamed McCormick Theological Seminary 1886; Presbyterian Theological Seminary 1928.
6. Jane Van Zandt; later spelled Vansant (?-1893).
7. China's ban on the importation of opium and destruction of British-owned supplies of the drug at Canton in 1839 served as a pretext for the first Opium War of 1839-42. The real object was the ending of Chinese restrictions on foreign trade, and the 1842 Treaty of Nanking opened five major ports south of the Yangtze (including Ningpo) to the British, and ceded Hong Kong. The second Opium War (1856-58), fought by both the British and French, opened ports from the Yangtze north to Manchuria.
8. William Bradford Reed (not Reid) (1806-76; University of Pennsylvania '25). Taught history at University of Pennsylvania 1850-57; appointed minister to China latter year, where he negotiated the treaty of June 13, 1858, ending the second Opium War. Returned to U.S. and became a journalist — notably U.S. correspondent of the *London Times* — and author.
9. Samuel Wells Williams (1812-84). Went to China as a mission printer 1833; acquired mastery of both Chinese and Japanese and translated numerous works into those languages, as well as publishing in them works of his own. From 1855-76 secretary and interpreter to the American legation at Peking; in 1853-54 interpreter for Commodore Perry. Held Yale's first lectureship in Chinese literature, and afterwards headed Yale's Department of Oriental Studies, created for him in 1877.

the aid of these two missionaries he negotiated the treaty of 1858, which for half a century regulated the intercourse of the United States and China. In reporting the result of his negotiations to his government, Minister Reid, referring to the aid given him by these missionaries, said, "I could not but for this aid have advanced a step in the discharge of my duties."

In this connection it may not be out of place to notice briefly the services which American missionaries in China have been able to render their own government in that empire. When our first diplomatic minister, Caleb Cushing,[10] was sent to China in 1843, Dr. Peter Parker,[11] a medical missionary, and Rev. E. C. Bridgman,[12] both of the American Board[13] stationed at Canton, were appointed secretaries, and it was entirely though them that intercourse with the Chinese was carried on. Afterwards Dr. Parker acted as charge' of the Legation. I have mentioned the invaluable services rendered by Dr. S. Wells Williams as interpreter and adviser to Commodore Perry in Japan. For many years he was attached to our legation at Peking as interpreter and chargé. Dr. Martin, as we shall see, was often a valuable adviser to our legation during his long residence at that capital. And throughout the empire the American consuls have found our missionaries of the greatest value in the discharge of their duties. At present two ex-missionaries occupy important posts under our government, one as the head of the Bureau of Far-Eastern Affairs in the Department of State,[14] and the other as Chinese Secretary of our legation at

10. Caleb Cushing (1800-79; Harvard '17 [date is correct]). Member U.S. House of Representatives 1835-43. Appointed commissioner, later envoy extraordinary and minister plenipotentiary, to China 1843. Returned to U.S. after having circumnavigated the globe, 1844. U.S. Attorney-General 1852-57; thereafter held various diplomatic posts. Author several books.

11. Peter Parker (1804-88; Yale '31, L.L.D. '33). Studied medicine; was appointed mission physician to China by American Board of Commissioners of Foreign Missions (ABCFM). One of founders of Medical Missionary Society of China. Appointed secretary and interpreter to American legation by Cushing 1844, ending his connection with ABCFM, but continued to do hospital work until 1855. In that year appointed U.S. commissioner with plenipotentiary powers to negotiate a treaty regulating trade arrangements. Returned to U.S. 1857. Became member ABCFM 1871; regent Smithsonian Institute 1868.

12. Elisha Coleman Bridgman (1801-61; Amherst '21; Amherst Theological Seminary '29). Became missionary to China 1829, spending rest of life there. The preaching of Christianity being forbidden, he worked as a pioneering organizer in various educational works; edited Chinese-language journals and translated Western books. Assisted in formation of various missionary societies, including Medical Missionary Society.

13. That is, local chapter of American Board of Commissioners for Foreign Missions, itself created in 1810 to unify and regulate missionary activity of various U.S. religious denominations.

14. Edward Thomas Williams (1854-1944; B.D. Bethany College, West Virginia, '83).

Peking.[15]

Following soon after the treaty of 1858, negotiated with Dr. Martin's assistance, the Presbyterian Mission Board established a station at Peking, and in 1863 he was transferred to it. His accomplishments as a Chinese scholar soon brought him into intimate contact with the Chinese authorities, and in 1868 he was asked by the imperial government to establish the Tung Wen College, a school for the education of selected Chinese youths in international law and customs and in European languages.[16] He remained in charge of this college for twenty-six years, and it was a high honor conferred upon him and a marked recognition of his ability that, at the age of forty-one, he should be called to such an important task by this proud people who esteemed age and wisdom as necessarily associated. The graduates of this college were assigned to duty abroad as secretaries and interpreters of legations. Some of them rose to be diplomatic ministers, and others became connected with the Imperial Foreign Office, and they exercised an important influence in bringing the country out of its seclusion into the road to modern progress. While engaged in this work he prepared the famous Marquis Tseng, though not a student, for the duties of his post as minister to London and St. Petersburg.[17] Marquis Tseng proved the most distinguished of Chinese diplomatic

---

China missionary 1887-96; beginning latter year held various posts in Peking embassy, including secretary. Appointed chief of the state department's Division of Far Eastern Affairs 1913. In August, 1919, Williams testified to a Senate committee as to the reasoning behind and general effect of Wilson's Shantung decision at Versailles, saying he personally thought it unwise.

15. Charles D. Tenney (1857-1930; Dartmouth '78; studied at Oberlin Theological Seminary), China missionary 1882-6, subsequently presided over many Chinese institutions of learning of all levels, including presidency of the Imperial Chinese University at Tientsin. Twice Chinese Secretary at Peking, the second stint beginning 1914.

16. Tung Wen Kuan, established 1863 according to the *Encyclopedia Sinica*, was founded as a language school for the Peking Office for General Management, which oversaw all matters connected with foreign relations, and originally intended as simply offering joint instruction in Chinese and Western tongues. Subjects such as mathematics and political science gradually were introduced, however; and the College's eventual importance lay in its work in disseminating knowledge from and about the West, in part through a wide-ranging translation program. Tung Wen Kuan was merged with Peking University in the year following the end of the Boxer Rebellion.

17. Chi-Tse Tseng (1837-?), son of Tseng Kuo-Fan, chief Chinese general opposing Taiping rebels. Thoroughly educated in Chinese history, literature, and music; also had substantial backgrounding in Western science and English-language studies. Inherited title of *hou* on father's death, translated *Marquis* in West. Appointed minister to England and France 1878; Russia 1880: most famous diplomatic accomplishment being the conclusion of the 1881 Treaty of St. Petersburg concerning Russo-Chinese border. Recalled 1885; held various administrative posts; appointed head of Tung Wen Kuan 1889.

representatives.

When I visited Peking in 1894, I was cordially welcomed by its president, Dr. Martin, and the students of the college, learning that I was a fellow alumnus of the same institution in America with their president, tendered me a public reception accompanied by a unique and very flattering address, which beautifully engrossed in silk I brought away with me, as one of the most highly prized of the souvenirs of my visit to the Far East.

During the period of his long service as president of the college he translated into Chinese Wheaton's International Law,[18] and prepared a number of other books to be used by the students of this and other Chinese schools as textbooks, such as works on geography, arithmetic, natural philosophy, a history of Greece and also one of Rome, Evidences of Christianity, and others. These books have had a wide circulation in Chinese, and some of them have been translated into Japanese and Korean.[19]

In these years of service as president of the college he was made an unofficial adviser of the Foreign Office, and his knowledge of international law and foreign affairs was constantly availed of by the imperial officials. He also acted in the double capacity of an adviser of the American Legation at Peking. He was an intense American and was ever ready to help his countrymen in any way. During his long residence in China he became better acquainted with that vast country from personal visitation than any other individual, Chinese or foreigner; and the American minister[20] gladly resorted to him on many occasions for information and advice.

As illustrative of his varied activity and usefulness during

18. *Elements of International Law* by American lawyer and diplomat Henry Wheaton (1785-1848), 1st edition London 1836, numerous subsequent editions and translations, including Martin's, Peking 1864. (One Ryushu Takatani made another Chinese translation in 1876.) In W.A.P. Martin's A Cycle of Cathay, he quotes the French chargé d'affaires in Peking saying to Ned Burlingame concerning the Wheaton translation: "Who is this man who is going to give the Chinese insight into our European international law? Kill him--choke him off; he'll make us endless trouble."

19. Martin's major books translated into English are: *The Analytical Reader: A Short Method for Learning to Read and Write Chinese* (Shanghai: Presbyterian Mission Press, 1863); *The Hanlin Papers* (two series), Shanghai, 1880, 1894); *The Chinese* (1881); *Siege in Peking* (NY: Revell, 1900); *The Awakening of China* (NY: Doubleday, Page and Co., 1907); and *The Lore of Cathay* Second edition. (NY: Revell, 1912). In addition, he wrote more than 100 magazine articles, and contributed sections to more than 20 books.

20. While Martin often served as translator for American ministers to China, one Anson Burlingame (1820-1870), minister to China when Martin moved to Peking in 1863, was a professional colleague as well as a personal friend—the Martin and Burlingame families often were together for holidays. When Burlingame's appointment to China was terminated in 1868, he was appointed by Imperial decree to become Minister Plenipotentiary of the Chinese Empire.

this period, the story is told of his efforts to introduce the use of the telegraph into China. He secured a set of instruments, learned how to operate them, and then invited the high government officials to see the working of the new wonder. They came and witnessed his exhibition of it with unconcealed wonder and awe. When he urged them to adopt it one of the dignitaries is reported to have replied that China had gotten along without it for four thousand years and did not need it now. But the Doctor's persistency was crowned with success, and before his death he saw it extended to the remotest corners of the broad empire.

In 1898 the Chinese government determined to establish a vast university on a complete modern basis, and Dr. Martin was put in charge of the evolution of the plan, the establishment of the institution, and its administration. But the Boxer uprising which for a time paralyzed the imperial government and declared for the extermination of all foreigners, destroyed for a time at least all hope of the projected university. Dr. Martin, with the other foreign residents at Peking, had to take refuge in the British legation grounds, which were speedily converted into a defensive fortification. Here he enrolled himself as a soldier, shouldered his musket, and did duty in repelling the assaults of the Boxers and standing guard through many long nights of the siege, notwithstanding his advanced years, until rescued by the relief army of the international powers.

After peace was restored[21] Dr. Martin accepted an employment from the viceroy Chang Chi-tung,[22] the greatest of the Chinese rulers after the death of Li Hung Chang,[23] to become the president of the government university at Wuchang,[24] under an

---

21. End of Boxer Rebellion in 1900.
22. (1837-1909), referee in Chinese civil service examinations in Szechuan Province 1867-77; 1877-81 chief editor of gazetteer of Peking region; appointed governor Shansi Province 1882, undertaking there many schemes of reform, including modern mint, institute of higher learning, and printing works. Later carried out similar programs as governor of Hupeh and Hunnan Provinces 1889-94. Opposed Boxers while remaining loyal to the Empress (who had of course backed them) during the uprising. In 1907 made Grand Secretary and councillor at Peking.
23. Li Hung Chang (1823-1901), principal leader of so-called Self-Strengthening Movement, concerned with military modernization and development of the Chinese industrial base following her defeat in the Opium Wars. Founder of Huai Army, which played an important part in the defeat of the Taiping rebels. After 1870 governor-general of Chihli and High Commissioner of Northern Ports, where he carried out extensive military and navigational works. Negotiated the Boxer Protocol with the Western powers 1900. Subject of a short biography by W.A.P. Martin. (see Section Nine - "Words I Had With Molly" and Section Thirteen - "Democracy's Crusaders."
24. Principal city of Hu Bei Province, central China. University founded at that time; W.A.P. Martin apparently its first president.

engagement for three years, to instruct the junior officials in international law and customs. When this service was concluded he returned to the United States for a brief vacation. He was then in his seventy-eighth year. He had resigned his appointment as a missionary of the Presbyterian Boards when he accepted employment under the Chinese government, but he now, notwithstanding his advanced age, asked a new appointment of his church Board, with a devotion which we may well admire and imitate, saying, "I am too young to quit the field." With an unselfishness rarely equaled he declined to accept any salary when the Board made him an honorary member of the North China station.

He returned to China for the last time, to finish his earthly career, for in bidding farewell to his friends in America he said, "I expect to die on the field." In this last period of his life, in addition to his aid and counsel to his missionary associates, the imperial government availed of his ripe experience and expert knowledge on several occasions in its disputes with foreign governments. As indicating the manner in which the evening of his life was spent in other ways, Rev. Dr. Brown,[25] senior secretary of the Presbyterian Board, writes: "When I saw him in Peking in 1909, the son of Yuan Chih Kai,[26] afterwards the famous president of the Chinese republic, was coming regularly three times a week to Dr. Martin's residence to receive special instruction in political economy and international law."

Many years of his long life were cheered by a faithful wife and co-worker, who died in 1893. The happiness of their domestic life may be inferred from the dedication of a book written by him some time after her death: "To the Memory of my Wife, whose love made life a poem, and whose presence was a constant inspiration."[27]

Notwithstanding a busy public life, engrossed with important labors, Dr. Martin was a prolific author. In addition to the eight or more books written by him in Chinese, he was the author of many

---

25. See Section thirteen - "Korean Christians."
26. Yuan Chih Kai (1859-1916), served in Korea as advisor to Korean armies in 1880's; afterwards prominent member of China's modernizing and reformist movement. Fought on side of court in Boxer Rebellion, but was subsequently instrumental in expelling the Manchu dynasty. Became premier 1911, succeeded Sun Yat Sen as president year following. Had himself declared emperor 1916, but reign lasted only a few months as China lapsed into warlord rule. Yuan Chih Kai had 30 children, including 16 sons; son in questions very likely Yuan Ko Ting (1887-sometime after 1971) who for a time hoped to succeed his father as monarch.
27. Possibly Chinese Legends and Other Poems (Shanghai 1896; expanded edition 1912).

more in English. They have had a wide-spread circulation both in China and in foreign lands, and constitute not the least potent influence of his useful life. In a centennial conference of scholars and missionaries recently held in Shanghai, his Evidences of Christianity was pronounced "the best single book published in Chinese".[28]

Distinguished as Dr. Martin became as an authority on the Chinese language, as an instructor of international law and Western learning, as an adviser of the imperial government, and as an author of Chinese and English books, it was as a missionary that he most desired to be known. He felt the great need of the Chinese people was Christianity. He was greatly devoted to that people. He regarded it in many respects as the greatest race the world has produced. It had maintained a government and civilized institutions through thousands of years, while that of Egypt, Chaldea, Greece, and Rome had risen to power and passed away. It had given to mankind some of the most useful of its inventions, as printing, the mariner's compass, and gunpowder. It had a literature older than any other in existence, and a philosophy antedating and rivaling that of Socrates and the other wise men of Greece. And it is today a race unsurpassed by any other in its habits of industry, thriftiness, and temperance.

It was to such a people that Dr. Martin gave the best services of a long life, to lead them to Christianity and the road to modern progress. If it should be asked who had been the most distinguished and useful foreigner in China during the last generation or more, the answer would be either Sir Robert Hart[29] or Dr. Martin. But Sir Robert's services were confined to finance and administration, while those of Dr. Martin were more varied, and more lasting in their influence upon the Chinese people.

Rev. Arthur H. Smith,[30] regarded as one of the highest authorities on modern China, in a recent book has written: "At some

---

28. Prepared as a text for students in Chinese schools; apparently never translated into English; does not appear in the *National Union Catalog* bibliography.
29. Sir Robert Hart (1835-1911), extended government service in British administration of China, culminating in the post of inspector-general of the imperial maritime customs at Shanghai, from which he resigned in 1906. Martin, at one time, was Hart's rumored successor. Hart failed to anticipate the collapse of China in the war with Japan 1894-5, but used every effort after its conclusion to induce the Chinese to introduce necessary reforms. See Section Fourteen - "Modern Haste on the Hilltops."
30. Arthur Henderson Smith (1845-1932; B.D. Union Theological Seminary '70), ordained to Congregational ministry 1872; sailed that same year for China. Stationed at Tientsin 1872-80; subsequently founded a Christian community in rural area in Shantung Province. Was in besieged Peking legation during Boxer Rebellion. From 1901-25 missionary-at-large. Author numerous books, all on China.

perhaps distant day, the Chinese will begin to get an idea of what it means to have a scholar of the West give the whole of a long and fruitful life to China for no other reward than the service of man and the glory of God. Dr. Martin is a 'pyramid' with the widest base and the highest peak that was ever seen in the ranks of at least American missionaries in China."[31] Hon. Charles Denby,[32] of Indiana, for so many years our able representative at Peking, has characterized him as "the foremost American in China." A Peking (Chinese) paper says: "Dr. Martin is dead, but he still lives, and may we not truly say that by his words, his writings, and the lives which he has touched, he will live on in China forever and forever?"

Our Alma Mater will do well to place the name of Dr. Martin first on the roll of its sons; and we, his brother alumni, should cherish his memory and follow his example of devotion and service for his fellow men.

*   *   *

### Dr. Martin.[33]

Among departures we cannot overlook that of Dr. Martin who has been one of the brightest ornaments of Peking, sinologically and intellectually, for the last thirty years. He is too well known in China to need any eulogium.... His contributions in prose and verse on subjects connected with China have neither been few nor unimportant. His books in Chinese on international law, natural philosophy, and religion, are in constant demand. It was his work on the first named subject the Wan kwah kung fah which first brought him to the notice of the Chinese officials and give him his position."

*   *   *

---

33. Excerpt from a newspaper column by Dr. Dudgeon in the *North Carolina Herald* June 22, 1884, on the occasion of W.A.P. Martin's departure from China to the United States for a year's leave.

## From the Preface to Martin's
*Elements of Natural Philosophy and Chemistry*
By Tung-Seun, Minister of War
translated by S. Wells Williams, L.L.D. of the U.S. Legation
[1868]

"The authors of the Sung dynasty, who wrote upon the nature of things did not very clearly discriminate the specific peculiarities of the objects described by them, inasmuch as they dealt too much in generals without taking pains to show wherein the differences consisted; yet those who have examined the writers of the Han dynasty upon these topics have been wont to commend them at the expense of the former. How unfair to both! Like the sun and moon which adorn the heavens, or the two great rivers which course through our land, so are both these schools; and during many ages of controversy down to the present day no one has been able to decide to which the palm belongs. But where shall one, unfamiliar with these subjects, lay out his strength to the best results?...

Our Imperial House whose thoughts include plans that are illimitable, and comprehend things not coming within the range of sight or hearing, thereupon founded the Tung Wan Kwan College of United Learning, to which were invited western scholars to teach these books and show their application.

Among those scholars is the Missionary, Dr. Martin, styled [by us], the Cap of the West*.[34] He is a man of varied learning and disciplined mind, who came to China many years since, and has mastered its language. He has in the present work brought together the principal facts in Western science...and put them into Chinese in the form of question and answer, in a style that can be clearly understood....

Students who test the experiments and master the principles here given will thereby obtain a full knowledge of these topics. Even without classing it with the writings of the Han and Sung dynasties, its important principles — so concisely expressed — enable one not only to solve the nature of things, but also to see their practical usufruct. In comparison, with this, I regard processes like those employed in bleaching and preparing silks (which I once thought to be very difficult) as remarkably simple.

Written in the seventh year of Tung-chi, in the first moon (February, 1868).

---

34. *Kwan-se*, a title conferred by Prince Kung.

"Early Years of the Central China Mission"[35]

The following year, 1850, the mission was reinforced by Rev. W. A. P. and Samuel Martin and their wives. The failing health of the latter, eight years later, obliged him to leave this field, since which he has done good service among one of our Indian tribes, and also as a Home Missionary. The former is the distinguished President of the Government College at Peking, having in 1869 resigned his connection with the [Missionary] Board on his appointment to that office.

🙢 🙢 🙢

A Veteran Missionary.[36]

Rev. W.A.P. Martin, D.D., LL.D., of Peking, China, who has been a missionary in China for over forty years, expects to attend the meeting of the Synod of South Carolina at rock Hill next week.... He has recently arrived and has in the New York press a book, China, North and South. As a student Dr. Martin was a prodigy, and in China he has attained the highest distinction as a Chinese scholar and for many years has been President of Tung Wen College, Peking, a government institution, founded on the progressive idea of introducing into China the sciences of the West. There never has a more gifted man gone from our country to the heathen world. The favorable disposition of the present Chinese Dynasty to Missions is believed to be largely due to the personal influence of Dr. Martin."

🙢 🙢 🙢

# Relations

*Some hints regarding Martin's relationship with his father toward the turn of the century are revealed in the following three letters. Martin's father enclosed in a letter to him a six-page essay on Christian doctrine entitled "Religion Quaerentis," the last five paragraphs of which appear here. Martin had saved (and copied) a letter from his father written on July 4, 1897, and a duplicate of a letter he wrote his father on July 15, 1897. These, in turn, were preserved by Martin's grandchildren.*

---

35. Excerpt from an article by William Rankin in *The New-York Evangelist*, Thursday, Jan. 14, 1892.
36. Headline and text from a preserved clipping from The Southern Presbyterian.

APPENDIX    491

Dear Newell, Pearl Grotto, Peking, June, 1897.

From an educational stand-point, the broadest view of the universe is the Christian. Compared with a spiritual world of boundless possibilities, what is this narrow dusty tread mill to which we are now condemned. Children should not be deprived of the glorious vision. It does them good to believe there are people on Mars. How much more to believe that there are saints in Heaven.

You and Laura owe the best elements of your character, not to heredity, but to Christian influences. If you neglect those influences, a deterioration will ensue in the next generation.

I am anxious that my grandchildren shall grow up Christians. Do you not think it better for them to follow the old paths than to sink into blank materialism?

The choice of a church is not a question at all in comparison with that of Christianity or practical atheism. It amounts to atheism, if, because you can't know everything about God, you refuse to believe anything.

I trust you will give these lines your most serious consideration; and that they may help to lead you to revise your practice for the sake of your children, if not for your own.

W.A.P.M.

Pearl Grotto, 4th July, 1897
(Sunday)
My dear Newell:-

Get the April No. of the "American Journal of Theology"; and consider it as my gift, cost 75/100. The Revells have it; or can get it for you. It is in its line the organ of the University of Chicago. This No. contains a paper of mine to which they give the place of honor -- also on p. 474 a good notice of my Cycle.[38] Still better it contains besides other papers giving Theology up to date a remarkable paper by Dr. Lyman Abbot on the need of a new Theology. It is for that, I send the book. Please read it carefully as expressing my views. Yet my views were not derived from it. You will find the same substantially in the accompany sheets, which I had written for you[39], before I saw Abbot's article, i.e. a week ago. The sheet entitled "Chance thoughts" is one of many fragments under that

---

38. *A Cycle of Cathay: or, China, South and North.* With personal reminiscences (N.Y.: F.H. Revell Co., 1896).
39. Underlining in original.

title, dating back some months.

Ponder these as well as Abbot's, and they will do you good. The occasion of my writing the paper entitled <u>Religion</u> was a remark in one of your last letters that you "agree with me in nine-tenths of my views". You did not specify; but as to the remaining tenth, I infer from our conversations you do not dissent; but suspend your assent. Now, absolute agreement is more than I expect, tho' with Paul I might say "I would that thou wert not only almost, but altogether such as I am, except" etc., etc.

Though Robert is not as earnest a Christian as I should like him to be; still I think he is what may be called a Christian. I would like him to see this confession of Faith; as also the book and articles referred to.

You need not send them to Europe, if he has gone there; but wait his return.

Your affectionate Father,
W.A.P. Martin.

A <u>sense</u>[40] of God's presence keeps me from feeling lonely.

Madison Square.
July 15, 1897.

My dear Father,

I have sent you a Forum, hoping that you will read the articles by Woolsey, Hamlin and Davidson and eschew the others. I may have written to you already about these 3 articles but I think not.

I write not to complain. It grieves me to rea d and re-read the letter in which you describe your new work. I fee. no gratitude to Mr. Reid for his drawing you into this work. The c irrying on of a mission, the editing of a magazine, the superintendence of a staff of a dozen assistants and the founding of a new University — which will be the 4th, at least, in your province — are heavy tasks to impose on a man who has already done enough work for te.1 men.

The new University is to be built up from nothing. The money, even, is to be raised. And, after the money is raised, it is to be taken as a favor if the authorities will let you have a piece of vacant land, to put the buildings on.

---

40. Underlining, as well as placement of statement, as in original.

I can well imagine the glee with which Mr. Reid seized the chance to hitch you to his car. I don't mean for a moment that your labor is wasted. Every man who comes to that mission will profit by talking to you.

But what I complain of is that here is a man organizing a new institution — or a team of them — and making such things out of nothing and into successes is not the work for emeriti, however hale. DeLesseps built a great canal — in middle age — and then made a botch of another when he retired.

How many estates I have seen squandered, how many businesses ruined by men who ventured back into business when they had once wisely retired.

Young men for action — old men for counsel.

I hope that you will lay down at an early day these tasks which Mr. Reid has thrust on you with so little regard for the rest you have earned by forty years of toil. The devil still walks when wise and aged men can be thus buncoed. I fancy Mr. Reid on his leisurely journey while you, with aching head, in a tropical summer, are trying to convert a mandarin, some skeptical mandarin, with one hand, so to speak, while you try to pacify the printer's devil with the other.

I would like to see you chuck up the whole thing to-morrow, and return to live with us in the Haines house. I gave Haines notice to quit yesterday. With your seven or more labors you will hardly have time to read this. So I shall have it type-written. That is the latest thing in filial respect.

One writes to his father with pen — to show that no trouble is spared by the writer — and a duplicate is then made by the type-writer — so that no trouble may be given to the reader.

Your affectionate son,
Newell Martin.

# Phelps Tribute to W.R. Martin [1]
[undated]

The following is an extract from the useful little book entitled

"TEACHING"
by Prof. William Lyon Phelps, of Yale.[2]

In many of our recitations at school and college we never expected to learn anything and we simply answered formal questions. So fixed was this idea in our minds that our first interview with a new instructor in the Hartford High School, Mr. Winfred R. Martin -- one of the greatest teachers I ever knew -- was not only disastrous to us but we nearly broke out into rebellion. He asked us things that were not in the notes. Later we found him a constant and powerful inspiration. Even at that early age we obtained from him a notion of the meaning of true scholarship. He was and is a profound and original scholar, a man of varied and amazing learning and we respected him for it.

*[Phelps had more to say about Winfred Martin in his autobiography, published in 1939.[3]*

I entered the Hartford Public High School in April 1878, and found it difficult to keep up with my studies. There was a printed monthly report, which gave the exact standing of every pupil in the school. This report was public, was sent to all the parents, so that the precise position in scholarship of every boy and girl in the school was known. If one's average fell below Five for three months, one was dropped into the lower classes; and if one was in the lowest class, one was dropped from the school. In the next Spring my average fell below Five. The Principal, Joseph Hall, sent for me, and told me I should have to go. I suggested we were nearly at the end of the school year, when everyone had to take the final examination; that I be allowed to try this. He immediately granted my request and to his amazement I successfully survived this ordeal and entered the

---

1. Typewritten sheet. Included with Martin's papers; preserved by Meyer family.
2. *Teaching* (N.Y.: Macmillan, 1912; 1918). See Section Nine - "Recommendation for Schuyler from Phelps."
3. William Lyon Phelps, *An Autobiography with Letters* (N.Y. Oxford University Press, 1939), pp. 100-103; 235.

next class.

But in the Autumn of the following year (1899) I fell so low in my studies that my case was hopeless. There seemed to be a cloud over my mind, so that I could not properly learn anything, though I tried hard. I became discouraged; and I had bad luck with one of my teachers who was anything but sympathetic. She thought I was a shirker and a loafer. I withdrew from the school in November, feeling my disgrace keenly. My parents must have been terribly disappointed, but they were unbelievably kind. Not a word of reproach; perhaps they saw how disconsolate I was.

In January I re-entered the High School, and in the lower class. For some weeks I suffered from a depression so profound that I should have been glad to die....But, by the mercy of God, I was assigned to a room presided over by Miss Mary Mather, a young and very attractive woman. She must have observed my sorrowful countenance, for while she never asked me what was the matter, her attitude was extremely sympathetic. She was kind; she was encouraging. Suddenly a cloud seemed to pass from my mind.

Studies that had seemed impossibly difficult became easily comprehensible; I obtained high marks with less than half the effort it had previously cost me to get low ones. I astounded my parents, teachers, and former classmates by going to the top row; my name frequently came to the head on the monthly reports...

In Junior and Senior year at the High School, we had a teacher who made a profound impression. This was Winfred R. Martin. six feet four, with a large red beard. He was the exact opposite of a routine hearer of recitations; and at first we boys rebelled against his methods, because 'he asked questions that were not in the notes.' He was one of the most learned men I have ever known and he never published a line. He had an overwhelming passion for the acquisition of knowledge; and had no other ambition. To publish would have taken time which he used to learn something more. Every Saturday he took the train to New Haven, to study Sanskrit with the greatest scholar in the world, William Dwight Whitney. And after he got to the point where he could not endure High School teaching any more, he went to Tubingen and stayed there until he had won his doctor's degree. Later he became Professor of Ancient and Modern Languages at Trinity College, Hartford, where he was happy. He taught Sanskrit, Arabic, the Semitic languages, Greek, Latin, French, German, and Italian. He was never married and his highest happiness was in learning.

Occasionally I went to his rooms in Hartford and called on him, something I never did with any other teacher. I bored him horribly, but I came away from those interviews feeling inspired. I can see him in my mind's eye as plainly as I saw him in the classroom nearly sixty years ago. I remember his translation of the famous passage in Virgil's eclogues. He spoke it just once in the classroom, and it printed on my mind in imperishable type. The passage begins

*Tale tuum carmen nobis, divine poeta*

"O divine poet, your song is to me as deep sleep upon the grass to the weary, as in summer's heat to slake one's thirst from a springing rivulet of clear water."

When I was an undergraduate at Yale, I became acquainted with Floyd R. Smith of the class above me, a famous half-mile runner. Fifty years later I met him in New Jersey, and discovered that before Martin came to the High School at Hartford, Smith had him as teacher of Latin and Greek in the High School at Jersey City. Replying to my request, he wrote me as follows:

"I remember well the day he told us that he was going to leave, to go to the Hartford High School. So you were the looters that pilfered our treasure chest. Boy, but he was a teacher, the best of all we met on our way. He embodied for me all of the romance and service of teaching.

"When, on one occasion, we were fed up on the Gallic Wars, he closed his textbook and turned to Froissart with some comment as this: 'Froissart would have described in detail each of these patriotic murders. Caesar disposed of all of them with one ablative absolute, onimbus occisis (I believe), and devoted the rest of his column to the glorification of Julius Caesar — a great reporter, that Caesar.' He took us with Froissart on his journey through England, Scotland, Italy and finally to Aquitaine in the retine of the Black Prince.

"Our reward for enduring the monotony of Xenophon's parasangs was his personally-conducted tour to Jane Austen's pre-Victorian England. *Sense and Sensibility*, *Pride and Prejudice* for a time at least, displaced *Diamond Dick* and *Murderous Moses*.

"One of the most dramatic and enduring by-products of that course in Latin and Greek was our introduction to the old Norse Vikings. Romance in golden trappings. I used to stare at him in a transport of admiration. He seemed to me to be one of them, which his six-foot stature, his commanding brow and his blond beard. We boys spoke of him as Old Man Martin, for he must have been at least thirty when we knew him — past ninety now if living. I wonder who else remembers him.

"I met him in my Freshman year [at Yale], on Chapel Street, and he took me to lunch. He was then taking a post-graduate course in Sanskrit, I believe. Why didn't Yale grab him?"

[*Phelps continues*] In Paris [in 1890] ... we went to the opera to hear Faust. Before the curtain rose a gentleman with a big beard whose seat was directly in front of us, turned around and said he recognized my voice. It was Doctor Winfred R. Martin, my inspiring teacher of Virgil in the Hartford High School nearly ten years before. He told us we were in luck that night, because a beautiful American girl from Maine, named Emma Eames, who had just made her debut and was the sensation of Paris, was to sing Marguerite. She was indeed passing fair to see and her glorious voice haunts me still.

❧ ❧ ❧

*The following biographical data on Winfred Robert Martin are taken from* The National Cyclopedia of American Biography (Vol. XV).

Orientalist, was born in Ningpo, China, Mar. 22, 1852, son of William Alexander Parsons and Jane (Vansant) Martin....was educated at Phillips Academy, Andover, Mass., and entering Princeton College was graduated in the class of 1872. He held the classical fellowship of his class at Princeton, and soon after graduation went abroad, spending one semester at Berlin and one at Leipsig.

Returning to the United States in 1874 he was for several years instructor in Latin and Greek at the Jersey City High School, and later in the Hartford (Conn.) High School. While teaching at the latter he took up the study of Sanskrit under Prof. Whitney, of Yale University, and made a second trip abroad in 1885 to pursue its further study.

He was professor of Oriental languages and co-ordinate professor of modern languages at Trinity College during 1888-1907, when he was appointed librarian of the Hispanic Society of America, which had recently been organized by Archer M. Huntington.[4]

Meanwhile he was also instructor of Sanskrit at the Hartford Theological Seminary. Prof. Martin was a member of the American Oriental Society, the American Philological Association, the Society of Biblical Literature and Exegesis, the American Geographical, the American Numismatic Society and the Hispanic Society of America, but he made it his business to promote the studies of these rather than to publish.

He received the degrees of A.M. from Princeton in 1875, LL.B. from the New York University in 1878, Ph.D. from the University of Tubingen in 1887, and LL.D. from Trinity College in 1907 in recognition of long educational service. As librarian of the Hispanic Society of America, a place of somewhat varied functions, he received the decoration of Knight of the Order of Isabella the Catholic.[5]

He was unmarried, and died in New York, Feb. 1, 1915.

---

4. Archer M. Huntington (1870-1955) founded the Hispanic Society of America in 1904 with the bestowal of a personal library of some 40,000 volumes, mostly collected in Spain by Huntington himself, together with a gift of land and money. The Society, located in Audubon Park, came to possess the greatest collection outside Spain of Spanish art in all categories; an official organ, the *Revue Hispanique*, was issued until 1937. Huntington also established a number of other art collections and bequests around the country, notably the Huntington Library in Pasadena, California.

5. The Order of Isabella the Catholic was founded by Ferdinand VII in 1815, and placed under the patronage of Isabella I (1451-1504), queen of Castile and Leon, and consort of Ferdinand V of Spain. The order was originally bestowed as a reward for loyalty to the Royal House, and especially for defense of Spanish possessions in America, but has come to serve as a distinction for all kinds of merit. It is divided into three classes, Knights of the Grand Cross, Commanders, and (W.R.M.) Knights. Nomination confers personal nobility. The costume, on gala days, consists of a mantle of yellow velvet, of a white velvet tunic trimmed with gold embroidery, white shoes with golden bows, and a Spanish hat with white and yellow feathers. The decoration is then suspended from a collar, and may be adorned with precious stones.

# Memorandum As To Rev. William W. Martin.[1]

5 Broad Street,
New York, December 1, 1905.

Prof. W. R. Martin, a grandson of Rev. William W. Martin, has found among his own papers a newspaper clipping containing a sketch of Rev. William W. Martin, the father of W.A.P. Martin. It purports to be written by Leroy J. Halsey, D. D., and appears to have been printed about 1870 in the "Interior," a paper published by the Western Presbyterian Publishing Company at Chicago. (W. S. Mills, publisher, Room 5, Monroe Building, Chicago.)

It was sent to Wm. R. Martin in 1899 from Charles City, Iowa, by Mrs. Susan Bruce, a daughter of Rev. S. N. D. Martin. I have had a few copies[2] made for the use of the great-grandchildren of Rev. William W. Martin.

Newell Martin.

❧ ❧ ❧

### A NOBLE PIONEER PREACHER OF INDIANA.

By Leroy J. Halsey, D. D.[3]

The name of William W. Martin, for many years familiarly called "Father Martin," is a household word of precious memory to

---

1. William Wilson Martin (1781-1850). As Martin wrote in his distinctive hand above the title: "One of Molly's 4 great-great-grandfathers."
2. An 8-page pamphlet 6" X 9", nicely typeset.
3. Leroy J. Halsey, D. D. (1812-1896; University of Nashville '36; Princeton seminary '39), theologian; pastorates in Kentucky 1840-1859; in that year accepted the chair of pastoral theology, church government, and homiletics at the newly-founded Presbyterian theological seminary in Chicago, subsequently called the McCormick Theological Seminary. Became professor emeritus 1881. Author seven books.

hundreds of Presbyterian families in Indiana, and to not a few in the adjacent States. He was a representative man of his times, and belonged to a class of ministers now almost gone from our midst, who should be held in perpetual honor, not only for the solid qualities which adorned them, but for the great and almost heroic hardships and labors they endured, in laying out the foundations of the Church in these broad, and, at that time wild domains. Though he has now been dead twenty years, yet to this day no fitting record of his life has ever been published; and it serves to illustrate how our best men at the West are permitted to toil, die, and be forgotten, that his name is not even mentioned in the voluminous work of Dr. Sprague on the Annals of the American Pulpit.[4] It is unjust both to the living and the dead, that such names should pass into oblivion.

"Tis to the virtues of such men, man owes
His portion in the good that heaven bestows."

Mr. Martin's ministry extended through thirty-eight years, the greater part of which he spent in Southern Indiana. He removed to the State in 1818, only two years after it was admitted into the Union, and when only three Presbyterian ministers, Scott, Robinson and Dickey, had preceded him. From this feeble beginning he lived to see the Presbyterian Church of Indiana swell into two Synods, eleven Presbyteries, one hundred and thirty ministers, two hundred churches, and nearly ten thousand members of the Old School Branch alone, not to mention a similar increase of the New. To this growth he had probably contributed more than any other man in the State.

Blest with no great vigor of health or strength of constitution, but fired with apostolic zeal, he made extended journeys on horseback in all directions, and performed an amount of service in planting new churches and preaching to the destitute, which would seem almost incredible to the railroad travelers of the present generation. Not only by preaching and pastoral labors did he extend his influence far and wide, but being a fine classical scholar he was also engaged, most of his life, in teaching young men and preparing them for the ministry; and thus, as a practical educator, performed a service for the Church and the country, not exceeded by any of his contemporaries in the State, with the single exception, perhaps, of

---

4. William Buell Sprague (1795-1876), *Annals of the American Pulpit,* 9 volumes (N.Y.: Carter, 1857-1869).

the venerable Dr. Crowe, of Hanover.[5]

Mr. Martin was of Scotch-Irish descent, being one of four children who all became useful and honored members of the Presbyterian Church. He was born in the year 1781, in Westmoreland county, Pa., but educated in Kentucky, to which State his parents removed in his boyhood. Having become a member of the Church, he determined, at the age of twenty-four, to prepare himself for the gospel ministry. For this purpose he entered the classical Academy of the Rev. John Lyle, at Paris, Ky., where he spent four years in study, and then, for two years more, pursued his theological course under the same instructor. He became a superior classical scholar, and excelled particularly in the Latin language. At the close of his literary course he was married to Miss Alexander,[6] whose three brothers, Thomas, Samuel and William, became widely known as able Presbyterian ministers — the last named, for nearly forty years a missionary of the American Board in the Sandwich Islands.

At the close of his theological studies he was licensed to preach by the *Presbytery of West Lexington* June, 1812. His trial sermon on the Perseverance of the Saints, (Phil. i., 6,) a masterly discourse, in which every position was clinched by an argument from Scripture, was memorized and delivered in Lexington, Ky., in the presence of the Presbytery and a large congregation, who listened to him with great satisfaction.

Mr. Martin's first settlement was in Winchester, Ky., where, in a short period he organized and built up a church at the same time teaching a high school and editing a newspaper. He was ordained to the full work of the ministry in 1814. He remained at Winchester about six years. He was regarded at this time as one of the most promising young ministers in Kentucky, and had tempting offers to settle in one or two of the best churches in the State. But he had set his heart on being a pioneer missionary in the new and free State of Indiana, to which he removed, as above stated, and became the regular supply of the two churches of Salem and Livonia.

At the latter of these places he soon fixed his residence. Here he built a dwelling for his family, and a school-house for his pupils.

---

5. John Finley Crowe (1787-1860), Presbyterian clergyman. Pastor at Hanover, Indiana 1823-1832, principal of Hanover Academy 1827-1833. Founded Hanover College and Indiana Theological Seminary; vice-president of the College and professor of rhetoric, logic, political economy, and history.

6. *Dictionary of American Biography*, Vol. 12, gives name of Wm. W. Martin's wife as Susan Depew, noting that both were "of frontier Scotch-Irish stock."

In this humble edifice, which might well be denominated a Log College, he taught for many years. Here he instructed his three sons and his seven daughters, some of whom were good Latin scholars, and read Virgil and other authors with the young men. Five of these daughters married Presbyterian ministers. His three sons are now in the ministry — two of them distinguished missionaries to China.[7] Seldom has any man been more blessed in his family, or more blessed in his work. By his children and his pupils he, being dead, yet speaks.

Mr. Martin changed his location a few times, but sill remained in the same Synod, in which he was ever regarded with the greatest affection by his ministerial brethren. He continued through life to preach with great acceptance, not only to his own churches, but to those at a distance whenever his services were called for. Besides his own sons, he lived to see many of the young men, whom he had taught, in the ministry and other useful professions. Amidst his multiplied avocations, he never neglected to prepare well for the pulpit. Occasionally he wrote out his discourses in full. But generally he prepared an outline or skeleton, studied it thoroughly, and then depended upon the occasion for the language. His sermons were for the most part long; but such was his fervor and earnestness that no audience ever became weary under his preaching. He was also remarkably gifted in prayer, <u>frequently praying for a half hour</u>,[8] and his congregation not aware of the length of time occupied in this solemn service. Those were the days of zeal and consecration, when the people of God were not afraid of long sermons or long prayers, for they felt that the house of God was the best place, and the service of God the best way in which to spend the Sabbath.

One of his nephews, the Rev. John L. Martin, of Toledo, Iowa,[9] who was prepared for college under his tuition, and for fifteen years was associated with him in the same Presbytery, bears the following decisive testimony to his excellence and ability as a preacher:

"Few ministers possessed so many and such rare excellences; an eloquent speaker — <u>often addressing a thousand people</u>, assembled in the grove, and holding his hearers enchained <u>for an hour and a half</u>.[10] His favorite theme was the love of Christ, and

---

7. W.A.P. (father of Newell; great-grandfather of Molly) and his brother, Samuel Newall.
8. "<u>Frequently praying for a half hour</u>" underlined in pencil, probably by Martin; Molly says not done by her.
9. Small city, 50 miles due west of Cedar Rapids.
10. Penciled underlining of: "<u>Addressing a thousand people and for an hour and a half</u>."

his discourses on communion occasions were overpowering. His descriptive powers were remarkable. He was a good poet, and very frequently, when he preached on particular subjects, made the hymns to be sung on that occasion. In short, he was a superior preacher, a good scholar, a fine writer, an indefatigable student, a successful teacher, and excellent pastor. His social qualities were excellent. He carried the popular feeling with him wherever he went."

Mr. Martin gave but few of his writings to the public through the press. An occasional article in the religious newspapers, and a few addresses delivered before literary associations, are all that he saw fit to publish. Had he been favored with more leisure he could easily have distinguished himself as a writer. His manuscript sermons which remain bear witness to his logical acumen, his theological ability, and his scholarly taste.[11] It was proposed at one time to publish a memoir of his life. Such a life is indeed worthy of a lasting remembrance.

This great and good man closed his earthly existence at his old home at Livonia, Ind., on the 10th of September, 1850, in the seventieth year of his age. The last act of his eventful life was to attend the Commencement at Hanover College in the latter part of August, 1850, at the time that his youngest son -- now Rev. C. B. Martin, of Evansville -- graduated. Up to the time of his death he preached with his usual power, and those who heard his last sermon at Hanover, the Sabbath preceding the commencement, declared that on this occasion he even surpassed himself. Though he never possessed a strong physical constitution, yet he is believed to have preached more than any other minister of his day. His form was slender, his complexion fair, in height six feet, inclining forward; when young a very handsome man, and beautiful even in age. He returned from his visit to Hanover somewhat exhausted by the heat and travel, took typhoid fever, and in three weeks exchanged earth for heaven. "Let me die the death of the righteous, and let my last end be like his."[12]

He has long ceased from his labors here, but his works do follow him. How it illustrates the deathless influence of character, and how it vindicates the claims of the ministry, and the wisdom of

---

11. Recently found in an old suitcase are two sets of what are apparently notes from which Reverend William W. Martin delivered "manuscript sermons." They date from 1838-39; are written in a minute hand, completely occupying both sides of sewn-together octavo sheets.
12. Numbers 23:10

consecrating one's life to the Lord, and consider, that this good man, when he was toiling in that log cabin in Indiana fifty years ago, was but laying foundations and starting influences which should preach the Gospel to the millions of Chinese on the other side of the Globe. His log cabin is gone, and he is gone; but his work remains, his influence lives, his example shines, and his very name is "to memory dear, and dear to God!"

# Rev. Dirck C. Lansing, D.D.[1]
(From a pamphlet, a 3 page printed memorial.)

Dr. Lansing died at Cincinnati. "His funeral was attended" on March 18, 1857, at Troy, New York, "in the vicinity of which city he spent his youth upon his father's manor. Lansingburgh derived its name from his paternal grandfather who was Patroon over a large tract of land in that neighborhood. In that village Dr. Lansing was born in 1785...He entered upon his ministry in Onondaga, which was then a settlement of log cabins in the wilderness...In 1816 he was settled in Auburn, and for twenty years he was a leading mind in...western New York. He was prominent as a preacher in the great revival period from 1825 to 1835 and was a chief agent in founding Auburn Seminary." Later he went to a church in New York City which became "the Thirteenth Street Presbyterian Church." He carried on "a brief but memorable ministry in Utica (New York). Ill health drove him to Illinois." From Chrystie Street in New York City he "removed to Clinton Avenue, in Brooklyn." There he "nursed an infant church to maturity and strength." He regarded the Clinton Avenue church as his greatest work. "In...50 years Dr. Lansing was actively concerned in more than 60 revivals." The pamphlet speaks of "his pure and noble character...logical faculty... severe analysis... spiritual vision... childlike... faith... and a most

---

1. Martin's wife, Laura (Grinnell) Martin, was a direct descendant (a granddaughter on her mother's side) of Dr. Lansing. Martin has reprinted and annotated excerpts from a memorial pamphlet dedicated to Lansing. Martin's typed text pages are without paragraph indentations.

heavenly charity...His heart never grew old." He had a "tall, vigorous, muscular frame, fitted for endurance."

Observe these 3:

| | |
|---|---|
| Dirck Cornelius Lansing | Already: |
| Mrs. George Blake Grinnell | 1939 |
| Laura Grinnell Martin | 154 |

Already these 3 lives span 154 years.

(Exodus, chap. 20 verse 12)[2]

Observe these lines of descent:
1. The patroon, Lansing, for whom "Lansingburgh" was named.
2. His son.
3. Dirck Cornelius Lansing
4. Helen Lansing Grinnell
5. Laura Grinnell Martin
6. Grinnell Martin
7. Laura Grinnell Martin and her 2 amiable and prepossessing sisters.

1. The "patroon", Lansing, grandfather of Dirck.
2. Lansing, the father of Dirck.
3. Rev. Dirck Cornelius Lansing, D.D.
4. Helen Lansing Grinnell, wife of George Blake Grinnell.
5. Laura Grinnell Martin, wife of Newell Martin.
6. Helen Meyer, wife of Schuyler M. Meyer.
7. Schuyler Merritt Meyer, Jr. and his 3 prepossessing and amiable sisters.

### Dirck C. Lansing, D.D.

Joseph P. Thompson,[3] Pastor of the Broadway Tabernacle Church of New York, preached in Brooklyn, on May 10, 1857, "A Discourse Commemorative" of Dr. Lansing. It was printed by

---

2. "Honour thy father and thy mother: that thy days may be long upon the land which the Lord thy God giveth thee."
3. Joseph P. Thompson (1819-1879; Yale '38), Congregational minister, pastor Chapel Street Congregational Church in New Haven 1840-1845, Broadway Tabernacle Church 1845-1871. Founded the reviews *New Englander* and *The Independent*. Became expert on Egyptology after trip there in 1853. Taught in England and Germany after retirement. Author numerous books.

Calkins and Stiles, 348 Broadway in 1857. "A holy life...active and conspicuous service"(8). "The father of this people." "Labors" of "51 years"(10). "The beginning of the present Century was a memorable era in the history of' Yale. "The French Revolution...had widely infected this country with infidelity and libertinism. The powerful influence of Thomas Jefferson and Thomas Paine...the former, the almost idolized head of the then rising democracy, the latter one of the most vigorous and trenchant writers upon popular rights -- gave currency...to the doctrines of Voltaire and the Encyclopedists: Popular freedom was associated with irreligion...'Down with the priest' was the echo of the cry 'down with the king.' Infidelity was open and fashionable...This spirit of skepticism was rife in Yale." (In the Colonies there had been a "great awakening", the work of Whitfield [sic], Edwards and Davenport, in 1740. N.M.)[4]

At the close of the eighteenth century "among more than 100 students in Yale college there were but 4 or 5 professors of religion; and at one communion season in the College church, only a single under-graduate was present..To be a Christian was far from popular in the public opinion of the College." (12). Jeremiah Evarts, a senior,[5] led in a revival (14). 80 students were converted and nearly half of these became preachers. "Among them" was Lansing (15). Lansing "entered Yale college in September, 1800, at the age of 15. " He was "of correct and amiable deportment, but of high spirit, and of such vivacity and heartiness...that he was peculiarly exposed to the temptations of College popularity." He was "sprung from an ancient, honorable and wealthy family—his grandfather being patroon or patentee of a large manor near Troy" (15). He spent "more than 50 years ...in unremitted toil, at much pecuniary sacrifice, in following the light" (16). He was "converted" in 1802. One classmate said of him: "Frank and cheerful, uniformly full of exhilaration and with abundant means for pleasurable indulgence,

---

4. A widespread and intense religious revival called the Great Awakening took place in the American colonies roughly 1720-1750. Martin names three of its leading figures: George Whitefield (1714-1770), English-born Calvinistic Methodist preacher who participated in both the General Assembly and Wesleyan movement in England; Jonathan Edwards (1703-1758; Yale '20), whose Calvinist theology furnished the intellectual backbone of the General Assembly; and James Davenport (1716-1757; Yale '32), one of Yale's youngest-ever graduates, was an itinerant preacher from 17139-1743 in New York, New Jersey, and Connecticut. His violent attacks on the regular clergy generated strong opposition. He later partially recanted his enthusiast views.

5. Jeremiah Evarts (1781-1831; Yale '98), lawyer in New Haven; subsequently Charlestown, Mass. Devoted himself extensively to religious and philanthropic works; his labors for the American Board of Commissioners for Foreign Missions considered to have played a part in bringing on his early death. Author of 24 essays on the rights of the Indian.

he won the hearts of all his associates" (18). Another classmate said of him: "His domestic education was a great embarrassment to him, inasmuch as, being of a Dutch family, he had not used the English language until he was a large boy...the distinction to which, as a man, and a minister of the Gospel, he attained in after life, was to me and his other companions, unexpected and a great gratification. For a discriminating mind, warm affections and well-directed enterprise, he took rank among the best of his fellows" (20). "Picture this young man of 21, reared amid the comforts of wealth, traversing the woods...in quest of materials for a Church" (21). He held 7 pastorates (22). We read of him as "the first pulpit orator in western New York" and of his "effective eloquence" (24). He went to a New York city pastorate in 1832.

(At page 31 Dr. Thompson makes this appropriate note of something that happened 45 years before Dr. Lansing was born:

"The great revival of religion in New England in 1740 was...bitterly assailed as a work of fanaticism" (31). Dr. Thompson contrasted John C. Calhoun[6] with his classmate Lansing, greatly to the advantage of Lansing; and well he might (51, 52).

ta ta ta

---

6. John C. Calhoun (1782-1850; Yale '04), U.S. Representative from South Carolina 1811-1817, Secretary of War 1817-1825, Vice-President 1825-1832; later U.S. Senator and Secretary of State. Noted defender of the Southern cause. Calhoun's character normally is described as "upright."

# SEVENTEEN

# A FINAL WORD


**Letter to Molly,
   August 12, 1939**  . . . . . . . . . . . . .510

# Letter to Molly, August 12, 1939

*Handwritten on typing paper; apparently last dated letter kept by Molly. Martin (Other Gomby to the Meyer grandchildren, and grandfather to Grinnell Martin family) died November 15, 1941, in Huntington due to arteriosclerosis.*

|  |  |
|---|---|
| Miss Molly Meyer | West Main St. |
|    Twin Birches | Route Two |
|    Lake Memphremagog | Huntington |
|      Newport | L. I. |
|       Vermont | New York |
|  | Aug. 12, 1939 |

Dear Molly

You have rain & we have dust. In my childhood I was told that the Lord rained on the just & the unjust. In my childhood I spent or rather lost about five years in learning a lot of things that were not so; & now, the golden years of my prime are to be destroyed.

Here I am, full to the brim with ripe & correct opinions; & nobody will ever hear them but my nurse & Beelzebub.

      Affectionately

      *Newell Martin*

# INDEX

511

Abbot, Dr. Lyman, 491-2
Adams, Henry, 438
Adirondack Mountains, 414-447
Angell, Dr. James R., 34-53, 216
Alexander, Robert, 114-5, 264
American Defense Society, 19
"American Journal of Theology", 491
Baker, Dr. O.E., 195
Bannard, Otto T., 59
Beede, Charles, 442-4
Betts, Samuel R., 450
Black, John D., 195
Bogle, Lieutenant Blythe, 120
Bowker, Richard Rodgers, 89, 202-3
Boxer Rebellion, 106, 485
Brown, George W., 238
Bruce, Susan, 499
Brusati, Renzo (Mrs. T. Lilley), 119, 237, 445-6
Bryn Mawr College, 464-6
Buchanan, Sir George W., 20
Buckner, Emory G., 54
Buckner, Mrs. Emory R., 55
Butler, Dr. Nicholas Murray, 51
Carson, Russell M.L., 433
Century Association, 289, 295-97, 455
    and University Clubs, 284
Cheney, John, 433, 442
Cheston, Galloway, 120
Choate, Joseph, 104
Coolidge, Calvin, 64
Crawford, Albert B., 36
Darwin Safety Razor Company, 131-2
Daily Neech, 195
Das, Taraknath, 21
Denison, Carmen, 237
Denison, Geraldine, 237
Denison, James, 237
Depew, Susan, 236
Dodd, Mead & Company, 284
East-West relations, 345-411
"English Merchants", 334-338
Evans, Madge, 266
Family Tree, 236
Father Martin, 499
Football and prayer, 221

## 512　　INDEX

Foster, Pell W., 289, 295-297
Fraser, George C., 289, 297-303
Germann, Helen, 237
Germann, Laurie, 237
    Germann, Michael, 237
    Gibbs, Emerson, 438-441
    Gibbs, Josiah 'Willard', 438-441
    Gibbs, William James, 438-441
    Gibbs, Wolcott, 438-441
    Gilliat, Captain, 119
    Gomby, (Laura Martin) 1, 237
    Gould, Charles W., 156
    Grant, Madison, 155
    Grinnell, Frank, 237
    Grinnell, George, 119-20, 236
    Grinnell, George Bird, 237
    Grinnell, George Blake, 236
    Grinnell, Helen Jesup, 237
    Grinnell, Helen Lansing, 236, 505
    Grinnell, Laura Griswold, 236
    Grinnell, Morton, 237
    Grinnell, William, 237
    Grinnell-Milne, Lieut. Douglas, 120
    Grinnell-Milne, Lieut. Duncan, 120
    Grinnell-Milne, Muriel, 119
    Grinnell-Milne, Violet, 119
    Griswold, W.E.S., 48-9, 52
    Groton School, 10
    Gundelfinger, 225-6
    Hallam, Oscar, 193
    Halsey D.D., Leroy J., 499
    Handy, Mrs. John I. (Jane), 236
    Hara, T., 378
    Hartford High School, 494-7
    Hathaway, Milford, 437
    Hazen, George, 130
    Higgenbotham, Thomas W., 123
    Hooten, Earnest Albert, 161, 165
    Hughes, Charles Evans, 130
    Huntington Water Works Corporation, 23-27
    Hyphenated-Americans, writings on, 141
    Indiana University, 480
    Introduction, 1
    Jews,
        and Philistines, 165-171
        in clubs, 145-152

# INDEX 513

Johnson, Ephraim, 131
Kamm, Dr. Oliver, 91-2
Keene Flats (Valley), 439
Kellog-Briand Pact, 98
Koehne, Mrs. Richard S. (Laura), 236
Kuropatkin, Alexi Nikolaevich, 101, 367
Lamb, Charles, 202
Lamb, Levi, 442
Lambert, Henri, 99
LaMotte, Ellen, 18, 340-5
Landon, Harold Morton, 120
Landon, Lucy, 119
Landon, William G., 120
Lansing, Dirck Cornelius, 236, 254, 458, 504-507
Legge, Alexander, 195
Letters,
    from Newell Martin to his brothers, 240-50
    to and about the family, 135, 251-7
    to Bear (Schuyler Merritt Meyer, Jr.), 223-4
    to Grinnell, 457
    to Jane, 254
    to Janet, 471
    to Laura, 458
    to Major-General Robert Alexander, 114
    to Molly, 28, 118, 134, 172, 199, 214-5, 228-233, 277, 280, 320, 459-71, 510
    to Myra, 251-254, 446, 451-6
    to Samuel R. Betts, 450
Lever, Samuel Hudson, 238
Lilley, Mrs. Theodore (Renzo Brusati), 237
Mann, Captain, 119
Martin, C.B., Reverend, 503
Martin, Claude, 236
Martin, Grinnell, 120, 236, 505
Martin, Helen (Mrs. Schuyler Merritt Meyer), 203, 236, 314, 505
Martin, Jacob, 236
Martin, Jane (Vansant), 497
Martin, Janet, 236
Martin, Laura Grinnell, 264
Martin, Myra Fraser, 236, 314
Martin, Pascal, 236
Martin, Robert, 236
Martin, Dr. William Alexander Parsons (W.A.P.), 1, 236, 480-90
Martin, William Wilson, 236, 499-504
Martin, Winifred R., 236, 494-8

# 514 INDEX

Mathers, Mrs. William H. (Myra), 236
McCullough, John Ramsay, 208-9
McIntyre, Dr. Archibald, 433
Meyer, Aileen, 237
Meyer, Allen, 237
Meyer, Charles John, 237
Meyer, Eugene Jr., 174-80
Meyer, Helen Martin, 203, 236, 314, 505
Meyer, Helen (Mrs. Oliver Germann), 236, 445
Meyer, Janet (Mrs. Howard Denison), 236
Meyer, Molly, (Mrs. Cathal O'Connor) 114-115, 134-6, 236-7, 266-9,
  will and testament, 270-1, 275,277-280
Meyer, Schuyler Merritt, 236, 272, 314
Meyer, Schuyler Merritt, Jr., 236-237, 274
Meyer, Scott, 237
Mills, Ogden Livingstone, 59
Missionaries in China, 482-3, 488
Mountain climbing, 414-431, 433
Muruts, 210-3
Nourse, E.G., 195
O'Connor, Christopher, 237
O'Connor, David, 237
O'Connor, Erin, 237
O'Connor, Jennifer, 237
O'Connor, Mrs. Cathal (Molly Meyer), 114-115, 134-6, 236-7, 266-9, 270-1,
  275,277-280
O'Connor, Peter, 237
"On Drinking Alone by Moonlight", 95
Osgood, Alfred, 289-94
O'Shaughnessy, James J., 123-124, 128-9
Other Gomby (Newell Martin), 1, 237, 510
Page, Donald, 237
Page, Frank L.G., 237
Page, Laura, L.G., 237
Page, Rutherford, 237
Page, Sylvia, 119, 237
Page, William Drummond, 237
Parson, William Alexander, 497
Peacock, Thomas Love, 202
Peking Dust, 340, 342, 344
Phelps, Professor William Lyon, 274-5, 442, 494-498
Prohibition, writings on, 15-96
Quinnipac Club, 450
Reid, John, 17

INDEX 515

Royal Gazette (Bermuda), 180
Sabbatis, Mitchell, 442
Schenck, A.A., 433
Shuster, William Morgan, 21, 289, 304-9, 345
Scott, Barbara, 236
"Seven Seas", 468
Smith, Arthur H. (Reverend), 487-488
Smith, Charles Robinson, 309-12, 324
Smith, Floyd R., 496
Smith, Jeannie, 324
Speed, Captain Ralph, 119
Siamese Royal Commission, 181-195
Spinach and Zweiback, 2, 130
Stoddard, Theodore Lothrop, 155-156
Stokes, Frederick A., 284
Stowe, Hilda, 29
Strong, Dr. Archibald McIntyre, 433
Strong, Benjamin, Sr., 433
Sturges, Captain Harry, 119
Sung Dynasty, 489
Tabert, Martin, 123
Thompson, Joseph P., 505, 507
Timeline, 5
Tredo, Max, 442
University Club, 144,153-4, 284
VanZandt, Jane, 236
Volstead Act, 34-95
Wadsworth, James Walcott, 59
Walpole, Horace, 328-9
War and Peace, 97
War Finance Corporation, 174-80
Watch & Ward Society, 86
Water Bill, The, 22
Weeks, Percy, 468
Whitney, Roger, 314-318
Wilson, Catherine, 236
Winslow, Sidney, 238
Wrigley's Cathedral, 227
Wright, Jr., William Burnett, 53
Yale Alumni Advisory Board, 47-8
Yale Alumni Weekly, 47-9, 196, 457
Yale University, 196, 506
    Commencement controversy, 34-53

## SPINACH AND ZWEIBACK

I thought of dedicating this monograph to Charles Evans Hughes, as Samuel Johnson once dedicated something heavy to Chesterfield; but, as that might savor of sycophancy, I address and dedicate it to George H. Hazen, who was one of the inventors of "trade propaganda" and who is "on a diet", at the Roosevelt Hospital.

Multitudes of us American men and women, and, above all, you and I, are "on a diet." Our food is weighed, measured and prescribed. The number and hours of our meals are ordered, like the stars in their courses, and at such times as are most irksome.

The glutton is given one meal a day and to him that is abstemious are given seven, that seem seventy times seven. Eac[h] must carry exactly so many vi[tamins,] ptomaines, chromosomes, hormones[, calo]ries, bacilli. What we like is cut o[ut and] what we dislike is put in. Our relu[ctance] to follow our regimens is enhanced [by] knowing that, for thousands of [years] doctors practiced letting out blood, [to save] life; and that, suddenly, they decid[ed in]stead, on transfusion, and now p[ut in] blood, to save life. We fear, therefor[e, that] with the swift march of medical sci[ence it] will be found, tomorrow, that all the[se cures] are wrong. Our sorrow's crown of [sorrow] is the fear that we are barking, at gr[eat dis]comfort, up the wrong tree. The [press] does not report how many are unde[r...]

THE

DUTY

OF

REBELLIO[N]

*REPRINTED FROM THE*
*GROTON SCHOOL QUAR[TERLY]*

BY
GEORGE W. MART[IN]